WRITING
SKILLS
WITH
READINGS

COLLEGE WRITING SKILLS WITH READINGS

Fourth Edition

JOHN LANGAN

Atlantic Community College

THE McGRAW-HILL COMPANIES, INC.

New York   St. Louis   San Francisco   Auckland   Bogotá   Caracas
Lisbon   London   Madrid   Mexico City   Milan   Montreal
New Delhi   San Juan   Singapore   Sydney   Tokyo   Toronto

McGraw-Hill

A Division of The **McGraw·Hill** *Companies*

COLLEGE WRITING SKILLS WITH READINGS

This book is printed on acid-free paper.

3 4 5 6 7 8 9 0   DOC   DOC   9 0 9 8 7

ISBN 0-07-036458-3

This book was set in Times Roman by Monotype Composition Company.
The editors were Tim Julet and Peggy Rehberger;
the design manager was Joan E. O'Connor and the text designer was Rafael Hernandez.
The production supervisor was Richard A. Ausburn.
The cover illustrator was Tina Hill and the cover was designed by John Hite;
R. R. Donnelley & Sons Company was printer and binder.

Library of Congress Cataloging-in-Publication Data

Langan, John. (date)
    College writing skills with readings / John Langan.—5th ed.
       p.   cm.
    Student ed.
    Includes index.
    ISBN 0-07-036458-3
    1. English language—Rhetoric.   2. English language—Grammar.
3. Academic writing.   4. College readers.   5. Essay.   I. Title.
PE1471.L34   1997
808'.0427—dc20   96-28159

http://www.mhcollege.com

ABOUT
THE AUTHOR

John Langan has taught reading and writing at Atlantic Community College near Atlantic City, New Jersey, for over twenty years. The author of a popular series of college textbooks on both subjects, he enjoys the challenge of developing materials that teach skills in an especially clear and lively way. Before teaching, he earned advanced degrees in writing at Rutgers University and in reading at Glassboro State College. He also spent a year writing fiction that, he says, "is now at the back of a drawer waiting to be discovered and acclaimed posthumously." While in school, he supported himself by working as a truck driver, machinist, battery assembler, hospital attendant, and apple packer. He now lives with his wife, Judith Nadell, near Philadelphia. Among his everyday pleasures are running, working on his Macintosh computer, and watching Philadelphia sports teams on TV. He also loves to read: newspapers at breakfast, magazines at lunch, and a chapter or two of a recent book ("preferably an autobiography") at night.

CONTENTS

PART FOUR

HANDBOOK OF SENTENCE SKILLS

READINGS LISTED BY RHETORICAL MODE

Note: Some selections are cross-listed because they illustrate more than one rhetorical method of development.

EXAMPLES

PROCESS

CAUSE AND EFFECT

COMPARISON-CONTRAST

TO
THE
INSTRUCTOR

Note: This Instructor's Edition of *College Writing Skills with Readings* is identical to the student textbook except that it also includes, at the end, a special section: "Instructor's Guide." (A separate *Instructor's Manual and Test Bank* is also available; it includes this guide along with supplementary activities and tests.)

College Writing Skills with Readings is a rhetoric with readings that will help students master the writing of the traditional five-paragraph essay. It is a very practical book with a number of special features to aid teachers and their students.

KEY FEATURES

- *Four principles are presented as keys to effective writing.* These four principles—unity, support, coherence, and sentence skills—are highlighted on page 127 and the inside front cover and reinforced throughout the book. Part One focuses on the first three principles; Part Four serves as a concise handbook of sentence skills. In Part Two, students learn how to apply the four principles within the different patterns of essay development; then, in Part Three, they apply the principles to such specialized types of writing as the exam essay and the research paper. Finally, the reading selections in Part Five generate assignments which encourage students to apply the four principles in a variety of well-developed essays.

- *Activities and assignments are numerous and varied.* For example, in the opening two chapters there are over twenty activities to help students learn how to advance and support a thesis. There are over one hundred activities in the entire book. Such activities serve as an essential step between the explanation of a skill and a student's full understanding of that skill.

A variety of writing assignments follows each of the types of essay development in Part Two. Some topics are highly structured, for students needing such support; others require more work on the part of the student. Instructors thus have the option of selecting those assignments most suited to the individual needs of their students.

- *Clear thinking is stressed throughout.* This focus on logic starts with the section "To the Student" on page xxi. Then, in an early chapter (see page 41), students are introduced to the two principles that are the bedrock of clear thinking: *making a point* and *providing support to back up that point.* The focus on these principles continues throughout the book: a section on outlining in Part One offers practice in distinguishing between main and supporting ideas; writing assignments in Part Two provide direction in planning papers that support and develop a central point; many other activities in the book require students to develop basic thinking skills; a form that will help students prepare a well-thought-out essay appears on page 9. In short, students learn that clear writing is inseparable from clear thinking.

- *The traditional essay is emphasized.* Students are asked to write formal essays with an introduction, three supporting paragraphs, and a conclusion. Anyone who has tried to write a solidly reasoned essay knows how much work is involved. A logical essay requires a great deal of mental discipline and close attention to a set of logical rules. Writing an essay in which there is an overall thesis statement and in which each of three supporting paragraphs begins with a topic sentence is more challenging than writing a free-form or expressive essay. The demands are significant, but the rewards are great.

  Such a rigorous approach may seem limiting. But students discover quickly enough on their own that the rules can be broken. Indeed, in the general media they are exposed to daily, they see those rules being broken all the time (at times to the detriment of clear communication and sound thinking). First-year college students do not need to work on breaking or going beyond the rules; they need to learn the rules thoroughly and practice using them. Freedom to move beyond the rules effectively is possible only when they know what the rules are. Mastering the rules is, in fact, the cornerstone that students can build on to become powerful and versatile writers.

- *Writing is treated as a process.* The second chapter, "Important Factors in Writing," discusses prewriting, rewriting, and editing. In addition, many writing assignments are accompanied by "Suggestions on How to Proceed" that give step-by-step directions in the process of writing a paper.

- *Lively models are provided.* One way (though by no means the only way) that students learn is by imitation. *College Writing Skills with Readings* thus provides several high-interest essays with each assignment. Students read and evaluate these essays in terms of the four standards: unity, support, coherence, and sentence skills. Student essays appear in place of professional ones, which typically run longer than five hundred words and vary widely from the regular five-paragraph format. The book assumes that students are especially interested in and challenged by the writing of their peers. After reading vigorous papers composed by other students and experiencing the power that good writing can have, students will be more encouraged to aim for similar honesty, realism, and detail in their own work.

- *The book is versatile.* Since no two people use an English text in exactly the same way, the material has been organized in a highly accessible manner. Each of the four parts of the book deals with a distinct area of writing. Instructors can therefore turn quickly and easily to the skills they want to present.

- *A number of prose readings are included in Part Five.* These readings deal with many contemporary concerns and will stimulate lively class discussions as well as individual thought. They will serve as a rich source of material for a wide range of writing assignments.

    There are two special features in Part Five. First is the emphasis placed on helping students become stronger readers. A brief introductory section offers tips on good reading, and ten questions after each selection help students practice key skills in effective comprehension. A second special feature is the detailed guidelines provided with many of the writing assignments. Students are shown how to start thinking about an assignment, and they are often given specific ideas on how to proceed.

- *Helpful learning aids accompany the book.* Instructors will find useful the checklist of the four steps in essay writing on page 127 and the inside front cover. Also helpful will be the form for planning an essay on page 9 and the list of correction symbols on the inside back cover. The *Instructor's Edition* is made up of the student text followed by an Instructor's Guide featuring hints to the instructor, a model syllabus, and answers for all the activities and tests in the text. An *Instructor's Manual and Test Bank* includes the material in the Instructor's Guide along with thirty supplementary activities and tests. These activities and tests offer practice in a wide range of skills covered in the book, from generating and narrowing a thesis to outlining essays to editing papers for such common mistakes as fragments, verb problems, and run-ons. Both the Instructor's Edition and the Instructor's Manual and Test Bank are available from the local McGraw-Hill representative or by writing to the College English Editor, The McGraw-Hill Companies, Inc., 1221 Avenue of the Americas, New York, New York 10020.

DIFFERENCES BETWEEN THIS BOOK
AND *COLLEGE WRITING SKILLS*

College Writing Skills with Readings includes a Part Five, made up of twenty-five professional reading selections. It also contains, at the end of each chapter in Part Two, an additional writing assignment titled "Writing about a Reading Selection"; this assignment asks students to respond to one of the professional essays in Part Five by writing a paper using the mode of development in question.

CHANGES IN THE FOURTH EDITION OF *COLLEGE WRITING SKILLS WITH READINGS*

Here are the major changes and additions in the new edition of *College Writing Skills with Readings:*

■   The treatment of prewriting in Part One has been enlarged by adding a section titled "Practice in Seeing the Entire Writing Process." The section illustrates and comments on the sequence of stages that a student writer goes through in preparing a paragraph.

■   "Introduction to Essay Development" at the start of Part Two has been revised, and the patterns of development have been rearranged into a more traditional sequence, beginning with description.

■   The chapter on argumentation in Part Two has been expanded to provide more background information on the nature of argument. Students now learn five strategies that they can use to win over readers with differing viewpoints.

■   Some chapters in the handbook in Part Four have been resequenced; a chapter on numbers and abbreviations has been added; and two more tests have been added to the popular editing activities that close the handbook.

■   Five of the readings are new: "Only Daughter," by Sandra Cisneros; "I Became Her Target," by Roger Wilkins; "Propaganda Techniques in Today's Advertising," by Ann McClintock; "How to Deal with a Difficult Boss," by Donna Brown Hogarty; and "Is Sex All That Matters?" by Joyce Garity.

■   Finally, the book is now available in this Instructor's Edition that features a convenient Instructor's Guide at the end of the student text. The guide includes hints to the instructor, a model syllabus, and answers for all the activities and tests in the book.

ACKNOWLEDGMENTS

Reviewers who have contributed to this edition through their helpful comments include Gale Aston, Roxbury Community College; Ellen H. Bell, Manatee Community College; Edna Boykin, Florida Agricultural and Mechanical University; Roseann Cacciola, Rancho Santiago College; Alice Cleveland, College of Marin; John Covolo, Lakeland Community College; Susan Day, Illinois State University; Jeannie Dobson, Greenville Technical College; Linda Wheeler Donahue, Mattatuck Community College; Evelyn Etheridge, Paine College; Elaine Fitzpatrick, Massasoit Community College; R. Douglas Fossek, Santa Barbara City College; Cara Fuchs, Fairleigh Dickinson University; Daniel B. Gallagher, Laredo Junior College; Jan Gerzema, Indiana University Northwest; Dabney Gray, Mississippi University for Women; Linda Eanes Jefferson, Richard Bland College of the College of William and Mary; Leslie K. King, SUNY College at Oswego; Cyril M. Leder, Mott Community College; Patricia Maida, University of the District of Columbia; Mary Mears, Macon College; Michelle Peterson, Santa Barbara City College; Kathleen L. Pickard, Cuyahoga Community College; Carolyn Russell, Rio Hondo College; Rachel Schaffer, Eastern Montana College; Betty Slifer, College of Southern Idaho; Linda Suddeth Smith, Midlands Technical College; and Edna Troiano, Charles County Community College.

I also thank my McGraw-Hill editors, Tim Julet and Peggy Rehberger, for their talented support, and my copyeditor, Sue Gamer, for her superb editing work. Finally, I am grateful to my wife and writing colleague, Judy Nadell, for the major role she played in expanding the chapter on argumentation.

TO
THE
STUDENT

The experience I had writing my first college essay has helped shape this book. I received a C— for the essay. Scrawled beside the grade was the comment, "Not badly written, but ill-conceived." I remember going to the instructor after class, asking about his comment as well as the word *Log* that he had added in the margin at various spots. "What are all these logs you put in my paper?" I asked, trying to make a joke of it. He looked at me a little wonderingly. "Logic, Mr. Langan," he answered, "logic." He went on to explain that I had not thought out my paper clearly. There were actually two ideas rather than one in my thesis, one supporting paragraph had nothing to do with either idea, another paragraph lacked a topic sentence, and so on. I've never forgotten his last words. "If you don't think clearly," he said, "you won't write clearly."

I was speechless, and I felt confused and angry. I didn't like being told that I didn't know how to think. I went back to my room and read over my paper several times. Eventually, I decided that my instructor was right. "No more logs," I said to myself. "I'm going to get these logs out of my papers."

My instructor's advice was invaluable. I learned that if you plan and think through an essay first, you'll have completed a major stage of the work. *College Writing Skills with Readings* develops this idea by breaking down the writing process into a series of easily followed steps.

Part One of the book presents the four basic steps or principles you'll need to write strong essays:

1   Begin with a clearly stated point or thesis.
2   Provide logical, detailed support for your thesis.
3   Organize your supporting material effectively.
4   Revise and edit carefully so that the material is presented in clear, error-free sentences.

Part Two describes a number of different ways you can organize and develop essays. Each chapter opens with a brief introduction followed by several essays written by students. Then comes a series of questions so that you can evaluate the essays in terms of the basic principles explained in Part One. Finally, a number of writing topics are presented, along with hints about prewriting to help you plan and write an effective paper.

Part Three helps with the many types of writing you will do in college: exam essays, summaries, reports, the résumé and job application letter, and the research paper. You will see that all these kinds of writing are variations of the essay form you have already learned.

Part Four offers review and practice in the skills needed to write sentences that are clear, error-free, and varied. Included is a series of selections to sharpen your proofreading and editing ability.

Finally, Part Five consists of a series of high-interest reading selections that will give you many ideas for writing. A special feature of Part Five is an introductory guide to effective reading. Each selection is then accompanied by comprehension questions that will give you practice in key reading skills. In addition, there are discussion questions and writing assignments that will help direct your thinking about each selection.

For your convenience, the book contains the following:

- On page 127 and the inside front cover, there is a checklist of the four basic steps in effective writing.
- On page 9, there is a diagram to use when planning an essay.
- On the inside back cover, there is a list of correction symbols.

Get into the habit of referring to these guides on a regular basis; they can help ensure that you'll produce clearly thought out, well-written essays.

College Writing Skills with Readings will help you learn, practice, and apply the thinking and writing skills you need to communicate effectively. But your starting point must be a determination to do the work needed to become a strong writer. The ability to express yourself clearly and logically can open doors for you, both in school and in your career. If you decide—and only you can decide— that you want this kind of power, this book will help you reach that goal.

John Langan

PART ONE

BASIC PRINCIPLES OF ESSAY WRITING

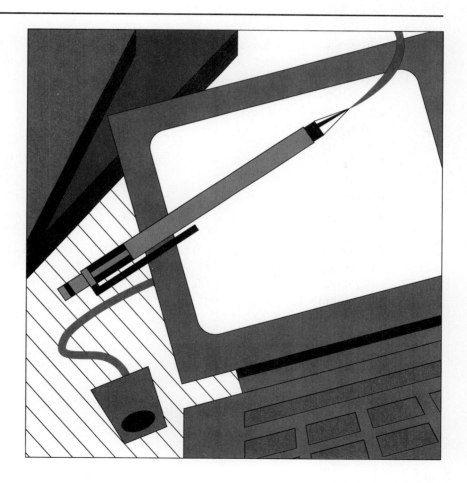

INTRODUCTION TO THE ESSAY FORM

This chapter will explain:

- The importance of supporting a point in writing
- The difference between a paragraph and an essay
- The general structure of an essay

POINT AND SUPPORT

An Important Difference between Writing and Talking

In your everyday conversation, you make all kinds of points or assertions. You say, for example, "It's not safe to walk in our neighborhood after dark"; "My boss is a hard person to work for"; or "Poor study habits keep getting me into trouble." The points that you make concern personal matters as well as, at times, outside issues: "That trade will be a disaster for the team"; "Lots of TV commercials are degrading to women"; "Students should have to work for a year before attending college."

The people you are talking with do not always challenge you to give reasons for your statements. They may know why you feel as you do, or they may already agree with you, or they simply may not want to put you on the spot; and so they do not always ask, "Why?" The people who read what you write, however, may not know you, agree with you, or feel in any way obliged to you. So if you want to communicate effectively with them, you must provide solid evidence for any point you make. An important difference, then, between writing and talking is this: *In writing, any idea that you advance must be supported with specific reasons or details.*

Think of your readers as reasonable persons. They will not take your views on faith, but they are willing to accept what you say as long as you support it. So remember to support with specific evidence any statement that you make.

Point and Support in a Paragraph

In conversation you might say to a friend who has suggested a movie, "No thanks. Going to the movies is just too much of a hassle. Parking, people, everything." From shared past experiences, your friend may know what you are talking about, so that you will not have to explain your statement. But in writing, your point would have to be backed up with specific reasons and details.

Below is a paragraph on why moviegoing is a nuisance. A *paragraph* is a short paper of around 150 words. It usually consists of an opening point called a *topic sentence* followed by a series of sentences which support that point.

The Hazards of Moviegoing

Although I love movies, going to see them drives me slightly crazy. First of all, getting to the movie can take a lot of time. I have a thirty-five-minute drive down a congested highway. Then, with a popular film, I usually have to wait in a long line at the ticket booth. Another problem is that the theater itself is seldom a pleasant place to be. A musty smell suggests that there has been no fresh air in the theater since it was built. Half the seats seem to be falling apart. And the floor often has a sticky coating that gets on your shoes. The worst problem of all is some of the other moviegoers. Kids run up and down the aisle. Teenagers laugh and shout at the screen. People of all ages loudly drop soda cups and popcorn tubs, cough and burp, and elbow you out of the armrest on either side of your seat. All in all, I would rather stay home and wait for the latest movie hits to appear on TV in the safety and comfort of my own living room.

Notice what the supporting evidence has done here. It has provided you, the reader, with a basis for understanding *why* the writer makes the point that is made. Through this specific evidence, the writer has explained and successfully communicated the idea that moviegoing can be a nuisance.

The evidence that supports the point in a paper often consists of a series of reasons followed by examples and details that support the reasons. That is true of the paragraph above: three reasons are provided, with examples and details that back up those reasons. Supporting evidence in a paper can also consist of anecdotes, personal experiences, facts, statistics, and the opinions of experts.

Activity

The paragraph on moviegoing, like almost any piece of effective writing, has two essential parts: (1) a point is advanced, and (2) that point is then supported. Taking a minute to outline the paragraph will help you understand these basic parts clearly. Write in the following space the point that has been advanced in the paragraph. Then add the words needed to complete the outline of the paragraph.

Point _____

_____

Support   1. *Time getting there* _____

        a. *Long drive* _____

        b. _____

   2. _____

        a. _____

        b. _____

        c. _____

   3. _____

        a. _____

        b. _____

        c. *People of all ages* _____

          (1) _____

          (2) *Cough and burp* _____

          (3) _____

Point and Support in an Essay

Much of your college writing will be in the form of five-hundred-word essays—
papers of several paragraphs that support a single point. An *essay* typically consists
of an introductory paragraph, three supporting paragraphs, and a concluding paragraph. The central idea, or point, developed in an essay is called a *thesis statement*
rather than, as in a paragraph, a topic sentence. A thesis appears in the introductory
paragraph, and the specific support for the thesis appears in the paragraphs that
follow. The supporting paragraphs allow for a fuller treatment of the evidence
that backs up the central point than would be possible in a single-paragraph paper.

GENERAL STRUCTURE OF AN ESSAY

A Model Essay

The following model should help you understand clearly the form of an essay.
The writer of the paragraph on moviegoing later decided to develop her subject
more fully. Here is the essay that resulted.

The Hazards of Moviegoing

I am a movie fanatic. When friends want to know what picture won the Oscar in 1980 or who played the police chief in *Jaws,* they ask me. My friends, though, have stopped asking me if I want to go out to the movies. The problems in getting to the theater, the theater itself, and the behavior of some patrons are all reasons why I often wait for a movie to show up on TV.

First of all, just getting to the theater presents difficulties. Leaving a home equipped with a TV and a video recorder isn't an attractive idea on a humid, cold, or rainy night. Even if the weather cooperates, there is still a thirty-minute drive to the theater down a congested highway, followed by the hassle of looking for a parking space. And then there are the lines. After hooking yourself to the end of a human chain, you worry about whether there will be enough tickets, whether you will get seats together, and whether many people will sneak into the line ahead of you.

Once you have made it to the box office and gotten your tickets, you are confronted with the problems of the theater itself. If you are in one of the run-down older theaters, you must adjust to the musty smell of seldom-cleaned carpets. Escaped springs lurk in the faded plush or cracked leather seats, and half the seats you sit in seem loose or tilted so that you sit at a strange angle. The newer twin and quad theaters offer their own problems. Sitting in an area only one-quarter the size of a regular theater, moviegoers often have to put up with the sound of the movie next door. This is especially jarring when the other movie involves racing cars or a karate war and you are trying to enjoy a quiet love story. And whether the theater is old or new, it will have floors that seem to be coated with rubber cement. By the end of a movie, shoes almost have to be pried off the floor because they have become sealed to a deadly compound of spilled soda, hardening bubble gum, and crushed Ju-Jubes.

Some of the patrons are even more of a problem than the theater itself. Little kids race up and down the aisles, usually in giggling packs. Teenagers try to impress their friends by talking back to the screen, whistling, and making what they consider to be hilarious noises. Adults act as if they were at home in their own living rooms and comment loudly on the ages of the stars or why movies aren't as good anymore. And people of all ages crinkle candy wrappers, stick gum on their seats, and drop popcorn tubs or cups of crushed ice and soda on the floor. They also cough and burp, squirm endlessly in their seats, file out for repeated trips to the rest rooms or concession stand, and elbow you out of the armrest on either side of your seat.

After arriving home from the movies one night, I decided that I was not going to be a moviegoer anymore. I was tired of the problems involved in getting to the movies and dealing with the theater itself and some of the patrons. The next day I arranged to have cable TV service installed in my home. I may now see movies a bit later than other people, but I'll be more relaxed watching box office hits in the comfort of my own living room.

"The Hazards of Moviegoing" is a good example of the standard short essay you will write in college English. It is a composition of slightly over five hundred words that consists of a one-paragraph introduction, a three-paragraph body, and a one-paragraph conclusion. The roles of these paragraphs are described and illustrated below.

Introductory Paragraph

The introductory paragraph of an essay should start with several sentences that attract the reader's interest. It should then advance the central idea or thesis that will be developed in the essay. The thesis often includes a plan of development— a ''preview'' of the major points that will support the thesis. These supporting points should be listed in the order in which they will appear in the essay. In some cases, the plan of development is presented in a sentence separate from the thesis; in other cases, it is omitted.

Activity

1. In ''The Hazards of Moviegoing,'' which sentences are used to attract the reader's interest?
   a. First sentence
   b. First two sentences
   c. First three sentences
2. The thesis in ''The Hazards of Moviegoing'' is presented in which sentence?
   a. Third sentence
   b. Fourth sentence
3. The thesis contains a plan of development.
   a. Yes
   b. No
4. Write down the words in the thesis that announce the three major supporting points in the essay:

   a. _____

   b. _____

   c. _____

Body: Supporting Paragraphs

Most essays have three supporting points, developed at length over three separate paragraphs. (Some essays will have two supporting points, others four or more. For the purposes of this book, your goal will be three supporting points for most essays.) Each of the supporting paragraphs should begin with a *topic sentence* that states the point to be detailed in that paragraph. Just as the thesis provides a focus for the entire essay, the topic sentences provide a focus for each supporting paragraph.

Activity

1. What is the topic sentence for the first supporting paragraph of the essay?

   _____

   _____

2. The first topic sentence is then supported by details about (*fill in the missing words*):

   a. _____

   b. _____

   c. *Long ticket line*
      _____

3. What is the topic sentence for the second supporting paragraph of the essay?

   _____

   _____

4. The second topic sentence is then supported by details about (*fill in the missing words*):

   a. *Problems of old theaters (mustiness and   )*

   b. *Problems of new theaters (and sound of adjoining movie)*

   c. *Problem of old and new theaters (   )*

5. What is the topic sentence for the third supporting paragraph of the essay?

   _____

   _____

6. The third topic sentence is then supported by details about (*fill in the missing words*):

   a. *Patrons (kids,   , and   )*

   b. *Distractions caused by people of all ages*

Concluding Paragraph

The concluding paragraph often summarizes the essay by restating briefly the thesis and, at times, the main supporting points of the essay. In addition, the writer often presents a concluding thought about the subject of the paper.

Activity

1. Which two sentences in the concluding paragraph restate the thesis and supporting points of the essay?

    a. First and second   b. Second and third   c. Third and fourth

2. Which sentence contains the concluding thought of the essay?

    a. First   b. Second   c. Third   d. Fourth

Diagram of an Essay

The following diagram shows you at a glance the different parts of a standard college essay, also known as a *one-three-one essay*. This diagram will serve as a helpful guide when you are writing or evaluating essays.

Title of the Essay

Introduction
Opening remarks to catch reader's interest
Thesis statement
Plan of development (optional)

Body
Topic sentence 1 (supporting point 1)
Specific evidence

Topic sentence 2 (supporting point 2)
Specific evidence

Topic sentence 3 (supporting point 3)
Specific evidence

Conclusion
Summary (optional)
General closing remarks
(Or both)

WHY WRITE ESSAYS?

Mastering the essay form will help, first of all, on a practical level. For other courses, you will write specific forms of essays, such as the report and research paper. Many of your written tests will be in the form of essay exams. In addition, the basic structure of an essay will help in career-related writing, from a job application letter to the memos and reports that may become part of your work.

On a more abstract level, essay writing serves other valuable purposes. It will make you a better reader. You will become more aware of other writers' ideas and the evidence they provide (or fail to provide) to support those ideas. Most important, essay writing will make you a better thinker. Writing an essay forces you to sort out and organize your ideas and think them through clearly. You will learn to identify just what your ideas are and what support exists to back them up. Essay writing, in short, will give you practice in the process of clear and logical reasoning. Your ability to recognize ideas and to measure their validity will help you make sound decisions not just in school and your career but in all phases of your everyday life.

IMPORTANT
FACTORS
IN WRITING

This chapter will discuss the importance of:

- Your attitude about writing
- Developing a subject
- Keeping a journal
- Prewriting
- Outlining
- Revising, editing, and proofreading

The previous chapter introduced you to the essay form, and the chapters that follow will explain the basic steps in writing an essay and the basic standards for evaluating it. The purpose of this chapter is to describe a number of important general factors that will help you create good papers. These factors include (1) having the right attitude about writing; (2) developing a subject; (3) keeping a journal; (4) prewriting, or having ways to get started in writing; (5) outlining; and (6) revising, editing, and proofreading.

11

Your Attitude about Writing

One way to wreck your chances of learning how to write competently is to believe that writing is a "natural gift." People with this attitude think that they are the only ones for whom writing is an unbearably difficult activity. They feel that everyone else finds writing easy or at least tolerable. Such people typically say, "I'm not any good at writing" or "English was not one of my good subjects." They imply that they simply do not have a talent for writing, while others do. The result of this attitude is that people do not do their best when they write— or, even worse, that they hardly ever try to write. Their attitude becomes a self-fulfilling prophecy: their writing fails chiefly because they have brainwashed themselves into thinking that they don't have the "natural talent" needed to write. Unless their attitude changes, they probably will not learn how to write effectively.

A realistic attitude about writing—to replace the mistaken notion of writing as a "natural gift"—should build on the following two ideas.

1   *Writing is hard work for almost everyone.* It is difficult to do the intense and active thinking that clear writing demands. (Perhaps television has made us all so passive that the active thinking necessary in both writing and reading now seems harder than ever.) It is frightening to sit down before a blank sheet of paper and know that an hour later, nothing on it may be worth keeping. It is frustrating to discover how much of a challenge it is to transfer thoughts and feelings from one's head onto a sheet of paper. It is upsetting to find that an apparently simple writing subject often turns out to be complicated. But writing is not an automatic process: we will not get something for nothing—and we should not expect to. Competent writing results only from plain hard work—from determination, sweat, and head-on battle.

2   *Writing is a skill.* Writing is a skill like driving, typing, or preparing a good meal. Like any skill, it can be learned—if you decide that you are going to learn and then really work at it. This book will give you the extensive practice needed to develop your writing skills.

Activity

Answering these questions will help you evaluate your attitude about writing.

1.   How much practice were you given writing compositions in high school?

_____ Much   _____ Some   _____ Little

2. How much feedback (positive or negative comments) from teachers were you given on your compositions?

_____ Much   _____ Some   _____ Little

3. How did your teachers seem to regard your writing?

_____ Good   _____ Fair   _____ Poor

4. Do you feel that some people have a gift for writing and others do not?

_____ Yes   _____ Sometimes   _____ No

5. When do you start writing a paper?

_____ Several days before it is due

_____ About a day before it is due

_____ At the last possible minute

Many people who answer *Little* to questions 1 and 2 also answer *Poor, Yes,* and *At the last possible minute* to the other questions. On the other hand, people who answer *Much* or *Some* to questions 1 and 2 tend to have more favorable responses to the other questions. People with little *experience* in writing often have understandably negative feelings about their writing *ability*. But they should realize that writing is a skill they can learn with practice.

Developing a Subject

CHOOSING AND LEARNING ABOUT YOUR SUBJECT

Whenever possible, try to write on a subject which interests you. You will then find it easier to put the necessary time into your work. Even more important, try to write on a subject that you already know something about. If you do not have direct experience with a subject, you should at least have indirect experience—knowledge gained through thinking, prewriting (to be explained on pages 17–26), reading, or talking about the subject.

If you are asked to write on a topic about which you have no experience or knowledge, you should do whatever research is required to gain the information you need. The chapter "Using the Library" on pages 268–285 will show you how to use the library to look up relevant information. Without direct or indirect experience, or information gained through research, you will not be able to provide the specific evidence needed to develop the point you are trying to make. Your writing will be starved for specifics.

DISCOVERING YOUR SUBJECT

At times you will not know your subject when you begin to write. Instead, you will discover it in the *process* of writing. For example, when the author of the paper on moviegoing in the previous chapter first sat down to write, her initial topic was all the things that bothered her about movies. As she began to accumulate details, she quickly realized that this topic was too broad. She then narrowed her topic down to the drawbacks of moviegoing. In other words, when she began to write, she only *thought* she knew what the focus of her paper was. In fact, she *discovered her subject in the course of writing*.

Another writer, without at first knowing his exact point, knew he wanted to write about a time when he had belonged to a gang and cruelly mugged someone. He began by getting down the grim details of the actual mugging. As he developed the details, he realized gradually what point he wanted to make. The paper that resulted, "A Night of Violence," appears on pages 139–140.

A third student author started with the idea that using computers in the classroom can be a real challenge. As she began getting details onto paper, her point became clearer, and she realized that she wanted to argue that computers in the classroom are a bad idea. Her paper, "A Vote against Computers," is on pages 222–223.

The moral of these examples is that sometimes you must write a bit in order to find out just what you want to write. Writing can help you think about and explore your topic and decide on the final direction of your paper. The techniques presented in the section ahead on ''Prewriting'' starting on page 17 will suggest specific ways to discover and develop a subject.

One related feature of the writing process bears mention. Do not feel that you must proceed in a straight line when you write. That is, do not assume that the writing process must be a railroad track on which you go directly from your central point to ''supporting detail one'' to ''supporting detail two'' to ''supporting detail three'' to your concluding paragraph. Instead, proceed in whatever way seems most comfortable as you draft the paper. You may want to start by writing the closing section of your paper or by developing your third supporting detail.

Do whatever is easiest—and as you get material down on the page, it will make what you have left to do a bit easier. Sometimes, of course, as you work on one section, it may happen that another focal point for your paper will emerge. That's fine: if your writing tells you that it wants to be something else, then revise or start over as needed to take advantage of that discovery. Your goal is to wind up with a paper that makes a point and supports it solidly. Be ready to change direction and to make whatever adjustments are needed to reach your goal.

Activity 1

Answer the following questions.

1. What are three ways to get the knowledge you need to write on a subject?

    a. _____

    b. _____

    c. _____

2. A student begins to write a paper about the best job he ever had. After writing for about half an hour, he realizes that his details are all about what a wonderful person his boss was. What has happened in the process of writing?

    _____

3. Suppose you want to write a paper about problems that come with a holiday season. You think you can discuss family, personal, and financial problems. You feel you have the most details about financial problems. Should you start with that area, or with one of the other two areas?

    _____

Activity 2

Write for five minutes about the house, dormitory, or apartment where you live. Simply write down whatever details come to you. Don't worry about being neat; just pile up as many details as you can.

Afterward, go through the material. Try to find a potential focus within all those details. Do the details suggest a simple point that you could make about the place where you live? If so, you've seen a small example of how writing about a topic can be an excellent way of discovering a point about that topic.

Keeping a Journal

Because writing is a skill, the more you practice it, the better you will become at it. One excellent way to get writing practice is to keep a daily (or ''almost daily'') journal.

At some point during the day—perhaps during a study period after your last class of the day, or right before dinner, or right before going to bed—spend fifteen minutes or so writing in your journal. Keep in mind that you do not have to plan what to write about, or be in the mood to write, or worry about making mistakes as you write; just write down whatever words come out. You should write at least one page in each session.

You may want to use a notebook that you can easily carry with you for on-the-spot writing. Or you may decide to write on loose-leaf paper that can be transferred later to a journal folder on your desk. No matter how you proceed, be sure to date all entries.

The content of your journal should be some of the specific happenings, thoughts, and feelings of the day. Your starting point may be a comment by an instructor, a classmate, or a family member; a gesture or action that has amused, angered, confused, or depressed you; something you have read or seen on television—anything, really, that has caught your attention and that you decide to explore a bit in writing. Some journal entries may focus on a single subject; others may wander from one topic to another.

Your instructor may ask you to make journal entries a specific number of times a week, for a specific number of weeks. He or she may have you turn in your journal every so often for review and feedback. If you are keeping the journal on your own, try to make entries three to five times a week every week of the semester.

Keeping a journal will help you develop the habit of thinking on paper, and it can help you make writing a familiar part of your life. Your journal can also serve as a source of ideas for possible papers.

Following is an excerpt from one student's journal. As you read, look for a general point and supporting material that could be the basis for an interesting paper.

September 6

My first sociology class was tonight. The parking lot was jammed when I got there. I thought I was going to be late for class. A guard had us park on a field next to the regular lot. When I got to the room, it had the usual painted-cinder-block construction. Every school I have ever been in since first grade seems to be made of cinder block. Everybody sat there without saying anything, waiting for the instructor to arrive. I think they were all a bit nervous like me. I hoped there wasn't going to be a ton of work in the course. I think I was also afraid of looking foolish somehow. This goes back to grade school, when I wasn't a very good student and teachers sometimes embarrassed me in class. I didn't like grade school, and I hated high school. Now here I am six years later in college of all places. Who would have thought that I would end up here? The instructor appeared—a woman who I think was a bit nervous herself. I think I like her. Her name is Barbara Hanlin. She says we should call her Barbara. We got right into it, but it was interesting stuff. I like the fact that she asks questions, but then she lets you volunteer. I always hated it when teachers would call on you whether you wanted to answer or not. I also like the fact that she answers the questions and doesn't just leave you hanging. She takes the time to write important ideas on the board. I also like the way she laughs. This class may be OK.

Activity

1. If the writer of the journal entry above was looking for ideas for an essay, he could probably find several in this single entry. For example, he might write a narrative about the roundabout way he apparently wound up in college. See if you can find in the entry an idea that might be the basis for an interesting essay, and write your point in the space below.

_____

2. Take fifteen minutes right now to write a journal entry on this day in your life. On a separate sheet of paper, just start writing about anything that you have seen, said, heard, thought, or felt today, and let your thoughts take you where they may.

Prewriting

If you are like many people, you may sometimes have trouble getting started with your writing. A mental block may develop when you sit down with a blank sheet of paper in front of you. You may not be able to think of a topic or an interesting slant on a topic. Or you may have trouble coming up with interesting and relevant details that you can use to support your topic. Even after starting a paper, you may hit snags or moments of wondering, "Where to go next?"

The following pages describe five techniques that will help you think about and develop a topic and get words down on paper. These techniques, which are often called *prewriting* techniques, are a central part of the writing process. They are (1) brainstorming, (2) freewriting, (3) diagramming, (4) making a list, and (5) preparing a scratch outline.

TECHNIQUE 1: BRAINSTORMING

In *brainstorming,* you generate ideas and details by asking as many questions as you can think of about your subject. Such questions include *What? When? Why? How? Where?* and *Who?*

Following is an example of how one student, Tim, used brainstorming to generate material for a paper. Tim felt he could write about a depressing diner he had visited, but he was having trouble getting started. So he asked himself a series of questions about the experience and, as a result, accumulated a series of details that provided the basis for the paper he finally wrote.

Here are the questions Tim asked and the answers he wrote:

<u>Why</u> did I stop at the diner?	I was on the way home after driving all day, and I was tired. I decided to get a cup of coffee at the next diner.
<u>How</u> do I feel about diners?	I've always liked diners. I was looking forward to a friendly waitress and talk with the customers at the counter.
<u>What</u> was the diner like?	It was lonely. There were only a few people, and it was very quiet. Only one waitress was on duty. Even the parking lot looked lonely—trash was blowing around, and it was raining.
<u>Who</u> was in the diner?	Two workmen were sitting at the counter. There was also a young man sitting by himself at the far end of the counter. He looked depressed. There was a middle-aged couple in a booth. They weren't talking to each other—one was doodling, the other staring.
<u>What</u> happened at the diner?	I got out of there as fast as possible. I just wanted to get away from that lonely place and reach my home.

After brainstorming, Tim's next step was to prepare a scratch outline. He then prepared several drafts of the paper. The effective essay that eventually resulted from Tim's prewriting techniques appears on pages 130–131.

Activity

To get a sense of the brainstorming process, use a sheet of paper to ask yourself a series of questions about a *pleasant* diner you have visited. See how many details you can accumulate about that diner in ten minutes.

TECHNIQUE 2: FREEWRITING

When you do not know what to write about a subject, or when you start to write but then become blocked, freewriting sometimes helps. In *freewriting,* you write without stopping for ten minutes or so. You do not worry about checking your spelling or punctuation, erasing mistakes, or finding exact words. If you get stuck, you write, ''I am looking for something to say,'' or repeat words until you get an idea. There is no need to feel inhibited, since mistakes do not count and you do not have to hand in your paper.

Freewriting will limber up your writing muscles and make you familiar with the act of writing. It is a way to break through mental blocks about writing and the fear of making errors. As you do not have to worry about making mistakes, you can concentrate on discovering what you want to say about a subject. Your initial ideas and impressions will often become clearer after you have gotten them down on paper. Through continued practice in freewriting, you will develop the habit of thinking as you write. And you will learn a technique that is a helpful way to get started on almost any paper.

Here is the freewriting that one student did to accumulate details for a paper on why she had decided to put her mother in a nursing home.

I'm still upset about the whole thing, but seeing everything going downhill really forced the decision. Mom just needed so much help with all the pills and dressing and bathing. She needed more help than Daddy could handle by himself. Hospital bills in this country are outrageous, and Medicare doesn't pay for everything. Mom needed someone to work out her special diet because it was so complicated. The wheelchair rental was expensive. The hardest thing was the fact that she was breaking down emotionally, saying things like, ''You don't care about me.'' We cared, but we worried about Dad. What an enormous strain he was under in all this. Mom really acted emotionally disturbed at times. She would call for an ambulance and tell them she was dying. Dad started to lose weight. The bills coming in started to fill an entire shopping bag. Some people think we were cruel, but we didn't have any other choice. My father doesn't drive, so he was walking all over town to get medicine and food.

This writer's next step was to use the freewriting as the basis for a scratch outline. The paper that eventually resulted from her freewriting, a scratch outline (see "Technique 5" below), and a good deal of rewriting appears on pages 167–168.

Activity

To get a sense of the freewriting process, take a sheet of paper and freewrite about some of your own everyday worries. See how many ideas and details you can accumulate in ten minutes.

TECHNIQUE 3: DIAGRAMMING

Diagramming, also known as *mapping* or *clustering,* is another prewriting activity that can help you generate ideas and details about a topic. In diagramming, you use lines, boxes, arrows, and circles to show relationships between the ideas and details that come to you.

Diagramming is especially helpful to people who like to do their thinking in a very visual way. Whether you use a diagram, and just how you proceed with it, is up to you.

Here is the diagram that one student, Todd, prepared for a paper on differences between McDonald's and a fancy restaurant. This diagram, with its clear picture of relationships, was especially helpful for the comparison-contrast paper that Todd was doing. His final essay appears on pages 179–180.

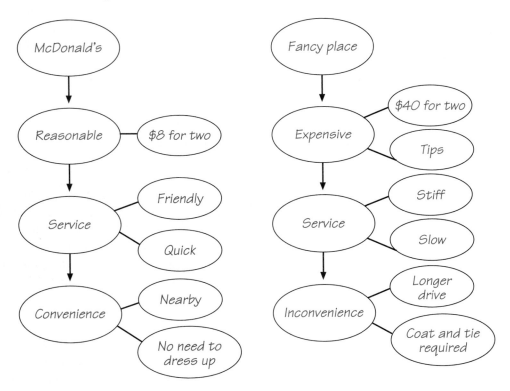

Activity

To get a sense of diagramming, use a sheet of paper to make a diagram of differences between two instructors or two jobs. See how many ideas and details you can accumulate in ten minutes.

TECHNIQUE 4: MAKING A LIST

Another prewriting technique is *making a list*. To get started on a paper, list as many different items as you can think of concerning your topic. Do not worry about repeating yourself, about sorting out major points from minor details, or about spelling or punctuating correctly. Simply make a list of everything about your subject that occurs to you. Your aim is to generate details and to accumulate as much raw material for writing as possible.

Following is a list prepared by one student, Jan, who was gathering details for an essay called "Benefits of Television." Her first step was simply to jot down thoughts and details that occurred to her.

> Entertainment
> Movies and sports events
> Video games
> Educational (important—save for last)
> Relaxing after work
> Covers major world events
> Can be used with computers
> Reduce stress (used for high-blood-pressure patients)
> Rent videocassettes
> Shows for children (Sesame Street)
> Special cable services (sports, concerts)
> College courses on TV

Notice that partway down her list Jan put in parentheses a note to herself that one thought (about the educational benefits of television) seems most important and should be saved for last. Very often, as you make a list, ideas about how to develop and organize a paper will occur to you. Jot them down.

Making a list is an excellent way to get started. Often, you then go on to make a scratch outline and write the first draft of your paper. (A scratch outline for Jan's list appears in the next section.)

Activity

To get a sense of making a list, use a sheet of paper to list specific problems you will face this semester. See how many ideas and details you can accumulate in ten minutes.

TECHNIQUE 5: PREPARING A SCRATCH OUTLINE

A scratch outline can often be the *single most helpful technique* for writing a good paper. It is an excellent complement to the prewriting techniques already mentioned. In a *scratch outline,* you think carefully about the exact point you are making, about the exact details you will use to support it, and about the exact order in which you will arrange them. The scratch outline is a plan or blueprint to help you achieve a unified, supported, and organized composition.

When you are planning an essay consisting of an introduction, three supporting paragraphs, and a conclusion (this is known as a *one-three-one* essay), a scratch outline is especially important. It may be only a few words, but it will be the bedrock on which your whole essay will rest.

Here is the scratch outline Jan prepared for her general list on television:

Television can have real benefits.
1. Relaxation
2. Entertainment
3. Education

This brief outline made it clear to Jan that she could develop her essay on the basis of three distinct supporting points. While the outline appears simple, it represents a good deal of thinking on Jan's part. In the essays that you write, you should always try to develop such a basic outline.

With this outline, Jan knew she had a solid plan and a workable paper. As the next step in her writing process, she then felt comfortable about developing her scratch outline further by detailing the items that fit under each benefit:

1. Relaxation
    a. After work
    b. Reduce stress
2. Entertainment
    a. Network programming
    b. Cable programming
    c. Videocassettes and videodisks
    d. Video games
3. Education
    a. Children's shows
    b. College courses
    c. World events
    d. Computer capability

These scratch outlines enabled Jan to decide what to put into the paper, and in what order. Without having to write actual sentences, she took a giant step toward a paper that is unified (she left out items that are not related), supported (she added items that develop her point), and organized (she arranged the items in a logical way). These criteria for an effective essay are discussed on pages 95–118; and the essay that resulted from Jan's list and outlines is on page 103.

Outlining is not only a prewriting technique; it is an important factor throughout the writing process. Beginning on page 26, outlining is described in more detail.

Activity

To get a sense of preparing a scratch outline, develop such an outline on reasons why you did or did not do well in high school. See how many ideas and details you can accumulate in ten minutes.

USING ALL FIVE PREWRITING TECHNIQUES

Very often a scratch outline follows brainstorming, freewriting, diagramming, and making a list. At other times, however, the scratch outline may substitute for the other four techniques. Also, you may use several techniques almost simultaneously when writing a paper. You may, for example, ask questions while making a list; you may diagram and outline a list as you write it; you may ask yourself questions and then freewrite answers to them. The five techniques are all ways to help you go about writing a paper.

Activity 1

Answer the following questions.

1. Which of the prewriting techniques do you already practice?

   _____ Brainstorming   _____ Making a list

   _____ Freewriting   _____ Preparing a scratch outline

   _____ Diagramming

2. Which prewriting technique involves asking questions about your topic?

   _____

3. Which prewriting technique shows in a very visual way the relationship between ideas and details?

   _____

4. Which prewriting technique involves writing quickly about your topic without being concerned about grammar or spelling?

_____

5. Which prewriting technique is almost always part of writing an essay?

_____

6. Which prewriting techniques do you think will work best for you?

_____

Activity 2

Below are examples of how the five prewriting techniques could be used to develop the topic "Problems of Combining Work and College." Identify each technique by writing B (for brainstorming), F (for freewriting), D (for the diagram), L (for the list), or SO (for the scratch outline) in the answer space.

_____

Never enough time
Miss campus parties
Had to study (only two free hours a night)
Give up activities with friends
No time to rewrite papers
Can't stay at school to play video games or talk to friends
Friends don't call me to go out anymore
Sunday no longer relaxed day—have to study
Missing sleep I should be getting
Grades aren't as good as they could be
Can't watch favorite TV shows
Really need the extra money
Tired when I sit down to study at nine o'clock

_____

What are some of the problems of combining work and school?

Schoolwork suffers because I don't have time to study or rewrite papers. I've had to give up things I enjoy, like sleep and touch football. I can't get into the social life at college, because I have to work right after class.

How have these problems changed my life?

My grades aren't as good as they were when I didn't work. Some of my friends have stopped calling me. My relationship with a girl I liked fell apart because I couldn't spend much time with her. I miss TV.

<u>What</u> do I do in a typical day?

I get up at 7 to make an 8 A.M. class. I have classes till 1:30, and then I drive to the supermarket where I work. I work till 7 P.M., and then I drive home and eat dinner. After I take a shower and relax for a half hour, it's about 9. This gives me only a couple of hours to study—read textbooks, do math exercises, write essays. My eyes start to close well before I go to bed at 11.

<u>Why</u> do I keep up this schedule?

I can't afford to go to school without working, and I need a degree to get the accounting job I want. If I invest my time now, I'll have a better future.

_____

Juggling a job and college has created major difficulties in my life.

1. Little time for studying
    a. Not reading textbooks
    b. Not rewriting papers
    c. Little studying for tests
2. Little time for enjoying social side of college
    a. During school
    b. After school
3. No time for personal pleasures
    a. Favorite TV shows
    b. Sunday football games
    c. Sleeping late

_____

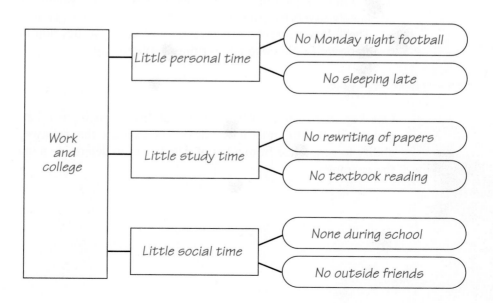

_____

It's hard working and going to school at the same time. I never realized how much I'd have to give up. I won't be quitting my job because I need the money and the people are friendly at the place where I work. I've had to give up a lot more than I thought. We used to play touch football games every Sunday. They were fun and we'd go out for drinks afterwards. Sundays now are for catch-up work with my courses. I have to catch up because I don't get home every day until 7, and I have to eat dinner first before studying. Sometimes I'm so hungry I just eat cookies or chips. Anyway, by the time I take a shower it's 9 P.M. or later and I'm already feeling tired. I've been up since 7 A.M. Sometimes I write an English paper in twenty minutes and don't even read it over. I feel that I'm missing out on a lot in college. The other day some people I like were sitting in the cafeteria listening to music and talking. I would have given anything to stay and not have to go to work. I almost called in sick. I used to get invited to parties but I don't much anymore. My friends know I'm not going to be able to make it, so they don't bother. I can't sleep late on weekends or watch TV during the week.

Outlining

As already mentioned (see page 22), outlining is central to writing a good paper. An outline lets you see, and work on, the bare bones of a paper, without the distraction of a clutter of words and sentences. It develops your ability to think in a clear and logical manner. Outlining provides a quick check on whether your paper will be *unified*. It also suggests right at the start whether your paper will be adequately *supported*. And it shows you how to plan a paper that is *well organized*.

The following series of exercises will help you develop the outlining skills so important to planning and writing a solid essay.

Activity 1

One key to effective outlining is the ability to distinguish between major ideas and details that fit under those ideas. The exercise that follows will develop your ability to generalize from a list of details and to determine a major thought. Note the examples.

Examples

Writing instruments

Pencil
Ball-point pen
Crayon
Felt-tip marker

Outer garments

Coat
Shawl
Jacket
Cape

1. _____

Spiderman
Superman
Wonder Woman
Batman

2. _____

Gas
Electricity
Water
Phone

3. _____

Boston Globe
The New York Times
Washington Post
Philadelphia Inquirer

4. _____

Tinsel
Mistletoe
Lights
Wreaths

5. _____

Chicken
Turkey
Cornish game hen
Duck

6. _____

Dictionary
Almanac
Encyclopedia
Atlas

7. _____

Chain
Handlebars
Gearshift
Wheel spokes

8. _____

Loans
Checking accounts
Savings accounts
Check cashing

9. _____

Wrinkles
Hearing loss
Brittle bones
Thinning hair

10. _____

Crutch
Cane
Metal walker
Artificial leg

Activity 2

Major and minor ideas are mixed together in the two lists below. Put the ideas into logical order by filling in the outlines that follow.

1. Thesis: My high school had three problem areas.

Involved with drugs	a. _____
Leaky ceilings	(1) _____
Students	(2) _____
Unwilling to help after class	
Formed cliques	b. _____
Teachers	(1) _____
Buildings	(2) _____
Ill-equipped gym	c. _____
Much too strict	(1) _____
	(2) _____

2. Thesis: Working as a dishwasher in a restaurant was my worst job.

Ten-hour shifts	a. _____
Heat in kitchen	(1) _____
Working conditions	(2) _____
Minimum wage	
Hours changed every week	b. _____
No bonus for overtime	(1) _____
Hours	(2) _____
Pay	c. _____
Noisy work area	(1) _____
	(2) _____

Activity 3

Again, major and minor ideas are mixed together in the two following lists. In addition, in each outline one of the three major ideas is missing and must be added. Put the ideas into a logical order by filling in the outlines that follow and adding a third major idea.

1. Thesis: Joining an aerobics class has many benefits.

Make new friends   a. _____

Reduces mental stress   (1) _____

Social benefits   (2) _____

Strengthens heart

Improves self-image   b. _____

Mental benefits   (1) _____

Tones muscles   (2) _____

Meet interesting instructors   c. _____

                           (1) _____

                           (2) _____

2. Thesis: My favorite times in school were the days before holiday vacations.

Lighter workload   a. _____

Teachers more relaxed   (1) _____

Pep rallies   (2) _____

Less work in class

Friendlier atmosphere   b. _____

Less homework   (1) _____

Holiday concerts   (2) _____

Students happy about vacation   c. _____

                           (1) _____

                           (2) _____

Activity 4

Read the essay on the following pages and outline it in the spaces provided. Write out the central point and topic sentences and summarize in a few words the supporting material that fits under each topic sentence. One item is summarized for you as an example.

Losing Touch

Steve, a typical American, stays home on workdays. He plugs into his   1
personal computer terminal in order to hook up with the office. After work, he
puts on his stereo headphones, watches a movie on his home video recorder, or
challenges himself to a game of electronic baseball. On many days, Steve doesn't
talk to any other human beings, and he doesn't see any people except those on
television. Steve is imaginary, but his lifestyle is very possible. The inventions of
modern technology seem to be cutting us off from contact with our fellow human
beings.

Thesis: _____

_____

The world of business is one area in which technology is isolating us. Many   2
people now work alone at home. With access to a large central computer, employees
such as secretaries, insurance agents, and accountants do their jobs at display
terminals in their own homes. They no longer actually have to see the people they're
dealing with. In addition, employees are often paid in an impersonal way. Workers'
salaries are automatically credited to their bank accounts, eliminating the need for
paychecks. Fewer people stand in line with their coworkers to receive their pay
or cash their checks. Finally, personal banking is becoming a detached process.
Customers interact with machines rather than people to deposit or withdraw money
from their accounts. Even some bank loans are approved or rejected, not in an
interview with a loan officer, but through a display on a computer screen.

First topic sentence: _____

_____

Support: 1. _Many people now work alone at home._____

2. _____

3. _____

a. _____

b. _____

Another area that technology is changing is entertainment. Music, for instance,   3
was once a group experience. People listened to music at concert halls or in small
social gatherings. For many people now, however, music is a solitary experience.
Walking along the street or sitting in their living rooms, they wear headphones to
build a wall of music around them. Movie entertainment is changing, too. Movies
used to be social events. Now, fewer people are going out to see a movie. Many
more are choosing to wait for a film to appear on cable television. Instead of being
involved with the laughter, applause, or hisses of the audience, viewers watch movies
in the isolation of their own living rooms.

Second topic sentence: _____

_____

Support: 1. _____

            2. _____

     Education is a third important area in which technology is separating us from others. From elementary schools to colleges, students spend more and more time sitting by themselves in front of computers. The computers give them feedback, while teachers spend more time tending the computers and less time interacting with their classes. A similar problem occurs in homes. As more families buy computers, increasing numbers of students practice their math and reading skills with software programs instead of with their friends, brothers and sisters, and parents. Last, alienation is occurring as a result of another high-tech invention, videotapes. People are buying videocassette tapes on subjects such as cooking, real estate investment, speaking, and speed-reading. They then practice their skills at home rather than by taking group classes in which a rich human interaction can occur.   4

Third topic sentence: _____

_____

Support: 1. _____

            2. _____

            3. _____

     Technology, then, seems to be driving human beings apart. Soon, we may no longer need to communicate with other human beings in order to do our work, entertain ourselves, or play the games we enjoy. Machines will be the coworkers and companions of the future.   5

Revising, Editing, and Proofreading

An effective paper is almost never written all at once. Rather, it is written in a step-by-step process in which you take it through a series of stages—from prewriting to final draft.

In the first stage, described above, you *prewrite,* getting your initial ideas and impressions about the subject down on paper. You accumulate raw material through brainstorming, freewriting, diagramming, and making lists and scratch outlines.

In the second stage, you *write and revise several drafts* of your paper. You fill out and shape your paper, adding and subtracting as needed to move it as close as you can to its final form. You work to make clear the single point of your paper, to develop fully the specific evidence needed to support that point, and to organize and connect the specific evidence. For example, in the second draft you may concentrate on adding details that will further support the central point of your paper. At the same time, you may also eliminate details that, you now realize, do not truly back up your thesis. In the third draft, you may work on reorganizing details and adding connections between supporting paragraphs so that your material will hold together more tightly.

Ideally, you should now set your paper aside for a while, so that you can move into the editing and proofreading stage with a fresh, rested mind. In this last stage, you first *edit* the next-to-final draft; that is, you check it carefully for sentence skills—for correct grammar, mechanics, punctuation, and usage. Then you *proofread* the final copy of the paper for any typing or handwriting mistakes. Editing and proofreading are important steps that some people neglect, often because they have worked too hard (or too little) on the previous stages.

Remember that correcting mistakes in the next-to-final and final versions can turn an average paper into a better one and a good paper into an excellent one. A later section of this book will give you practice in editing and proofreading in the form of a series of editing tests (pages 487–499).

Practice in Seeing the Entire Writing Process

This section will show you the stages that are often involved in writing an effective paper. You will see what one student, Diane, does in preparing her paragraph on the hazards of moviegoing.

There is no single sequence that all people follow in writing a composition. However, the various stages that Diane goes through in writing her paragraph should give you some idea of what to expect. As you'll see, Diane does not just sit down and proceed neatly from start to middle to finish, in one easy draft. Writing almost never works like that.

STAGE 1:
THINKING AND PREWRITING ABOUT YOUR TOPIC

In retrospect, here is what Diane says about her initial writing topic and her reaction to it:

"The assignment was to write about some problem or annoyance in everyday life. I thought of various problems but kept looking; I wanted something I really felt strongly about. Then I thought of movies and all the things that bother me about movies. There were plenty of things to scribble notes about. I wrote about the poor quality of many 'big name' movies, about how directors seem to think famous stars will make up for a bad script. I wrote about how I hate what Hollywood does when it turns books into movies. It simplifies the plot and slaps on a happy ending until the movie bears no resemblance to the book it was based on. I wrote about the fact that many foreign films I want to see almost never come to my local theaters. I wrote about the poor sound quality in the big multiscreen theaters; the high prices at theater concession stands; the inconsiderate behavior of other moviegoers. I wrote about directors who throw needless violence and explicit sex into their movies.

"By the time I had written down all my complaints about movies, I had covered almost two pages. When I read over my notes, I realized, 'It would be hard to turn this into a focused, well-organized paper. I'm trying to cover too much ground.' I then decided to narrow my topic down and write only about the annoyances involved in seeing a movie in a theater. Now I had a focus for my paper."

Comments and Activity

Fill in the missing word: The result of Diane's thinking and prewriting is that she discovers a topic—movies—and then successfully _____ her topic. Instead of writing about "all the things that bother me about movies," she decides to focus on "annoyances involved in seeing a movie in a theater."

STAGE 2: MAKING A LIST

At this point, Diane makes up an initial list of details about the problems of going to the theater. Her list is shown on the following page.

Going to the theater—what bugs me

Smelly theaters
Expensive food and drink
Wasting time on bad movies that have gotten a lot of publicity
Little kids running around
Audience members talking loudly
Unexpected amounts of sex or violence in films
Noise from adjacent theaters
Other viewers blurting out plot developments before they happen
Sticky floors
Others in theater inconsiderate
High ticket prices
Parking problems

Comments and Activity

Fill in the missing words: Diane is fortunate enough to know almost from the start what the _____ of her paper will be. Most of her work can thus go into developing details to support the point. Details seldom come automatically; they must be dug for, and Diane's list of annoyances of moviegoing is an early stage in the development of her subject. Making a _____ is an excellent way to get started.

Note that, in her list, Diane is not concerned about ordering the details in any way, or about deciding whether any detail really fits, or even about repeating herself. She is just doing first things first: getting raw material down on paper. In the second stage, Diane will also concentrate on accumulating raw material and will start to give attention to shaping that material.

STAGE 3: FURTHER PREWRITING

After making a list, Diane continues on to make a partial draft of her paper.

Note: To keep Diane's drafts as readable as possible, her spelling and sentence-skills mistakes have been corrected. Ordinarily, a number of such mistakes might be present, and editing a paper for them would be a part of the writing process.

Although I love movies, I hate going to the movie theater. Going to the theater is unpleasant because the theater itself is nasty. It's uncomfortable, dirty, and noisy. I also hate it because of inconsiderate people in the theater. They make it impossible to concentrate on the movie being shown.

What are problems with theater?	What are problems with other people?
Too far away	Children run up and down aisles
Traffic/parking problems	Teenagers talk and yell
Dirty, sticky floors	Adults carry on conversations
Uncomfortable seats	Everybody squirms in seats
Long lines	People going in and out to bathroom
Noise comes in from movie in next room	
Theater is smelly	

   3   People noisy and inconsiderate
   1   Difficulties in getting to theater
   2   Theater is uncomfortable (seats, smell, etc.)

Comments and Activity

Fill in the missing words: The second stage of Diane's paper is a mix of freewriting, brainstorming, and a scratch _____ . Diane uses all these techniques as she continues to draw out and accumulate _____ . At the same time, she has realized how to organize her details. She decides not to focus on the quality of the movies themselves; rather, she will write only about the experience of being in the movie theater. In a rough scratch outline, she lists three reasons (difficulty in getting there, uncomfortable theaters, inconsiderate people) for hating to go to the theater. She then tentatively decides on inconsiderate audience members as the worst part of going to the theater and numbers the reasons 1, 2, 3 in the order in which she might develop them. Keep in mind as you accumulate and develop details that you should, like Diane, be thinking of a way to _____ them.

STAGE 4: WRITING SEVERAL DRAFTS

Diane puts her work aside for the day and then continues writing the next morning. She now moves to a fuller draft:

> Although I love movies, I hate to see them in movie theaters. Getting to the theater is a pain. The drive to the theater ~~is long~~ takes thirty-five minutes. ~~When I lived just ten minutes from the theater, I didn't mind the drive so much.~~ Usually you have to wait in a long line to buy your ticket. The theater itself is ~~unpleasant~~ physically uncomfortable. ~~I don't like the way they smell~~ Many of the

theaters smell A musty smell is present in many theaters. Some of the seats are falling apart. The floor is gross has a sticky coating on it. Some of the audience members other moviegoers are the worst problem of all. Little kids race up and down. Older people talk and laugh as if they were in their own living rooms. They wriggle around, crowd you in your chair, and cough and sneeze. No more . . . wait for movies on TV . . . be more comfortable, less hassled.

Comments and Activity

Fill in the missing words: At this stage, Diane has enough details to write the initial draft of her paper. Notice that she continues to accumulate specific supporting details as she writes her draft. For instance, she crosses out and replaces *is*

long with the more specific _____ ; she crosses out and replaces

gross with _____ . She also works to improve some of her sentences (for instance, she writes three different versions of the sentence about

the _____ in many theaters). In addition, she crosses out and

eliminates a sentence about _____ because, as she realizes, it does not develop her first supporting point that getting to the theater is difficult.

Toward the end of her paper, Diane either can't find the right words to say what she wants or isn't yet sure what she wants to say. So she freewrites (shown by the ellipses . . .), putting down on paper all the impressions that come into

her head. She knows the technique of _____ may help her move closer to the right thought and the right words.

In a second draft and a third draft, Diane continues to work on and improve her paper. She then carefully edits her next-to-final draft, and the result is the final draft that follows.

The Hazards of Moviegoing

Although I love movies, going to see them drives me slightly crazy. First of all, getting to the movie can take a lot of time. I have a thirty-five-minute drive down a congested highway. Then, with a popular film, I usually have to wait in a long line at the ticket booth. Another problem is that the theater itself is seldom a pleasant place to be. A musty smell suggests that there has been no fresh air in the theater since it was built. Half the seats seem to be falling apart. And the floor often has a sticky coating that gets on your shoes. And finally there is the worst problem of all: other moviegoers. Kids run up and down the aisle. Teenagers laugh and shout at the screen. People of all ages loudly drop soda cups and popcorn tubs, cough and burp, and elbow you out of the armrest on either side of your seat. All in all, I would rather stay home and wait for the latest movie hits to appear on TV in the safety and comfort of my own living room.

Comments and Activity

Fill in the missing words: Notice the many improvements that Diane has made as a result of her second and third drafts. She has added transitional words that mark clearly the first two supporting points of her paper. The transitional words are _____ and _____ . Her third supporting point is also marked clearly with the words *the worst problem of all.* She has sharpened her details, improved the phrasing of her sentences, and found the words needed to complete the last section of her paper. She has also edited and proofread her paper carefully, checking the spelling of words she was unsure about and correcting several sentence-skills mistakes.

Almost every effective writer, like Diane, is engaged in a continuing process of moving toward a completely realized paper. The final version is seldom— almost never—attained all at once. Instead, it is the end result of a series of _____ . All too often, people stop writing when they are only partway through the writing process; they turn in a paper that is really only an early draft. They have the mistaken notion that a paper is something they should be able to do "all at once." But for almost everyone, writing means hard work and lots of _____ . Be sure, then, to take your paper through the entire series of drafts that you probably will need to write an effective composition.

■ Additional Activities

Activity 1

Answering the questions below will help you evaluate your attitude about revising, editing, and proofreading.

1. When do you typically start work on a paper?

   _____ Several nights before it's due

   _____ Night before it's due

   _____ Day it's due

2. How many drafts do you typically write when doing a paper?

   _____ One   _____ Two   _____ Three   _____ Four or more

3. How would you describe your editing (checking the next-to-final draft for errors in grammar, punctuation, mechanics, and usage)?

   _____ Do little or no editing

   _____ Look quickly for and correct obvious errors

   _____ Consult a grammar handbook and a dictionary about all possible errors

4. How would you describe your proofreading (checking the final draft for typing or handwriting errors)?

_____ Do not look at the paper again after the last word is written

_____ May glance quickly through the paper

_____ Read the paper over carefully to find mistakes

5. Do you ever get back papers marked for obvious errors?

_____ Frequently _____ Sometimes _____ Almost never _____ Never

Activity 2

Following is a supporting paragraph from an essay called ''Problems of Combining School and Work.'' The paragraph is shown in four different stages of development: (1) first full draft, (2) second draft, (3) next-to-final draft, (4) final draft. The four stages appear in scrambled order. Write the number 1 in the answer blank for the first full draft and number the remaining stages in sequence.

_____

I have also given up some special personal pleasures in my life. On Sundays, for example, I used to play softball or football, now I use the entire day to study. Another pleasure Ive had to give up is good old-fashioned sleep. I never get as much as I like because their just isnt time. Finally I miss having the chance to just sit in front of the TV, on weeknights. In order to watch the whole lineup of movies and sports that I used to watch regularly. These sound like small pleasures, but you realize how important they are when you have to give them up.

_____

I've had to give up special personal pleasures in my life. I use to spend Sundays playing pick-up games, now I have to study. Im the sort of person who needs alot of sleep, but I dont have the time for that either. Sleeping nine or ten hours a night woul'dnt be unusual. Psychologists have shown that each individual need a different amount of sleep, some people as little as five hours, some as much as nine or ten. So I'm not unusual in that. But I've given up that pleasure too. The third thing is that I can't watch the TV shows I use to enjoy. This is another personal pleasure I've had to give up trying to balence work and school. These sound like small pleasures, but you realize how important they are when you have to give them up.

_____

Besides missing the social side of college life, I've also had to give up some of my special personal pleasures. I used to spend Sunday afternoons, for example, playing lob-pitch softball or touch football, depending on the season. Now, I use Sunday as a catch-up day for my studies. Another pleasure I've lost is sleeping late on days off and weekends. I once loved mornings when I could check the clock, bury my head in the pillow, and drift off for another hour. These days I'm forced to crawl out of bed the minute the alarm lets out its piercing ring. Finally, I no longer have the chance to just sit, for three or four hours at a time, watching the movies and sports programs I enjoy. A leisurely night of <u>Monday Night Football</u> or a network premiere of a Clint Eastwood movie is a pleasure of the past for me now.

Besides missing the social side of college life, I've also had to give up some of my special personal pleasures. I used to spend Sunday afternoons, for example, playing lob-pitch softball or touch football, depending on the season. Now I use Sunday as a day for my studies. Another pleasure I've had to give up is sleeping late on days off and weekends. I once loved mornings when I could check the clock, bury my head in the pillow, and drifting off for another hour. These days I'm forced to get out of bed the minute the alarm lets out it's piercing ring. Finally, I no longer have the chance to just sit watching the movies and sports programs I enjoy. A liesurely night of <u>Monday Night Football</u> or a network premere of a Clint Eastwood movie is a pleasure of the past for me now.

Activity 3

Fill in the missing words in the following summary of this chapter.

Having the Right Attitude: Some people feel that in order to be a good writer, writing must come easily. This idea is false and can interfere with the ability to make progress in writing. A more realistic and productive attitude includes the

understanding that, for most people, writing is _____ . In addition,

it helps to realize that, like driving or typing, writing is a _____

that can be learned with lots of _____ .

Developing a Subject: It is best to write about a subject that _____ you and that you know something about, either directly or indirectly. When you must write on a topic about which you have little or no background, you should

do _____ to gain the necessary knowledge. The library is one good place to do that.

There are times, however, when you won't know your exact subject until after you have written for a while. Writing will help you think about and explore your material. On occasion you will write for a page or two and discover that it

makes sense to change the _____ of your paper.

As you work on a paper, remember that it is not necessary to write a paper

straight through from _____ to end. You should proceed in whatever way seems easiest, including starting at the middle or even the end. Make whatever adjustments are needed to reach your goal of writing a paper that makes

and _____ a point.

Prewriting: There are five prewriting techniques. One technique, called

_____ , is a process of generating ideas by asking questions about your subject. Such questions include *What? When?* and *Why?*

Freewriting is a second prewriting technique. It involves writing on your topic

for ten minutes without _____ or worrying about being correct. In this process, your thoughts about your paper often become clearer.

Making a _____ is a third excellent prewriting technique for getting started on a paper. The goal is to generate many possible details for your paper and maybe even ways of developing that paper.

Diagramming, also known as _____ or _____ , is a fourth prewriting activity. Here you use lines, boxes, arrows, and circles to show relationships among the ideas and details that come to you.

Fifth, perhaps the most helpful technique for writing a good paper is preparing a scratch outline. It is an excellent follow-up to the other prewriting techniques. Sometimes you may even skip the other techniques and concentrate on this one. In a scratch outline, you think about the specific point you will make in your

paper, the exact _____ that will support that point, and the ex-

act _____ in which you will arrange those items.

Outlining: Often the best way to write an effective paragraph is to _____ it. Outlining develops your ability to think clearly and logically. It helps you see and work with the fundamental ideas of a paper, and it helps you focus on producing a paper that is unified, well supported, and well organized.

Revising, Editing, and Proofreading: Writing a paper is usually a step-by-step process. It begins with prewriting, during which you accumulate raw material. In the second stage, you shape your paper by writing and revising it several times. Finally, you edit and proofread. Editing involves checking your paper for mistakes

in sentence _____ . Proofreading involves checking the final copy

of your paper for typing or handwriting _____ .

THE FIRST
AND SECOND
STEPS
IN ESSAY
WRITING

This chapter will show you how to:

- **Start an essay with a point or thesis**
- **Support that point or thesis with specific evidence**

Now that you have a sense of the general structure of an essay, it is time to consider the basic steps involved in writing such a paper. The four steps are as follows:

1   Begin with a point or thesis.
2   Support the thesis with specific evidence.
3   Organize and connect the specific evidence.
4   Write clear, error-free sentences.

This chapter will describe the first and second steps; the chapter that follows (see page 69) will present the third and fourth.

Step 1:
Begin with a Point or Thesis

Your first step in writing is to decide what point you want to make and to write out that point in a single sentence. Formulating your point or thesis right at the start will help in two ways. First, you will find out at once whether you have a clear and workable thesis. Second, you will be able to use the thesis as a guide while writing your essay. You will know what material to include by frequently asking yourself, ''Does this support my thesis?'' With the thesis as a guide, the danger of drifting away from the point of the essay is greatly reduced.

WRITING A GOOD THESIS

To write a good thesis, you must begin with a subject that is neither too broad nor too narrow. Suppose, for example, that an instructor asks you to write a paper on some aspect of marriage. Such a topic is obviously too broad to cover in a five-hundred-word essay. You would have to write a book to support adequately any point you might make about the general subject of marriage. What you need to do, then, is limit your subject. Narrow it down until you have a thesis that you can deal with specifically in four hundred to five hundred words. In the box that follows are examples of narrowed subjects.

General Subject	Limited Subject	Thesis
Marriage	Honeymoon	A honeymoon is perhaps the worst way to begin a marriage.
Family	Older sister	My older sister helped me overcome my shyness.
Television	TV preachers	TV evangelists use sales techniques to promote their messages.
Children	Disciplining of children	My husband and I have several effective ways of disciplining our children.
Sports	Players' salaries	High players' salaries are bad for the game, for the fans, and for the values our children are developing.

Activity

Sometimes a subject must go through several stages of limiting before it is narrow enough to write about. Below are four lists reflecting several stages that writers went through in moving from a general subject to a narrow thesis statement. Number the stages in each list from 1 to 5, with 1 marking the broadest stage and 5 marking the thesis.

List 1

_____ Teachers

_____ Education

_____ Math teacher

_____ My high school math
teacher was incompetent.

_____ High school math teacher

List 2

_____ Bicycles

_____ Dangers of bike riding

_____ Recreation

_____ Recreational vehicles

_____ Bike riding in the city is
a dangerous activity.

List 3

_____ Financial institutions

_____ Bank

_____ Dealing with customers

_____ Working in a bank

_____ I've learned how to
handle unpleasant bank
customers.

List 4

_____ Camping

_____ First camping trip

_____ Summer vacation

_____ My first camping trip was
a disastrous experience.

_____ Vacations

Later in this chapter, you will get more practice in narrowing general subjects to thesis statements.

COMMON ERRORS IN WRITING A THESIS

When writing thesis statements, people often make mistakes that undermine their chances of producing an effective essay. One mistake is to substitute an announcement of the subject for a true thesis idea. A second mistake is to write a thesis that is too broad, and a third is to write a thesis that is too narrow. A fourth mistake is to write a thesis containing more than one idea. Following are examples of these four errors.

1   Announcements Rather Than Statements

> The subject of this paper will be my parents.
>
> I want to talk about the crime wave in our country.
>
> The "baby boom" generation is the concern of this essay.

In this first group, the sentences are not thesis statements but just announcements of a topic idea. For instance, "The subject of this paper will be my parents" does not make a point but merely tells, in a rather weak and unimaginative way, the writer's general subject. A thesis statement must advance a point about a limited subject.

2   Statements That Are Too Broad

> My parents have been the most influential people in my life.
>
> Crime is a major concern of everyone in our country.
>
> The "baby boom" generation has changed history.

In this second group, all the statements are too broad to be supported adequately. For example, "My parents have been the most influential people in my life" could not be supported with specific details in five hundred words or less. There are many autobiographies in which authors have devoted entire chapters to detailing the influence of their mothers or fathers on their lives.

3   Statements That Are Too Narrow

> My parents had only one child.
>
> In the last year there have been over twenty robberies in our neighborhood.
>
> The members of the post–World War II "baby boom" make up the largest single age group in the United States.

In this third group, there is no room in any of the three statements for support to be given. For instance, "My parents had only one child" is too narrow to be expanded into a paper. It is a simple fact that does not lend itself to much discussion. Such a statement is sometimes called a *dead-end statement*; there is no place to go with it. On the other hand, "My parents helped me grow in three important ways" is a point that you could go on to write about in an essay.

4   Statements That Contain More Than One Idea

My parents helped me grow in important ways, although in other respects I was limited.

The problem of overcrowded American prisons must be solved, and judges must start handing out tougher sentences.

The ''baby boom'' generation has had many advantages, but it also faces many problems.

In this fourth group, each of the statements contains more than one idea. For instance, ''My parents helped me grow in important ways, although in other respects I was limited'' appears to have two separate ideas (''parents helped me grow'' *and* ''in other respects I was limited''). Thus the reader does not know what the real focus will be.

Activity

Part A: Write TN in the space next to each statement that is too narrow to be developed in an essay. Write TB beside each statement that is too broad to be covered in an essay.

_____   1.   The way our society treats elderly people is unbelievable.

_____   2.   The first car that I owned was a Ford.

_____   3.   Computers have changed our society.

_____   4.   People who eat a lot of red meat are almost three times more likely to get colon cancer than people who eat mostly fish and chicken.

_____   5.   Action must be taken against drugs.

Part B: Write A beside each sentence that is an announcement rather than a thesis statement. Write 2 beside each statement that contains more than one idea.

_____   6.   My last car was dependable, but many American cars are poorly made.

_____   7.   The subject of this essay is daily prayer in our public schools.

_____   8.   Soap operas show many stereotyped characters, although they also portray real problems in American life.

_____   9.   I am going to write on my ideas concerning ''F'' grades.

_____   10.   The hardest teacher I ever had taught me a lesson I will never forget.

Step 2:
Support the Thesis
with Specific Evidence

The first essential step in writing a successful essay is to formulate a clearly stated thesis. The second basic step is to support the thesis with specific reasons or details.

To ensure that your essay will have adequate support, you may find an informal outline very helpful. Write down a brief version of your thesis idea and then work out and jot down the three points that will support that thesis.

Here is the informal outline that was prepared by the author of the essay on moviegoing:

Moviegoing is a problem.
1. Getting there
2. Theater itself
3. Patrons

An informal outline like this one looks simple, but developing it often requires a great deal of careful thinking. The time spent, though, on developing a logical outline is invaluable. Once you have planned out the steps that logically support your thesis, you will be in an excellent position to go on to write an effective essay.

Activities in this chapter will give you practice in the crucial skill of planning an essay clearly.

Activity

Complete any five of the six informal outlines that follow by adding a third logical supporting point (*c*) that will parallel the two already provided (*a* and *b*).

1. The first day on a new job can be nerve-wracking.
   a. Meeting new people
   b. Finding your way around a new place

   c. _____
2. My stepmother has three qualities I admire.
   a. Patience
   b. Thoughtfulness

   c. _____

3. At our school, the library is the worst place to study.
   a. Uncomfortable chairs and tables
   b. Little privacy

   c. _____

4. College students should live at home.
   a. Stay in touch with family
   b. Avoid distractions of dorm or apartment life

   c. _____

5. _____ is the worst job I've ever had.
   a. Difficult boss
   b. Poor pay

   c. _____

6. College is a stressful situation for many people.
   a. Worry about grades
   b. Worry about being accepted

   c. _____

THE IMPORTANCE OF SPECIFIC DETAILS

Just as a thesis must be developed with three supporting points, those supporting points must be developed with specific details. Specific details have two key values. First of all, details excite the reader's interest. They make writing a pleasure to read, for we all enjoy learning particulars about people, places, and things. Second, details serve to explain a writer's points. They give the evidence needed for us to see and understand general ideas.

All too often, the body paragraphs in essays contain vague generalities rather than the specific supporting details that are needed to engage and convince a reader. Here is what one of the paragraphs in "The Hazards of Moviegoing" would have looked like if the writer had not detailed her supporting evidence vividly.

> Some of the other patrons are even more of a problem than the theater itself. Many people in the theater often show themselves to be inconsiderate. They make noises and create disturbances at their seats. Included are people in every age group, from the young to the old. Some act as if they were at home in their own living rooms watching the TV set. And people are often messy, so that you're constantly aware of all the food they're eating. People are also always moving around near you, creating a disturbance and interrupting your enjoyment of the movie.

The following box contrasts the vague support in the preceding paragraph with the specific support in the essay.

Vague Support	*Specific Support*
1. Many people in the theater show themselves to be inconsiderate. They make noises and create disturbances at their seats. Included are people in every age group, from the young to the old. Some act as if they were at home in their own living rooms watching the TV set.	1. Little kids race up and down the aisles, usually in giggling packs. Teenagers try to impress their friends by talking back to the screen, whistling, and making what they consider to be hilarious noises. Adults act as if they were at home in their own living rooms and comment loudly on the ages of the stars or why movies aren't as good anymore.
2. And people are often messy, so that you're constantly aware of all the food they're eating.	2. And people of all ages crinkle candy wrappers, stick gum on their seats, and drop popcorn tubs or cups of crushed ice and soda on the floor.
3. People are also always moving around near you, creating a disturbance and interrupting enjoyment of the movie.	3. They also cough and burp, squirm endlessly in their seats, file out for repeated trips to the rest rooms or concession stand, and elbow you out of the armrest on either side of your seat.

The effective paragraph from the essay provides details that make vividly clear the statement that the patrons are a problem in the theater. The writer specifies the exact age groups (little kids, teenagers, and adults) and the offenses of each (giggling, talking and whistling, and loud comments). She specifies the various food excesses (crinkled wrappers, gum on seats, dropped popcorn and soda containers). Finally, she provides concrete details that enable us to see and hear other disturbances (coughs and burps, squirming, constant trips to bathroom, jostling for elbow room). The ineffective paragraph asks us to guess about these details; in the effective paragraph, we see and hear them vividly.

In the strong paragraph, then, sharp details capture our interest and enable us to share in the writer's experiences. They provide pictures that make each of us feel, ''I am there.'' The particulars also enable us to understand clearly the writer's point that patrons are a problem. You should aim to make your own writing equally convincing by providing detailed support in your papers.

Activity

Write S in front of the two selections below that provide specific evidence to support their opening points. Write X in front of the two selections that follow their opening points with vague, general, and wordy sentences.

_____ 1. Building a wooden deck can be an enjoyable project only if you take certain precautions.

Get a building permit before you start. If you don't have one, you may have to tear down everything you've built when the town's building inspector learns of your project. Also, purchase pressure-treated lumber for any posts that will be set into the ground. Ordinary wood, not treated with preservatives, will eventually rot from contact with soil and moisture.

_____ 2. My mother was a harsh disciplinarian.

When I did something wrong, no matter how small, she would inflict serious punishment. She had expectations that I was to live up to, and she never changed her attitude. When I did not behave as I should, I was dealt with severely. There were no exceptions as far as my mother was concerned.

_____ 3. Some things are worse when they're "improved."

A good cheesecake, for one thing, is perfect. It doesn't need pineapple, cherries, blueberries, or whipped cream smeared all over it. Plain old American blue jeans, the ones with five pockets and copper rivets, are perfect too. Manufacturers only made them worse when they added flared legs, took away the pockets, tightened the fit, and plastered white logos and designers' names all over them.

_____ 4. Pets can be more trouble than children.

My dog, unlike my children, has never been completely housebroken. When he's excited or nervous, he still has an occasional problem. My dog, unlike my children, has never learned how to take care of himself when we're away, despite the fact that we've given him plenty of time to do so. We don't have to worry about our grown children anymore. However, we still have to hire a dog-sitter.

THE IMPORTANCE OF ADEQUATE DETAILS

One of the most common and most serious problems in students' writing is inadequate development. You must provide *enough* specific details to support fully the point in a body paragraph of an essay. You could not, for example, include a paragraph about a friend's unreliability and provide only a short example. You would have to extend the example or add several other examples showing your friend as an unreliable person. Without such additional support, your paragraph would be underdeveloped.

Students may try to disguise unsupported paragraphs through repetition and generalities. Do not fall into this ''wordiness trap.'' Be prepared to do the plain hard work needed to ensure that each paragraph has solid support.

Activity 1

Both of the following body paragraphs were written on the same topic, and both have clear opening points. Which one is adequately developed? Which one, on the other hand, has only several particulars and uses mostly vague, general, wordy sentences to conceal the fact that it is starved for specific details?

Eternal Youth?—No Thanks

I wouldn't want to be a teenager again, first of all, because I wouldn't want to worry about talking to girls. I still remember how scary it was to call up a girl and ask her out. My heart would race, my pulse would pound, and perspiration would trickle down my face, adding to my acne by the second. I never knew whether my voice would come out deep and masculine, like Dan Rather's, or squeaky, like Pee Wee Herman's. Then there were the questions: Would she be at home? If she was, would she want to talk to me? And if she did, what would I say? The one time I did get up the nerve to take a girl in my homeroom to a movie, I was so tongue-tied that I stared silently at the box of popcorn in my lap until the feature finally started. Needless to say, I wasn't very interesting company.

Terrors of My Teenage Years

I wouldn't want to be a teenager again, first of all, because I wouldn't want to worry about talking to girls. Calling up a girl to ask her out was something that I completely dreaded. I didn't know what words to express or how to express them. I would have all the symptoms of nervousness when I got on the phone. I worried a great deal about how I would sound, and I had a lot of doubts about the girl's reaction. Once, I managed to call up a girl to go out, but the evening turned out to be a disaster. I was too unsure of myself to act in a confident way. I couldn't think of anything to say and just kept quiet. Now that I look back on it, I really made a fool of myself. Agonizing over my attempts at relationships with the opposite sex made adolescence a very uncomfortable time.

The first paragraph offers a series of well-detailed examples of the author's nerve-wracking experiences, as a teenager, with girls. The second paragraph, on the other hand, is underdeveloped. It speaks only of the ''torture'' of calling up a girl, whereas the first paragraph supplies such particulars as ''My heart would race, my pulse would pound, and perspiration would trickle down my face.''

The second paragraph describes in a general way being "worried about my voice," whereas in the first paragraph, the author wonders if his voice will "come out deep and masculine, like Dan Rather's, or squeaky, like Pee Wee Herman's." And there is no specific description in the second paragraph of the evening that turned into a disaster. In summary, the second paragraph lacks the full detailed support needed to develop its opening point convincingly.

Activity 2

Take a few minutes to write a paragraph supporting the point that "My room is a mess." Afterward, you and your classmates (or the other students in the small group you may be working with) should all read your paragraphs aloud. The best-received paragraphs will be those with plenty of specific details.

Practice in Advancing and Supporting a Thesis

You now know the two most important steps in competent essay writing: (1) advancing a point or thesis and (2) supporting that thesis. The purpose of this section is to expand and strengthen your understanding of these two basic steps. You will first work through a series of activities on *developing* a thesis:

1 Identifying the parts of an essay
2 Evaluating thesis statements
3 Completing thesis statements
4 Writing a thesis statement
5 Limiting a topic and writing a thesis

You will then sharpen your understanding of how to *support* a thesis effectively by working through the following activities:

6 Making words and phrases specific
7 Making sentences specific
8 Providing specific evidence
9 Identifying adequate supporting evidence
10 Adding details to complete an essay

1 IDENTIFYING THE PARTS OF AN ESSAY

Activity

This activity will sharpen your sense of the parts of an essay. "Coping with Old Age" has no indentations between paragraphs. Read this essay carefully, and then double-underline the thesis and single-underline the topic sentence for each of the three supporting paragraphs and the first sentence of the conclusion. Write the numbers of those sentences in the spaces provided at the end.

Coping with Old Age

[1]I recently read about an area of the former Soviet Union where many people live to be well over a hundred years old. [2]Being 115 or even 125 isn't considered unusual there, and these old people continue to do productive work right up until they die. [3]The United States, however, isn't such a healthy place for older people. [4]Since I retired from my job, I've had to cope with the physical, mental, and emotional stresses of being "old." [5]For one thing, I've had to adjust to physical changes. [6]Now that I'm over sixty, the trusty body that carried me around for years has turned traitor. [7]Aside from the deepening wrinkles on my face and neck, and the wiry gray hairs that have replaced my brown hair, I face more frightening changes. [8]I don't have the energy I used to. [9]My eyes get tired. [10]Once in a while, I miss something that's said to me. [11]My once-faithful feet seem to have lost their comfortable soles, and I sometimes feel I'm walking on marbles. [12]In order to fight against this slow decay, I exercise whenever I can. [13]I walk, I stretch, and I climb stairs. [14]I battle constantly to keep as fit as possible. [15]I'm also trying to cope with mental changes. [16]My mind was once as quick and sure as a champion gymnast. [17]I never found it difficult to memorize answers in school or to remember the names of people I met. [18]Now, I occasionally have to search my mind for the name of a close neighbor or favorite television show. [19]Because my mind needs exercise, too, I challenge it as much as I can. [20]Taking a college course like this English class, for example, forces me to concentrate. [21]The mental gymnast may be a little slow and out of shape, but he can still do a back flip or turn a somersault when he has to. [22]Finally, I must deal with the emotional impact of being old. [23]Our society typecasts old people. [24]We're supposed to be unattractive, senile, useless leftovers. [25]We're supposed to be the crazy drivers and the cranky customers. [26]At first, I was angry and frustrated that I was considered old at all. [27]And I knew that people were wrong to stereotype me. [28]Then I got depressed. [29]I even started to think that maybe I was a cast-off, one of those old animals that slow down the rest of the herd. [30]But I have now decided to rebel against these negative feelings. [31]I try to have friends of all ages and to keep up with what's going on in the world. [32]I try to remember that I'm still the same person who sat at a first-grade desk, who fell in love, who comforted a child, who got a raise at work. [33]I'm not "just" an old person. [34]Coping with the changes of old age has become my latest full-time job. [35]Even though it's a job I never applied for, and one for which I had no experience, I'm trying to do the best I can.

Thesis statement in "Coping with Old Age": _____

Topic sentence of first supporting paragraph: _____

Topic sentence of second supporting paragraph: _____

Topic sentence of third supporting paragraph: _____

First sentence of the conclusion: _____

2   EVALUATING THESIS STATEMENTS

As was explained on pages 43–44, some writers substitute an announcement of a subject for a true thesis idea. Others write dead-end thesis statements that are too narrow to need support or development. Contrasting with such dead-end statements are statements that are wide open—too broad to be adequately supported in the limited space of a five-hundred-word essay. Finally, some thesis statements are vague, often containing more than one idea. They suggest that the writer has not thought out the main point sufficiently.

Activity 1

Write A beside the sentences that are announcements rather than thesis statements. Write OK beside the statement in each pair that is a clear, limited point which could be developed in an essay.

1. _____ a.   This essay will discuss the people you meet in exercise class.

   _____ b.   The kinds of workout clothes worn in my aerobics class identify ''jocks,'' ''strugglers,'' and ''princesses.''

2. _____ a.   I made several mistakes in the process of trying to win the respect and affection of my teenage stepson.

   _____ b.   My thesis in this paper is relationships between stepparents and stepchildren.

3. _____ a.   A period of loneliness can teach you to use your creativity, sort out your values, and feel empathy for others.

   _____ b.   Loneliness is the subject of this paper.

4. _____ a.   This paper will be about sharing housework.

   _____ b.   Deciding who will perform certain unpleasant household chores can be the crisis that makes or breaks a marriage.

5. _____ a.   My concern here is to discuss ''near-death'' experiences reported by some patients.

   _____ b.   There are several possible explanations for the similar ''near-death'' experiences reported by some patients.

Activity 2

Write TN beside statements that are too narrow to be developed in an essay. Write OK beside the statement in each pair that is a clear, limited point.

1. _____ a. I had squash, tomatoes, and corn in my garden last summer.

   _____ b. Vegetable gardening can be a frustrating hobby.

2. _____ a. The main road into our town is lined with billboards.

   _____ b. For several reasons, billboards should be abolished.

3. _____ a. There are more single-parent households in our country than ever.

   _____ b. Organization is the key to being a successful single parent.

4. _____ a. In my first job, I learned that I had several bad work habits.

   _____ b. Because I was late for work yesterday, I lost an hour's pay and was called in to see the boss.

5. _____ a. Americans abuse alcohol because it has become such an important part of our personal and public celebrations.

   _____ b. Consumption of wine, beer, and hard liquor increases in the United States every year.

Activity 3

Write TB beside statements that are too broad to be developed in an essay. Write OK beside the statement in each pair that is a clear, limited point.

1. _____ a. In many ways, sports are an important part of American life.

   _____ b. Widespread gambling has changed professional football for the worse.

2. _____ a. Modern life makes people suspicious and unfriendly.

   _____ b. A succession of frightening news stories has made me lose my trust in strangers.

3. _____ a. Toy ads on television teach children to be greedy, competitive, and snobbish.

   _____ b. Advertising has a bad influence on the values that children develop in life.

4. _____ a. Learning new skills can be difficult and frustrating.

     _____ b. Learning a skill like writing takes work, patience, and a sense of humor.

5. _____ a. I didn't get along with my family, so I did many foolish things.

     _____ b. Running away from home taught me that my parents weren't as terrible as I thought.

Activity 4

For each pair, write 2 beside the statement that contains more than one idea. Write OK beside the statement in each pair that is a clear, limited point.

1. _____ a. Working with old people changed my stereotyped ideas about the elderly.

     _____ b. My life has moved in new directions since the rewarding job I had working with older people last summer.

2. _____ a. The new architecture on this campus is very unpleasant, although the expansion was desperately needed.

     _____ b. Our new college library building is ugly, intimidating, and inefficient.

3. _____ a. Among the most entertaining ads on TV today are those for mail-order products.

     _____ b. Although ads on TV for mail-order products are often misleading, they can still be very entertaining.

4. _____ a. My roommate and I are compatible in most ways, but we still have conflicts at times.

     _____ b. My roommate has his own unique systems for studying, writing term papers, and cleaning his room.

5. _____ a. Although some good movies have come out lately, I prefer to watch old movies because they're more interesting.

     _____ b. Movies of the thirties and forties had better plots, sets, and actors than the ones made today.

3 COMPLETING THESIS STATEMENTS

Activity

Complete the following thesis statements by adding a third supporting point that will parallel the two already provided. You might want to check first the section on parallelism (pages 392–395) to make sure you understand parallel form.

1. Because I never took college preparatory courses in high school, I entered college deficient in mathematics, study skills, and _____ .

2. A good salesperson needs to like people, to be aggressive, and _____
   _____ .

3. Rather than blame myself for failing the course, I blamed the instructor, my adviser, and even _____ .

4. Anyone who buys an old house planning to fix it up should be prepared to put in a lot of time, hard work, and _____ .

5. Our old car eats gas, makes funny noises, and _____ .

6. My mother, my boss, and my _____ are three people who are very important in my life right now.

7. Getting married too young was a mistake because we hadn't finished our education, we weren't ready for children, and _____
   _____
   _____ .

8. Some restaurant patrons seem to leave their honesty, their cleanliness, and their _____ at home.

9. During my first semester at college, I had to learn how to manage my time, how to manage my diet, and _____ .

10. Three experiences I wish I could forget are the time I fell off a ladder, the time I tried to fix my parents' lawn mower, and _____
    _____
    _____ .

4 WRITING A THESIS STATEMENT

Activity

This activity will give you practice in writing an effective essay thesis—one that is neither too broad nor too narrow for the supporting points. An added value of the activity is that sometimes you will construct your thesis after you have decided what your supporting points will be. You will need to know, then, how to write a thesis that will exactly match the points that you have developed.

1. Thesis: _____
   a. My first car was a rebellious-looking one which matched the way I felt and acted as a teenager.
   b. My next car reflected my more mature and practical adult self.
   c. My latest car seems to tell me that I'm aging; it shows my growing concern with comfort and safety.

2. Thesis: _____
   a. Going to a two-year college can save up to $20,000 dollars in tuition.
   b. If the college is nearby, there are no costs for room and board.
   c. All the course credits that are accumulated can be transferred to a four-year school.

3. Thesis: _____
   a. First, I tried simply avoiding the snacks aisle of the supermarket.
   b. Then I started limiting myself to only five units of any given snack.
   c. Finally, in desperation, I began keeping the cellophane bags of snacks in a padlocked cupboard.

4. Thesis: _____
   a. The holiday can be frightening for little children and can encourage vandalism in older ones.
   b. Children can be struck by cars while wearing vision-obstructing masks and dark costumes.
   c. More and more incidents of deadly treats filled with razor blades or contaminated with poisons are occurring.

5. Thesis: _____
   a. First of all, I was a typical ''type A'' personality: anxious, impatient, and hard-driving.
   b. I also had a family history of relatives with heart trouble.
   c. My unhealthy lifestyle, though, was probably the major factor.

5   LIMITING A TOPIC AND WRITING A THESIS

The following two activities will give you practice in distinguishing general from limited subjects and in writing a thesis.

Activity 1

Look carefully at the ten general and ten limited subjects below. Then see if you can write a thesis for any five of them.

Hint: To create a thesis for a limited subject, ask yourself, "What point do I want to make about _____ (*my limited subject*)?"

General Subject	*Limited Subject*
1. Apartment	1. Sharing an apartment with a roommate
2. Self-improvement	2. Behavior toward others
3. Family	3. My mother
4. Eating out	4. Fast-food restaurants
5. Automobiles	5. Bad driving habits
6. Health	6. Regular exercise
7. Owning a house	7. Do-it-yourself home repairs
8. Baseball	8. Free-agent system
9. Parenthood	9. Being a single parent
10. Pollution	10. Noise pollution

Thesis statements for five of the limited subjects:

_____

_____

_____

_____

_____

_____

_____

_____

_____

_____

Activity 2

Here is a list of ten general subjects. Limit five of the subjects. Then write theses about those five limited subjects.

General Subject	Limited Subject
1. Pets	_____
2. Teenagers	_____
3. Television	_____
4. Work	_____
5. College	_____
6. Doctors	_____
7. Vacations	_____
8. Cooking	_____
9. Money	_____
10. Shopping	_____

Thesis statements for five of the limited subjects:

_____

_____

_____

_____

_____

_____

_____

_____

_____

_____

6   MAKING WORDS AND PHRASES SPECIFIC

To be an effective writer, you must use specific rather than general words. Specific words create pictures in the reader's mind. They help capture interest and make your meaning clear.

Activity

This activity will give you practice at changing vague, indefinite words into sharp, specific ones. Add three or more specific words to replace the general word or words italicized in each sentence. Make changes in the wording of a sentence as necessary.

Example   *Several of our appliances* broke down at the same time.

Our washer, refrigerator, and television broke down at the same

time.

1.   *Salty snacks* are my diet downfall.

_____

_____

2.   *Several sections* of the newspaper were missing.

_____

_____

3.   *Various gifts for men* were displayed in the department-store window.

_____

_____

4.   *Several items in my purse* had been crushed.

_____

_____

5.   I swept aside the *things* on my desk in order to spread out the road map.

_____

_____

6.   The waitress told us we could have *several types of potatoes.*

_____

_____

7. The doctor examined *various parts of my body* before diagnosing my illness as bronchitis.

   _____

   _____

   _____

8. The *food choices* in the cafeteria were unappetizing.

   _____

   _____

   _____

9. Terry threw all the *junk* from the bottom of her closet into a large cardboard carton.

   _____

   _____

   _____

10. Our neighbor's family room has *a lot of electronic equipment.*

    _____

    _____

    _____

7 MAKING SENTENCES SPECIFIC

Again, you will practice changing vague, indefinite writing into lively, image-filled writing that helps capture the reader's interest and makes your meaning clear. Compare the following sentences:

General	Specific
She walked down the street.	Anne wandered slowly along Rogers Lane.
Animals came into the space.	Hungry lions padded silently into the sawdust-covered arena.
The man signed the paper.	The biology teacher hastily scribbled his name on the course withdrawal slip.

The specific sentences create clear pictures in our minds. The details *show* us exactly what has happened. Here are four ways to make your sentences specific.

1   Use exact names.

He sold his *camper.*   *Vince* sold his *Winnebago.*

2   Use lively verbs.

The flag *moved* in the breeze.   The flag *fluttered* in the breeze.

3   Use descriptive words (modifiers) before nouns.

A man strained to lift the crate.

A *heavyset, perspiring* man strained to lift the *heavy wooden* crate.

4   Use words that relate to the senses—sight, hearing, taste, smell, touch.

That woman jogs five miles a day.
That *fragile-looking, gray-haired* woman jogs five miles a day.   (*sight*)

A noise told the crowd that there were two minutes left to play.
A *piercing whistle* told the *cheering* crowd that there were two minutes left to play.   (*hearing*)

When he returned, all he found in the refrigerator was bread and milk.
When he returned, all he found in the refrigerator was *stale* bread and *sour* milk.   (*taste*)

Neil stroked the kitten's fur until he felt its tiny claws on his hand.
Neil stroked the kitten's *velvety* fur until he felt its tiny, *needle-sharp* claws on his hand.   (*touch*)

Fran placed a sachet in her bureau drawer.
Fran placed a *lilac-scented* sachet in her bureau drawer.   (*smell*)

Activity

With the help of the methods described above, add specific details to any ten of the twelve sentences that follow. Use separate paper. Note the two examples.

Example   The person got off the bus.

> *The teenage boy bounded down the steps of the shiny yellow school bus.*

Example   She worked hard all summer.

All summer, Eva sorted peaches and blueberries in the hot, noisy

canning factory.

1. The car would not start.
2. The test was difficult.
3. The boy was tired.
4. My room needs cleaning.
5. The student was bored.
6. The game was exciting.
7. A fire started.
8. A vehicle blocked traffic.
9. A large rock fell.
10. The salesperson was obnoxious.
11. The child started to cry.
12. The lounge area was busy.

8   PROVIDING SPECIFIC EVIDENCE

Activity

Provide three details that logically support each of the following points. Your details can be drawn from your own experience or they can be invented. In each case, the details should show *specifically* what the point expresses only generally. State your details briefly in several words rather than in complete sentences.

Example   We quickly spruced up the apartment before our guest arrived.

1. Hid toys and newspapers in spare closet

2. Vacuumed pet hairs off sofa

3. Sprayed air freshener around living room

1. The dinner was a disaster.

_____

_____

_____

2. My seven-year-old nephew has some disgusting habits.

_____

_____

_____

3. There are several reasons why I put off studying.

_____

_____

_____

4. My parents never allowed me to think for myself.

_____

_____

_____

5. I have several ways in which I can earn extra cash.

_____

_____

_____

6. My car needs repairs.

_____

_____

_____

7. Friday evening, I didn't sit still for a minute.

_____

_____

_____

8. Mr. or Ms. _____ was the worst teacher I ever had.

_____

_____

_____

9   IDENTIFYING ADEQUATE SUPPORTING EVIDENCE

Activity

The following body paragraphs were taken from student essays. Two of the paragraphs provide sufficient details to support their topic sentences convincingly. Write AD for *adequate development* beside those paragraphs. Three paragraphs use vague, wordy, general, or irrelevant sentences instead of real supporting details. Write U for *underdeveloped* beside those paragraphs.

_____ 1.   Another consideration in adopting a dog is the cost. Initial fees for shots and a license might add up to $40. Annual visits to the vet for heartworm pills, rabies or distemper shots, and general checkups could cost $50 or more. Then, there is the cost of food. A twenty-five-pound bag of dry food (the cheapest kind) costs around $10. A large dog can eat that much in a couple of weeks.

_____ 2.   People can be cruel to pets simply by being thoughtless. They don't think about a pet's needs or simply ignore the needs. It never occurs to them that their pet can be experiencing a great deal of discomfort as a result of their failure to be sensitive. The cruelty is a result of the basic lack of attention and concern— qualities that should be there, but aren't.

_____ 3.   If I were in charge of the nighttime programming on a TV network, I would make changes. I would completely eliminate some shows. In fact, all of the shows that proved of little interest would be canceled. Commercials would also change, so that it would be possible to watch them without wanting to turn off the TV set. I would expand the good shows so that people would come away with an even better experience. My ideal network would be a great improvement over the average lineup we see today on any of the major networks.

_____ 4.   A friend's rudeness is much more damaging than a stranger's. When a friend says sharply, "I don't have time to talk to you just now," you feel hurt instead of angry. When a friend shows up late for lunch or a shopping trip, with no good reason, you feel that you're being taken for granted. Worst, though, is a friend who pretends to be listening to you but whose wandering eyes reveal a lack of attention. Then you feel betrayed. Friends, after all, are supposed to make up for the thoughtless cruelties of strangers.

_____ 5.   Giving my first shampoo and set to a real person, after weeks of practicing on wigs, was a nerve-wracking experience. The customer was a woman who was very set in her ways. She tried to describe what she wanted, and I tried without much success to understand what she had in mind. Every time I did something, she seemed to be indicating in one way or another that it was not what she wanted. I got more and more nervous as I worked on her hair, and the nervousness showed. The worst part of the ordeal happened at the very end, when I added the final touches. Nothing, to this woman, had turned out right.

10 ADDING DETAILS TO COMPLETE AN ESSAY

Activity

The following essay needs specific details to back up the ideas in its supporting paragraphs. In the spaces provided, add a sentence or two of clear, convincing details for each idea. This activity will give you practice at supplying specific details and an initial feel for writing an essay.

Introduction

Life without Television

When my family's only television set went to the repair shop the other day, my parents, my sister, and I thought we would have a terrible week. How could we get through the long evenings in such a quiet house? What would it be like without all the shows to keep us company? We soon realized, though, that living without television for a while was a stroke of good fortune. It became easy for each of us to enjoy some activities alone, to complete some postponed chores, and to spend rewarding time with each other and friends.

First supporting paragraph

First of all, with no television to compete for our time, we found plenty of hours for personal interests. We all read more that week than we had read during the six months before. _____

_____

_____

We each also enjoyed some hobbies we had ignored for ages. _____

_____

_____

In addition, my sister and I both stopped procrastinating with our homework. _____

_____

_____

_____

Second supporting paragraph

  Second, we did chores that had been hanging over our heads for too long. There were many jobs around the house that had needed attention for some time. _____

_____

_____

We also had a chance to do some long-postponed shopping. _____

_____

_____

_____

And each of us also did some letter writing or other paperwork that was long overdue. _____

_____

_____

Third supporting paragraph

  Finally, and probably most important, we spent time with each other. Instead of being in the same room together while we stared at a screen, we actually talked for many pleasant hours. _____

_____

Moreover, for the first time in years my family played some games together. _____

_____

And because we didn't have to worry about missing this or that show, we had some family friends over a couple of evenings and spent an enjoyable time with them. _____

_____

_____

Conclusion

> Once our television set returned, we were not prepared to put it in the attic. But we had a sense of how it can take over our lives if we are not careful. We are now more selective. We turn on the set for our favorite shows, certain sports events, and the news, but we don't leave it running all night. As a result, we find we can enjoy television and still have time left over for other activities and interests.

THE THIRD
AND FOURTH
STEPS
IN ESSAY
WRITING

This chapter will show you how to:

- **Organize and connect specific evidence in the body paragraphs of an essay**
- **Begin and end an essay with effective introductory and concluding paragraphs**
- **Write clear, error-free sentences**

You know from the previous chapter that the first two steps in writing an effective essay are advancing a thesis and supporting it with specific evidence. The third step is to organize and connect the specific evidence, which appears in the supporting paragraphs of the essay. Most of this chapter will deal with the chief ways to organize and connect this supporting information in a paper. The chapter will also discuss how to start the essay smoothly with a suitable introductory paragraph and how to finish it effectively with a well-rounded concluding paragraph. Finally, the chapter will look briefly at the sentence skills that make up the fourth and final step in writing a successful paper.

69

Step 3:
Organize and
Connect the Specific Evidence

At the same time that you are generating the specific details needed to support a thesis, you should be thinking about ways to organize and connect those details. All the details in your essay must cohere, or stick together, so that your reader will be able to move smoothly and clearly from one bit of supporting information to the next. This section will discuss the following ways to organize and connect supporting details: (1) common methods of organization, (2) transitions, and (3) other connecting words.

COMMON METHODS OF ORGANIZATION

Two common methods used to organize the supporting material in an essay are time order and emphatic order. (You will learn more specific methods of development in Part Two of this book.)

Time, or *chronological*, *order* simply means that details are listed as they occur in time. *First* this is done; *next* this; *then* this; *after* that, this; and so on. Here is an outline of an essay in this book in which time order is used.

Thesis: However, for success in exercise, you should follow a simple plan consisting of arranging the time, making preparations, and following the sequence with care.

1. To begin with, set aside a regular hour for exercise.
2. Next, prepare for your exercise session.
3. If this is your first attempt at exercising, start slowly.

Fill in the missing word: The topic sentences in the essay use the words ___To begin with___ and ___Next___ to help show time order.

Here is one supporting paragraph from the essay:

Next, prepare for your exercise session. You do this, first, by not eating or drinking anything for an hour before the session. Why risk an upset stomach? Then, dress comfortably in something that allows you to move freely. Since you'll be in your own home, there's no need to invest in a high-fashion dance costume.

A loose T shirt and shorts are good. A bathing suit is great in summer, and in winter a set of long underwear is warm and comfortable. If your hair tends to flop in your eyes, pin it back or wear a headband or scarf. After dressing, prepare the exercise area. Turn off the phone and lock the door to prevent interruptions. Shove the coffee table out of the way so you won't bruise yourself on it. Finally, get out the simple materials you'll need to exercise on.

Fill in the missing words: The paragraph uses the following words to help show time order: _____ *Next* _____, _____ *First* _____, _____ *Then* _____, _____ *After* _____, and _____ *Finally* _____.

Emphatic order is sometimes described as "save the best till last." It means that the most interesting or important detail is placed in the last part of a paragraph or in the final supporting paragraph of an essay. (In cases where all the details seem equal in importance, the writer should impose a personal order that seems logical or appropriate to the details in question.) The last position in a paper is the most emphatic position because the reader is most likely to remember the last thing read. *Finally, last of all,* and *most important* are typical words showing emphasis. Here is an outline of an essay in the book that uses emphatic order:

Thesis: Celebrities lead very stressful lives; for, no matter how glamorous or powerful they are, they have too little privacy, too much pressure, and no safety.

1. For one thing, celebrities don't have the privacy an ordinary person does.
2. In addition, celebrities are under constant pressure.
3. Most important, celebrities must deal with the stress of being in constant danger.

Fill in the missing words: The topic sentences in the essay use the words _____ *For one thing* _____, _____ *In addition* _____, and _____ *Most Important* _____ to help show emphatic order.

Here is the third supporting paragraph from the essay:

Most important, celebrities must deal with the stress of being in constant danger. The friendly grabs, hugs, and kisses of enthusiastic fans can quickly turn into uncontrolled assaults on a celebrity's hair, clothes, and car. Celebrities often get strange letters from people who become obsessed with their idols or from people who threaten to harm them. Worst of all, threats can turn into deeds. The attempt to kill Ronald Reagan and the murder of John Lennon came about because two unbalanced people tried to transfer the celebrity's fame to themselves. Famous people must live with the fact that they are always fair game—and never out of season.

Fill in the missing words: The words ___most important___ are used to mark the most emphatic detail in the paragraph.

Some essays use a combination of time order and emphatic order. For example, the essay on moviegoing in the first chapter includes time order: The writer first talks of getting to the theater, then of the theater itself, and finally of the behavior of patrons during the movie. At the same time, the writer uses emphatic order, ending with the most important reason for her dislike of moviegoing: ''Some of the other patrons are even more of a problem than the theater itself.''

Activity

Part A: Read the essays referred to below and identify their method of organizing details—time order, emphatic order, or a combination of both.

1. "My First Professional Performance" (page 137)

    _____

2. "A Vote for McDonald's (page 179)

    _____

3. "Everyday Cruelty" (page 147)

    _____

Part B: See if you can now complete the explanations that follow.

The essay titled "My First Professional Performance" uses (*add the missing word*) _____ order. The writer begins with the problems she experienced when she arrived at the carnival grounds, moves on to problems during the performance, and ends with the concert's rather abrupt finish. "A Vote for McDonald's" uses (*add the missing word*) _____ order. The writer presents three advantages of eating at McDonald's and ends with the most important one: reasonable prices. "Everyday Cruelty" uses a combination of (*add the missing words*) _____ order and _____ order. It moves from the beginning to the end of a particular workday. It also ends with the "worst incident of mean-spiritedness" that the writer witnessed that day.

TRANSITIONS

Transitions are signals that help readers follow the direction of the writer's thought. They are like signposts on the road that guide travelers. In the box that follows are some common transitional words and phrases, grouped according to the kind of signal they give to readers. Note that certain words provide more than one kind of signal.

Addition signals: one, first of all, second, the third reason, also, next, another, and, in addition, moreover, furthermore, finally, last of all

Time signals: first, then, next, after, as, before, while, meanwhile, soon, now, during, finally

Space signals: next to, across, on the opposite side, to the left, to the right, above, below, nearby

Change-of-direction signals: but, however, yet, in contrast, although, otherwise, still, on the contrary, on the other hand

Illustration signals: for example, for instance, specifically, as an illustration, once, such as

Conclusion signals: therefore, consequently, thus, then, as a result, in summary, to conclude, last of all, finally

Activity

1. Underline the four *addition* signals in the following selection:

Another way that animals are abused is through their use in unnecessary lab and medical experiments. One instance is the use of rabbits in lab tests for cosmetic companies. The helpless animals are locked into neck restraints resembling the old-fashioned stocks used by the Puritans. Moreover, their eyes are pinned open with metal clamps. Solutions of experimental hair dye are dripped continuously into each rabbit's eyes to test the solution for possible irritation or cancer-causing effects. A second example of needless animal abuse involves the endless repetition of previously done experiments. Every year, science and medical students destroy thousands of monkeys, cats, dogs, and rabbits simply for practice. They repeat experiments whose results are well known and which they could learn from books and scientific reports. These are cases not of worthwhile advances in science but of the thoughtless destruction of life.

2. Underline the three *time* signals in the following selection:

Once you've snagged the job of TV sports reporter, you have to begin working on the details of your image. First, invest in two or three truly loud sports jackets. Look for gigantic plaid patterns in odd color combinations like purple and green or orange and blue. These should become familiar enough to viewers so that they will associate that crazy jacket with that dynamic sportscaster. Next, try to cultivate a distinctive voice that will be just annoying enough to be memorable. A nasal whine or a gravelly growl will do it. Be sure to speak only in tough, punchy sentences that seem to be punctuated with imaginary exclamation points. Finally, you must share lots of pompous, obnoxious opinions with your viewers. Your tone of voice must convey the hidden message, "I dare anyone to disagree with me." When the home teams lose, call them bums. When players strike, talk sarcastically about the good old days. When a sports franchise leaves town, say, "Good riddance."

3. Underline the three *space* signals in the following selection:

The vegetable bin of my refrigerator contained an assortment of weird-looking items. Next to a shriveled, white-coated lemon was a pair of oranges covered with blue fuzz. To the right of the oranges was a bunch of carrots that had begun to sprout points, spikes, knobs, and tendrils. The carrots drooped into U shapes as I picked them up with the tips of my fingers. Near the carrots was a net bag of onions; each onion had sent curling shoots through the net until the whole thing resembled a mass of green spaghetti. The most horrible item, though, was a head of lettuce that had turned into a pool of brown goo. It had seeped out of its bag and coated the bottom of the bin with a sticky, evil-smelling liquid.

4. Underline the two *change-of-direction* signals in the following selection:

Taking small children on vacation, for instance, sounds like a wonderful experience for the entire family. But vacations can be scary or emotionally overwhelming times for children. When children are taken away from their usual routine and brought to an unfamiliar place, they can become very frightened. That strange bed in the motel room or the unusual noises in Grandma's spare bedroom may cause nightmares. On vacations, too, children usually clamor to do as many things in one day as they can and to stay up past their usual bedtime. And, since it is vacation time, parents may decide to give in to the children's demands. A parental attitude like this, however, can lead to problems. After a sixteen-hour day of touring the amusement park, eating in a restaurant, and seeing a movie, children can experience sensory and emotional overload. They become cranky, unhappy, or even rebellious and angry.

5.   Underline the two *illustration* signals in the following selection:

Supermarkets also use psychology to encourage you to buy. For example, in most supermarkets, the milk and the bread are either at opposite ends of the store or located far away from the first aisle. Even if you've stopped at the market only for staples like these, you must pass hundreds of items in order to reach them. The odds are that instead of leaving with just a quart of milk, you'll leave with additional purchases as well. Special displays, such as a pyramid of canned green beans in an aisle or a large end display of cartons of paper towels, also increase sales. Because you assume that these items are a good buy, you may pick them up. However, they may not even be on sale! Store managers know that the customer is automatically attracted to a display like this, and they will use it to move an overstocked product.

6.   Underline the two *conclusion* signals in the following selection:

Finally, my grandmother was extremely thrifty. She was one of those people who hoard pieces of used aluminum foil after carefully scraping off the cake icing or beef gravy. She had a drawer full of old eyeglasses that dated back at least thirty years. The lens prescriptions were no longer accurate, but Gran couldn't bear to throw away "a good pair of glasses." She kept them "just in case," but we could never figure out what situation would involve a desperate need for a dozen pairs of old eyeglasses. We never realized the true extent of Gran's thriftiness, though, until after she died. Her house was to be sold, and therefore we cleaned out its dusty attic. In one corner was a cardboard box filled with two- and three-inch pieces of string. The box was labeled, in Gran's spidery hand, "String too short to be saved."

TRANSITIONAL SENTENCES

Transitions occur not only *within* the supporting paragraphs in an essay but also *between* the paragraphs. *Transitional,* or *linking, sentences* are used to help tie together the supporting paragraphs in an essay. They enable the reader to move smoothly and clearly from one idea and paragraph in an essay to the next idea and paragraph.

Here is one of the two linking sentences in the essay on moviegoing:

Once you have made it to the box office and gotten your tickets, you're confronted with the problems of the theater itself.

The words *made it to the box office* remind us of the point of the first supporting paragraph, while *confronted with the problems of the theater itself* presents the point to be developed in the second supporting paragraph.

Here is the second linking sentence:

Some of the other patrons are even more of a problem than the theater itself.

The words *the theater itself* echo the point of the second supporting paragraph, while *some of the other patrons* announces the topic of the third supporting paragraph.

Activity

Given below is a brief sentence outline of an essay. In the outline, the second and third topic sentences serve as transitional or linking sentences. They both remind us of the point in the preceding paragraph and announce the point to be developed in the present paragraph. In the space provided, add the words needed to complete the second and third topic sentences.

Thesis

The most important values I learned from my parents are the importance of family support, of hard work, and of a good education.

First supporting paragraph

First, my parents taught me that family members should stick together, especially in times of trouble. . . .

Second supporting paragraph

In addition to teaching me about the importance of _____ family support _____,
my parents taught me the value of ____hard   work_____
_____. . . .

Third supporting paragraph

Along with the value of ____hard   work_____,
my parents emphasized the benefits of ____a   good   education__
_____. . . .

OTHER CONNECTING WORDS

In addition to transitions, there are three other kinds of connecting words that help tie together the specific evidence in a paper: repeated words, pronouns, and synonyms. Each will be discussed in turn.

Repeated Words

Many of us have been taught by English instructors—correctly so—not to repeat ourselves in our writing. On the other hand, repeating *key* words can help tie together the flow of thought in a paper. Below is a selection that uses repeated words to remind readers of the key idea on which the discussion is centered:

One reason for studying psychology is to help you deal with your children. Perhaps your young daughter refuses to go to bed when you want her to and bursts into tears at the least mention of "lights out." A little knowledge of psychology comes in handy. Offer her a choice of staying up until 7:30 with you or going upstairs and playing until 8:00. Since she gets to make the choice, she does not feel so powerless and will not resist. Psychology is also useful in rewarding a child for a job well done. Instead of telling your ten-year-old son what a good boy he is when he makes his own bed, tell him how neat it looks, how happy you are to see it, and how proud of him you are for doing it by himself. The psychology books will tell you that being a good boy is much harder to live up to than doing one job well.

Pronouns

Pronouns (*he, she, it, you, they, this, that,* and others) are another way to connect ideas as you develop a paper. Using pronouns to take the place of other words or ideas can help you avoid needless repetition in a paper. (Note, however, that although pronouns are helpful, they should be used with care in order to avoid the unclear or inconsistent pronoun references described in this book on pages 364–371.) Here is a selection that makes use of pronouns:

Another way for people to economize at an amusement park is to bring their own food. If they pack a nourishing, well-balanced lunch of cold chicken, carrot sticks, and fruit, they will avoid having to pay high prices for hamburgers and hot dogs. They will also save on calories. Also, instead of filling up on soft drinks, they should bring a thermos of iced tea. It is more refreshing than soda, and it is a great deal cheaper. Every dollar that is not spent at a refreshment stand is one that can be spent on another ride.

Synonyms

Using synonyms (that is, words which are alike in meaning) can also help move the reader clearly from one step in the thought of a paper to the next. In addition, the use of synonyms increases variety and interest by avoiding needless repetition of the same words.

Note the synonyms for *method* in the following selection:

There are several methods of fund-raising that work well with small organizations. One technique is to hold an auction, with everyone either contributing an item from home or obtaining a donation from a sympathetic local merchant. Because all the merchandise, including the services of the auctioneer, has been donated, the entire proceeds can be placed in the organization's treasury. A second fund-raising procedure is a car wash. Club members and their children get together on a Saturday and wash all the cars in the neighborhood for a few dollars apiece. A final, time-tested way to raise money is to give a bake sale, with each family contributing homemade cookies, brownies, layer cakes, or cupcakes. Sold by the piece or by the box, these baked goods will satisfyingly fill both the stomach and the pocketbook.

Activity

Read the selection below and then answer the questions about it that follow:

[1]When I think about my childhood in the 1930s, today's energy crisis and lowered thermostats don't seem so bad. [2]In our house, we had only a wood-burning cookstove in the kitchen to keep us warm. [3]In the morning, my father would get up in the icy cold, go downstairs, and light a fire in the black iron range. [4]When he called us, I would put off leaving my warm bed until the last possible minute and then quickly grab my school clothes. [5]The water pitcher and washing basin in my room would be layered with ice, and my breath would come out as white puffs as I ran downstairs. [6]My sisters and I would all dress—as quickly as possible—in the chilly but bearable air of the kitchen. [7]Our schoolroom, once we had arrived, didn't provide much relief from the cold. [8]Students wore woolen mitts which left their fingers free but covered their palms and wrists. [9]Even with these, we occasionally suffered chilblains. [10]The throbbing patches on our hands made writing a painful process. [11]When we returned home in the afternoon, we spent all our indoor hours in the warm kitchen. [12]We hated to leave it at bedtime in order to make the return trip to those cold bedrooms and frigid sheets. [13]My mother made up hot-water bottles and gave us hot bricks to tuck under the covers, but nothing could eliminate the agony of that penetrating cold when we first slid under the bedclothes.

1. How many times is the key word *cold* repeated? _____

2. Write here the pronoun that is used for *father* (sentence 4): _____;
    mitts (sentence 9): _____; *kitchen* (sentence 12): _____.

3. Write here the words that are used as a synonym for *cookstove* in sentence 3:
    _____; write in the words that are used as a synonym for
    chilblains in sentence 10: _____; write in the word that is
    used as a synonym for *cold* in sentence 12: _____ .

INTRODUCTIONS, CONCLUSIONS, AND TITLES

So far, this chapter has been concerned with ways to organize the supporting
paragraphs of an essay. A well-organized essay, however, should also have a
strong introductory paragraph, an effective concluding paragraph, and a good title.

Introductory Paragraph

A well-written introductory paragraph will perform several important roles:

1   It will attract the reader's interest, encouraging him or her to go on and
    actually read the essay. Using one of the methods of introduction described
    below can help draw the reader into your paper.

2   It will supply any background information needed to understand the essay.
    Such information is sometimes needed so that the reader has a context in
    which to understand the ideas presented in the essay.

3   It will present a thesis statement. This clear, direct statement of the main idea
    to be developed in the paper usually occurs near the end of the introduc-
    tory paragraph.

4   It will indicate a plan of development. In this "preview," the major points
    that will support the thesis are listed in the order in which they will be
    presented in the essay. In some cases, the thesis and plan of development
    may appear in the same sentence. In some cases, though, the plan of develop-
    ment may be omitted.

Common Methods of Introduction: Here are some common methods of introduction. Use any one method, or a combination of methods, to introduce your
subject in an interesting way to the reader.

1 *Begin with a broad, general statement of your topic and narrow it down to your thesis statement.* Broad, general statements ease the reader into your thesis statement by providing a background for it. In the example below, the writer talks generally about diets and then narrows down to comments on a specific diet.

> Bookstore shelves today are crammed with dozens of different diet books. The American public seems willing to try any sort of diet, especially the ones that promise instant, miraculous results. And authors are more than willing to invent new fad diets to cash in on this craze. Unfortunately, some of these fad diets are ineffective or even unsafe. One of the worst is the "Palm Beach diet." It is impractical, doesn't achieve the results it claims, and is a sure route to poor nutrition.

2 *Start with an idea or situation that is the opposite of the one you will develop.* This approach works because your readers will be surprised, and then intrigued, by the contrast between the opening idea and the thesis that follows it.

> When I decided to return to school at age thirty-five, I wasn't at all worried about my ability to do the work. After all, I was a grown woman who had raised a family, not a confused teenager fresh out of high school. But when I started classes, I realized that those "confused teenagers" sitting around me were in much better shape for college than I was. They still had all their classroom skills in bright, shiny condition, while mine had grown rusty from disuse. I had totally forgotten how to locate information in a library, how to write a report, and even how to speak up in class discussions.

3 *Explain the importance of your topic to the reader.* If you can convince your readers that the subject in some way applies to them, or is something they should know more about, they will want to keep reading.

> Diseases like scarlet fever and whooping cough used to kill more young children than any other cause. Today, however, child mortality due to disease has been almost completely eliminated by medical science. Instead, car accidents are the number one killer of our children. And most of the children fatally injured in car accidents were not protected by car seats, belts, or restraints of any kind. Several steps must be taken to remedy this serious problem.

4 *Use an incident or brief story.* Stories are naturally interesting. They appeal to a reader's curiosity. In your introduction, an anecdote will grab the reader's attention right away. The story should be brief and should be related to your main idea. The incident in the story can be something that happened to you, something you have heard about, or something you have read about in a newspaper or magazine.

Early Sunday morning the young mother dressed her little girl warmly and gave her a candy bar, a picture book, and a well-worn stuffed rabbit. Together, they drove downtown to a Methodist church. There the mother told the little girl to wait on the stone steps until children began arriving for Sunday school. Then the young mother drove off, abandoning her five-year-old because she couldn't cope with being a parent anymore. This incident is one of thousands of cases of child neglect and abuse that occur annually. Perhaps the automatic right to become a parent should no longer exist. Would-be parents, instead, should be forced to apply for licenses granting them the privilege of raising children.

5   *Ask one or more questions.* But remember that questions need answers. You may simply want the reader to think about possible answers, or you may plan to answer the questions yourself later in the paper.

What is love? How do we know that we are really in love? When we meet that special person, how can we tell that our feelings are genuine and not merely infatuation? And, if they are genuine, will these feelings last? Love, as we all know, is difficult to define. But most people agree that true and lasting love involves far more than mere physical attraction. It involves mutual respect, the desire to give rather than take, and the feeling of being wholly at ease.

6   *Use a quotation.* A quotation can be something you have read in a book or article. It can also be something that you have heard: a popular saying or proverb (''Never give advice to a friend''); a current or recent advertising slogan (''Reach out and touch someone''); a favorite expression used by friends or family (''My father always says . . .''). Using a quotation in your introductory paragraph lets you add someone else's voice to your own.

''Fish and visitors,'' wrote Benjamin Franklin, ''begin to smell after three days.'' Last summer, when my sister and her family came to spend their two-week vacation with us, I became convinced that Franklin was right. After only three days, I was thoroughly sick of my brother-in-law's corny jokes, my sister's endless complaints about her boss, and their children's constant invasions of our privacy.

Activity

The box on the next page summarizes the six kinds of introduction. Read the introductions that follow it and, in the space provided, write the letter of the kind of introduction used in each case.

A. General to narrow	D. Incident or story
B. Starting with an opposite	E. Questions
C. Stating importance of topic	F. Quotation

_____ 1.   The ad, in full color on a glossy magazine page, shows a beautiful kitchen with gleaming counters. In the foreground, on one of the counters, stands a shiny new food processor. Usually, a feminine hand is touching it lovingly. Around the main picture are other, smaller shots. They show mounds of perfectly sliced onion rings, thin rounds of juicy tomatoes, heaps of matchstick-sized potatoes, and piles of golden, evenly grated cheese. The ad copy tells you how wonderful, how easy, food preparation will be with a processor. Don't believe it. My processor turned out to be expensive, difficult to operate, and very limited in its use.

_____ 2.   People say, "You can't tell a book by its cover." Actually, you can. When you're browsing in the drugstore or supermarket and you see a paperback featuring an attractive young woman in a low-cut dress fleeing from a handsome dark figure in a shadowy castle, you know exactly what you're getting. Every romance novel has the same elements: an innocent heroine, an exotic setting, and a cruel but fascinating hero.

_____ 3.   We Americans are incredibly lazy. Instead of cooking a simple, nourishing meal, we pop a frozen dinner into the oven. Instead of studying a daily newspaper, we are contented with the capsule summaries on the network news. Worst of all, instead of walking even a few blocks to the local convenience store, we jump into our cars. This dependence on the automobile, even for short trips, has robbed us of a valuable experience—walking. If we drove less and walked more, we would save money, become healthier, and discover fascinating things about our surroundings.

Concluding Paragraph

A concluding paragraph is your chance to remind the reader of your thesis idea. Also, the conclusion brings the paper to a natural and graceful end, sometimes leaving the reader with a final thought on the subject.

Common Methods of Conclusion: Any one of the methods below, or a combination of methods, may be used to round off your paper.

1   *End with a summary and final thought.* When army instructors train new recruits, each of their lessons follows a three-step formula:

a   Tell them what you're going to tell them.

b   Tell them.

c   Tell them what you've told them.

An essay that ends with a summary is not very different. After you have stated your thesis ("Tell them what you're going to tell them") and supported it ("Tell them"), you restate the thesis and supporting points ("Tell them what you've told them"). Don't, however, use the exact wording you used before. Here is a summary conclusion:

> Catalog shopping at home, then, has several advantages. Such shopping is convenient, saves you money, and saves you time. It is not surprising that growing numbers of devoted catalog shoppers are welcoming those full-color mail brochures that offer everything from turnip seeds to televisions.

Note that the summary is accompanied by a final comment that "rounds off" the paper and brings the discussion to a close. This combination of a summary and a final thought is the most common method of concluding an essay.

2   *Include a thought-provoking question or short series of questions.* A question grabs the reader's attention. It is a direct appeal to your reader to think further about what you have written. A question should follow logically from the points you have already made in the paper. A question must deal with one of these areas:

a   Why the subject of your paper is important

b   What might happen in the future

c   What should be done about this subject

d   Which choice should be made

In your conclusion, you may provide an answer to your question. Be sure, though, that the question is closely related to your thesis. Here is an example:

> What, then, will happen in the twenty-first century when most of the population will be over sixty years old? Retirement policies could change dramatically, with the age-sixty-five testimonial dinner and gold watch postponed for five or ten years. Even television would change as the Geritol generation replaces the Pepsi generation. Glamorous gray-haired models would sell everything from toilet paper to televisions. New soap operas and situation comedies would reveal the secrets of the "sunset years." It will be a different world indeed when the young finally find themselves outnumbered.

3   *End with a prediction or recommendation.* Like questions, predictions and recommendations also involve your readers. A prediction states what will or may happen in the future:

> If people stopped to think before acquiring pets, there would be fewer instances of cruelty to animals. Many times, it is the people who adopt pets without considering the expense and responsibility involved who mistreat and neglect their animals. Pets are living creatures. They do not deserve to be acquired as carelessly as one would acquire a stuffed toy.

A recommendation suggests what should be done about a situation or problem:

> Stereotypes such as the helpless homemaker, harried executive, and dotty grandparent are insulting enough to begin with. In magazine ads or television commercials, they become even more insulting. Now these unfortunate characters are not just being laughed at; they are being turned into hucksters to sell products to an unsuspecting public. Consumers should boycott companies whose advertising continues to use such stereotypes.

Activity

In the space provided, note whether each concluding paragraph ends with a summary and final thought (write S in the space), ends with a prediction or recommendation (write P/R), or ends with a question (write Q).

_____ 1.   Disappointments are unwelcome, but regular, visitors to everyone's life. We can feel depressed about them, or we can try to escape from them. The best thing, though, is to accept a disappointment and then try to use it somehow: step over the unwelcome visitor and then get on with life.

_____ 2.   Holidays, it is clear, are often not the fulfilling experiences they are supposed to be. They can, in fact, be nerve-wracking. How can one deal with the problem? Most experts agree that a person should schedule plenty of activities: more time with family, volunteer work, even overtime on the job. Staying active is preferable to the depressing time one might spend at home with only the hollow and flickering images on the TV for company.

_____ 3.   Some people dream of starring roles, their names in lights, and their pictures on the cover of People magazine. I'm not one of them, though. A famous person gives up private life, feels pressured all the time, and is never completely safe. So let someone else have that cover story. I'd rather lead an ordinary, but calm, life than a stress-filled one.

Titles

A title is usually a very brief summary of what your paper is about. It is often no more than several words. You may find it easy to write the title *after* you have completed your paper.

Following are the introductory paragraphs for two of the essays in this text, along with the titles of the essays.

Introductory Paragraph

I'm not just a consumer—I'm a victim. If I order a product, it is sure to arrive in the wrong color, size, or quantity. If I hire people to do repairs, they never arrive on the day scheduled. If I owe a bill, the computer is bound to overcharge me. Therefore, in self-defense, I have developed the following consumer's guide to complaining effectively.

Title: How to Complain

Introductory Paragraph

Schools divide people into categories. From first grade on up, students are labeled "advanced" or "deprived" or "remedial" or "antisocial." Students pigeonhole their fellow students, too. We've all known the "brain," the "jock," the "dummy," and the "teacher's pet." In most cases, these narrow labels are misleading and inaccurate. But there is one label for a certain type of college student that says it all. That is, of course, "zombie."

Title: Student Zombies

Note that you should not underline the title. Nor should you put quotation marks around it. On the other hand, you should capitalize all but small connecting words in the title. Also, you should skip a space between the title and the first line of the text. (See "Manuscript Form," pages 396–397.)

Activity

Write an appropriate title for each of the introductory paragraphs that follow.

1.   For my birthday this month, my wife has offered to treat me to dinner at the restaurant of my choice. I think she expects me to ask for a meal at the Chalet, the classiest, most expensive restaurant in town. However, I'm going to eat my birthday dinner at McDonald's. When I compare the two restaurants, the advantages of eating at McDonald's are clear.

   Title: _____

2.   I've been in lots of diners, and they've always seemed to be warm, busy, friendly, happy places. That's why, on a recent Monday night, I stopped at a diner for a cup of coffee. I was returning home after an all-day car trip and needed something to help me make the last forty-five miles. A diner at midnight, however, was not the place I had expected. It was different—and lonely.

Title: _____

3.   If you see rock-concert audiences only on television or in newspaper photos, the people at these events may all seem to be excited teenagers. However, if you attended a few rock shows, you would see that several kinds of people make up the crowd. At any concert, you would find the typical fan, the out-of-place person, and the troublemaker.

Title: _____

Step 4: Write Clear, Error-Free Sentences

The fourth step in writing an effective paper is to follow the agreed-upon rules or conventions of written English. These conventions—or, as they are called in this book, *sentence skills*—must be followed if your sentences are to be clear and error-free. A paper that contains a number of errors in grammar, mechanics, punctuation, or usage will not make a favorable impression on a reader. Even if the paper is otherwise well written, the reader will be disposed against it because of the sentence-skills mistakes.

Here are the most common of the conventions you'll need to follow:

1 Write complete sentences rather than fragments.
2 Do not write run-ons.
3 Use verb forms correctly.
4 Make sure that subject, verbs, and pronouns agree.
5 Eliminate faulty parallelism.
6 Eliminate faulty modifiers.
7 Use pronoun forms correctly.
8 Use capital letters where needed.

9 Use the following marks of punctuation correctly: apostrophe, quotation marks, comma, semicolon, colon, hyphen, dash, parentheses.

10 Use correct paper format.

11 Eliminate wordiness.

12 Choose words carefully.

13 Check for possible spelling errors.

14 Eliminate careless errors.

15 Vary your sentences.

These sentence skills are treated in detail in Part Four of this book, and they can be referred to easily as needed. Note that both the list of sentence skills on page 127 and the inside front cover (item 4) and the correction symbols on the inside back cover give references, so that you can turn quickly to those skills which give you problems.

Practice in Organizing and Connecting Specific Evidence

You now know the third step in effective writing: organizing the specific evidence used to support the thesis of a paper. You also know that the fourth step—writing clear, error-free sentences—will be treated in detail in Part Four. This closing section will expand and strengthen your understanding of the third step in writing. You will work through the following series of activities:

1 Organizing through time or emphatic order
2 Providing transitions
3 Identifying transitions and other connecting words
4 Completing transitional sentences
5 Identifying introductions and conclusions

1 ORGANIZING THROUGH TIME OR EMPHATIC ORDER

Activity 1

Use time order to organize the scrambled lists of supporting ideas below. Write 1 beside the supporting idea that should come first in time, 2 beside the idea that logically follows, and 3 beside the idea that comes last in time.

1. Thesis: When I was a child, Disney movies frightened me more than any other kind.

    _____ As a five-year-old, I found the story of *Pinocchio,* a boy transformed into a puppet, terrifying.

    _____ Although I saw *Bambi* when I was old enough to begin poking fun at "baby movies," the scene during which Bambi's mother is killed has stayed with me to this day.

    _____ About a year after *Pinocchio,* I gripped my seat in fear as the witches and goblins of *Fantasia* flew across the screen.

2. Thesis: Beware of these pitfalls if you want to make the perfect cheesecake.

    _____ There's only one way to remove the cake cleanly and easily from its pan.

    _____ Plan in advance to have your equipment ready and the ingredients at room temperature.

    _____ Remember to time the baking process and regulate the oven temperature while the cake is baking.

3. Thesis: Applying for unemployment benefits was a confusing, frustrating experience.

    _____ It was difficult to find both the office and a place to park.

    _____ When I finally reached the head of the line after four hours of waiting, the clerk had problems processing my claim.

    _____ There was no one to direct or help me when I entered the large office, which was packed with people.

Activity 2

Use emphatic order (order of importance) to arrange the following scrambled lists of supporting ideas. For each thesis, write 1 in the blank beside the point that is perhaps less important or interesting than the other two, 2 beside the point that appears more important or interesting, and 3 beside the point that should be most emphasized.

1. Thesis: My after-school job has been an invaluable part of my life this year.

    _____ Better yet, it has taught me how to get along with many kinds of people.

    _____ Since it's in the morning, it usually keeps me from staying up too late.

    _____ Without it, I would have had to drop out of school.

2. Thesis: We received some odd gifts for our wedding.

_____ The winner in the odd-gift category was a large wooden box with no apparent purpose or function.

_____ Someone gave us a gift certificate for a massage.

_____ Even stranger, my uncle gave me his favorite bowling ball.

3. Thesis: Donna is my most loyal friend.

_____ She has even taken time off from work to do special favors for me.

_____ She's always there in real emergencies or emotional crises.

_____ She once lent me her favorite necklace to wear on a date.

2   PROVIDING TRANSITIONS

Activity

In the spaces provided, add appropriate transitions to tie together the sentences and ideas in the following essay. Draw from the words given in the boxes above the paragraphs. Use each word only once.

Annoying People

Former President Richard Nixon used to keep an "enemies list" of all the   1
people he didn't especially like. I'm ashamed to confess it, but I, too, have an enemies list—a mental one. On this list are all the people I would gladly live without, the ones who cause my blood pressure to rise to the boiling point. The top three places on the list go to people with annoying nervous habits, people who talk in movie theaters, and people who smoke in restaurants.

For example	First of all	Another	However

_____, there are the people with nervous habits.   2

_____, there are the ones who make faces. When in deep thought, they twitch, squint, and frown, and they can be a real distraction when

I'm trying to concentrate during an exam. _____ type of nervous character makes useless designs. These people bend paper clips into abstract sculptures as they talk or string the clips into necklaces.

_____, neither of these groups is as bad as the people who make noises. These individuals, when they are feeling uncomfortable, bite their fingernails or crack their knuckles. If they have a pencil in their hands, they tap it rhythmically against whatever surface is handy—a desk, a book, a head.

Lacking a pencil to play with, they jingle the loose change or keys in their pockets. These people make me wish I were hard of hearing.

On the contrary   Then   As a result   After   second

A _____ category of people I would gladly do away with is   3
the ones who talk in movie theaters. These people are not content to sit back,

relax, and enjoy the film they have paid to see. _____, they feel compelled to comment loudly on everything from the hero's hairstyle to the appropriateness of the background music.

_____, no one hears a word of any dialog except theirs.

_____ they have been in the theater for a while, their interest in

the movie may fade. _____ they will start discussing other things, and the people around them will be treated to an instant replay of the last family scandal or soap opera episode. These stories may be entertaining, but they don't belong in a movie theater.

Otherwise   But   Last of all

_____, there are the restaurant smokers. If I have ordered   4
an expensive dinner, I don't appreciate having another diner's smelly cigar smoke compete with the aroma of my sirloin steak. Even the appetizing smell of a Big Mac or Whopper can be spoiled by the sharp fumes sent out by a nearby cigarette smoker. Often, I have to lean over to the next table and ask the offender

to stop smoking. _____, it is impossible for me to taste my food.

So long as murder remains illegal, the nervous twitchers, movie talkers, and   5

restaurant smokers of the world are safe from me. _____ if ever I am granted the power of life or death, these people had better think twice about annoying me. They might not have long to live.

3   IDENTIFYING TRANSITIONS AND OTHER CONNECTING WORDS

Activity

The following items use connecting words to help tie ideas together. The connecting words you are to identify are set off in italics. In the space, write T for *transition,* RW for *repeated word,* S for *synonym,* or P for *pronoun.*

_____   1.   Kate wears a puffy, quilted, down-filled jacket. In this *garment,* she resembles a stack of inflated inner tubes.

_____   2.   Plants like poinsettias and mistletoe are pretty. *They* are also poisonous.

_____   3.   A strip of strong cloth can be used as an emergency fan-belt replacement. *In addition,* a roll of duct tape can be used to patch a leaky hose temporarily.

_____   4.   Newspapers may someday be brought to your home, not by paper carriers, but by computers. Subscribers will simply punch in a code, and the *machines* will display the desired pages.

_____   5.   I'm always losing my soft contact lenses, which resemble little circles of thick Saran Wrap. One day I dropped both of *them* into a cup of hot tea.

_____   6.   The molded plastic chairs in the classrooms are hard and uncomfortable. When I sit in one of these *chairs,* I feel as if I were sitting in a bucket.

_____   7.   One way to tell if your skin is aging is to pinch a fold of skin on the back of your hand. If *it* doesn't smooth out quickly, your skin is losing its youthful tone.

_____   8.   I never eat sloppy joes. *They* look as if they've already been eaten.

_____   9.   Clothing intended just for children seems to have vanished. *Instead,* children wear scaled-down versions of everything adults wear.

_____   10.   Some successful salespeople use voice tones and hand gestures that are almost hypnotic. Customers are not conscious of this *hypnotic* effect but merely feel an urge to buy.

_____   11.   The giant cockroaches in Florida are the subject of local legends. A visitor, according to one tale, saw one of the *insects,* thought it was a Volkswagen, and tried to drive it away.

_____   12.   Some thieves scour garbage cans for credit-card receipts. *Then,* they use the owner's name and card number to order merchandise by phone.

_____   13.   When the phone rang, I dropped the garden hose. *It* whipped around crazily and squirted water through the kitchen screen door.

_____   14.   There are many phobias other than the ones described in psychology textbooks. I have *phobias,* for instance, about toasters and lawn mowers.

_____   15.   My mother believes that food is love. *Therefore,* when she offers homemade cookies or cupcakes, I hate to hurt her feelings by refusing them.

4   COMPLETING TRANSITIONAL SENTENCES

Activity

Following are brief sentence outlines from two essays. In each outline, the second and third topic sentences serve as transitional, or linking, sentences. They both remind us of the point in the preceding paragraph and announce the point to be developed in the present paragraph. In the space provided, add the words needed to complete the second and third topic sentences.

Thesis 1

In order to set up a day-care center in your home, you must make sure your house will conform to state regulations, obtain the necessary legal permits, and advertise your service in the right places.

First supporting paragraph

First of all, as a potential operator of a home day-care center, you must make sure your house will conform to state regulations. . . .

Second supporting paragraph

After making certain that _____ _____, you must obtain _____ . . . .

Third supporting paragraph

Finally, once you have the necessary _____ you can begin to _____.

Thesis 2   Cheaper cost, greater comfort, and superior electronic technology make watching football at home more enjoyable than attending a game at the stadium.

First supporting paragraph

> For one thing, watching the game on TV eliminates the cost of attending the game. . . .

Second supporting paragraph

> In addition to saving me money, watching the game at home is more _____ than sitting in a stadium. . . .

Third supporting paragraph

> Even more important than _____ and _____, though, is the _____ which makes a televised game better than the "real thing." . . .

5   IDENTIFYING INTRODUCTIONS AND CONCLUSIONS

Activity

The box below lists six common kinds of introductions and three common kinds of conclusions. Read the three pairs of introductory and concluding paragraphs that follow on the next page. Then, in the space provided, write the letter of the kind of introduction and conclusion used in each case.

Introductions	Conclusions
A. General to narrow	G. Summary and final thought
B. Starting with an opposite	H. Question(s)
C. Stating importance of topic	I. Prediction or recommendation
D. Incident or story	
E. Question(s)	
F. Quotation	

Pair 1

_____   Shortly before Easter, our local elementary school sponsored a fund-raising event at which classroom pets and their babies—hamsters, guinea pigs, and baby chicks—were available for adoption. Afterward, as I was driving home, I saw a hand drop a baby hamster out of the car ahead of me. I couldn't avoid running over the tiny creature. One of the parents had taken the pet, regretted the decision, and decided to get rid of it. Such people have never stopped to consider the real obligations involved in owning an animal. . . .

_____   A pet cannot be thrown onto a trash heap when it is no longer wanted or tossed into a closet if it begins to bore its owner. A pet, like us, is a living thing that needs physical care, affection, and respect. Would-be owners, therefore, should think seriously about their responsibilities before they acquire a pet.

Pair 2

_____   What would life be like if we could read each other's minds? Would communications be instantaneous and perfectly clear? These questions will never be answered unless mental telepathy becomes a fact of life. Until then, we will have to make do with less-perfect means of communication, such as letters, telephone calls, and face-to-face conversations. Each of these has its drawbacks. . . .

_____   Neither letters, phone calls, nor conversations guarantee perfect communication. With all our sophisticated skills, we human beings often communicate less effectively than howling wolves or chattering monkeys. Even if we <u>were</u> able to read each other's minds, we'd probably still find some way to foul up the message.

Pair 3

_____   "Few things are harder to put up with," said Mark Twain, "than the annoyance of a good example." Twain obviously knew the problems faced by siblings cursed with older brothers or sisters who are models of perfection. All our lives, my older sister Shelley and I have been compared. Unfortunately, my looks, talents, and accomplishments always ended up on the losing side. . . .

_____   Although our looks, talents, and accomplishments were constantly compared, Shelley and I have somehow managed not to turn into deadly enemies. Feeling like the Edsel of the family, in fact, helped me to develop a drive to succeed and a sense of humor. In our sibling rivalry, we both managed to win.

FOUR BASES
FOR EVALUATING
ESSAYS

This chapter will show you how to evaluate an essay for:

- Unity
- Support
- Coherence
- Sentence skills

In the preceding chapters, you learned four essential steps in writing an effective paper. The box below shows how the steps lead to four standards, or bases, you can use in evaluating an essay.

Four Steps $\longrightarrow$	*Four Bases*
1 If you advance a single point and stick to that point,	your paper will have *unity*.
2 If you support the point with specific evidence,	your paper will have *support*.
3 If you organize and connect the specific evidence,	your paper will have *coherence*.
4 If you write clear, error-free sentences,	your paper will demonstrate effective *sentence skills*.

This chapter will discuss these four bases—unity, support, coherence, and sentence skills—and will show how the four bases can be used to evaluate a paper.

Base 1: Unity

Activity

The following student essays are on the topic ''Problems or Pleasures of My Teenage Years.'' Which one makes its point more clearly and effectively, and why?

Essay 1

Teenage Pranks

Looking back at some of the things I did as a teenager makes me break out in a sweat. The purpose of each adventure was fun, but occasionally things got out of hand. In my search for good times, I was involved in three notable pranks, ranging from fairly harmless to fairly serious.   1

The first prank proved that good, clean fun does not have to be dull. As a high school student, I was credited with making the world's largest dessert. With several friends, I spent an entire year collecting boxes of Jell-O. Entering our school's indoor pool one night, we turned the water temperature up as high as it would go and poured in box after box of the strawberry powder. The next morning, school officials arrived to find the pool filled with thirteen thousand gallons of the quivering, rubbery stuff. No one was hurt by the prank, but we did suffer through three days of a massive cleanup.   2

Not all my pranks were harmless, and one involved risking my life. As soon as I got my driver's license, I wanted to join the ''Fliers' Club.'' Membership in this club was limited to those who could make their cars fly a distance of at least ten feet. The qualifying site was an old quarry field where friends and I had built a ramp made of dirt. I drove my battered Ford Pinto up this ramp as fast as it would go. The Pinto flew ten feet, but one of the tires exploded when I landed. The car rolled on its side, and I luckily escaped with only a bruised arm.   3

Risking my own life was bad enough, but there was another prank where other people could have been hurt, too. On this occasion, I accidentally set a valley on fire. Two of my friends and I were sitting on a hill sharing a few beers. It was a warm summer night, and there was absolutely nothing to do. The idea came like a thunderclap. We collected a supply of large plastic trash bags, emergency highway flares, and the half tank of helium left over from a science-fair experiment. Then we began to construct a fleet of UFOs. Filling the bags with helium, we tied them closed with wire and suspended several burning flares below each bag. Our UFOs leaped into the air like an army of invading Martians. Rising and darting in the blackness, they convinced even us. Our fun turned into horror, though, as we watched the balloons begin to drop onto the wooded valley of expensive homes below. Soon, a brush fire started and, quickly sobered, we hurried off to call the fire department anonymously.   4

Every so often, I think back on the things that I did as a teenager. I chuckle   5
at the innocent pranks and feel lucky that I didn't harm myself or others with the not-so-innocent ones. Those years were filled with wild times. Today I'm older, wiser—and maybe just a little more boring.

Essay 2

Problems of My Adolescence

In the unreal world of television situation comedies, teenagers are carefree, smart, funny, wisecracking, secure kids. In fact, most of them are more "together" than the adults on the shows. This, however, isn't how I recall my teenage years at all. As a teen, I suffered. Every day, I battled the terrible physical, family, and social troubles of adolescence.   1

For one thing, I had to deal with a demoralizing physical problem—acne. Some days, I would wake up in the morning with a red bump the size of a taillight on my nose. Since I worried constantly about my appearance anyway, acne outbreaks could turn me into a crying, screaming maniac. Plastering on a layer of orange-colored Clearasil, which didn't fool anybody, I would slink into school, hoping that the boy I had a crush on would be absent that day. Within the last few years, however, treatments for acne have improved. Now, skin doctors prescribe special drugs that clear up pimples almost immediately. An acne attack could shatter whatever small amount of self-esteem I had managed to build up.   2

In addition to fighting acne, I felt compelled to fight my family. As a teenager, I needed to be independent. At that time, the most important thing in life was to be close to my friends and to try out new, more adult experiences. Unfortunately, my family seemed to get in the way. My little brother, for instance, turned into my enemy. We're close now, though. In fact, Eddie recently painted my new apartment for me. Eddie used to barge into my room, listen to my phone conversations, and read my secret letters. I would threaten to tie him up and leave him in a garbage dumpster. He would scream, my mother would yell, and all hell would break loose. My parents, too, were enemies. They wouldn't let me stay out late, wear the clothes I wanted to wear, or hang around with the friends I liked. So I tried to get revenge on them by being miserable, sulky, and sarcastic at home.   3

Worst of all, I had to face the social traumas of being a teenager. Things that were supposed to be fun, like dates and dances, were actually horrible. On the few occasions when I had a real date, I agonized over everything—my hair, my weight, my pimples. After a date, I would come home, raid the kitchen, and drown my insecurities in a sea of junk food. Dances were also stressful events. My friends and I would sneak a couple of beers just to get up the nerve to walk into the school gym. Now I realize that teenage drinking is dangerous. I read recently that the number one killer of teenagers is drunk driving. At dances, I never relaxed. It was too important to look exactly right, to act really cool, and to pretend I was having fun.   4

I'm glad I'm not a teenager anymore. I wouldn't ever want to feel so unattractive, so confused, and so insecure again. I'll gladly accept the crow's-feet and stomach bulge of adulthood in exchange for a little peace of mind.   5

Essay _____ makes its point more clearly and effectively because

_____

_____

_____

UNDERSTANDING UNITY

Essay 1 is more effective because it is unified. All the details in this essay are on target; they support and develop each of its three topic sentences ("The first prank proved that good, clean fun does not have to be dull''; "Not all my pranks were harmless, and one involved risking my life''; and "Risking my own life was bad enough, but there was another prank where other people could have been hurt, too'').

On the other hand, essay 2 contains some details irrelevant to its topic sentences. In the first supporting paragraph (paragraph 2), the sentences, "Within the last few years, however, treatments for acne have improved. Now, skin doctors prescribe special drugs that clear up pimples almost immediately,'' do not support the writer's topic statement that she had to deal with the physical problem of acne. Such details should be left out in the interest of unity. Go back to essay 2 and cross out the two sentences in the second supporting paragraph (paragraph 3) and the two sentences in the third supporting paragraph (paragraph 4) that are off target and do not help support their topic sentences.

You should have crossed out the following two sentences: "We're close now . . . apartment for me'' and "Now I realize . . . drunk driving.''

The difference between these first two essays leads us to the first base or standard of effective writing: *unity*. To achieve unity is to have all the details in your paper related to your thesis and three supporting topic sentences. Each time you think of something to put into your paper, ask yourself whether it relates to your thesis and supporting points. If it does not, leave it out. For example, if you were writing a paper about the problems of being unemployed and then spent a couple of sentences talking about the pleasures of having a lot of free time, you would be missing the first and most essential base of good writing.

Base 2: Support

Activity

The following essays were written on ''Dealing with Disappointment.'' Both are unified, but one communicates more clearly and effectively. Which one, and why?

Essay 1

Dealing with Disappointment

One way to look at life is as a series of disappointments. Life can certainly appear that way because disappointment crops up in the life of everyone more often, it seems, than satisfaction. How disappointments are handled can have a great bearing on how life is viewed. People can react negatively by sulking or by blaming others, or they can try to understand the reasons behind the disappointment.   1

Sulking is one way to deal with disappointment. This ''Why does everything always happen to me?'' attitude is common because it is an easy attitude to adopt, but it is not very productive. Everyone has had the experience of meeting people who specialize in feeling sorry for themselves. A sulky manner will often discourage others from wanting to lend support, and it prevents the sulker from making positive moves toward self-help. It becomes easier just to sit back and sulk. Unfortunately, feeling sorry for oneself does nothing to lessen the pain of disappointment. It may, in fact, increase the pain. It certainly does not make future disappointments easier to bear.   2

Blaming others is another negative and nonproductive way to cope with disappointment. This all-too-common response of pointing the finger at someone else doesn't help one's situation. This posture will lead only to anger, resentment, and, therefore, further unhappiness. Disappointment in another's performance does not necessarily indicate that the performer is at fault. Perhaps expectations were too high, or there could have been a misunderstanding as to what the performer actually intended to accomplish.   3

A positive way to handle disappointment is to try to understand the reasons behind the disappointment. An analysis of the causes for disappointment can have an excellent chance of producing desirable results. Often understanding alone can help alleviate the pain of disappointment and can help prevent future disappointments. Also, it is wise to try to remember that what would be ideal is not necessarily what is reasonable to expect in any given situation. The ability to look disappointment squarely in the face and then go on from there is the first step on the road back.   4

Continuous handling of disappointment in a negative manner can lead to a negative view of life itself. Chances for personal happiness in such a state of being are understandably slim. Learning not to expect perfection in an imperfect world and keeping in mind those times when expectations were actually surpassed are positive steps toward allowing the joys of life to prevail.   5

Essay 2

Reactions to Disappointment

Ben Franklin said that the only sure things in life are death and taxes. He [1]
left something out, however: disappointment. No one gets through life without
experiencing many disappointments. Strangely, though, most people seem
unprepared for disappointment and react to it in negative ways. They feel
depressed or try to escape their troubles instead of using disappointment as an
opportunity for growth.

One negative reaction to disappointment is depression. A woman trying to [2]
win a promotion, for example, works hard for over a year in her department.
Helen is so sure she will get the promotion, in fact, that she has already picked
out the car she will buy when her salary increase comes through. However, the
boss names one of Helen's coworkers to the spot. The fact that all the other
department employees tell Helen that she is the one who really deserved the
promotion doesn't help her deal with the crushing disappointment. Deeply
depressed, Helen decides that all her goals are doomed to defeat. She loses her
enthusiasm for her job and can barely force herself to show up every day. Helen
tells herself that she is a failure and that doing a good job just isn't worth the
work.

Another negative reaction to disappointment, and one that often follows [3]
depression, is the desire to escape. Kevin fails to get into the college his brother
is attending, the college that was the focus of all his dreams, and decides to
escape his disappointment. Why worry about college at all? Instead, he covers up
his real feelings by giving up on his schoolwork and getting completely involved
with friends, parties, and "good times." Or Linda doesn't make the varsity
basketball team—something she wanted very badly—and so refuses to play
sports at all. She decides to hang around with a new set of friends who get high
every day; then she won't have to confront her disappointment and learn to live
with it.

The positive way to react to disappointment is to use it as a chance for [4]
growth. This isn't easy, but it's the only useful way to deal with an inevitable part
of life. Helen, the woman who wasn't promoted, could have handled her
disappointment by looking at other options. If her boss doesn't recognize talent
and hard work, perhaps she could transfer to another department. Or she could
ask the boss how to improve her performance so that she would be a shoo-in for
the next promotion. Kevin, the boy who didn't get into the college of his choice,
should look into other schools. Going to another college may encourage him to be
his own person, step out of his brother's shadow, and realize that being turned
down by one college isn't a final judgment on his abilities or potential. Rather
than escape into drugs, Linda could improve her basketball skills for a year or
pick up another sport—like swimming or tennis—that would probably turn out to
be more useful to her as an adult.

Disappointments are unwelcome, but regular, visitors to everyone's life. We   5
can feel depressed about them or we can try to escape from them. The best
thing, though, is to accept a disappointment and then try to use it somehow:
step over the unwelcome visitor on the doorstep and get on with life.

Essay _____ makes its point more clearly and effectively because

_____

_____

_____

UNDERSTANDING SUPPORT

Here, essay 2 is more effective, for it offers specific examples of the ways people
deal with disappointment. We see for ourselves the kinds of reactions people have
to disappointment.

Essay 1, on the other hand, gives us no specific evidence. The writer tells us
repeatedly that sulking, blaming others, and trying to understand the reasons
behind a disappointment are the reactions people have to a letdown. However,
the writer never *shows* us any of these responses in action. Exactly what kinds
of disappointments is the writer talking about? And how, for instance, does
someone analyze the causes of disappointment? Would a person make up a list
of causes on a piece of paper, or review the causes with a concerned friend, or
speak to a professional therapist? In an essay like this, we would want to see
examples of how sulking and blaming others are negative ways of dealing with
disappointment.

Consideration of these two essays leads us to the second base of effective
writing: *support.* After realizing the importance of specific supporting details, one
student writer revised a paper she had done on being lost in the woods as the
worst experience of her childhood. In the revised paper, instead of talking about
"the terror of being separated from my parents," she referred to such specifics
as "tears streamed down my cheeks as I pictured the faces I would never see
again" and "I clutched the locket my parents had given me as if it were a lucky
charm that could help me find my way back to the campsite." All your papers
should include such vivid details!

Base 3: Coherence

Activity

The following two essays were written on the topic ''Positive or Negative Effects of Television.'' Both are unified, and both are supported. However, one communicates more clearly and effectively. Which one, and why?

Essay 1

Harmful Effects of Watching Television

In a recent cartoon, one character said to another, ''When you think of the awesome power of television to educate, aren't you glad it doesn't?'' It's true that television has the power to educate and to entertain, but unfortunately, these benefits are outweighed by the harm it does to dedicated viewers. Television is harmful because it creates passivity, discourages communication, and presents a false picture of reality.   1

Television makes viewers passive. Children who have an electronic baby-sitter spend most of their waking hours in a semiconscious state. Older viewers watch tennis matches and basketball games with none of the excitement of being in the stands. Even if children are watching Sesame Street or The Electric Company, they are being educated passively. The child actors are going on nature walks, building crafts projects, playing with animals, and participating in games, but the little viewers are simply watching. Older viewers watch a studio audience discuss issues with Phil Donahue, but no one will turn to the home viewers to ask their opinion.   2

Worst of all, TV presents a false picture of reality that leaves viewers frustrated because they don't have the beauty or wealth of characters on television. Viewers absorb the idea that everyone else in the United States owns a lavish apartment, suburban house, sleek car, and expensive wardrobe. Every detective, police officer, oil baron, and lawyer, male or female, is suitable for a pinup poster. The material possessions on TV shows and commercials contribute to the false image of reality. News anchors and reporters, with their perfect hair and makeup, must fit television's standard of beauty. From their modest homes or cramped apartments, many viewers tune in daily to the upper-middle-class world that TV glorifies.   3

Television discourages communication. Families watching television do very little talking except for brief exchanges during commercials. If Uncle Bernie or the next-door neighbors drop in for a visit, the most comfortable activity for everyone may be not conversation but watching Wide World of Sports. The family may not even be watching the same set; instead, in some households, all the family members head for their own rooms to watch their own sets. At dinner, plates are plopped on the coffee table in front of the set, and the meal is wolfed down during CBS Nightly News. During commercials, the only communication a family has all night may consist of questions like ''Do we have any popcorn?'' and ''Where's the TV Guide?''   4

Television, like cigarettes or saccharine, is harmful to our health. We are   5
becoming isolated, passive, and frustrated. And, most frightening, the average
viewer spends more time watching television than ever.

Essay 2

The Benefits of Television

We hear a lot about the negative effects of television on the viewer. Obviously,   1
television can be harmful if it is watched constantly to the exclusion of other
activities. It would be just as harmful to listen to records or to eat constantly.
However, when television is watched in moderation, it is extremely valuable, as it
provides relaxation, entertainment, and education.

First of all, watching TV has the value of sheer relaxation. Watching television   2
can be soothing and restful after an eight-hour day of pressure, challenges, or
concentration. After working hard all day, people look forward to a new episode of
a favorite show or yet another showing of Casablanca or Red River. This period of
relaxation leaves viewers refreshed and ready to take on the world again. Watching
TV also seems to reduce stress in some people. This benefit of television is just
beginning to be recognized. One doctor, for example, advises his patients with high
blood pressure to relax in the evening with a few hours of television.

In addition to being relaxing, television is entertaining. Along with the standard   3
comedies, dramas, and game shows that provide enjoyment to viewers, television
offers a variety of movies and sports events. Moreover, in many areas, viewers can
pay a monthly fee and receive special cable programming. With this service, viewers
can watch first-run movies, rock and classical music concerts, and specialized sports
events, like European soccer and Grand Prix racing. Viewers can also buy or rent
movies to show on their television sets through videodisk players or videocassette
players. Still another growing area of TV entertainment is video games. Cartridges
are available for everything from electronic baseball to Pac-man, allowing the owner
to have a video game arcade in the living room.

Most important, television is educational. Preschoolers learn colors, numbers,   4
and letters from public television programs, like Sesame Street, that use animation
and puppets to make learning fun. Science shows for older children, like 1-2-3
Contact, go on location to analyze everything from volcanoes to rocket launches.
Adults, too, can get an education (college credits included) from courses given on
television. Also, television widens our knowledge by covering important events and
current news. Viewers can see and hear presidents' speeches, state funerals, natural
disasters, and election results as they are happening. Finally, a television set hooked
up to a home computer can help its owner learn how to manage the household
budget, invest in the stock market, or master a foreign language.

Perhaps because television is such a powerful force, we like to criticize it and   5
search for its flaws. However, the benefits of television should not be ignored. We
can use television to relax, to have fun, and to make ourselves smarter. This electronic
wonder, then, is a servant, not a master.

Essay _____ makes its point more clearly and effectively because

_____

_____

_____

_____

UNDERSTANDING COHERENCE

In this case, essay 2 is more effective because the material is organized clearly and logically. Using emphatic order, the writer develops three positive uses of television, ending with the most important use: television as an educational tool. The writer includes transitional words that act as signposts, making movement from one idea to the next easy to follow. The major transitions include *First of all, In addition,* and *Most important;* transitions within paragraphs include such words as *Moreover, Still another, too, Also,* and *Finally.* And this writer also uses a linking sentence (''In addition to being relaxing, television is entertaining'') to tie the first and second supporting paragraphs together clearly.

Although essay 1 is unified and supported, the writer does not have any clear and consistent way of organizing the material. The most important idea (signaled by the phrase *Worst of all*) is discussed in the second supporting paragraph instead of being saved for last. None of the supporting paragraphs organizes its details in a logical fashion. The first supporting paragraph, for example, discusses older viewers, then goes to younger viewers, then jumps back to older people again. The third supporting paragraph, like the first, leaps from an opening idea (families talking only during commercials) to several intervening ideas and then back to the original idea (talking during commercials). In addition, essay 1 uses practically no transitional devices to guide the reader.

These two essays lead us to the third base of effective writing: *coherence.* All the supporting ideas and sentences in a paper must be organized so that they cohere, or ''stick together.'' As has already been mentioned, key techniques for tying together the material in a paper include a clear method of organization (such as time order or emphatic order), transitions, and other connecting words.

Base 4: Sentence Skills

Activity

Following are two versions of an essay. Both are unified, supported, and organized, but one version communicates more clearly and effectively. Which one, and why?

Essay 1

"revenge"

[1]Revenge is one of those things that everyone enjoy. [2]People don't like to talk about it, though. [3]Just the same, there is nothing more tempting, more satisfying, or more rewarding than revenge. [4]The purpose is not to harm your victims. [5]But to let them know that I am upset about something they are doing. [6]Careful plotting can provide you with relief from bothersom coworkers, gossiping friends, or nagging family members.

[7]Coworkers who make comments about the fact that you are always fifteen minutes late for work can be taken care of very simply. [8]All you have to do is get up extra early one day. [9]Before the sun comes up, drive to each coworker's house, reach under the hood of his car, and disconnected the center wire that leads to the distrib. cap. [10]The car will be unharmed, but it will not start, and your friends at work will all be late for work on the same day. [11]If youre lucky, your boss might notice that you are the only one there and will give you a raise. [12]Later if you feel guilty about your actions you can call each person anonymously and tell them how to get the car running.

[13]Gossiping friends at school are also perfect targets for a simple act of revenge. [14]A way to trap either male or female friends are to leave phony messages on their lockers. [15]If the friend that you want to get is male, leave a message that a certain girl would like him to stop by her house later that day. [16]With any luck, her boyfriend will be there. [17]The girl won't know what's going on, and the victim will be so embarrassed that he probably won't leave his home for a month. [18]The plan works just as well for female friends, too.

[19]When Mom and Dad and your sisters and brothers really begin to annoy you, harmless revenge may be just the way to make them quite down for a while. [20]The dinner table, where most of the nagging probably happens, is a likely place. [21]Just before the meal begins, throw a handful of raisins into the food. [22]Wait about 5 minutes and, after everyone has began to eat, clamp your hand over your mouth and begin to make odd noises. [23]When they ask you what the matter is, point to a raisin and yell, Bugs. [24]Dumping the food in the disposal, the car will make a beeline for mcdonald's. [25]That night, you'll have your first quiet, peaceful meal in a long time.

[26]A well-planned revenge does not have to hurt anyone. [27]The object is simply to let other people know that they are beginning to bother you. [28]You should remember, though, to stay on your guard after completing your revenge. [29]The reason for this is simple, coworkers, friends, and family can also plan revenge on you.

Essay 2

Revenge

Revenge is one of those things that everyone enjoys. People don't like to talk   1
about it, though. Just the same, there is nothing more tempting, more satisfying,
or more rewarding than revenge. The purpose is not to harm your victims but to
let them know that you are upset about something that they are doing to you.
Careful plotting can provide you with relief from bothersome coworkers, gossiping
friends, or nagging family members.

Coworkers who make comments about the fact that you are always fifteen   2
minutes late for work can be taken care of very simply. All you have to do is get
up extra early one day. Before the sun comes up, drive to each coworker's house.
Reach under the hood of your coworker's car and disconnect the center wire that
leads to the distributor cap. The car will be unharmed, but it will not start, and
your friends at work will all be late for work on the same day. If you're lucky, your
boss might notice that you are the only one there and will give you a raise. Later,
if you feel guilty about your actions, you can call your coworkers anonymously
and tell them how to get their cars running again.

Gossiping friends at school are also perfect targets for a simple act of   3
revenge. A way to trap either male or female friends is to leave phony messages
on their lockers. If the friend that you want to get is male, leave a message that a
certain girl would like him to stop by her house later that day. With any luck, her
boyfriend will be there. The girl won't know what's going on, and the victim will
be so embarrassed that he probably won't leave his home for a month. The plan
works just as well for female friends, too.

When Mom and Dad and your sisters and brothers really begin to annoy you,   4
harmless revenge may be just the way to make them quiet down for a while. The
dinner table, where most of the nagging probably happens, is a likely place. Just
before the meal begins, throw a handful of raisins into the food. Wait about five
minutes and, after everyone has begun to eat, clamp your hand over your mouth
and begin to make odd noises. When they ask you what the matter is, point to a
raisin and yell, "Bugs!" They'll all dump their food in the disposal, jump into the
car, and head for McDonald's. That night, you'll have your first quiet, peaceful
meal in a long time.

A well-planned revenge does not have to hurt anyone. The object is simply to   5
let other people know that they are beginning to bother you. You should
remember, though, to stay on your guard after completing your revenge. The
reason for this is simple. Coworkers, friends, and family can also plan revenge on
you.

Essay _____ makes its point more clearly and effectively because

_____

_____

_____

UNDERSTANDING SENTENCE SKILLS

Essay 2 is more effective because it uses *sentence skills,* the fourth base of competent writing. See if you can find and explain briefly the twenty sentence-skills mistakes in essay 1; use the spaces provided below. The first mistake is described for you as an example. Note that comparing essays 1 and 2 will help you locate the mistakes.

1. _Title should not be set off with quotation marks._
2. _____
3. _____
4. _____
5. _____
6. _____
7. _____
8. _____
9. _____
10. _____
11. _____
12. _____
13. _____
14. _____
15. _____
16. _____
17. _____
18. _____
19. _____
20. _____

Practice in Using the Four Bases

You are now familiar with four standards, or bases, of effective writing: *unity*, *support*, *coherence*, and *sentence skills*. In this section you will expand and strengthen your understanding of the four bases as you evaluate essays for each of them.

1   EVALUATING ESSAYS FOR UNITY

Activity

Both of the following essays contain irrelevant sentences that do not relate to the thesis of the essay or support the topic sentence of the paragraph in which they appear. Cross out the irrelevant sentences and write the numbers of those sentences in the spaces provided.

Playing on the Browns

[1]For the past three summers, I have played first base on a softball team known as the Browns. [2]We play a long schedule, including play-offs, and everybody takes the games pretty seriously. [3]In that respect, we're no different from any other of the thousand or so teams in our city. [4]But in one respect, we are different. [5]In an all-male league, we have a woman on the team—me. [6]Thus I've had a chance to observe something about human nature by seeing how the men have treated me. [7]Some have been disbelieving; some have been patronizing; and fortunately, some have simply accepted me.

[8]One new team in the league was particularly flabbergasted to see me start the game at first base. [9]Nobody on the Comets had commented one way or the other when they saw me warming up, but playing in the actual game was another story. [10]The Comet first-base coach leaned over to me with a disbelieving grin and said, "You mean, you're starting, and those three guys are on the bench?" [11]I nodded and he shrugged, still amazed. [12]He probably thought I was the manager's wife. [13]When I came up to bat, the Comet pitcher smiled and called to his outfielders to move way in on me. [14]Now, I don't have a lot of power, but I'm not exactly feeble. [15]I used to work out on the exercise machines at a local health club until it closed, and now I lift weights at home a couple of times a week. [16]I wiped the smirks off their faces with a line drive double over the left fielder's head.

The number of the irrelevant sentence: _____

[17]The next game, we played another new team, and this time their attitude was a patronizing one. [18]The Argyles had seen me take batting practice, so they didn't do anything so rash as to draw their outfield way in. [19]They had respect for my ability as a player. [20]However, they tried to annoy me with phony concern. [21]For example, a redheaded Argyle got on base in the first inning and said to me, "You'd better be careful, Hon. [22]When you have your foot on the bag, somebody might step on it. [23]You can get hurt in this game." [24]I was mad, but I have worked out several mental techniques to control my anger because it interferes with my playing ability. [25]Well, this delicate little girl survived the season without injury, which is more than I can say for some of the "he-men" on the Argyles.   3

The number of the irrelevant sentence: _____

[26]Happily, most of the teams in the league have accepted me, just as the Browns did. [27]The men on the Browns coached and criticized me (and occasionally cursed me) just like anyone else. [28]Because I'm a religious person, I don't approve of cursing, but I don't say anything about it to my teammates. [29]They are not amazed when I get a hit or stretch for a wide throw. [30]My average this year was higher than the averages of several of my teammates, yet none of them acted resentful or threatened. [31]On several occasions I was taken out late in a game for a pinch runner, but other slow players on the team were also lifted at times for pinch runners. [32]Every woman should have a team like the Browns!   4

The number of the irrelevant sentence: _____

[33]Because I really had problems only with the new teams, I've concluded that it's when people are faced with an unfamiliar situation that they react defensively. [34]Once a rival team has gotten used to seeing me on the field, I'm no big deal. [35]Still, I suspect that the Browns secretly feel we're a little special. [36]After all, we won the championship with a woman on the team.   5

How to Con an Instructor

[1]Enter college, and you'll soon be reminded of an old saying: "The pen is mightier than the sword." [2]That person behind the instructor's desk holds your future in his or her ink-stained hands. [3]So your first important assignment in college has nothing to do with required readings, examinations, or even the hazards of registration. [4]It is, instead, how to con an instructor.   1

[5]The first step in conning an instructor is to use body language. [6]You may be able to convince your instructor you are special without even saying a word. [7]When you enter the classroom, be sure to sit in the front row. [8]That way, the instructor can't possibly miss you. [9]Then, as the instructor lectures, take notes frantically. [10]The instructor will be flattered that you think so much of his or her words that you want to write them all down. [11]Using a felt-tip pen is superior to a   2

pen or pencil; it will help you write faster and prevent aching wrists. [12]While you are writing, be sure to smile at the instructor's jokes and nod violently in agreement with every major point. [13]Most important of all, as class continues, sit with your body pitched forward and your eyes wide open, fixed firmly, as if hypnotized, on your instructor's face. [14]Make your whole body suggest that you are watching a star.

The number of the irrelevant sentence: _____

3

[15]Once you have mastered body language, it is time to move on to the second phase of conning the instructor: class participation. [16]Everyone knows that the student who is most eager to learn is the one who responds to the questions that are asked and even comes up with a few more. [17]Therefore, be sure to be responsive. [18]Questions such as "How does this affect the future of the United States?" or "Don't you think that someday all of this will be done by computer?" can be used in any class without prior knowledge of the subject matter. [19]Many students, especially in large classes, get lost in the crowd and never do anything to make themselves stand out. [20]Another good participation technique is to wait until the instructor has said something that sounds profound and then ask him or her to repeat it slowly so you can get it down word for word in your notes. [21]No instructor can resist this kind of flattery.

The number of the irrelevant sentence: _____

4

[22]However, the most advanced form of conning an instructor happens after class is over. [23]Don't be like the others who slap their notebooks closed, snatch up their books, and rush out the door before the echoes of the final bell have died away. [24]Did you ever notice how students begin to get restless about five minutes before class ends, even if there's no clock on the wall? [25]Instead, be reluctant to leave. [26]Approach the instructor's desk hesitantly, almost reverently. [27]Say that you want to find out more about the topic. [28]Is there any extra reading you can do? [29]Even better, ask if the instructor has written anything on the topic—and whether you could borrow it. [30]Finally, compliment your instructor by saying that this is the most interesting course you've ever taken. [31]Nothing beats the personal approach for making an instructor think you care.

The number of the irrelevant sentence: _____

5

[32]Body language, questions, after-class discussions—these are the secrets of conning an instructor that every college student should know. [33]These kinds of things go on in high school, too, and they're just as effective on that level. [34]Once you master these methods, you won't have to worry about a thing—until the final exam.

The number of the irrelevant sentence: _____

2 EVALUATING ESSAYS FOR SUPPORT

Activity

Both of the essays below lack supporting details at certain key points. Identify the spots where details are needed in each essay.

Formula for Happiness

1 [1]Everyone has his or her own formula for happiness. [2]As we go through life, we discover the activities that make us feel best. [3]I've already discovered three keys for my happiness. [4]I depend on karate, music, and self-hypnosis.

2 [5]Karate helps me feel good physically. [6]Before taking karate lessons, I was tired most of the time, my muscles felt like foam rubber, and I was twenty pounds overweight. [7]After three months of these lessons, I saw an improvement in my physical condition. [8]Also, my endurance has increased. [9]At the end of my workday, I used to drag myself home to eat and watch television all night. [10]Now, I have enough energy to play with my children, shop, or see a movie. [11]Karate has made me feel healthy, strong, and happy.

The spot where supporting details are needed occurs after sentence _____ .

3 [12]Singing with a chorus has helped me achieve emotional well-being by expressing my feelings. [13]In situations where other people would reveal their feelings, I would remain quiet. [14]Since joining the chorus, however, I have an outlet for joy, anger, or sadness. [15]When I sing, I pour my emotions into the music and don't have to feel shy. [16]For this reason, I enjoy singing certain kinds of music the most, since they demand real depth of feeling.

The first spot where supporting details are needed occurs after sentence _____ .

The second spot occurs after sentence _____ .

4 [17]Self-hypnosis gives me peace of mind. [18]This is a total relaxation technique which I learned several years ago. [19]Essentially I breathe deeply and concentrate on relaxing all my muscles. [20]I then repeat a key suggestion to myself. [21]Through self-hypnosis, I have gained control over several bad habits that have long been haunting me. [22]I have also learned to reduce the stress that goes along with my secretarial job. [23]Now I can handle the boss's demands or unexpected work without feeling tense.

The first spot where supporting details are needed occurs after sentence _____ .

The second spot occurs after sentence _____ .

5 [24]In short, my physical, emotional, and mental well-being have been greatly increased through karate, music, and self-hypnosis. [25]These activities have become important elements in my formula for happiness.

Problems of a Foreign Student

[1]About ten months ago I decided to leave my native country and come to the United States to study. [2]When I got here, I suddenly turned into someone labeled "foreign student." [3]A foreign student, I discovered, has problems. [4]Whether from Japan, like me, or from some other country, a foreign student has to work twice as hard as Americans do to succeed in college.

1

[5]First of all, there is the language problem. [6]American students have the advantage of comprehending English without working at it. [7]But even they complain that some professors talk too fast, mumble, or use big words. [8]As a result, they can't take notes fast enough to keep up, or they misunderstand what was said. [9]Now consider my situation. [10]I'm trying to cope with a language that is probably one of the hardest in the world to learn. [11]Dozens of English slang phrases—"mess around," "hassle," "get into"—were totally new to me. [12]Other language problems gave me trouble, too.

2

The spot where supporting details are needed occurs after sentence _____ .

[13]Another problem I face has to do with being a stranger to American culture. [14]For instance, the academic world is much different in Japan. [15]In the United States, instructors seem to treat students as equals. [16]Many classes are informal, and the relationship between instructor and student is friendly; in fact, students call some instructors by their first names. [17]In Japan, however, the instructor-student relationship is different. [18]Lectures, too, are more formal, and students show respect by listening quietly and paying attention at all times. [19]This more casual atmosphere occasionally makes me feel uncomfortable in class.

3

The spot where supporting details are needed occurs after sentence _____ .

[20]Perhaps the most difficult problem I face is social. [21]American students may have some trouble making new friends or may feel lonely at times. [22]However, they usually manage to find other people with the same backgrounds, interests, or goals. [23]It is twice as hard to make friends, though, if a person has trouble making the small talk that can lead to a relationship. [24]I find it difficult to become friends with other students because I don't understand some aspects of American life. [25]Students would rather talk to someone who is familiar with these things.

4

The spot where supporting details are needed occurs after sentence _____ .

[26]Despite all the handicaps that I, as a foreign student, have to overcome, I wouldn't give up this chance to go to school in the United States. [27]Each day, the problems seem a little bit less overwhelming. [28]Like a little child who is finally learning to read, write, and make sense of things, I am starting to enjoy my experience of discovering a brand-new world.

5

3   EVALUATING ESSAYS FOR COHERENCE

Activity

Both of the essays that follow could be revised to improve their coherence. Answer the questions about coherence that come after each essay.

Noise Pollution

[1]Natural sounds—waves, wind, bird songs—are so soothing that companies sell tapes of them to anxious people seeking a relaxing atmosphere in their homes or cars. [2]One reason why "environmental sounds" are big business is the fact that ordinary citizens—especially city dwellers—are bombarded by noise pollution. [3]On the way to work, on the job, and on the way home, the typical urban resident must cope with a continuing barrage of unpleasant sounds.

[4]The noise level in an office can be unbearable. [5]From nine o'clock to five, phones ring, typewriters clack and clatter, intercoms buzz, and Xerox machines thump back and forth. [6]Every time the receptionists can't find people, they resort to a nerve-shattering public address system. [7]And because the managers worry about the employees' morale, they graciously provide the endless droning of canned music. [8]This effectively eliminates any possibility of a moment of blessed silence.

[9]Traveling home from work provides no relief from the noisiness of the office. [10]The ordinary sounds of blaring taxi horns and rumbling buses are occasionally punctuated by the ear-piercing screech of car brakes. [11]Taking a shortcut through the park will bring the weary worker face to face with chanting religious cults, freelance musicians, screaming children, and barking dogs. [12]None of these sounds can compare with the large radios many park visitors carry. [13]Each radio blasts out something different, from heavy-metal rock to baseball, at decibel levels so strong that they make eardrums throb in pain. [14]If there are birds singing or wind in the trees, the harried commuter will never hear them.

[15]Even a trip to work at 6 or 7 A.M. isn't quiet. [16]No matter which route a worker takes, there is bound to be a noisy construction site somewhere along the way. [17]Hard hats will shout from third-story windows to warn their coworkers below before heaving debris out and sending it crashing to earth. [18]Huge front-end loaders will crunch into these piles of rubble and back up, their warning signals letting out loud, jarring beeps. [19]Air hammers begin an ear-splitting chorus of rat-a-tat-tat sounds guaranteed to shatter sanity as well as concrete. [20]Before reaching the office, the worker is already completely frazzled.

[21]Noise pollution is as dangerous as any other kind of pollution. [22]The endless pressure of noise probably triggers countless nervous breakdowns, vicious arguments, and bouts of depression. [23]And imagine the world problems we could solve, if only the noise stopped long enough to let us think.

1. In "Noise Pollution," what is the number of the sentence to which the transition word *Also* could be added in paragraph 2? ———

2. In the last sentence of paragraph *2*, to what does the pronoun *This* refer?
   _____

3. What is the number of the sentence to which the transition word *But* could be added in paragraph 3? ———

4. What is the number of the sentence to which the transition word *Then* could be added in paragraph 4? ———

5. What is the number of the sentence to which the transition word *Meanwhile* could be added in paragraph 4? ———

6. What word is used as a synonym for *debris* in paragraph 4?
   _____

7. How many times is the key word *sounds* repeated in the essay? ———

8. The time order of the three supporting paragraphs is confused. Which supporting paragraph should come first? ——— Second? ——— Third? ———

Weight Loss

1. ¹The big fraternity party turned out to be the low point of my first year at college. ²I was in heaven until I discovered that my date with handsome Greg, the fraternity vice president, was a hoax: he had used me to win the "ugliest date" contest. ³I ran sobbing back to the dorm, wanting to resign from the human race. ⁴Then I realized that it was time to stop kidding myself about my weight. ⁵Within the next two years, I lost forty-two pounds and turned my life around. ⁶Losing weight gave me self-confidence socially, emotionally, and professionally.

2. ⁷I am more outgoing socially. ⁸Just being able to abandon dark colors, overblouses, and tent dresses in favor of bright colors, T shirts, and designer jeans made me feel better in social situations. ⁹I am able to do more things. ¹⁰I once turned down an invitation for a great camping trip with my best friend's family, making up excuses about sun poisoning and allergies. ¹¹Really, I was too embarrassed to tell them that I couldn't fit in the bathroom in their Winnebago! ¹²I made up for it last summer when I was one of the organizers of a college backpacking trip through the Rockies.

3. ¹³Most important, losing weight helped me seek new professional goals. ¹⁴When I was obese, I organized my whole life around my weight, as if it were a

defect I could do nothing about. ¹⁵With my good grades, I could have chosen almost any major the college offered, but I had limited my goal to teaching kindergarten because I felt that little children wouldn't judge how I looked. ¹⁶Once I was no longer fat, I realized that I love working with all sorts of people. ¹⁷I became a campus guide and even had small parts in college theater productions. ¹⁸As a result, last year I changed my major to public relations. ¹⁹The area fascinates me, and I now have good job prospects there.

²⁰I have also become more emotionally honest. ²¹Rose, at the college counseling center, helped me see that my "fat and jolly" personality had been false. ²²I was afraid others would reject me if I didn't always go along with their suggestions. ²³I eventually put Rose's advice to the test. ²⁴My roommates were planning an evening at a Greek restaurant. ²⁵I loved the restaurant's atmosphere, but there wasn't much I liked on the menu. ²⁶Finally, in a shaky voice I said, "Actually, I'm not crazy about lamb. ²⁷How about Italian or Chinese food?" ²⁸They scolded me for not mentioning it before, and we had dinner at a Chinese restaurant and ended with coffee, dessert, and entertainment at the Greek restaurant. ²⁹We all agreed it was one of our best evenings out.   4

³⁰Fortunately, the low point of my first year turned out to be the turning point leading to what promises to be an exciting senior year. ³¹Greg's cruel joke became a strange sort of favor, and I've gone from wanting to resign from the human race to welcoming each day as a source of fresh adventure and self-discovery.   5

1. In "Weight Loss," what is the number of the sentence to which the transition words *For one thing* could be added in paragraph 2? _____
2. What is the number of the sentence to which the transition word *Also* could be added in paragraph 2? _____
3. What is the number of the sentence to which the transition word *But* could be added in paragraph 2? _____
4. In sentence 11, to what does the pronoun *them* refer? _____
5. What is the number of the sentence to which the transition word *However* could be added in paragraph 3? _____
6. What word is used as a synonym for *obese* in paragraph 4? _____
7. How many times is the key word *weight* repeated in the essay? _____
8. Which supporting paragraph should be placed in the emphatic final position? _____

4   EVALUATING ESSAYS FOR ALL FOUR BASES: UNITY, SUPPORT, COHERENCE, AND SENTENCE SKILLS

Activity

In this activity, you will evaluate two essays in terms of all four bases: unity, support, coherence, and sentence skills. Comments follow each supporting paragraph. Circle the letter of the *one* statement that applies in each case.

Chiggers

1   I had lived my whole life not knowing what chiggers are. I thought they were probably a type of insect Humphrey Bogart encountered in <u>The African Queen</u>. I never had any reason to really care, until one day last summer. Within twenty-four hours, I had vividly experienced what chigger bites are, learned how to treat them, and learned how to prevent them.

2   First of all, I learned that chiggers are the larvae of tiny mites found in the woods and that their bites are always multiple and cause intense itching. A beautiful summer day seemed perfect for a walk in the woods. I am definitely not a city person, for I couldn't stand to be surrounded by people, noise, and concrete. As I walked through the ferns and pines, I noticed what appeared to be a dusting of reddish seeds or pollen on my slacks. Looking more closely, I realized that each speck was a tiny insect. I casually brushed off a few and gave them no further thought. I woke up the next morning feeling like a settler staked to an anthill by an Indian wise in the ways of torture. Most of my body was speckled with measlelike bumps that at the slightest touch burned and itched like a mosquito bite raised to the twentieth power. When antiseptics and calamine lotion failed to help, I raced to my doctor for emergency aid.

a.   Paragraph 2 contains an irrelevant sentence.
b.   Paragraph 2 lacks supporting details at one key spot.
c.   Time order in paragraph 2 is confused.
d.   Paragraph 2 contains two run-ons.

3   Healing the bites of chiggers, as the doctor diagnosed them to be, is not a simple procedure. It seems there is really no wonder drug or commercial product to help the cure. The victim must rely on a harsh and primitive home remedy and mostly wait out the course of the painful bites. First, the doctor explained, the skin must be bathed carefully in alcohol. An antihistamine spray applied several hours later will soothe the intense itching and help prevent infection. Before using the spray, I had to saturate each bite with gasoline or nail polish to kill any remaining chiggers. A few days after the treatment, the bites finally healed. Although I was still in pain, and desperate for relief, I followed the doctor's instructions. I carefully applied gasoline to the bites and walked around for an hour smelling like a filling station.

a. Paragraph 3 contains an irrelevant sentence.
b. Paragraph 3 lacks supporting details at one key spot.
c. Time order in paragraph 3 is confused.
d. Paragraph 3 contains one fragment.

Most important of all, I learned what to do to prevent getting chigger bites in the future. Mainly, of course, stay out of the woods in the summertime. But if the temptation is too great on an especially beautiful day, I'll be sure to wear the right type of clothing, like a long-sleeved shirt, long pants, knee socks, and closed shoes. In addition, I'll cover myself with clouds of superstrength insect repellent. I will then shower thoroughly as soon as I get home, I also will probably burn all my clothes if I notice even one suspicious red speck.   4

a. Paragraph 4 contains an irrelevant sentence.
b. Paragraph 4 lacks supporting details at one key spot.
c. Paragraph 4 lacks transitional words.
d. Paragraph 4 contains a run-on and a fragment.

I will never forget my lessons on the cause, cure, and prevention of chigger bites. I'd gladly accept the challenge of rattlesnakes and scorpions in the wilds of the West but will never again confront a siege of chiggers in the pinewoods.   5

The Hazards of Being an Only Child

Many people who have grown up in multichild families think that being an only child is the best of all possible worlds. They point to such benefits as the only child's annual new wardrobe and lack of competition for parental love. But single-child status isn't as good as people say it is. Instead of having everything they want, only children are sometimes denied certain basic human needs.   1

Only children lack companionship. An only child can have trouble making friends, since he or she isn't used to being around other children. Often, the only child comes home to an empty house; both parents are working, and there are no brothers or sisters to play with or to talk to about the day. At dinner, the single child can't tell jokes, giggle, or throw food while the adults discuss boring adult subjects. An only child always has his or her own room but never has anyone to whisper to half the night when sleep doesn't come. Some only children thrive on this isolation and channel their energies into creative activities like writing or drawing. Owing to this lack of companionship, an only child sometimes lacks the social ease and self-confidence that come from being part of a closely knit group of contemporaries.   2

a. Paragraph 2 contains an irrelevant sentence.
b. Paragraph 2 lacks supporting details at one key spot.
c. Paragraph 2 lacks transitional words.
d. Paragraph 2 contains one fragment and one run-on.

> Second, only children lack privacy. An only child is automatically the center   3
> of parental concern. There's never any doubt about which child tried to sneak in
> after midnight on a weekday. And who will get the lecture the next morning.
> Also, whenever an only child gives in to a bad mood, runs into his or her room,
> and slams the door, the door will open thirty seconds later, revealing an anxious
> parent. Parents of only children sometimes don't even understand the child's
> need for privacy. For example, they may not understand why a teenager wants a
> lock on the door or a personal telephone. After all, the parents think, there are
> only the three of us, there's no need for secrets.

a. Paragraph 3 contains an irrelevant sentence.
b. Paragraph 3 lacks supporting details at one key spot.
c. Paragraph 3 lacks transitional words.
d. Paragraph 3 contains one fragment and one run-on.

> Most important, only children lack power. They get all the love; but if   4
> something goes wrong, they also get all the punishment. When a bottle of
> perfume is knocked to the floor or the television is left on all night, there's no
> little sister or brother to blame it on. Moreover, an only child has no recourse
> when asking for a privilege of some kind, such as permission to stay out to a late
> hour or to take an overnight trip with friends. There are no older siblings to point
> to and say, "You let them do it. Why won't you let me?" With no allies their own
> age, only children are always outnumbered, two to one. An only child hasn't a
> chance of influencing any major family decisions, either.

a. Paragraph 4 contains an irrelevant sentence.
b. Paragraph 4 lacks supporting details at one key spot.
c. Paragraph 4 lacks transitional words.
d. Paragraph 4 contains one fragment and one run-on.

> Being an only child isn't as special as some people think. It's no fun being   5
> without friends, without privacy, and without power in one's own home. But the
> child who can triumph over these hardships grows up self-reliant and strong.
> Perhaps for this reason alone, the hazards are worth it.

PART TWO

TYPES OF ESSAY DEVELOPMENT

INTRODUCTION TO ESSAY DEVELOPMENT

This chapter will discuss

- Nine patterns of essay development
- Point of view
- Writing for a specific purpose and audience
- Peer review of your papers
- The order of each chapter
- A personal checklist for your papers

NINE PATTERNS OF ESSAY DEVELOPMENT

Traditionally, essay writing has been divided into the following patterns of development:

- Description
- Narration
- Exposition

Examples	Comparison and contrast
Process	Definition
Cause and effect	Division and classification

- Argumentation

A *description* is a verbal picture of a person, place, or thing. In *narration*, a writer tells the story of something that happened.

In *exposition*, the writer provides information about and explains a particular subject. Patterns of development within exposition include giving *examples*, detailing a *process* of doing or making something, analyzing *causes and effects, comparing and/or contrasting, defining* a term or concept, and *dividing* something into parts or *classifying* it into categories.

Finally, in *argumentation*, a writer attempts to support a controversial point or defend a position on which there is a difference of opinion.

121

The pages ahead present individual chapters on each pattern. You will have a chance, then, to learn nine different patterns or methods for organizing material in your papers. Each pattern has its own internal logic and provides its own special strategies for imposing order on your ideas. As you practice each pattern, you should keep two points in mind.

First, while each essay that you write will involve one predominant pattern, very often one or more additional patterns may be involved as well. For example, consider the three model essays in the chapter on ''Examples.'' The first essay there, ''Everyday Cruelty'' (page 147), is developed through a series of *examples*. But there is also an element of *narration*, as the writer presents examples that occur as he proceeds through his day. In the second essay, ''Altered States'' (page 148), use of *examples* is again the predominant pattern, but in a lesser way the author is also explaining the *causes* of altered states of mind. The third essay, ''Childhood Fears'' (page 149), also presents a series of *examples* but to a lesser degree relies on *narration* and *cause and effect*.

Second, no matter which pattern or patterns you use, each essay must advance a point and then go on to support that point. In "Everyday Cruelty," for instance, the author uses *examples* to support his point that people inflict little cruelties on each other. In an essay that appears earlier in Part Two, a writer supports the point that a particular diner is depressing by providing a number of *descriptive details* (see page 130). Another writer claims that a certain experience in her life was embarrassing and then uses a *narrative* to persuade us of the truth of this statement (see page 137). And yet another author states that a fast-food restaurant can be preferable to a fancy one and then supplies *comparative information* about both to support his statement (see page 179).

POINT OF VIEW IN WRITING

When you write, you can take any of three approaches, or points of view: first-person, second-person, or third-person.

First-Person Approach

In the first-person approach—a strongly individualized point of view—you draw on your own experience and speak to your audience in your own voice, using pronouns like *I, me, mine, we, our,* and *us.*

The first-person approach is most common in narrative essays based on personal experience. It also suits other essays where most of the evidence presented consists of personal observation.

Here is a first-person supporting paragraph from an essay on camping:

First of all, I like comfort when I'm camping. My GMC motor home, with its completely equipped kitchen, shower stall, toilet, double bed, and color television, resembles a mobile motel room. I can sleep on a real mattress, clean sheets, and fluffy pillows. Next to my bed are devices that make me feel at home: a radio, an alarm clock, and a TV remote-control unit. Unlike the poor campers huddled in tents, I don't have to worry about cold, rain, heat, or annoying insects. After a hot shower, I can slide into my best nightgown, sit comfortably on my down-filled quilt, and read the latest best-seller while a thunderstorm booms outside.

Second-Person Approach

In the second-person approach, the writer speaks directly to the reader, using the pronoun *you.* The second-person approach is considered appropriate for giving direct instructions and explanations to the reader. That is why *you* is used throughout this book.

You should expect to use the second-person approach only when writing a process essay. Otherwise, as a general rule, *never* use the word *you* in writing. (If doing so has been a common mistake in your writing, you should review the rule about pronoun point of view on pages 368–369.)

Third-Person Approach

The third-person approach is by far the most common point of view in academic writing. In the third person, the writer includes no direct references to the reader (*you*) or the self (*I, me*). Third person gets its name from the stance it suggests—that of an outsider or "third person" observing and reporting on matters of public rather than private importance. In this approach, you draw on information that you have gotten through observation, thinking, or reading.

Here is the paragraph on camping, recast in the third person. Note the third-person pronouns *their, them,* and *they,* which all refer to *campers* in the first sentence.

First of all, modern campers bring complete bedrooms with them. Winnebagoes, GMC motor homes, and Airstream trailers lumber into America's campgrounds every summer like mobile motel rooms. All the comforts of home are provided inside. Campers sleep on real mattresses with clean sheets and fluffy pillows. Next to their beds are the same gadgets that litter their night tables at home—radios, alarm clocks, and TV remote-control units. It's not necessary for them to worry about annoyances like cold, heat, rain, or buzzing insects, either. They can sit comfortably in bed and read the latest best-sellers while a thunderstorm booms outside.

WRITING FOR A SPECIFIC PURPOSE AND AUDIENCE

The three most common purposes of writing are to *inform,* to *entertain,* and to *persuade.* Most of the writing you will do in this book will involve some form of persuasion. You will advance a point or thesis and then support it in a variety of ways. To some extent, also, you will write papers that provide readers with information about a particular subject.

Your audience will be primarily your instructor, and sometimes other students as well. Your instructor is really a symbol of the larger audience you should see yourself as writing for—an educated, adult audience that expects you to present your ideas in a clear, direct, organized way. If you can learn to persuade or inform such an audience through your writing, you will have accomplished a great deal.

However, it will also be helpful for you to write some papers for a more specific audience. By so doing, you will develop an ability to choose words and adopt a tone of voice for a given purpose and a given group of readers.

In this part of the book, then, there is an assignment at or near the end of each chapter that asks you to write with a very specific purpose in mind and for a very specific audience. You will be asked, for example, to imagine yourself as a college sophomore making a presentation to incoming students about how to prepare for college life, as a client of a video dating service introducing himself or herself to potential dates, as a reader of a local newspaper writing a letter responding to a recent editorial, and as an author of a campus newspaper column giving advice on romance. Through these and other assignments, you will learn how to adjust your style and tone of voice to a given writing situation.

HOW TO PROCEED

Using Part Two: The Progression in Each Chapter

In the following chapters, after each type of essay development is explained, student papers illustrating that type are presented, and then there are questions about the papers. The questions relate to unity, support, and coherence—three principles of effective writing explained earlier.

You are then asked to write your own essay. In most cases, the first assignment is fairly structured and provides a good deal of guidance for the writing process. The other assignments offer a wide and interesting choice of writing topics. In each case, the last or next-to-last assignment involves writing an essay with a specific purpose and for a specific audience. And in three instances (examples, cause-effect, and comparison or contrast), the final assignments require outside reading of literary works; a student model is provided for each of these assignments.

Using Peer Review

In addition to your instructor, you will benefit by having another student in your class as an audience for your writing. On the day a paper is due, or on a day when you are writing papers in class, your instructor may ask you to pair up with another student. That student will read your paper, and you will read his or her paper.

Ideally, read the other paper aloud while your peer listens. If that is not practical, read it in a whisper while your peer looks on. As you read, both you and your peer should look and listen for spots where the paper does not read smoothly and clearly. Check or circle the trouble spots where your reading snags. Your peer should then read your paper, marking possible trouble spots.

Then, each of you should do three things.

1 Identification: On a separate sheet of paper, write at the top the title and author of the paper you have read. Under it, write your own name as the reader of the paper.

2 Outline: ''X-ray'' the paper for its inner logic by making up a scratch outline. The scratch outline need be no more than twenty words or so, but it should show clearly the logical foundation on which the essay is built. It should identify and summarize the overall point of the paper and the three areas of support for the point. Your outline can look as follows:

Point: _____

Support:

(1) _____

(2) _____

(3) _____

For example, here is a scratch outline of the essay on moviegoing on page 6:

Point: *Going out to the movies presents too many problems.*

Support: *(1) Getting to the theater*

(2) Dealing with theater itself

(3) Putting up with other patrons

3   **Comments:**   Under the outline, write the heading "Comments." Then make some useful comments.

Here is what you should comment on:

- Look at the spots where your reading of the paper snagged. Are words missing or misspelled? Is parallel structure lacking? Are there mistakes with punctuation? Is the meaning of a sentence confused? Try to figure out what the problems are and suggest ways of fixing them.
- Are there spots in the paper where you see problems with *unity, support,* or *coherence?* If so, offer comments. For example, you might say, "More details are needed in the first supporting paragraph," or "Some of the details in the last supporting paragraph don't really back up your point."
- Finally, note something you really liked about the paper. You might, for instance, mention good use of transitions or a specific detail that is especially realistic or vivid.

After you have completed your evaluation of the paper, give it to your classmate. Your instructor may offer you the option of rewriting a paper in light of "peer feedback." Whether or not you rewrite, be sure to hand in the "peer evaluation form" with your paper.

Using a Personal Checklist

After you have completed a paper, there are three ways you should check it yourself. You should *always* do the first two checks, which take only a few minutes. Ideally, you should then take the time to do the detailed third check as well.

1   Read the paper *out loud.* If it does not sound right—if it does not read smoothly and clearly—then make the changes needed to ensure that it will be smooth and clear.
2   Make sure you can answer two basic questions clearly and concisely: "What is the point of my essay? What are the three distinct bits of support for my point?"
3   Last, evaluate your paper in terms of the following detailed checklist. (This checklist is repeated on the inside front cover of the book.) The numbers in parentheses refer to the pages of this book that discuss each skill.

Checklist of the Four Steps in Writing an Effective Essay

1   Unity
- Clearly stated thesis in the introductory paragraph of your paper (pages 7; 42–45; 53–59)
- All the supporting paragraphs on target in backing up your thesis (96–98; 108–110)

2   Support
- Three separate supporting points for the thesis (7–8; 22; 26–31; 46–47)
- *Specific* evidence for each of the three supporting points (46–51; 59–64; 99–101)
- *Plenty of* specific evidence for each supporting point (49–51; 65–68; 111–112)

3   Coherence
- Clear method of organization (70–72; 87–89; 102–104; 113–115)
- Transitions and other connecting words (73–79; 89–92)
- Effective introduction, conclusion, and title (5–9; 79–86)

4   Sentence Skills
- Fragments eliminated (314–327)
- Run-ons eliminated (328–340)
- Correct verb forms (341–349; 356–363)
- Subject and verb agreement (350–355)
- Faulty modifiers and faulty parallelism eliminated (384–395)
- Faulty pronouns eliminated (364–376)
- Adjectives and adverbs used correctly (378–383)
- Capital letters used correctly (398–405)
- Punctuation marks where needed:
    - a Apostrophe (410–416)
    - b Quotation marks (417–423)
    - c Comma (424–433)
    - d Colon; Semicolon (434–435)
    - e Dash; Hyphen (435–437)
    - f Parentheses (436)
- Correct paper format (396–397)
- Needless words eliminated (472–474)
- Correct word choices (467–476)
- Possible spelling errors checked (447–451)
- Careless errors eliminated through proofreading (31–32; 487–499)
- Sentences varied (477–486)

DESCRIPTION

When you describe someone or something, you give your readers a picture in words. To make the word picture as vivid and real as possible, you must observe and record specific details that appeal to your readers' senses (sight, hearing, taste, smell, and touch). More than any other type of essay, a descriptive paper needs sharp, colorful details.

Here is a sentence in which there is almost *no* appeal to the senses: "In the window was a fan." In contrast, here is a description rich in sense impressions: "The blades of the rusty window fan clattered and whirled as they blew out a stream of warm, soggy air." Sense impressions in this second example include sight (*rusty window fan, whirled*), hearing (*clattered*), and touch (*warm, soggy air*). The vividness and sharpness provided by the sensory details give us a clear picture of the fan and enable us to share the writer's experience.

In this section, you will be asked to describe a person, place, or thing sharply, by using words rich in sensory details. To prepare for the assignment, first read the three essays ahead and then answer the questions that follow.

ESSAYS TO CONSIDER

Family Portrait

My mother, who is seventy years old, recently sent me a photograph of herself that I had never seen before. While cleaning out the attic of her Florida home, she came across a studio portrait she had had taken about a year before she married my father. This picture of my mother as a twenty-year-old girl has fascinated me from the moment I began to study it closely.

The young woman in the picture has a face that resembles my own in many ways. Her face is a bit more oval than mine, but the softly waving brown hair around it is identical. The small, straight nose is the same model I was born with. My mother's mouth is closed, yet there is just the slightest hint of a smile on her full lips. I know that if she had smiled, she would have shown the same wide grin and downcurving "smile lines" that appear in my own snapshots. The most haunting features in the photo, however, are my mother's eyes. They are exact duplicates of my own large, dark brown ones. Her brows are plucked into thin lines, which are like two pencil strokes added to highlight those fine, luminous eyes.

I've also carefully studied the clothing and jewelry in the photograph. My
mother is wearing a blouse and skirt that, although the photo was taken fifty
years ago, could easily be worn today. The blouse is made of heavy eggshell-
colored satin and reflects the light in its folds and hollows. It has a turned-down
cowl collar and smocking on the shoulders and below the collar. The smocking
(tiny rows of gathered material) looks hand-done. The skirt, which covers my
mother's calves, is straight and made of light wool or flannel. My mother is
wearing silver drop earrings. They are about two inches long and roughly shield-
shaped. On her left wrist is a matching bracelet. My mother can't find this
bracelet now, despite the fact that we spent hours searching through the attic for
it. On the third finger of her left hand is a ring with a large, square-cut stone.

3

The story behind the picture is as interesting to me as the young woman it
captures. Mom, who was earning twenty-five dollars a week as a file clerk,
decided to give her boyfriend (my father) a picture of herself. She spent almost
two weeks' salary on the skirt and blouse, which she bought at a fancy
department store downtown. She borrowed the earrings and bracelet from her
older sister, my aunt Dorothy. The ring she wore was a present from another
young man she was dating at the time. Mom spent another chunk of her salary to
pay the portrait photographer for the hand-tinted print in old-fashioned tones of
brown and tan. Just before giving the picture to my father, she scrawled at the
lower left, "Sincerely, Beatrice."

4

When I study this picture, I react in many ways. I think about the trouble
that Mom went to in order to impress the young man who was to be my father. I
laugh when I look at the ring that was probably worn to make my father jealous. I
smile at the serious, formal inscription my mother used in this stage of the
budding relationship. Sometimes, I am filled with a mixture of pleasure and
sadness when I look at this frozen long-ago moment. It is a moment of beauty, of
love, and—in a way—of my own past.

5

My Fantasy Room

Recently, the comic strip "Peanuts" had a story about Lucy's going to camp
for two weeks. At Camp Beanbag, Lucy tells Charlie Brown, there is no flag
raising or required activity. All the campers do is lie in a room in beanbag chairs
and eat junk food. This idea appealed to me, and I began to think. If I could
spend two weeks in just one place, what would that place be like? I began to
imagine the room of my dreams.

1

First of all, my fantasy room would be decorated in a way that would make
me feel totally at ease. The walls would be painted a tasteful shade of pale
green, the color supposed to be the most soothing. Psychologists have conducted
studies proving that color can affect a person's mood. Also, a deep plush carpet
in an intense blue would cover the floor from wall to wall—the perfect foundation
for padding silently around the room. In the entryway, huge closets with sliding
doors would contain my wardrobe of size-eight designer originals. The closets I
have now are always messy and crowded, stuffed with old shoes and other kinds

2

of junk. Lastly, on the walls, silver frames would hold my memories: pictures of me with my sports star and musician friends, news clippings reporting on my social life, a poster advertising the movie version of my most recent best-selling novel. Everything would be quiet and tasteful, of course.

I'd have a king-sized bed with a headboard full of buttons that would allow me to turn on lights, start music playing, or run hot water for my Jacuzzi bath without getting up. Tall bookcases with enough shelf space for all the souvenirs from my world travels would line an entire wall. Against the opposite wall would be a chrome and glass desk topped with lined pads and a rainbow of felt-tipped pens. They would await the moment when I became inspired enough to begin writing my next best-seller. And for my purebred Persian cat, there would be a lavender satin pillow.

Finally, my fantasy room would have the latest technological advances. The air-conditioning or heating, depending on the season, would function at a whisper. A telephone, operated by a push button from my bed, would put me in touch with the world. Or, if I were feeling antisocial, I could flick on my quadraphonic stereo system and fill the room with music. I could select a movie from my library of videocassette tapes to play on my giant-screen projection TV. Or I could throw a switch, and the satellite dish on my roof would bring me my choice of television programs from all over the world.

It's probably good that my fantasy room exists only in my mind. If it were real, I don't think two weeks would be long enough. I might stay in it forever.

The Diner at Midnight

I've been in lots of diners, and they've always seemed to be warm, busy, friendly, happy places. That's why, on a recent Monday night, I stopped in a diner for a cup of coffee. I was returning home after an all-day car trip and needed something to help me make the last forty-five miles. A diner at midnight, however, was not the place I had expected. It was different—and lonely.

My Toyota pulled to a halt in front of the dreary gray aluminum building that looked like an old railroad car. A half-lit neon sign sputtered the message, "Fresh baked goods daily," on the surface of the rain-slick parking lot. Only a half dozen cars and a battered pickup were scattered around the lot. An empty paper coffee cup made a hollow scraping sound as it rolled in small circles on one cement step close to the diner entrance. I pulled hard at the balky glass door, and it banged shut behind me.

The diner was quiet when I entered. As there was no hostess on duty, only the faint odor of stale grease and the dull hum of an empty refrigerated pastry case greeted me. I looked around for a place to sit. The outside walls were lined with empty booths which squatted back to back in their orange vinyl upholstery. On each speckled beige-and-gold table were the usual accessories. The kitchen hid mysteriously behind two swinging metal doors with round windows. I glanced through these windows but could see only a part of the large, apparently deserted cooking area. Facing the kitchen doors was the counter. I approached the length of Formica and slid onto one of the cracked vinyl seats bolted in soldierlike straight lines in front of it.

The people in the diner seemed as lonely as the place itself. Two men in   4
rumpled work shirts sat at the counter, on stools several feet apart, staring
wearily into cups of coffee and smoking cigarettes. Their faces sprouted what
looked like daylong stubbles of beard. I figured they were probably shift workers
who, for some reason, didn't want to go home. Three stools down from the
workers, I spotted a thin young man with a mop of black, curly hair. He was
dressed in brown Levi cords with a checked western-style shirt unbuttoned at the
neck. He wore a blank expression as he picked at a plate of limp french fries. I
wondered if he had just returned from a disappointing date. At the one occupied
booth was a middle-aged couple. They hadn't gotten any food yet. He was staring
off into space, idly tapping his spoon against the table, while she drew aimless
parallel lines on her paper napkin with a bent dinner fork. Neither said a word to
the other.

Finally, a tired-looking waitress approached me with her thick order pad. I   5
ordered the coffee, but I wanted to drink it fast and get out of there. My car, and
the solitary miles ahead of me, would be lonely. But they wouldn't be as lonely
as that diner at midnight.

■ **Questions**

About Unity

1. Which supporting paragraph in ''My Fantasy Room'' lacks a topic sentence?

    _____

2. Which two sentences in paragraph 2 of ''My Fantasy Room'' should be
    omitted in the interest of paragraph unity? (*Write the opening words of
    each.*) _____   _____

3. Which sentence in paragraph 3 of ''Family Portrait'' should be omitted in

    the interest of paragraph unity?   _____

About Support

4. How many examples support the topic sentence, ''The people in the diner
    seemed as lonely as the place itself,'' in ''The Diner at Midnight''?
    a. One   b. Two   c. Three

5. Label as *sight, touch, hearing,* or *smell* all the sensory details in the following
    sentences taken from the three essays. The first one is done for you as
    an example.

a.   *sight*   *smell*
       "As there was no hostess on duty, only the faint odor of stale grease
              hearing   *sight*
       and the dull hum of an empty refrigerated pastry case greeted me."

b.   "He was staring off into space, idly tapping his spoon against the table,
       while she drew aimless parallel lines on her paper napkin with a bent
       dinner fork."

c.   "Also, a deep plush carpet in an intense blue would cover the floor
       from wall to wall—the perfect foundation for padding silently around
       the room."

d.   "The blouse is made of heavy eggshell-colored satin and reflects the
       light in its folds and hollows."

6.   After which sentence in paragraph 3 of "The Diner at Midnight" are more
       details needed? _____

About Coherence

7.   Which method of organization (time order or emphatic order) is used in
       paragraph 2 of "Family Portrait"? _____
8.   Which sentence in this paragraph indicates the method of organization?

       _____

9.   Which of the following topic sentences in "The Diner at Midnight" is a
       linking sentence?
       a.   "My Toyota pulled to a halt in front of the dreary gray aluminum
              building that looked like an old railroad car."
       b.   "The diner was quiet when I entered."
       c.   "The people in the diner seemed as lonely as the place itself."
10.   In paragraph 2 of "My Fantasy Room," what are the major transition words?
       a. _____   b. _____   c. _____

WRITING A DESCRIPTIVE ESSAY

■ Writing Assignment 1

Write an essay describing a place that you can observe carefully or that you already know well. It might be one of the following, or some other place:

Pet shop
Exam room
Laundromat
Bar or nightclub
Video arcade
Corner store
Library study area
Basement or garage
Hotel or motel lobby
Your bedroom or the bedroom of someone you know
Waiting room at a train station or bus terminal
Winning or losing locker room after an important game
Antique shop or other small shop

How to Proceed

a   Remember that, like all essays, a descriptive essay must have a thesis. Your thesis should state a dominant impression about the place you are describing. In a single short sentence, state what place you want to describe and what dominant impression you want to make. The sentence can be refined later. For now, you just want to find and express a workable topic. You might write, for example, a sentence like one of the following:

The study area was noisy.
The exam room was tense.
The pet shop was crowded.
The bar was cozy.
The video arcade was confusing.
The bus terminal was frightening.
The corner store was cheerful.
The antique shop was lonely.
The bedroom was very organized.
The motel lobby was restful.
The winners' locker room was chaotic.

b Now make a list of as many details as you can that support the general impression. For example, the writer of ''A Diner at Midnight'' made this list:

Tired workers at counter
Rainy parking lot
Empty booths
Quiet
Few cars in lot
Dreary gray building
Lonely young man
Silent middle-aged couple
Out-of-order neon sign
No hostess
Couldn't see anyone in kitchen
Tired-looking waitress

c Organize your paper according to one or a combination of the following:

Physical order—move from left to right, or far to near, or in some other consistent order
Size—begin with large features or objects and work down to smaller ones
A *special order*—use an order that is appropriate to the subject

For instance, the writer of ''The Diner at Midnight'' builds his essay around the dominant impression of loneliness. The paper is organized in terms of physical order (from the parking lot to the entrance to the interior); a secondary method of organization is size (large parking lot to smaller diner to still smaller people).

d Use as many senses as possible in describing a scene. Chiefly, you will use sight, but to an extent you may be able to use touch, hearing, smell, and perhaps even taste as well. Remember that it is through the richness of your sense impressions that the reader will form a picture of the scene.

e As you work on the drafts of your descriptive essay, refer to the checklist on page 127 and the inside front cover. Make sure you can answer *Yes* to the questions about unity, support, and coherence.

■ **Writing Assignment 2**

Write a descriptive essay about a family photograph. You may want to use an order similar to the one in ''A Family Portrait,'' where the first supporting paragraph deals with the subject's face, the second with clothing and jewelry, and the third with the story behind the picture. Another possible order might be (1) people in the photo (and how they look), (2) relationships among the people (and what they are doing in the picture), and (3) the story behind the picture (time, place, occasion, relationships, or feelings). Use whatever order seems appropriate.

■ **Writing Assignment 3**

Write an essay describing a person. First, decide on your dominant impression of the person, and then use only those details which will add to it. Here are some examples of interesting types of people you might want to write about:

Campus character	Enemy	Drunk
Dentist	Clergyman	Employer
Bus driver	Clergywoman	TV or movie personality
Close friend	Teacher	Street person
Rival	Child	Older person

■ **Writing Assignment 4**

In this descriptive essay, you will write with a specific purpose, for a specific audience.

Option 1:   You have just attended a richly satisfying event, such as a concert, a sports contest, a stage show, or even a family gathering. Now you want to share your experience with a good friend who lives in another city. Write a letter in which you enthusiastically describe the event. Include vivid details so that your friend will be able to see, hear, and feel the event as if he or she had been there in person.

Option 2:   You have subscribed to a video dating service. Clients of the service are asked to make a five-minute presentation which will be recorded on videotape. Prepare such a presentation in which you describe yourself in terms of your attitudes and beliefs, your interests, and your personal habits. Your purpose is to give interested members of the dating service a good sense of what you are like.

■ **Writing Assignment 5:
Writing about a Reading Selection**

Read the selection titled "On Being a Mess" on pages 522–524. Then write an essay describing a messy indoor place. You might consider writing about one of the following:

Room in a house or apartment
Cafeteria or restaurant
Instructor's office
Rest room
Basement or attic
Waiting room
Refrigerator
Closet
Shop
Area where you study
Inside of a bus, a subway, a train, or your own car

In your introductory paragraph, you might explain where the place is and why you are familiar with it, if necessary. (For example, you may have spent several hours during the semester conferring with your instructor in his or her office.) Be sure that you state in the thesis that messiness is the dominant impression you have of the place.

To organize your supporting paragraphs, use any order that you feel is appropriate (left to right, near to far, top to bottom, or other). Use vivid images, as the author of "On Being a Mess" does, to capture your messy place on paper.

NARRATION

At times we make a statement clear by relating in detail something that has happened to us. In the story we tell, we present the details in the order in which they happened. A person might say, for example, "I was really embarrassed the day I took my driver's test," and then go on to develop that statement with an account of the experience. If the story is sharply detailed, we will be able to see and understand just why the speaker felt that way.

In this section, you'll be asked to tell a story that illustrates some point. The essays ahead all present narrative experiences that support a thesis. Read them and then answer the questions that follow.

ESSAYS TO CONSIDER

My First Professional Performance

I was nineteen, and the invitation to play my guitar and sing at the County Rescue Squad Carnival seemed the "big break" aspiring performers dream about. I would be sharing the program with well-known professionals. My spirits were not even dampened by the discovery that I would not be paid. I had no reason to suspect then that my first professional performance was to be the scene of the most embarrassing experience of my life.

I arrived at the carnival grounds early, which proved fortunate. The manager knew that, in addition to the amplifier and speakers, I needed an extra microphone for my guitar and a high stool. However, when I checked the stage, I found the amplifier and speakers but nothing else. I also couldn't find the manager. The drunks who would hassle me later, after I had gotten started, became another problem. Since I couldn't perform without all the equipment, I was ready to call the whole thing off. Only the large potential audience milling around the carnival grounds influenced me to go through with it. One eye on my watch, I drove to the music store, told the owner my story, borrowed the needed equipment, and got back just as the Stone Gravel Rock Band, which preceded me on the program, was finishing its set. The band plays bluegrass music in some local clubs, and the lead singer was recently offered a professional recording contract.

I had some attentive listeners for my first song, but then problems   3
developed. A voice boomed, "Play 'Mister Bojangles.' " A group of noisy drunks,
surrounded by empty beer cans, half-eaten hot dogs, and greasy paper plates,
were sprawled on picnic tables to one side of the stage. "We want to hear 'Mister
Bojangles,' " roared the others, laughing. "Not today," I answered pleasantly,
"but if you like 'Bojangles,' you'll like this tune." I quickly slid into my next
number. Unfortunately, my comment only encouraged the drunks to act in an
even more outrageous manner. As they kept up the disturbance, my audience
began drifting away to escape them.

I was falsely cheered by the arrival of a uniformed policeman and several   4
older men in work clothes. "Fans," I thought hopefully. Then I gave a start as a
large engine roared very close to me, filling the air with choking diesel fumes.
Only then did I realize that my "stage" was really a huge flatbed truck and that
the older men in work clothes were in the cab warming up the engine. As I
played a song, the policeman approached me. "Hey, lady," he said, "you're
going to have to get down from there with all that stuff. They've got to take this
rig away now." "I can't do that," I said. "I'm a professional musician in the
middle of a performance. Tell him to turn that engine off." (In my confusion, I
left the mike open, transmitting this exchange to the entire carnival grounds.)
"Sorry, lady, he has to take it now," insisted the policeman. The drunks happily
entered into the spirit of the thing, yelling, "Take her away. We don't want her.
Yeah, haul her away." To save a small amount of self-respect, I played one more
chorus before I began packing up my gear.

Fortunately, in conversations I eventually had with other performers, I heard   5
similar stories of experiences they had when starting out. Then I would tell them
about the stage that nearly rolled away with me on it, and we would laugh. Now I
see that it's all part of becoming a professional.

Adopting a Handicap

My church recently staged a "Sensitivity Sunday" to make our congregation   1
aware of the problems faced by people with physical handicaps. We were asked
to "adopt a handicap" for several hours one Sunday morning. Some members
chose to be confined to wheelchairs; others stuffed cotton in their ears, hobbled
around on crutches, or wore blindfolds.

Wheelchairs had never seemed like scary objects to me before I had to sit in   2
one. A tight knot grabbed hold in my stomach when I first took a close look at
what was to be my only means of getting around for several hours. I was struck
by the irrational thought, "Once I am in this wheelchair, the handicap might
become real, and I might never walk again." This thought, as ridiculous as it
was, frightened me so much that I needed a large dose of courage just to sit
down.

After I overcame my fear of the wheelchair, I had to learn how to cope with   3
it. I wiggled around to find a comfortable position and thought I might even enjoy
being pampered and wheeled around. I glanced over my shoulder to see who
would be pushing me. It was only then that I realized I would have to navigate
the contraption all by myself! My palms reddened and started to sting as I tugged
at the heavy metal wheels. I could not seem to keep the chair on an even course
or point the wheels in the direction I wanted to go. I kept bumping into doors,
pews, and other people. I felt as though everyone were staring at me and
commenting on my clumsiness.

When the service started, more problems cropped up to frustrate me even   4
further. Every time the congregation stood up, my view was blocked. I could not
see the minister, the choir, or the altar. Also, as the church's aisles were narrow,
I seemed to be in the way no matter where I parked myself. For instance, the
ushers had to step around me in order to pass the collection plate. This made me
feel like a nuisance. Thanks to a new building program, however, our church will
soon have the wide aisles and well-spaced pews that will make life easier for the
handicapped. Finally, if people stopped to talk to me, I had to strain my neck to
look up at them. This made me feel like a little child being talked down to and
added to my sense of helplessness.

My few hours as a disabled person left a deep impression on me. Now, I no   5
longer feel resentment at large tax expenditures for ramp-equipped buses, and I
wouldn't dream of parking my car in a space marked "Handicapped Only."
Although my close encounter with a handicap was short-lived, I can now
understand the challenges, both physical and emotional, that people who use
wheelchairs must overcome.

A Night of Violence

According to my history instructor, Adolf Hitler once said that he wanted to   1
sign up "brutal youths" to help him achieve his goals. If Hitler were still alive, he
wouldn't have any trouble recruiting the brutal youths he wanted; he could get
them right here in the United States. I know, because I was one of them. As a
teenager, I ran with a gang. And it took a terrible incident to make me see how
violent I had become.

One Thursday night, I was out with my friends. I was still going to school   2
once in a while, but most of my friends weren't. We spent our days on the
streets, talking, showing off, sometimes shoplifting a little or shaking people
down for a few dollars. My friends and I were close, maybe because life hadn't
been very good to any of us. On this night, we were drinking wine and vodka on
the corner. For some reason, we all felt tense and restless. One of us came up
with the idea of robbing one of the old people who lived in the high-rise close by.
We would just knock him or her over, grab the money, and party with it.

After about an hour, and after more wine and vodka, we spotted an old man.   3
He came out of the glass door of the building and started up the street. Stuffing
our bottles in our jacket pockets, we closed in behind him. Victor, the biggest of
us, said, "We want your money, old man. Hand it over." Suddenly, the old man
whipped out a homemade wooden club from under his coat and began swinging.
The club thudded against the side of Victor's head, making bright-red blood spurt
out of his nose. When we saw this, we went crazy. We smashed our bottles over
the old man's head. Then Victor ground the jagged edges of a broken bottle into
the old man's skull. As we ran, I kept seeing the bottom of that bottle sticking up
out of the man's head. It looked like a weird glass crown.

Later, at home, I threw up. I wasn't afraid of getting caught; in fact, we   4
never did get caught. I just knew I had gone over some kind of line. I didn't know
if I could step back, now that I had gone so far. But I knew I had to. I had seen
plenty of people in my neighborhood turn into the kind who hated their lives,
people who didn't care about anything, people who wound up penned in jail or
ruled by drugs. I didn't want to become one of them.

That night, I realize now, I decided not to become one of Hitler's "brutal   5
youths." I'm proud of myself for that, even though life didn't get any easier and
no one came along to pin a medal on me. I just decided, quietly, to step off the
path I was on. I hope my parents and I will get along better now, too. Maybe the
old man's pain, in some terrible way, had a purpose.

■ Questions

About Unity

1. Which sentence in paragraph 4 of "Adopting a Handicap" should be omitted
    in the interest of paragraph unity? (*Write the opening words.*)

    _____

2. Which sentence in paragraph 2 of "My First Professional Performance"
    should be omitted in the interest of paragraph unity? _____

3. Which essay lacks a thesis statement?

    _____

About Support

4. Label as *sight, touch, hearing,* or *smell* all the sensory details in the following
    sentences taken from the three essays.

    a. "Then I gave a start as a large engine roared very close to me, filling
        the air with choking diesel fumes."

b. "The club thudded against the side of Victor's head, making bright-red blood spurt out of his nose."

c. "My palms reddened and started to sting as I tugged at the heavy metal wheels."

d. "A group of noisy drunks, surrounded by empty beer cans, half-eaten hot dogs, and greasy paper plates, were sprawled on picnic tables to one side of the stage."

5. In "Adopting a Handicap," how many examples support the topic sentence "When the service started, more problems cropped up to frustrate me even further"? _____

6. After which sentence in paragraph 3 of "My First Professional Performance" are more specific details needed? _____

7. Which supporting paragraphs in "My First Professional Performance" use dialog to help recreate the event?

_____

About Coherence

8. The first stage of the writer's experience in "Adopting a Handicap" might be called *sitting down in the wheelchair*. What are the other two stages of the experience?

   a. _____

   b. _____

9. In paragraph 2 of "My First Professional Performance," which detail is out of chronological (time) order?

_____

About the Conclusion

10. Which sentence in the conclusion of "A Night of Violence" makes the mistake of introducing a completely new idea? _____

WRITING A NARRATIVE ESSAY

■ **Writing Assignment 1**

Write an essay narrating an experience in which a certain emotion was predominant. The emotion might be disappointment, embarrassment, happiness, frustration, or any of the following:

Fear	Shock	Nervousness	Loss
Pride	Love	Hate	Sympathy
Jealousy	Anger	Surprise	Violence
Sadness	Nostalgia	Shyness	Bitterness
Terror	Relief	Silliness	Envy
Regret	Greed	Disgust	Loneliness

The experience should be limited in time. Note that the three essays presented in this chapter all describe experiences that occurred within relatively short periods. One writer described her embarrassing musical debut; another described her frustration in acting as a disabled person at a morning church service; the third described the terror of a minute's mugging that had lifelong consequences. See "How to Proceed," below.

How to Proceed

a   Think of an experience or event in your life in which you felt a certain emotion strongly. Then spend at least ten minutes freewriting about that experience. Do not worry at this point about such matters as spelling or grammar or putting things in the right order; instead, just try to get down as many details as you can think of that seem related to the experience.

b   This preliminary writing will help you decide whether your topic is promising enough to continue working on. If it is not, choose another emotion. If it is, do two things:

First, write out your thesis in a single sentence, underlining the emotion you will focus on. For example, "My first day in kindergarten was one of the <u>scariest</u> days of my life."

Second, make up a list of all the details involved in the experience. Then arrange those details in chronological (time) order.

c   Using the list as a guide, prepare a rough draft of your paper. Use time signals such as *first, then, next, after, while, during,* and *finally* to help connect details as you move from the beginning to the middle to the end of your narrative.

d   See if you can divide your story into separate stages (what happened first, what happened next, what finally happened). Put each stage into a separate paragraph. In narratives, it is sometimes difficult to write a topic sentence for each supporting paragraph. You may, therefore, want to start new paragraphs at points where natural shifts or logical breaks in the story seem to occur.

e   One good way to recreate an event is to include some dialog, as does the writer of ''My First Professional Performance.'' Repeating what you have said or what you have heard someone else say helps make a situation come alive. And, in general, try to provide as many vivid, exact details as you can to help your readers experience the event as it actually happened.

f   As you work on the drafts of your narrative essay, refer to the checklist on page 127 and the inside front cover to make sure that you can answer *Yes* to the questions about unity, support, and coherence. Also, use the checklist to proofread your next-to-final draft for sentence-skills mistakes, including spelling.

■ **Writing Assignment 2**

Think of an experience in your life that supports one of the statements below.

■   ''Before I got married I had six theories about bringing up children; now I have six children and no theories.''—John Wilmot, Earl of Rochester

■   ''The chains of habit are too weak to be felt until they are too strong to be broken.''—Samuel Johnson

■   ''Peter's Law—The unexpected always happens.''—Laurence J. Peter

■   ''Haste makes waste.''—popular saying

■   ''Good people are good because they've come to wisdom through failure.'' —William Saroyan

■   ''Lying is an indispensable part of making life tolerable.''—Bergen Evans

■   ''The key to everything is patience. You get the chicken by hatching the egg—not by smashing it.''—Arnold Glasgow

■   ''A good scare is worth more to a man than good advice.''—Ed Howe

■   ''A fool and his money are soon parted.''—popular saying

■   ''Like its politicians and its wars, society has the teenagers it deserves.'' —J. B. Priestley

■   ''It's what you learn after you know it all that counts.''—John Wooden

■   ''Wise sayings often fall on barren ground; but a kind word is never thrown away.''—Arthur Helps

■   ''What a tangled web we weave/When first we practice to deceive.'' —Walter Scott

- "All marriages are happy. It's the living together afterward that causes all the trouble."—Raymond Hull
- "We lie loudest when we lie to ourselves."—Eric Hoffer
- "The worst country to be poor in is America."—Arnold Toynbee
- "Criticism—a big bite out of someone's back."—Elia Kazan
- "Work is what you do so that sometime you won't have to do it anymore." —Alfred Polgar
- "Hoping and praying are easier but do not produce as good results as hard work."—Andy Rooney
- "A little learning is a dangerous thing."—Alexander Pope
- "Nothing is so good as it seems beforehand."—George Eliot
- "Give a pig a finger, and he'll take the whole hand."—folk saying

Write a narrative essay using one of the statements as a thesis. Refer to the suggestions in "How to Proceed" on pages 142–143. Remember that the point of your story is to *support* your thesis. Feel free to select from and even add to your experience so that your story truly supports the thesis.

■ Writing Assignment 3

In this narrative essay, you will write with a specific purpose and for a specific audience.

Option 1: Imagine that you are in a town fifty miles from home, that your car has broken down several miles from a gas station, and that you are carrying no money. You're afraid you are going to have a terrible time, but the friendly people who help you turn your experience into a positive one. It is such a good day, in fact, that you don't want to forget what happened.

Write a narrative of the day's events in your diary, so that you can read it ten years from now and remember exactly what happened. Begin with the moment you realize your car has broken down and continue until you're safely back home. Include a thesis at either the beginning or the end of your narration.

Option 2: Imagine that a friend or sister or brother has to make a difficult decision of some kind. Perhaps he or she must decide how to deal with a troubled love affair, or a problem with living at home, or a conflict with a boss or coworker. Write a narrative from your own experience that will teach him or her something about the decision that must be made.

- **Writing Assignment 4:**
  Writing about a Reading Selection

Read the selection titled "The Ambivalence of Abortion" on pages 540–543. Then write a narrative essay about a time when you did something that you later regretted. The action may be an important one that lends itself to a serious tone. For example, you might write about a topic such as the following:

> punishing a child
> dropping a course
> being mean, unkind, or rude to someone
> quitting a job
> getting married or divorced

Or the action that you took may be written about in a light, humorous tone. Some possibilities might include:

> going out on a particular date
> getting a new hairstyle
> wearing a certain outfit
> eating in a strange restaurant
> trying a new sport

In your introduction, provide a few sentences of background information to prepare your readers for the narrative. State your thesis in a general way, so as not to give away too much of what happened too soon. Use your concluding paragraph to underline the significance of your narrative from your point of view—then, now, or both. Finally, let the nature of your story help you decide how to break it up into paragraphs.

EXAMPLES

In our daily conversations, we often provide *examples*—that is, details, particulars, specific instances—to explain statements that we make. Here are several statements and supporting examples:

The first day of school was frustrating.	My sociology course was canceled. Then, I couldn't find the biology lab. And the lines at the bookstore were so long that I went home without buying my textbooks.
That washing machine is unreliable.	The water temperature can't be predicted; it stops in midcycle; and it sometimes shreds my clothing.
My grandfather is a thrifty person.	He washes and reuses aluminum foil. He wraps gifts in newspaper. And he's worn the same Sunday suit for twenty years.

In each case, the examples help us see for ourselves the truth of the statement that has been made. In essays, too, explanatory examples help your audience fully understand your point. Lively, specific examples also add interest to your paper.

In this section, you will be asked to provide a series of examples to support your thesis. First read the essays ahead; they all use examples to develop their points. Then answer the questions that follow.

ESSAYS TO CONSIDER

Everyday Cruelty

Last week, I found myself worrying less about problems of world politics and national crime and more about smaller evils. I came home one day with a bad taste in my mouth, the kind I get whenever I witness the little cruelties that people inflict on each other. On this particular day, I had seen three especially mean-spirited things happen.

I first thought about mean-spirited people as I walked from the bus stop to the office where I work. I make this walk every day, and it's my first step away from the comforts of home and into the tensions of the city. For me, a landmark on the route is a tiny patch of ground that was once strewn with rubbish and broken glass. The city is trying to make a "pocket park" out of it by planting trees and flowers. Every day this spring, I watched the skinny saplings put out tiny leaves. When I walked past, I always noted how big the tulips were getting and made bets with myself on when they would bloom. But last Wednesday, as I reached the park, I felt sick. Someone had knocked the trees to the ground and trampled the budding tulips into the dirt. Someone had destroyed a bit of beauty for no reason.

At lunchtime on Wednesday, I witnessed more meanness. Along with dozens of other hungry, hurried people, I was waiting in line at McDonald's. Also in line was a young mother with two tired, impatient children clinging to her legs. The mother was trying to calm the children, but it was obvious that their whining was about to give way to full-fledged tantrums. The lines barely moved, and the lunchtime tension was building. Then, one of the children began to cry and scream. The little boy's bloodcurdling yells resounded through the restaurant, and people stared angrily at the helpless mother. Finally, one man turned to her and said, "Lady, you shouldn't bring your kids to a public place if you can't control them." The woman was exhausted and hungry. Someone in line could have helped her with her problem. Instead, even though many of the customers in the restaurant were parents themselves, they treated her like a criminal.

The worst incident of mean-spiritedness that I saw that day happened after I left work. As I walked to the bus stop, I approached an old woman huddled in a doorway. She was wrapped in a dirty blanket and clutched a cheap vinyl bag packed with her belongings. She was one of the "street people" our society leaves to fend for themselves. The United States, the richest country on earth, should not allow such suffering. Some of these victims even live in cardboard boxes during the coldest winters. Approaching the woman from the opposite direction were three teenagers who were laughing and talking in loud voices. When they saw the old woman, they began to shout crude remarks at her. One of them grabbed her shopping bag and pretended to throw it out into the street. The woman stared helplessly at them, like a wounded animal surrounded by hunters. Then, having had their fun, the teenagers went on their way.

I had seen enough of the world's coldness that day and wanted to leave it behind. At home, I huddled in the warmth of my family. I wondered why we all contribute to the supply of petty cruelty. There's enough of it already.

Altered States

Most Americans are not alcoholics. Most of us do not smoke marijuana to get   1
high. LSD trips went out of style along with the flower children of the sixties.
Nevertheless, many Americans <u>are</u> walking and driving around with their minds
slightly out of kilter. In its attempt to cope with modern life, the human mind
seems to have evolved some defense strategies. Confronted with inventions like
the automobile, the television, and the shopping center, for example, the mind
will slip—all by itself—into an altered state.

First of all, the mind must now cope with the automobile. In the past, no   2
human being ever sat for hours at a time, in the same position, staring at endless
white lines and matched pairs of small red taillights. In order to deal with this
unnatural situation, the mind goes on automatic pilot. A primitive, less-developed
region of the brain takes over the actual driving. It tells the foot when to apply
pressure to the brake and gas pedal and directs the eyes to stay open.
Meanwhile, the rest of the brain continues on with higher functions. It devises
excuses for being late for work. It replays, better than any video system,
yesterday's Cowboys game. Or it creates a pleasant imaginary world where its
owner wins all arguments, tells hilarious jokes, and attracts the opposite sex like
a magnet. By splitting into two halves, the mind deals with the boredom of
driving.

The mind has defenses not only against the auto but also against television.   3
Since too much staring at flickering images of police officers, detectives, and
talk-show hosts can be dangerous to human sanity, the mind automatically goes
into a TV hypnosis state. The eyes see the sitcom or the dog food commercial,
but the mind goes into a holding pattern. None of the televised images or sounds
actually enters the brain. This is why, when questioned, people cannot remember
commercials they have seen five seconds before or why the TV cops are chasing a
certain suspect. In this hypnotic, trancelike state, the mind resembles an
armored armadillo. It rolls up in self-defense, letting the stream of televised
information pass by harmlessly.

Perhaps the most dangerous threat to the mind, however, is the shopping   4
center. In the modern mall, dozens of stores, restaurants, and movie theaters
compete for the mind's attention. There are hundreds of questions to be
answered. Should I start with the upper or lower mall level? Which stores should
I look in? Should I bother with the sweater sale at J. C. Penney? Should I eat
fried chicken or a burger for lunch? Where is my car parked? To combat this
mental overload, the mind goes into a state resembling the white-out experienced
by mountain climbers trapped in a blinding snowstorm. Suddenly, everything
looks the same. The shopper is unsure where to go next and cannot remember
what he or she came for in the first place. The mind enters this state
deliberately, so that the shopper has no choice but to leave.

Therefore, the next time you see drivers, TV viewers, or shoppers with eyes as   5
glazed and empty as polished doorknobs, you'll know these people are in a
protective altered state. Be gentle with them. They are merely trying to cope with
the mind-numbing inventions of modern life.

Childhood Fears

I remember my childhood as being generally happy and can recall   1
experiencing some of the most carefree times of my life. But I can also
remember, even more vividly, moments of being deeply frightened. As a child, I
was truly terrified of the dark and of getting lost; these fears were very real and
caused me some extremely uncomfortable moments.

Maybe it was the strange way things looked and sounded in my familiar room   2
at night that scared me so much. There was never total darkness, but a
streetlight or passing car lights made clothes hung over a chair take on the shape
of an unknown beast. Out of the corner of my eye, I saw curtains seem to move
when there was no breeze. A tiny creak in the floor would sound a hundred times
louder than in the daylight, and my imagination would take over, creating
burglars and monsters on the prowl. Darkness always made me feel so helpless,
too. My heart would pound, and I would lie very still so that the "enemy"
wouldn't discover me.

Another of my childhood fears was that I would get lost, especially on the   3
way home from school. Every morning I got on the school bus right near my
home—that was no problem. After school, though, when all the buses were lined
up along the curb, I was terrified that I'd get on the wrong one and be taken to
some unfamiliar neighborhood. I would scan the bus for the faces of my friends,
make sure the bus driver was the same one that had been there in the morning,
and even then ask the others over and over again to be sure I was on the right
bus. On school or family trips to an amusement park or a museum, I wouldn't let
the leaders out of my sight. And of course, I was never very adventurous when it
came to taking walks or hikes, because I would go only where I was sure I could
never get lost.

Perhaps one of the worst fears of all I had as a child was that of not being   4
liked or accepted by others. First of all, I was quite shy. Second, I worried
constantly about my looks, thinking people wouldn't like me because I was too
fat or wore braces. I tried to wear the "right" clothes and even had intense
arguments with my mother over the importance of wearing "flats" instead of
saddle shoes to school. I'm sorry that we had these arguments now, especially
since my mother is quite sickly and has spent the last year in and out of the
hospital. Being popular was so important to me then, and the fear of not being
liked was a powerful one.

One of the processes of evolving from a child to an adult is being able to   5
recognize and overcome or outgrow our fears. I've learned that darkness does not
have to take on a life of its own, that others can help me when I'm lost, and that
friendliness and sincerity will encourage people to like me. Understanding the
things that scared us as children helps us to cope with our lives as adults.

■ **Questions**

About Unity

1. Which sentence in paragraph 4 of "Childhood Fears" should be omitted in the interest of paragraph unity? (*Write the opening words.*)

   _____

2. Which two sentences in paragraph 4 of "Everyday Cruelty" should be omitted in the interest of paragraph unity?

   _____   _____

3. Which thesis statement fails to mention all three of its supporting points in its plan of development? _____

About Support

4. After which sentence in paragraph 4 of "Childhood Fears" are more supporting details needed? _____

5. Which essay uses a single extended example in each of its supporting paragraphs? _____

About Coherence

6. Which words in paragraph 4 of "Altered States" signal that the most important idea was saved for last? _____

7. What are the two transition words in paragraph 4 of "Childhood Fears"?

   _____   _____

8. Which topic sentence in "Altered States" functions as a linking sentence between paragraphs? _____

About the Introduction and Conclusion

9. What kind of introduction is used in "Childhood Fears"? Circle the appropriate letter.
   a. Broad, general statement narrowing to thesis
   b. Idea that is the opposite of the one to be developed
   c. Quotation   d. Anecdote   e. Questions

10. What transition word signals the conclusion of "Altered States"?

    _____

WRITING AN EXAMPLES ESSAY

■ Writing Assignment 1

For this assignment, you will complete an unfinished essay by adding appropriate supporting examples. Here is the incomplete essay:

Problems with My Apartment

> When I was younger, I fantasized about how wonderful life would be when I moved into my own apartment. Now I'm a bit older and wiser, and my fantasies have turned into nightmares. My apartment has given me nothing but headaches. From the day I signed the lease, I've had to deal with an uncooperative landlord, an incompetent janitor, and inconsiderate neighbors.

> First of all, my landlord has been uncooperative. . . .

> I've had a problem not only with my landlord but also with an incompetent janitor. . . .

> Perhaps the worst problem has been with the inconsiderate neighbors who live in the apartment above me. . . .

> Sometimes, my apartment seems like a small, friendly oasis surrounded by hostile enemies. I never know what side trouble is going to come from next: the landlord, the janitor, or the neighbors. Home may be where the heart is, but my sanity is thinking about moving out.

Note: If you do not have experience with an apartment, write instead on problems of living in a dormitory, or problems of living at home. Revise the introduction and conclusion so that they fit your topic. Problems of living in a dorm might include:

Restrictive dorm regulations
Inconsiderate students on your floor
A difficult roommate

Problems of living at home might include:

Lack of space
Inconsiderate brothers and sisters
Conflict with your parent or parents

How to Proceed

a   Brainstorm by making up answers to the following questions. Use separate paper.

How has the landlord been uncooperative?
In what ways have you been inconvenienced?
Has he (or she) been uncooperative more than once?
What has been your reaction?
What has been the landlord's reaction?
What kinds of things have you said to each other?

Who is the janitor?
What has he (or she) tried to fix in the apartment?
In what ways has the janitor been incompetent?
How has the janitor inconvenienced you?
Has the janitor's incompetence cost you money?
What is the worst example of the janitor's incompetence?

Who are the neighbors?
How long have they lived upstairs?
What kinds of hassles have you had?
Have these incidents happened several times?
If you have spoken to the neighbors, what did they say?
What is the worst problem with these neighbors?

The answers to these questions should serve as an excellent source of details for the essay.

b   Keep in mind that you may use one extended example in each paragraph (as in the essay "Everyday Cruelty") or two or three short examples (as in "Childhood Fears").

c   As you are writing drafts of your three supporting paragraphs, ask yourself repeatedly:

Do my examples truly show my landlord as *uncooperative*?
Do my examples truly show the janitor as *incompetent*?
Do my examples truly show my neighbors as *inconsiderate*?

Your aims in this assignment are twofold: (1) to provide *adequate* specific details for the three qualities in question and (2) to provide *enough* specific details so that you solidly support each quality.

d   When you are satisfied that you have provided effective examples, proofread your paragraphs carefully for the sentence skills listed on page 127 and the inside front cover. Then write out the full essay on separate paper and submit it to your instructor.

■ Writing Assignment 2

Write an examples essay on the good or bad qualities (or habits) of a person you know well. The person might be a member of your family, a friend, a roommate, a boss or supervisor, a neighbor, an instructor, or someone else. Listed below are some descriptive words that can be applied to people. They are only suggestions; you can write about other qualities as well.

Honest	Persistent	Irresponsible	Spineless
Bad-tempered	Shy	Stingy	Good-humored
Ambitious	Sloppy	Trustworthy	Cooperative
Bigoted	Hardworking	Aggressive	Disciplined
Considerate	Supportive	Courageous	Sentimental
Argumentative	Suspicious	Compulsive	Defensive
Softhearted	Open-minded	Jealous	Dishonest
Energetic	Lazy	Modest	Insensitive
Patient	Independent	Sarcastic	Unpretentious
Reliable	Stubborn	Self-centered	Neat
Generous	Flirtatious		

In assignment 2, you may want to write about three related qualities of one person (for example, "My brother is stubborn, bad-tempered, and suspicious") or about one quality that is apparent in different aspects of a person's life (for example,"My wife's sensitivity is apparent in her relationships with her friends at work, my parents, and our teenage son").

■ Writing Assignment 3

Write an essay that uses examples to develop one of the following statements or a related statement of your own.

> If you look hard enough, you can see complete strangers being kind to one another.
>
> The gossip tabloids sold at supermarket checkouts use several techniques to lure consumers into buying them.
>
> The Super Bowl is superhype, not supersport.
>
> The best things in life are definitely not free.
>
> Living with a roommate can help you learn honesty, tolerance, and consideration.
>
> There's more joy in simple pleasures than in life's great events.
>
> Looking for a job can be a stressful process.
>
> Pets in the United States are treated like surrogate children.
>
> Our lives would be improved without the automobile.
>
> American culture is infatuated with violence.

Be sure to choose examples that actually support your thesis. They should be relevant facts, statistics, personal experiences, or incidents you have heard or read about.

Organize each paragraph by grouping several examples that support a particular point. Or use one extended example—an incident or story that may take up a full paragraph.

Save the paragraph containing the most vivid, convincing, or important examples for last.

■ Writing Assignment 4

In this examples essay, you will write with a specific purpose and for a specific audience. Imagine that you have completed a year of college and have agreed to take part in your college's summer orientation program for incoming students. You will be meeting with a small group of new students to help them get ready for college life.

Prepare a brief presentation to the new students in which you make the point that they must be ready to take on more responsibility than they may have had in high school. Make vividly clear—using several hypothetical students as examples—just what the consequences of inappropriate behavior can be. To organize your presentation, you might want to focus on three of the following areas: instructors, class attendance, time control, class note-taking, textbook study, establishing regular times and places for study, and getting help when needed. Each area could be developed with detailed examples in a separate supporting paragraph.

■ Writing Assignment 5

Write an examples essay based on an outside reading. It might be a selection in one of the following books (most should be available in your college library) or another selection recommended by your instructor.

Dave Barry, *Greatest Hits**
John Chancellor, *Peril and Promise*
Ellen Goodman, *Making Sense**
Bob Greene, *Cheeseburgers**
Sue Hubbell, *A Country Year*
Maxine Hong Kingston, *The Woman Warrior*
Harold S. Kushner, *When All You've Ever Wanted Isn't Enough*
Anne Morrow Lindbergh, *Gift from the Sea*
William Least Heat Moon, *Blue Highways*
George Orwell, *Shooting an Elephant and Other Essays*
Richard Rodriguez, *Hunger of Memory*
Andy Rooney, *Not That You Asked**
Al Santoli, *New Americans*
Phyllis Theroux, *Night Lights*
Calvin Trillin, *If You Can't Say Something Nice**
Alice Walker, *Living by the Word**
Marie Winn, *The Plug-In Drug*

Base your essay on some idea in the selection you have chosen and provide a series of examples to back up your idea. A student model is given on the following page.

*Or any other collection of essays by the same author.

Paying Attention to a Death

In "A Hanging," George Orwell describes the execution of a man in a Burmese prison. The prisoner, a Hindu, is marched from his cell, led to a gallows, and killed when the drop opens and the noose tightens. The entire procedure takes eight minutes. As he depicts this incident, Orwell uses a series of details that make us sharply aware of the enormity of killing a human being.

The moments leading up to the hanging are filled with tension. Six tall guards, two of them armed with rifles, surround the prisoner, "a puny wisp of a man." The guards not only handcuff the man but also chain his handcuffs to their belts and lash his arms to his sides. The guards, nervous about fulfilling their duty, treat the Hindu like "a fish which is still alive and may jump back into the water." Meanwhile, the jail superintendent prods the head jailer to get on with the execution. The superintendent's irritability is a mask for his discomfort. Then, the procession toward the gallows is interrupted by the appearance of a friendly dog, "wagging its whole body, wild with glee at finding so many human beings together." This does not ease the tension but increases it. The contrast of the lively dog licking the doomed man's face momentarily stuns the guards and arouses in the superintendent a sense of angry urgency.

Next, in the gallows scene, Orwell uses vivid details that emphasize the life within the man who is about to die. The condemned prisoner, who has been walking steadily up to this point, moves "clumsily" up the ladder. And until now, he has been utterly silent. But, after the noose is placed around his neck, he begins "crying out to his god." The repeated cry of "Ram! Ram! Ram!" is "like the tolling of a bell," a death knell. The dog begins to whine at the sound, and the guards go "grey," their bayonets trembling. It is as if the hooded, faceless man on the wooden platform has suddenly become a human being, a soul seeking aid and comfort. The superintendent, who has been hiding his emotions behind a stern face, gives the execution order "fiercely." The living man of moments ago simply ceases to be.

After the hanging, Orwell underscores the relief people feel when the momentous event is over. The jail superintendent checks to be sure that the prisoner is dead and then blows out "a deep breath" and loses his "moody look." "One felt an impulse," Orwell says, "to sing, to break into a run, to snigger." Suddenly, people are talking and chattering, even laughing. The head jailer's story about a condemned prisoner who clung to the bars of his cell so tightly that it took six men to move him sets off a gale of laughter. On the road outside the prison, everyone who participated in the execution has a whiskey. The men, having been so close to death, need to reassure themselves of the fact that they are alive. They must laugh and drink, not because they are insensitive, but because they are shaken. They must try to forget that the dead man is only a hundred yards away.

"A Hanging" sets out to create a picture of death in the midst of life. Orwell tries to make us see, through the details he chooses, that killing a person results in "one mind less, one world less." Such an act—"cutting a life short when it is in full tide"—violates the laws of life and nature.

■ **Writing Assignment 6:**
  Writing about a Reading Selection

Read the selection titled "Seven Ways to Keep the Peace at Home" on pages 647–653. Then write an essay about three ways that would be most appropriate for keeping peace at your home. Following are examples of how the three supporting paragraphs in your essay might begin:

First Supporting Paragraph:

> One way our family would benefit is if we would stop playing the game of telephone. All too often, one family member uses another to . . .

Second Supporting Paragraph:

> Another step our family should take is to "Tell it like you feel it." My mother, for instance, sometimes hides her true feelings about . . .

Third Supporting Paragraph:

> Perhaps most important, our family needs to stop the "Good-Guy/Bad-Guy" routine. Two people in my family seem to have been cast in these roles . . .

Develop the ways you choose with specific examples that involve actual members of your family. In the interest of privacy you may, of course, change the names of the members of your family or alter some of the details.

PROCESS

Every day we perform many activities that are *processes,* that is, series of steps carried out in a definite order. Many of these processes are familiar and automatic: for example, loading film into a camera, diapering a baby, or making an omelet. We are thus seldom aware of the sequence of steps making up each activity. In other cases—for example, when someone asks us for directions to a particular place, or when we try to read and follow directions for a new table game that someone has given us—we may be painfully conscious of the whole series of steps involved in the process.

In this section, you will be asked to write a *process essay*—one that explains clearly how to do or make something. To prepare for this assignment, you should first read the student process papers that are presented and then answer the questions that follow them.

ESSAYS TO CONSIDER

Successful Exercise

Regular exercise is something like the weather—we all talk about it, but we 1
tend not to do anything about it! Television exercise classes, records and tapes, and new videocassettes and disks, as well as the instructions in books, magazines, and pamphlets, now make it easy to have a personal, low-cost exercise program without leaving home. However, for success in exercise, you should follow a simple plan consisting of arranging the time, making preparations, and following the sequence with care.

To begin with, set aside a regular time for exercise. If you have a heavy 2
schedule at work or school, this may be difficult, since you're rushed in the morning and exhausted at night, and you have no time in between. However, one solution is simply to get up half an hour earlier in the morning. Look at it this way: If you're already getting up too early, what's an extra half hour? Of course, that time could be cut to fifteen minutes earlier if you could lay out your clothes, set the breakfast table, fill the coffee maker, and gather your books and materials for the next day before you go to bed.

Next, prepare for your exercise session. To begin with, get yourself ready by not eating or drinking anything before exercising. Why risk an upset stomach? Then, dress comfortably in something that allows you to move freely. Since you'll be in your own home, there's no need to invest in a high-fashion dance costume. A loose T shirt and shorts are good. A bathing suit is great in summer, and in winter a set of long underwear is warm and comfortable. If your hair tends to flop in your eyes, pin it back or wear a headband or scarf. Prepare the exercise area, too. Turn off the phone and lock the door to prevent interruptions. Shove the coffee table out of the way so you won't bruise yourself on it or other furniture. Finally, get out the simple materials you'll need to exercise on. 3

If this is your first attempt at exercising, start slowly. You do not need to do each movement the full number of times at first, but you should <u>try</u> each one. After five or six sessions, you should be able to do each one the f<u>ull</u> number of times. Try to move in a smooth, rhythmic way; doing so will help prevent injuries and pulled muscles. Pretend you're a dancer and make each move graceful, even if it's just climbing up off the floor. After the last exercise, give yourself five minutes to relax and cool off—you have earned it. Finally, put those sore muscles under a hot shower and get ready for a great day. 4

Establishing an exercise program isn't difficult, but it can't be achieved by reading about it, talking about it, or watching models exercise on television. To begin with, you're going to have to get up off that couch and do something about it. Otherwise, as my doctor likes to say, "If you don't use it, you'll lose it." 5

How to Complain

I'm not just a consumer—I'm a victim. If I order a product, it is sure to arrive in the wrong color, size, or quantity. If I hire people to do repairs, they never arrive on the day scheduled. If I owe a bill, the computer is bound to overcharge me. Therefore, in self-defense, I have developed the following consumer's guide to complaining effectively. 1

The first step is getting organized. I save all sales slips and original boxes. Also, I keep a special file for warranty cards and appliance guarantees. This file does not prevent a product from falling apart the day after the guarantee runs out. One of the problems in our country is the shoddy workmanship that goes into many products. However, these facts give me the ammunition I need to make a complaint. I know the date of the purchase, the correct price (or service charge), where the item was purchased, and an exact description of the product, including model and serial numbers. When I compose my letter of complaint, I find it is not necessary to exaggerate. I just stick to the facts. 2

The next step is to send the complaint to the person who will get results 3
quickly. My experience has shown that the president of a company is the best
person to contact. I call the company to find out the president's name and make
sure I note the proper spelling. Then I write directly to that person, and I usually
get prompt action. For example, the head of AMF arranged to replace my son's
ten-speed "lemon" when it fell apart piece by piece in less than a year. Another
time, the president of a Philadelphia department store finally had a twenty-dollar
overcharge on my bill corrected after three months of arguing with the computer
had brought no results.

If I get no response to a written complaint within ten days, I follow through 4
with a personal telephone call. When I had a new bathtub installed a few years
ago, the plumber left a gritty black substance on the bottom of the tub. No
amount of scrubbing could remove it. I tried every cleanser on the supermarket
shelf, but I still had a dirty tub. The plumber shrugged off my complaints and
said to try Fantastik. The manufacturer never answered my letter. Finally, I made
a personal phone call to the president of the firm. Within days a well-dressed
executive showed up at my door. In a business suit, white shirt, striped tie, and
rubber gloves, he cleaned the tub. Before he left, he scolded in an angry voice,
"You didn't have to call the president." The point is, I did have to call the
president. No one else cared enough to solve the problem.

Therefore, my advice to consumers is to keep accurate records, and when 5
you have to complain, go right to the top. It has always worked for me.

How to Pick the Perfect Class Schedule

As you look at the punch cards or computer printout that lists your courses 1
for next semester, do you experience a terrible sinking feeling in the pit of your
stomach? Have you gotten stuck with unwanted courses or a depressing time
schedule that cannot be changed? If so, you obviously don't know how to select
the perfect schedule. But by following a few simple procedures, you can begin
any semester with the right courses at the most convenient times.

First, you must find the right courses. These are the ones that combine the 2
least amount of work with the fewest tests and the most lenient professors. Ask
your friends and acquaintances about courses in which they received A's after
attending only 25 percent of the classes. Ask around, too, to see which
instructors have given the same tests for the last fifteen years. Photocopies of
these tests are usually cheap and widely available. Then, pick up a copy of the
master schedule and study it carefully. Find the telltale course titles that signal
an easy glide through a painless subject. Look for titles like "History of the
Animated Cartoon," "Arts and Crafts for Beginners," and "Rock Music of the
1950s."

Next, when you have accumulated lists of easy instructors and subjects, you can begin to block out time periods. The ideal schedule will vary according to your individual needs. If you stay up late in order to watch old movies or work the graveyard shift, you may want a daily schedule that begins no sooner than noon. You should schedule only afternoon courses, too, if you're one of those people who would rather be tortured than forced to leave a warm, cozy bed in the morning. On the other hand, if you are a "lark" who bounds out of bed at dawn, you may want to get your classes out of the way as early as possible. That way you have the rest of the day free. Morning classes are also necessary if you are a soap opera fanatic who can't miss one day's events in Pine Valley or Port Charles. 3

Finally, you must outsmart the registration process. You want your ideal schedule to pass through official channels untouched. The main way to do this is to register early. Ignore things like registration by first letter of last name or by number of accumulated credits. Desperate stories about dying relatives or heartless employers will get you quickly through a registration line. If a course does happen to be closed because you simply couldn't register at 7:00 A.M., you may still be able to get in. Talk to the professor and convince him or her that a serious, ambitious, hardworking student like yourself would be a shining asset to the class. Be sure to carry a list of backup courses to registration, though, just in case one of your chosen classes switches professors or changes time periods. Be ready to fill in vacant slots with courses that meet your strict requirements. 4

By following these suggestions, any student can pick the perfect class schedule. College can thus become a nonirritating, almost pleasant activity that disrupts your real life as little as possible. And you never know—you might even learn something in "Creative TV Watching." 5

■ **Questions**

About Unity

1. Which supporting paragraph in "Successful Exercise" lacks a topic sentence? _____

2. Which sentence in paragraph 2 of "How to Complain" should be omitted in the interest of paragraph unity? (*Write the opening words.*)

   _____

About Support

3. After which sentence in paragraph 3 in "Successful Exercise" are more specific details needed? _____

4. Which paragraph in "How to Complain" uses a single extended example to support its topic sentence? _____

5.   What are the three key stages in the process of ''How to Complain''?

a.   _____

b.   _____

c.   _____

6.   What are the three key stages in "How to Pick the Perfect Class Schedule"?

a.   _____

b.   _____

c.   _____

About Coherence

7.   What are the four main transition words in paragraph 3 of ''Successful Exercise''?   _____   _____   _____   _____

8.   Which topic sentence in ''How to Pick the Perfect Class Schedule'' functions as a linking sentence between paragraphs?   _____

About the Introduction and Conclusion

9.   Which method of introduction is used in ''How to Pick the Perfect Class Schedule''?

_____

10.   Which essay ends with a recommendation?

_____

WRITING A PROCESS ESSAY

■   ## Writing Assignment 1

Choose one of the following ten topics that you think you can write about in a process paper.

How to do grocery shopping in a minimum of time
How to select a car (new or used), apartment, or home
How to do household cleaning efficiently
How to drive defensively

How to protect a home from burglars

How to gain or lose weight

How to relax

How to study for an important exam

How to play a position (third base, guard, goalie, etc.) in a team sport

How to plan an event (party, wedding, garage sale, etc.)

How to Proceed

a   Now freewrite for ten minutes on the topic you have tentatively chosen. Do not worry about spelling, grammar, organization, or other matters of correct form. Just write whatever comes into your head regarding the topic. Keep writing for more than ten minutes if any additional details about the topic occur to you.

This freewriting will give you a base of raw material that you can draw on in the next phase of your work on your process essay. After freewriting for ten minutes, you should have a sense of whether there is enough material available for you to write a process essay about the topic. If so, continue as explained below. If not, choose another topic and freewrite about this new topic for ten minutes.

b   State your thesis in a single clear sentence. In your thesis, you can (1) say it is important that your audience know about this process (''Knowing how to register a complaint can save time and frustration'') or (2) state your opinion of this process (''Growing your own tomatoes is easier than you might think'').

c   Make a list of all the steps that you are describing. Here, for example, is the list prepared by the author of ''How to Complain'':

Save sales slips and original boxes

Engrave items with ID number in case of burglary

Write letter of complaint

Make photocopy of letter

Create file of warranties and guarantees

Send complaint letter directly to president

Call company for president's name

Follow through with telephone call if no response

Make thank-you call after action is taken

d   Number your items in time order; strike out items that do not fit in the list; add others you can think of. Thus:

1 Save sales slips and original boxes
~~Engrave items with ID number in case of burglary~~
4 Write letter of complaint
~~Make photocopy of letter~~
2 Create file of warranties and guarantees
5 Send complaint letter directly to president
3 Call company for president's name
6 Follow through with telephone call if no response
~~Make thank-you call after action is taken~~

e   After making the list, decide how the items can be grouped into a minimum of three steps. For example, with ''How to Complain,'' you might divide the process into (1) getting organized, (2) sending the complaint to the president, and (3) following up with further action. Or, with a topic like ''How to Grow Tomatoes,'' you might divide the process into (1) soil preparation, (2) planting, and (3) care.

f   Use your list as a guide to write the first rough draft of your paper. As you write, try to think of additional details that will develop your opening sentence. Do not expect to finish your paper in one draft. You should, in fact, be ready to write a series of lists and drafts as you work toward the goals of unity, support, and coherence.

g   Be sure to use transitions such as *first, next, also, then, after, now, during,* and *finally* so that your paper moves smoothly and clearly from one step in the process to the next.

h   While working on your process paper, refer to the checklist on page 127 and the inside front cover to make sure you can answer *Yes* to the questions about unity, support, and coherence. Also, refer to the checklist when you proofread your next-to-final draft for sentence-skills mistakes, including spelling.

■ ## Writing Assignment 2

Any one of the topics below and on the next page can be written as a process paper. Follow the steps suggested for writing assignment 1.

How to break a bad habit
How to live with a two-year-old, a teenager, or a parent
How to make someone like you

How to make excuses
How to fall out of love
How to improve reading skills
How to do well at a job interview
How to care for an aging relative
How to stay young
How to improve a school or a place of work

■ Writing Assignment 3

Everyone is an expert at something. Write a process essay on some skill that you can perform very well. Write from the point of view that "This is how _____ *should* be done." (Remember that a skill can be anything from "starting a fire" to "setting up a new stereo system" to "dealing with unpleasant customers" to "using a personal computer.")

■ Writing Assignment 4

In this process essay, you will write with a specific purpose and for a specific audience. Imagine that you are "Val Valentine," a columnist in the campus newspaper who gives advice on romance. A reader has written to you asking how to get to know someone he or she has admired from afar.

In your reply, suggest a process for meeting and getting to know another person on campus. You may describe a realistic process or a humorous one, in which you exaggerate the steps involved.

■ Writing Assignment 5

Write an essay in which you summarize, in your own words, the steps involved in doing a research paper or in preparing for and taking an essay exam. Both of these processes are explained in Part Three of this book. Before starting this paper, you should read "Writing a Summary" on pages 247–256.

■ **Writing Assignment 6:
Writing about a Reading Selection**

Do *either* of the following.

Option 1: Read the selection titled "Brett Hauser: Supermarket Box Boy" on pages 584–586. Then write a process essay on how you perform a certain task at a present job (or did at some past job)—how to ring up a charge slip, take inventory, make french fries, load a truck, or do any other task you know how to do. (If you have never had a job, describe how you do a certain household chore.)

You could start by imagining how you would train someone else to perform the task: break it down into a series of clear steps. Then follow steps *d* through *h* under "How to Proceed" on pages 163–164.

Think of your audience for the paper as someone who is going to take over the job for you. Make your essay detailed enough so that it can serve as a brief training guide for that person.

Option 2: Read the selection titled "How to Make It in College, Now That You're Here" on pages 632–637. Then write a process essay with the thesis, "Here are the tips that will help a student succeed in _____" (name a course in which you are now enrolled or one that you have taken in the past). To get started, think of the advice you would like to have had *before* you took that particular course: What would you have wanted to know about the professor? The assignments? The exams? Policies about attendance, lateness, and so on? Pick three tips that you believe would be most helpful to another student about to enroll in the class, and discuss each one in a separate supporting paragraph. Model your introduction after the one in "How to Make It in College" by telling your readers that, on the basis of your own experience, you are going to pass on the secrets for succeeding in this course.

Below are three sample topic sentences for an essay on "How to Succeed in Communications 101."

First topic sentence: First of all, a student who wants a good grade in Communications 101 should be prepared at every class meeting for a surprise quiz.

Second topic sentence: In addition, students should speak up during class discussion, for Professor Knox adds "participation" into final grades.

Third topic sentence: Most important, students should start early on term papers and turn them in on time.

CAUSE
AND
EFFECT

Why did Janet decide to move out of her parents' house? What made you quit a well-paying job? Why are horror movies so popular? Why has Ben acted so depressed lately? Why did our team fail to make the league play-offs?

Every day we ask questions similar to those above and look for answers. We realize that many actions do not occur without causes, and we realize also that a given action can have a series of effects—for good or bad. By examining causes or effects of an action, we seek to understand and explain things that happen in our lives.

You will be asked in this section to do some detective work by examining the cause of something or the effects of something. First read the three essays that follow and answer the questions about them. All three essays support their thesis statements by explaining a series of causes or a series of effects.

ESSAYS TO CONSIDER

A Necessary Decision

Have you ever seen a supermarket bag crammed full of medical bills for just one person? Well, I have. I had known that my mother was sick as a result of a failing kidney, but I had not realized how much trouble my parents were having in dealing with that sickness. Only when I had saved enough money to visit them in Florida did I discover just how critical the situation had become. The problems were so serious, in fact, that I had to make the decision to put my mother in a nursing home.

1

First, there were countless bills. Many were for drugs, since Mother was   2
taking about twenty-four pills a day along with receiving insulin injections. Then
there were hospital bills for the initial diagnosis, for batteries of tests, and for the
operation that prepared her for kidney dialysis. Next, there were the ambulance
bills for my mother's trips three times a week to the dialysis clinic. And finally,
there were clinic bills for $350 for each of the dozen or so treatments she had
already had. Unable to contend with the insurance paperwork needed to pay for
the bills, my father had stuffed all incoming bills into a Winn-Dixie shopping bag
in the closet.

She was confined to a wheelchair and needed help moving around. She had   3
to have assistance in getting dressed and undressed, going to the bathroom, and
getting into and out of bed. She also needed a very specialized diet involving a
combination of foods for renal, diabetic, and gallbladder patients. In addition,
she required emotional support. Sometimes she was so depressed, she wouldn't
eat unless she was urged to. "I'm going to die; just let me die in peace," she
would say, or "You don't love me anymore now that I'm sick." These constant
needs, I concluded, would benefit from professional care.

Finally, I was concerned not only with my mother's needs but also with my   4
father's welfare. He assumed total responsibility for my mother. Since he doesn't
drive, he walked everywhere, including to the grocery store, drugstore,
laundromat, hospital, and clinic. Also, he did all the housework; he fed, dressed,
bathed, and medicated my mother; and he prepared her special meals and
snacks. In addition, her behavior was a strain on him. She would wait until he
was in the kitchen, and then she would call the police or ambulance to say she
was dying. Or she would wait until 3 A.M. and telephone each of her children to
say good-bye. Never robust, my father dropped from 125 pounds to 98 pounds
under the strain, caught a bad cold, and finally telephoned me for help.

I conferred with a social worker, found a nursing home, and signed my   5
mother in. My father is able to get a bus that takes him, within twenty minutes,
right to the nursing home door. He has gained weight and has gotten back in
control of things to the point where he can handle the paperwork again. Even my
mother has recovered to the extent that she is making my daughter a quilt. My
decision was not easy, but it has turned out to be the best one for both of my
parents.

The Joys of an Old Car

Some of my friends can't believe my car still runs. Others laugh when they   1
see it parked outside the house and ask if it's an antique. But they aren't being
fair to my fourteen-year-old Honda Civic. In fact, my "antique" has opened my
eyes to the rewards of owning an old car.

One obvious reward is economy. Fourteen years ago, when my husband and I   2
were newly married and nearly broke, we bought the car—a shiny, red, year-old
leftover—for a mere $1,800. Today it would cost five times as much. We save

money on insurance, since it's no longer worthwhile for us to have collision coverage. Old age has even been kind to the Civic's engine, which required only three major repairs in the last several years. And it still delivers twenty-six miles per gallon in the city and thirty-eight on the highway—not bad for a senior citizen.

The second benefit is dependability. If a Civic passes the twenty-thousand-mile mark with no major problems, it will probably go on forever. Our Civic breezed past that mark many years ago and has run almost perfectly ever since. Even on the coldest, snowiest mornings, I can count on my car to sputter to life and roll surefootedly down the driveway. The only time it didn't start, unfortunately, was the day I had a final exam. The Civic may have the body of an old car, but beneath its elderly hood hums the engine of a teenager.   3

Last of all, there is the advantage of familiarity. When I open the door and slide into the driver's seat, the soft vinyl envelops me like a well-worn glove. I know to the millimeter exactly how much room I have when I turn a corner or back into a streetside parking space. When my gas gauge is on empty, I know that 1.3 gallons are still in reserve and I can plan accordingly. The front wheels invariably begin to shake when I go more than fifty-five miles an hour, reminding me that I am exceeding the speed limit. With the Civic, the only surprises I face are the ones from other drivers.   4

I prize my fourteen-year-old Civic's economy and dependability, and most of all, its familiarity. It is faded, predictable, and comfortable, like a well-worn pair of jeans. And, like a well-worn pair of jeans, it will be difficult to throw away.   5

Stresses of Being a Celebrity

Last week, a woman signing herself "Want the Truth in Westport" wrote to Ann Landers with a question she just had to have answered. "Please find out for sure," she begged the columnist, "whether or not Oprah Winfrey has had a face-lift." Fortunately for Ms. Winfrey's privacy, Ann Landers refused to answer the question. But the incident disturbed me. How awful it would be to be a celebrity, I thought, and always be in the public eye. Celebrities lead very stressful lives, for no matter how glamorous or powerful they are, they have too little privacy, too much pressure, and no safety.   1

For one thing, celebrities don't have the privacy an ordinary person has. The most personal details of their lives are splashed all over the front pages of the National Enquirer and the Globe so that bored supermarket shoppers can read about "Roseanne and Her New Love" or "Letterman's Deepest Fear." Even a celebrity's family is hauled into the spotlight. A teenage son's arrest for pot possession or a wife's drinking problem becomes the subject of glaring headlines. Photographers hound celebrities at their homes, in restaurants, and on the street, hoping to get a picture of a Cindy Crawford in curlers or a Bruce Willis guzzling a beer. When celebrities try to do the things that normal people do, like eat out or attend a football game, they run the risk of being interrupted by thoughtless autograph hounds or mobbed by aggressive fans.   2

In addition, celebrities are under constant pressure. Their physical   3
appearance is always under observation. Famous women, especially, suffer from
the "she really looks old" or the "boy, has she put on weight" spotlight.
Unflattering pictures of celebrities are photographers' prizes to be sold to the
highest bidder; this increases the pressure on celebrities to look good at all
times. Famous people are also under pressure to act calm and collected under
any circumstances. There's no freedom to blow off steam or to do something just
a little crazy. Therefore, people who forget this must suffer the consequences.

Most important, celebrities must deal with the stress of being in constant   4
danger. The friendly grabs, hugs, and kisses of enthusiastic fans can quickly turn
into uncontrolled assaults on a celebrity's hair, clothes, and car. Celebrities often
get strange letters from people who become obsessed with their idols or from
people who threaten to harm them. Worst of all, threats can turn into deeds. The
attempt to kill Ronald Reagan and the murder of John Lennon came about
because two unbalanced people tried to transfer the celebrity's fame to
themselves. Famous people must live with the fact that they are always fair
game—and never out of season.

Some people dream of starring roles, their names in lights, and their pictures   5
on the cover of People magazine. I'm not one of them, though. A famous person
gives up private life, feels pressured all the time, and is never completely safe.
So let someone else have that cover story. I'd rather lead an ordinary, but calm,
life than a stress-filled public one.

■ Questions

About Unity

1. Which supporting paragraph in "A Necessary Decision" lacks a topic
   sentence? _____

2. Which sentence in paragraph 3 of "The Joys of an Old Car" should be
   omitted in the interest of paragraph unity? (*Write the opening
   words.*) _____

3. Rewrite the thesis statement of "The Joys of an Old Car" to include a plan
   of development.

   _____

   _____

   _____

   _____

About Support

4. How many effects are given to develop the thesis in "Stresses of Being a Celebrity"? (*Check the right answer.*)

   _____ 1   _____ 2   _____ 3   _____ 4

   How many are given in "The Joys of an Old Car"?

   _____ 1   _____ 2   _____ 3   _____ 4

5. After which sentence in paragraph 3 of "Stresses of Being a Celebrity" are more specific details needed? _____

6. How many examples are given to support the topic sentence "One obvious reward is economy" in "The Joys of an Old Car"?

   _____

About Coherence

7. Which topic sentence in "A Necessary Decision" functions as a linking sentence between paragraphs? _____

8. What are the three main transition words in paragraph 3 of "Stresses of Being a Celebrity"?

   _____   _____   _____

9. What are the three transition words in "The Joys of an Old Car" that signal the three major points of support for the thesis?

   _____   _____   _____

About the Introduction

10. What two methods of introduction are combined to form the first paragraph of "Stresses of Being a Celebrity"? Circle the appropriate letters.

    a. Broad, general statement narrowing to thesis
    b. Idea that is the opposite of the one to be developed
    c. Quotation
    d. Anecdote
    e. Questions

Activity 1

Complete the following outline of "A Necessary Decision." The effect is the author's decision to put her mother in a nursing home; the causes of that decision are what make up each supporting paragraph. Summarize each cause in a few words. The first cause and one detail are given for you as an example.

Thesis: The problems were so serious, in fact, that I had to make the decision to put my mother in a nursing home.

1. *Countless bills*
   a. *Bills for drugs*
   b. _____
   c. _____
   d. _____
2. _____
   a. _____
   b. _____
   c. _____
3. _____
   a. _____
   b. _____
   c. _____

Activity 2

In scratch-outline form on separate paper, provide brief causes or effects for at least four of the ten statements below. Note the example. Make sure that you have three *separate* and *distinct* items for each statement. Also, indicate whether you have listed three causes or three effects.

Example Many youngsters are terrified of school.

1. *Afraid of not being liked by other students* ⎫
2. *Fearful of failing tests*   ⎬ *Causes*
3. *Intimidated by teachers*   ⎭

1. Fast-food outlets have changed the eating habits of many Americans.
2. I would recommend (*or* not recommend) _____ (*name a certain course*) to other students.
3. The women's movement has had an enormous impact on women's lives.
4. Congress should take several steps to make automobile driving safer.
5. Exercise has changed my life.
6. Students often have trouble adjusting to college for several reasons.
7. Videocassette recorders have changed the way we watch television.
8. _____ is a popular sport for several reasons.
9. Computers have begun to affect the lives of many families.
10. There are several advantages (*or* drawbacks) to living at home while going to school.

WRITING A CAUSE-EFFECT ESSAY

■ ### Writing Assignment 1

Decide, perhaps through discussion with your instructor or classmates, which of the outlines prepared above would be most promising to develop into an essay. Make sure that your supporting reasons are logical ones that actually back up your thesis statement. Ask yourself in each case, ''Does this reason truly support my thesis idea?'' See ''How to Proceed,'' below.

How to Proceed

a   On separate paper, make a list of details that might go under each of the supporting points. Provide more details than you can actually use. Here, for example, are the details generated by the writer of ''The Joys of an Old Car'' when she was working on her third supporting paragraph:

Car's familiarity:

Know how much space I have to park
Front wheels shake at fifty-five miles per hour
Know what's in glove compartment
Worn seat—comfortable
Know tire inflation (pounds of pressure)
Can turn corners expertly (space)
Gas tank has reserve
Radio push buttons are set for favorite stations
Know how hard to press brake
Know that reverse gear is over, <u>then</u> down

b   Decide which details you will use to develop each of your supporting paragraphs. Then, number the details in the order in which you will present them. Here is how the writer of ''The Joys of an Old Car'' made decisions about the details in her final supporting paragraph:

2   Know how much space I have to park
4   Front wheels shake at fifty-five miles per hour
~~Know what's in glove compartment~~
1   Worn seat—comfortable
~~Know tire inflation (pounds of pressure)~~
2   Can turn corners expertly (space)
3   Gas tank has reserve
~~Radio push buttons are set for favorite stations~~
~~Know how hard to press brake~~
~~Know that reverse gear is over, then down~~

c   As you are working on the drafts of your cause-effect paper, refer to the checklist on page 127 and the inside front cover. Make sure that you answer *Yes* to the questions about unity, support, and coherence.

d   You may also want to refer to pages 79–84 for suggestions on writing an effective introduction and conclusion to your essay.

e   Finally, use the checklist on page 127 and the inside front cover when you are proofreading your next-to-final draft for sentence-skills mistakes, including spelling.

■ Writing Assignment 2

Below are six thesis statements for a ''cause'' paper and six for an ''effect'' paper. In scratch-outline form, provide brief supporting points for four of the twelve.

List Causes

1. Americans tend to get married later in life than they used to.
2. Childhood is the unhappiest time of life.
3. Being young is better than being old. (*Or vice versa.*)
4. _____ is the most difficult course I have ever taken.
5. My relationship with _____ (name a relative, employer, or friend) is better than ever.
6. It is easy to fall into an unhealthy diet in our society.

List Effects

7. Punishment for certain crimes should take the form of community service.
8. Growing up in the family I have has influenced my life in important ways.
9. The average workweek should be no more than thirty hours long.
10. A bad (*or* good) instructor can affect students in significant ways.
11. The drinking age should be raised to twenty-one in every state.
12. The fact that both parents often work has led to a number of changes in the typical family household.

■ **Writing Assignment 3**

If friendly aliens from a highly developed civilization decided to visit our planet, they would encounter a contradictory race of beings—us. We human beings would have reasons to feel both proud and ashamed of the kind of society the aliens would encounter. Write an essay explaining whether you would be proud or ashamed of the state of the human race today. Give reasons for your feeling.

■ **Writing Assignment 4**

In this cause-effect essay, you will write with a specific purpose and for a specific audience. Imagine that a friend of yours is having a hard time learning anything in a class taught by Professor X. You volunteer to attend the class and see for yourself. You also get information from your friend about the course requirements.

Afterward, you write a letter to Professor X, calling attention to what you see as causes of the learning problems that students are having in the class. To organize your essay, you might develop each of these causes in a separate supporting paragraph. In the second part of each supporting paragraph, you might suggest changes that Professor X could make to deal with each problem.

■ **Writing Assignment 5**

Write a cause-effect essay in which you advance an idea about a poem, story, play, literary essay, or novel. The work you choose may be assigned by your instructor or may require your instructor's approval. To develop your idea, use a series of two or more reasons and specific supporting evidence for each reason. A student model follows.

Paul's Suicide

Paul, the main character in Willa Cather's short story "Paul's Case," is a   1
young man on a collision course with death. As Cather reveals Paul's story, we
learn about elements of Paul's personality that inevitably come together and
cause his suicide. Paul takes his own life as a result of his inability to conform to
his society, his passive nature, and his emotional isolation.

First of all, Paul cannot conform to the standards of his own society. At   2
school, Paul advertises his desire to be part of another, more glamorous world by
wearing fancy clothes that set him apart from the other students. At home on
Cordelia Street, Paul despises everything about his middle-class neighborhood.
He hates the houses "permeated by kitchen odors," the "ugliness and
commonness of his own home," and the respectable neighbors sitting on their
front stoops every Sunday, "their stomachs comfortably protruding." Paul's father
hopes that Paul will settle down and become like the young man next door, a
nearsighted clerk who works for a corporate steel magnate. Paul, however, is
repelled by the young man and all he represents. It seems inevitable, then, that
Paul will not be able to cope with the office job his father obtains for him at the
firm of Denny & Carson; and this inability to conform will, in turn, lead to Paul's
theft of $1,000.

Paul's suicide is also due, in part, to his passive nature. Throughout his life,   3
Paul has been an observer and an onlooker. Paul's only escape from the prison of
his daily life comes from his job as an usher at Pittsburgh's Carnegie Hall; he
lives for the moments when he can watch the actors, singers, and musicians.
However, Paul has no desire to be an actor or musician. As Cather says, ". . .
What he wanted was to see, to be in the atmosphere, float on the wave of it, to
be carried out . . . away from everything." Although Paul steals the money and
flees to New York, these uncharacteristic actions underscore the desperation he
feels. Once at the Waldorf in New York, Paul is again content to observe the
glamorous world he has craved for so long: "He had no especial desire to meet or
to know any of these people; all he demanded was the right to look on and
conjecture, to watch the pageant." During his brief stay in the city, Paul enjoys
simply sitting in his luxurious rooms, glimpsing the show of city life through a
magical curtain of snow. At the end, when the forces of ordinary life begin to
close in again, Paul kills himself. But it is typical that he does not use the gun
he has bought. Rather, more in keeping with his passive nature, Paul lets himself
fall under the wheels of a train.

Finally, Paul ends his life because he is emotionally isolated. Throughout the   4
story, not one person makes any real contact with Paul. His teachers do not
understand him and merely resent the attitude of false bravado that he uses as a
defense. Paul's mother is dead; he cannot even remember her. Paul is
completely alienated from his father, who obviously cares for him but who cannot
feel close to his withdrawn, unhappy son. To Paul, his father is only the man

waiting at the top of the stairs, "his hairy legs sticking out of his nightshirt," who will greet him with "inquiries and reproaches." When Paul meets a college boy in New York, they share a night on the town. But the "champagne friendship" ends with a "singularly cool" parting. Paul is not the kind of person who can let himself go or confide in one of his peers. For the most part, Paul's isolation is self-imposed. He has drifted so far into his fantasy life that people in the "real" world are treated like invaders. As he allows no one to enter his dream, there is no one Paul can turn to for understanding.

The combination of these personality factors—inability to conform, passivity, and emotional isolation—makes Paul's tragic suicide inevitable. Before he jumps in front of the train, Paul scoops a hole in the snow and buries the carnation that he has been wearing in his buttonhole. Like a hothouse flower in the winter, Paul has a fragile nature that cannot survive its hostile environment.   5

■ Writing Assignment 6:
Writing about a Reading Selection

Read the essay titled "The Plug-In Drug" on pages 662–667. Then write an essay that develops *either* of the following statements:

- There are three reasons why people watch so much television.
- There are three reasons why people should not watch as much television as they do.

Use specific examples to support each reason—either examples based on your observations of real households or hypothetical examples using fictionalized typical households.

To get started, you may find it helpful to freewrite for several minutes on the topic of television: the needs it satisfies, the pleasures it gives us, the problems it hides, the purposes it serves in the household.

COMPARISON AND CONTRAST

Comparison and contrast are two thought processes we constantly perform in everyday life. When we *compare* two things, we show how they are similar; when we *contrast* two things, we show how they are different. We may compare or contrast two brand-name products (for example, Sony versus Zenith TV), two television shows, two cars, two teachers, two jobs, two friends, or two courses of action we can take in a given situation. The purpose of comparing or contrasting is to understand each of the two things more clearly and, at times, to make judgments about them.

You will be asked in this section to write a paper of comparison or contrast. To prepare for this assignment, first read the three essays ahead. Then answer the questions and do the activities that follow the essays.

ESSAYS TO CONSIDER

Second Marriage

Married people live "happily ever after" in fairy tales, but they do so less   1
and less often in real life. I, like many of my friends, got married, divorced, and
remarried. I suppose, to some people, I'm a failure. After all, I broke my first
solemn promise to "love and cherish until death us do part." But I feel that I'm
finally a success. I learned from the mistakes I made in my first marriage. This
time around, the ways my husband and I share our free time, make decisions,
and deal with problems are very different.

I learned, first of all, not to be a clinging vine. In my first marriage, I felt that every moment we spent apart was wasted. If Ray wanted to go out to a bar with his friends to watch a football game, I felt rejected and talked him into staying home. I wouldn't accept an offer to go to a movie or join an exercise class if it meant that Ray would be home alone. I realize now that we were often on edge or angry with each other just because we spent too much time together. In contrast, my second husband and I spend some of our free time apart and try to have interests of our own. I have started playing racquetball at a health club, and David sometimes takes off to go to the local auto races with his friends. When we are together, we aren't bored with each other; our separate interests make us more interesting people.

I learned not only to be apart sometimes but also to work together when it's time to make decisions. When Ray and I were married, I left all the important decisions to him. He decided how we would spend money, whether we should sell the car or fix it, and where to take a vacation. I know now that I went along with this so that I wouldn't have to take the responsibility when things went wrong. I could always end an argument by saying, "It was your fault!" With my second marriage, I am trying to be a full partner. We ask each other's opinions on major decisions and try to compromise if we disagree. If we make the wrong choice, we're equally guilty. When we rented an apartment, for example, we both had to take the blame for not noticing the drafty windows and the "no pets" clause in our lease.

Maybe the most important thing I've learned is to be a grown-up about facing problems. David and I have made a vow to face our troubles like adults. If we're mad at each other or worried and upset, we say how we feel. Rather than hide behind our own misery, we talk about the problem until we discover how to fix it. Everybody argues or has to deal with the occasional crisis, but Ray and I always reacted like children to these stormy times. I would lock myself in the spare bedroom and pout. Ray would stalk out of the house, slam the door, and race off in the car. Then I would cry and worry till he returned.

I wish that my first marriage hadn't been the place where I learned how to make a relationship work, but at least I did learn. I feel better now about being an independent person, about making decisions, and about facing problems. My second marriage isn't perfect, but it doesn't have the deep flaws that made the first one fall apart.

A Vote for McDonald's

For my birthday this month, my wife has offered to treat me to dinner at the restaurant of my choice. I think she expects me to ask for a meal at the Chalet, the classiest, most expensive restaurant in town. However, I'm going to eat my birthday dinner at McDonald's. When I compare the two restaurants, the advantages of eating at McDonald's are clear.

For one thing, going to the Chalet is more difficult than going to McDonald's. 2
The Chalet has a jacket-and-tie rule, which means I have to dig a sport coat and
tie out of the back of my closet, make sure they're semiclean, and try to steam
out the wrinkles somehow. The Chalet also requires advance reservations. Since
it is downtown, I have to leave an hour early to give myself time to find a parking
space within six blocks of the restaurant. The Chalet cancels reservations if a
party is more than ten minutes late. Going to McDonald's, on the other hand, is
easy. I can feel comfortable wearing jeans or a warm-up suit. I don't have to do
any advance planning. I can leave my house whenever I'm ready and pull into a
doorside parking space within fifteen minutes.

The Chalet is a dimly lit, formal place. While I'm struggling to see what's on 3
my plate, I worry that I'll knock one of the fragile glass vases off the table. The
waiters at the Chalet can be uncomfortably formal, too. As I awkwardly
pronounce the French words on the menu, I get the feeling that I don't quite live
up to their standards. Even though the food at the Chalet is gourmet, I prefer
simpler meals. I don't like unfamiliar food swimming in dead-white sauce or
covered with pie pastry. Eating at the Chalet is, to me, less enjoyable than eating
at McDonald's. McDonald's is a pleasant place where I feel at ease. It is well
lighted, and the bright-colored decor is informal. The employees serve with a
smile, and the food is easy to pronounce and identify. I know what I'm going to
get when I order a certain type of sandwich.

The most important difference between the Chalet and McDonald's, though, 4
is the price difference. Dinner for two at the Chalet, even one without appetizers
or desserts, would easily cost $50. And the $50 doesn't include the cost of
parking the car and tipping the waiter, which can come to an additional $10.
Once, I forgot to bring enough money. At McDonald's, a filling meal for two will
cost around $10. With the extra $50, my wife and I can eat at McDonald's five
more times, or go to the movies five times, or buy play-off tickets to a football
game.

So, for my birthday dinner celebration, or any other time, I prefer to eat at 5
McDonald's. It is convenient, friendly, and cheap. And with the money my wife
saves by taking me to McDonald's, she can buy me what I really want for my
birthday—a new Sears power saw.

Studying: Then and Now

One June day, I staggered into a high school classroom to take my final exam 1
in United States History IV. Bleary-eyed from an all-night study session, I
checked my "cheat sheets," which were taped inside the cuffs of my long-
sleeved shirt. I had made my usual desperate effort to cram the night before,
with the usual dismal results—I had made it only to page seventy-five of a four-
hundred-page textbook. My high school study habits, obviously, were a mess.
But, in college, I've made an attempt to reform my note-taking, studying, and
test-taking skills.

Taking notes is one thing I've learned to do better since high school days. I used to lose interest and begin doodling, drawing Martians, or seeing what my signature would look like if I married the cute guy in the second row. Now, however, I try not to let my mind wander, and I pull my thoughts back into focus when they begin to go fuzzy. In high school, my notes often looked like something written in Arabic. In college, I've learned to use a semiprint writing style that makes my notes understandable. When I would look over my high school notes, I couldn't understand them. There would be a word like "Reconstruction," then a big blank, then the word "important." Weeks later, I had no idea what Reconstruction was or why it was important. I've since learned to write down connecting ideas, even if I have to take the time to do it after class. 2

Ordinary during-the-term studying is another area where I've made changes. In high school, I let reading assignments go. I told myself that I'd have no trouble catching up on two hundred pages during a fifteen-minute bus ride to school. College courses have taught me to keep pace with the work. Otherwise, I feel as though I'm sinking into a quicksand of unread material. When I finally read the high school assignment, my eyes would run over the words but my brain would be plotting how to get the car for Saturday night. Now, I use several techniques that force me to really concentrate on my reading. 3

In addition to learning how to cope with daily work, I've also learned to handle study sessions for big tests. My all-night study sessions in high school were experiments in self-torture. Around 2:00 A.M., my mind, like a soaked sponge, simply stopped absorbing things. Now, I space out exam study sessions over several days. That way, the night before can be devoted to an overall review rather than raw memorizing. Most important, though, I've changed my attitude toward tests. In high school, I thought tests were mysterious things with completely unpredictable questions. Now, I ask instructors about the kinds of questions that will be on the exam, and I try to "psych out" which areas or facts instructors are likely to ask about. These practices really work, and for me they've taken much of the fear and mystery out of tests. 4

Since I've reformed, note-taking and studying are not as tough as they once were. And one benefit makes the work worthwhile: my college grade sheets look much different from the red-splotched ones of high school days. 5

■ ## Questions

About Unity

1. In which supporting paragraph of "A Vote for McDonald's" is the topic sentence in the middle rather than, more appropriately, at the beginning? _____

2. Which sentence in paragraph 4 of "A Vote for McDonald's" should be omitted in the interest of paragraph unity? (*Write the opening words.*) _____

About Support

3. After which sentence in paragraph 3 of "Studying: Then and Now" are more supporting details needed? _____

4. In which sentence in paragraph 3 of "A Vote for McDonald's" are more supporting details needed? _____

About Coherence

5. What transition signal is used in "Second Marriage" to indicate emphatic order? _____

6. What are the transition signals used in paragraph 2 of "Second Marriage"?

   _____

7. What are the three points of contrast in paragraph 2 ("taking notes") of "Studying: Then and Now"?

   a. _____

   b. _____

   c. _____

8. Which supporting paragraph in "Second Marriage" fails to follow the pattern of organization set by the other two? _____

About the Introduction and Conclusion

9. What method of introduction is used in "Studying: Then and Now"? Circle the appropriate letter.

   a. Broad, general statement narrowing to thesis
   b. Idea that is the opposite of the one to be developed
   c. Quotation
   d. Anecdote
   e. Questions

10. What conclusion technique is used in "Second Marriage"? Circle the appropriate letter.

    a. Summary
    b. Prediction or recommendation
    c. Question

METHODS OF DEVELOPMENT

Two methods of development are possible in a comparison or contrast essay. Details can be presented in a *one-side-at-a-time* format or in a *point-by-point* format. Each format is illustrated below.

One Side at a Time

Look at the following supporting paragraph from ''A Vote for McDonald's'':

> For one thing, going to the Chalet is more difficult than going to McDonald's. The Chalet has a jacket-and-tie rule, which means that I have to dig a sport coat and tie out of the back of my closet, make sure they're semiclean, and try to steam out the wrinkles somehow. The Chalet also requires advance reservations. Since it is downtown, I have to leave an hour early to give myself time to find a parking space within six blocks of the restaurant. The Chalet cancels reservations if a party is more than ten minutes late. Going to McDonald's, on the other hand, is easy. I can feel comfortable wearing jeans or a warm-up suit. I don't have to do any advance planning. I can leave my house whenever I'm ready and pull into a doorside parking space within fifteen minutes.

The first half of the paragraph explains fully one side of the contrast; the second half of the paragraph deals entirely with the other side. When you use this method, be sure to follow the same order of points of contrast (or comparison) for each side. An outline of the paragraph shows how the points for each side are developed in a consistent sequence.

Outline (One Side at a Time)

Going to the Chalet is more difficult than going to McDonald's.

1. Chalet
   a. Dress code
   b. Advance reservations
   c. Leave an hour early
   d. Find parking space
2. McDonald's
   a. Casual dress
   b. No reservations
   c. Leave only fifteen minutes ahead of time
   d. Plenty of free parking

Point by Point

Now look at the supporting paragraph below, which is from "Studying: Then and Now":

> Taking notes is one thing I've learned to do better since high school days. I used to lose interest in what I was doing and begin doodling, drawing Martians, or seeing what my signature would look like if I married the cute guy in the second row. Now, however, I try not to let my mind wander, and I pull my thoughts back into focus when they begin to go fuzzy. In high school, my notes often looked like something written in Arabic. In college, I've learned to use a semiprint writing style that makes my notes understandable. When I would look over my high school notes, I couldn't understand them. There would be a word like "Reconstruction," then a big blank, then the word "important." Weeks later, I had no idea what Reconstruction was or why it was important. I've since learned to write down connecting ideas, even if I have to take the time to do it after class.

The paragraph contrasts the two methods of note-taking point by point. The outline below illustrates this method.

Outline (Point by Point)

Taking notes is one thing I've learned to do better since high school days.

1. Level of attention in class
   a. High school
   b. College
2. Handwriting
   a. High school
   b. College
3. Completeness of notes
   a. High school
   b. College

When you begin a comparison or contrast paper, you should decide right away whether you are going to use the one-side-at-a-time format or the point-by-point format. An outline is an essential step in writing and planning a clearly organized paper.

Activity 1

Complete the partial outlines given for the supporting paragraphs that follow.

Paragraph A

The most important difference between the Chalet and McDonald's, though, is the price difference. Dinner for two at the Chalet, even one without appetizers or desserts, would easily cost $50. And the $50 doesn't include the cost of parking the car and tipping the waiter, which can come to an additional $10. At McDonald's a filling meal for two will cost around $10. With the extra $50, my wife and I can eat at McDonald's five more times, or go to the movies five times, or buy play-off tickets to a football game.

The most important difference between the Chalet and McDonald's is the price difference.

1. Chalet

    a. _____

    b. Additional costs of parking and tipping

2. _____

    a. $10 for dinner for two

    b. _____

Complete the following statement: Paragraph A uses a _____

_____ method of

development.

Paragraph B

In addition to learning how to cope with daily work, I've also learned to handle study sessions for big tests. My all-night study sessions in high school were experiments in self-torture. Around 2:00 A.M., my mind, like a soaked sponge, simply stopped absorbing things. Now, I space out exam study sessions over several days. That way, the night before can be devoted to an overall review rather than raw memorizing. Most important, though, I've changed my attitude toward tests. In high school, I thought tests were mysterious things with completely unpredictable questions. Now, I ask instructors about the kinds of questions that will be on the exam, and I try to "psych out" which areas or facts instructors are likely to ask about. These practices really work, and for me they've taken much of the fear and mystery out of tests.

In addition to learning how to cope with daily work, I've also learned to handle study sessions for big tests.

1. Planning study time

    a. _____ (all-night study sessions)

    b. College (spread out over several days)

2. _____

    a. High school (tests were mysterious)

    b. _____ (_____)

Complete the following statement: Paragraph B uses a _____

_____ method of

development.

Paragraph C

I learned not only to be apart sometimes but also to work together when it's time to make decisions. When Ray and I were married, I left all the important decisions to him. He decided how we would spend money, whether we should sell the car or fix it, and where to take a vacation. I know now that I went along with this so that I wouldn't have to take the responsibility when things went wrong. I could always end an argument by saying, "It was your fault!" With my second marriage, I am trying to be a full partner. We ask each other's opinions on major decisions and try to compromise if we disagree. If we make the wrong choice, we're equally guilty. When we rented an apartment, for example, we both had to take the blame for not noticing the drafty windows and the "no pets" clause in our lease.

I learned not only to be apart sometimes but also to work together when it's time to make decisions.

1. First marriage
    a. Husband made decisions
    b. Husband took responsibility and blame

2. _____

    a. _____

    b. Share responsibility and blame

Complete the following statement: Paragraph C uses a _____

_____ method of

development.

Activity 2

Following is a contrast essay about two sisters. The sentences in each supporting paragraph of the essay are scrambled. For each supporting paragraph, put a number 1 beside the point that all the other scrambled sentences support. Then number the rest of the sentences in a logical order. To do this, you will have to decide whether the sentences should be arranged according to the order of one side at a time or the order of point by point.

Introduction

> When my sister and I were growing up, we shared the same bedroom. It wasn't hard to tell which half of the room was mine and which was Kathy's. My side was always as tidy as if a Holiday Inn chambermaid had just left. Kathy's side always looked like the aftermath of an all-night party. Back then, we argued a lot. Kathy said that I was a neatness nut, and I called her a slob. Today we get along just fine, since we have our own homes and don't have to share a room anymore. But Kathy's approach to housekeeping is still much different from mine.

First supporting paragraph

_____ Kathy, on the other hand, believes that a kitchen should look lived-in and not like a hospital operating room.

_____ I treat my kitchen as if a health inspector were waiting to close it down at the least sign of dirt.

_____ I wipe counters with Fantastik while I wait for bread to toast.

_____ She scrambles eggs and leaves the dirty pan on the stove until the nightly cleanup.

_____ She forgets to put the bread away.

_____ When I leave the kitchen, it's usually cleaner than it was before I started to cook.

_____ The kitchen is one room that points up the contrasts between us.

_____ I wrap leftovers in neat packages of aluminum foil or seal them tightly in Tupperware.

_____ Kathy doesn't mind leaving a messy kitchen behind if she has more interesting things to do.

_____ Leftovers go naked into the refrigerator, without covers or foil.

_____ Even as I'm scrambling a couple of eggs, I begin to wash the bowl I used to mix them.

Second supporting paragraph

_____ The clothes in my closet are carefully arranged.

_____ My bedroom is a place of rest, and I can rest only when everything is in order.

_____ A peek into Kathy's bedroom in midmorning might reveal last night's cheese and crackers growing stale on the night table and several magazines hiding under the rumpled bedcovers.

_____ Some clothes are hung haphazardly in the closet, but many more are under the bed, behind the drapes, or on the deck.

_____ When I leave my bedroom in the morning, the bed is made and there are no clothes lying on the floor or over the chairs.

_____ Plastic bags cover out-of-season items, and shoes are lined up on racks.

_____ We still treat our bedrooms differently.

_____ In contrast, Kathy feels that her bedroom is a private place where she can do as she pleases.

Third supporting paragraph

_____ After I brush my hair, I check the sink for stray hairs.

_____ The spot that shows our differences the most, though, is the bathroom.

_____ My bathroom must be sanitized and germ-free.

_____ She cleans her mirror only when she gets tired of the polka-dot effect of hardened toothpaste.

_____ I clean the tub with Ajax before and after taking a bath.

_____ Needless to say, her makeup and toiletries litter every available surface.

_____ Once in a while, she points her hair dryer at the sink to blow away the accumulation of hairs in it.

_____ She cleans the tub, but only after a clearly defined brown ring has formed around it.

_____ I wipe off any spots of toothpaste or soap from the mirror and put all my cosmetics and cleaners in their proper places.

_____ Kathy, however, thinks that Americans worry too much about germs.

Conclusion

> As adults, Kathy and I can joke about the habits that caused us so much trouble as adolescents. We can, at times, even see the other's point of view when it comes to housecleaning. But I'm afraid the patterns are pretty much set. It's too late for this "odd couple" to change.

Complete the following statement: The sentences in each supporting paragraph can be organized using a _____

_____ method of development.

WRITING A COMPARISON-CONTRAST ESSAY

■ Writing Assignment 1

Write an essay of comparison or contrast on one of the topics below:

Two courses	Two singers
Two teachers	Two dates
Two jobs	Two popular magazines
Two bosses	Two games
Two family members	Two vacations
Two friends	Two hobbies
Two pets	Two leisure activities
Two vacations	Two stores
Two sports	Two public figures

How to Proceed

a   You must begin by making two decisions: (1) what your topic will be and (2) whether you are going to do a comparison or a contrast. Many times, students choose to do essays centered on the differences between two things. For example, you might write about how a math instructor you have in college differs from a math teacher you had in high school. You might discuss important differences between your mother and your father, or between two of your friends. You might contrast a factory job you had packing vegetables with a white-collar job you had as a salesperson in a shoe store.

b   After you choose a tentative topic, write a simple thesis statement expressing that topic. Then see what kind of support you can generate for that topic. For instance, if you plan to contrast two restaurants, see if you can think of and jot down three distinct ways they differ. *In other words, prepare a brief outline.* An outline is an excellent prewriting technique for any essay; it is almost indispensable when you are planning a comparison or contrast essay. Here is a brief outline prepared by the author of the essay titled ''A Vote for McDonald's'':

Thesis: The advantages of McDonald's over the Chalet are clear.
1. Going to the restaurants
2. Eating at the restaurants
3. Prices at the restaurants

Keep in mind that this planning stage is probably the most important single phase of work you will do on your paper. Without clear planning, you are not likely to write an effective essay.

c   After you have decided on a topic and the main lines of support, you must decide whether to use a one-side-at-a-time or a point-by-point method of development. Both methods are explained and illustrated in this chapter.

d   Now, freewrite for ten minutes on the topic you have chosen. Do not worry about punctuation, spelling, or other matters relating to correct form. Just get as many details as you can onto the page. You want a base of raw material that you can add to and select from as you now work on the first draft of your paper.

After you do a first draft, try to put it aside for a day or at least several hours. You will then be ready to return with a fresh perspective on the material and build upon what you have already done.

e   As you work on a second draft, be sure that each of your supporting paragraphs has a clear topic sentence.

f   Use transition words like *first, in addition, also, in contrast, another difference, on the other hand, but, however,* and *most important* to link together points in your paper.

g   As you continue working on your paper, refer to the checklist on page 127 and the inside front cover. Make sure that you can answer *Yes* to the questions about unity, support, and coherence.

h   Finally, use the checklist on page 127 and the inside front cover to proofread your next-to-final draft for sentence-skills mistakes, including spelling.

■ Writing Assignment 2

Write a comparison or contrast essay on college versus high school life. Narrow the focus of your paper to a particular aspect of school—teachers and instructors, classes, sports, social life, or students' attitudes, for example. *Or* you may write a paper on dormitory or apartment life versus living at home.

■ Writing Assignment 3

Write an essay that contrasts two attitudes on a controversial subject. The subject might be abortion, marijuana, capital punishment, homosexuality, euthanasia, prostitution, coed prisons, busing, school prayer, nuclear power plants, the social security system, or some other matter on which there are conflicting feelings and opinions. You may want to contrast your views with someone else's or to contrast the way you felt at some point in the past with the way you feel now.

■ Writing Assignment 4

In this comparison-contrast essay, you will write with a specific purpose and for a specific audience.

Option 1:   Your boyfriend or girlfriend wants to get married this year, but you think you'd rather just live together for a while. To help both of you think through the issue, write him or her a letter in which you compare and contrast the advantages and disadvantages of each approach. Use a one-side-at-a-time method in making your analysis.

Option 2:   Write a letter to your boss in which you compare your abilities with those of the ideal candidate for a position to which you'd like to be promoted. Use a point-by-point method in which you discuss each ideal requirement and then describe how well you measure up to it. Use the requirements of a job you're relatively familiar with, perhaps even a job you would really like to apply for one day.

■ Writing Assignment 5

Write an essay that contrasts two characters or two points of view in one or more poems, stories, plays, or novels. The work you choose may be assigned by your instructor, or it may require your instructor's approval. For this assignment, your essay may have two supporting paragraphs, with each paragraph representing one side of the contrast. A student model follows.

Warren and Mary

In "Death of the Hired Man," Robert Frost uses a brief incident—the return   1
of Silas, an aging farmhand—to dramatize the differences between a husband
and wife. As Warren and Mary talk about Silas and reveal his story, the reader
learns their story, too. By the end of the poem, Warren and Mary emerge as
contrasting personalities; one is wary and reserved, while the other is open and
giving.

Warren is a kindly man but one whose basic decency is tempered by a sense   2
of practicality and emotional reserve. Warren is upset with Mary for sheltering
Silas, who is barely useful and sometimes unreliable: "What use he is there's no
depending on." Warren feels that he has already done his duty toward Silas by
hiring him the previous summer and that he is under no obligation to care for
him now. "Home," says Warren, "is the place where, when you have to go there/
They have to take you in." Warren's home is not Silas' home, so Warren does not
have a legal or moral duty to keep the shiftless old man. Warren's temperament,
in turn, influences his attitude toward Silas' arrival. Warren hints to Mary—
through a condescending smile—that Silas is somehow playing on her emotions
or faking his illness. Warren considers Silas' supposed purpose in coming to the
farm—to ditch the meadow—nothing but a flimsy excuse for a free meal. The
best that Warren can find to say about Silas is that he does have one practical
skill: the ability to build a good load of hay.

Mary, in contrast, is distinguished by her giving nature and her concentration   3
on the workings of human emotion. In caring for Silas, Mary sees not his lack of
ability or his laziness but the fact that he is "worn out" and needs help. To Mary,
home represents not obligation ("They have to take you in") but unconditional
love: "I should have called it/Something you somehow haven't to deserve." Mary
is observant, not only of outer appearance but also of the inner person; this is
why she thinks not that Silas is trying to trick them but that he is a desperate
man trying to salvage a little self-respect. She realizes, too, that he will never
ditch the meadow, and she knows that Silas' insecurity prompted his arguments
with the college boy who helped with the haying. Mary is also perceptive enough
to see that Silas could never humble himself before his estranged brother. Mary's
attitude is more sympathetic than Warren's; whereas Warren wonders why Silas
and his brother don't get along, Mary thinks about how Silas "hurt my heart the
way he lay/And rolled his old head on that sharp-edged chairback."

In describing Silas, Warren and Mary describe themselves. We see a   4
basically good man, one whose spirit has been toughened by a hard life. Warren,
we learn, would have liked to pay Silas a fixed wage but simply couldn't afford
to. Life has taught Warren to be practical and to rein in his emotions. In
contrast, we see a nurturing woman, alert to human feelings, who could never
refuse to care for a lonely, dying man. Warren and Mary are both decent people.
This is the reason why, as Mary instinctively feels, Silas chooses their home for
his final refuge.

■ Writing Assignment 6:
Writing about a Reading Selection

Read the selection titled "Smash Thy Neighbor" on pages 547–551. Pay special attention to how the author compares and contrasts football and war in paragraphs 5–8 and compares football and the rest of society in paragraph 14. Notice how he makes the comparisons and contrast in order to describe football more fully. Then write an essay in which you use a comparison to describe more fully three aspects of an activity, place, or person. You may use serious or humorous supporting details.

Following are some suggestions that you might consider for a thesis for this assignment.

Thesis: In a few significant ways,

going to college is like working at a career.
the high-school hallways between classes are like a three-ring circus.
getting divorced is like getting married.
caring for a pet is like caring for a child.
meditation is like exercise.
shopping for Christmas gifts is like playing professional football.
teachers should be like parents.
hate is like love.
raising a family is like caring for a garden.

These are only suggestions; feel free to use any other thesis that makes a comparison in order to fill out a description of an activity, person, or place. (Note that a comparison that points out similarities between things that are otherwise quite different is called an *analogy*.)

In your introduction, you might state your general thesis as well as the three points of comparison. Here, for example, is a possible introduction for an essay on meditation:

On the surface, meditation may seem to be very different from exercise. A person who meditates is usually very still, while someone who exercises is very active. Yet the two activities are more alike than they might seem. Both require discipline, both bestow physical and mental benefits, and both can be habit-forming.

At the same time as you develop your introduction, you should prepare a general outline for your essay. The outline for the essay started by the introduction above would be as follows:

Thesis: Meditation is like exercise in three ways.
A. Both require discipline.
   1. Exercise
   2. Meditation
B. Both have physical and mental rewards.
   1. Exercise
   2. Meditation
C. Both can be habit-forming.
   1. Exercise
   2. Meditation

(Note that this outline uses the point-by-point method of development. Other topics might, of course, be more suited to the one-side-at-a-time method.)

As you work on your supporting paragraphs, *be sure to outline them first.* Such planning is very helpful in organizing and maintaining control over a comparison or contrast essay. Here, for example, is a sample scratch outline for a paragraph in a point-by-point essay comparing raising children to gardening.

Topic sentence: Just as a garden benefits from both sun and rain, so do children.
A. Benefits of sun and rain to a garden
   1. Both sun and rain required for life
   2. Increase growth
B. Benefits of sunny and rainy times to children
   1. Ups and downs natural over a life
   2. Personal growth

Each of your supporting paragraphs should be outlined in this way.

In your conclusion, you might round off the essay by summarizing the three areas of comparison and leaving your readers with a final thought. Do not, however, make the mistake of introducing a completely *new* idea ("Every couple should have children," for example) in your conclusion.

DEFINITION

In talking with other people, we sometimes offer informal definitions to explain just what we mean by a particular term. Suppose, for example, we say to a friend, "Bob is really an inconsiderate person." We might then explain what we mean by "inconsiderate" by saying, "He borrowed my accounting book 'overnight,' but didn't return it for a week. And when I got it back, it was covered with coffee stains." In a written definition, we make clear in a more complete and formal way our own personal understanding of a term. Such a definition typically starts with one meaning of a term. The meaning is then illustrated with a series of details.

You will be asked in this section to write an essay in which you define a term. The three student essays ahead are all examples of definition essays. Read them and then answer the questions that follow.

ESSAYS TO CONSIDER

Definition of a Baseball Fan

What is a baseball fan? The word <u>fan</u> is an abbreviation of <u>fanatic</u>, meaning "insane." In the case of baseball fans, the term is appropriate. They behave insanely, they are insane about trivia, and they are insanely loyal.   1

Baseball fans wear their official team T shirts and warm-up jackets to the mall, the supermarket, the classroom, and even—if they can get away with it—to work. Then, whenever the team offers a giveaway item, the fans rush to the ball park to get the roll-up hat or tote bag that is being offered that day. Baseball fans behave insanely, especially between April and October. In addition, baseball fans cover the walls with items of every kind. When they go to a game, which they do as often as possible, the true baseball fans put on their team colors, grab their pennants, pin on their team buttons, and even bring along hand-lettered bedsheet signs proudly proclaiming "Go Dodgers" or "Braves Are Number One." At the game, these fans form a rooting section, constantly encouraging their favorite players and obediently echoing every cheer flashed on the electronic scoreboard.   2

Baseball fans, in addition to behaving insanely, are also insanely fascinated   3
by trivia. Every day, they turn to the sports page and study last night's statistics.
They simply have to see who has extended his hitting streak and how many
strikeouts the winning pitcher recorded. Their bookshelves are crammed with
record books, team yearbooks, and baseball almanacs. They delight in
remembering such significant facts as who was the last left-handed third
baseman to hit into an inning-ending double play in the fifth game of the play-
offs. And if you do not show equal interest or enthusiasm, they look at you as if
they were doubting your sanity.

Last of all, baseball fans are insanely loyal to the team of their choice.   4
Should the home team lose eight in a row, their fans may begin to call them
"bums." They may even suggest, vocally, that the slumping cleanup hitter be
sent to the minors or the manager be fired. But these reactions only hide their
broken hearts. They still check the sports pages and tune in to get the score.
Furthermore, this intense loyalty makes fans dangerous, for anyone who dares to
say to a loyal fan that some other team has sharper fielding or a better attitude
could be risking permanent physical damage. Incidents of violence on the
baseball field have increased in recent years and are a matter of growing
concern.

From mid-October through March, baseball fans are like any other human   5
beings. They pay their taxes, take out the garbage, and complain about the high
cost of living or the latest home repair. But when April comes, the colors and
radios go on, the record books come off the shelves, and the devotion returns.
For the true baseball fan, another season of insanity has begun.

Stupidity

Although stupidity is commonly defined as "lack of normal intelligence,"   1
stupid behavior is not the behavior of a person lacking intelligence but the
behavior of a person not using good judgment or sense. In fact, stupidity comes
from a Latin word that means "senseless." Therefore, stupidity can be defined as
the behavior of a person of normal intelligence who is acting in a particular
situation as if he or she weren't very bright. Stupidity exists on three levels of
seriousness.

First is the simple, relatively harmless level. Behavior on this level is often   2
amusing. It is humorous when someone places the food from a fast-food
restaurant on the roof of the car while unlocking the door and then drives away
with the food still on the roof. We call this absentminded. The person's good
sense or intelligence was temporarily absent. On this level, other than passing
inconvenience or embarrassment, no one is injured by the stupid behavior.

More dangerous than simple stupidity is the next type—potentially serious   3
stupidity. Practical jokes such as putting sugar in the restaurant salt shakers are

on this level. The intent is humorous, but there is a potential for harm. Irresponsible advice given to others is also serious stupidity. An example is the person who plays psychiatrist on the basis of an introductory psychology course or a TV program on psychiatry. The intent may be to help, but if the victims really need psychiatric help, an amateur telling them that they "have no ego" or characterizing them as "neurotic" will only worsen the situation.

Even worse is the third kind of stupidity, which is always harmful. Otherwise 4 kind persons, who would never directly injure another living thing, stupidly dump off a box of six-week-old kittens along a country road. Lacking the heart to have "the poor things put to sleep," they sentence them to almost certain death from parasites, upper respiratory infections, exposure, other animals, or the wheels of a passing vehicle. Yet they are able to tell themselves that "they will find nice homes" or "animals can get along in the wild." Another example of this kind of stupidity is the successful local businessman who tries to have as many office affairs as he can get away with. He risks the loss of his job, his home, his wife and children, and the goodwill of his parents and friends. He fails to see, though, that there is anything wrong with what he is doing. His is the true moral stupidity of a person not willing to think about the results of his actions or to take responsibility for them.

The common defense of the person guilty of stupidity is, "But I didn't 5 think. . . ." This, however, is an inadequate excuse, especially when serious or harmful stupidity is involved. We are all liable when we do not think about the consequences of our actions.

Student Zombies

Schools divide people into categories. From first grade on up, students are 1 labeled "advanced" or "deprived" or "remedial" or "antisocial." Students pigeonhole their fellow students, too. We've all known the "brain," the "jock," the "dummy," and the "teacher's pet." In most cases, these narrow labels are misleading and inaccurate. But there is one label for a certain type of college student that says it all. That is, of course, "zombie."

Most of us haven't known many real zombies personally, but we do know how 2 they act. Horror movies have given us portraits of zombies, the living dead, for years. They stalk around graveyards, their eyes glued open by Hollywood makeup artists, bumping like cheap toy robots into living people. The special effects in horror movies are much better now. Zombie students in college do just about the same thing. They stalk around campus, eyes glazed, staring off into space. They wander into classrooms, sit down mechanically, and contemplate the ceiling. Zombie students rarely eat, play sports, or toss Frisbees on campus lawns. Instead, they mysteriously disappear when classes are over and return only when they next feel the urge to drift into a classroom. The urge may not return, however, for weeks.

Where student zombies come from is as weird as the origin of the original   3
zombies of the voodoo cults. According to voodoo legend, zombies are corpses
that have come alive again. They have been reanimated by supernatural spells.
Student zombies, too, are directed by a strange power. They continue to attend
school although they have no apparent motivation to do so. They are completely
uninterested in college-related activities like tests, grades, papers, and projects.
They seem to be propelled by some inner force that compels them to wander
forever through the halls of higher education.

All zombies, unfortunately, have a similar fate. In the movies, they are   4
usually shot, stabbed, or electrocuted, all to no avail. Then the hero or heroine
finally realizes that a counterspell is needed. Once the counterspell is cast, with
the appropriate props of chicken legs, human hair, and bats' eyeballs, the
zombie-corpse can return peacefully to its coffin. Student zombies, if they are to
change at all, must undergo a similar traumatic experience. Sometimes the evil
spell can be broken by a grade transcript decorated with "F" grades. Sometimes
a professor will hold a private, intensive exorcism session. Sometimes, though,
the zombies blunder around for years until they are gently persuaded by the
college administration to head for another institution that accepts zombies. Then,
they enroll in a new college or get a job in the family business.

Every college student knows that it's not necessary to see Night of the Living   5
Dead or Voodoo Island in order to see zombies in action. Forget the campus
movie theater or the late late show. Just sit in a classroom and wait for the
students who walk in without books or papers of any kind and sit in the farthest
seats in the rear. Day of the Living Dead is showing every day at a college near
you.

■ Questions

About Unity

1. Which essay places the topic sentence for its first supporting paragraph
    within the paragraph rather than, more appropriately, at the beginning?

    _____

2. Which sentence in paragraph 2 of "Student Zombies" should be omitted
    in the interest of paragraph unity? (*Write the opening words.*)

    _____

3. Which sentence in paragraph 4 of "Definition of a Baseball Fan" should

    be omitted in the interest of unity? _____

About Support

4. Which supporting paragraph in the essay on stupidity needs more supporting details? _____

5. Which essay develops its definition through a series of comparisons?

_____

6. Which sentence in paragraph 2 of the essay on baseball needs supporting details? _____

About Coherence

7. Which essay uses emphatic order, saving its most important idea for last?

_____

8. Which two essays use linking sentences between their first and second supporting paragraphs?

_____   _____

9. What are five major transition words that appear in the three supporting paragraphs of "Definition of a Baseball Fan"?

a. _____

b. _____

c. _____

d. _____

e. _____

About the Introduction

10. What kind of introduction is used for "Student Zombies"? Circle the appropriate letter.
    a. Broad, general statement narrowing to thesis
    b. Idea that is the opposite of the one to be developed
    c. Quotation
    d. Anecdote
    e. Questions

WRITING A DEFINITION ESSAY

- ### Writing Assignment 1

    Shown below are an introduction, a thesis, and supporting points for an essay that defines the word *maturity*. Using separate paper, plan out and write the supporting paragraphs and a conclusion for the essay. Refer to the suggestions on "How to Proceed" on page 201.

    The Meaning of Maturity

    > Being a mature student does not mean being an old-timer. Maturity is not measured by the number of years a person has lived. Instead, the yardstick of maturity is marked by the qualities of self-denial, determination, and dependability.

    > Self-denial is an important quality in the mature student. . . .

    > Determination is another characteristic of a mature student. . . .

    > Although self-denial and determination are both vital, probably the most important measure of maturity is dependability. . . .

How to Proceed

a   Prepare examples for each of the three qualities of maturity. For each quality, you should have one extended example that takes up an entire paragraph or two or three shorter examples that together form enough material for a paragraph.

b   To generate these details, ask yourself questions like these:

What could I do, or have I done, that would be an example of self-denial?

What has someone I know ever done that could be described as self-denial?

What kind of behavior on the part of a student could be considered self-denial?

Write down quickly whatever answers occur to you. Don't worry about writing correct sentences; just concentrate on getting down as many details relating to self-denial as you can think of. Then repeat the questioning and writing process with the qualities of determination and dependability as well.

c   Draw from and add to this material as you work on the drafts of your essay. Also, refer to the checklist on page 127 and the inside front cover to make sure you can answer *Yes* to the questions about unity, support, and coherence.

d   Write a conclusion for the essay by adding a summarizing sentence or two and a final thought about the subject. See page 83 for an example.

e   Finally, use the checklist on page 127 and the inside front cover to proofread your next-to-final draft for sentence-skills mistakes, including spelling.

■ Writing Assignment 2

Write an essay that defines one of the terms below. Each term refers to a certain kind of person.

Snob	Optimist	Slob
Cheapskate	Pessimist	Tease
Loser	Team player	Practical joker
Good neighbor	Scapegoat	Black sheep of a family
Busybody	Bully	Procrastinator
Complainer	Religious person	Loner
Con artist	Hypocrite	Straight arrow

Refer to "How to Proceed," on the next page.

How to Proceed

a   In assignment 2, if you start with a dictionary definition, be sure to choose just one meaning of a term. (A dictionary often provides several different meanings associated with a word.) Also, *don't* begin your paper with the overused line, "According to Webster, . . ."

b   Remember that the thesis of a definition essay is actually some version of "What _____ means to me." The thesis presents what *you* think the term actually means.

c   You may want to organize the body of your paper around three different parts or qualities of your term. Here are the three-part divisions of the four essays considered in this chapter:

Maturity "is marked by qualities of self-denial, determination, and dependability."

"Stupidity exists on three levels of seriousness."

Baseball fans are fanatics in terms of "their behavior, their fascination with trivia, and their loyalty."

Student zombies usually have the same kind of behavior, origin, and fate.

Each division in a three-part breakdown should be supported by either a series of examples or a single extended example.

d   Be sure to outline the essay before you begin to write. As a guide, put your thesis and three supporting points in the spaces below.

Thesis: _____

_____

Support: 1. _____

2. _____

3. _____

e   While writing your paper, use as a guide the checklist of the four bases on page 127 and the inside front cover. Make sure you can answer *Yes* to the questions about unity, support, coherence, and sentence skills.

■ Writing Assignment 3

Write an essay that defines one of the terms below.

Persistence	Responsibility	Fear
Rebellion	Insecurity	Arrogance
Sense of humor	Assertiveness	Conscience
Escape	Jealousy	Class
Laziness	Practicality	Innocence
Danger	Nostalgia	Freedom
Curiosity	Gentleness	Violence
Common sense	Depression	Shyness
Soul	Obsession	Idealism
Family	Self-control	Christianity

As a guide, use the suggestions in "How to Proceed" for writing assignment 2.

■ Writing Assignment 4

In this definition essay, you will write with a specific purpose and for a specific audience.

Option 1:   You work in a doctor's office and have been asked to write a brochure that will be placed in the patients' waiting room. The brochure is intended to tell patients what a healthy lifestyle is. Write a definition of *healthy lifestyle* for your readers, using examples wherever appropriate. Your definition might focus on both mental and physical health and might include eating, sleeping, exercise, and recreational habits.

Alternatively, you might decide to take a playful point of view and write a brochure defining an *unhealthy lifestyle*.

Option 2:   Your Spanish class will be hosts to some students from Mexico. The class is preparing a minidictionary of slang for the visitors. Your job is to write a paragraph in which you define the phrase *to gross out*. In your paper, include a general definition as well as several examples showing how the phrase is used and the circumstances in which it would be appropriate. By way of providing background, you may also want to include the nonslang meaning of *gross* which led to the slang usage. To find the information, consult a dictionary.

Alternatively, you may write about any other slang term. If necessary, first get the approval of your instructor.

■ Writing Assignment 5:
Writing about a Reading Selection

Read the selection titled "Shame" on pages 515–518. Then write an essay in which you define a term, as Dick Gregory does in "Shame," through narration. You can use one of the terms listed in Writing Assignment 3 or think up one of your own. In your introduction, fill in a brief background for your readers—when and where the experience happened. Your thesis should express the idea that because of this experience, you (or the person or people you are writing about) learned the meaning of the word _____ (fill in the term you have chosen). Break the narrative at logical points to create three supporting paragraphs. You might first want to look at the examples of narrative essays given on pages 137–140.

Alternatively, you might develop your definition with three experiences that seem to embody the word you have chosen. These could be experiences of your own, ones you know about, or ones you have read about. Develop each in a separate supporting paragraph.

DIVISION AND CLASSIFICATION

When you return home from your weekly trip to the supermarket with five bags packed with your purchases, how do you sort them out? You might separate food items from nonfood items (like toothpaste, paper towels, and detergent). Or you might divide and classify the items into groups intended for the freezer compartment, the refrigerator, and the kitchen cupboards. You might even put the items into groups like "to be used tonight," "to be used soon," and "to be used last." Sorting supermarket items in such ways is just one small example of how we spend a great deal of our time organizing our environment in one manner or another.

In this section, you will be asked to write an essay in which you divide or classify a subject according to a single principle. To prepare for this assignment, first read the division and classification essays below and then work through the questions and the activity that follow.

ESSAYS TO CONSIDER

Mall People

Having fun can exhaust one's bank account. By the time a person drives to the city and pays the tired-looking parking attendant the hourly fee to park, there is little money left to buy movie tickets, let alone popcorn and soft drinks to snack on. As a result, people have turned from wining, dining, and moviegoing to the nearby free-parking, free-admission shopping malls. Teenagers, couples on dates, and the nuclear family can all be observed having a good time at this alternative recreation spot. 1

Teenagers are the largest group of mallgoers. The guys saunter by in sneakers, T shirts, and blue jeans, complete with a package of cigarettes sticking out of their pockets. The girls stumble along in high-heeled shoes and daring tank tops, with hairbrushes tucked snugly in the rear pockets of their tight-fitting designer jeans. Traveling in a gang that resembles a wolf pack, the teenagers make the shopping mall their hunting ground. Their raised voices, loud laughter, and occasional shouted obscenities can be heard from as far as half a mall away. They come to "pick up chicks," to "meet guys," and just to "hang out." 2

205

Couples are now spending their dates at shopping malls. The young lovers are easy to spot because they walk hand in hand, stopping to sneak a quick kiss after every few steps. They first pause at jewelry store windows so they can gaze at diamond engagement rings and gold wedding bands. Then, they wander into furniture departments in the large mall stores. Whispering happily to each other, they imagine how that five-piece living room set or brass headboard would look in their future home. Finally, they drift away, their arms wrapped around each other's waists. 3

Mom, Dad, little Jenny, and Fred, Jr., visit the mall on Friday and Saturday evenings. Jenny wants to see some of the special mall exhibits geared toward little children. Fred, Jr., wants to head for the places that young boys find appealing. Mom walks around looking at various things until she discovers that Jenny is no longer attached to her hand. She finally finds her in a favorite hiding place. Meanwhile, Dad has arrived at a large store and is admiring the products he would love to buy. Indeed, the mall provides something special for every member of the family. 4

The teenagers, the couples on dates, and the nuclear family make up the vast majority of mallgoers. These folks need not purchase anything to find pleasure at the mall. They are shopping for inexpensive recreation, and the mall provides it. 5

Movie Monsters

Dracula rises from the grave—again. Mutant insects, the product of underground nuclear testing, grow to the size of boxcars and attack our nation's cities. Weird-looking aliens from beyond the stars decide to invade our planet. None of these events, if they ever happened, would surprise horror-movie fans. For years, such moviegoers have enjoyed being frightened by every type of monster Hollywood has managed to dream up, whether it be natural, artificial, or extraterrestrial. 1

One kind of movie monster is a product of nature. These monsters may be exaggerated versions of real creatures, like the single-minded shark in <u>Jaws</u> or the skyscraper-climbing gorilla in <u>King Kong</u>. They may be extinct animals, like the dinosaurs that terrorize cave dwellers and explorers in movies. Actually, cave dwellers and dinosaurs would never have met, for some unexplained event caused the dinosaurs to become extinct before the cave dwellers existed. "Natural" monsters sometimes combine human and animal features. Cat people, werewolves, and vampires fit into this category; so do Bigfoot and the Abominable Snowman. All these monsters seem to frighten us because they represent nature at its most threatening. We may have come a long way since the stone age, but we're still scared of what's out there beyond the campfire. 2

The second type of movie monster is a product of humans. Every giant lobster or house-sized spider that attacks Tokyo or Cleveland is the result of a mad scientist's meddling or a dose of radiation. In these cases, humans interfere with nature, and the results are deadly. Frankenstein's monster, for example, is put together out of spare parts stolen from graveyards. His creator, an insane scientist in love with his own power, uses a jolt of electricity to bring the monster to life. The scientist, along with lots of innocent villagers, dies as a result of his pride. In dozens of other monster movies, creatures grow to enormous proportions after wandering too close to atomic bomb sites. Our real fears about the terrors of technology are given the shape of giant scorpions and cockroaches that devour people.

The third type of movie monster comes from outer space. Since the movies began, odd things have been crawling or sliding down the ramps of spaceships. To modern movie fans, the early space monsters look suspiciously like actors dressed in rubber suits and metal antennas. Now, thanks to special effects, these creatures can horrify the bravest moviegoer. The monster in Alien, for example, invades a spaceship piloted by humans. The monster, which resembles a ten-pound raw clam with arms, clamps onto a crew member's face. Later, it grows into a slimy six-footer with a double jaw and long, toothed tongue. Movies like Alien reflect our fear of the unfamiliar and the unknown. We don't know what's out there in space, and we're afraid it might not be very nice.

Movie monsters, no matter what kind they are, sneak around the edges of our imaginations long after the movies are over. They probably play on fears that were there already. The movies merely give us the monsters that embody those fears.

Selling Beer

The other night, my six-year-old son turned to me and asked for a light beer. My husband and I sat there for a moment, stunned, and then explained to him that beer was only for grown-ups. I suddenly realized how many, and how often, beer ads appear on television. To my little boy, it must seem that every American drinks beer after work, or after playing softball, or while watching a football game. Beer makers have pounded audiences with all kinds of campaigns to sell beer. Each type of ad, however, seems to be targeted toward a different economic level of the TV viewing audience.

The first type of ad appeals to working-class people. There is the "this Bud's for you" approach, which shows the "boys" headed down to the neighborhood tavern after a tough day on the job at the auto plant or the construction site. The Budweiser jingle congratulates them on a job well done and encourages them to reward themselves—with a Bud. Miller beer uses a slightly different approach to appeal to workers. Men are shown completing a tough and unusual job and then relaxing during "Miller time." "Miller time" jobs might be called fantasy blue-collar jobs. Some Miller men, for example, fly helicopters to round up cattle or manage to cap blazing oil well fires.

The second kind of ad aims not at working-class people but at an upper-middle-class audience. The actors in these ads are shown in glamorous or adventurous settings. Some ads show a group of friends in their thirties and forties getting together to play a fancy sport, like tennis or rugby. One Lowenbrau ad, featuring a group of compatible couples at a clambake, is aimed at those rich enough to have a costly beach house.   3

The third type of ad appeals to people with a weight problem. These are the ads for the light beers, and they use sports celebrities and indirect language to make their points. For example, they never use the phrase "diet beer." Instead, they use phrases like "tastes great, and is less filling." In the macho world of beer commercials, men don't admit that they're dieting—that's too sissy. But if former football coaches and baseball greats can order a Lite without being laughed out of the bar, why can't the ordinary guy?   4

To a little boy, it may well seem that beer is necessary to every adult's life. After all, we need it to recover from a hard day at work, to celebrate our pleasurable moments, and to get rid of the beer bellies we got by drinking it in the first place. At least, that's what advertisers tell him—and us.   5

■ Questions

About Unity

1.   Which paragraph in "Mall People" lacks a topic sentence? _____
     Write a topic sentence for the paragraph:

     _____

2.   Which sentence in paragraph 2 of "Movie Monsters" should be omitted in the interest of paragraph unity? (*Write the opening words.*)

     _____

3.   Which paragraph in "Selling Beer" does not logically support the thesis statement? _____

About Support

4.   Which supporting paragraph in "Movie Monsters" uses a single extended example? _____

5.   After which sentence in paragraph 3 of "Selling Beer" are more supporting details needed? _____

6.   Which paragraph in "Mall People" lacks specific details? _____

About Coherence

7. What are the transition words used in the second supporting paragraph of "Mall People"?

   a. _____   b. _____   c. _____

8. Which topic sentence in "Selling Beer" functions as a linking sentence between paragraphs? _____

About the Introduction and Conclusion

9. What kind of introduction is used in "Selling Beer"? Circle the appropriate letter.
   a. Broad, general statement narrowing to thesis
   b. Idea that is the opposite of the one to be developed
   c. Quotation
   d. Anecdote
   e. Questions

10. Which two essays have conclusions that include brief summaries of their supporting points?
   a. "Movie Monsters"
   b. "Mall People"
   c. "Selling Beer"

Activity

This activity will sharpen your sense of the classifying process. In each of the following groups, cross out the one item that has not been classified on the same basis as the other four. Also, indicate in the space provided the single principle of classification used for the four items. Note the examples.

Example   Shirts
   a. Flannel
   b. Cotton
   c. ~~Tuxedo~~
   d. Denim
   e. Silk

   (Unifying principle: _material_)

Example   Sports
a.   Swimming
b.   Sailing
c.   ~~Basketball~~
d.   Water polo
e.   Scuba diving

(Unifying principle: *water sports*)

1.   School subjects
   a.   Algebra
   b.   History
   c.   Geometry
   d.   Trigonometry
   e.   Calculus

(Unifying principle: _____)

2.   Movies
   a.   *The Sound of Music*
   b.   *My Fair Lady*
   c.   *Dracula*
   d.   *Cabaret*
   e.   *The Wizard of Oz*

(Unifying principle: _____)

3.   Clothing
   a.   Sweat shirt
   b.   Shorts
   c.   T shirt
   d.   Evening gown
   e.   Sweat pants

(Unifying principle: _____)

4.   Fasteners
   a.   Staples
   b.   Buttons
   c.   Zippers
   d.   Snaps
   e.   Velcro

(Unifying principle: _____)

5.   Sources of information
   a.   *Newsweek*
   b.   *The New York Times*
   c.   *People*
   d.   *TV Guide*
   e.   *Life*

(Unifying principle: _____)

6.   Fibers
   a.   Wool
   b.   Acrylic
   c.   Cotton
   d.   Silk
   e.   Linen

(Unifying principle: _____)

7. Tapes
   a. Cellophane
   b. Recording
   c. Masking
   d. Duct
   e. Electrical

   (Unifying principle: _____)

8. Fairy-tale characters
   a. Witch
   b. King
   c. Fairy godmother
   d. Wicked queen
   e. Princess

   (Unifying principle: _____)

9. Immigrants
   a. Haitian
   b. Irish
   c. Mexican
   d. Illegal
   e. German

   (Unifying principle: _____)

10. Famous buildings
    a. Lincoln Memorial
    b. Empire State Building
    c. White House
    d. Capitol Building
    e. Washington Monument

    (Unifying principle: _____)

11. Emotions
    a. Depression
    b. Anger
    c. Jealousy
    d. Despair
    e. Affection

    (Unifying principle: _____)

12. Crimes
    a. Rape
    b. Murder
    c. Robbery
    d. Prostitution
    e. Mugging

    (Unifying principle: _____)

WRITING A DIVISION-CLASSIFICATION ESSAY

■ Writing Assignment 1

Shown on the next page are an introduction, a thesis, and supporting points for a classification essay on college stress. Using separate paper, plan out and write the supporting paragraphs and a conclusion for the essay. Refer to the suggestions on ''How to Proceed'' that follow on page 213.

College Stress

Jack's heart pounds as he casts panicked looks around the classroom. He doesn't recognize the professor, he doesn't know any of the students, and he can't even figure out what the subject is. In front of him is a test. At the last minute his roommate awakens him. It's only another anxiety dream. The very fact that dreams like Jack's are common suggests that college is a stressful situation for young people. The causes of this stress can be academic, financial, and personal.

Academic stress is common. . . .

In addition to academic stress, the student often feels financial pressure. . . .

Along with academic and financial worries, the student faces personal pressures. . . .

How to Proceed

a   To develop some ideas for the division-classification essay in assignment 1, freewrite for five minutes apiece on (1) *academic,* (2) *financial,* and (3) *personal* problems of college students.

b   Add to the material you have written by asking yourself these questions:

What are some examples of academic problems that are stressful for students?
What are some examples of financial problems that students must contend with?
What are some examples of personal problems that create stress in students?

Write down quickly whatever answers occur to you for the questions. As with the freewriting, do not worry at this stage about writing correct sentences. Instead, concentrate on getting down as much information as you can think of that supports each of the three points.

c   Now go through all the material you have accumulated. Perhaps some of the details you have written down may help you think of even better details that would fit. If so, write down these additional details. Then make decisions about the exact information that you will use in each supporting paragraph. List the details (1, 2, 3, and so on) in the order in which you will present them.

d   As you work on the drafts of your paper, refer to the checklist on page 127 and the inside front cover to make sure you can answer *Yes* to the questions about unity, support, and coherence.

e   Write a conclusion for the essay by adding a summarizing sentence or two and a final thought about the subject. See page 83 for an example.

f   Finally, use the checklist on page 127 and the inside cover to proofread your next-to-final draft for sentence-skills mistakes, including spelling.

■ Writing Assignment 2

Write a division-classification essay on one of the following subjects:

Crimes	Advertisements	Clothes
Dates	Churchgoers	Attitudes toward life
Teachers	Junk food	Eating places
Bosses	Jobs	Marriages
Friends	Shoppers	TV watchers
Sports fans	Soap operas	College courses
Parties	Bars	

How to Proceed

a   The first step in writing a division-classification essay is to divide your tentative topic into three reasonably complete parts. *Always use a single principle of division when you form your three parts.* For example, if your topic is "Automobile Drivers" and you divide them into slow, moderate, and fast drivers, your single basis for division will be "rate of speed." It would be illogical, then, to have as a fourth type "teenage drivers" (the basis of such a division would be "age") or "female drivers" (the basis of such a division would be "sex"). You could probably classify automobile drivers on the basis of age or sex or another division, for almost any subject can be analyzed in more than one way. What is important, however, is that in any single paper, you choose only one basis for division and stick to it. Be consistent.

In "Movie Monsters," the single basis for dividing monsters into natural, artificial, and extraterrestrial is *origin*. It would have been illogical, then, to have a fourth category dealing with vampires. In "Selling Beer," the intended basis for the types of beer ads was *economic level*. The writer's first group was working-class people; his second group was upper-middle-class people. To be consistent, his third group should have been, perhaps, lower-middle-class people. Instead, the writer confusingly shifted to ads that appeal to people with a weight problem.

b   To avoid such confusion in your own essay, fill in the outline below before starting your paper and make sure you can answer *Yes* to the questions that follow. You should expect to do a fair amount of thinking before coming up with a logical plan for your paper.

Topic: _____
Three-part division of the topic:

1.   _____

2.   _____

3.   _____

Is there a single basis of division for the three parts? _____

Is the division reasonably complete? _____

c   Refer to the checklist of the four bases on page 127 and the inside front cover while writing the drafts of your paper. Make sure you can answer *Yes* to the questions about unity, support, coherence, and sentence skills. Also, use the checklist when you proofread your next-to-final draft for sentence-skills mistakes, including spelling.

■ Writing Assignment 3

In this division-classification essay, you will write with a specific purpose and for a specific audience.

Option 1: Your younger sister or brother has moved to another city and is about to choose a roommate. Write her or him a letter about what to expect from different types of roommates. Label each type of roommate (''The Messy Type,'' ''The Neatnik,'' ''The Loud-Music Lover,'' etc.) and explain what it would be like to live with each.

Option 2: Unsure about your career direction, you have gone to a vocational counseling service. To help you select the type of work you are best suited for, a counselor has asked you to write a detailed description of your ''ideal job.'' You will present this description to three other people who are also seeking to make a career choice.

To describe your ideal job, divide work life into three or more elements, such as:

Activities done on the job
Skills used on the job
Physical environment
People you work with and under
How the job affects society

In your paper, explain your ideals for each element. Use specific examples where possible to illustrate your points.

■ Writing Assignment 4: Writing about a Reading Selection

Read the selection titled "Five Parenting Styles" on pages 603–605. Then write an essay in which you divide and classify a group of people. The group you classify should be *one* of the following:

- Instructors
- Friends
- Coworkers

Following are suggestions about how to write your essay.

To begin, you must think of a way—a principle of division—to divide the group you have chosen. If you were considering "coworkers," for example, you could probably imagine several principles of division, such as these:

Ways they treat the boss
Efficiency at work
Punctuality at work
Level of neatness (desks, lockers, work turned in)

Once you have a useful principle of division, you will find that you can easily divide the people you are writing about into groups. If you decided, for instance, to use "ways they treat the boss" as your principle of division, you might write about these three groups:

(1) Coworkers who "butter up" the boss
(2) Coworkers who get along with the boss
(3) Coworkers who dislike the boss

Here are some suggested principles of division for "instructors" and "friends." You should feel free, of course, to come up with your own approach.

Instructors

Teaching methods
Methods of classroom control
Clothing styles
Testing methods
Level of dedication to the job

Friends

Level of loyalty
Where or how you first met them
Length of time you've been friends
Level of emotional closeness
Attitudes toward something (money, college, drugs, and so on)

To complete the essay, follow the suggestions on "How to Proceed" on page 214.

ARGUMENTATION

Most of us know someone who enjoys a good argument. Such a person usually challenges any sweeping statement we might make. "Why do you say that?" he or she will ask. "Give your reasons." Our questioner then listens carefully as we state our case, waiting to see if we really do have solid evidence to support our point of view. Such a questioner may make us feel uncomfortable, but we may also feel grateful to him or her for helping us clarify our opinions.

The ability to advance sound and compelling arguments is an important skill in everyday life. You can use argumentation to make a point in a class discussion, persuade a friend to lend you money, or talk an employer into giving you a day off. Becoming skilled in clear, logical reasoning can also help you see through the sometimes faulty arguments in advertisements, newspaper articles, political speeches, and the other persuasive appeals you see and hear every day.

In this section, you will be asked to write essays in which you defend a position with a series of solid reasons. In a general way, you have done the same thing—making a point and then supporting it—with all the essays in the book. The key difference here is that argumentation advances a *controversial* point— one that at least some of your readers will not be inclined to accept.

When you state your thesis, it's important to keep in mind that not all your readers are likely to agree with the position you take. Don't, then, express your thesis as a fact; since a fact can be shown to be true, it doesn't allow for differences of opinion. Instead, write a thesis that takes a disputable position on a controversial issue. Consider the differences between the factual statement and the effective thesis statement below:

Fact

People often get drunk at bars, parties, and other places away from their own homes.

Thesis

Anyone—a bartender, server, or party host—who provides alcohol to a person who later causes an alcohol-related car accident should share legal responsibility for that accident.

In the preceding example, the first statement is true. People do often get drunk away from home. Because there is no arguing against such an obvious fact, such a statement cannot serve as a thesis for an argumentation essay. The second statement, however, takes a controversial point of view on the issue of drinking and driving. It is the kind of statement that can serve as an effective thesis for an argumentation essay.

STRATEGIES FOR ARGUMENTATION

Because argumentation assumes controversy, you have to work especially hard to convince readers of the validity of your position. Here are five strategies you can use to help win over readers whose viewpoint may differ from yours.

1   Use Tactful, Courteous Language

In an argumentation essay, you are attempting to persuade readers to accept your viewpoint. It is important, therefore, not to anger them by referring to them or their opinions in rude or belittling terms. Stay away from sweeping statements like "Everybody knows that . . . " or "People with any intelligence agree that . . . " Also, keep the focus on the issue you are discussing, not on the people involved in the debate. Don't write, "*My opponents* say that orphanages cost less than foster care." Instead, write, "*Supporters of orphanages* say they cost less than foster care." Terms like *my opponents* imply that the argument is between you and the "bad guys"—an attitude that puts more distance between you and anyone who disagrees with you. By contrast, a term such as *supporters of orphanages* suggests that those who don't agree with you are nevertheless reasonable people who are willing to consider differing opinions.

2   Point Out Common Ground

Another way to persuade readers to consider your opinion is to point out common ground that you share. Find points on which people on all sides of the argument can agree. Perhaps you are arguing that there should be an 11 P.M. curfew for juveniles in your town. Before going into detail about your proposal, remind readers who oppose such a curfew that you and they share certain goals: a safer city, a lower crime rate, and fewer gang-related tragedies. Readers will be more receptive to your idea once they have considered the ways in which you and they think alike.

3   Acknowledge Differing Viewpoints

It is a mistake to simply ignore points of view that conflict with yours. Acknowledging other viewpoints strengthens your position in several ways. First, it helps you spot flaws in the opposing position—as well as in your own argument. Second, and equally important, it gives the impression that you are a reasonable person, willing to look at an issue from all sides. Readers will be more likely to consider your point of view if you indicate a willingness to consider theirs.

At what point in your essay should you acknowledge opposing arguments? The earlier the better—ideally, in the introduction. By quickly establishing that you recognize the other side's position, you get your readers "on board" with you, ready to hear what else you have to say.

One effective technique is to *cite the opposing viewpoint in your thesis statement*. You do this by dividing your thesis into two parts. In the first part, you acknowledge the other side's point of view; in the second, you state your opinion, suggesting that yours is the stronger viewpoint. In the example below, the opposing viewpoint is underlined once; the writer's own position is underlined twice:

> Although some students believe that studying a foreign language is a waste of time, two years of foreign-language study should be required of all college graduates.

For another example of a thesis that acknowledges an opposing viewpoint, look at this thesis statement, taken from the essay entitled "Once Over Lightly: Local TV News" (page 223):

> While local TV newscasts can provide a valuable community resource, too often such programs provide mere entertainment at the expense of solid news.

Another effective technique is to use one or two sentences (separate from the thesis) in the introduction to *acknowledge the alternative position*. Such sentences briefly state the "other side's" argument. To see this technique at work, look at the introduction to the essay "Teenagers and Jobs" (page 221), noting the sentence "Many people argue that working can be a valuable experience for the young." The essay "A Vote against Computers" (page 222) also uses this strategy in the opening paragraph. But rather than stating the opposing opinion in a single sentence, the author of this essay uses a slightly more sophisticated approach: in several sentences, he describes how he, like most people, was initially enthusiastic about writing on a computer. Then, having acknowledged that common attitude, he goes on to state how experience has dampened his original enthusiasm.

A third technique is to *use a paragraph within the body of your essay to summarize opposing opinions in greater detail.* To do this successfully, you must spend some time researching those opposing arguments. A fair, evenhanded summary of the other side's ideas will help convince readers that you have looked at the issue from all angles before deciding where you stand. Imagine, for instance, that you are writing an essay arguing that the manufacture and sale of handguns should be outlawed. You would begin by doing some library research to find information on both sides of the issue, making sure to pay attention to material that argues against your viewpoint. You might also talk with local representatives of the National Rifle Association or other organizations that support gun ownership. Having done your research, you would be in a good position to write a paragraph summarizing the opposing viewpoints. In this paragraph, you might mention that many citizens believe that gun ownership is a right guaranteed by the Constitution and that gun owners fear that outlawing handguns would deprive law-abiding people of protection against gun-toting criminals. Once you had demonstrated that you understood opposing views, you would be in a stronger position to present your own point of view.

4 When Appropriate, Grant the Merits of Differing Viewpoints

Sometimes an opposing argument contains a point whose validity you cannot deny. What should you do then? The strongest strategy is to admit that the point is a good one. You will lose credibility if you argue against something that clearly makes sense. Admit the merit of one aspect of the other argument while making it clear that you still believe your argument to be stronger overall. The author of "A Vote against Computers" (page 222) takes this approach when discussing the merits of using computers in writing classes. The sentence "Granted, students who are already accustomed to computers can use them to write papers quickly and efficiently" admits that the other side has a valid point. But the author quickly follows this admission with several statements making her own viewpoint clear: "But for students like me who have not used computers in the past, a computer is more a hindrance than a help; it requires too much time and trouble to use, and it changes an instructor from a teacher to a technician."

5 Rebut Differing Viewpoints

Sometimes it may not be enough simply to acknowledge other points of view and present your own argument. When you are dealing with an issue that your readers feel strongly about, you may need to *rebut* the opposing arguments. To *rebut* means to point out problems with an opposing view, to show where an opponent's argument breaks down.

Imagine that you are writing an essay arguing that your college should use money intended to build a campus health and fitness center to upgrade the library instead. From reading the school paper, you know that supporters of the center say it will help attract new students to the college. You rebut that point by citing a study conducted by the admissions office which shows that most students choose a college because they can afford it and because they like its academic programs and facilities. You also emphasize that many students, already financially strapped, would have trouble paying the proposed fee for using the center.

A rebuttal can take two forms. (1) You can first mention all the points raised by the other side and then present your counterargument to each of those points. (2) You can present the first point raised by the opposition and rebut that point, then move on to the second opposing point and rebut that, and so on.

ESSAYS TO CONSIDER

Teenagers and Jobs

"The pressure for a teenager to work is great, and not just because of the economic plight in the world today. Much of it is peer pressure to have a little bit of freedom and independence, and to have their own spending money. The concern we have is when the part-time work becomes the primary focus," says Roxanne Bradshaw, educator and officer of the National Education Association. Many people argue that working can be a valuable experience for the young. However, working more than about fifteen hours a week is harmful to adolescents because it reduces their involvement with school, encourages a materialistic and expensive lifestyle, and increases the chance of having problems with drugs and alcohol.

Schoolwork and the benefits of extracurricular activities tend to go by the wayside when adolescents work long hours. As more and more teens have filled the numerous part-time jobs offered by fast-food restaurants and mall stores, teachers have faced increasing difficulties. They must both keep the attention of tired pupils and give homework to students who simply don't have time to do it. In addition, educators have noticed less involvement in the extracurricular events many consider healthy influences on young people. School bands and athletic teams are losing players to work, and sports events are poorly attended by working students. Those teenagers who try to do it all—homework, extracurricular activities, and work—may find themselves exhausted and prone to illness. A recent newspaper story, for example, described a girl in Pennsylvania who came down with mononucleosis as a result of aiming for good grades, playing on two school athletic teams, and working thirty hours a week.

Another drawback of too much work is that it may promote materialism and   3
an unrealistic lifestyle. Some parents say that work teaches adolescents the value
of a dollar. Undoubtedly, it can, and it's true that some teenagers work to help
out with the family budget or save for college. However, surveys have shown that
the majority of working teens use their earnings to buy luxuries—stereos, tape
decks, clothing, even cars. These young people, some of whom earn $300 and
more a month, don't worry about spending wisely—they can just about have it
all. In many cases, experts point out, they are becoming accustomed to a
lifestyle they won't be able to afford several years down the road, when they'll no
longer have parents to pay for car insurance, food and lodging, and so on. At that
point, they'll be hard pressed to pay for necessities as well as luxuries.

Finally, teenagers who work a lot are more likely than others to get involved   4
with alcohol and drugs. Teens who put in long hours may seek a quick release
from stress, just like the adults who need to drink a couple of martinis after a
hard day at work. Stress is probably greater in our society today than it has been
at any time in the past. Also, teens who have money are more likely, for various
obvious reasons, to get involved with drugs.

Teenagers can enjoy the benefits of work while avoiding its drawbacks simply   5
by limiting their work hours during the school year. As is often the case, a
moderate approach will be the most healthy and rewarding.

A Vote against Computers

I was excited when my English composition instructor announced that   1
computers would be a major part of our writing course. "Half of the classes will
be held in the computer lab," she said, "and all required work will be done on
the computer." I was thrilled while touring the new computer lab to see all the
magical-looking machines with their glowing screens. The machines hummed as
if they were alive. I thought to myself excitedly, "We're living in the middle of
the computer revolution, and here's my chance to get on board." But three
months later, I've had some second thoughts. I now believe that computers are a
bad idea in the writing classroom. Granted, students who are already accustomed
to computers can use them to write papers quickly and efficiently. But for
students like me, who have not used computers in the past, a computer is more
a hindrance than a help; it requires too much time and trouble to use, and it
changes my instructor from a teacher to a technician.

To begin with, the computer does not help me go about writing a paper. When   2
I start an essay, I like to use a yellow pad and scribble out my ideas. I may write
a couple of sentences, scratch them out, and then write a few more. I may make
a couple of rough outlines, and then cross out parts of them, and then combine
those leftover parts to make a third outline. I may go back to some idea I
rejected at first and write another idea in the margin. I may circle something
from one part of the page and join it with something on another part. At any one
time, I want to see everything I'm doing in front of me. With a computer, I can't

do that. If I delete something, I can't look back at it later. If I write too much, I have to scroll back and forth, since not everything can fit on the screen at once. There's no room in the margin for questions. And I can't circle things on the computer screen and connect them the way I can on a sheet of paper. I want a chance to see and change everything at once when planning a paper, and a computer does not let me do that.

3   Next, the mechanics involved in using a computer are complicated and time-consuming. Before I can get down to some honest-to-goodness writing, I have to show the computer lab technician my student ID card and sign out the appropriate software. Then I have to find an open terminal, turn on my computer and monitor, insert the proper disks, create or find a file, and set the required format. When I'm finished writing, I have to make sure that my work is properly saved, that there's paper in the printer, and that the printer is on-line. And at any point, when I have mechanical problems or questions about the computer, I have to wait five or ten minutes or more for the instructor or a student technician to come to help me. Worst of all, I'm not a good typist. I spend half of my time hunting and pecking for the proper letters on the keyboard. If I had wanted to get a lot of typing practice, I would have taken a typing course, but this is supposed to be a writing course.

4   Finally, when we meet in the computer lab, the instructor spends most of the class walking around and helping students log on and off the computer, handing out and collecting software, and trying to locate and retrieve lost documents. I sat here the other day watching the class trying to write on computers, and my impression was that 75 percent of what the instructor did involved computers rather than writing. I've had other writing courses, before computers, where the instructor spent a lot of time going over students' work on a one-on-one basis or in a class discussion. It was in these workshop settings that I believe my writing improved the most. Now, my instructor has much less time to devote to individual help and feedback. She's too busy being a computer troubleshooter.

5   In conclusion, it may be wise to take another look at the use of the computer in college writing courses. At first glance the computer offers excitement and a world of promise, but I think there's a serious question about whether it actually improves students' writing.

Once Over Lightly: Local TV News

1   Are local television newscasts a reliable source of news? Do they provide in-depth coverage and analysis of important local issues? Unfortunately, all too often they do not. While local TV newscasts can provide a valuable community resource, too often such programs provide mere entertainment at the expense of solid news. In their battle for high ratings, local programs emphasize news personalities at the expense of stories. Visual appeal has a higher priority than actual news. And stories and reports are too brief and shallow.

Local TV newscasters are as much the subject of the news as are the stories they present. Nowhere is this more obvious than in weather reports. Weatherpersons spend valuable news time joking, drawing cartoons, chatting about weather fronts as "good guys" and "bad guys," and dispensing weather trivia such as statistics about relative humidity and record highs and lows for the date. Reporters, too, draw attention to themselves. Rather than just getting the story, we are shown the reporters jumping into or getting out of helicopters to get the story. When reporters interview crime victims or the residents of poor neighborhoods, the camera angle typically includes them and their reaction as well as their subjects. When they report on a storm, they stand outside in the storm, their styled hair blowing, so we can admire how they "brave the elements." Then there are the anchorpersons, who are chosen as much for their looks as for their skills. They too dilute the news by putting their personalities on center stage.

Often the selection of stories and the way they are presented are based on visual impact rather than news value. If a story is not accompanied by an interesting film clip, it is unlikely to be shown on the local news. The result is an overemphasis on fires and car crashes and little attention to such important issues as the local employment situation. As much as possible, every story is presented with a reporter standing "live" in front of something. If City Hall has passed a resolution, for instance, then the reporter will be shown standing live in front of City Hall. Very often, cars are zooming by or neighborhood kids are waving at the camera or passersby are recognizing suddenly that they are being filmed. Most people are natural hams, and they love to discover that they are on stage. Such background happenings are so distracting that viewers may not even listen to what the reporter is saying. And even if a story is not live, the visuals that accompany a story are often distracting. A recent story on falling oil prices, for example, was accompanied by footage of a working oil well that drew away attention from the important economic information in the report.

Finally, the desire of the local stations to entertain viewers is demonstrated in short news stories and shallow treatment. On the average, about half a minute is devoted to a story. Clearly, stories that take less than half a minute are superficial. Even the longest stories, which can take up several minutes, are not accompanied by meaningful analysis. Instead, the camera jumps from one location to another and the newscaster simplifies and trivializes the issues. For instance, one recent "in-depth" story about the homeless consisted of a glamorous reporter talking to a homeless person and asking him what should be done about the problem. The poor man was in no condition to respond intelligently. The story then cut to an interview with a city bureaucrat who mechanically rambled on about the need for more government funding. There were also shots of homeless people sleeping in doorways and on top of heating vents, and there were interviews with people on the street, all of whom said something should be done about the terrible problem of the homeless. There was, in all of this, no real exploration of the issue and no proposed solutions. It was also apparent that the homeless were just the issue-for-the-week. After the week's coverage was over, the topic was not mentioned again.

Because of the emphasis on newscasters' personalities and on the visual 　　5
impact of stories and the short time span for stories, local news shows provide
little more than diversion. What viewers need instead is news that has real
significance. Rather than being amused and entertained, we need to deal with
complex issues and learn uncomfortable truths that will help us become more
responsible consumers and citizens.

■ Questions

About Unity

1. Which sentence in paragraph 4 of ''Teenagers and Jobs'' should be
    omitted in the interest of paragraph unity? (*Write the opening words.*)

    _____

2. Which supporting paragraph in ''A Vote against Computers'' lacks a topic
    sentence? _____
    Write a topic sentence for the paragraph:

    _____

    _____

    _____

    _____

About Support

3. Which paragraph in ''Teenagers and Jobs'' develops its point by citing and
    then refuting an opposing point of view? _____
4. After which sentence in paragraph 4 of ''Teenagers and Jobs'' are specific
    details needed? _____
5. After which sentence in paragraph 2 of ''Once Over Lightly: Local TV
    News'' is support needed? _____
6. Which supporting paragraph of which essay uses the longest single sup-
    porting example?

    _____

About Coherence

7. What three transition words are used to introduce the three supporting paragraphs in "A Vote against Computers"?

    a. _____

    b. _____

    c. _____

8. What are the two main transition words in paragraph 2 of "Once Over Lightly: Local TV News"?

    a. _____

    b. _____

About the Introduction and Conclusion

9. Which method of introduction is used in "Teenagers and Jobs"? _____ "A Vote against Computers"? _____ "Once Over Lightly: Local TV News"? _____

    a. Broad, general statement narrowing to thesis
    b. Idea that is the opposite of the one to be developed
    c. Quotation
    d. Anecdote
    e. Questions

10. Which essay has a conclusion that briefly summarizes the supporting points? _____

Activity

In scratch-outline form on separate paper, provide brief supporting reasons for at least five of the twelve statements that follow. Note the example. Make sure that you have three *separate* and *distinct* reasons for each statement.

Example   Recycling of newspapers, cans, and bottles should be mandatory.

   a. Towns sell recycled items rather than pay for dumping.
   b. Natural resources are protected.
   c. Respect for the environment is encouraged.

1. Couples should be required to live together for six months before marriage.
2. High schools should give birth control devices and information to students.
3. All instructors should be graded by their students.
4. TV commercials are often particularly insulting to women.
5. Professional boxing should be outlawed.
6. Attendance at college classes should be optional.
7. Cigarette companies should not be allowed to advertise.
8. Television does more harm than good.
9. Killing animals for food is wrong.
10. School does not prepare you for life.
11. Governments should not pay ransom for terrorist kidnappings.
12. All companies should be required to have day-care centers.

WRITING AN ARGUMENTATION ESSAY

■ Writing Assignment 1

Decide, perhaps through discussion with your instructor or classmates, which of the outlines prepared in the preceding activity would be the most promising to develop into an argumentation essay. Make sure that your supporting reasons are logical ones that actually back up your thesis statement. Ask yourself in each case, "Does this reason truly support my thesis idea?"

How to Proceed

a On separate paper, make a list of details that might go under each of the supporting points. Provide more details than you can actually use. Here, for example, are the details generated by the writer of "Teenagers and Jobs" when she was working on her first supporting paragraph:

School problems:

Less time for sports and other activities
Lower attendance at games
Students leave right after school
Students sleep in class and skip homework
Teachers are angry and frustrated
More time buying things like clothing and compact disks
More stress for students and less concentration
Some students try to do it all and get sick
Students miss school to go to work
Some drop out of school

b Decide which reasons and details you will use to develop each of your supporting paragraphs. Also, number the items in the order in which you will present them. Here is how the writer of "Teenagers and Jobs" made decisions on what to develop:

School problems

2 Less time for sports and other activities
~~Lower attendance at games~~
~~Students leave right after school~~
1 Students sleep in class and skip homework
~~Teachers are angry and frustrated~~
~~More time buying things like clothing and compact disks~~
~~More stress for students and less concentration~~
3 Some students try to do it all and get sick
~~Students miss school to go to work~~
~~Some drop out of school~~

c As you are working on the drafts of your paper, refer to the checklist on page 127 and the inside front cover. Make sure that you can answer *Yes* to the questions about unity, support, and coherence.

d You may also want to refer to pages 79–84 for suggestions on writing an effective introduction and conclusion to your essay.

e Finally, use the checklist on page 127 and the inside front cover when you are proofreading your next-to-final draft for sentence-skills mistakes, including spelling.

■ Writing Assignment 2

Write a paper in which you argue *for* or *against* any *one* of the three comments below (options 1–3). Support and defend your argument by drawing on your reasoning ability and general experience. Remember that your thesis should express an opinion rather than state a fact. Use some of the strategies described on pages 218–221 to help win over readers whose viewpoint may differ from your own. To guide your work, refer to "How to Proceed" on pages 229–231.

Option 1

In some ways, television has proved to be one of the worst inventions of recent times. All too often, television is harmful because of the shows it broadcasts and the way it is used in the home.

Option 2

College athletes devote a lot of time and energy to teams that sometimes make a great deal of money for their schools. Often athletes stress a sport at the expense of their education. And their efforts rarely give these young men and women experiences and skills that are useful after college. It is only fair, therefore, that college athletes be paid for their work.

Option 3

Many of society's worst problems with drugs result from the fact that they are illegal. During Prohibition, Americans discovered that making popular substances unlawful causes more problems than it solves. Like alcohol, drugs should be legal in this country.

How to Proceed

a   Take several minutes to think about the three options. Which one in particular are you for or against—and *why*?

b   On a sheet of paper, make up a brief outline of support for *your* position on one of the options. Preparing the outline will give you a chance to think further about your position. And the outline will show whether you have enough support for your position. (If you don't, choose another position, and prepare another outline.)

   This initial thinking and outlining will be the key to preparing a solid paper. Your goal should be to decide on a position for which you can provide the most convincing evidence.

   The writer of the model essay on computers was originally asked to take a position for or against the use of computers in the classroom. After a good deal of thinking, he came up with the following brief outline:

I am against the use of computers.
1. Don't help me plan a paper.
2. Are complicated to use.
3. Take up instructor's time.

While he had not yet written his first draft, he had already done the most important work on the paper.

c   Next, decide how you will develop each of your three supporting points. Make up brief outlines of the three points. Here, for example, is what the author of the essay on computers did:

1. Don't help me plan a paper:
   Like to scribble.
   Use margins.
   Circle details on different parts of paper.
   See whole thing at once.
2. Are complicated to use:
   Sign out software.
   Get machine started.
   Wait for help.
   Type slowly.
3. Take up instructor's time:
   Helps students use computers.
   Has less time for writing feedback.

Such preliminary work is vital; to write a good paper, you must *think, plan,* and *prewrite.* In addition to preparing brief outlines, you may also find that other prewriting techniques are useful. You may, variously, want to freewrite, brainstorm, and make up lists—all of which are described on pages 18–21.

d   Decide in what order you want to present your paragraphs. Often, emphatic order (in which you end with the most important reason) is an effective way to organize an argument, for the final reason is the one your reader is most likely to remember.

e   Provide as many convincing details as possible. For example, in the essay on computers, the writer includes such supportive details as the following:

"If I write too much [on the computer], I have to scroll back and forth, since not everything can fit on the screen at once."

"I spend half of my time hunting and pecking for the proper letters on the keyboard."

"I sat here the other day watching the class trying to write on computers, and my impression was that 75 percent of what the instructor did involved computers rather than writing."

f   As you write, think of your audience as a jury that will ultimately believe or disbelieve your argument. Have you presented a convincing case? Do you need more details? If *you* were on the jury, would you be favorably impressed with this argument?

g   As you are working on the drafts of your paper, keep the four bases in mind: unity, support, coherence, and sentence skills.

h   Finally, proofread your next-to-final draft for sentence-skills mistakes, including spelling.

■ Writing Assignment 3

Write a paper in which you argue *for* or *against* any *one* of the three comments that follow (options 1–3). Support and defend your argument by drawing on your reasoning ability and general experience.

Option 1

While it is now well known that smoking is very unhealthy, it would be very difficult in our society to make it illegal. But this does not mean that smoking should be encouraged. On the contrary, cigarette advertising should be banned.

Option 2

By the time many students reach high school, they have learned the basics in most subjects. Some still have much to gain from the education that high schools offer, but others might be better off spending the next four years in other ways. For their benefit, high school attendance should be voluntary, not compulsory.

Option 3

It is sad but true that some of the most miserable days in many people's lives are their last days. It is also true there is no way to avoid dying. But establishing centers where people can choose to end their lives in peace can eliminate the long suffering that many fatal illnesses cause. The government should take an active role in creating such centers.

Remember that the best way to get started is *to think, plan,* and *prewrite.* Which comment do you feel most strongly for or against? What are three solid reasons you can give to support your position? After you work out a satisfactory scratch outline, go on to follow the rest of the steps described in writing assignment 2.

■ Writing Assignment 4

Write a paper in which you argue *for* or *against* any *one* of the three comments below (options 1–3). Support and defend your argument by drawing on your reasoning ability and general experience.

Option 1

Giving students grades does more harm than good. Schools should replace grades with evaluations, which would benefit both students and parents.

Option 2

Because our jails are overcrowded and expensive, the fewer people sentenced to jail the better. Of course, it is necessary to put violent criminals in jail in order to protect others. Society, however, would benefit if nonviolent criminals received punishments other than jail sentences.

Option 3

Physical punishment is often a successful way of disciplining children. After all, no child wants to experience pain. But adults who frequently spank and hit are also teaching the lesson that violence is a good method of accomplishing a goal. Nonviolent methods are a more effective way of training children.

■ Writing Assignment 5

Write a paper in which you argue *for* or *against* any *one* of the three comments below (options 1–3). Support and defend your argument by drawing on your reasoning ability and general experience.

Option 1

Junk food is available in school cafeterias and school vending machines, and the cafeteria menus do not encourage the best of eating habits. But good education should include good examples as well as classwork. Schools should practice what they preach about a healthy diet and stop providing junk food.

Option 2

The sale of handguns to private citizens should be banned throughout the United States. It is true that the Constitution guarantees the right to bear arms, but that does not necessarily mean any type of arms. Some weapons, including handguns, are simply too dangerous to be legal.

Option 3

Many of today's young people are mainly concerned with prestigious careers, making money, and owning things. It seems we no longer teach the benefits of spending time and money to help the community, the country, or the world. Our country can strengthen these human values and improve the world by requiring young people to spend a year working in some type of community service.

■ Writing Assignment 6

In this argumentation essay, you will write with a specific purpose, for a specific audience.

Option 1:   Your town is one of the few in the state that hasn't developed a recycling program. Write a speech to give at a city council meeting in which you argue for establishing a local recycling program. Include in your speech the environmental benefits of recycling. And, since we are more likely to persuade others of something if they feel they will benefit, note also how the town will benefit economically and otherwise.

Option 2:   You'd like to live in a big city, but your spouse or parent refuses to budge from the suburbs. Write him or her a letter in which you argue the advantages of city life. Since the success of your argument will depend to some degree on how well you overcome the other person's objections to city life, be sure to address those as well. Use specific, colorful examples wherever possible.

Option 3:   Write a letter to the editor of your local newspaper, responding to an issue that was discussed in a recent editorial. Agree or disagree with the position taken by the paper, and provide several short paragraphs of supporting evidence for your position. Actually send your letter to the newspaper. Turn in a copy to your instructor, with the editorial you responded to.

■ Writing Assignment 7

Write an argumentation paper in which you use research findings to help support one of the twelve statements in the activity on pages 226–227. Research the topic in one or both of these ways:

- Look up the topic in the subject section of your library book file. (You may want to review pages 269–271 of "Using the Library.") Subject headings might include *Birth control, Materialism, Day care, Marriage contracts, Animal rights, Advertising, Smoking, Retirement,* and *Terrorism.* Select books that seem likely to give you information about your topic. Then find the books in the library stacks.
- Look up the topic in recent issues of *Magazine Index* or *Readers' Guide to Periodical Literature.* (Again, you may want to review "Using the Library" first.) Try some of the same headings noted above. Select articles that appear most likely to provide information on your topic. Then see if you can find some of these articles in your library's magazine storage area.

Reading about your topic will help you think about it. See if you can organize your paper in the form of three reasons that support the topic. Put these reasons into a scratch outline, and use it as a guide. Here is an example:

Prayer should not be allowed in the public schools:
a. Children who are not religious will feel excluded.
b. Children may still pray silently whenever they please.
c. Not all schools and teachers would keep prayer nondenominational.

Note that statistical information, results of studies, and advice from experts may all help develop supporting reasons for your thesis. Do not hesitate to cite such information in a limited way; it helps make your argument more objective and compelling.

■ **Writing Assignment 8:
Writing about a Reading Selection**

Read the selection titled "College Lectures: Is Anybody Listening?" on pages 641–643. Notice how the author gives reasons *against* lectures and *for* interactive classes. Then write an essay in which you try to persuade your readers that a particular classroom activity, method, or policy is good or bad by presenting reasons for or against it. You may wish, for instance, to argue for or against one of the following:

> Weekly quizzes
> Grades
> Evaluations instead of grades
> Class discussions
> Mandatory attendance

Choose a subject for which you can find three strong reasons pro or con. Each of your reasons or points will form a topic sentence for one supporting paragraph. Following, for example, is a brief outline for an essay persuading readers of the benefits of weekly quizzes. Each of the three reasons is a topic sentence for one supporting paragraph.

> Thesis: Weekly quizzes can be a useful part of students' education.
> 1. They help motivate students to keep up with classwork.
> 2. They give students frequent feedback on their work.
> 3. They give instructors frequent insight into students' progress.

Develop your supporting paragraphs by explaining each topic sentence, using examples to illustrate your points.

PART THREE

SPECIAL
SKILLS

TAKING
ESSAY
EXAMS

Essay exams are perhaps the most common type of writing you will do in school. They include one or more questions to which you must respond in detail, writing your answers in a clear, well-organized manner. Many students have trouble with essay exams because they do not realize there is a sequence to follow that will help them do well on such tests. This section describes five basic steps needed to prepare adequately for an essay test and to take the test. It is assumed, however, that you are already doing two essential things: first, attending class regularly and taking notes on what happens in class; second, reading your textbook and other assignments and taking notes on them. If you are *not* consistently going to class, reading your text, and taking notes in both cases, you are likely to have trouble with essay exams and other tests as well.

To write an effective exam essay, follow these five steps:

Step 1: Anticipate ten probable questions.

Step 2: Prepare and memorize an informal outline answer for each question.

Step 3: Look at the exam carefully and do several things.

Step 4: Prepare a brief, informal outline before writing your essay answer.

Step 5: Write a clear, well-organized essay.

The following pages explain and illustrate these steps.

STEP 1: ANTICIPATE TEN PROBABLE QUESTIONS

Because exam time is limited, the instructor can give you only several questions to answer. He or she will, reasonably, focus on questions dealing with the most important areas of the subject. You can probably guess most of them.

Go through your class notes with a colored pen and mark off those areas where your instructor has spent a good deal of time. The more time spent on any one area, the better the chance you will get an essay question on it. If the instructor spent a week talking about present-day changes in the traditional family structure, or the importance of the carbon molecule, or the advantages of capitalism, or key early figures in the development of psychology as a science, you can reasonably expect that you will get a question on the emphasized area.

In both your class notes and your textbooks, pay special attention to definitions and examples and to basic lists of items (enumerations). Enumerations in particular are often a key to essay questions. For instance, if your instructor spoke at length about causes of the Great Depression, effects of water pollution, or advantages of capitalism, you should probably expect a question such as ''What were the causes of the Great Depression?'' or ''What are the effects of water pollution?'' or ''What are the advantages of capitalism?''

If your instructor has given you study guides, look for probable essay questions there. (Some instructors choose essay questions from those listed in a study guide.) Look for clues to essay questions on any short quizzes that you may have been given. Finally, consider very carefully any review that the instructor provides. Always write down such reviews—your instructor has often made up the test or is making it up at the time of the review and is likely to give you valuable hints about it. Take advantage of them! Note also that if the instructor does not offer to provide a review, do not hesitate to *ask* for one in a friendly way. Essay questions are likely to come from areas the instructor may mention.

An Illustration of Step 1

A psychology class was given one day to prepare for an essay exam on stress—a subject that had been covered in class and comprised a chapter in the textbook for the course. One student, Mark, read carefully through his class notes and the textbook chapter. On the basis of the headings, major enumerations, and definitions he noted, he decided that there were five likely essay questions:

1. What are the common sources of stress?
2. What are the types of conflict?
3. What are the defense mechanisms that people use to cope with stress?
4. What effects can stress have on people?
5. What are the characteristics of the well-adjusted person?

STEP 2: PREPARE AND MEMORIZE AN INFORMAL OUTLINE ANSWER FOR EACH QUESTION

Write out each question you have made up and, under it, list the main points that need to be discussed. Put important supporting information in parentheses after each main point. You now have an informal outline that you can memorize.

Pick out a *key word* in each point, and then create a *catchphrase* to help you remember the key words.

Note: If you have spelling problems, make up a list of words you might have to spell in writing your answers. For example, if you are having a psychology test on the principles of learning, you might want to study such terms as *conditioning, reinforcement, Pavlov, reflex, stimulus,* and so on.

An Illustration of Step 2

After identifying the likely questions on the exam, Mark made up an outline answer for each of the questions. For example, here is the outline answer that he made up for the first question:

Common sources of stress:
1. (Pressure) (internal and external)
2. (Anxiety) (sign of internal conflict)
3. (Frustration) (can't reach desired goal)
4. (Conflict) (three types of approach-avoidance)

   P A F C (People are funny creatures.)

Activity

See whether you can complete the following explanation of what Mark has done in preparing for the essay question.

First, Mark wrote down the heading and then numbered the sources of stress under it. Also, in parentheses beside each point he added _____

_____ . Then he circled the four key words, and he wrote down

the first _____ of each word underneath his outline. Mark then used the first letter in each key word to make up a catchphrase that he could

easily remember. Finally, he _____ himself over and over until he could recall all four of the sources of stress that the first letters stood for. He also made sure that he recalled the supporting material that went with each idea.

STEP 3: LOOK AT THE EXAM CAREFULLY AND DO SEVERAL THINGS

1   Get an overview of the exam by reading *all* the questions on the test.

2   Note *direction words* (*compare, illustrate, list,* and so on) for each question. Be sure to write the kind of answer that each question requires. For example, if a question says "illustrate," do not "compare." The list on the opposite page will help clarify the distinctions among various direction words.

3   Budget your time. Write in the margin the number of minutes you should spend for each essay. For example, if you have three essays worth an equal number of points and a one-hour time limit, figure twenty minutes for each one. Make sure you are not left with only a couple of minutes to do a high-point essay.

4   Start with the easiest question. Getting a good answer down on paper will help build up your confidence and momentum. Number your answers plainly so your instructor knows what question you are answering first.

An Illustration of Step 3

When Mark received the exam, the question was, "Describe the four common sources of stress in our lives." Mark circled the direction word *describe,* which meant that he should explain in detail each of the four causes of stress. He also jotted a "30" in the margin when the instructor said that students would have a half hour to write the answer.

Activity

Complete the short matching quiz below. It will help you review the meanings of some of the direction words listed on the opposite page.

1. List _____
2. Contrast _____
3. Define _____
4. Summarize _____
5. Describe _____

a. Tell in detail about something.
b. Give a series of points and number them 1, 2, 3, etc.
c. Give a condensed account of the main points.
d. Show differences between two things.
e. Give the normal meaning of a term.

Direction Words

Term	Meaning
Compare	Show similarities between things.
Contrast	Show differences between things.
Criticize	Give the positive and negative points of a subject as well as evidence for those positions.
Define	Give the formal meaning of a term.
Describe	Tell in detail about something.
Diagram	Make a drawing and label it.
Discuss	Give details and, if relevant, the positive and negative points of a subject as well as evidence for those positions.
Enumerate	List points and number them 1, 2, 3, etc.
Evaluate	Give the positive and negative points of a subject as well as your judgment about which outweighs the other and why.
Illustrate	Explain by giving examples.
Interpret	Explain the meaning of something.
Justify	Give reasons for something.
List	Give a series of points and number them 1, 2, 3, etc.
Outline	Give the main points and important secondary points. Put main points at the margin and indent secondary points under the main points. Relationships may also be described with logical symbols, as follows:

    1. _____

        a. _____

        b. _____

    2. _____

Term	Meaning
Prove	Show to be true by giving facts or reasons.
Relate	Show connections among things.
State	Give the main points.
Summarize	Give a condensed account of the main points.
Trace	Describe the development or history of a subject.

STEP 4: PREPARE A BRIEF, INFORMAL OUTLINE BEFORE WRITING YOUR ESSAY ANSWER

Use the margin of the exam or a separate piece of scratch paper to jot down quickly, as they occur to you, the main points you want to discuss in each answer. Then decide in what order you want to present these points in your response. Put 1 in front of the first item, 2 beside the second, and so on. You now have an informal outline to guide you as you answer your essay question.

If there is a question on the exam which is similar to the questions you anticipated and outlined at home, quickly write down the catchphrase that calls back the content of the outline. Below the catchphrase, write the key words represented by each letter in the catchphrase. The key words, in turn, will remind you of the concepts they represent. If you have prepared properly, this step will take only a minute or so, and you will have before you the guide you need to write a focused, supported, organized answer.

An Illustration of Step 4

Mark immediately wrote down his catchphrase, ''People are funny creatures.'' He next jotted down the first letters in his catchphrase and then the key words that went with each letter. He then filled in several key details and was ready to write his essay answer. Here is what his brief outline looked like:

People are funny creatures.

P   Pressure (internal and external)
A   Anxiety (internal conflict)
F   Frustration (prevented from reaching goal)
C   Conflict (approach-avoidance)

STEP 5: WRITE A CLEAR, WELL-ORGANIZED ESSAY

If you have followed steps 1 through 4, you have done all the preliminary work needed to write an effective essay. Now, be sure not to wreck your chance of getting a good grade by writing carelessly. Keep in mind the principles of good writing: unity, support, coherence, and clear, error-free sentences.

First, start your essay with a sentence that clearly states what your answer will be about. Then make sure that everything in your paper relates to your opening statement.

Second, though you must obviously take time limitations into account, provide as much support as possible for each of your main points.

Third, use transitions to guide your reader through your answer. Words such as *first, next, then, however,* and *finally* make it easy to follow your thought.

Last, leave time to proofread your essay for sentence-skills mistakes you may have made while you concentrated on writing your answer. Look for words omitted, miswritten, or misspelled (if it is possible, bring a dictionary with you); for awkward phrasings or misplaced punctuation marks; and for whatever else may prevent the reader from understanding your thought. Cross out any mistakes and make your corrections neatly above the errors. If you want to change or add to some point, insert an asterisk at the appropriate spot, put another asterisk at the bottom of the page, and add the corrected or additional material there.

An Illustration of Step 5

Read Mark's answer, reproduced below, and then do the activity that follows.

There are four common sources of stress in our lives. The first one is pressure, which can be internal or external. Internal pressure occurs when a person tries to live up to his or her own goals and standards. This kind of pressure can help (when a person strives to be a better musician, for instance) or hurt (as when someone tries to reach impossible standards of beauty). External pressure occurs when people must compete, deal with rapid change, or cope with outside demands. Another source of stress is anxiety. People who are ~~anxous~~ *anxious* often don't know why they feel this way. Some psychologists think anxiety comes from some internal conflict, like feeling angry and trying hard to repress this ~~angry feeling~~ anger. A third source of stress is frustration, which occurs when people are prevented from reaching goals or obtaining certain needs. For example, a woman may do poorly on an *important* exam because she has a bad cold. She feels angry and frustrated because she could not reach her goal of an A or B grade. The most common source of stress is conflict. Conflict results when a person is faced with two incompatible ~~goals~~ *desires.* The person may want both goals (a demanding career and motherhood, for instance). This is called approach/approach. Or a person may want to avoid both choices (avoidance/avoidance). Or a person may be both attracted to and repelled by a desire (as a woman *who* wants to marry a gambler). This is approach/avoidance.

Activity 1

The following sentences comment on Mark's essay. Fill in the missing word or words in each case.

1. Mark begins with a sentence that clearly states what his paper _____ _____ . Always begin with such a clear statement!

2. Notice the _____ that Mark made when writing and proofreading his paper. He neatly crossed out miswritten or unwanted words, and he used insertion signs (∧) to add omitted words.

3. The four signal words that Mark used to guide his readers, and himself, through the main points of his answer are _____, _____ , _____ , and _____ .

Activity 2

1. Make up five questions you might be expected to answer on an essay exam for a course in a social or physical science (sociology, psychology, biology, or other).

2. For each of the five questions, make up an outline answer comparable to the one on anxiety.

3. Finally, write a full essay answer, in complete sentences, to one of the questions. Your outline will serve as your guide.

Be sure to begin your essay with a statement that makes clear the direction of your answer. An example might be, "The six major defense mechanisms are defined and illustrated below." If you are explaining in detail the different causes of, reasons for, or characteristics of something, you may want to develop each point in a separate paragraph. For example, if you were answering a question in sociology about the primary functions of the family unit, you could start with the statement "There are three primary functions of the family unit," and go on to develop and describe each function in a separate paragraph.

You will turn in the essay answer to your English instructor, who will evaluate it using the standards for effective writing applied to your other written assignments.

WRITING
A SUMMARY

At some point in a course, your instructor may ask you to write a summary of a book, article, TV show, or the like. In a *summary* (also referred to as a *précis* or an *abstract*), you reduce material in an original work to its main points and key supporting details. Unlike an outline, however, a summary does not use symbols such as I, A, 1, 2, etc., to indicate the relations among parts of the original material.

A summary may consist of a single word, a phrase, several sentences, or one or more paragraphs. The length of any summary you prepare will depend on your instructor's expectations and the length of the original work. Most often, you will be asked to write a summary of one or more paragraphs.

Writing a summary brings together a number of important reading, study, and writing skills. To condense the original assigned material, you must preview, read, evaluate, organize, and perhaps outline it. Summarizing, then, can be a real aid to understanding; you must "get inside" the material and realize fully what is being said before you can reduce its meaning to a few words.

HOW TO SUMMARIZE AN ARTICLE

To write a summary of an article, follow the steps described below. If the assigned material is a TV show or film, adapt the suggestions accordingly.

1   Take a few minutes to preview the work. You can preview an article in a magazine by taking a quick look at the following:

   a   *Title.* A title often summarizes what an article is about. Think about the title for a minute, and about how it may condense the meaning of the article.

   b   *Subtitle.* A subtitle, if given, is a short summary appearing under or next to the title. For example, in a *Newsweek* article entitled ''Growing Old, Feeling Young,'' the following caption appeared: ''Not only are Americans living longer, they are staying active longer—and their worst enemy is not nature, but the myths and prejudices about growing old.'' In short, the subtitle, the caption, or any other words in large print under or next to the title often provide a quick insight into the meaning of an article.

   c   *First and last several paragraphs.* In the first several paragraphs, the author may introduce you to the subject and state the purpose of the article. In the last several paragraphs, the writer may present conclusions or a summary. These previews or summaries can give you a quick overview of what the entire article is about.

   d   *Other items.* Note any heads or subheads that appear in the article. They often provide clues to the article's main points and give an immediate sense of what each section is about. Look carefully at any pictures, charts, or diagrams that accompany the article. Page space in a magazine or journal is limited, and such visual aids are generally used only when they help illustrate important points in the article. Note any words or phrases set off in *italic type* or **boldface print;** such words have probably been emphasized because they deal with important points in the article.

2   Read the article for all you can understand the first time through. Do not slow down or turn back. Check or otherwise mark main points and key supporting details. Pay special attention to all the items noted in the preview. Also, look for definitions, examples, and enumerations (lists of items), as they often indicate key ideas. You can also identify important points by turning any heads into questions and reading to find the answers to the questions.

3   Go back and reread more carefully the areas you have identified as most important. Also, focus on other key points you may have missed in your first reading.

4   Take notes on the material. Concentrate on getting down the main ideas and the key supporting points.

5   Prepare the first draft of your summary, keeping these points in mind:

   a   Identify at the start of the summary the title and author of the work. Include in parentheses the date of publication. For example, ''In 'Parents, Take Heart' (*Newsweek,* April 8, 1996), Laura Shapiro states . . .''

   b   Do not write an overly detailed summary. Remember that the purpose of a summary is to reduce the original work to its main points and essential supporting details.

   c   Express the main points and key supporting details in your own words. Do not imitate the style of the original work.

   d   Quote from the material only to illustrate key points. Also, limit your quotations. A one-paragraph summary should not contain more than one or two quoted sentences.

   e   Preserve the balance and proportion of the original work. If the original devoted 70 percent of its space to one idea and only 30 percent to another, your summary should reflect that emphasis.

   f   Revise your first draft, paying attention to the principles of effective writing (*unity, support, coherence,* and *clear, error-free sentences*) explained in Part One.

   g   Write the final draft of the paper.

A Model Summary of an Article

Here is a model summary of a magazine article.

In "Crime Time Bomb" (U.S. News & World Report, March 25, 1996), Ted Gest reports that there is a growing epidemic of drug use, weapons violations, and murders by juveniles. Cities, states, and Congress are seeking the right balance of punishment and prevention to combat the problem. Conservatives demand that the most violent offenders be tried as adults and given longer prison terms. Liberals insist that the answer lies with prevention programs. In the meanwhile, criminologists have concluded that trying the most violent teens as adults doesn't work as expected: Prison terms of young defendants tried in adult courts tend to be shorter. In addition, Gest writes, a new study shows that "youths tried as adults commit even more crimes after release than do those who remain in the juvenile system." Now some communities are trying a combination of the preventive and tough approaches, including escalating punishments for teens who continue to commit crimes. Although some programs show promise, juvenile crime appears to be growing faster than solutions. Gest concludes that "it may take an even greater bloodbath to force effective crime solutions to the top of the nation's agenda."

Activity 1

Write an essay-length summary of the following article. Include a short introductory paragraph that states the thesis of the article. Then summarize in your three supporting paragraphs the three important areas in which study skills can be useful. Your conclusion might be a single sentence restating the thesis.

POWER LEARNING

Jill had not done as well in high school as she had hoped. Since college involved even more work, it was no surprise that she didn't do better there. 1

The reason for her so-so performance was not a lack of effort. She attended most of her classes and read her textbooks. And she never missed handing in any assignment, even though it often meant staying up late the night before homework was due. Still, she just got by in her classes. Before long, she came to the conclusion she simply couldn't do any better. 2

Then one day, one of her instructors said something to make her think otherwise. "You can probably build some sort of house by banging a few boards together," he said. "But if you want a sturdy home, you'll have to use the right techniques and tools. Building carefully takes work, but it gets better results. The same can be said of your education. There are no shortcuts, but there are some proven study skills that can really help. If you don't use them, you may end up with a pretty flimsy education." 3

Jill signed up for a study-skills course and found out a crucial fact—that learning how to learn is the key to success in school. There are certain dependable skills that have made the difference between disappointment and success for generations of students. These techniques won't free you from work, but they will make your work far more productive. They include three important areas: time control, classroom note-taking, and textbook study. 4

TIME CONTROL

Success in college depends on time control. *Time control* means that you deliberately organize and plan your time, instead of letting it drift by. Planning means that you should never be faced with a night-before-the-test "cram" session or an overdue term paper. 5

There are three steps involved in time control. *First,* you should prepare a large monthly calendar. Buy a calendar with a large white block around each date, or make one yourself. At the beginning of the college semester, circle important dates on this calendar. Circle the days on which tests are scheduled; circle the days papers are due. This calendar can also be used to schedule study plans. You can jot down your plans for each day at the beginning of the week. An alternative method would be to make plans for each day the night before. On Tuesday night, for example, you might write down "Read Chapter 5 in psychology" in the Wednesday block. Hang this calendar where you will see it every day—your kitchen, your bedroom, even your bathroom! 6

The *second step* in time control is to have a weekly study schedule for the   7
semester—a chart that covers all the days of the week and all the waking hours in
each day.

Time	Mon.	Tues.	Wed.	Thurs.	Fri.	Sat.	Sun.
6:00 A.M.							
7:00	B	B	B	B	B		
8:00	Math	STUDY	Math	STUDY	Math		
9:00	STUDY	Biology	STUDY	Biology	STUDY	Job	
10:00	Psychology	↓	Psychology	↓	Psychology		
11:00	STUDY	English		English			
12:00	L		L	↓	L	↓	

Above is part of one student's schedule. On your own schedule, mark in all the fixed
hours in each day—hours for meals, classes, job (if any), and travel time. Next, mark
in time blocks that you can *realistically* use for study each day. Depending on the
number of courses you are taking and the demands of the courses, you may want to
block off five, ten, or even twenty or more hours of study time a week. Keep in mind
that you should not block off time for study that you do not truly intend to use for
study. Otherwise, your schedule will be a meaningless gimmick. Also, remember that
you should allow time for ''rest and relaxation.'' You will be happiest, and able to
accomplish the most, when you have time for both work and play.

The *third step* in time control is to make a daily or weekly ''to do'' list. This   8
may be the most valuable time control method you ever use. On this list, you write
down the things you need to do for the following day or the following week. If you
choose to write a weekly list, do it on Sunday night. If you choose to write a daily
list, do it the night before. Here is part of one student's daily list:

> *To Do*   *Tuesday*
>
> *1. Review biology notes before class
> *2. Proofread English paper due today
> 3. See Dick about game on Friday
> *4. Gas for car
> 5. Read next chapter of psychology text

You may use a three- by five-inch note pad or a small spiral-bound notebook for this list. Carry the list around with you during the day. Always concentrate on doing first the most important items on your list. To make the best use of your time, mark high-priority items with an asterisk and give them precedence over low-priority items. For instance, you may find yourself wondering what to do after dinner on Thursday evening. Among the items on your list are ''Clean inside of car'' and ''Review chapter for math quiz.'' It is obviously more important for you to review your notes at this point; you can clean the car some other time. As you complete items on your ''to do'' list, cross them out. Do not worry about unfinished items. They can be rescheduled. You will still be accomplishing a great deal and making more effective use of your time.

CLASSROOM NOTE-TAKING

One of the most important single things you can do to perform well in a college course is to take effective class notes. The following hints should help you become a better note-taker.   9

First, attend class faithfully. Your alternatives—reading the text, reading someone   10
else's notes, or both—cannot substitute for the experience of hearing ideas in person as someone presents them to you. Also, in class lectures and discussions, your instructor typically presents and develops the main ideas and facts of the course—the ones you will be expected to know on exams.

Another valuable hint is to make use of abbreviations while taking notes. Using   11
abbreviations saves time when you are trying to get down a great deal of information. Abbreviate terms that recur frequently in a lecture and put a key to your abbreviations at the top of your notes. For example, in sociology class, *eth* could stand for *ethnocentrism;* in a psychology class, STM could stand for *short-term memory.* (When a lecture is over, you may want to go back and write out the terms you have abbreviated.) In addition, abbreviate words that often recur in any lecture. For instance, use *e* for *example; def* for *definition; info* for *information;* + for *and*; and so on. If you use the same abbreviations all the time, you will soon develop a kind of personal shorthand that makes taking notes much easier.

A third hint for taking notes is to be on the lookout for signals of importance.   12
Write down whatever your instructor puts on the board. If he or she takes the time to put material on the board, it is probably important, and the chances are good that it will come up later on exams. Always write down definitions and enumerations. Enumerations are lists of items. They are signaled in such ways as: ''The four steps in the process are . . .''; ''There were three reasons for . . .''; ''The two effects were . . .''; ''Five characteristics of . . . ''; and so on. In your notes, always number (1, 2, 3, etc.) such enumerations in your notes. They will help you understand relationships among ideas and organize the material of the lecture. Watch for emphasis words—words your instructor may use to indicate that something is important. Examples of such words are ''This is an important reason . . .''; ''A point that will keep coming up later . . .''; ''The chief cause was . . .''; ''The basic idea here is . . .''; and so on.

Always write down the important statements announced by these and other emphasis words. Finally, if your instructor repeats a point, you can assume that it is important. You might put an R for *repeated* in the margin, so that later you will know that your instructor stressed it.

Next, be sure to write down the instructor's examples and mark them with an *e*. The examples help you understand abstract points. If you do not write them down, you are likely to forget them later, when they are needed to help make sense of an idea. 13

Also, be sure to write down the connections between ideas. Too many students merely copy terms the instructor puts on the board. They forget that, as time passes, the details that serve as connecting bridges between ideas quickly fade. You should, then, write down the relationships and connections in class. That way you'll have them to help tie together your notes later on. 14

Review your notes as soon as possible after class. You must make them as clear as possible while they are fresh in your mind. A day later may be too late, because forgetting sets in very quickly. Make sure that punctuation is clear, that all words are readable and correctly spelled, and that unfinished sentences are completed (or at least marked off so that you can check your notes with another student's). Add clarifying or connecting comments wherever necessary. Make sure important ideas are clearly marked. Improve the organization if necessary, so that you can see at a glance main points and relationships among them. 15

Finally, try in general to get down a written record of each class. You must do this because forgetting begins almost immediately. Studies have shown that within two weeks you are likely to have forgotten 80 percent or more of what you have heard. And in four weeks you are lucky if 5 percent remains! This is so crucial that it bears repeating: To guard against the relentlessness of forgetting, it is absolutely essential that you write down what you hear in class. Later on you can concentrate on working to understand fully and to remember the ideas that have been presented in class. And the more complete your notes are at this time of study, the more you are likely to learn. 16

TEXTBOOK STUDY

In many college courses, success means being able to read and study a textbook skillfully. For many students, unfortunately, textbooks are heavy going. After an hour or two of study, the textbook material is as formless and as hard to understand as ever. But there is a way to attack even the most difficult textbook and make sense of it. Use a sequence in which you preview a chapter, mark it, take notes on it, and then study the notes. 17

Previewing

Previewing a selection is an important first step to understanding. Taking the time to preview a section or chapter can give you a bird's-eye view of the way the material is organized. You will have a sense of where you are beginning, what you will cover, and where you will end. 18

There are several steps in previewing a selection. First, study the title. The title   19
is the shortest possible summary of a selection and will often tell you the limits of
the material you will cover. For example, the title "FDR and the Supreme Court"
tells you to expect a discussion of President Roosevelt's dealings with the Court.
You know that you will probably not encounter any material dealing with FDR's
foreign policies or personal life. Next, read over quickly the first and last paragraphs
of the selection; these may contain important introductions to, and summaries of, the
main ideas. Then examine briefly the headings and subheadings in the selection.
Together, the headings and subheadings are a mini-outline of what you are reading.
Headings are often main ideas or important concepts in capsule form; subheadings
are breakdowns of ideas within main areas. Finally, read the first sentence of some
paragraphs, look for words set off in **boldface** or *italics,* and look at pictures or
diagrams. After you have previewed a selection in this way, you should have a good
general sense of the material to be read.

Marking

You should mark a textbook selection at the same time that you read it through   20
carefully. Use a felt-tip highlighter to shade material that seems important, or use a
ballpoint pen and put symbols in the margin next to the material: stars, checks, or
NB (*nota bene,* Latin for "note well"). What to mark is not as mysterious as some
students believe. You should try to find main ideas by looking for clues: definitions
and examples, enumerations, and emphasis words.

1   *Definitions and examples:* Definitions are often among the most important ideas   21
in a selection. They are particularly significant in introductory courses in almost
any subject area, where much of your learning involves mastering the specialized
vocabulary of that subject. In a sense, you are learning the "language" of psychology or business or whatever the subject might be.

Most definitions are abstract, and so they usually are followed by one or   22
more examples to help clarify their meaning. Always mark off definitions and at
least one example that makes a definition clear to you. In a psychology text, for
example, we are told that "rationalization is an attempt to reduce anxiety by
deciding that you have not really been frustrated." Several examples follow,
among them: "A young man, frustrated because he was rejected when he asked
for a date, convinces himself that the girl is not very attractive or interesting."

2   *Enumerations:* Enumerations are lists of items (causes, reasons, types, and so   23
on) that are numbered 1, 2, 3, . . . or that could easily be numbered. They are
often signaled by addition words. Many of the paragraphs in this book, for instance,
use words like *First of all, Another, In addition,* and *Finally* to signal items in a
series. Other textbooks also use this very common and effective organizational
method.

3   *Emphasis words:* Emphasis words tell you that an idea is important. Common   24
emphasis words include phrases such as *a major event, a key feature, the chief
factor, important to note, above all,* and *most of all.* Here is an example: "The
most significant contemporary use of marketing is its application to nonbusiness
areas, such as political parties."

Note-Taking

Next, you should take notes. Go through the chapter a second time, rereading the   25
most important parts. Try to write down the main ideas in a simple outline form. For
example, in taking notes on a psychology selection, you might write down the heading
"Kinds of Defense Mechanisms." Below the heading you would number and describe
each kind and give an example of each.

> Defense Mechanisms
> a. Definition: unconscious attempts to reduce anxiety
> b. Kinds:
>   (1) Rationalization: An attempt to reduce anxiety by deciding that
>   you have not really been frustrated
>   Example: A man turned down for a date decides that the woman
>   was not worth going out with anyway
>   (2) Projection: Projecting onto other people motives or thoughts of
>   one's own
>   Example: A wife who wants to have an affair accuses her husband
>   of having one

Studying Notes

To study your notes, use the method of repeated self-testing. For example, look at   26
the heading "Kinds of Defense Mechanisms" and say to yourself, "What are the
kinds of defense mechanisms?" When you can recite them, then say to yourself,
"What is rationalization?" "What is an example of rationalization?" Then ask
yourself, "What is projection?" "What is an example of projection?" After you
learn each section, review it, and then go on to the next section.

Do not simply read your notes; keep looking away and seeing if you can recite   27
them to yourself. This self-testing is the key to effective learning.

Summary: Textbook Study

In summary, remember this sequence in order to deal with a textbook: previewing,   28
marking, taking notes, studying the notes. Approaching a textbook in this methodical
way will give you very positive results. You will no longer feel bogged down in a
swamp of words, unable to figure out what you are supposed to know. Instead, you
will understand exactly what you have to do, and how to go about doing it.

Take a minute now to evaluate your own study habits. Do you practice many of the   29
above skills in order to take effective classroom notes, control your time, and learn
from your textbooks? If not, perhaps you should. The skills are not magic, but they
are too valuable to ignore. Use them carefully and consistently, and they will make
academic success possible for you. Try them, and you won't need convincing.

Activity 2

Write an essay-length summary of a broadcast of the CBS television show *Sixty Minutes*. In your first sentence, include the date of the show. For example, "The December 8, 1995, broadcast of CBS's *Sixty Minutes* dealt with three subjects most people would find of interest. The first segment of the show centered on . . . ; the second segment examined . . . ; the final segment discussed. . . ." Be sure to use parallel form in describing the three segments of the show. Then summarize each segment in the three supporting paragraphs that follow.

Activity 3

Write an essay-length summary of a cover story of interest to you in a recent issue of *Time, Newsweek,* or *U.S. News & World Report.*

HOW TO SUMMARIZE A BOOK

To write a summary of a book, first preview the book by briefly looking at:

1   *Title.* A title is often the shortest possible summary of what a book is about. Think about the title and how it may summarize the whole book.

2   *Table of contents.* The contents will tell you the number of chapters in the book and the subject of each chapter. Use the contents to get a general sense of how the book is organized. You should also note the number of pages in each chapter. If thirty pages are devoted to one episode or idea and an average of fifteen pages to other episodes or ideas, you should probably give more space to the contents of the longer chapter in your summary.

3   *Preface.* Here you will probably find out why the author wrote the book. Also, the preface may summarize the main ideas developed in the book and may describe briefly how the book is organized.

4   *First and last chapters.* In these chapters, the author may preview or review important ideas and themes developed in the book.

5   *Other items.* Note how the author has used headings and subheadings to organize information in the book. Check the opening and closing paragraphs of each chapter to see if they contain introductions or summaries. Look quickly at charts, diagrams, and pictures in the book, since they are probably there to illustrate key points. Note any special features (index, glossary, appendixes) that may appear at the end of the book.

Next, adapt steps 2 through 5 for summarizing an article on pages 248–249.

Activity

Write an essay-length summary of a book you have read.

WRITING
A REPORT

Each semester, you will probably be asked by at least one instructor to read a book or an article and to write a paper recording your response to the material. In these reports or reaction papers, your instructor will most likely expect you to do two things: *summarize the material* and *detail your reaction to it*. The following pages explain both parts of a report.

PART 1 OF A REPORT: A SUMMARY OF THE WORK

To develop the first part of a report, do the following. (An example follows, on page 259.)

1 Identify the author and title of the work and include in parentheses the publisher and publication date. With magazines, give the date of publication.

2 Write an informative summary of the material. Condense the content of the work by highlighting its main points and key supporting points. (See pages 247–256 for a complete discussion of summarizing techniques.) Use direct quotations from the work to illustrate important ideas.

   Do *not* discuss in great detail any single aspect of the work while neglecting to mention other equally important points. Summarize the material so that the reader gets a general sense of *all* key aspects of the original work. Also, keep the summary objective and factual. Do not include in the first part of the paper your personal reaction to the work; your subjective impression will form the basis of the second part of the paper.

257

PART 2 OF A REPORT: YOUR REACTION TO THE WORK

To develop the second part of a report, do the following:

1 Focus on any or all of the questions that follow. (Check with your instructors to see if they want you to emphasize specific points.)

 a How is the assigned work related to ideas and concerns discussed in the course? For example, what points made in the course textbook, class discussions, or lectures are treated more fully in the work?

 b How is the work related to problems in our present-day world?

 c How is the work related to your life, experiences, feelings, and ideas? For instance, what emotions did it arouse in you? Did it increase your understanding of an issue or change your perspective?

2 Evaluate the merit of the work: the importance of its points; its accuracy, completeness, and organization; and so on. You should also indicate here whether you would recommend the work to others, and why.

POINTS TO KEEP IN MIND WHEN WRITING A REPORT

Here are some important matters to consider as you prepare a report.

1 Apply the four basic standards of effective writing (unity, support, coherence, and clear, error-free sentences).

 a Make sure each major paragraph presents and then develops a single main point. For example, in the model report that follows, a paragraph summarizes the book, and the three paragraphs that follow detail three separate reactions that the student writer had. The student then closes the report with a short concluding paragraph.

 b Support with specific reasons and details any general points or attitudes you express. Statements such as ''I agreed with many ideas in this article'' and ''I found the book very interesting'' are meaningless without specific evidence that shows why you feel as you do. Look at the model report to see how the main point or topic sentence of each paragraph is developed by specific supporting evidence.

 c Organize the material in the paper. Follow the basic *plan of organization* already described: an introduction, a summary of one or more paragraphs, a reaction of two or more paragraphs, and a conclusion. Use *transitions* to connect the parts of the paper.

 d Proofread the paper for grammar, mechanics, punctuation, and word use.

2   Document quotations from all works by placing the page number in parentheses after the quoted material (see the model report). You may use quotations in the summary and reaction parts of the paper, but do not overrely on them. Use them only to emphasize key ideas.

A MODEL REPORT

Here is a report written by a student in an introductory sociology course. Look at the paper closely to see how it follows the guidelines for report writing described in this chapter.

A Report on I Know Why the Caged Bird Sings

Introductory paragraph

In I Know Why the Caged Bird Sings (New York: Bantam Books, 1971), Maya Angelou tells the story of her earliest years. Angelou, a dancer, poet, and television producer as well as a writer, has continued her life story in three more volumes of autobiography. I Know Why the Caged Bird Sings is the start of Maya Angelou's story; in this book, she writes with crystal clarity about the pains and joys of being black in America.

PART 1: SUMMARY Topic sentence for summary paragraph

I Know Why the Caged Bird Sings covers Maya Angelou's life from age three to age sixteen. We first meet her as a gawky little girl in a white lady's cut-down lavender silk dress. She has forgotten the poem she had memorized for the Easter service, and all she can do is rush out of the church. At this point, Angelou is living in Stamps, Arkansas, with her grandmother and uncle. The town is heavily segregated: "People in Stamps used to say that the whites in our town were so prejudiced that a Negro couldn't buy vanilla ice cream" (40). Yet Angelou has some good things in her life: her adored older brother Bailey, her success in school, and her pride in her grandmother's quiet strength and importance in the black community. There is laughter, too, as when the preacher is interrupted in midsermon by an overly enthusiastic woman shouting, "Preach it, I say preach it!" The woman, in a frenzied rush of excitement, hits the preacher with her purse, making his false teeth fly out of his mouth and land at Angelou's feet. Shortly after this incident, Angelou and her brother are taken by her father to live in California with their mother. Here, at age eight, she is raped by her mother's boyfriend, who is mysteriously murdered after receiving only a suspended sentence for his crime. She returns, silent and withdrawn, to Stamps, where the gloom is broken when a friend of her mother introduces her to the magic of great books. Later, at age thirteen, Angelou returns to California. She learns how to dance. She runs away after a violent family fight and lives for a month in a junkyard. She becomes the first black female to get a job on the San Francisco streetcars. She graduates from high school eight months pregnant. And she survives.

PART 2:
REACTION

Topic
sentence
for first
reaction
paragraph

I was impressed with the vividness of Maya Angelou's writing style. For example, she describes the lazy dullness of her life in Stamps: "Weekdays revolved in a sameness wheel. They turned into themselves so steadily and inevitably that each seemed to be the original of yesterday's rough draft" (93). She also knows how to bring a scene to life, as when she describes her eighth-grade graduation. For months, she has been looking forward to this event, knowing she will be honored for her academic successes. She is even happy with her appearance: her hair has become pretty, and her yellow dress is a miracle of hand-sewing. But the ceremony is spoiled when the speaker—a white man—implies that the only success available to blacks is in athletics. Angelou remembers: "The man's dead words fell like bricks around the auditorium and too many settled in my belly. . . . The proud graduating class of 1940 had dropped their heads" (152). Later, Angelou uses a crystal-clear image to describe her father's mistress sewing: "She worked the thread through the flowered cloth as if she were sewing the torn ends of her life together" (208). With such vivid details and figures of speech, Maya Angelou recreates her life for her readers.

Topic
sentence
for second
reaction
paragraph

I also reacted strongly to the descriptions of injustices suffered by blacks two generations ago. I was as horrified as the seven-year-old Maya when some "powhitetrash" girls torment her dignified grandmother, calling her "Annie" and mimicking her mannerisms. In another incident, Mrs. Cullinan, Angelou's white employer, decides that Marguerite (Angelou's real name) is too difficult to pronounce and so renames her Mary. This loss of her name—a "hellish horror" (91)—is another humiliation suffered at white hands, and Angelou leaves Mrs. Cullinan's employ soon afterward. Later, Angelou encounters overt discrimination when a white dentist tells her grandmother, "Annie, my policy is I'd rather stick my hand in a dog's mouth than in a nigger's" (160)—and only slightly less obvious prejudice when the streetcar company refuses to accept her application for a conductor's job. We see Angelou over and over as the victim of a white society.

Topic
sentence
for third
reaction
paragraph

Although I was saddened to read about the injustices, I rejoiced in Angelou's triumphs. Angelou is thrilled when she hears the radio broadcast of Joe Louis' victory over Primo Carnera: "A Black boy. Some Black mother's son. He was the strongest man in the world" (114). She weeps with pride when the class valedictorian leads her and her fellow eighth-graders in singing the Negro National Anthem. And there are personal victories, too. One of these comes after her father has gotten drunk in a small Mexican town. Though she has never driven before, she manages to get her father into the car and drives fifty miles through the night as he lies intoxicated in the backseat. Finally, she rejoices in the birth of her son: "He was beautiful and mine. Totally mine. No one had bought him for me" (245). Angelou shows us, through these examples, that she is proud of her race—and of herself.

Concluding → I Know Why the Caged Bird Sings is a remarkable book. Angelou could have
paragraph   been just another casualty of race prejudice. Yet by using her intelligence,
sensitivity, and determination, she succeeds in spite of the odds against her. And
by writing with such power, she makes us share her defeats and joys. She also
teaches us a vital lesson: with strength and persistence, we can all escape our
cages—and sing our songs.

Activity 1

Read a magazine article that interests you. Then write a report on the article.
Include an introduction, a one-paragraph summary, a reaction (consisting of one
or more paragraphs), and a brief conclusion. You may, if you like, quote briefly
from the article. Be sure to enclose the words that you take from the article
in quotation marks and put the page number in parentheses at the end of the
quoted material.

Activity 2

Read a book suggested by your instructor. Then write a report on the book. Include
an introduction, a one-paragraph summary, a reaction consisting of one or more
paragraphs, and a brief conclusion. Make sure that each major paragraph in your
report develops a single main point. You may quote some sentences from the
book, but they should be only a small part of your report. When you quote
material, follow the directions in Activity 1 above.

WRITING
A RÉSUMÉ
AND
JOB APPLICATION
LETTER

When applying for a job through the mail, you should ordinarily send (1) a résumé and (2) a letter of application.

RÉSUMÉ

A *résumé* is a summary of your personal background and your qualifications for a job. It helps your potential employer see at a glance whether you are suited for a job opening. A sample job résumé follows.

SARAH BECKETT
27 Hawkins Road
Clarksboro, New Jersey 08020
609-723-2166

Professional objective	A challenging position in the computer technology field.
Education	1993 to present: Glassboro State College, Glassboro, New Jersey 08028
	Degree: B.S. (in June)

Major courses:
Computer Programming I and II
Basic Computer Languages
Introduction to Microprocessors
Communications Circuits and Systems
Word Processing Systems
Advanced Computer Technologies

Related courses:
College Math I and II
Trigonometry
Calculus I and II
Small Business Management
Business Law
Organizational Systems Management

Special school project

As part of a class project, I chaired a study group which advised a local business about the advantages of installing a computerized payroll system. We projected comparative cost figures, developed a time-sharing purchase plan, and prepared a budget. The fifteen-page report received the highest grade in the class.

Work experience

1993 to present: As a salesperson at Radio Shack, I am involved in sales, inventory control, repairs, and customer relations. I have designed a computer program that our store uses to demonstrate the Radio Shack TRS-80 microcomputer. This program, written in BASIC, demonstrates ways the TRS-80 can be used in the home and small businesses.

1991–1993: My temporary jobs included waitress, theater usher, and child care aide.

Skills

I am experienced in the following computer languages: PASCAL, BASIC, and COBOL. I have sales experience, am good with figures, relate easily to people, have initiative, and am dependable.

References

My references are available on request from Glassboro State College Placement Office, Glassboro, New Jersey 08028.

Points to Note about the Résumé

1 Your résumé, along with your letter of application, is your introduction to a potential employer. First impressions count, *so make the résumé neat!*

    a Type the résumé on good-quality letter (8½ by 11 inches) paper. If possible, use a word processor to prepare your résumé; if you don't have a word processor, you can use a résumé service listed in the yellow pages of the telephone directory.

    b Proofread *very carefully* for sentence-skills and spelling mistakes. A potential employer may regard such mistakes as signs of carelessness in your character. You might even want to get someone else to proofread the résumé for you. If you are working with a word processor, see if it has a "spell-check" feature.

    c Be brief and to the point: use only one page if possible.

    d Use a format like that of the model résumé (see also the variations described ahead). Balance your résumé on the page so that you have roughly the same margin on all sides.

    e Note that you should start with your most recent education or employment and work backward in time.

2 Your résumé should point up strengths, not weaknesses. Don't include "Special Training" if you have had none. Don't refer to your grade point average if it's a low C.

    On the other hand, include a main heading like "Extracurricular Activities" if the activities or awards seem relevant. For example, if Sarah Beckett had been a member of the Management Club or vice president of the Science Club in high school or college, she should have mentioned those facts.

    If you have no work experience related to the job for which you're applying, then list the jobs you have had. Any job that shows a period of responsible employment may favorably impress a potential employer.

3 You can list the names of your references directly on the résumé. Be sure to get the permission of people you cite before listing their names.

    You can also give the address of a placement office file that holds references, as shown on the model résumé.

    Or you can simply say that you will provide references on request.

JOB APPLICATION LETTER

The purpose of the letter of application that goes with your résumé is to introduce yourself briefly and to try to make an employer interested in you. You should include only the high points of the information about yourself given in the résumé.

Following is the letter of application that Sarah Beckett sent with her résumé:

27 Hawkins Road
Clarksboro, New Jersey 08020
May 13, 1995

Mr. George C. Arline
Personnel Manager, Indesco Associates
301 Sharptown Road
White Plains, New York 10019

Dear Mr. Arline:

I would like to be considered as a candidate for the assistant computer programmer position advertised in the Philadelphia Inquirer on April 28, 1995.

I am currently finishing my degree in Computer Technology at Glassboro State College. I have taken every computer course offered at the college and have a solid background in the following computer languages: PASCAL, BASIC, and COBOL. In addition to my computer background, I have supplemented my education with business and mathematics courses.

My knowledge of computers and the business field goes beyond my formal classroom education. For the past two years I have worked part-time at Radio Shack, where I have gained experience in sales and inventory control. Also, on my own initiative, I designed a demonstration program for Radio Shack's TRS-80 microcomputer and developed promotional fliers about the program.

In short, I believe I have the up-to-date computer background and professional drive needed to contribute to your organization. I have enclosed a copy of my résumé to give you further details about my experience. Some time next week, I'll plan to give you a call to see whether I can come in for an interview at your convenience. I look forward to speaking with you then.

Sincerely,
Sarah Beckett
Sarah Beckett

Points to Note about
the Job Application Letter

1 Your letter should do the following:

a In the first paragraph, state that you are an applicant for a job and identify the source through which you learned about the job.

Here is how Sarah Beckett's letter might have opened if her source had been the college placement office. "I learned through the placement office at Glassboro State College of the assistant computer programmer position at your company. I would like to be considered as a candidate for the job."

Sometimes an ad will list only a box number (Y 172) to reply to. Your inside address should then be:

Y 172
Philadelphia Inquirer
Philadelphia, Pennsylvania 19101

Dear Sir or Madam:

b In the second paragraph, state briefly your qualifications for the job and refer the reader to your résumé.

c In the last paragraph, state your willingness to come for an interview. If you can be available for an interview only at certain times, indicate this.

2 As with the résumé, neatness is crucial. Follow the same hints for the letter that you did for the résumé:

a Type the letter on good paper.

b Proofread *very carefully* for sentence-skills mistakes and spelling mistakes. Use the checklist of sentence skills on page 127 and the inside front cover.

c Be brief and to the point: use no more than one page.

d Use a format like the model letter. Keep roughly the same margin on all sides.

e Use punctuation and spelling in the model letter as a guide. For example:

(1) Skip two spaces between the inside address and the salutation ("Dear Mr. Arline").

(2) Use a colon after the salutation.

(3) Sign your name at the bottom, in addition to typing it.

Activity

Clip a job listing from a newspaper or copy a job description posted in your school placement office. The job should be one that you feel you are qualified for or that you would one day like to have.

Write a résumé and a letter of application for the job. Use the models already considered as guides.

Use the checklist of the four bases on page 127 and the inside front cover as a guide in your writing.

USING
THE
LIBRARY

This chapter provides the basic information you need to use your college library with confidence. It also describes the basic steps you should follow in researching a topic.

Most students know that libraries provide study space, typing facilities, and copying machines. They are also aware that a library has a reading area, which contains recent copies of magazines and newspapers. But the true heart of a library consists of the following: a *main desk,* a *book file, book stacks,* a *magazine file,* and a *magazine storage area.* Each of these will be discussed in turn. A note will then be added about computer online databases.

PARTS OF THE LIBRARY

Main Desk

The main desk is usually located in a central spot. Check at the main desk to see if there is a brochure that describes the layout and services of the library. You might also ask if the library staff provides tours of the library. If not, explore the library on your own to find each of the areas described below.

Activity

Make up a floor plan of your college library. Label the main desk, card file, book stacks, magazine file, and magazine storage area.

Book File

The book file will be your starting point for almost any research project. The book file is a list of all the books in the library. It may be an actual card catalog: a file of cards alphabetically arranged in drawers. Often, however, the book file is computerized, and it appears on a number of computer terminals located at different spots in the library.

Finding a Book—Author, Title, and Subject: Whether you use an actual file of cards or a computer terminal, it is important for you to know that there are three ways to look up a book: according to *author, title,* or *subject.*

For example, suppose you wanted to see if the library had *Read with Me,* by Walter Anderson. You could check for the book in any of three ways:

1   You could go to the *title* section of the book file and look it up there under *R.* Note that you always look up a book under the first "significant" word in the title, excluding the word *A, An,* or *The.*

2   You could go to the *author* section of the book file and look it up there under *A.* An author is always listed under his or her last name. Here is the author entry in a card catalog for Anderson's book *Read with Me:*

LC151
A64   **Anderson, Walter**
           Read with me / by Walter Anderson
           — Boston: Houghton, Mifflin, 1990.
           vi, 320 p.
           Includes bibliographical references.

           1. Literacy—United States.   2. Functional Literacy—United
           States—Case studies. 3. Volunteer workers in education—
           United States—Case studies.   4. Reading (Adult
           education)—United States—Case studies.

---

3   Or, since you know the subject of the book—in this case, "literacy"—you could go to the *subject* section of the book file and look it up under L.

Generally, if you are looking for a particular book, it is easier to use the *author* or *title* section of the book file.

On the other hand, if you hope to find other books about literacy, then the *subject* section is where you should look. You will get a list of all the books in the library that deal with literacy. You'll also be given related subject headings under which you might find additional books about the subject.

■   In the catalog card shown on page 269, how many subject headings are listed under which you might find books about literacy? _____

Using a Computerized Book File: Several years ago, I visited a local library that had just been computerized. The card catalog was gone, and in its place was a table with ten computer terminals. I approached a terminal and looked at the instructions placed nearby. The instructions told me that if I wanted to look up the author of a book, I should type "A =" on the keyboard in front of the terminal and then the name of the author. I typed "A = Anderson, Walter," and then (following the directions) I hit the Enter/Return key on the keyboard.

In seconds a new screen appeared, showing me a numbered list of several books by Walter Anderson, one of which was *Read with Me*. This title was numbered "2" on the list, and at the bottom of the screen was a direction to type the number of the title I wanted more information about. So I typed the number "2" and hit the Enter/Return key. I then got the following screen:

AUTHOR:	Anderson, Walter
TITLE:	Read with Me
PUBLISHER:	Houghton, Mifflin, 1990.
SUBJECTS:	1. Literacy—United States. 2. Functional Literacy—United States—Case studies. 3. Volunteer workers in education—United States—Case studies. 4. Reading (Adult education)—United States—Case studies.

Call Number	Material	Location	Status
374.012And	Book	Cherry Hill	Available

I was impressed. The terminal was easier and quicker to use than a card catalog. The screen gave me the basic information I needed to know about the book, including where to find it. In addition, the screen told me that the book was "Available" on the shelves. (A display card nearby explained that if the book was not on the shelves, the message under "Status" would be "Out on loan.") I noticed other options. If the book was not on the shelves at the Cherry Hill location of the library, I would be told if it was available at other libraries nearby, by means of interlibrary loan.

The computer gave me two other choices. I could type "T =" plus a name to look up the title of a book. Or I could type "S =" plus the subject to get the names of any books that the library had dealing with the subject of literacy.

Using Subject Headings to Research a Topic: Whether your library has a card catalog or a computer terminal, it is the *subject section* that will be extremely valuable to you when you are researching a topic. If you have a general topic, the subject section will help you find books on that general topic and will also suggest more specialized topics.

For example, I typed ''S = Literacy'' to see how many book titles there were dealing with the subject of literacy. In seconds a screen came up showing me fifteen different titles. In addition, the screen informed me of related subject headings under which I could find other books about literacy. These related headings included the ones shown on the catalog card for *Read with Me* plus several others. With the help of the book titles and the subject headings in the book file (as well as the article titles and the subject headings suggested in the magazine file, which will be explained later in this chapter), a student could really begin to think about a limited research topic within the general subject of literacy.

There are three points to remember here: (1) Start researching a topic by using the subject section of the book file. (2) Look at the book titles as well; they sometimes suggest specific directions in which you might develop a paper. (3) Keep trying to narrow your topic. Chances are, you will be asked to do a paper of five to fifteen pages or so. You do not want to choose a topic so broad that covering it would require an entire book or more. Instead, you want to come up with a limited topic that can be dealt with adequately in a relatively short paper.

Activity

Part A: Answer the following questions about the card catalog.

1. Is your library's book file an actual file of cards in drawers, or is the book file on computer terminals?

    _____

2. What are the three ways of looking up a book in the library?

    a. _____

    b. _____

    c. _____

3. Which section of the book file will help you research and limit a topic?

    _____

Part B: Use your library book file to answer the following questions.

1.   What is the title of one book by Alice Walker?

_____

2.   What is the title of one book by Andy Rooney?

_____

3.   Who is the author of *The White House Years?* (Remember to look up the title under *White,* not *The.*)

_____

4.   Who is the author of *The Woman Warrior?* _____

5.   List two books dealing with the subject of stress reduction, and note their authors.

a.   _____

b.   _____

6.   List two books dealing with the subject of Martin Luther King, and note their authors.

a.   _____

b.   _____

7.   Look up a book titled *The Immense Journey* or *Passages* or *The Lives of a Cell* and give the following information about it:

a.   Author _____

b.   Publisher _____

c.   Date of publication _____

d.   Call number _____

e.   Subject headings _____

8.   Look up a book written by Carl Sagan, Ellen Goodman, or Calvin Trillin and give the following information about it:

a.   Title _____

b.   Publisher _____

c.   Date of publication _____

d.   Call number _____

e.   Subject headings _____

Book Stacks

The book stacks are the library shelves where books are arranged according to their call numbers. The call number, as distinctive as a social security number, appears on a call file for any book and is printed on the spine of the book.

If your library has *open stacks* (ones that you are permitted to enter), follow these steps to find a book. Suppose you are looking for *Read with Me,* which has the call number LC151.A64 in the Library of Congress system. (Libraries using the Dewey decimal system have call letters made up entirely of numbers rather than letters and numbers. However, you use the same basic method to locate a book.) First you go to the section of the stacks that holds the L's. After you locate the L's, you look for the LC's. After that, you look for LC151. Finally, you look for LC151/A64, and you have the book.

If your library has *closed stacks* (ones you are not permitted to enter), you write down title, author, and call number on a slip of paper. (Such paper will be available near the card catalog or computer terminals.) You'll give the slip to a library staff person, who will locate the book and bring it to you.

Activity

Use the book stacks to answer one of the following sets of questions. Choose the questions related to the system of classifying books (Library of Congress or Dewey Decimal) used by your library.

Option 1:
Library of Congress System (Letters and Numbers)

1. Books in the E184.6-E185.9 area deal with
   a. Benjamin Franklin.
   b. American presidents.
   c. American Indians—history and writings.
   d. African Americans—history and writings.
2. Books in the HM-HN65 area deal with
   a. sociology.   b. economics.   c. history.   d. psychology.
3. Books in the M1-M220 area deal with
   a. painting.   b. music.   c. sculpture.   d. architecture.
4. Books in the PR4553-PR4595.H3 area deal with
   a. Thomas Hardy.
   b. George Eliot.
   c. Charles Dickens.
   d. Samuel Coleridge.

Option 2:
Dewey Decimal System (Numbers)

1. Books in the 200–299 area deal with
   a. language.   b. religion.   c. philosophy.   d. sports.
2. Books in the 370–372 area deal with
   a. education.   b. the military.   c. death.   d. waste disposal.
3. Books in the 613 area deal with
   a. wildflowers.   b. drugs.   c. health.   d. the solar system.
4. Books in the 916 area deal with
   a. Japan.   b. Israel.   c. China.   d. Africa.

Magazine File

The magazine file is also known as the *periodicals* file. *Periodicals* (from the word *periodic,* which means ''at regular periods'') are magazines, journals, and newspapers. In this chapter, the word *magazine* stands for any periodical.

The magazine file often contains recent or very specialized information about a subject, which may not be available in a book. It is important, then, to check magazines as well as books when you are doing research.

Just as you use the book file to find books on your subject, you use the magazine file to find articles on your subject in magazines and other publications. Your library probably has one or more of the following magazine files: *Readers' Guide to Periodical Literature, InfoTrac,* and *Academic Search.*

Readers' Guide to Periodical Literature: The familiar green volumes of *Readers' Guide,* found in just about every library, list articles published in almost two hundred popular magazines, such as *Newsweek, Health, People, Ebony, Redbook,* and *Popular Science.* Articles are listed alphabetically under both subject and author. For example, if you wanted to learn the titles of articles published on the subject of child abuse within a certain time span, you would look under the heading ''Child abuse.'' Here is a typical entry from *Readers' Guide:*

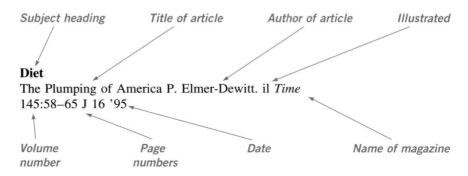

Note the sequence in which information is given about the article:

1   Subject heading.
2   Title of the article. In some cases, there will be bracketed words [like these] after the title that help make clear just what the article is about.
3   Author (if it is a signed article). The author's first name is always abbreviated.
4   Whether the article has a bibliography (*bibl*) or is illustrated with pictures (*il*). Other abbreviations sometimes used are shown in the front of *Readers' Guide.*
5   Name of the magazine. A short title like *Time* is not abbreviated, but longer titles are. For example, the magazine *Popular Science* is abbreviated *Pop Sci.* Refer to the list of magazines in the front of the index to identify abbreviations.
6   Volume number of the magazine (preceding the colon).
7   Page numbers on which the article appears (after the colon).
8   Date when the article appeared. Dates are abbreviated: for example, *Mr* stands for *March, Ag* for *August, N* for *November.* Other abbreviations are shown in the front of *Readers' Guide.*

Readers' Guide is published in monthly supplements. At the end of a year, a volume is published covering the entire year. You will see in your library large green volumes that say, for instance, *Readers' Guide 1990* or *Readers' Guide 1994.* You will also see the small monthly supplements for the current year.

Readers' Guide is now often available on a computer terminal hooked up to a CD-ROM (compact disk, read-only memory) player. Such a disk may contain seven years or more of entries in *Readers' Guide.* You can then quickly search for all the articles that have been published on a given subject in those seven years. Searching the compact disk is much easier than having to page your way through seven paper volumes of *Readers' Guide.*

InfoTrac: *InfoTrac* is a general index on CD-ROM that lists articles published in over one thousand publications. In a matter of seconds you can search ten years of back issues to locate articles on the subject in which you are interested. Obviously, this can greatly reduce your initial research time.

Academic Search: Popular in an increasing number of libraries, *Academic Search* is another general index on CD-ROM. It lists articles published over the last ten years or so in more than two thousand publications, including *The New York Times.* Given this and other CD-ROM databases, it is no wonder that hardcover copies of *Readers' Guide to Periodical Literature* are beginning to gather dust in many libraries.

Activity 1

At this point in the chapter, you know the two basic steps in researching a topic in the library. What are the steps?

1. _____

2. _____

Activity 2

Use the excerpt below from *Readers' Guide* to answer the following questions.

1. Who is the author of an article titled ''A Potent Brew: Booze and Crime''?

   _____

2. What is the title of an article by W. Richards?

   _____

3. How many articles are listed that deal with alcohol and youth?

   _____

4. In what issue of *Consumer's Research Magazine* is there an article about moderate alcohol drinking?

   _____

5. On what pages of *USA Today* is there an article titled ''Dieting Coeds More Likely to Drink''?

   _____

Excerpt from Readers' Guide

ALCOHOL

   See also

   Prohibition

   Physiological effects

   See also

   Fetal alcohol syndrome

Ask Mr. Statistics [Normative Aging Study on death rates of heavy drinkers] D. Seligman. il *Fortune* v128 p127-8 S 6 '93

A drink for your oysters [having alcohol with raw oysters may decrease risk of hepatitis] I. Springer. il *American Health* v12 p89-90 Mr '93

The drinking man's diet [under supervision of Heidi Skolnik] T. Sullivan. il *Gentlemen's Quarterly* v63 p 142-5 Ja '93

Low alcoholism/low tension. *Society* v30 p3 Ja/F '93

Moderate alcohol drinking: benefits and risks. B. T. Hunter. *Consumer's Research Magazine* v76 p8-9 My '93

Proof against heart attacks [benefits of moderate drinking] il *Time* v142 p66 D 27 '93

This could be your brain on booze [GABA receptors; research by Peter H. Seeburg] C. Ezzell. il *Science News* v143 p 70 Ja 30 '93

A toast to lower cholesterol [moderate drinking] *Newsweek* v122 p44 D 27 '93

Wishful thinking [moderate drinking] S. Jennings. il *Forbes* v152 p2267 S 13 '93

ALCOHOL AND AIR PILOTS

Random alcohol tests proposed. J. Ott. il *Aviation Week & Space Technology* v138 p33 Ja 11 '93

ALCOHOL AND ATHLETES

In the rough [J. Daly's drinking problem] W. Plummer. il pors *People Weekly* v 39 p75-6 Ja 18 '93

Outstanding in his field [pitcher D. Eckersley uses running to help overcome drinking problem] D. Hanson. il pors *Runner's World* v28 p38-40 My '93

Sweet redemption [golfer J. Daly overcomes drinking problem] R. Reilly. il pors *Sports Illustrated* v78 p66-72+ Je 7 '93

ALCOHOL AND AUTOMOBILE DRIVERS

The car-seizure idea: it's catching [Portland, Or. remedies drunk driving and prostitute solicitation] J. Ponessa. *Governing* v6 p15-16 Ja '93

The drunk driver and the detour [lawsuits brought against engineers] D. Frum. il *Forbes* v 152 p53 N 22 '93

From fame to shame [retired jockey B. Shoemaker files multiple lawsuits over alcohol-related accident that left him a quadriplegic] W. Nack. il pors *Sports Illustrated* v78 p70-82 Ap 19 '93

I drove drunk. W. Richards. il por *Seventeen* v52 p56+ N '93

Look out! P. Bedard. Il *Car and Driver* v39 p17 N '93

Pickett to perform in concert to settle dispute with mayor. por *Jet* v83 p60 Mr 15 '93

Youth and booze: no easy answer [bush parties in Canada] T. Fennell. il *Maclean's* v106 p 16-17 My 24 '93

ALCOHOL AND BLACKS

A potent brew: booze and crime [L.A. riots expose alcohol problem of blacks] D. Whitman. il map *U.S. News & World Report* v114 p57-9 My 31 '93

ALCOHOL AND CELEBRITIES

Dark voyage [G. L. Whitney] C. Sanz. il pors *People Weekly* v40 p105-7 D 13 '93

A matter of time [P. Summerall] C. Smith, il por *Golf Magazine* v35 p54-5 F '93

ALCOHOL AND CRIME

A potent brew: booze and crime [L.A. riots expose alcohol problem of blacks] D. Whitman. il map *U.S. News & World Report* v114 p57-9 My 31 '93

ALCOHOL AND EMPLOYMENT

Exxon loses again [Theodore Ellenwood's suit to retain position as tanker chief engineeer despite history of alcoholism] D. Seligman. il *Fortune* v127 p103-4 My 3 '93

ALCOHOL AND GAMBLING

Invoking the Fifth [L. Tose's suit against the Sands Hotel for plying him with alcohol while gambling] W. Plummer. il pors *People Weekly* v39 p87-8 Mr 29 '93

Know when to hold 'em, know when to fold 'em [L. Tose's suit against Sands Hotel for plying him with alcohol while gambling] D. A. Kaplan. il por *Newsweek* v121 p68 Mr 15 '93

ALCOHOL AND INDIANS (AMERICAN)

See also

Poundmaker's Lodge (Alta.)

ALCOHOL AND MUSICIANS

Pickett to perform in concert to settle dispute with mayor, por *Jet* v83 p60 Mr 15 '93

ALCOHOL AND PREGNANCY

See also

Fetal alcohol syndrome

ALCOHOL AND PRISONERS

Bars of another kind [drug and alcohol abuse programs at Dorchester Penitentiary, N.B.] J. DeMont. *Maclean's* v1067 p 39 Jl 19 '93

ALCOHOL AND SEAMEN

Exxon loses again [Theodore Ellenwood's suit to retain position as tanker chief engineer despite history of alcoholism] D. Seligman. il *Fortune* v127 p103-4 My 3 '93

ALCOHOL AND SPORTS *See* Alcohol and athletes

ALCOHOL AND THE AGED

Ask Mr. Statistics [Normative Aging Study on death rates of heavy drinkers] D. Seligman. il *Fortune* v128 p127-8 S 6 '93

ALCOHOL AND WOMEN

See also

Fetal alcohol syndrome

The best years of my life. B. Ford. il pors *McCall's* v120 p90+ My '93

Dieting coeds more likely to drink [study by Dean Krahn] il *USA Today (Periodical)* v121 p11 D '92

ALCOHOL AND YOUTH

See also

Alcohol education

Alcohol & tobacco advertising [address, February 8, 1993] A. Novello. *Vital Speeches of the Day* v59 p454-8 My 15 '93

Dieting coeds more likely to drink [study by Dean Krahn] il *USA Today (Periodical)* v121 p11 D '92

Gateway drugs. A. M. Brooks. il *Current Health 2* v19 p6-11 Ja '93

Helping kids learn right from wrong. L. Elliott. il *Washingtonian* v28 p83-6 S '93

I drove drunk. W. Richards. il por *Seventeen* v52 p56+ N '93

Police pop their tops over beer-test ruling [hindrance to underage drinking convictions in Pennsylvania] L. E. Briggs. *Governing* v6 p15-16 N '92

The pub report [Univ of Western Ontario] J. Chidley and S. Steele. il *Maclean's* v106 p49-50 N 15 '93

Saturday night [Washington's suburban teens; cover story] L. Milk and H. Jaffe. il *Washingtonian* v28 p78-82+ S '93

True stories: teens with drinking problems. J. Monahan. il *Teen* v38 p14+ Ap '93

Youth and booze: no easy answer [bush parties in Canada] T. Fennell. il *Maclean's* v106 p16-17 My 24 '93

Activity 3

1. Look up a recent article on date rape in *Readers' Guide* or another general magazine index and fill in the following information:

   a.   Article title _____

   b.   Author (if given) _____

   c.   Name of magazine _____

   d.   Pages _____

   e.   Date _____

2. Look up a recent article on unemployment in *Readers' Guide* or another general magazine index and fill in the following information:

   a.   Article title _____

   b.   Author (if given) _____

   c.   Name of magazine _____

   d.   Pages _____

   e.   Date _____

Specialized Indexes: Once you know how to use *Readers' Guide,* you will find it easy to use some of the more specialized indexes in most libraries. Here are some helpful ones:

- *New York Times Index.* This is an index to articles published in *The New York Times.* After you look up a subject, you'll get a list of articles published on that topic, with a short summary of each article.

- *Business Periodical Index.* The articles here are from over three hundred publications that generally treat a subject in more detail than it would receive in the popular magazines indexed in *Readers' Guide.* At the same time, the articles are usually not *too* technical or hard to read.

- *Social Sciences Index.* This is an index to articles published by journals in the areas of anthropology, environmental science, psychology, and sociology. Your instructors in these areas may expect you to consult this index while doing a research project on any of these subjects.

Other specialized indexes that your library may have include the following:

Art Index
Applied Science and Technology Index
Biography Index
Book Review Index
Education Index
General Science Index
Humanities Index
Nursing Index
Religion Index

Depending on the subject area you are researching, you may want to consult the appropriate index above. Note that many libraries now have these specialized periodical indexes on compact disks.

Activity

1. Check the magazine area in your library. (It might be known as the *Periodicals* area.) Place a check by each of the indexes that it includes:

    _____ *Readers' Guide* (in paperbound volumes)

    _____ *Readers' Guide* (on CD-ROM)

    _____ *InfoTrac*

    _____ *Social Sciences Index* (in paperbound volumes)

    _____ *Social Sciences Index* (on CD-ROM)

2. What are three other indexes in this area of your library besides the ones mentioned above?

    _____

    _____

    _____

A Note on Other Reference Materials: Every library has a reference area, often close to the place where *Readers' Guide* is located, in which other reference materials can be found. Such general resource materials include dictionaries, encyclopedias, atlases, yearbooks, almanacs, a subject guide to books in print (this can help in locating books on a particular subject), anthologies of quotations, and other items.

You may also find in the reference area a series of filing cabinets called the *pamphlet file.* These cabinets are full of pamphlets, booklets, and newsletters on a multitude of topics. One file drawer, for example, may include all the pamphlets and the like for subjects that start with A. I looked in the A drawer of the pamphlet file in my library and found lots of small pieces about subjects like abortion, adoption, and animal rights, along with many other topics starting with A. On top of these filing cabinets may be a booklet titled ''Pamphlet File Subject Headings''; it will quickly tell you if the file includes material on your subject of interest.

Activity

1. What is one encyclopedia that your library has?

    _____

2. What unabridged dictionary does your library have?

    _____

3. Where is your library's pamphlet file located?

    _____

4. Is there a booklet or small file that tells you what subject headings are included

    in the pamphlet file? _____

    Where is it? _____

Magazine Storage Area

Near your library's *Readers' Guide* and other magazine indexes, you'll probably notice slips of paper. Shown at the top of the opposite page is a copy of the slip used in my local library. As you locate each magazine and journal article that you would like to look at, fill out a slip. Take the slips to a library staff person working nearby. Don't hesitate to do this: helping you obtain the articles you want is part of his or her job.

PERIODICAL REQUEST

Name of Magazine _____

Date of Magazine _____

(For your reference: Title and pages of article:)

_____

Here's what will probably happen next:

- If a magazine that you want is very recent, it may be on open shelves in the library. The staff member will tell you, and you can go find it yourself.
- If the magazine you want is up to a year or so old, it may be kept in a closed area. The staff person will go find it and bring it to you.
- Sometimes you'll ask to see a magazine that the library does not carry. You'll then have to plan to use other articles, or go to a larger library. However, most college libraries or large county libraries should have what you need.
- In many cases, especially with older issues, the magazine will be on microfilm or microfiche. (*Microfilm* is a roll of film on which articles have been reproduced in greatly reduced size; *microfiche* is the same thing but on easily handled sheets of film rather than on a roll.) The staff person will bring you the film or fiche and at your request will then show you how to load this material onto a microfiche or microfilm machine nearby.

Faced with learning how to use a new machine, many people are intimidated and nervous. I know I was. What is important is that you ask for as much help as you need. Have the staff person demonstrate the machine and then watch you as you do it. (Remember that this person is being paid by the library to help you learn how to use the resources in the library, including the machine.) While the machine may seem complex at first, in fact most of the time it turns out to be easy to use. Don't be afraid to insist that the person give you as much time as you need to learn the machine.

After you are sure you can use the machine to look up any article, check to see if the machine will make a copy of the article. Many will. Make sure you have some change to cover the copying fee, and then go back to the staff person and ask him or her to show you how to use the print option on the machine. You'll be amazed at how quickly and easily you can get a printed copy of almost any article you want.

Activity

1. Use *Readers' Guide* or another general magazine index to find an article on divorce that was published in the last three months. Write the name of the magazine and the date on a slip of paper and give it to a library staff person. Is the article available in the actual magazine? _____ If so, is it on an open shelf or is it in a closed area where a staff person must bring it to you? _____

2. Use *Readers' Guide* or another general magazine index to find an article on divorce that was published more than one year ago. Write down the name of the magazine and the date on a slip of paper and give it to a library staff person. Is the article available in the actual magazine, or is it on microfiche or microfilm? _____

3. Write in a check if your library has:

    _____ Microfiche machine   _____ with a print option

    _____ Microfilm machine   _____ with a print option

A Note on Computer Online Databases

Some libraries now provide computer online databases. You can sit down at a computer and connect with an online service such as CompuServe. (Note that if you own a computer and a modem—a device that hooks your computer up to your telephone—you can subscribe to an online service for about $10 a month. You can have many of the resources of the library available within your own home!)

Once you are online, you can go to the reference section of the service and select the newspaper or magazine database you wish to search. For example, I recently did a search on CompuServe to see what information it would provide about the subject of adult literacy. Within the reference section, I chose a database called Magazine Database Plus, selected "QuickSearch," and typed the word *literacy* and then the word *adult* to narrow the search. Within a minute or so I was given the titles of twelve articles on literacy. I chose the five whose titles seemed most promising for my purposes and had them "downloaded"—sent to the computer—so that I could print them right out. In little more than ten minutes, I had in my hand five articles on adult literacy. It is obvious, then, that using an online database can be an incredibly quick and convenient way to do research. Just remember that you will probably have to pay for the time you spend using such a database and for downloading articles; be sure that you understand the pricing policies in advance.

A Summary of Library Areas

You have reviewed the six areas of the library that may be most useful to you in doing research:

1 *Main desk.*
2 *Book file.* In particular, you can use the *subject* section of the card file to get the names of books on your subject, as well as suggestions about other subject headings under which you might find books. It is by exploring your general subject in books and then in magazine articles that you will gradually be able to decide upon a subject limited enough to cover in your research paper.
3 *Book stacks.* Here you will get the books themselves.
4 *Magazine files and indexes.* Once again, you can use the *subject* sections of these files to get the names of magazine and journal articles on your subject.
5 *Magazine storage area.* Here you will get the articles themselves.
6 *Online databases.* You can sit at a computer and connect with an online service to use its reference section.

PRACTICE IN USING THE LIBRARY

Activity

Use your library to research a subject that interests you. Select one of the following areas, or (with your instructor's permission) one of your own choice:

Date rape	Censorship in the 1990s
Problems of retirement	New prison reforms
Organ donation	Drug treatment programs
Medical care for the aged	Sudden infant death syndrome
Pro-choice movement	New treatments for insomnia
Pro-life movement	Greenhouse effect
Health insurance reform	Safe sex
Drinking water pollution	Voucher system in schools
Food poisoning (salmonella)	Self-help groups
Cremation	Indoor air pollution
Fertility drugs	Gambling and youth
Acid rain	Nongraded schools
Drug treatment programs for adolescents	Earthquake forecasting
	Ethical aspects of hunting
Air bags	Video display terminals— health aspects
Witchcraft in the 1990s	
New treatments for AIDS	Recent consumer frauds
Changes in immigration policy	Stress reduction in the workplace
Euthanasia	Sex in television
Hazardous substances in the home	Everyday addictions
Day-care programs that work	Toxic waste disposal
Capital punishment	Sexual harassment in business
Prenatal care	Telephone crimes
Noise control	Heroes for the 1990s
New aid for the handicapped	New programs for the homeless
New remedies for allergies	Marriage contracts

Research the topic first through the *subject* section of the book file and then through the *subject* section of one or more magazine indexes.

On a separate sheet of paper, provide the following information:

1. Topic.
2. Three books that cover the topic directly or at least touch on the topic in some way. Include these items:

   Author
   Title
   Place of publication
   Publisher
   Date of publication

3. Three articles on the topic published in 1994 or later from *Readers' Guide* or another general magazine index. Include these items:

   Title of article
   Author (if given)
   Title of magazine
   Date
   Page(s)

4. Finally, include a photocopy of one of the three articles. Note whether the source of the copy was the article on paper, on microfiche, or on microfilm.

WRITING
A
RESEARCH
PAPER

The process of writing a research paper can be divided into six steps:

1   Select a topic that you can readily research.
2   Limit your topic and make the purpose of your paper clear.
3   Gather information on your limited topic.
4   Plan your paper and take notes on your limited topic.
5   Write the paper.
6   Use an acceptable format and method of documentation.

This chapter explains and illustrates each of these steps and then provides a model research paper.

STEP 1: SELECT A TOPIC
THAT YOU CAN READILY RESEARCH

First of all, go to the *subject* section of your library book file (as described on page 269) and see whether there are at least three books on your general topic. For example, if you initially choose the topic ''day care,'' see if you can find at least three books on day care. Make sure that the books are actually available on the library shelves.

Next, go to *Readers' Guide* (see pages 274–275), and try to find five or more articles on your subject.

If both books and articles are at hand, pursue your topic. Otherwise, you may have to choose another topic. You cannot write a paper on a topic for which research materials are not readily available.

STEP 2: LIMIT YOUR TOPIC AND
MAKE THE PURPOSE OF YOUR PAPER CLEAR

A research paper should develop a *limited* topic. It should be narrow and deep rather than broad and shallow. Therefore, as you read through books and articles on your general topic, look for ways to limit the topic.

For instance, in reading through materials on the general topic ''adoption,'' you might decide to limit your topic to the problems that single people have in adopting a child. The general topic ''drug abuse'' might be narrowed to successful drug treatment programs for adolescents. After doing some reading on the world-wide problem of overpopulation, you might decide to limit your paper to the birth-control policies of the Chinese government. The broad subject ''death'' could be reduced to unfair pricing practices in funeral homes; ''divorce'' might be limited to its most damaging effects on the children of divorced parents; ''stress in everyday life'' could be narrowed to methods of reducing stress in the workplace.

The subject headings in the book file and the magazine file will give you helpful ideas about how to limit your subject. For example, under the subject heading ''Adoption'' in the *book file* at one library were several related headings, such as ''Intercountry adoption'' and ''Interracial adoption.'' In addition, there was a list of eighteen books, with several of the titles suggesting limited directions for research: the tendency toward adopting older children; problems faced by the adopted child; problems faced by foster parents. Under the subject heading ''Adoption'' in the *magazine file* at the same library were subheadings and titles of many articles which suggested additional limited topics that a research paper might explore: corrupt practices in adoption; the increase in mixed-race adoptions; ways to find a child for adoption. The point is that *subject headings and related headings, as well as book and article titles, may be of great help to you in narrowing your topic.* Take advantage of them.

Do not expect to limit your topic and make your purpose clear all at once. You may have to do quite a bit of reading as you work out the limited focus of your paper. Note that many research papers have one of two general purposes. Your purpose might be to *make and defend a point* of some kind. (For example, your purpose in a paper might be to provide evidence that gambling should be legalized.) Or, depending on the course and the instructor, your purpose might simply be to *present information* about a particular subject. (For instance, you might be asked to write a paper describing the latest scientific findings about what happens when we dream.)

STEP 3: GATHER INFORMATION
ON YOUR LIMITED TOPIC

After you have a good sense of your limited topic, you can begin gathering information that is relevant to it.

A helpful way to proceed is to sign out the books you need from your library—or to use the copier in your library to duplicate the pages you need from those books. In addition, make copies of all the articles you need from magazines, journals, or other reference materials. Remember that, as described in ''Using the Library'' on pages 281–282, you should be able to make copies even of articles on microfiche or microfilm.

In other words, take the steps needed to get all your key source materials together in one place. You can then sit and work on these materials in a quiet, unhurried way in your home or some other place of study.

STEP 4: PLAN YOUR PAPER AND
TAKE NOTES ON YOUR LIMITED TOPIC

Preparing a Scratch Outline

As you carefully read through the material you have gathered, think constantly about the specific content and organization of your paper. Begin making decisions about exactly what information you will present and how you will arrange it. Prepare a scratch outline of your paper that shows both its thesis and the areas of support for the thesis. It may help to try to plan at least three areas of support.

Thesis: _____

Support: (1) _____

          (2) _____

          (3) _____

Here, for example, is the brief outline that one student, Jodi Harris, prepared for her paper on a national family policy:

Thesis: *The United States should establish a national policy for the family.*

Support: *(1)   National parental-leave policy*

          (2)   National day-care policy

          (3)   National policy for school-age children

Note-Taking

With a tentative outline in mind, you can begin taking notes on the information that you expect to include in your paper. Write your notes on four- by six-inch or five- by eight-inch cards or on sheets of loose-leaf paper. The notes you take should be in the form of *direct quotations, summaries in your own words,* or both. (At times you may also *paraphrase*—use an equal number of your own words in place of someone else's words. Since most research involves condensing information, you will summarize much more than you will paraphrase.)

A *direct quotation* must be written *exactly* as it appears in the original work. But as long as you don't change the meaning, you may omit words from a quotation if they are not relevant to your point. Show such an omission with three spaced periods known as *ellipses* in place of the deleted words:

Original passage

We cannot guarantee that bad things will happen, but we can argue that good things are not happening. It is the contention of this report that increasing numbers of young people are left to their own devices at a critical time in their development.

Direct quotation with ellipses

"We cannot guarantee that bad things will happen, but we can argue that good things are not happening. . . . Increasing numbers of young people are left to their own devices at a critical time in their development."

(Note that there are four dots in the above example, with the first dot indicating the period at the end of the sentence.)

In a *summary,* you condense the original material by expressing it in your own words. Summaries may be written as lists, as brief paragraphs, or both. Following is one of Jodi Harris' summary note cards:

Maternity leave

The United States is an undeveloped country when it comes to programs for working parents. Unlike over one hundred other countries, we do not always grant mothers the right to a leave of absence after the birth of a child. In France, mothers receive sixteen weeks' maternity leave at 84 percent of their salary. In Sweden, mothers get twenty-six weeks' leave at 90 percent of their salary. In Russia, mothers get about four months' fully paid leave.

Wallis, 60

Keep in mind the following points about your research notes:

- Write on only one side of each card or sheet of paper.
- Write only one kind of information, from one source, on any one card or sheet. For example, the sample card on page 289 has information on only one idea (maternity leave) from one source (Wallis).
- Include at the top of each card or sheet a heading that summarizes its content. This will help you organize the different kinds of information you gather.
- Identify the source and page number at the bottom.

Whether you quote or summarize, be sure to record the exact source and page from which you take each piece of information. In a research paper, you must document all information that is not common knowledge or a matter of historical record. For example, the birth and death dates of Martin Luther King are established facts and do not need documenting. On the other hand, the number of adoptions granted to single people in 1994 is a specialized fact that should be documented. As you read several sources on a subject, you will develop a sense of what authors regard as generally shared or common information about a subject and what is more specialized information that must be documented.

If you do not document specialized information or ideas that are not your own, you will be stealing (the formal term is *plagiarizing*—presenting someone else's work as your own work). A good deal of the material in research writing, it can usually be assumed, will need to be documented.

STEP 5: WRITE THE PAPER

After you have finished your reading and note-taking, you should have a fairly clear idea of the plan of your paper. Make a *final outline* and use it as a guide to write your first full draft. If your instructor requires an outline as part of your paper, you should prepare either a *topic outline*, which contains your thesis plus words and phrases; or a *sentence outline*, which contains all complete sentences. In the model paper shown on pages 295–305, a topic outline appears on page 296. You will note that roman numerals are used for first-level headings, capital letters for second-level headings, and numbers for third-level headings.

In your *introductory paragraph*, include a thesis statement expressing the purpose of your paper and indicate the plan of development that you will follow. The section on writing an introductory paragraph for an essay (pages 79–82) is also appropriate for the introductory section of the research paper. Note also the opening paragraph in the model research paper on page 297.

As you move from introduction to *main body* to *summary, conclusion,* or both, strive for unity, support, and coherence so that your paper will be clear and effective. Repeatedly ask, "Does each of my supporting paragraphs develop the thesis of my paper?" Use the checklist on page 127 and the inside front cover to make sure that your paper touches all four bases of effective writing.

STEP 6: USE AN ACCEPTABLE FORMAT AND METHOD OF DOCUMENTATION

Format

The model paper on pages 295–305 shows an acceptable format for a research paper. Comments and directions are set in small print in the margins of each page; be sure to note these.

Documentation of Sources

You must tell the reader the sources (books, articles, and so on) of the borrowed material in your paper. Whether you quote directly or summarize ideas in your own words, you must acknowledge your sources. In the past, you may have used footnotes and a bibliography to cite your sources. Now, you will learn a simplified documentation style used by the Modern Language Association. This easy-to-learn style resembles the documentation used in the social sciences and natural sciences.

Citations within a Paper: When citing a source, you must mention the author's name and the relevant page number. The author's name may be given either in the sentence you are writing or in parentheses following the sentence. Here are two examples:

> "There is, at present, no centralized program to provide quality day care to all children in the United States," states Angela Browne Miller (4).

> One expert states, "There is, at present, no centralized program to provide quality day care to all children in the United States" (Miller 4).

There are several points to note about citations within the paper:

- When the author's name is provided within the parentheses, only his or her last name is given.
- There is no punctuation between the author's name and the page number.
- The parenthetical citation is placed after the borrowed material but before the period at the end of the sentence.
- If you are using more than one work by the same author, include a shortened version of the title within the parenthetical citation. For example, suppose you were using several books by Angela Browne Miller and you included the quotation above, which is from Miller's book *The Day Care Dilemma.* Your citation within the text would be:

(Miller, Day Care, 4).

Note that commas separate the author's last name and the page number from the abbreviated title.

Citations at the End of a Paper: Your paper should end with a list of "Works Cited" which includes all the sources actually used in the paper. (Don't list any other sources, no matter how many you have read.) Look at "Works Cited" in the model research paper (pages 304–305) and note the following points:

- The list is organized alphabetically according to authors' last names. Entries are not numbered.
- Entries without an author (such as "Child Care News") are listed alphabetically by the first word.
- When more than one work by the same author or authors is listed, three hyphens followed by a period should be substituted for the author's or authors' names after the first entry.
- Entries are double-spaced, with no extra space between entries.
- After the first line of each entry, there is an indentation for each additional line in the entry.

Model Entries for a List of "Works Cited":   Model entries for "Works Cited" are given below. Use these entries as a guide when you prepare your own list.

Book by One Author

Rhodes, Richard. A Hole in the World: An American Boyhood. New York: Simon & Schuster, 1990.

Always give the complete title, including any subtitle. Separate a subtitle from the title with a colon.

Two or More Entries by the Same Author

———. The Making of the Atomic Bomb. New York: Simon & Schuster, 1986.

If you cite two or more entries by the same author (in the example above, a second book by Richard Rhodes is cited), do not repeat the author's name. Instead, begin with a line made up of three hyphens followed by a period. Then give the remaining information as usual. Arrange the works by the same author alphabetically by title. Note in the examples above that the words *A, An,* and *The* are ignored in alphabetizing by title.

Book by Two or More Authors

Bassis, Michael A., Richard J. Gelles, and Ann Levine. Sociology: An Introduction. New York: Random House, 1991.

For a book with two or more authors, give all the authors' names but reverse only the first name.

Magazine Article

Quinn, Jane Bryant. "How to Lose." <u>Newsweek</u> 8 Apr. 1996:55.

Write the date of the issue as follows: day, month (abbreviated in most cases to three letters), and year. The final number or numbers refer to the page or pages of the issue in which the article appears.

Newspaper Article

Lopez, Steve. "Give the Schools a Break." <u>The Philadelphia Inquirer</u> 21 Jan. 1996:A2.

The final letter and number refer to section A, page 2.

Editorial

"The Ugly Side of a Tax Cut." Editorial. <u>The New York Times</u> 20 Jan. 1995, sec. A:28.

List an editorial as you would any signed or unsigned article, but indicate the nature of the piece by adding *Editorial* or *Letter* after the article's title.

Encyclopedia Article

Foulkes, David, and Rosalind D. Cartwright. "Sleep and Dreams." <u>Encyclopaedia Britannica.</u> 1989 ed.

Selection in an Edited Collection

Moody, Harry R. "Education as a Lifelong Process." <u>Our Aging Society.</u> Eds. Alan Pifer and Lydia Bronte. New York: Norton, 1986.

Revised or Later Edition

Quinn, Virginia Nichols. <u>Applying Psychology.</u> 3d ed. New York: McGraw-Hill, 1995.

Note that the abbreviations *Rev. ed., 2d ed., 3d ed.,* and so on are placed right after the title.

Pamphlet

<u>Heart and Stroke Facts.</u> American Heart Association, 1995.

Television Program

"Is There Poison in Your Mouth?" Narr. Morley Safer. Prod. Patti Hassler. <u>60 Minutes.</u> CBS. 16 Dec. 1990.

Film

The Jungle Book. Dir. Stephen Sommers. Universal, 1995.

Recording

Turner, Tina. "Paradise Is Here." Break Every Rule. Capitol Records CD
    7463232.

Personal Interview

Thornton, Dr. Roger K. Personal interview. 19 Nov. 1995.

Material from an Online Database

Musto, David F. "Alcohol in American History." Scientific American Apr. 1996:
    78–83. Scientific American Online. Online. CompuServe. 4 Apr. 1996.

In a citation for an electronic source also available in print, provide the same information you would for the printed source. Also provide the database title, underlined (Scientific American Online), the medium of the publication (Online), the name of the computer service (CompuServe), and the date the material was accessed (April 4, 1996).

For an electronic source available only online, provide the author's name (if given), the title, and the date the material was "published" online, in addition to the information in the previous sentence.

Activity

On a separate sheet of paper, convert the information in each of the following references into the correct form for a list of "Works Cited." Use the appropriate model on pages 292–294 as a guide.

1. A book by Theodore Zeldin called An Intimate History of Humanity and published in New York by HarperCollins in 1995.
2. An article by Katie Hafer titled "Wiring the Campuses" on pages 62–66 of the January 30, 1995, issue of Newsweek.
3. An article by Anita Manning titled "Abortion Pill: An Answer or New Problem?" on page 1A of the January 24, 1995, issue of USA Today.
4. A book by Diane Papalia and Sally Wendkos Olda titled Human Development and published in a sixth edition by McGraw-Hill in New York in 1995.

The title should be centered and about one-third down the page.

Your name, the title of your course, your instructor's name, and the date should all be double-spaced and centered.

AMERICA'S NEGLECTED CHILDREN:
HOW THE GOVERNMENT CAN HELP

by

Jodi Harris

English 101
Professor Lessig

20 December 1995

OUTLINE

Thesis: The United States should establish a national family policy that supports parental leaves, day care, and after-school care.

I. Great need for child care
    A. Great numbers of children with working mothers
    B. Predicted increase of children with working mothers
II. Comparison of our national commitment to child care with that of other countries
    A. Commitment of other countries
    B. Our own failure
III. Solution: Establishment of a three-part national family policy
    A. National parental leave program
        1. Problem: financial consequences to women who leave work to have a baby
        2. Solution:
            a. Two-part policy
                (1) Unpaid leave
                (2) Full restoration to job and benefits
            b. State programs as evidence such policies can work
    B. National day-care policy
        1. Problems
            a. Lack of facilities
            b. Low-quality facilities
            c. High cost of day care
            d. Government's hands-off policy and its effects
        2. Solutions for families and employers
            a. Tax breaks for companies with day-care centers
            b. Encouragement of day-care centers for government employees
            c. Denial of federal funding to states without stringent standards for child care facilities
    C. National policy for after-school child care
        1. Problems
            a. Great numbers of school-age children needing care
            b. Problems of latchkey children
        2. Solution
            a. Use of schools for before- and after-school care
            b. Model example in Independence, Missouri

*Your last name and the page number should go
in the upper-right-hand corner of each page.*

Harris 1

Double-space between lines of the text. Leave about a one-inch margin all the way around the page.

Thesis, with plan of development.

Parenthetic citations, with author and page number but no comma.

The abbreviation qtd. *means quoted.*

With both Mom and Dad at work in today's world, child care has become a wrenching personal problem for millions of America's families (Wallis 54). The overriding question for most expectant American mothers—rich, middle-class, or working poor—is how to take time off from work to have the baby. Soon after the birth, parents must cope with the problem of how to find care for their baby when they are both back at work. And later, parents must face the question of who will watch their older children when the school day is over. To help working families properly care for their children, the United States should establish a national family policy that supports parental leave, day care, and after-school care.

The need for such a policy is great and continues to grow. Only a minority of families fit the traditional "Dick and Jane" mold, with a breadwinner father and homemaker mother. Today, more than two-thirds of all mothers with children under the age of eighteen work outside the home (Papalia and Olds 329). Twelve million children under age six have working mothers (Weber 65). In the 1990s, an estimated 75 percent of all mothers with children under six will be employed outside their homes (Miller 6). Elinor Guggenheimer, president of the Child Care Action Campaign, says, "We are in the midst of an explosion," and predicts that within ten years, the number of children under six needing daytime supervision will grow by more than 50 percent (qtd. in Wallis 55).

Compared with other industrialized nations, the United States is an underdeveloped country when it comes to policies and programs for working parents. Ours, for instance, is the only Western industrialized nation that does not guarantee a mother the right to a leave of absence after she has a child (Wallis 56). In France, Sweden, and Denmark, mothers <u>and</u> fathers are guaranteed the right to take time off to be with their newborns (Wallis 60).

We also rate poorly when it comes to day care. Many European nations with a high percentage of working women have invested in public nurseries and subsidize in-home care (Dreskin and Dreskin 138). In Germany, for example, parents can deduct the cost of child care from their taxes. In Japan, the government and most companies subsidize parents whose children require day care (Gibbs 45).

Clearly, our national commitment to child care lags notably. When Democratic Representative Pat Schroeder arrived in Washington from Colorado in 1973 with her two small children, she expected it would take only a year or so for Congress to pass an all-inclusive child care bill. Yet today, almost twenty years later, the United States is still without a national family policy (Mernit 65). "Under our laws," observes Congresswoman Schroeder, "a business woman can deduct a new Persian rug for her office but can't deduct most of her costs for child care" (qtd. in Gibbs 45).

Recent efforts to persuade Congress to pass a parental leave bill have been unsuccessful. The most recent failure occurred in the summer of 1990 when Congress did not override President Bush's veto of the Family and Medical Leave Act (Lewin A8).

The absence of a national policy to help working parents reflects our antiquated attitudes toward motherhood. For the most part, the workplace still operates as if workers had no families and women were not half of the entire labor force (Kantrowitz 57). Jay Belsky, a professor of human development at Pennsylvania State University, reminds us, "We are as much

Harris 3

a society dependent on female labor, and thus in need of a child-care system, as we are a society dependent on the automobile, and thus in need of roads" (qtd. in Wallis 55).

An important first step toward a strong child care system in the United States would be the development of a policy helping parents take leave for birth and for the care of newborns. At present, women lose one-fifth of their earning power when they leave a job to have a baby (Hewlett 194). Speaking for the Women's Legal Defense Fund at a hearing on family leave before the House Committee on Education and Labor, Donna Lenhoff said, "Children of course suffer whenever either of their parents is too pressured by work and financial considerations to spend time with them. . . . This problem becomes acute at certain times . . . such as birth." She continued, "[Family leave] would be an essential first step toward meeting the needs and realities of American families today" (Sweeney 146–148).

Because most women work out of economic necessity, we must create a parental leave policy with two requirements. First, employers would have to grant men and women as much as eighteen weeks of unpaid leave after the birth or adoption of a child. Second, employers would have to restore those persons to the same job or an equivalent job with continued benefits and seniority when they return. As John J. Sweeney, International President of the Service Employees International Union, AFL-CIO, said at a Congressional committee hearing on family leave, "No one should have to choose between being a breadwinner and being a caring family member" (Sweeney 140).

That such a program can work is evidenced by the fact that fifteen states have adopted some form of job protection for parents requesting leave, and

Brackets mark words inserted to clarify a quotation.

thirty others have considered similar legislation in the past year (Lewin A8). The legislation permits mothers and fathers at least six weeks of leave with continued health benefits and a guarantee of employment at the end of the leave (Parents 38).

The second component of a national family policy should be day care. Our present day-care system is clearly inadequate. First of all, we do not have enough facilities to meet the demand. Long waiting lists at child care centers are routine. In addition, many day-care facilities have marginal standards of health and safety and are short of qualified help (Traver 17).

Moreover, finding an acceptable day-care arrangement is just the beginning of the problems parents face. With the average cost of day care at $3,000 a child, parents must struggle to pay for a suitable program once they have found it. The high price is a real financial strain for middle-class families and is beyond the reach of the working poor (Traver 17).

"There is, at present, no centralized program to provide quality day care to all children in the United States," Angela Browne Miller states in her book The Day Care Dilemma (4). Instead, the prevailing belief is that parents alone should finance the cost of day care. An editorial in Glamour (84) reports that, according to Yale professor Edwin Zigler and researcher Susan Muenchen, the result of this belief is that in this country the issue is seen as a problem for mothers. Therefore, the editorial continues, "the care of America's most precious resource — her children — is left to chance, luck, or geography." The editorial concludes that, on the whole, the government, employers, and society have chosen the ostrich approach to the issue of day care: "Ignore the need and maybe it will go away" (Glamour 84).

Harris 5

This attitude has had profound effects. Most American employers expect parents to behave in the same way as childless workers (Dreskin and Dreskin 138). Yet both parents and employers would benefit from a more enlightened attitude. As the Glamour editorial states, "The overwhelming burdens on working mothers must be relieved, not only for the health of the American family but for the increased productivity in the workplace. . . . Parents miss an average of 7.2 work days per year because of child care difficulties" (Glamour 84). Businesses that have made an investment in child care say that it pays off handsomely in reduced turnover and absenteeism (Wallis 60). Thus a national policy encouraging more high-quality day-care centers would help both working families and employers.

The government could stimulate the development of more good child care centers by giving larger tax breaks for companies that establish day-care centers for their employees. Furthermore, since the government is the nation's largest employer (Glamour 84), all levels of government should be encouraged to establish day-care centers for their employees.

Finally, states without stringent health, safety, and teaching standards for child care facilities should lose whatever federal funding they have. This will encourage a day-care system that provides children with enriching programs, well-paid teachers, and a safe environment.

To be complete, a national family policy must also include comprehensive after-school care for children. A child's entry into the school system is too often equated with the end of the struggle for child care. But the battle is not over. It is just different—the need is now for a few hours of care instead of a full day (Quindlen E17).

Harris 6

Indeed, for working parents, those few hours can become the trickiest of all child care problems. According to recent estimates, there may be in the United States today as many as twelve million latchkey children, those children regularly left without direct adult supervision before or after school (Quindlen E17). Their parents are trying to make ends meet while worrying about where the children are after school hours (Lipsitz 5). These parents would obviously prefer to have their children participate in organized after-school activities, but that kind of program is not always available or affordable.

No one denies that latchkey children are at risk—of loneliness, negative behavior, mistreatment, and actual physical harm. Recognition of these risks must be translated into programs. In the words of educational researcher Joan Lipsitz:

> We cannot guarantee that bad things will happen, but we can argue that good things are not happening. . . . Increasing numbers of young people are left to their own devices at a critical time in their development. They are losing opportunities to be culturally enriched, to interact positively with peers and adults, and to contribute to their communities. (qtd. in Landers 7)

Such opportunities could be provided at our nation's schools, natural sites for before- and after-school care. The most obvious benefits of school-based programs are the convenience and security they offer. Also, schools provide a well-equipped environment with excellent facilities for day care

Direct quotations of four lines or more are indented ten spaces from the left margin. Quotation marks are not used. The spaced periods (ellipses) show that material has been omitted from the quotation.

Harris 7

(Egan 27). Dr. Gwendolyn C. Baker, president of the New York City Board of Education, would like to see schools open from early in the morning until six o'clock at night "for enrichment activities, for sports, for all kinds of things we don't have time for during the school day" (qtd. in Quindlen E17).

Such a program works well in Independence, Missouri, where elementary schools now stay open twelve hours a day. Corporate and public subsidies help keep costs low. School Superintendent Robert L. Henley says, "Most parents work today, and we feel that we are providing a good service" (qtd. in Garland 68).

His attitude reflects the fact that child care is no longer just a women's issue. Rather, it is a family issue and, as such, a national issue. The economic needs of parents and employers will certainly cause a change in the attitude of the business community (Wallis 60). Our government can make the struggle less painful by instituting a national family policy which will relieve the stresses on working parents and improve the lives of their children. If we are serious about our nation's future, we must demand no less.

Harris 8

Works Cited

"Child Care News." <u>Parents</u> Feb. 1990:38.

"Day-Care Center Slots." Editorial. <u>Glamour</u> Apr. 1985:84.

Dreskin, William, and Wendy Dreskin. "The Family Here and Abroad." <u>The Day Care Decision</u>. New York: Evans, 1983. 126–154.

Egan, Leslie A., and Barbara A. Lowe. "Debate." <u>NEA Today</u> Dec. 1984:27.

Garland, Susan B. "America's Child-Care Crisis: The First Tiny Steps toward Solutions." <u>Business Week</u> 10 July 1989:64–66.

Gibbs, Nancy. "Shameful Bequests to the Next Generation." <u>Time</u> 8 Oct. 1990:42–46.

Hewlett, Sylvia Ann. "Why We Need a National Policy to Help Working Mothers." <u>Glamour</u> Nov. 1986:194.

Kantrowitz, Barbara, et al. "Changes in the Workplace." <u>Newsweek</u> 31 Mar. 1986:57.

Landers, Susan. "Latchkey Kids." <u>The Monitor</u> Dec. 1986:1, 6–7.

Lewin, Tamar. "Battle for Family Leave Will Be Fought in States." <u>The New York Times</u> 27 July 1990:A8.

Lipsitz, Joan. "3:00 to 6:00 P.M.: Programs for Young Adolescents." <u>Report on School Age Day Care</u>. New Jersey: Cherry Hill Public Schools, 1987.

Mernit, Susan. "The Day-Care Deadline." <u>Harper's Bazaar</u> July 1989:65, 130.

Miller, Angela Browne. <u>The Day Care Dilemma</u>. New York: Plenum, 1990.

Papalia, Diane E., and Sally Wendkos Olds. "Intellectual Development in Early Childhood." <u>A Child's World: Infancy through Adolescence</u>. 6th ed. New York: McGraw-Hill, 1993. 311–345.

Works cited should be double-spaced. The second and following lines of an entry should be indented five spaces. Titles of books, magazines, and the like should be underlined.

Harris 9

Quindlen, Anne. "Latchkey Summer." The New York Times 8 July
    1990:E17.

Sweeney, John J., Donna Lenhoff, and Karen Nussbaum. "Should the
    Proposed 'Family and Medical Leave Act' Be Approved?" Congressional
    Digest May 1988:136–152.

Traver, Nancy. "The ABCs of Child Care." Time 3 July 1989:17.

Wallis, Claudia. Time 22 June 1987:54–60.

Weber, Joseph. "Why Day Care Is Still Mostly Mom and Pop." Business
    Week 10 July 1989:65.

A Note on the First Page of a Research Paper Using MLA Style

If your instructor prefers that you follow the MLA style for the opening of a research paper, omit the title page and the outline page. Start your first page as follows:

Jodi Harris

Professor Lessig

English 101

20 December 1995

    America's Neglected Children: How the Government Can Help

    With both Mom and Dad at work in today's world, child care has become

a wrenching personal problem for millions of America's families (Wallis 54).

PART FOUR

HANDBOOK
OF SENTENCE
SKILLS

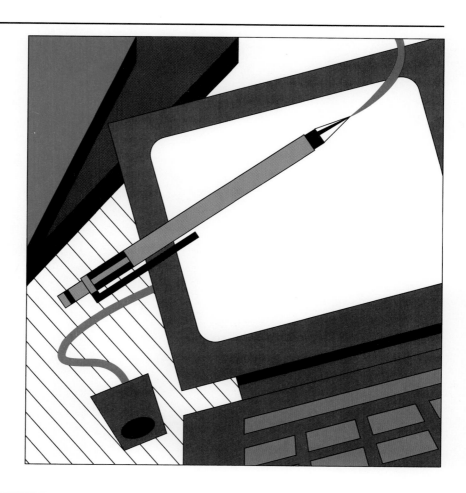

SUBJECTS
AND
VERBS

The basic building blocks of English sentences are subjects and verbs. Understanding them is an important first step toward mastering a number of sentence skills.

Every sentence has a subject and a verb. Who or what the sentence speaks about is called the *subject;* what the sentence says about the subject is called the *verb.* In the following sentences, the subject is underlined once and the verb twice:

The boy cried.

That fish smells.

Many people applied for the job.

The show is a documentary.

A SIMPLE WAY TO FIND A SUBJECT

To find a subject, ask *who* or *what* the sentence is about. As shown below, your answer is the subject.

Who is the first sentence about?   The boy

What is the second sentence about?   That fish

Who is the third sentence about?   Many people

What is the fourth sentence about?   The show

A SIMPLE WAY TO FIND A VERB

To find a verb, ask what the sentence *says about* the subject. As shown below, your answer is the verb.

What does the first sentence *say about* the boy?   He <u>cried</u>.
What does the second sentence *say about* the fish?   It <u>smells</u>.
What does the third sentence *say about* the people?   They <u>applied</u>.
What does the fourth sentence *say about* the show?   It <u>is</u> a documentary.

A second way to find the verb is to put *I, you, he, she, it,* or *they* in front of the word you think is a verb. If the result makes sense, you have a verb. For example, you could put *he* in front of *cried* in the first sentence above, with the result, *he cried,* making sense. Therefore, you know that *cried* is a verb. You could use the same test with the other three verbs as well.

Finally, it helps to remember that most verbs show action. In the sentences already considered, the three action verbs are *cried, smells,* and *applied.* Certain other verbs, known as *linking verbs,* do not show action. They do, however, give information about the subject. In "The show is a documentary," the linking verb *is* tells us that the show is a documentary. Other common linking verbs include *am, are, was, were, feel, appear, look, become,* and *seem.*

Activity

In each of the following sentences, draw one line under the subject and two lines under the verb.

1.   The ripening tomatoes glistened on the sunny windowsill.
2.   Biofeedback reduces the pain of my headaches.
3.   Elena nervously twisted a strand of hair around her fingers.
4.   My brother made our stereo cabinet from inexpensive particleboard.
5.   A jackrabbit bounds up to fifteen feet in one leap.
6.   The blind woman knits woolen caps for Christmas presents.
7.   The amateur astronomer set his alarm for 3 A.M. to view the lunar eclipse.
8.   On St. Patrick's Day, our neighborhood tavern serves green beer.
9.   Children sometimes eat the dangerous lead-based paint found in old houses.
10.   During my parents' divorce, I felt like a rag doll being torn between two people.

MORE ABOUT SUBJECTS AND VERBS

1   A sentence may have more than one verb, more than one subject, or several
    subjects and verbs.

The <u>engine</u> <u>coughed</u> and <u>sputtered</u>.
Broken <u>glass</u> and empty <u>cans</u> <u>littered</u> the parking lot.
<u>Joyce</u>, <u>Brenda</u>, and <u>Robert</u> <u>met</u> after class and <u>headed</u> downtown.

2   The subject of a sentence never appears within a prepositional phrase. A
    prepositional phrase is simply a group of words that begins with a preposition.
    Following is a list of common prepositions:

about	before	by	inside	over
above	behind	during	into	through
across	below	except	of	to
among	beneath	for	off	toward
around	beside	from	on	under
at	between	in	onto	with

Cross out prepositional phrases when looking for the subject of a sentence.

The weathered old <u>house</u> <u>perched</u> unsteadily ~~on its rotted foundation~~.
The <u>label</u> ~~on that mayonnaise jar~~ <u>can</u> <u>be</u> easily <u>removed</u> ~~with hot water~~.
The color <u>picture</u> ~~on our TV set~~ <u>turns</u> black and white ~~during a storm~~.
The murky <u>waters</u> ~~of the polluted lake~~ <u>spilled</u> ~~over the dam~~.
The amber <u>lights</u> ~~on its sides~~ <u>outlined</u> the tractor-trailer ~~in the hazy dusk~~.

3   Many verbs consist of more than one word. Here, for example, are some of
    the many forms of the verb *work*:

work	worked	should work
works	were working	will be working
does work	have worked	can work
is working	had worked	could be working
are working	had been working	must have worked

Notes

a   Words like *not, just, never, only,* and *always* are not part of the verb although they may appear within the verb.

Rebecca <u>has</u> just <u>finished</u> filling out her tax form.

The intersection <u>has</u> not always <u>been</u> this dangerous.

b   No verb preceded by *to* is ever the verb of a sentence.

At night, my son <u>likes</u> to read under the covers.

Evelyn <u>decided</u> to separate from her husband.

c   No *-ing* word by itself is ever the verb of a sentence. (It may be part of the verb, but it must have a helping verb in front of it.)

They going on a trip this weekend.
(not a sentence, because the verb is not complete)

They <u>are</u> <u>going</u> on a trip this weekend.   (a sentence)

Activity

Draw a single line under subjects and a double line under verbs. Crossing out prepositional phrases may help you find the subjects.

1. The top of our refrigerator is covered with dusty pots and pans.
2. A new muffler and tailpipe were just installed in my car.
3. The people in the all-night coffee shop seemed weary and lost.
4. Every plant in the dim room bent toward the small window.
5. A glaring headline about the conviction of a local congressman attracted my attention.
6. Two of the biggest stores on our main shopping street are going out of business.
7. The glow of the stereo's tiny red light always reminds me to turn off the amplifier.
8. Both private wells and public reservoirs in our area are contaminated with deadly chemicals.
9. The jar of peppercorns tumbled from the spice shelf and shattered on the floor.
10. The scar in the hollow of Brian's throat is the result of an emergency operation to clear his windpipe.

■ **Review Test**

Draw a single line under subjects and a double line under verbs. Crossing out prepositional phrases may help you find the subjects.

1. With one graceful motion, the shortstop fielded the grounder and threw to first base.

2. Forty-seven czars are buried within the walls of Moscow's Kremlin.

3. Before class, Barbara and Aaron rushed to the coffee machine in the hall.

4. I punched and prodded my feather pillow before settling down to sleep.

5. Waiting in the long ticket line, Matt shifted his weight from one foot to the other.

6. Cattle branding was practiced by ancient Egyptians over four thousand years ago.

7. Lilacs and honeysuckle perfume our yard on summer nights.

8. The mail carrier abruptly halted her Jeep and backed up toward the mailbox.

9. During the American Revolution, some brides rejected white wedding gowns and wore red as a symbol of rebellion.

10. The little girl's frantic family called a psychic to help locate the child.

FRAGMENTS

Every sentence must have a subject and a verb and must express a complete thought. A word group that lacks a subject or a verb and that does not express a complete thought is a *fragment*. Following are the most common types of fragments that people write:

1   Dependent-word fragments
2   *-ing* and *to* fragments
3   Added-detail fragments
4   Missing-subject fragments

Once you understand what specific kinds of fragments you might write, you should be able to eliminate them from your writing. The following pages explain all four types.

DEPENDENT-WORD FRAGMENTS

Some word groups that begin with a dependent word are fragments. Following is a list of common dependent words. Whenever you start a sentence with one of these words, you must be careful that a fragment does not result.

Dependent Words		
after	if, even if	when, whenever
although, though	in order that	where, wherever
as	since	whether
because	that, so that	which, whichever
before	unless	while
even though	until	who
how	what, whatever	whose

In the example below, the word group beginning with the dependent word *After* is a fragment:

After I cashed my paycheck. I treated myself to dinner.

A *dependent statement*—one starting with a dependent word like *After*—cannot stand alone. It depends on another statement to complete the thought. *After I cashed my paycheck* is a dependent statement. It leaves us hanging. We expect in the same sentence to find out *what happened after* the writer cashed the check. When a writer does not follow through and complete a thought, a fragment results.

To correct the fragment, simply follow through and complete the thought:

After I cashed my paycheck, I treated myself to dinner.

Remember, then, that *dependent statements by themselves are fragments.* They must be attached to a statement that makes sense standing alone.

Here are two other examples of dependent-word fragments.

I won't leave the house. Until I hear from you.

Rick finally picked up the socks. Which he had thrown on the floor days ago.

Until I hear from you is a fragment; it does not make sense standing by itself. We want to know in the same statement *what cannot happen* until I hear from you. The writer must complete the thought. Likewise, *Which he had thrown on the floor days ago* is not in itself a complete thought. We want to know in the same statement what *which* refers to.

How to Correct a Dependent-Word Fragment

In most cases you can correct a dependent-word fragment by attaching it to the sentence that comes after it or the sentence that comes before it:

After I cashed my paycheck, I treated myself to dinner.
(The fragment has been attached to the sentence that comes after it.)

I won't leave the house until I hear from you.
(The fragment has been attached to the sentence that comes before it.)

Rick finally picked up the socks which he had thrown on the floor days ago.
(The fragment has been attached to the sentence that comes before it.)

Another way of correcting a dependent-word fragment is simply to eliminate the dependent word by rewriting the sentence.

I cashed my paycheck and then treated myself to dinner.
I will wait to hear from you.
He had thrown them on the floor days ago.

Notes

a   Use a comma if a dependent word group comes at the *beginning* of a sentence (see also page 426):

After I cashed my paycheck, I treated myself to dinner.

However, do not generally use a comma if the dependent word group comes at the *end* of a sentence:

I won't leave the house until I hear from you.
Rick finally picked up the socks which he had thrown on the floor days ago.

b   Sometimes the dependent words *who, that, which,* or *where* appear not at the very start but *near* the start of a word group. A fragment often results:

I drove slowly past the old brick house. The place where I grew up.

The place where I grew up is not in itself a complete thought. We want to know in the same statement *where was the place* the writer grew up. The fragment can be corrected by attaching it to the sentence that comes before it:

I drove slowly past the old brick house, the place where I grew up.

Activity 1

Turn each of the following dependent word groups into a sentence by adding a complete thought. Use a comma after the dependent word group if a dependent word starts the sentence. Note the examples.

Examples   Although I felt miserable
Although I felt miserable, I tried to smile for the photographer.

          The man who found my wallet
The man who found my wallet returned it the next day.

1. If I have to work late

   _____

   _____

2. Because it was raining

   _____

   _____

3. When I heard the news

   _____

   _____

4. Because I couldn't find the car keys

   _____

   _____

5. The restaurant that we tried

   _____

   _____

Activity 2

Underline the dependent-word fragment in each item. Then rewrite the items, correcting each fragment by attaching it to the sentence that comes before or the sentence that comes after it—whichever sounds more natural. Use a comma after the dependent word group if it starts the sentence.

1. Whenever I spray deodorant. My cat arches her back. She thinks she is hearing a hissing enemy.

   _____

   _____

2. My father, a salesman, was on the road all week. We had a great time playing football in the house. Until he came home for the weekend.

    _____

    _____

3. If Kim takes too long saying good-bye to her boyfriend. Her father will start flicking the porch light. Then he will come out with a flashlight.

    _____

    _____

4. I bought a calendar watch. Which is running fast. Last week had sixteen days.

    _____

    _____

5. Before I move, I scrub both my old and new apartments. After all the apartments I've left spick-and-span. I think it's my turn to move into a clean one.

    _____

    _____

-ING AND *TO* FRAGMENTS

When an *-ing* word appears at or near the start of a word group, a fragment may result. Such fragments often lack a subject and part of the verb. In the items below, underline the word groups that contain *-ing* words. Each is a fragment.

1. Ellen walked all over the neighborhood yesterday. Trying to find her dog Bo. Several people claimed they had seen him only hours before.
2. We sat back to watch the movie. Not expecting anything special. To our surprise, we clapped, cheered, and cried for the next two hours.
3. I telephoned the balloon store. It being the day before our wedding anniversary. I knew my wife would be surprised to receive a dozen heart-shaped balloons.

People sometimes write *-ing* fragments because they think the subject in one sentence will work for the next word group as well. Thus, in item 1 they think the subject *Ellen* in the opening sentence will also serve as the subject for *Trying to find her dog Bo.* But the subject must actually be *in* the sentence.

How to Correct *-ing* Fragments

1   Attach the fragment to the sentence that comes before or the sentence that comes after it, whichever makes sense. Item 1 could read: ''Ellen walked all over the neighborhood yesterday trying to find her dog Bo.''

2   Add a subject and change the *-ing* verb part to the correct form of the verb. Item 2 could read: ''We didn't expect anything special.''

3   Change *being* to the correct form of the verb *be* (*am, are, is, was, were*). Item 3 could read: ''It was the day before our wedding anniversary.''

How to Correct *to* Fragments

When *to* appears at or near the start of a word group, a fragment sometimes results:

At the Chinese restaurant, Tim used chopsticks. To impress his date. He spent one hour eating a small bowl of rice.

The second word group is a fragment and can be corrected by adding it to the preceding sentence:

At the Chinese restaurant, Tim used chopsticks to impress his date.

Activity 1

Underline the *-ing* fragment in each of the following items. Then make it a sentence by rewriting it, using the method described in parentheses.

Example   Stepping hard on the accelerator. Stan tried to beat the truck to the intersection. He lost by a hood.
(Add the fragment to the sentence that comes after it.)
Stepping hard on the accelerator, Stan tried to beat the truck to

the intersection.

1.   Marble-sized hailstones fell from the sky. Flattening the young plants in the cornfield. A year's work was lost in an hour.
(Add the fragment to the preceding sentence.)

_____

_____

2. My grandmother, who is seventy, delivers papers by car every morning. Then returning home to make breakfast for my grandfather. She has more energy than I do.
   (Correct the fragment by adding the subject *she* and changing *returning* to the proper form of the verb, *returns*.)

   _____

   _____

3. My phone doesn't ring. Instead, a light on it blinks. The reason for this being that I am partially deaf.
   (Correct the fragment by changing *being* to the proper form of the verb, *is*.)

   _____

   _____

Activity 2

Underline the *-ing* or *to* fragment in each item. Then rewrite each item, correcting the fragments by using one of the three methods described above.

1. Flora scratched her mosquito bites. Trying to stop the itching. Instead, they began to bleed.

   _____

   _____

2. I put a box of baking soda in the freezer. To get rid of the musty smell. However, my ice cubes still taste like old socks.

   _____

   _____

3. Staring at the clock on the far wall. I nervously began my speech. I was afraid to look at any of the people in the room.

   _____

   _____

4. Larry sat quietly at his desk. Fantasizing about the upcoming weekend. He might meet the girl of his dreams at Saturday night's party.

   _____

   _____

5. To get to the bus station from here. You have to walk two blocks out of your way. The sidewalk is torn up because of construction work.

   _____

ADDED-DETAIL FRAGMENTS

Added-detail fragments lack a subject and a verb. They often begin with one of the following words:

also	especially	except	for example	including	such as

Underline the one added-detail fragment in each of the following items:

1. Before a race, I eat starchy foods. Such as bread and spaghetti. The carbohydrates provide quick energy.
2. Bob is taking a night course in auto mechanics. Also, one in plumbing. He wants to save money on household repairs.
3. My son keeps several pets in his room. Including hamsters, mice, and gerbils.

People often write added-detail fragments for much the same reason they write *-ing* fragments. They think the subject and verb in one sentence will serve for the next word group. But the subject and verb must be in *each* word group.

How to Correct Added-Detail Fragments

1 Attach the fragment to the complete thought that precedes it. Item 1 could read: "Before a race, I eat starchy foods such as bread and spaghetti."

2 Add a subject and a verb to the fragment to make it a complete sentence. Item 2 could read: "Bob is taking a night course in auto mechanics. Also, he is taking one in plumbing."

3 Change words as necessary to make the fragment part of the preceding sentence. Item 3 could read: "My son keeps several pets, including hamsters, mice, and gerbils, in his room."

Activity 1

Underline the fragment in each of the following items. Then make it a sentence by rewriting it, using the method described in parentheses.

Example My mother likes watching daytime television shows. Especially old movies and soap operas. She says that daytime television is less violent. (Add the fragment to the preceding sentence.)

My mother likes watching daytime television shows, especially old

movies and soap operas.

1. Luis works evenings in a video store. He enjoys the fringe benefits. For example, seeing the new movies first.
   (Correct the fragment by adding the subject and verb *he sees*.)

   _____

   _____

2. Bob's fingernails are ragged from years of working as a mechanic. And his fingertips are always black. Like ink pads.
   (Add the fragment to the preceding sentence.)

   _____

   _____

3. Schools are beginning to use advanced technology. For instance, computers and word processors. Tomorrow's students will be ''computer-literate.''
   (Correct the fragment by adding the subject and verb *they are using*.)

   _____

   _____

Activity 2

Underline the added-detail fragment in each item. Then rewrite to correct the fragment. Use one of the three methods described above.

1. Left-handed students face problems. For example, right-handed desks. Spiral notebooks can also be uncomfortable to use.

   _____

   _____

2. Mrs. Daly always wears her lucky clothes to bingo. Such as a blouse printed with four-leaf clovers. She also carries a rhinestone horseshoe.

   _____

   _____

3. With all the moths swarming around the stadium lights. I almost thought it was snowing. The eighty-degree weather, though, made this unlikely.

   _____

   _____

4. Jack buys and sells paper collectors' items. For instance, baseball cards and movie posters. He sets up a display at local flea markets and county fairs.

   _____

   _____

5. I wonder now why I had to learn certain subjects. Such as geometry. No one has ever asked me about the hypotenuse of a triangle.

_____

_____

MISSING-SUBJECT FRAGMENTS

In each item below, underline the word group in which the subject is missing:

1. Alice loved getting wedding presents. But hated writing thank-you notes.
2. Mickey has orange soda and potato chips for breakfast. Then eats more junk food, like root beer and cookies, for lunch.

How to Correct Missing-Subject Fragments

1 Attach the fragment to the preceding sentence. Item 1 could read: ''Alice loved getting wedding presents but hated writing thank-you notes.''

2 Add a subject (which can often be a pronoun standing for the subject in the preceding sentence). Item 2 could read: ''Then he eats more junk food, like root beer and cookies, for lunch.''

Activity

Underline the missing-subject fragment in each selection. Then rewrite that part of the selection needed to correct the fragment. Use one of the two methods of correction described above.

1. Every other day, Karen runs two miles. Then does fifty sit-ups. She hasn't lost weight, but what she had has been redistributed.

_____

_____

_____

2. I like all kinds of fresh pizza. But refuse to eat frozen pies. The sauce on them is always dried out, and the crust tastes like leather.

_____

_____

_____

3. Scientists have invented a computerized doctor. It takes every Wednesday off. And plays video golf.

_____

_____

_____

4. To be a defensive driver, you must assume the worst. Every other driver on the road is incompetent. And is out there trying to kill you.

_____

_____

_____

5. Last semester, I took six courses. And worked part-time in a discount drugstore. Now that the term is all over, I don't know how I did it.

_____

_____

A Review: How to Check for Sentence Fragments

1 Read your paper aloud from the *last* sentence to the *first*. You will be better able to see and hear whether each word group you read is a complete thought.

2 Ask yourself of any word group you think is a fragment: Does this contain a subject and a verb and express a complete thought?

3 More specifically, be on the lookout for the most common fragments:

- Dependent-word fragments (starting with words like *after, because, since, when,* and *before*)
- *-ing* and *to* fragments (*-ing* or *to* at or near the start of a word group)
- Added-detail fragments (starting with words like *for example, such as, also,* and *especially*)
- Missing-subject fragments (a verb is present but not the subject)

■ **Review Test 1**

Each word group in the following student paragraph is numbered. In the space provided, write C if a word group is a complete sentence; write F if it is a fragment. You will find eight fragments in the paragraph.

_____	1. ¹I'm starting to think that there is no safe place left. ²To ride a bicycle.
_____	2. ³When I try to ride on the highway, in order to go to school. ⁴I feel like a rabbit
_____	3. being pursued by predators. ⁵Drivers whip past me at high speeds. ⁶And try to
_____	4. see how close they can get to my bike without actually killing me. ⁷When they
_____	5. pull onto the shoulder of the road or make a right turn. ⁸Drivers completely
_____	6. ignore my vehicle. ⁹On city streets, I feel more like a cockroach than a rabbit.
_____	7. ¹⁰Drivers in the city despise bicycles. ¹¹Regardless of an approaching bike rider.
_____	8. ¹²Street-side car doors will unexpectedly open. ¹³Frustrated drivers who are
_____	9. stuck in traffic will make nasty comments. ¹⁴Or shout out obscene propositions.
_____	10. ¹⁵Even pedestrians in the city show their disregard for me. ¹⁶While jaywalking
_____	11. across the street. ¹⁷The pedestrian will treat me, a law-abiding bicyclist, to a
_____	12. withering look of disdain. ¹⁸Pedestrians may even cross my path deliberately.
_____	13. ¹⁹As if to prove their higher position in the pecking order of the city streets.
_____	14. ²⁰Today, bicycling can be hazardous to the rider's health.
_____	15.
_____	16.
_____	17.
_____	18.
_____	19.
_____	20.

Now (on separate paper) correct the fragments you have found. Attach the fragments to sentences that come before or after them or make whatever other change is needed to turn each fragment into a sentence.

■ **Review Test 2**

Underline the two fragments in each item below. Then make whatever changes are needed to turn the fragments into sentences.

Example   Sharon was going to charge her new suit_x <u>$\overset{b}{B}$ut then decided to pay</u> <u>cash instead.</u> She remembered her New Year's resolution_x <u>$\overset{t}{T}$o cut down</u> <u>on her use of credit cards.</u>

1. We both began to tire. As we passed the halfway mark in the race. But whenever I'd hear Reggie's footsteps behind me. I would pump my legs faster.

2. I have a few phobias. Such as fear of heights and fear of dogs. My nightmare is to be trapped in a hot-air balloon. With three German shepherds.

3. My children joke that we celebrate "Hanumas." With our Jewish neighbors. We share Hanukkah and Christmas activities. Including making potato pancakes at their house and decorating our tree.

4. Punching all the buttons on his radio in sequence. Phil kept looking for a good song. He was in the mood to cruise down the highway. And sing at the top of his voice.

5. I noticed two cartons of cigarettes. Sticking up out of my neighbor's trash bag. I realized he had made up his mind. To give up smoking for the fifth time this year.

6. I've decided to leave home. And rent an apartment. By being away from home and on my own. I will get along better with my parents.

7. The alley behind our house was flat. Except for a wide groove in the center. We used to sail paper boats down the groove. Whenever it rained hard enough to create a "river" there.

8. Don passed the computer school's aptitude test. Which qualifies him for nine months of training. Don kidded that anyone could be accepted. If he or she had $4,000.

■ **Review Test 3**

Turn each of the following word groups into a complete sentence.

Examples With trembling hands

With trembling hands, I headed for the front of the classroom.

As the race wore on

Some runners dropped out as the race wore on.

1. After the storm passed

2. Such as fresh fruits and vegetables

3. During the mystery movie

4. But soon grew frustrated

5. Norma, who hates housework

6. To get to class on time

7. The ants swarming over the lollipop

8. Hurrying to get dressed

9. Up in the attic

10. Losing my temper

RUN-ONS

WHAT ARE RUN-ONS?

A *run-on* is two complete thoughts that are run together with no adequate sign given to mark the break between them.*

Some run-ons have no punctuation at all to mark the break between the thoughts. Such run-ons are known as *fused sentences*: they are fused or joined together as if they were only one thought.

Fused Sentences

Tim told everyone in the room to be quiet his favorite show was on.

My blow-dryer shorted out I showed up for work with Harpo Marx hair.

In other run-ons, known as *comma splices,* a comma is used to connect or "splice" together the two complete thoughts. However, a comma alone is *not enough* to connect two complete thoughts. Some stronger connection than a comma alone is needed.

Comma Splices

Tim told everyone in the room to be quiet, his favorite show was on.

My blow-dryer shorted out, I showed up for work with Harpo Marx hair.

Comma splices are the most common kind of run-on. Students sense that some kind of connection is needed between two thoughts, and so they often put a comma at the dividing point. But the comma alone is *not sufficient.* A stronger, clearer mark is needed between the two thoughts.

*Note: Some instructors refer to each complete thought in a run-on as an *independent clause.* A *clause* is simply a group of words having a subject and a verb. A clause may be *independent* (expressing a complete thought and able to stand alone) or *dependent* (not expressing a complete thought and not able to stand alone). Using this terminology, we'd say that a run-on is two independent clauses run together with no adequate sign given to mark the break between them.

A Warning—Words That Can Lead to Run-Ons: People often write run-ons when the second complete thought begins with one of the following words:

I	we	there	now
you	they	this	then
he, she, it	that	next	

Remember to be on the alert for run-ons whenever you use one of these words in writing a paper.

HOW TO CORRECT RUN-ONS

Here are three common methods of correcting a run-on:

1   Use a period and a capital letter to break the two complete thoughts into separate sentences.

Tim told everyone in the room to be quiet. His favorite show was on.
My blow-dryer shorted out. I showed up for work with Harpo Marx hair.

2   Use a comma plus a joining word (*and, but, for, or, nor, so, yet*) to connect the two complete thoughts:

Tim told everyone in the room to be quiet, for his favorite show was on.
My blow-dryer shorted out, and I showed up for work with Harpo Marx hair.

3   Use a semicolon to connect the two complete thoughts:

Tim told everyone in the room to be quiet; his favorite show was on.
My blow-dryer shorted out; I showed up for work with Harpo Marx hair.

A fourth method of correcting a run-on is to use *subordination.* The following activities will give you practice in the first three methods. Subordination will be described fully on page 479, in a section of the book that deals with sentence variety.

Method 1: Period and a Capital Letter

One way of correcting a run-on is to use a period and a capital letter at the break between the two complete thoughts. Use this method especially if the thoughts are not closely related or if another method would make the sentence too long.

Activity

Locate the split in each of the following run-ons. Each is a *fused sentence*—that is, each consists of two sentences fused or joined together with no punctuation at all between them. Reading each sentence aloud will help you "hear" where a major break or split in the thought occurs. At such a point, your voice will probably drop and pause.

Correct the run-on by putting a period at the end of the first thought and a capital letter at the start of the next thought.

Example   Bev's clock radio doesn't work anymore $\overset{S}{\cancel{s}}$he spilled a glass of soda on it.

1.   The telephone salesman offered a deal on vinyl siding he wanted to drop by and give us a free estimate.

2.   Joyce, a paralegal, helps some people write wills she assists others in divorce and child custody proceedings.

3.   Vicky has her own unique style of dressing she wore a man's tuxedo with a red bow tie to her cousin's wedding.

4.   In the summer, ants are attracted to water they will often enter a house through the dishwasher.

5.   Humans have managed to adapt to any environment they can survive in Arctic wastes, tropical jungles, and barren deserts.

6.   A five-year-old child knows over six thousand words he or she has also learned more than one thousand rules of grammar.

7.   I rummaged around the crowded drawer looking for a pair of scissors then it suddenly stabbed me in the finger.

8.   Squirrels like to jump from trees onto our roof their footsteps sound like ghosts running around our attic.

9. Today I didn't make good time driving to work every traffic light along the way was red.

10. As a result of a cable hookup, we now receive over forty stations on our television I sometimes waste an entire evening just clicking from one channel to the next.

Method 2: Comma and a Joining Word

Another way of correcting a run-on is to use a comma plus a joining word to connect the two complete thoughts. Joining words (also called *conjunctions*) include *and, but, for, or, nor, so,* and *yet*. Here is what the four most common joining words mean:

and in addition to, along with

Teresa works full time for an accounting firm, and she takes evening classes.

(*And* means *in addition:* Teresa works full time for an accounting firm; *in addition,* she takes evening classes.)

but however, except, on the other hand, just the opposite

I turned to the want ads, but I knew my dream job wouldn't be listed.

(*But* means *however:* I turned to the want ads; *however,* I knew my dream job wouldn't be listed.)

for because, the reason why, the cause for something

Lizards become sluggish at night, for they need the sun's warmth to maintain an active body temperature.

(*For* means *because* or *the reason why:* Lizards become sluggish at night; *the reason why* is that they need the sun's warmth to maintain an active body temperature.)

so as a result, therefore

The canoe touched bottom, so Dave pushed it toward deeper water.

(*So* means *as a result:* The canoe touched bottom; *as a result,* Dave pushed it toward deeper water.)

Activity 1

Insert the joining word (*and, but, for, so*) that logically connects the two thoughts in each sentence.

1. Napoleon may have been a brave general, _____ he was afraid of cats.

2. The large dog was growling at me, _____ there were white bubbles of foam around his mouth.

3. The library had just closed, _____ I couldn't get any of the reserved books.

4. He checked on the new baby every five minutes, _____ he was afraid something would happen to her.

5. Kate thought the milk was fresh, _____ it broke up into little sour flakes in her coffee.

6. An infant elephant has no thumbs, _____ it sucks its trunk.

7. Lew heard a noise and looked out the window, _____ the only thing there was his reflection.

8. Have you noticed that one of our English instructor's eyes is green, _____ the other is brown?

9. My sister saves all her empty wine bottles, _____ she likes to make lamps out of them.

10. A young woman in our neighborhood recently tried to kill herself, _____ her friends are afraid that she will try it again.

Activity 2

Add a complete and closely related thought to go with each of the following statements. Use a comma plus the italicized joining word when you write the second thought.

Example *for* I decided to leave school an hour early, *for I had a pounding headache.*

but 1. The corner store is convenient _____
_____

for 2. Leo attended night class _____
_____

and   3. Brenda studied for an hour before dinner _____

_____

so   4. Our field trip had been canceled _____

_____

but   5. I needed a haircut _____

_____

Activity 3

Correct each run-on with either (1) a period and a capital letter or (2) a comma and a logical joining word. Do not use the same method of correction for every sentence.

Some of the run-ons are fused sentences (there is no punctuation between the two complete thoughts) and some are comma splices (there is only a comma between the two complete thoughts). One sentence is correct.

Example   There was a strange odor in the house, ^so Burt called the gas company immediately.

1. Jackie smeared cream cheese on the bagel half, then she popped it into her mouth.

2. Cockroaches adapt to any environment they have even been found living inside nuclear reactors.

3. My dog was panting from the heat I decided to wet him down with the garden hose.

4. The college installed a dish antenna outside the science building it picks up satellite broadcasting from all over the world.

5. The best-selling items in the zoo gift shop are the stuffed pandas and the polar bear T shirts the profits from these items help support the real animals in the zoo.

6. The bristles of the paintbrushes were very stiff, soaking them in turpentine made them soft again.

7. Tran bought cassettes to listen to on the way to work, some of them were recordings of best-selling books.

8. Last week, Rita's two boys chased the baby-sitter out of the house, now the girl won't come back.

9. We knew a power failure had occurred, for all the clocks in the building were forty-seven minutes slow.

10. I volunteered to run the ''Meals on Wheels'' service in our city we deliver hot meals to sick or housebound people.

Method 3: Semicolon

A third method of correcting a run-on is to use a semicolon to mark the break between two thoughts. A *semicolon* (;) looks like a period above a comma and is sometimes called a *strong comma*. A semicolon signals more of a pause than a comma alone but not quite the full pause of a period. When it is used to correct run-ons, the semicolon can be used alone or with a transitional word.

Semicolon Alone: Here are some earlier sentences that were connected with a comma plus a joining word. Now they are connected by a semicolon alone. Notice that the semicolon alone—unlike the comma alone—can be used to connect the two complete thoughts in each sentence:

Lew heard a noise and looked out the window; the only thing there was his reflection.

He checked on the new baby every five minutes; he was afraid something would happen to her.

Lizards become sluggish at night; they need the sun's warmth to maintain an active body temperature.

The large dog was growling at me; there were white bubbles of foam around his mouth.

We knew a power failure had occurred; all the clocks in the building were forty-seven minutes slow.

Using semicolons can add to sentence variety. For some people, however, the semicolon is a confusing mark of punctuation. Keep in mind that if you are not comfortable using it, you can and should use one of the first two methods of correcting run-ons.

Activity

Insert a semicolon where the break occurs between the two complete thoughts in each of the following sentences.

Example   The plumber gave me an estimate of $60; I decided to repair the faucet myself.

1.   The children stared at the artichokes on their plates they didn't know how to eat the strange vegetable.
2.   I changed that light bulb just last week now it's blown again.
3.   The "no-frills" supermarket doesn't sell perishables like milk or meat customers must bring their own bags or boxes to pack their bargains.
4.   Elaine woke up at 3 A.M. to the smell of sizzling bacon her husband was having another insomnia attack.
5.   Jamie curled up under the covers she tried to get warm by grasping her icy feet with her chilly hands.
6.   Three single mothers rent one house they share bills and help each other out.
7.   Ice had formed on the inside edge of our window Joey scratched a J in it with his finger.
8.   Charles peered into the microscope he saw only his own eyelashes.
9.   Guests were laughing and drinking at the party my uncle was doing his John Wayne imitation.
10. I angrily punched a hole in the wall with my fist later I covered the hole with a picture.

Semicolon with a Transitional Word   A semicolon can be used with a transitional word and a comma to join two complete thoughts. Here are some examples:

Larry believes in being prepared for emergencies; therefore, he stockpiles canned goods in his basement.

I tried to cash my paycheck; however, I had forgotten to bring identification.

Athletic shoes must fit perfectly; otherwise, the wearer may injure the feet or ankles.

A short nap at the end of the day relaxes me; in addition, it gives me the energy to spend the evening on my homework.

Some zoo animals have not learned how to be good parents; as a result, baby animals are sometimes brought up in zoo nurseries and even in private homes.

People use seventeen muscles when they smile; on the other hand, they use forty-three muscles when they frown.

Following is a list of common transitional words (also known as *adverbial conjunctions*), with brief meanings.

Transitional Word	Meaning
however	but
nevertheless	however
on the other hand	however
instead	as a substitute
meanwhile	in the intervening time
otherwise	under other conditions
indeed	in fact
in addition	also, and
also	in addition
moreover	in addition
furthermore	in addition
as a result	thus, therefore
thus	as a result
consequently	as a result
therefore	as a result

Activity

For each sentence, choose a logical transitional word from the box above and write it in the space provided. Use a semicolon *before* the connector and a comma *after* it.

Example   I dread going to parties; <u>*however*</u>, my husband loves meeting new people.

1. Jackie suffers from migraine headaches _____ her doctor has advised her to avoid caffeine and alcohol.

2. Ray's apartment is always neat and clean _____ the interior of his car looks like the aftermath of a tornado.

3. I try to attend all my math classes _____ I'll get too far behind to pass the weekly quizzes.

4. Dan was singing Whitney Houston tunes in the shower _____ his toast was burning in the kitchen.

5. The reporter was tough and experienced _____ even he was stunned by the tragic events.

A Note on Subordination

A fourth method of joining related thoughts is to use subordination. *Subordination* is a way of showing that one thought in a sentence is not as important as another thought. (Subordination is explained in full on page 479.) Here are three earlier sentences, recast so that one idea is subordinated to (made less important than) the other idea:

Because the library had just closed, I couldn't get any of the reserved books.

When the canoe touched bottom, Dave pushed the craft toward deeper water.

I didn't make good time driving to work today, because every traffic light was red.

A Review: How to Check for Run-Ons

1 To see if a sentence is a run-on, read it aloud and listen for a break marking two complete thoughts. Your voice will probably drop and pause at the break.

2 To check an entire paper, read it aloud from the *last* sentence to the *first*. Doing so will help you hear and see each complete thought.

3 Be on the lookout for words that can lead to run-on sentences:

I	he, she, it	they	this	then
you	we	there	that	next

4 Correct run-ons by using one of the following methods:

- Period and a capital letter
- Comma and a joining word (*and, but, for, or, nor, so, yet*)
- Semicolon
- Subordination (as explained on page 479)

■   ## Review Test 1

Correct each run-on with either (1) a period and a capital letter or (2) a comma (if needed) and the joining word *and, but, for,* or *so.* Do not use the same method of correction for every sentence.

Some of the run-ons are fused sentences (there is no punctuation between the two complete thoughts), and some are comma splices (there is only a comma between the two complete thoughts). One sentence is correct.

1.   Our boss expects us to work four hours without a break, he wanders off to a vending machine at least once an hour.

2.   By late afternoon the bank had closed its front doors for the day I moved my car into a long line waiting to use the bank's drive-in window.

3.   Chuck bent over and lifted the heavy tray then he heard an ominous crack in his back.

4.   The branches of the tree were bare they made a dark feathery pattern against the orange-pink sunset.

5.   In the grimy bakery window, cobwebs were in every corner, a rat was crawling over a birthday cake.

6.   Our class wanted to do something for the earthquake victims, we sent a donation to the Red Cross.

7.   My ex-husband hit me just once in our marriage five minutes later I was packed and walking out the door.

8.   The boys dared each other to enter the abandoned building then they heard a strange rustling noise coming from the murky interior.

9.   The average American teenager spends thirty-eight hours a week on schoolwork the average Japanese teenager spends about sixty.

10.   We stocked our backpacks with high-calorie candy bars, and we also brought bags of dried apricots and peaches.

■ Review Test 2

Correct each run-on by using (1) a period and a capital letter, (2) a comma and a joining word, or (3) a semicolon. Do not use one method exclusively.

1. The magazine had lain in the damp mailbox for two days its pages were blurry and swollen.

2. With a groan, Margo pried off her high heels, then she plunged her swollen feet into a bucket of baking soda and hot water.

3. At 2 A.M. the last customer left the diner, a busboy began stacking chairs on the tables for the night.

4. Hypnosis has nothing to do with the occult it is merely a state of deep relaxation.

5. Many young adults today live at home with their parents this allows them to save money for the future.

6. I waited for the clanking train to clear the intersection rusty boxcars just kept rolling slowly along the rails.

7. Science will soon produce tomatoes that are more nutritious, they will also be square-shaped for easier packing.

8. Originally, horses were too small to carry riders very far larger horses had to be bred for use in warfare.

9. Suitcases circled on the conveyor belt at the airline baggage claim loose oranges from a broken carton tumbled along with them.

10. The broken soda machine dispensed either a cup or a soda, it would not provide both at the same time.

■ **Review Test 3**

Locate and correct the five run-ons in the passage that follows.

My worst experience of the week was going home for lunch, rather than eating at work. My children didn't know I was coming, they had used most of the bread on hand. All I had to make a sandwich with were two thin, crumpled pieces of crust. I sat there eating my tattered sandwich and trying to relax, then the telephone rang. It was for my daughter, who was in the bathroom, she called down to me that I should get the person's name and number. As soon as I sat down again, someone knocked on the door, it was a neatly dressed couple with bright eyes who wanted to talk with me about a higher power in life. I politely got rid of them and went back to finish lunch. I thought I would relax over my coffee I had to break up a fight between my two young sons about which television channel to watch. As a last bit of frustration, my daughter came downstairs and asked me to drive her over to a friend's house before I went back to work.

■ **Review Test 4**

Write quickly for five minutes about what you did this past weekend. Don't worry about spelling, punctuation, finding exact words, or organizing your thoughts. Just focus on writing as many words as you can without stopping.

After you have finished, go back and correct any run-ons in your writing.

REGULAR AND IRREGULAR VERBS

REGULAR VERBS

A Brief Review of Regular Verbs

Every verb has four principal parts: *present, past, past participle,* and *present participle.* These parts can be used to build all the verb tenses (the times shown by a verb).

Most verbs in English are regular. The past and past participles of a regular verb are formed by adding *-d* or *-ed* to the present. The *past participle* is the form of the verb used with the helping verbs *have, has,* or *had* (or some form of *be* with passive verbs). The *present participle* is formed by adding *-ing* to the present.

Here are the principal parts of some regular verbs:

Present	Past	Past Participle	Present Participle
shout	shouted	shouted	shouting
prepare	prepared	prepared	preparing
surprise	surprised	surprised	surprising
tease	teased	teased	teasing
frighten	frightened	frightened	frightening

Nonstandard Forms of Regular Verbs

Many people have grown up in communities where nonstandard forms of regular verbs are used in everyday speech. Instead of saying, for example, "That girl *looks* tired," a person using a community dialect might say, "That girl *look* tired." Instead of saying, "Yesterday I *fixed* the car," a person using a community dialect might say, "Yesterday I *fix* the car." Community dialects have richness and power but are a drawback in college and in the world of work, where regular English verb forms must be used.

The chart below compares the nonstandard and the regular verb forms of the verb *work*.

Nonstandard Verb Form (Do *not* use in your writing)		Regular Verb Form (Use for clear communication)	
Present tense			
I works	we works	I work	we work
you works	you works	you work	you work
he, she, it work	they works	he, she, it works	they work
Past tense			
I work	we work	I worked	we worked
you work	you work	you worked	you worked
he, she, it work	they work	he, she, it worked	they worked

To avoid nonstandard usage, memorize the forms shown above for the regular verb *work*. Then use the activities that follow to help make the inclusion of standard verb endings a writing habit.

Present Tense Endings: The verb ending -*s* or -*es* is needed with a regular verb in the present tense when the subject is *he, she, it,* or any *one person or thing.*

He reads every night.

She watches television every night.

It appears they have little in common.

Activity

Some verbs in the sentences that follow need *-s* or *-es* endings. Cross out each nonstandard verb form and write the standard form in the space provided.

———————   1.   My radio wake me up every morning with soft music.

———————   2.   Lyle always clown around at the start of the class.

———————   3.   My wife watch our baby in the morning, and I take over afternoons.

———————   4.   Brenda want to go to nursing school next year.

———————   5.   My brain work much better at night than it does in early morning.

Past Tense Endings: The verb ending *-d* or *-ed* is needed with a regular verb in the past tense.

This morning I completed my research paper.
The recovering hospital patient walked slowly down the corridor.
Some students hissed when the new assignment was given out.

Activity

Some verbs in the sentences that follow need *-d* or *-ed* endings. Cross out each nonstandard verb form and write the standard form in the space provided.

———————   1.   One of my teeth cave in when I bit on the hard pretzel.

———————   2.   The accident victim complain of dizziness right before passing out.

———————   3.   We realize a package was missing when we got back from shopping.

———————   4.   I burn a hole in my shirt while ironing it.

———————   5.   The driver edge her car into the intersection while the light was still red.

IRREGULAR VERBS

Irregular verbs have irregular forms in past tense and past participle. For example, the past tense of the irregular verb *choose* is *chose*; its past participle is *chosen*.

Almost everyone has some degree of trouble with irregular verbs. When you are unsure about the form of a verb, you can check the list of irregular verbs on the following pages. (The present participle is not shown on this list because it is formed simply by adding *-ing* to the base form of the verb.) Or you can check a dictionary, which gives the principal parts of irregular verbs.

A List of Irregular Verbs

Present	Past	Past Participle
arise	arose	arisen
awake	awoke *or* awaked	awoken *or* awaked
be (am, are, is)	was (were)	been
become	became	become
begin	began	begun
bend	bent	bent
bite	bit	bitten
blow	blew	blown
break	broke	broken
bring	brought	brought
build	built	built
burst	burst	burst
buy	bought	bought
catch	caught	caught
choose	chose	chosen
come	came	come
cost	cost	cost
cut	cut	cut
do (does)	did	done
draw	drew	drawn
drink	drank	drunk
drive	drove	driven
eat	ate	eaten
fall	fell	fallen
feed	fed	fed
feel	felt	felt
fight	fought	fought
find	found	found
fly	flew	flown
freeze	froze	frozen
get	got	got *or* gotten
give	gave	given
go (goes)	went	gone
grow	grew	grown
have (has)	had	had
hear	heard	heard
hide	hid	hidden
hold	held	held
hurt	hurt	hurt
keep	kept	kept

Present	*Past*	*Past Participle*
know	knew	known
lay	laid	laid
lead	led	led
leave	left	left
lend	lent	lent
let	let	let
lie	lay	lain
light	lit	lit
lose	lost	lost
make	made	made
meet	met	met
pay	paid	paid
ride	rode	ridden
ring	rang	rung
run	ran	run
say	said	said
see	saw	seen
sell	sold	sold
send	sent	sent
shake	shook	shaken
shrink	shrank	shrunk
shut	shut	shut
sing	sang	sung
sit	sat	sat
sleep	slept	slept
speak	spoke	spoken
spend	spent	spent
stand	stood	stood
steal	stole	stolen
stick	stuck	stuck
sting	stung	stung
swear	swore	sworn
swim	swam	swum
take	took	taken
teach	taught	taught
tear	tore	torn
tell	told	told
think	thought	thought
wake	woke *or* waked	woken *or* waked
wear	wore	worn
win	won	won
write	wrote	written

Activity

Cross out the incorrect verb form in each of the following sentences. Then write the correct form of the verb in the space provided.

flown   **Example**   After it had ~~flew~~ into the picture window, the dazed bird huddled on the ground.

_____ 1. As graduation neared, Michelle worried about the practicality of the major she'd chose.

_____ 2. Before we could find seats, the theater darkened and the opening credits begun to roll.

_____ 3. To be polite, I drunk the slightly sour wine that my grandfather poured from his carefully hoarded supply.

_____ 4. With a thunderous crack, the telephone pole breaked in half from the impact of the speeding car.

_____ 5. The inexperienced nurse shrunk from touching the patient's raw, burned skin.

_____ 6. After a day on the noisy construction site, Sam's ears rung for hours with a steady hum.

_____ 7. Sheila had forgot to write her social security number on the test form, so the computer rejected her answer sheet.

_____ 8. If I had went to work ten minutes earlier, I would have avoided being caught in the gigantic traffic snarl.

_____ 9. After the bicycle hit a patch of soft sand, the rider was throwed into the thorny bushes by the roadside.

_____ 10. Prehistoric people blowed paint over their outstretched hands to stencil their handprints on cave walls.

Nonstandard Forms of Three Common Irregular Verbs

People who use nonstandard forms of regular verbs also tend to use nonstandard forms of three common irregular verbs: *be, have,* and *do.* Instead of saying, for example, "My neighbors *are* nice people," a person using a nonstandard form might say, "My neighbors *be* nice people." Instead of saying, "She doesn't agree," they might say, "She *don't* agree." Instead of saying, "We have tickets," they might say, "We *has* tickets."

The following charts compare the nonstandard and the standard forms of *be, have,* and *do.*

Be

Community Dialect (Do not use in your writing)		Standard English (Use for clear communication)	
Present tense			
I be (*or* is)	we be	I am	we are
you be	you be	you are	you are
he, she, it be	they be	he, she, it is	they are
Past tense			
I were	we was	I was	we were
you was	you was	you were	you were
he, she, it were	they was	he, she, it was	they were

Have

Community Dialect (Do not use in your writing)		Standard English (Use for clear communication)	
Present tense			
I has	we has	I have	we have
you has	you has	you have	you have
he, she, it have	they has	he, she, it has	they have
Past tense			
I has	we has	I had	we had
you has	you has	you had	you had
he, she, it have	they has	he, she, it had	they had

Do

Community Dialect		Standard English	
(Do not use in your writing)		(Use for clear communication)	
Present tense			
I does	we do	I do	we do
you does	you does	you do	you do
he, she, it do	they does	he, she, it does	they do
Past tense			
I done	we done	I did	we did
you done	you done	you did	you did
he, she, it done	they done	he, she, it did	they did

Note: Many people have trouble with one negative form of *do.* They will say, for example, "He don't agree" instead of "He doesn't agree," or they will say "The door don't work" instead of "The door doesn't work." Be careful to avoid the common mistake of using *don't* instead of *doesn't.*

Activity

Cross out the nonstandard verb form in each sentence. Then write the standard form of *be, have,* or *do* in the space provided.

_____ 1. My cat, Tugger, be the toughest animal I know.

_____ 2. He have survived many close calls.

_____ 3. Three years ago, he were caught inside a car's engine.

_____ 4. He have one ear torn off and lost the sight in one eye.

_____ 5. We was surprised that he lived through the accident.

_____ 6. Within weeks, though, he were back to normal.

_____ 7. Then, last year, we was worried that we would lose Tugger.

_____ 8. Lumps that was growing on his back turned out to be cancer.

_____ 9. But the vet done an operation that saved Tugger's life.

_____ 10. By now, we know that Tugger really do have nine lives.

■ **Review Test 1**

Cross out the incorrect verb form in each sentence. Then write the correct form in the space provided.

_____ 1. The health inspectors walk into the kitchen as the cook was picking up a hamburger off the floor.

_____ 2. The thieves would have stole my stereo, but I had had it engraved with a special identification number.

_____ 3. At the Chinese restaurant, Dave choose his food by the number.

_____ 4. He had tore his girl friend's picture into little pieces and tossed them out the window.

_____ 5. Because I has asthma, I carry an inhaler to use when I lose my breath.

_____ 6. Baked potatoes doesn't have as many calories as I thought.

_____ 7. The grizzly bear, with the dart dangling from its side, begun to feel the effects of the powerful tranquilizer.

_____ 8. Yesterday I check my bank balance and saw my money was getting low.

_____ 9. Many childhood diseases has almost vanished in the United States.

_____ 10. Nancy sticked notes on the refrigerator with fruit-shaped magnets.

■ **Review Test 2**

Write short sentences that use the form requested for the following verbs.

Example Past of _grow_ _I grew my own tomatoes last year._

1. Past of _know_ _____

2. Present of _take_ _____

3. Past participle of _give_ _____

4. Past participle of _write_ _____

5. Past of _do_ _____

6. Past of _talk_ _____

7. Present of _begin_ _____

8. Past of _go_ _____

9. Past participle of _see_ _____

10. Present of _drive_ _____

SUBJECT-VERB AGREEMENT

A verb must agree with its subject in number. A *singular subject* (one person or thing) takes a singular verb. A *plural subject* (more than one person or thing) takes a plural verb. Mistakes in subject-verb agreement are sometimes made in the following situations:

1   When words come between the subject and the verb
2   When a verb comes before the subject
3   With compound subjects
4   With indefinite pronouns

Each of these situations is explained on the following pages.

WORDS BETWEEN SUBJECT AND VERB

Words that come between the subject and the verb do not change subject-verb agreement. In the sentence

The crinkly <u>lines</u> *around Joan's eyes* <u>give</u> her a friendly look.

the subject (*lines*) is plural and so the verb (*give*) is plural. The words *around Joan's eyes* that come between the subject and the verb do not affect subject-verb agreement.

To help find the subject of certain sentences, you should cross out prepositional phrases.

The lumpy <u>salt</u> ~~in the shakers~~ <u>needs</u> to be changed.
An old <u>television</u> ~~with a round screen~~ <u>has sat</u> in our basement for years.

Activity

Underline the subject and lightly cross out any words that come between the subject and the verb. Then double-underline the verb choice in parentheses that you believe is correct.

1. Some members of the parents' association (want, wants) to ban certain books from the school library.

2. The rising costs of necessities like food and shelter (force, forces) many elderly people to live in poverty.

3. Misconceptions about apes like the gorilla (has, have) turned a relatively peaceful animal into a terrifying monster.

4. Chuck's trench coat, with its big lapels and shoulder flaps, (make, makes) him feel like a tough private eye.

5. The high-pressure saleswomen in the designer dresses department (make, makes) me feel intimidated.

VERB BEFORE SUBJECT

A verb agrees with its subject even when the verb comes *before* the subject. Words that may precede the subject include *there, here,* and, in questions, *who, which, what,* and *where.*

Here are some examples of sentences in which the verb appears before the subject:

There are wild dogs in our neighborhood.
In the distance was a billow of black smoke.
Here is the newspaper.
Where are the children's coats?

If you are unsure about the subject, ask *who* or *what* of the verb. With the first example above, you might ask, "*What* are in our neighborhood?" The answer, *wild dogs,* is the subject.

Activity

Write the correct form of the verb in the space provided.

(is, are)   1. There _____ dozens of frenzied shoppers waiting for the store to open.

(is, are)   2. Here _____ the notes from yesterday's anthropology lecture.

(do, does)   3. When _____ we take our break?

(was, were)   4. There _____ scraps of yellowing paper stuck between the pages of the book.

(was, were)   5. At the very bottom of the grocery list _____ an item that meant a trip all the way back to aisle 1.

COMPOUND SUBJECTS

Subjects joined by *and* generally take a plural verb.

A patchwork quilt and a sleeping bag cover my bed in the winter.
Clark and Lois are a contented couple.

When subjects are joined by *either . . . or, neither . . . nor, not only . . . but also,* the verb agrees with the subject closer to the verb.

Neither the negotiator nor the union leaders want the strike to continue.
The nearer subject, *leaders,* is plural, and so the verb is plural.

Activity

Write the correct form of the verb in the space provided.

(sit, sits)   1. A crusty baking pan and a greasy plate _____ on the countertop.

(cover, covers) 2. Spidery cracks and a layer of dust _____ the ivory keys on the old piano.

(know, knows)   3. Not only the assistant manager but also the secretaries _____ that the company is folding.

(was, were)   4. In eighteenth-century France, makeup and high heels _____ worn by men.

(make, makes)   5. For women, a dark suit or dress and a pair of plain, closed shoes _____ the best impression at a job interview.

INDEFINITE PRONOUNS

The following words, known as *indefinite pronouns,* always take singular verbs:

(*-one* words)	(*-body* words)	(*-thing* words)	
one	nobody	nothing	each
anyone	anybody	anything	either
everyone	everybody	everything	neither
someone	somebody	something	

Note: *Both* always takes a plural verb.

Activity

Write the correct form of the verb in the space provided.

(suit, suits)   1. Neither of those hairstyles _____ the shape of your face.

(mention, mentions)   2. Somebody without much sensitivity always _____ my birthmark.

(give, gives)   3. Something in certain kinds of aged cheese _____ me a headache.

(enter, enters)   4. Everyone _____ the college kite-flying contest in the spring.

(fall, falls)   5. One of these earrings constantly _____ off my ear.

■ Review Test 1

In the space provided, write the correct form of the verb shown in the margin.

(is, are)   1. Some wheelchair-bound patients, as a result of a successful experiment, _____ using trained monkeys as helpers.

(was, were)   2. Each of their children _____ given a name picked at random from a page of the Bible.

(seem, seems)   3. Many of the headlines in the *National Enquirer* _____ hard to believe.

(is, are)   4. Envelopes, file folders, and a telephone book _____ jammed into Karen's kitchen drawers.

(contains, contain)   5. Neither of the textbooks _____ the answer to question 5 of the "open-book" exam.

(damage, damages)   6. The use of metal chains and studded tires _____ roadways by chipping away at the paved surface.

(was, were)   7. Next to the cash register _____ a can for donations to the animal protection society.

(makes, make)   8. A metal grab bar bolted onto the tiles _____ it easier for elderly people to get in and out of the bathtub.

(cleans, clean)   9. In exchange for a reduced rent, Karla and James _____ the dentist's office beneath their second-floor apartment.

(is, are)   10. One of the hospital's delivery rooms _____ furnished with bright carpets and curtains to resemble a room at home.

■ **Review Test 2**

Cross out the incorrect verb form in each sentence. In addition, underline the subject or subjects that go with the verb. Then write the correct form of the verb in the space provided.

_____   1. Why is Martha and her mother digging a hole in their garden so late at night?

_____   2. Neither of my children look like me.

_____   3. Several packages and a supermarket circular was lying on the porch mat.

_____   4. The little balls all over my pink sweater looks like woolen goose bumps.

_____   5. Here is the low-calorie cola and the double-chocolate cake you ordered.

_____   6. The odor of those perfumed ads interfere with my enjoyment of a magazine.

_____   7. One of my roommates are always leaving wet towels on the bathroom floor.

_____   8. A tiny piece of gum and some tape is holding my old glasses together.

_____   9. A man in his forties often begin to think about making a contribution to the world and not just about himself.

_____   10. Each of the players on the school's teams plan to give a uniform shirt to the charity auction.

■ Review Test 3

Complete each of the following sentences using *is, are, was, were, have,* or *has.*
Then underline the subject.

Example For me, <u>popcorn</u> at the movies *is like coffee at breakfast.* _____

1. Under my roommate's bed _____

2. The car with the purple fenders _____

3. My boss and her secretary _____

4. Neither of the football players _____

5. Here are _____

CONSISTENT VERB TENSE

Do not shift verb tenses unnecessarily. If you begin writing a paper in the present tense, do not shift suddenly to the past. If you begin in the past, do not shift without reason to the present. Notice the inconsistent verb tenses in the following example:

Jean *punched* down the risen yeast dough in the bowl. Then she *dumps* it onto the floured worktable and *kneaded* it into a smooth, shiny ball.

The verbs must be consistently in the present tense:

Jean *punches* down the risen yeast dough in the bowl. Then she *dumps* it onto the floured worktable and *kneads* it into a smooth, shiny ball.

Or the verbs must be consistently in the past tense:

Jean *punched* down the risen yeast dough in the bowl. Then she *dumped* it onto the floured worktable and *kneaded* it into a smooth, shiny ball.

Activity

Make the verbs in each sentence consistent with the *first* verb used. Cross out the incorrect verb and write the correct form in the space at the left.

ran　　**Example**　Aunt Helen tried to kiss her little nephew, but he ~~runs~~ out of the room.

_____ 1. An aggressive news photographer knocked a reporter to the ground as the movie stars arrive for the Oscar awards.

_____ 2. As we leafed through the old high school yearbook, we laugh at our outdated clothes and hairstyles.

_____ 3. "My husband is so dumb," said Martha, "that when he went to Las Vegas he tries to play the stamp machines."

_____ 4. In a zero-gravity atmosphere, water breaks up into droplets and floated around in space.

_____ 5. Elliot lights the oven pilot and then stands back as the blue gas flames flared up.

■ **Review Test 1**

Make the verbs in each item consistent with the *first* verb used. Cross out each incorrect verb and write the correct form in the space at the left.

recharge　　**Example**　Several times a year, I like to take a day off, go away by myself, and ~~recharged~~ my mental batteries.

_____ 1. Shampooing the plaid sofa upholstery, he was shocked as the colors fade before his eyes.

_____ 2. The jeep swerved around the corner, went up on two wheels, and tips over on its side.

_____ 3. On the TV commercial for mail-order kitchen knives, an actor cuts a tree branch in half and sliced an aluminum can into ribbons.

_____ 4. Ralph ripped open the bag of cheese puffs with his teeth and stuffs handfuls of the salty orange squiggles into his mouth.

_____ 5. The winning wheelchair racer in the marathon slumped back in exhaustion and asks for some ice to soothe his blistered hands.

_____ 6. From his perch high up on the rocky cliff, the eagle spots a white-tailed rabbit and swooped down toward his victim.

_____ 7. Earl wets his fingers and skimmed the rim of his water glass, producing an eerie whistling noise.

_____   8.   When the great earthquake struck San Francisco in 1906, the entire city burns to the ground in less than twenty-four hours.

_____   9.   Exploring the cloudy pond, the students collected a jar of tadpoles and gather some aquatic plants to grow in the school aquarium.

_____   10.   After the first Russian satellite was launched in 1957, American schools gear up their science programs to compete in the space race.

■ **Review Test 2**

Change verbs where needed in the following selection so that they are consistently in the past tense. Cross out each incorrect verb and write the correct form above it, as shown in the example. You will need to make ten corrections.

My uncle's shopping trip last Thursday was discouraging to him. First of all, he had to drive around for fifteen minutes until he ~~finds~~ *found* a parking space. There was a half-price special on paper products in the supermarket, and every spot is taken. Then, when he finally got inside, many of the items on his list were not where he expected. For example, the pickles he wanted are not on the same shelf as all the other pickles. Instead, they were in a refrigerated case next to the bacon. And the granola was not on the cereal shelves, but in the health food section. Shopping thus proceeds slowly. About halfway through his list, he knew there would not be time to cook dinner and decides to pick up a barbecued chicken. The chicken, he learned, was available at the end of the store he had already passed. So he parks his shopping cart in an aisle, gets the chicken, and came back. After adding half a dozen more items to his cart, he suddenly realizes it contained someone else's food. So he retraced his steps, found his own cart, transfers the groceries, and continued to shop. Later, when he began loading items onto the checkout counter, he notices that the barbecued chicken was missing. He must have left it in the other cart, certainly gone by now. Feeling totally defeated, he returned to the deli counter and says to the clerk, ''Give me another chicken. I lost the first one.'' My uncle told me that when he saw the look on the clerk's face, he felt as if he'd flunked Shop-O-Rama.

ADDITIONAL INFORMATION ABOUT VERBS

The purpose of this special section is to provide additional information about verbs. Some people will find the grammatical terms here a helpful reminder of what they've learned earlier, in school, about verbs. For them, the terms will increase their understanding of how verbs function in English. Other people may welcome more detailed information about terms used elsewhere in the text. In either case, remember that the most common mistakes that people make when writing verbs have been treated in previous sections of the book.

VERB TENSE

Verbs tell us the time of an action. The time that a verb shows is usually called *tense*. The most common tenses are the simple present, past, and future. In addition, there are nine other tenses that enable us to express more specific ideas about time than we could with the simple tenses alone. Shown on the next page are the twelve verb tenses and examples of each tense. Read them over to increase your sense of the many different ways of expressing time in English.

Tenses	*Examples*
Present	I *work*.
	Tony *works*.
Past	Ellen *worked* on her car.
Future	You *will work* on a new project next week.
Present perfect	He *has worked* on his term paper for a month.
	They *have worked* out a compromise.
Past perfect	The nurse *had worked* two straight shifts.
Future perfect	Next Monday, I *will have worked* here exactly two years.
Present progressive	I *am working* on my speech for the debate.
	You *are working* too hard.
	The tape recorder *is* not *working* properly.
Past progressive	He *was working* in the basement.
	The contestants *were working* on their talent routines.
Future progressive	My son *will be working* in our store this summer.
Present perfect progressive	Sarah *has been working* late this week.
Past perfect progressive	Until recently, I *had been working* nights.
Future perfect progressive	My mother *will have been working* as a nurse for forty-five years by the time she retires.

Activity

On separate paper, write twelve sentences using the twelve verb tenses.

HELPING VERBS

There are three common verbs that can either stand alone or combine with (and "help") other verbs. Here are the verbs and their forms:

be (am, are, is, was, were, being, been)
have (has, having, had)
do (does, did)

Here are examples of the helping verbs:

Used Alone	*Used as Helping Verbs*
I *was* angry.	I *was growing* angry.
Sue *has* the key.	Sue *has forgotten* the key.
He *did* well in the test.	He *did fail* the previous test.

There are nine helping verbs (traditionally known as *modals,* or *modal auxiliaries*) that are always used in combination with other verbs. Here are the nine verbs and sentence examples of each:

can	I *can see* the rainbow.
could	I *could* not *find* a seat.
may	The game *may be postponed.*
might	Cindy *might resent* your advice.
shall	I *shall see* you tomorrow.
should	He *should get* his car serviced.
will	Tony *will want* to see you.
would	They *would* not *understand.*
must	You *must visit* us again.

Note from the examples that these verbs have only one form. They do not, for instance, add an *-s* when used with *he, she, it,* or any one person or thing.

Activity

On separate paper, write nine sentences using the nine helping verbs.

VERBALS

Verbals are words formed from verbs. Verbals, like verbs, often express action. They can add variety to your sentences and vigor to your writing style. The three kinds of verbals are *infinitives, participles,* and *gerunds.*

Infinitive

An infinitive is *to* plus the base form of the verb.

I love *to dance.*
Lina hopes *to write* for a newspaper.
I asked the children *to clean* the kitchen.

Participle

A participle is a verb form used as an adjective (a descriptive word). The present participle ends in *-ing*. The past participle ends in *-ed* or has an irregular ending.

Peering into the cracked mirror, the *crying* woman wiped her eyes.
The *astounded* man stared at his *winning* lottery ticket.
Swinging a sharp ax, Bob split the *rotted* beam.

Gerund

A gerund is the *-ing* form of a verb used as a noun.

Swimming is the perfect exercise.
Eating junk food is my diet downfall.
Through *doodling,* people express their inner feelings.

Activity

On separate paper, write three sentences using infinitives, three sentences using participles, and three sentences using gerunds.

ACTIVE AND PASSIVE VERBS

When the subject of a sentence performs the action of a verb, the verb is in the *active voice.* When the subject of a sentence receives the action of a verb, the verb is in the *passive voice.*

The passive form of a verb consists of a form of the verb *be* plus the past participle of the main verb. Look at the following active and passive forms.

Active	*Passive*
Jan *sewed* the curtains. (The subject, *Jan,* is the doer of the action.)	The curtains *were sewn* by Jan. (The subject, *curtains,* does not act. Instead, something happens to them.)
The repairman *fixed* the air conditioner. (The subject, *repairman,* is the doer of the action.)	The air conditioner *was fixed* by the repairman. (The subject, *air conditioner,* does not act. Instead, something happens to it.)

In general, active verbs are more effective than passive ones. Active verbs give your writing a simpler and more vigorous style. At times, however, the passive form of verbs is appropriate when the performer of the action is unknown or is less important than the receiver of the action. For example:

The tests were graded yesterday.
(The performer of the action is unknown.)

Alan was very hurt by your thoughtless remark.
(The receiver of the action, Alan, is being emphasized.)

Activity

Change the following sentences from the passive to the active voice. Note that you may have to add a subject in some cases.

Examples   The dog was found by a police officer.

A police officer found the dog.

The baseball game was called off.

The officials called off the baseball game.

(Here a subject had to be added.)

1. Most of our furniture was damaged by the fire.

_____

2. Marsha's new dress was singed by a careless smoker.

_____

3. The problem was solved by the quiet student in the back of the room.

_____

4. The supermarket shelves were restocked after the truckers' strike.

_____

5. The children were mesmerized by the magician's sleight of hand.

_____

PRONOUN AGREEMENT, REFERENCE, AND POINT OF VIEW

Pronouns are words that take the place of *nouns* (persons, places, or things). In fact, the word *pronoun* means "for a noun." Pronouns are shortcuts that keep you from unnecessarily repeating words in writing. Here are some examples of pronouns:

> Eddie left *his* camera on the bus.   (*His* is a pronoun that takes the place of *Eddie's*.)
>
> Elena drank the coffee even though *it* was cold.   (*It* replaces *coffee*.)
>
> As I turned the newspaper's damp pages, *they* disintegrated in my hands. (*They* is a pronoun that takes the place of *pages*.)

This section presents rules that will help you avoid three common mistakes people make with pronouns. The rules are:

1   A pronoun must agree in number with the word or words it replaces.
2   A pronoun must refer clearly to the word it replaces.
3   Pronouns should not shift point of view unnecessarily.

PRONOUN AGREEMENT

A pronoun must agree in number with the word or words it replaces. If the word a pronoun refers to is singular, the pronoun must be singular; if that word is plural, the pronoun must be plural. (Note that the word a pronoun refers to is known as the *antecedent.*)

Marie showed me her antique wedding band.

Students enrolled in the art class must provide their own supplies.

In the first example, the pronoun *her* refers to the singular word *Marie;* in the second example, the pronoun *their* refers to the plural word *Students.*

Activity

Write the appropriate pronoun (*their, they, them, it*) in the blank space in each of the following sentences.

Example   I opened the wet umbrella and put _____*it*_____ in the bathtub to dry.

1. Kate and Bruce left for the movies earlier than usual, because _____ knew the theater would be packed.

2. The clothes were still damp, but I decided to fold _____ anyway.

3. Young adults often face a difficult transition period when _____ leave home for the first time.

4. Paul's grandparents renewed _____ marriage vows at a huge fiftieth wedding anniversary celebration.

5. The car's steering wheel began to pull to one side, and then _____ started to shimmy.

Indefinite Pronouns

The following words are always singular.

(*-one* words)	(*-body* words)	
one	nobody	each
anyone	anybody	either
everyone	everybody	neither
someone	somebody	

If a pronoun in a sentence refers to one of these singular words (also known as *indefinite pronouns*), the pronoun should be singular.

Somebody left (her) shoulder bag on the back of a chair.

One of the busboys just called and said (he) would be an hour late.

Everyone in the club must pay (his) dues next week.

Each circled pronoun is singular because it refers to an indefinite pronoun.

Note: There are two important points to remember about indefinite pronouns:

1   In the last example, if everyone in the club was a woman, the pronoun would be *her*. If the club had women and men, the pronoun would be *his or her:*

Everyone in the club must pay his or her dues next week.

Some writers follow the traditional practice of using *his* to refer to both women and men. Some now use *his or her* to avoid an implied sexual bias. To avoid using *his* or the somewhat awkward *his or her,* a sentence can often be rewritten in the plural:

Club members must pay their dues next week.

2   In informal spoken English, *plural* pronouns are often used with the indefinite pronouns. We would probably not say:

Everybody has his or her own opinion about the election.

Instead, we are likely to say:

Everybody has their own opinion about the election.

Here are other examples:

Everyone in the choir must buy their robes.
Everybody in the line has their ticket ready.
No one in the class remembered to bring their books.

In such cases, the indefinite pronouns are clearly plural in meaning, and using them helps people avoid the awkward *his or her.* In time, the plural pronoun may be accepted in formal speech or writing. Until then, however, you should use the grammatically correct singular form in your writing.

Activity

Underline the correct pronoun.

1. Neither of the potential buyers had really made up (her, their) mind.
2. Not one of the new cashiers knows what (he, they) should be doing.
3. Each of these computers has (its, their) drawbacks.
4. Anyone trying to reduce (his or her, their) salt intake should avoid canned and processed foods.
5. If anybody calls when I'm out, tell (him, them) I'll return in an hour.

PRONOUN REFERENCE

A sentence may be confusing and unclear if a pronoun appears to refer to more than one word or does not refer to any specific word. Look at this sentence:

Miriam was annoyed when they failed her car for a faulty turn signal.

Who failed her car? There is no specific word that *they* refers to. Be clear:

Miriam was annoyed when the inspectors failed her car for a faulty turn signal.

Here are sentences with other faulty pronoun references. Read the explanations of why they are faulty and look carefully at how they are corrected.

Faulty	*Clear*
Peter told Alan that his wife was unhappy. (Whose wife is unhappy: Peter's or Alan's? Be clear.)	Peter told Alan, ''My wife is unhappy.''
Sue is really a shy person, but she keeps it hidden. (There is no specific word that *it* refers to. It would not make sense to say, ''Sue keeps shy hidden.'')	Sue is really a shy person, but she keeps her shyness hidden.
Marsha attributed her success to her husband's support, which was generous. (Does *which* mean that Marsha's action was generous or that her husband's support was generous?)	Generously, Marsha attributed her success to her husband's support. *Or:* Marsha attributed her success to her husband's generous support.

Activity

Rewrite each of the following sentences to make clear the vague pronoun reference. Add, change, or omit words as necessary.

Example   Susan and her mother wondered if she was tall enough to be a model.
Susan's mother wondered if Susan was tall enough to be a model.

1. Dad spent all morning bird-watching but didn't see a single one.

    _____

2. At that fast-food restaurant, they give you free glasses with your soft drinks.

    _____

3. Ruth told Annette that her bouts of depression were becoming serious.

    _____

4. Dipping her spoon into the pot of simmering spaghetti sauce, Helen felt it slip out of her hand.

    _____

5. Pete visited the tutoring center because they can help him with his economics course.

    _____

PRONOUN POINT OF VIEW

Pronouns should not shift point of view unnecessarily. When writing a paper, be consistent in your use of first-, second-, or third-person pronouns.

	Singular	*Plural*
First-person pronouns	I (my, mine, me)	we (our, us)
Second-person pronouns	you (your)	you (your)
Third-person pronouns	he (his, him)	they (their, them)
	she (her)	
	it (its)	

Note: Any person, place, or thing, as well as any indefinite pronoun like *one, anyone, someone,* and so on (page 365), is a third-person word.

For instance, if you start writing in the first person, *I*, do not jump suddenly to the second person, *you.* Or if you are writing in the third person, *they,* do not shift unexpectedly to *you.* Look at the examples.

Inconsistent	*Consistent*
One of the fringe benefits of my job is that *you* can use a company credit card for gasoline.	One of the fringe benefits of my job is that *I* can use a company credit card for gasoline.
(The most common mistake people make is to let a *you* slip into their writing after they start with another pronoun.)	
In this course, a person can be in class for weeks before the professor calls on *you.*	In this course, a person can be in class for weeks before the professor calls on *him.*
(Again, the *you* is a shift in point of view.)	(See also the note on *his or her* references on page 366.)

Activity

Cross out inconsistent pronouns in the following sentences and write the correct form of the pronoun above each crossed-out word.

Example   When I examined the used car, ~~you~~ could see where a dent in the door panel had been repaired.

1. Ron refuses to eat pepperoni pizza because he says it gives you indigestion.

2. When I buy lipstick or nail polish, you never know how the color will actually look.

3. All you could hear was the maddening rattle of the heating registers, even though I buried my face in the pillow.

4. Hank searched the roadside mailboxes for the right name, but you couldn't see much in the pouring rain.

5. As we pulled on the heavy door, you could tell it wasn't going to budge.

■   **Review Test**

Cross out the pronoun error in each of the following sentences and write the correction in the space provided at the left. Then circle the letter that correctly describes the type of error that was made.

Examples

his or her

Anyone without a ticket will lose their place in the line.
Mistake in: a. pronoun reference   (b.) pronoun agreement

Ellen
(or Cara)

When Ellen takes her daughter Cara to the park, she enjoys herself.
Mistake in: (a.) pronoun reference   b. pronoun point of view

we

From where we stood on the mountain, you could see three states.
Mistake in: a. pronoun agreement   (b.) pronoun point of view

1.   Many people are ignorant of side effects that diets can have on your health.
_____   *Mistake in:* a. pronoun reference   b. pronoun point of view

2.   Could someone volunteer their services to clean up after the party?
_____   *Mistake in:* a. pronoun reference   b. pronoun agreement

3.   At the city council meeting, we asked them to provide better police protection for our neighborhood.
_____   *Mistake in:* a. pronoun reference   b. pronoun agreement

4.   During the border crisis, each country refused to change their aggressive stand.
_____   *Mistake in:* a. pronoun reference   b. pronoun agreement

5.   Darlene tried to take notes during class, but she didn't really understand it.
_____   *Mistake in:* a. pronoun reference   b. pronoun agreement

6.   If people don't like what the government is doing, you should let Congress know.
_____   *Mistake in:* a. pronoun reference   b. pronoun point of view

7.   Neither of those girls appreciates their parents' sacrifices.
_____   *Mistake in:* a. pronoun reference   b. pronoun agreement

8.   There wasn't much to do on Friday nights after they closed the only movie theater in town.
_____   *Mistake in:* a. pronoun reference   b. pronoun agreement

9. Rita never buys a dress with horizontal stripes because she knows that stripes make you look fat.
    Mistake in: a. pronoun reference   b. pronoun point of view

10. Any student who is working full-time and going to school knows that you need at least a twenty-five-hour day.
    Mistake in: a. pronoun agreement   b. pronoun point of view

■ Review Test 2

Underline the correct word or words in parentheses.

1. The referee watched the basketball game closely to make sure (they, the players) didn't commit any fouls.

2. After my husband and I had been running for two months, (you, we) could really see the difference in our strength and stamina.

3. If a job hunter wants to make a good impression at an interview, (they, he or she, you) should be sure to arrive on time.

4. From reading your short stories, I would say you are quite talented in (it, writing).

5. Each of the litle girls may choose one prize for (her, their) own.

6. I find vacations exhausting because (you, I) try so hard to have a good time before going back to work.

7. I asked at the body shop how quickly (they, the shop employees) could fix my car.

8. I picked up the can of fishing worms and carried (them, it) down to the lake.

9. The coaches told each member of the football team that (his, their) position was the most important in the game.

10. When someone has a cold, (they, he or she, you) should take extra vitamin C and drink a lot of fluids.

PRONOUN TYPES

This section describes some common types of pronouns: subject and object pronouns, possessive pronouns, and demonstrative pronouns.

SUBJECT AND OBJECT PRONOUNS

Pronouns change their form depending on what place they occupy in a sentence. In the box that follows is a list of subject and object pronouns.

Subject Pronouns	Object Pronouns
I	me
you	you (no change)
he	him
she	her
it	it (no change)
we	us
they	them

Subject Pronouns

Subject pronouns are subjects of verbs.

He is wearing an artificial arm. (*He* is the subject of the verb *is wearing*.)

They are moving into our old apartment. (*They* is the subject of the verb *are moving*.)

We students should have a say in the decision. (*We* is the subject of the verb *should have*.)

Several rules for using subject pronouns—and several kinds of mistakes people sometimes make with subject pronouns—are explained below.

Rule 1: Use a subject pronoun in spots where you have a compound (more than one) subject.

Incorrect	*Correct*
My brother and *me* are Bruce Springsteen fanatics.	My brother and *I* are Bruce Springsteen fanatics.
Him and *me* know the lyrics to all of Bruce's songs.	*He* and *I* know the lyrics to all of Bruce's songs.

Hint for Rule 1: If you are not sure what pronoun to use, try each pronoun by itself in the sentence. The correct pronoun will be the one that sounds right. For example, "Him knows the lyrics to all of Bruce's songs" does not sound right; "He knows the lyrics to all of Bruce's songs" does.

Rule 2: Use a subject pronoun after forms of the verb *be*. Forms of *be* include *am, are, is, was, were, has been, have been,* and others.

It was *I* who left the light on.

It may be *they* in that car.

It is *he*.

The sentences above may sound strange and stilted to you because they are seldom used in conversation. When we speak with one another, forms such as "It was me," "It may be them," and "It is him" are widely accepted. In formal writing, however, the grammatically correct forms are still preferred.

Hint for Rule 2: You can avoid having to use the subject pronoun form after *be* by simply rewording a sentence. Here is how the preceding examples could be reworded:

I was the one who left the light on.

They may be in that car.

He is here.

Rule 3: Use subject pronouns after *than* or *as*. The subject pronoun is used because a verb is understood after the pronoun.

You play better than I (play).   (The verb *play* is understood after *I*.)

Jenny is as bored as I (am).   (The verb *am* is understood after *I*.)

We don't need the money as much as they (do).   (The verb *do* is understood after *they*.)

Hint for Rule 3: Avoid mistakes by mentally adding the "missing" verb at the end of the sentence.

Object Pronouns

Object pronouns (*me, him, her, us, them*) are the objects of verbs or prepositions. (*Prepositions* are connecting words like *for, at, about, to, before, by, with,* and *of*. See also page 311.)

Tony helped me.   (*Me* is the object of the verb *helped*.)

We took *them* to the college.   (*Them* is the object of the verb *took*.)

Leave the children with *us*.   (*Us* is the object of the preposition *with*.)

I got in line behind *him*. (*Him* is the object of the preposition *behind*.)

People are sometimes uncertain about what pronoun to use when two objects follow the verb.

Incorrect	*Correct*
I gave a gift to Ray and *she*.	I gave a gift to Ray and *her*.
She came to the movie with Bobbie and *I*.	She came to the movie with Bobbie and *me*.

Hint: If you are not sure what pronoun to use, try each pronoun by itself in the sentence. The correct pronoun will be the one that sounds right. For example, "I gave a gift to she" does not sound right; "I gave a gift to her" does.

Activity

Underline the correct subject or object pronoun in each of the following sentences. Then show whether your answer is a subject or object pronoun by circling the S or O in the margin. The first one is done for you as an example.

S (O) 1. The sweaters Mom knitted for Victor and (I, me) are too small.
S O 2. The umpire and (he, him) started to argue.
S O 3. No one has a quicker temper than (she, her).
S O 4. Your grades prove that you worked harder than (they, them).
S O 5. (We, Us) runners train indoors when the weather turns cold.
S O 6. (She, Her) and Betty never put the cap back on the toothpaste.
S O 7. Chris and (he, him) are the most energetic kids in the first grade.
S O 8. Arguing over clothes is a favorite pastime for my sister and (I, me).
S O 9. The rest of (they, them) will be arriving in about ten minutes.
S O 10. The head of the ticket committee asked Linda and (I, me) to help with sales.

POSSESSIVE PRONOUNS

Here is a list of possessive pronouns:

my, mine	our, ours
your, yours	your, yours
his	their, theirs
her, hers	
its	

Possessive pronouns show ownership or possession.

Clyde revved up *his* motorcycle and blasted off.
The keys are *mine*.

Note: A possessive pronoun *never* uses an apostrophe. (See also page 413.)

Incorrect	*Correct*
That coat is *hers'*.	That coat is *hers*.
The card table is *theirs'*.	The card table is *theirs*.

Activity

Cross out the incorrect pronoun form in each of the sentences below. Write the correct form in the space at the left.

Example ___*hers*___ Those gloves are hers'.

_____ 1. I discovered that my car had somehow lost its' rear license plate.

_____ 2. Are those seats theirs'?

_____ 3. I knew the sweater was hers' when I saw the monogram.

_____ 4. The dog in that cage is our's.

_____ 5. These books are yours' if you want them.

DEMONSTRATIVE PRONOUNS

Demonstrative pronouns point to or single out a person or thing. There are four demonstrative pronouns:

this	these
that	those

Generally speaking, *this* and *these* refer to things close at hand; *that* and *those* refer to things farther away. The four pronouns are commonly used in the role of demonstrative adjectives as well.

Is anyone using *this* spoon?

I am going to throw away *these* magazines.

I just bought *that* white Volvo at the curb.

Pick up *those* toys in the corner.

Note: Do not use *them, this here, that there, these here,* or *those there* to point out. Use only *this, that, these,* or *those.*

Activity

Cross out the incorrect form of the demonstrative pronoun and write the correct form in the space provided.

Example _Those_ ~~Them~~ tires look worn.

_____ 1. This here map is out of date.

_____ 2. Leave them keys out on the coffee table.

_____ 3. I've seen them girls somewhere before.

_____ 4. Jack entered that there dog in an obedience contest.

_____ 5. Where are them new knives?

■ Review Test

Underline the correct word in the parentheses.

1. If the contract negotiations are left up to (they, them), we'll have to accept the results.
2. (Them, Those) student crafts projects have won several awards.
3. Our grandmother told David and (I, me) to leave our muddy shoes outside on the porch.
4. The judge decided that the fault was (theirs', theirs) and ordered them to pay the damages.
5. I gave the money to (she, her) and asked her to put it in the bank's night deposit slot.
6. The black-masked raccoon stared at Rudy and (I, me) for an instant and then ran quickly away.
7. When we saw the smashed window, Lynn and (I, me) didn't know whether to enter the house.
8. (This here, This) is my cousin Manuel.
9. This coat can't be (hers, her's); it's too small.
10. Because we weren't wearing shoes, Tara and (I, me) had a hard time walking on the sharp gravel.

ADJECTIVES
AND ADVERBS

ADJECTIVES

What Are Adjectives?

Adjectives describe nouns (names of persons, places, or things) or pronouns.

> Polly is a *wise* woman. (The adjective *wise* describes the noun *woman*.)
>
> She is also *funny*. (The adjective *funny* describes the pronoun *she*.)
>
> I'll carry the *heavy* bag of groceries. (The adjective *heavy* describes the noun *bag*.)
>
> It is *torn*. (The adjective *torn* describes the pronoun *it*.)

Adjectives usually come before the word they describe (as in *wise* woman and *heavy* bag). But they also come after forms of the verb *be* (*is, are, was, were,* and so on). They also follow verbs such as *look, appear, seem, become, sound, taste,* and *smell*.

> That road is *slippery*. (The adjective *slippery* describes the road.)
>
> The dogs are *noisy*. (The adjective *noisy* describes the dogs.)
>
> Those customers were *impatient*. (The adjective *impatient* describes the customers.)
>
> Your room looks *neat*. (The adjective *neat* describes the room.)

Using Adjectives to Compare

For all one-syllable adjectives and some two-syllable adjectives, add *-er* when comparing two things and *-est* when comparing three or more things.

> Phil's beard is *longer* than mine, but Lee's is the *longest.*
>
> Meg may be the *quieter* of the two sisters; but that's not saying much, since they're the *loudest* girls in school.

For some two-syllable adjectives and all longer adjectives, add *more* when comparing two things and *most* when comparing three or more things.

> Liza Minnelli is *more famous* than her sister; but their mother, Judy Garland, is still the *most famous* member of the family.
>
> The red letters on the sign are *more noticeable* than the black ones, but the Day-Glo letters are the *most noticeable.*

You can usually tell when to use *more* and *most* by the sound of a word. For example, you can probably tell by its sound that "carefuller" would be too awkward to say and that *more careful* is thus correct. In addition, there are many words for which both *-er* or *-est* and *more* or *most* are equally correct. For instance, either "a more fair rule" or "a fairer rule" is correct.

To form negative comparisons, use *less* and *least.*

> During my first dance class, I felt *less graceful* than an injured elephant.
>
> When the teacher came to our house to complain to my parents, I offered her the *least* comfortable chair in the room.

Points to Remember about Comparing

Point 1: Use only one form of comparison at a time. In other words, do not use both an *-er* ending and *more* or both an *-est* ending and *most:*

Incorrect	*Correct*
My mother's suitcase is always *more heavier* than my father's.	My mother's suitcase is always *heavier* than my father's.
Rosemary's Baby is still the *most frighteningest* movie I've ever seen.	*Rosemary's Baby* is still the *most frightening* movie I've ever seen.

Point 2: Learn the irregular forms of the words shown below.

	Comparative *(for comparing* *two things)*	*Superlative* *(for comparing three* *or more things)*
bad	worse	worst
good, well	better	best
little (in amount)	less	least
much, many	more	most

Do not use both *more* and an irregular comparative or *most* and an irregular superlative.

Incorrect	*Correct*
It is *more better* to give than to receive.	It is *better* to give than to receive.
Last night I got the *most worst* snack attack I ever had.	Last night I got the *worst* snack attack I ever had.

Activity

Add to each sentence the correct form of the word in the margin.

bad **Examples** The _____ worst _____ job I ever had was baby-sitting for spoiled four-year-old twins.

wonderful The _____ most wonderful _____ day of my life was when my child was born.

good 1. The _____ chocolate cake I ever ate had bananas in it.

young 2. Aunt Sonja is the _____ of the three sisters.

bad 3. A rain that freezes is _____ than a snowstorm.

unusual 4. That's the _____ home I've ever seen—it's shaped like a teapot.

little 5. Being painfully shy has made Leon the _____ friendly person I know.

ADVERBS

What Are Adverbs?

Adverbs describe verbs, adjectives, or other adverbs. They usually end in -*ly*.

The father *gently* hugged the sick child. (The adverb *gently* describes the verb *hugged.*)

Newborns are *totally* innocent. (The adverb *totally* describes the adjective *innocent.*)

The lecturer spoke so *terribly* fast that I had trouble taking notes. (The adverb *terribly* describes the adverb *fast.*)

A Common Mistake with Adverbs and Adjectives

People often mistakenly use an adjective instead of an adverb after a verb.

Incorrect	*Correct*
Sam needs a haircut *bad.*	Sam needs a haircut *badly.*
I laugh too *loud* when I'm embarrassed.	I laugh too *loudly* when I'm embarrassed.
You might have won the race if you hadn't run so *slow* at the beginning.	You might have won the race if you hadn't run so *slowly* at the beginning.

Activity

Underline the adjective or adverb needed. (Remember that adjectives describe nouns, and adverbs describe verbs or other adverbs.)

1. As Mac danced, his earring bounced (rapid, rapidly).
2. A drop of (thick, thickly) pea soup dripped down his chin.
3. I hiccupped (continuous, continuously) for fifteen minutes.
4. The detective opened the door (careful, carefully).
5. All she heard when she answered the phone was (heavy, heavily) breathing.

Well and *Good*

Two words that are often confused are *well* and *good*. *Good* is an adjective; it describes nouns. *Well* is usually an adverb; it describes verbs. *Well* (rather than *good*) is also used when referring to a person's health.

Activity

Write *well* or *good* in each of the sentences that follow.

1. If you girls do a _____ job of cleaning the garage, I'll take you for some ice cream.
2. If I organize the office records too _____, my bosses may not need me anymore.
3. After eating a pound of peanuts, I didn't feel too _____.
4. When Ernie got AIDS, he discovered who his _____ friends really were.
5. Just because brothers and sisters fight when they're young doesn't mean they won't get along _____ as adults.

■ Review Test 1

Underline the correct word in the parentheses.

1. The waitress poured (littler, less) coffee in my cup than in yours.
2. Humid air seems to make Sid's asthma (more worse, worse).
3. The movie is so interesting that the three hours pass (quick, quickly).
4. The talented boy sang as (confident, confidently) as a seasoned performer.
5. Our band played so (good, well) that a local firm hired us for its annual dinner.
6. Tri Lee is always (truthful, truthfully), even when it might be better to tell a white lie.
7. The driver stopped the bus (sudden, suddenly) and yelled, ''Everybody out!''
8. Shirt and pants in one color make you look (more thin, thinner) than ones in contrasting colors.
9. Your intentions may have been (good, well), but I'd prefer that you ask before arranging a blind date for me.
10. Our cat likes to sit in the (warmest, most warm) spot in any room—by a fireplace, on a windowsill in the sunshine, or on my lap.

■ **Review Test 2**

Write a sentence that uses each of the following adjectives and adverbs correctly.

1. careless _____

2. angrily _____

3. well _____

4. most relaxing _____

5. best _____

MISPLACED MODIFIERS

Misplaced modifiers are words that, because of awkward placement, do not describe what the writer intended them to describe. Misplaced modifiers often confuse the meaning of a sentence. To avoid them, place words as close as possible to what they describe.

Misplaced Words	*Correctly Placed Words*
George couldn't drive to work in his small sports car *with a broken leg.* (The sports car had a broken leg?)	With a broken leg, George couldn't drive to work in his small sports car. (The words describing George are now placed next to "George.")
The toaster was sold to us by a charming salesman *with a money-back guarantee.* (The salesman had a money-back guarantee?)	The toaster with a money-back guarantee was sold to us by a charming salesman. (The words describing the toaster are now placed next to it.)
He *nearly* brushed his teeth for twenty minutes every night. (He came close to brushing his teeth, but in fact did not brush them at all?)	He brushed his teeth for nearly twenty minutes every night. (The meaning—that he brushed his teeth for a long time—is now clear.)

Activity

Underline the misplaced word or words in each sentence. Then rewrite the sentence, placing related words together and thereby making the meaning clear.

Examples   Frozen shrimp lay in the steel pans <u>that were melting rapidly</u>.

Frozen shrimp that were melting rapidly lay in the steel pans.

The speaker discussed the problem of crowded prisons <u>at the college</u>.

At the college, the speaker discussed the problem of crowded prisons.

1. The patient talked about his childhood on the psychiatrist's couch.

2. The crowd watched the tennis players with swiveling heads.

3. Vonnie put four hamburger patties on the counter which she was cooking for dinner.

4. Steve carefully hung the new suit that he would wear to his first job interview in the bedroom closet.

5. Anne ripped the shirt on a car door that she made in sewing class.

6. The latest Arnold Schwarzenegger movie has almost opened in 2,200 theaters across the country.

7. The newscaster spoke softly into a microphone wearing a bulletproof vest.

8. The tenants left town in a dilapidated old car owing two months' rent.

9. The woman picked up a heavy frying pan with arthritis.

10. I discovered an unusual plant in the greenhouse that oozed a milky juice.

■ Review Test 1

Write MM for *misplaced modifier* or C for *correct* in the space provided for each sentence.

_____ 1. I nearly napped for twenty minutes during the biology lecture.

_____ 2. I napped for nearly twenty minutes during the biology lecture.

_____ 3. Ron paused as the girl he had been following stopped at a shop window.

_____ 4. Ron paused as the girl stopped at a shop window he had been following.

_____ 5. Marta dropped out of school after taking ten courses on Friday.

_____ 6. On Friday, Marta dropped out of school after taking ten courses.

_____ 7. Under his shirt, the player wore a good luck charm which resembled a tiny elephant.

_____ 8. The player wore a good luck charm under his shirt which resembled a tiny elephant.

_____ 9. I ordered a new telephone from the mail-order catalog shaped like a cartoon character.

_____ 10. I ordered from the mail-order catalog a new telephone shaped like a cartoon character.

■ Review Test 2

Make the changes needed to correct the misplaced modifier in each sentence.

1. Henry Wadsworth Longfellow wrote that rainbows are the flowers that have died and gone to heaven in a poem.

   _____

2. I almost filled an entire notebook with biology lab drawings.

   _____

3. The apprentice watched the carpenter expertly fit the door with envious eyes.

   _____

4. The photographer pointed the camera at the shy deer equipped with a special night-vision scope.

   _____

5. The people on the bus stared at the ceiling or read newspapers with tired faces.

   _____

DANGLING
MODIFIERS

A modifier that opens a sentence must be followed immediately by the word it is meant to describe. Otherwise, the modifier is said to be dangling, and the sentence takes on an unintended meaning. For example, in the sentence

> While reading the newspaper, my dog sat with me on the front steps.

the unintended meaning is that the *dog* was reading the paper. What the writer meant, of course, was that *he* (or *she*), the writer, was reading the paper. The writer should have said,

> While reading the newspaper, *I* sat with my dog on the front steps.

The dangling modifier could also be corrected by placing the subject within the opening word group:

> While *I* was reading the newspaper, my dog sat with me on the front steps.

Here are other sentences with dangling modifiers. Read the explanations of why they are dangling and look carefully at the ways they are corrected.

Dangling	*Correct*
Shaving in front of the steamy mirror, the razor nicked Ed's chin. (*Who* was shaving in front of the mirror? The answer is not *razor* but *Ed.* The subject *Ed* must be added.)	Shaving in front of the steamy mirror, *Ed* nicked his chin with the razor. *Or:* When *Ed* was shaving in front of the steamy mirror, he nicked his chin with the razor.
While turning over the bacon, hot grease splashed my arm. (*Who* is turning over the bacon? The answer is not *hot grease,* as it unintentionally seems to be, but *I.* The subject *I* must be added.)	While *I* was turning over the bacon, hot grease splashed my arm. *Or:* While turning over the bacon, *I* was splashed by hot grease.
Taking the exam, the room was so stuffy that Paula almost fainted. (*Who* took the exam? The answer is not *the room* but *Paula.* The subject *Paula* must be added.)	Taking the exam, *Paula* found the room so stuffy that she almost fainted. *Or:* When *Paula* took the exam, the room was so stuffy that she almost fainted.
To impress the interviewer, punctuality is essential. (*Who* is to impress the interviewer? The answer is not *punctuality* but *you.* The subject *you* must be added.)	To impress the interviewer, *you* must be punctual. *Or:* For *you* to impress the interviewer, punctuality is essential.

The preceding examples make clear two ways of correcting a dangling modifier. Decide on a logical subject and do one of the following:

1   Place the subject *within* the opening word group:

When *Ed* was shaving in front of the steamy mirror, he nicked his chin.

Note: In some cases an appropriate subordinating word such as *when* must be added, and the verb may have to be changed slightly as well.

2   Place the subject right *after* the opening word group:

Shaving in front of the steamy mirror, *Ed* nicked his chin.

Activity

Ask *Who?* of the opening words in each sentence. The subject that answers the question should be nearby in the sentence. If it is not, provide the logical subject by using either method of correction described above.

Example   While pitching his tent, a snake bit Tony on the ankle.

While Tony was pitching his tent, a snake bit him on the ankle.

Or: *While pitching his tent, Tony was bitten on the ankle by a snake.*

1. Dancing on their hind legs, the audience cheered wildly as the elephants paraded by.

   _____

   _____

2. Last seen wearing dark glasses and a blond wig, the police spokesperson said the suspect was still being sought.

   _____

   _____

3. Pouring out the cereal, a coupon fell into my bowl of milk.

   _____

   _____

4. Escorted by dozens of police motorcycles, I knew the limousine carried someone important.

   _____

   _____

5. Tired and exasperated, the fight we had was inevitable.

   _____

   _____

6. Packed tightly in a tiny can, Fran had difficulty removing the anchovies.

   _____

   _____

7. Kicked carelessly under the bed, Marion finally found her sneakers.

_____

_____

8. Working at the Xerox machine, the morning dragged on.

_____

_____

9. Sitting at a sidewalk café, all sorts of interesting people passed by.

_____

_____

10. Though somewhat warped, Uncle Zeke played his records from the forties.

_____

_____

■ **Review Test 1**

Write DM for *dangling modifier* or C for *correct* in the space provided for each sentence.

_____ 1. While riding the bicycle, a vicious-looking German shepherd snapped at Tim's ankles.

_____ 2. While Tim was riding the bicycle, a vicious-looking German shepherd snapped at his ankles.

_____ 3. Afraid to look his father in the eye, Howard kept his head bowed.

_____ 4. Afraid to look his father in the eye, Howard's head remained bowed.

_____ 5. Boring and silly, I turned the TV show off.

_____ 6. I turned off the boring and silly TV show.

_____ 7. Munching leaves from a tall tree, the giraffe fascinated the children.

_____ 8. Munching leaves from a tall tree, the children were fascinated by the giraffe.

_____ 9. At the age of twelve, several colleges had already accepted the boy genius.

_____ 10. At the age of twelve, the boy genius had already been accepted by several colleges.

■ **Review Test 2**

Make the changes needed to correct the dangling modifier in each sentence.

1. Not having had much sleep, my concentration during class was weak.

   _____

2. Joined at the hip, a team of surgeons successfully separated the Siamese twins.

   _____

3. Wading in the shallow surf, a baby shark brushed past my leg.

   _____

4. While being restrained by federal marshals, the judge sentenced the kidnapper.

   _____

5. In a sentimental frame of mind, the music brought tears to Beth's eyes.

   _____

■ **Review Test 3**

Complete the following sentences. In each case, a logical subject should follow the opening words.

Example Looking through the door's peephole, *I couldn't see who rang the*
                                                    doorbell.

1. Noticing the light turn yellow, _____

2. Being fragile, _____

3. While washing the car, _____

4. Although very expensive, _____

5. Driving by the cemetery, _____

FAULTY PARALLELISM

Words in a pair or a series should have parallel structure. By balancing the items in a pair or a series so that they have the same kind of structure, you will make the sentence clearer and easier to read. Notice how the parallel sentences that follow read more smoothly than the nonparallel ones.

Nonparallel (Not Balanced)	*Parallel (Balanced)*
My job includes checking the inventory, initialing the orders, and *to call* the suppliers.	My job includes checking the inventory, initialing the orders, and calling the suppliers. (A balanced series of *-ing* words: *checking, initialing, calling*)
The game-show contestant was told to be cheerful, charming, and *with enthusiasm.*	The game-show contestant was told to be cheerful, charming, and enthusiastic. (A balanced series of descriptive words: *cheerful, charming, enthusiastic*)
Lola likes to ride her moped, to do needlepoint, and *playing* games on her personal computer.	Lola likes to ride her moped, to do needlepoint, and to play games on her personal computer. (A balanced series of *to* verbs: *to ride, to do, to play*)
We painted the trim in the living room; *the wallpaper was put up by a professional.*	We painted the trim in the living room; a professional put up the wallpaper. (Balanced verbs and word order: *We painted . . . ; a professional put up . . .*)

Balanced sentences are not a skill you need worry about when writing first drafts. But when you rewrite, you should try to put matching words and ideas into matching structures. Such parallelism will improve your writing style.

Activity 1

The unbalanced part of each of the following sentences is italicized. Rewrite the unbalanced part so that it matches the rest of the sentence. The first one is done for you as an example.

1. Chocolate makes me gain weight, lose my appetite, and *breaking out in hives.* _____break out in hives_____

2. Adam convinced most of the audience because he argued logically, calmly, and *was reasonable.* _____

3. If I didn't have to clean the garage and *an English paper that needed finishing,* I could really enjoy my weekend. _____

4. Ed's last job offered security; *a better chance for advancement is offered by his new job.* _____

5. A sale on electrical appliances, *furniture for the patio,* and stereo systems begins this Friday. _____

6. Steven prefers books that are short, scary, and *filled with suspense.* _____

7. The novelty shop sells hand buzzers, plastic fangs, and *insects that are fake.* _____

8. Because the dying woman was dignified and *with courage,* she won everyone's respect. _____

9. The politician trusted no one, rewarded loyalty, and *was dependent only on his own instincts.* _____

10. The chickens travel on a conveyor belt, where they are plucked, washed, rinsed, and *bags are put on them.* _____

Activity 2

Following are "plan of development" sentences from student essays. Rewrite the sentences as needed so that the three points in each plan of development appear in parallel form.

1. To escape the stresses of everyday life, I rely upon watching television, reading books, and my kitchen.

   _____

   _____

2. If we're not careful, we'll leave the next generation polluted air, contaminated water, and forests that are dying.

   _____

   _____

3. Qualities that I look for in friends are a sense of humor, being kind, and dependability.

   _____

   _____

4. My three favorite jobs were veterinary assistant, gardener, and selling toys.

   _____

   _____

5. Many people have the same three great fears: being in high places, working with numbers, and speeches.

   _____

   _____

6. Housekeeping shortcuts will help you do a fast job of doing laundry, cleaning rooms, and food on the table.

   _____

   _____

7. The keys to improving grades are to take effective notes in class, to plan study time, and preparing carefully for exams.

   _____

   _____

8. To decide on a career, people should think closely about their interests, hobbies, and what they are skilled at.

   _____

   _____

9. The best programming on television includes news programs, shows on science, and children's series.

   _____

   _____

10. People in today's world often try to avoid silence, whether on the job, in school, or when relaxing at home.

   _____

   _____

■ **Review Test 1**

Draw a line under the unbalanced part of each sentence. Then rewrite the unbalanced part so that it matches the other item or items in the sentence. The first one is done for you as an example.

1. Curling overgrown vines, <u>porch furniture that was rotted</u>, and sagging steps were my first impressions of the neglected house.

   rotting porch furniture

2. In many ways, starting college at forty is harder than to start at eighteen.

   _____

3. The little girl came home from school with a tear-streaked face, a black eye, and her shirt was torn.

   _____

4. Studying a little every day is more effective than to cram.

   _____

5. At the body shop, the car was sanded down to the bare metal, painted with primer, and red enamel was sprayed on.

   _____

6. There are two ways to the top floor: climb the stairs or taking the elevator.

   _____

7. While waiting for the exam to start, small groups of nervous students glanced over their notes, drank coffee, and were whispering to each other.

   _____

8. In order to become a dancer, she is taking lessons, working in amateur shows, and auditioned for professional companies.

   _____

9. The "bag lady" shuffled along the street, bent over to pick something up, and was putting it in her shopping bag.

   _____

10. A teamsters' strike now would mean interruptions in food deliveries, a slowdown in the economy, and losing wages for workers.

    _____

■ **Review Test 2**

On separate paper, write five sentences of your own that use parallel structure.

MANUSCRIPT FORM

When you hand in a paper for any course, it will probably be judged first by its format. It is important, then, to make the paper look attractive, neat, and easy to read. Here is a checklist you should use when preparing a paper for an instructor:

_____ ■ Is the paper full-sized paper, 8½ by 11 inches?

_____ ■ Are there wide margins (1 to 1½ inches) all around the paper? In particular, have you been careful not to crowd the right-hand or bottom margin?

_____ ■ If the paper is handwritten, have you:

Used a blue or black pen?

Been careful not to overlap letters or to make decorative loops on letters?

Made all your letters distinct, with special attention to *a, e, i, o,* and *u*—five letters that people sometimes write illegibly?

Kept all your capital letters clearly distinct from small letters?

_____ ■ Have you centered the title of your paper on the first line of page 1? Have you been careful *not* to put quotation marks around the title or to underline it? Have you capitalized all the words in the title except for short connecting words like *of, for, the, and, in,* and *to*?

_____   ■ Have you skipped a line between the title and the first line of your paper?

_____   ■ Have you indented the first line of each paragraph about five spaces (half an inch) from the left-hand margin?

_____   ■ Have you made commas, periods, and other punctuation marks firm and clear? If typing, have you left a double space after a period?

_____   ■ If you have broken any words at the end of a line, have you been careful to break only between syllables?

_____   ■ Have you put your name, the date, and other information at the end of the paper (or wherever your instructor has specified)?

Also ask yourself these important questions about the title and the first sentence of your paper:

_____   ■ Is your title made up of several words that tell what the paper is about? (The title should be just several words, *not* a complete sentence.)

_____   ■ Does the first sentence of your paper stand independent of the title? (The reader should *not* have to use the words in the title to make sense of the opening sentence.)

Activity

Use the checklist to locate the seven mistakes in format in the following lines from a student paper. Explain the mistakes in the spaces provided. One mistake is described for you as an example.

	"Being alone"
	This is something that I simply cannot tolerate, and I will predi-
	ctably go to great lengths to prevent it. For example, if I know that

1. Hyphenate only between syllables (*predict-ably, not predi-ctably*).

2. _____

3. _____

4. _____

5. _____

6. _____

7. _____

CAPITAL
LETTERS

MAIN USES OF CAPITAL LETTERS

Capital letters are used with:

1 First word in a sentence or direct quotation
2 Names of persons and the word *I*
3 Names of particular places
4 Names of days of the week, months, and holidays
5 Names of commercial products
6 Titles of books, magazines, newspapers, articles, stories, poems, films, television shows, songs, papers that you write, and the like
7 Names of companies, associations, unions, clubs, religious and political groups, and other organizations

Each use is illustrated on the pages that follow.

First Word in a Sentence or Direct Quotation

The corner grocery was robbed last night.

The alien said, "Take me to your leader."

"If you feel lonely," said Carla, "call me. I'll be over in no time."

Note: In the third example above, *If* and *I'll* are capitalized because they start new sentences. But *call* is not capitalized, because it is part of the first sentence.

Names of Persons and the Word *I*

Last night, I saw a hilarious movie starring Stan Laurel and Oliver Hardy.

Names of Particular Places

Although Bill dropped out of Port Charles High School, he eventually earned his degree and got a job with Atlas Realty Company.

But: Use small letters if the specific name of a place is not given.

Although Bill dropped out of high school, he eventually earned his degree and got a job with a real estate company.

Names of Days of the Week, Months, and Holidays

On the last Friday afternoon in May, the day before Memorial Day, my boss is having a barbecue for all the employees.

But: Use small letters for the seasons—summer, fall, winter, spring.

Most people feel more energetic in the spring and fall.

Names of Commercial Products

My little sister knows all the words to the jingles for Oscar Mayer hot dogs, Diet Pepsi, Meow Mix cat food, and McDonald's hamburgers.

But: Use small letters for the *type* of product (hot dogs, cat food, hamburgers, and so on).

Titles of Books, Magazines, Newspapers, Articles, Stories, Poems, Films, Television Shows, Songs, Papers That You Write, and the Like

We read the book *Hiroshima,* by John Hersey, for our history class.

In the doctor's waiting room, I watched *All My Children,* read an article in *Reader's Digest,* and leafed through the *Miami Herald.*

Names of Companies, Associations, Unions, Clubs, Religious and Political Groups, and Other Organizations

Joe Naples is a Roman Catholic, but his wife is a Methodist.

The Hilldale Square Dancers' Club has won many competitions.

Brian, a member of Bricklayers Local 431 and the Knights of Columbus, works for Ace Construction.

Activity

Underline the words that need capitals in the following sentences. Then write the capitalized form of the words in the spaces provided. The number of spaces tells you how many corrections to make in each case.

Example   In our biology class, each student must do a report on an article in the magazine *scientific american.*   Scientific American

1. Leon's collection of beatles souvenirs includes a pair of tickets from their last concert in candlestick park, San Francisco.

    _____   _____   _____

2. Yumi read in *psychology today* magazine that abraham lincoln suffered from severe depression.

    _____   _____   _____   _____

3. When i have a cold, I use vick's ointment and chew listerine lozenges.

    _____   _____   _____

4. This spring, the boy scouts and the jaycees will clean up madison Park.

    _____   _____   _____

5. A nature trail for the blind in cape cod, massachusetts, has signs written in braille which encourage visitors to smell and touch the plants.

    _____   _____   _____

6. At a restaurant on Broad street called Joe's italian palace, the chefs use pasta machines to make fresh noodles right in the dining room.

    _____   _____   _____

7. My father is a confirmed Dallas cowboys fan, though he lives in boston.

    _____   _____

8. Martha bought a sugar-free tab to wash down her hostess twinkie.

    _____   _____   _____

9. Vince listened to a Billy Joel album called *The Stranger* while Donna read an article in *glamour* entitled ''What Do men Really want?''

    _____   _____   _____

10. After having her baby, joan received a card from one of her friends that read, ''congratulations, we all knew you had it in you.''

    _____   _____

OTHER USES OF CAPITAL LETTERS

Capital letters are also used with:

1 Names that show family relationships
2 Titles of persons when used with their names
3 Specific school courses
4 Languages
5 Geographic locations
6 Historical periods and events
7 Races, nations, and nationalities
8 Opening and closing of a letter

Each use is illustrated on the pages that follow.

Names That Show Family Relationships

All his life, Father has been addicted to gadgets.
I browsed through Grandmother's collection of old photographs.
Aunt Florence and Uncle Bill bought a mobile home.

But: Do not capitalize words like *mother, father, grandmother, grandfather, uncle, aunt,* and so on when they are preceded by a possessive word (*my, your, his, her, our, their*).

All his life, my father has been addicted to gadgets.
I browsed through my grandmother's collection of old photographs.
My aunt and uncle bought a mobile home.

Titles of Persons When Used with Their Names

I contributed to Senator McGrath's campaign fund.

Is Dr. Gregory on vacation?

Professor Adams announced that there would be no tests in the course.

But: Use small letters when titles appear by themselves, without specific names.

I contributed to my senator's campaign fund.

Is the doctor on vacation?

The professor announced that there would be no tests in the course.

Specific School Courses

The college offers evening sections of Introductory Psychology I, Abnormal Psychology, Psychology and Statistics, and Educational Psychology.

But: Use small letters for general subject areas.

The college offers evening sections of many psychology courses.

Languages

My grandfather's Polish accent makes his English difficult to understand.

Geographic Locations

He grew up in the Midwest but moved to the South to look for a better job.

But: Use small letters in directions.

Head west for five blocks and then turn south on State Street.

Historical Periods and Events

During the Middle Ages, the Black Death killed over one-quarter of Europe's population.

Races, Nations, and Nationalities

The census questionnaire asked if the head of our household was Caucasian, African American, Asian, or Native American.

Linda has lived on army bases in Germany, Italy, and Spain.

Denise's beautiful features are the result of her Chinese and Mexican parentage.

Opening and Closing of a Letter

Dear Sir: Sincerely yours,
Dear Ms. Henderson: Truly yours,

Note: Capitalize only the first word in a closing.

Activity

Underline the words that need capitals in the following sentences. Then write the capitalized forms of the words in the spaces provided. The number of spaces tells you how many corrections to make in each case.

1. During world war II, many americans were afraid that the japanese would invade California.

   _____ _____ _____ _____

2. Many college students are studying spanish and french to help them in their business careers.

   _____ _____

3. When uncle harvey got the bill from his doctor, he called the American Medical Association to complain.

   _____ _____

4. Dr. Freeling of the business department is offering a new course called introduction to word processing.

   _____ _____ _____

5. A new restaurant featuring vietnamese cuisine has just opened on the south side of the city.

   _____

UNNECESSARY USE OF CAPITALS

Activity

Many errors in capitalization are caused by using capitals where they are not needed. Underline the incorrectly capitalized letters in the following sentences and write the correct forms in the spaces provided. The number of spaces tells you how many corrections to make in each sentence.

1. James Garfield—the last President to be born in a log cabin—was also the first to use a Telephone.

   _____   _____

2. While she cleans and cooks, my Mother wears a pair of Sony Stereo Head-phones.

   _____   _____   _____

3. Americans were shocked when several members of the Chicago White Sox Baseball Team accepted bribes to ''fix'' the 1919 World Series.

   _____   _____

4. The Voyager spacecraft sent back pictures of Saturn's Rings which prove that they are made up of Millions of Small, icy Particles.

   _____   _____   _____   _____

5. Einstein's theory of relativity, which he developed when he was only twenty-six, led to the invention of the Electron Microscope, Television, and the Atomic bomb.

   _____   _____   _____   _____

■ **Review Test 1**

Add capitals where needed in the following sentences.

Example In an injured tone, Mary demanded, ''why wasn't uncle Lou invited to the party?''

1. To keep warm, a homeless old man sits on a steam vent near the sears building on tenth street.

2. Silent movie stars of the twenties, like charlie chaplin and gloria swanson, earned more than a million tax-free dollars a year.

3. Insects living in mammoth cave, in kentucky, include blind crickets, spiders, and flies.

4. Fidel Castro, the cuban leader, once tried out for the washington senators, a professional baseball team.

5. In the marx brothers movie, an attractive young lady invited groucho to join her.

6. ''why?'' asked groucho. ''are you coming apart?''

7. I was halfway to the wash & dry Laundromat on elm street when i realized that my box of tide was still home on the kitchen counter.

8. Every november, I make another vow that I will not gain weight between thanksgiving and new year's day.

9. *Rolling stone* magazine features an article about the making of the latest *star trek* sequel and a review of a new paul mccartney album.

10. Celebrities earn big money for endorsing items like polaroid cameras, trident gum, and jell-O pudding.

■ **Review Test 2**

On separate paper, write:

1. Seven sentences demonstrating the seven main uses of capital letters
2. Eight sentences demonstrating the eight other uses of capital letters

NUMBERS AND ABBREVIATIONS

NUMBERS

Here are three helpful rules for using numbers.

Rule 1: Spell out numbers that take no more than two words. Otherwise, use the numbers themselves.

> In Jody's kitchen is her collection of seventy-two cookbooks.
> It will take about six weeks to fix the computer.
> Only twelve students have signed up for the field trip.
> Jody has a file of 350 recipes.
> Since several people use the computer, we'll lose over 150 work days.
> Nearly 250 students came to the lecture.

Rule 2: Be consistent when you use a series of numbers. If some numbers in a sentence or paragraph require more than two words, then use numbers in every case throughout the selection.

> After the storm, maintenance workers unclogged 46 drains, removed 123 broken tree limbs, and rescued 3 kittens who were stuck in a rain pipe.

Rule 3: Use numbers to show dates, times, addresses, percentages, and parts of a book.

The burglary was committed on October 30, 1995, but not discovered until January 2, 1996.

Before I went to bed, I set my alarm for 6:45 A.M. (*But:* Spell out numbers before *o'clock*. For example: I didn't get out of bed until seven o'clock.)

The library is located at 45 West 52d Street.

When you take the skin off a piece of chicken, you remove about 40 percent of the fat.

The name of the murderer is revealed in Chapter 8 on page 236.

Activity

Cross out the mistakes in numbers and write the corrections in the spaces provided.

1. Sally and I will meet at 3 o'clock in front of the building at twenty-two South Fifteenth Street.

   _____   _____   _____

2. It took 4 hours to proofread all 75 pages of the manuscript.

   _____   _____

3. We expect to have fifty percent of the work completed by March tenth.

   _____   _____

ABBREVIATIONS

Using abbreviations can save you time when you take notes. In formal writing, however, you should avoid most abbreviations. Listed below are some of the few abbreviations that are considered acceptable in compositions. Note that a period is used after most abbreviations.

1 Mr., Mrs., Ms., Jr., Sr., Dr. when used with proper names:

   Mrs. Johnson   Dr. Findley   Howard Kelley, Jr.
2 Time references:

   A.M. or a.m.   P.M. or p.m.   B.C., A.D.

3   Initials in a person's name:

J. Edgar Hoover   John F. Kennedy   Michael J. Fox

4   Organizations, technical words, and trade names known primarily by their initials:

IBM   UNICEF   ABC   IRS   NBA   AIDS

Activity

Cross out the words that should not be abbreviated and correct them in the spaces provided.

1. Between Sept. 1 and Oct. 15, six people in my fam. have birthdays.

    _____   _____   _____

2. I had such a bad headache this aftern. that I called my doc. for an appt.

    _____   _____   _____

3. I stopped at the p.o. at about twenty min. past ten and bought five dol. worth of stamps.

    _____   _____   _____

    _____

■ Review Test

Cross out the mistakes in numbers and abbreviations and correct them in the spaces provided.

1. Our dept. has received over two hundred and thirty applications for the position.

    _____   _____

2. Grandpa lived to be ninety-nine despite smoking 3 packs of cigs. every day.

    _____   _____

3. Although the 2 girls are twins, they have different birthdays: one was born just before midnight on Feb. twenty-fifth, and the other a few minutes later after midnight.

    _____   _____   _____

4. In their first week of Span. class, students learned to count from 1 to twenty-one and studied Chapter One in their textbook.

_____ _____ _____

5. When I cleaned out the junk drawer in the kitch., I found twelve rubber bands, thirty-seven paper clips, and 3 used-up batteries.

_____ _____

APOSTROPHE

The two main uses of the apostrophe are:

1   To show the omission of one or more letters in a contraction
2   To show ownership or possession

Each use is explained on the pages that follow.

APOSTROPHE IN CONTRACTIONS

A contraction is formed when two words are combined to make one word. An apostrophe is used to show where letters are omitted in forming the contraction. Here are two contractions:

have + not = haven't (the *o* in *not* has been omitted)
I + will = I'll (the *wi* in *will* has been omitted)

Following are some other common contractions:

I + am = I'm	it + is = it's
I + have = I've	it + has = it's
I + had = I'd	is + not = isn't
who + is = who's	could + not = couldn't
do + not = don't	I + would = I'd
did + not = didn't	they + are = they're

Note: Will + not has an unusual contraction: won't.

Activity

Write the contractions for the words in parentheses. One is done for you.

1. (Are not) _____*Aren't*_____ the reserve books in the library kept at the circulation desk?

2. If (they are) _____ coming over, (I had) _____ better cook more hot dogs.

3. (I am) _____ the kind of student (who is) _____ extremely nervous before tests.

4. (We are) _____ hoping to find out (who is) _____ responsible for this error; (it is) _____ important to us to keep our customers happy.

5. I (can not) _____ remember if (there is) _____ gas in the car or not.

Note: Even though contractions are common in everyday speech and in written dialog, it is usually best to avoid them in formal writing.

APOSTROPHE TO SHOW OWNERSHIP OR POSSESSION

To show ownership or possession, we can use such words as *belongs to, possessed by, owned by,* or (most commonly) *of.*

the umbrella that *belongs to* Mark
the tape recorder *owned by* the school
the gentleness *of* my father

But the apostrophe plus *s* (if the word does not end in *s*) is often the quickest and easiest way to show possession. Thus we can say:

Mark's umbrella
the school's tape recorder
my father's gentleness

Points to Remember

1   The *'s* goes with the owner or possessor (in the examples given, *Mark, the school, my father*). What follows is the person or thing possessed (in the examples given, *the umbrella, the tape recorder, gentleness*).

2   There should always be a break between the word and the *'s*.

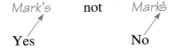

        Mark's   not   Marks

        Yes   No

Activity 1

Rewrite the *italicized* part of each of the sentences below, using the *'s* to show possession. Remember that the *'s* goes with the owner or possessor.

Example   *The wing of the bluejay* was broken.

        The bluejay's wing was broken.

1.   *The baton owned by the twirler* bounced on the ground.

_____

2.   *The performance of the quarterback* is inconsistent.

_____

3.   *The thin hand belonging to the old lady* felt as dry as parchment.

_____

4.   In *the window of the truck stop* is a sign: ''Five Hundred Mile Coffee.''

_____

5.   A fly flew into *the mouth of the TV weatherperson*.

_____

6.   *The new denim shirt belonging to Lamont* was as scratchy as sandpaper.

_____

7.   *The granite steps of the post office* were covered with green plastic turf.

_____

8.   *The bowl of cereal belonging to James* refused to snap, crackle, or pop.

_____

9.   *The Honda owned by Donna* was crammed with boxes and furniture.

_____

10.   *The previous tenant of the apartment* had painted all the walls bright green.

_____

Activity 2

Add *'s* to each of the following words to make them the possessors or owners of something. Then write sentences using the words. The first one is done for you.

1. rock star   *rock star's*
   The rock star's limousine pulled up to the curb.

2. Arnold _____

   _____

3. pilot _____

   _____

4. neighbor _____

   _____

5. school _____

   _____

6. gunslinger _____

   _____

Apostrophe versus Possessive Pronouns

Do not use an apostrophe with possessive pronouns. They already show ownership. Possessive pronouns include *his, hers, its, yours, ours,* and *theirs.*

Incorrect	Correct
The sun warped his' albums.	The sun warped his albums.
The restored Model T is theirs'.	The restored Model T is theirs.
The decision is yours'.	The decision is yours.
The plaid suitcase is ours'.	The plaid suitcase is ours.
The lion charged its' prey.	The lion charged its prey.

Apostrophe versus Simple Plurals

When you want to make a word plural, just add an *s* at the end of the word. Do *not* add an apostrophe. For example, the plural of the word *movie* is *movies,* not *movie's* or *movies'.*

Look at this sentence:

Tim coveted his roommate's collection of cassette tapes and compact disks.

The words *tapes* and *disks* are simple plurals, meaning more than one tape, more than one disk. The plural is shown by adding *s* only. On the other hand, the *'s* after *roommate* shows possession—that the roommate owns the tapes and disks.

Activity

Insert an apostrophe where needed to show possession in the following sentences. Write *plural* above words where the *s* ending simply means more than one thing.

Example   Arlene s tinted contact lenses protect her eyes from glare.
                       plural   *plural*

1. Harry grasped his wifes arm as she stood up on skates for the first time.

2. Vonettes decision to study computer science is based on predictions of good opportunities for women in that field.

3. The fires extreme heat had melted the telephones in the office and welded the metal chairs into a twisted heap.

4. Maria tried her sisters fad diet, which forbids eating any food that is white.

5. At the doctors request, Jim pulled up his shirt and revealed the zipperlike scars from his operation.

6. At the end of the day, Cals shirt and pants smelled like gasoline, and his fingernails were rimmed with grease.

7. Most peoples fear of flying is based on their fear of giving control over their destinies to someone else—in this case, the pilot.

8. Tinas camping handbook suggests that we bring water purification tablets and nylon ropes.

9. Carmens leaky pen had stained her fingers a deep blue.

10. The rattlesnakes head has a sensitive pit below the eyes, capable of detecting the body heat of warm-blooded prey.

Apostrophe with Plurals Ending in *-s*

Plurals that end in *-s* show possession simply by adding the apostrophe, rather than an apostrophe plus *s*.

the Thompsons' porch
the players' victory
her parents' motor home
the Rolling Stones' last album
the soldiers' hats

Activity

Add an apostrophe where needed.

1. Several campers tents collapsed during the storm.
2. The Murrays phone bill is over $200 a month.
3. Many buildings steep steps make it difficult for wheelchair-bound people to negotiate them.
4. The twins habit of dressing alike was started by their mother when they were children.
5. All the neighbors lawns are as parched as straw.

■ Review Test

In each sentence underline the two words that need apostrophes. Then write the words correctly in the spaces provided.

_____ 1. Although I hadnt met him before, Donalds voice sounded familiar to me.
_____

_____ 2. A shaky rope ladder led from the barns wooden floor to the haylofts dusty shadows.
_____

_____ 3. The paperback books glaring purple and orange cover was designed to attract the hurrying customers eye.
_____

_____ 4. Phils essay was due in a matter of hours, but he suffered a writers block that emptied his brain.
_____

_____   5. While he waited in his boss office, Charlies nervous fingers shredded a Styrofoam coffee cup into a pile of jagged white flakes.

_____   6. Jacks son stepped cautiously along the top of the farmyards splintery wooden fence.

_____   7. Members of the parents association constructed a maze made of old tires for the childrens playground.

_____   8. Barrys greatest accomplishment was conquering his addiction to his mothers chocolate pecan pie.

_____   9. The suns rays beat down until the streets blacktopped surface softened with the heat.

_____   10. The rivers swirling floodwaters lapped against the Thompsons porch.

QUOTATION MARKS

The two main uses of quotation marks are:

1   To set off the exact words of a speaker or writer
2   To set off the titles of short works

Each use is explained on the pages that follow.

QUOTATION MARKS TO SET OFF THE WORDS OF A SPEAKER OR WRITER

Use quotation marks to show the exact words of a speaker or writer.

''I feel as though I've been here before,'' Angie murmured to her husband.
(Quotation marks set off the exact words that Angie spoke to her husband.)

Ben Franklin once wrote, ''To lengthen thy life, lessen thy meals.''
(Quotation marks set off the exact words that Ben Franklin wrote.)

''Did you know,'' said the nutrition expert, ''that it's healthier to be ten pounds overweight?''
(Two pairs of quotation marks are used to enclose the nutrition expert's exact words.)

The biology professor said, ''Ants are a lot like human beings. They farm their own food and raise smaller insects as livestock. And, like humans, ants send armies to war.''
(Note that the end quotation marks do not come until the end of the biology professor's speech. Place quotation marks before the first quoted word and after the last quoted word. As long as no interruption occurs in the speech, do not use quotation marks for each new sentence.)

Punctuation Hint: In the four examples on the preceding page, notice that a comma sets off the quoted part from the rest of the sentence. Also observe that commas and periods at the end of a quotation always go *inside* quotation marks.

Complete the following statements that explain how capital letters, commas, and periods are used in quotations. Refer to the four examples as guides.

1. Every quotation begins with a _____ letter.
2. When a quotation is split (as in the sentence of the nutrition expert), the second part does not begin with a capital letter unless it is a _____ sentence.
3. _____ are used to separate the quoted part of a sentence from the rest of the sentence.
4. Commas and periods that come at the end of a quotation go _____ quotation marks.

The answers are *capital, new, Commas,* and *inside.*

Activity 1

Place quotation marks around the exact words of a speaker or writer in the sentences that follow.

1. I'll worry about that tomorrow, Scarlett said to Rhett.
2. Beatrice asked, Do you give a discount to senior citizens?
3. This hamburger is raw! cried Leon.
4. The bumper sticker on the rear of the battered old car read, Don't laugh— it's paid for.
5. I know why Robin Hood robbed only the rich, said the comedian. The poor don't have any money.
6. These records, proclaimed the television announcer, are not sold in any store.
7. When chefs go to great lengths, the woman at the reducing center said, I go to great widths.
8. Did you know, the counselor said to my husband and me, that it now costs $150,000 to raise a child to the age of eighteen?
9. On a tombstone in a Maryland cemetery are the words, Here lies an atheist, all dressed up and no place to go.
10. The advice columnist advised, Be nice to people on your way up because you'll meet them on your way down.

Activity 2

1. Write a sentence in which you quote a favorite expression of someone you know. Identify the relationship of the person to you.

   Example *My grandfather's favorite expression is, "It can't be as bad as all that."*

   _____

   _____

2. Write a quotation that contains the words *Nick asked Fran.* Write a second quotation that includes the words *Fran replied.*

   _____

   _____

   _____

   _____

   _____

   _____

3. Write down a sentence or two that interests you from a book or magazine. Identify the title and author of the work.

   Example *In And More by Andy Rooney, the author writes, "Any line you choose to stand in during your life will usually turn out to be the one that moves the slowest."*

   _____

   _____

   _____

   _____

   _____

   _____

Indirect Quotations

An indirect quotation is a rewording of someone else's comments rather than a word-for-word direct quotation. The word *that* often signals an indirect quotation.

Direct Quotation	*Indirect Quotation*
The nurse said, ''Some babies cannot tolerate cows' milk.'' (The nurse's exact spoken words are given, so quotation marks are used.)	The nurse said that some babies cannot tolerate cows' milk. (We learn the nurse's words indirectly, so no quotation marks are used.)
Vicky's note to Dan read, ''I'll be home by 7:30.'' (The exact words that Vicky wrote in the note are given, so quotation marks are used.)	Vicky left a note for Dan that said she would be home by 7:30. (We learn Vicky's words indirectly, so no quotation marks are used.)

Activity

Rewrite the following sentences, changing words as necessary to convert the sentences into direct quotations. The first one has been done for you as an example.

1. Teddy asked Margie if she wanted to see his spider collection.
   Teddy asked, "Margie, do you want to see my spider collection?"

2. Andy said that his uncle looks just like a large basset hound.

   _____

   _____

3. Nathan said that he wanted a box of the extra-crispy chicken.

   _____

   _____

4. My boss told me that I could make mistakes as long as I didn't repeat them.

   _____

   _____

5. The announcer said that tonight's regular TV programs have been canceled.

   _____

   _____

QUOTATION MARKS TO SET OFF
TITLES OF SHORT WORKS

Titles of short works are usually set off by quotation marks, while titles of long works are underlined. Use quotation marks to set off titles of such short works as articles in books, newspapers, or magazines; chapters in a book; short stories; poems; and songs. But you should underline titles of books, newspapers, magazines, plays, movies, record albums, and television shows. Following are some examples.

Quotation Marks	*Underlines*
the essay "On Self-Respect"	in the book Slouching towards Bethlehem
the article "The Problem of Acid Rain"	in the newspaper The New York Times
the article "Living with Inflation"	in the magazine Newsweek
the chapter "Chinese Religion"	in the book Paths of Faith
the story "Hands"	in the book Winesburg, Ohio
the poem "When I Have Fears"	in the book Complete Poems of John Keats
the song "Ziggy Stardust"	in the album Changes
	the television show Sixty Minutes
	the movie High Noon

Note: In printed works, including papers that are prepared on a word processor, italic type—slanted type that looks *like this*—is used instead of underlining.

Activity

Use quotation marks or underlines as needed.

1. In his short story entitled A Mother's Tale, James Agee describes a slaughter-house from the cow's point of view.
2. I bought the National Enquirer to read an article entitled How Video Games Are Hazardous to Your Mental Health.
3. We read the chapter Pulling Up Roots in Gail Sheehy's book Passages.
4. Jane used an article titled Ten Ways to Unplug Your Kid's TV Habit in her research paper for developmental psychology.

5. The movie Casablanca, which starred Humphrey Bogart, was originally cast with Ronald Reagan in the leading role.
6. My favorite old TV show was Thriller, a horror series hosted by Boris Karloff, the man who starred in the 1931 movie Frankenstein.
7. When the Beatles' movie A Hard Day's Night was first shown, fans screamed so much that no one could hear the songs or the dialog.
8. On my father's wall is a framed front page of The New York Times of February 25, 1940—the day he was born.
9. The sociology test will cover the first two chapters: Culture and Diversity and Social Stratification.
10. An article in Consumer Reports called Which Cereal for Breakfast? claims that children can learn to like low-sugar cereals like Cheerios and Wheaties.

OTHER USES OF QUOTATION MARKS

Quotation marks are also used as follows:

1   To set off special words or phrases from the rest of a sentence:

In grade school, we were taught a little jingle about the ''i before e'' spelling rule.
What is the difference between ''it's'' and ''its''?
(In this book, *italics* are often used instead of quotation marks to set off words.)

2   To mark off a quotation within a quotation:

The physics professor said, ''Do the problems at the end of Chapter Five, 'Work and Energy,' for class on Friday.''
Elliot remarked, ''Did you know that Humphrey Bogart never actually said, 'Play it again, Sam' in the movie *Casablanca*?''

Note: A quotation within a quotation is indicated by *single* quotation marks, as shown above.

■ Review Test 1

Insert quotation marks where needed in the sentences that follow.

1. The psychology class read a short story called Silent Snow, Secret Snow about a young boy who creates his own fantasy world.
2. When asked for advice on how to live a long life, the old man said, Don't look back; something may be gaining on you.
3. I'm against grade school students using pocket calculators, said Fred. I spent three years learning long division, and so should they.
4. One updated version of an old saying goes, Absence makes the heart grow fonder—of somebody else.
5. When I gagged while taking a foul-tasting medicine, my wife said, Put an ice cube on your tongue first, and then you won't taste it.
6. I looked twice at the newspaper headline that read, Man in River Had Drinking Problem.
7. Gene reported to his business class on an article in *Money* magazine entitled Cashing In on the Energy Boom.
8. When a guest at the wedding was asked what he was giving the couple, he replied, About six months.
9. Theodore Roosevelt, a pioneer in conservation, once said, When I hear of the destruction of a species, I feel as if all the works of some great writer had perished.
10. If you're ever in trouble, said the police officer, you'll have a better chance of attracting aid if you shout Fire instead of Help.

■ Review Test 2

Go through the comics section of a newspaper to find a comic strip that amuses you. Be sure to choose a strip where two or more characters are speaking to each other. Write a full description that will enable people who have not read the comic strip to visualize it clearly and appreciate its humor. Describe the setting and action in each panel and enclose the words of the speakers in quotation marks.

COMMA

SIX MAIN USES OF THE COMMA

Commas are used mainly as follows:

1 To separate items in a series
2 To set off introductory material
3 On both sides of words that interrupt the flow of thought in a sentence
4 Between two complete thoughts connected by *and, but, for, or, nor, so, yet*
5 To set off a direct quotation from the rest of a sentence
6 For certain everyday material

You may find it helpful to remember that the comma often marks a slight pause or break in a sentence. Read aloud the sentence examples given for each rule, and listen for the minor pauses or breaks that are signaled by commas.

1 Comma between Items in a Series

Use commas to separate items in a series.

The street vendor sold watches, necklaces, and earrings.
The pitcher adjusted his cap, pawed the ground, and peered over his shoulder.
The exercise instructor told us to inhale, exhale, and relax.
Joe peered into the hot, still-smoking engine.

Notes

a   The final comma in a series is optional, but it is often used.

b   A comma is used between two descriptive words in a series only if *and* inserted between the words sounds natural. You could say:

Joe peered into the hot *and* still-smoking engine.

But notice in the following sentence that the descriptive words do not sound natural when *and* is inserted between them. In such cases, no comma is used.

Tony wore a pale green tuxedo. (A pale *and* green tuxedo does not sound right, so no comma is used.)

Activity

Place commas between items in a series.

1. The old kitchen cabinets were littered with dead insects crumbs and dust balls.
2. Rudy stretched out on the swaying hammock popped open a frosty can of soda and balanced it carefully on his stomach.
3. The children splashed through the warm deep swirling rainwater that flooded the street.
4. The freezer was crammed with mysterious foil-wrapped lumps boxes of frozen french fries and empty ice cube trays.
5. The musty shadowy cellar with the crumbling cement floor was our favorite playground.

2   Comma after Introductory Material

Use a comma to set off introductory material.

> Just in time, Sherry slid a plastic tray under the overwatered philodendron.
>
> Muttering under his breath, Ken reviewed the terms he had memorized.
>
> In a wolf pack, the dominant male holds his tail higher than the other pack members.
>
> Although he had been first in the checkout line, Dave let an elderly woman go ahead of him.
>
> After the fire, we slogged through the ashes of the burned-out house.

Note: If the introductory material is brief, the comma is sometimes omitted. In the activities here, you should include the comma.

Activity

Place commas after introductory material.

1. As Patty struggled with the stuck window gusts of cold rain blew in her face.
2. Before taking a blood sample the nurse taped Jake's arm to make a large vein stand out.
3. Along the once-pretty river people had dumped old tires and loads of household trash.
4. When the movie still hadn't come on well after dusk the occupants of the cars parked at the drive-in began beeping their horns.
5. Setting down a smudged glass of murky water the waitress tossed Dennis a greasy menu and asked if he'd care to order.

3   Comma around Words Interrupting the Flow of Thought

Use a comma on both sides of words or phrases that interrupt the flow of thought in a sentence.

> The vinyl car seat, sticky from the heat, clung to my skin.
>
> Marty's personal computer, which his wife got him as a birthday gift, occupies all of his spare time.
>
> The hallway, dingy and dark, was illuminated by a bare bulb hanging from a wire.

Usually you can "hear" words that interrupt the flow of thought in a sentence by reading it aloud. In cases where you are not sure if certain words are interrupters, remove them from the sentence. If it still makes sense without the words, you know that the words are interrupters and that the information they give is nonessential. *Such nonessential or extra information is set off with commas.*

In the following sentence,

Sue Dodd, who goes to aerobics class with me, was in a serious car accident.

the words *who goes to aerobics class with me* are extra information not needed to identify the subject of the sentence, *Sue Dodd.* Commas go around such nonessential information. On the other hand, in the sentence

The woman who goes to aerobics class with me was in a serious accident.

the words *who goes to aerobics class with me* supply essential information—information needed for us to identify the woman being spoken of. If the words were removed from the sentence, we would no longer know who was in the accident. Here is another example:

Watership Down, a novel by Richard Adams, is the most thrilling adventure story I've ever read.

Here the words *a novel by Richard Adams* could be left out, and we would still know the basic meaning of the sentence. Commas are placed around such nonessential material. But in the sentence

Richard Adams's novel *Watership Down* is the most thrilling adventure story I've ever read.

the title of the novel is essential. Without it the sentence would read, "Richard Adams's novel is the most thrilling adventure story I've ever read." We would not know which of Richard Adams's novels was so thrilling. Commas are not used around the title, because it provides essential information.

Most of the time you will be able to "hear" words that interrupt the flow of thought in a sentence and will not have to think about whether the words are essential or nonessential.

Activity

Use commas to set off interrupting words.

1. A slight breeze muggy with heat ruffled the bedroom curtains.
2. The defrosting chickens loosely wrapped in plastic left a pool on the counter.
3. Lenny's wallet which he kept in his front pants pocket was linked to his belt with a metal chain.
4. Mr. Delgado who is an avid Yankees fan remembers the great days of Mickey Mantle and Yogi Berra.
5. The fleet of tall ships a majestic sight made its way into the harbor.

4 Comma between Complete Thoughts

Use a comma between two complete thoughts connected by *and, but, for, or, nor, so, yet.*

Sam closed all the windows, but the predicted thunderstorms never arrived.
I like wearing comfortable clothing, so I buy oversized shirts and sweaters.
Peggy doesn't envy the skinny models in magazines, for she is happy with her own well-rounded body.

Notes

a   The comma is optional when the complete thoughts are short.

The ferris wheel started and Wilson closed his eyes.
Irene left the lecture hall for her head was pounding.
I made a wrong turn so I doubled back.

b   Be careful not to use a comma in sentences having one subject and a double verb. The comma is used only in sentences made up of two complete thoughts (two subjects and two verbs). In this sentence,

The doctor stared over his bifocals and lectured me about smoking.

there is only one subject (*doctor*) and a double verb (*stared* and *lectured*). No comma is needed. Likewise, the sentence

Frank switched the lamp on and off and then tapped it with his fingers.

has only one subject (*Frank*) and a double verb (*switched* and *tapped*); therefore, no comma is needed.

Activity

Place a comma before a joining word that connects two complete thoughts (two subjects and two verbs). Remember, do *not* place a comma within a sentence that has only one subject and a double verb. (Some items may be correct as given.)

1. The television sitcom was interrupted for a special news bulletin and I poked my head out of the kitchen to listen to the announcement.
2. The puppy was beaten by its former owner and cringes at the sound of a loud voice.
3. The eccentric woman brought all her own clips and rollers to the hairdresser's for she was afraid to use the ones in the shop.
4. The tuna sandwich in my lunch is crushed and the cream-filled cupcake is plastered to the bottom of the bag.
5. Lynn unscrewed the front panel of the air conditioner and removed the plastic foam filter in order to clean it.
6. Ruth was tired of summer reruns so she visited the town library to pick up some interesting books.
7. Debbie tried to trap the jumbo bumblebee bumping along the ceiling but the angry insect stayed just out of reach.
8. Carl strolled among the exhibits at the comic book collectors' convention and stopped to look at a rare first edition of *Superman.*
9. Our neighborhood crime patrol escorts elderly people to the local bank and installs free dead-bolt locks on their apartment doors.
10. Brendan tapped the small geraniums out of their pots and carefully planted them on his grandfather's grave.

5   Comma with Direct Quotations

Use a comma to set off a direct quotation from the rest of a sentence.

The carnival barker cried, "Step right up and win a prize!"

"Now is the time to yield to temptation," my horoscope read.

"I'm sorry," said the restaurant hostess. "You'll have to wait."

"For my first writing assignment," said Scott, "I have to turn in a five-hundred-word description of a stone."

Note: Commas and periods at the end of a quotation go inside quotation marks. See also page 418.

Activity

Use commas to set off direct quotations from the rest of the sentence.

1. The coach announced ''In order to measure your lung capacity, you're going to attempt to blow up a plastic bag with one breath.''
2. ''A grapefruit'' said the comedian ''is a lemon that had a chance and took advantage of it.''
3. The psychology professor said ''Dreams about feeling paralyzed in emergencies can represent a real-life inability to cope with stressful situations.''
4. ''Speak louder'' a man in the back row said to the guest speaker. ''I paid five dollars to hear you talk, not whisper.''
5. The zookeeper explained to the visitors ''We can't tell the sex of a giant tortoise for almost ten years after its birth.''

6 Comma with Everyday Material

Use a comma with certain everyday material.

Persons Spoken to

If you're the last to leave, Paul, please switch off the lights.

Fred, I think we're on the wrong road.

Did you see the play-off game, Lisa?

Dates

June 30, 1997, is the day I make the last payment on my car.

Addresses

I buy discount children's clothing from Isaacs Baby Wear Factory, Box 900, Chicago, Illinois 60614.

Note: No comma is used to mark off a zip code.

Openings and Closings of Letters

Dear Santa,	Sincerely yours,
Dear Larry,	Truly yours,

Note: In formal letters, a colon is used after the opening: Dear Sir: *or* Dear Madam: *or* Dear Allan: *or* Dear Ms. Mohr:.

Numbers

The insurance agent sold me a $50,000 term life insurance policy.

Activity

Place commas where needed.

1. Would you mind George if we borrowed your picnic cooler this weekend?
2. The enchiladas served at Los Amigos 5607 Pacific Boulevard are the best in town.
3. On August 23 1963 over 200000 blacks and whites marched for civil rights in Washington D.C.
4. The mileage chart shows Elaine that we'll have to drive 1231 miles to get to Sarasota Florida.
5. The coupon refund address is 2120 Industrial Highway Great Plains Minnesota 55455.

■ Review Test 1

Insert commas where needed. In the space provided below each sentence, summarize briefly the rule that explains the comma or commas used.

1. "Kleenex tissues" said the history professor "were first used as gas mask filters in World War I."

    _____

2. Dee ordered a sundae with three scoops of rocky road ice cream miniature marshmallows and raspberry sauce.

    _____

3. While waiting to enter the movie theater we studied the faces of the people just leaving to see if they had liked the show.

    _____

4. I had left my wallet on the store counter but the clerk called me at home to say that it was safe.

    _____

5. The demonstrators protesting nuclear arms carried signs reading "Humans have never invented a weapon that they haven't used."

    _____

6. Large cactus plants which now sell for very high prices are being stolen from national parks and protected desert areas.

    _____

7. On March 3 1962 Wilt Chamberlain scored one hundred points in a game against the New York Knicks.

_____

8. Tom watched nervously as the dentist assembled drills mirrors clamps picks and cylinders of cotton on a tray next to the reclining chair.

_____

9. The talk show guest a former child star said that one director threatened to shoot her dog if she didn't cry on cue.

_____

10. Cats and dogs like most animals love the taste of salt and will lick humans' hands to get it.

_____

■ Review Test 2

Insert commas where needed. Mark the one sentence that is correct with a C.

1. Before leaving for the gym Ellen added extra socks and a tube of shampoo to the gear in her duffel bag.
2. My father said ''Golf isn't for me. I can't afford to buy lots of expensive sticks so that I can lose lots of expensive white balls.''
3. Clogged with soggy birds' nests the chimney had allowed dangerous gases to accumulate in our house.
4. Bill took a time-exposure photo of the busy highway and the cars' taillights appeared in the developed print as winding red ribbons.
5. The graduating students sweltering in their hot black gowns fanned their faces with commencement programs.
6. Puffing a cigarette twitching his lips and adjusting his hat Bogie sized up the dangerous situation.
7. On May 31 1889 a flood in Johnstown Pennsylvania killed 2200 people.
8. ''When I was little'' said Ernie ''my brother told me it was illegal to kill praying mantises. I still don't know if that's true or not.''
9. A huge side of beef its red flesh marbled with streaks of creamy fat hung from a razor-sharp steel hook.
10. A line of dancing numerals on *Sesame Street* kicked across the screen like a chorus line.

■ **Review Test 3**

In the following passage, there are ten missing commas. Add the commas where needed. The types of mistakes to look for are shown in the box below.

> 2 commas missing between items in a series
> 1 comma missing after introductory material
> 4 commas missing around interrupting words
> 2 commas missing between complete thoughts
> 1 comma missing with a direct quotation

When I was about ten years old I developed several schemes to avoid eating liver, a food I despise. My first scheme involved my little brother. Timmy too young to realize what a horrible food liver is always ate every bit of his portion. On liver nights, I used to sit next to Tim and slide my slab of meat onto his plate when my parents weren't paying attention. This strategy worked until older and wiser Tim decided to reject his liver along with the rest of us. Another liver-disposal method I used was hiding the meat right on the plate. I'd cut the liver into tiny squares half the size of postage stamps and then I would carefully hide the pieces. I'd put them inside the skin of my baked potato beneath some mashed peas, or under a crumpled paper napkin. This strategy worked perfectly only if my mother didn't look too closely as she scraped the dishes. Once she said to me "Do you know you left a lot of liver on your plate?" My best liver trick was to hide the disgusting stuff on a three-inch-wide wooden ledge that ran under our dining-room table. I'd put little pieces of liver on the ledge when Mom wasn't looking; I would sneak the dried-up scraps into the garbage early the next day. Our dog would sometimes smell the liver try to get at it, and bang his head noisily against the bottom of the table. These strategies seemed like a lot of work but I never hesitated to take whatever steps I could. Anything was better than eating a piece of meat that tasted like old socks soaked in mud.

■ **Review Test 4**

On separate paper, write six sentences, one illustrating each of the six main comma rules.

OTHER PUNCTUATION MARKS

COLON (:)

Use the colon at the end of a complete statement to introduce a list, a long quotation, or an explanation.

1 A list:

The store will close at noon on the following dates: November 26, December 24, and December 31.

2 A long quotation:

The scientist Stephen Jay Gould wrote: ''I am, somehow, less interested in the weight and convolutions of Einstein's brain than in the near certainty that people of equal talent have lived and died in cotton fields and sweatshops.''

3 An explanation:

Here's a temporary solution to a dripping faucet: tie a string to it and let the drops slide down the string to the sink.

Activity

Place colons where needed in the sentences below:

1. Bring these items to registration a ballpoint pen, your student ID card, and a check made out to the college.
2. In our veterinarian's office is a grisly item a real dog's heart removed from an animal infested with heartworms.
3. Willa Cather, the American author, once wrote ''There are only two or three human stories, and they go on repeating themselves as fiercely as if they had never happened before.''

SEMICOLON (;)

The main use of the semicolon is to mark a break between two complete thoughts, as explained on pages 334–336. Another use is to mark off items in a series when the items themselves contain commas. Here are some examples:

> Sharon's children are named Melantha, which means ''black flower''; Yonina, which means ''dove''; and Cynthia, which means ''moon goddess.''
>
> My favorite albums are *Rubber Soul,* by the Beatles; *Songs in the Key of Life,* by Stevie Wonder; and *Bridge over Troubled Water,* by Simon and Garfunkel.

Activity

Place semicolons where needed in the sentences below.

1. Strange things happen at very low temperatures a rose will shatter like glass.
2. My sister had a profitable summer: by mowing lawns, she earned $125 by washing cars, $85 and by walking the neighbors' dogs, $110.
3. The salad bar was well stocked it included fresh spinach and sliced almonds.

DASH (—)

A dash signals a degree of pause longer than a comma but not as complete as a period. Use a dash to set off words for dramatic effect:

> I was so exhausted that I fell asleep within seconds—standing up.
>
> He had many good qualities—sincerity, honesty, and thoughtfulness—yet he had few friends.
>
> The pardon from the governor finally arrived—too late.

Notes

a   A dash is formed on a keyboard by striking the hyphen twice (- -). In hand-writing, a dash is as long as two letters would be.

b   Be careful not to overuse dashes.

Activity

Place dashes where needed in the following sentences.

1.   The victim's leg broken in three places lay twisted at an odd angle on the pavement.
2.   With a shriek, Jeannette dropped the hot iron pan on her toe.
3.   After I had seen every exhibit and ride at Disney World, there was only one other thing I wanted to see my motel room.

PARENTHESES (   )

Parentheses are used to set off extra or incidental information from the rest of a sentence:

> In 1913, the tax on an annual income of $4,000 (a comfortable wage at that time) was one penny.
>
> A small mirror (a double-faced one) is useful to a camper for flashing signals or starting fires.

Note: Do not use parentheses too often in your writing.

Activity

Add parentheses where needed.

1.   Though the original *Star Trek* series originally ran for only three seasons 1965–1968, it can still be seen on many stations around the country.
2.   Whenever Jack has too much to drink even one drink is sometimes too much, he gets loud and abusive.
3.   When I opened the textbook, I discovered that many pages mostly ones in the first chapter were completely blank.

HYPHEN (-)

1   Use a hyphen with two or more words that act as a single unit describing a noun.

The light-footed burglar silently slipped open the sliding glass door.

While being interviewed on the late-night talk show, the quarterback announced his intention to retire.

With a needle, Rich punctured the fluid-filled blister on his toe.

2   Use a hyphen to divide a word at the end of a line of writing or typing. When you need to divide a word at the end of a line, divide it between syllables. Use your dictionary to be sure of correct syllable divisions (see also page 440).

Mark's first year at college was a time filled with numerous new pressures and responsibilities.

Notes

a   Do not divide words of one syllable.

b   Do not divide a word if you can avoid dividing it.

Activity

Place hyphens where needed.

1. The record breaking summer temperatures coincided with an upsurge of assaults and murders in the city.
2. My father, who grew up in a poverty stricken household, remembers putting cardboard in his shoes when the soles wore out.
3. The well written article in *Newsweek* described the nerve wracking experiences of a company of men who had fought in Vietnam.

■ **Review Test**

At the appropriate spot, place the punctuation mark shown in the margin.

—   1. A bad case of flu, a burglary, the death of an uncle it was not what you would call a pleasant week.

( )   2. My grandfather who will be ninety in May says that hard work and a glass of wine every day are the secrets of a long life.

:   3. Mark Twain once wrote "The difference between the right word and the nearly right word is the difference between lightning and the lightning bug."

-    4. The passengers in the glass bottomed boat stared at the colorful fish in the water below.

( )   5. Ellen's birthday December 27 falls so close to Christmas that she gets only one set of presents.

;   6. The police officer had spotted our broken headlight consequently, he stopped us at the next corner.

—   7. I feel I have two chances of winning the lottery slim and none.

-    8. Well stocked shelves and friendly service are what Mrs. Dale demands of her staff.

;   9. Some people need absolute quiet in order to study they can't concentrate with the soft sounds of a radio, air conditioner, or television in the background.

:   10. There are three work habits my boss hates taking long coffee breaks, making personal phone calls, and missing staff meetings.

USING
THE
DICTIONARY

The dictionary is a valuable tool. To take advantage of it, you need to understand the main kinds of information that a dictionary gives about a word. Look at the information provided for the word *tattoo* in the following entry from *Random House Webster's Dictionary,* paperback edition.*

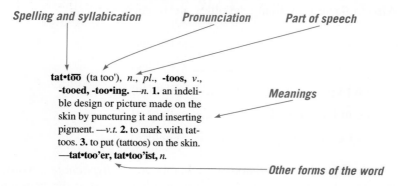

Spelling and syllabication   *Pronunciation*   *Part of speech*

tat•too (ta too'), *n., pl.,* **-toos,** *v.,*
-tooed, -too•ing. —*n.* **1.** an indelible design or picture made on the skin by puncturing it and inserting pigment. —*v.t.* **2.** to mark with tattoos. **3.** to put (tattoos) on the skin.
—**tat•too'er, tat•too'ist,** *n.*

Meanings

Other forms of the word

*Random House Webster's Dictionary (Ballantine Paperback edition). Copyright © 1993 by Random House, Inc.

SPELLING

The first bit of information, in the **boldface** (heavy type) entry itself, is the spelling of *tattoo*. Get into the habit of using the dictionary for spelling. When you write a paper, allow yourself time to look up the spelling of all those words you are unsure about.

Use your dictionary to correct the spelling of the following words:

accomodate	_____	intermitent	_____
crediter	_____	privlege	_____
decimel	_____	recesion	_____
unanamous	_____	propasition	_____
fulfil	_____	jepardy	_____
equivilent	_____	transmitt	_____
embarass	_____	adolesent	_____

SYLLABICATION

The second bit of information that the dictionary gives, also in the **boldface** entry, is the syllabication of *tattoo*. Note that a dot separates the syllables of the word.

Use your dictionary to mark the syllable divisions in the following words. Also indicate how many syllables are in each word.

f r u g a l	(_____ syllables)
t r a n s l u c e n t	(_____ syllables)
a n t i p a t h y	(_____ syllables)
s e m i a n n u a l	(_____ syllables)
i n f e r i o r i t y	(_____ syllables)

Noting syllable divisions will enable you to *hyphenate* a word, that is, divide it at the end of one line of writing and complete it at the beginning of the next line. You can correctly hyphenate a word only at a syllable division, and you may have to check your dictionary to make sure of the syllable divisions of a particular word.

PRONUNCIATION

The third bit of information in the dictionary entry is the pronunciation of *tattoo* (*ta tōo'*). You already know how to pronounce *tattoo,* but if you did not, the information within the parentheses would serve as your guide. Use your dictionary to complete the following exercises that relate to pronunciation.

Vowel Sounds

You will probably use the pronunciation key in your dictionary mainly as a guide to pronouncing different vowel sounds (vowels are the letters *a, e, i, o,* and *u*). Here is part of the pronunciation key in *The Random House Dictionary:*

a bat / ā way / e ebb / ē equal / i if

The key tells you, for example, that the sound of the short *a* is like the *a* in *bat,* the sound of the long *a* is like the *a* in *way,* and the sound of the short *e* is like the *e* in *ebb.*

Look at the pronunciation key in your dictionary. It is probably located in the front of the dictionary or at the bottom of every page. What common word in the key tells you how to pronounce each of the following sounds?

ī   _____

o   _____

ō   _____

u   _____

ŏŏ   _____

ōō   _____

Note: The long vowel always has the sound of its own name.

The Schwa ( )

The symbol ə looks like an upside-down *e*. It is called a *schwa,* and it stands for the unaccented sound in such words as *ago, item, easily, gallop,* and *circus.* More approximately, it stands for the sound *uh*—like the *uh* that speakers sometimes make when they hesitate. It is helpful to remember that *uh,* as well as ə, could be used to represent the schwa sound.

Here are some of the many words in which this sound appears: *credential* (kri-den' shəl); *horrify* (hôr'ə-fī); *signature* (sig'nə-choor). Open your dictionary to any page and you will almost surely be able to find three words with a schwa in their pronunciation (in parentheses after the main entry). Write three such words and their pronunciations in the spaces below.

1. _____   (_____)

2. _____   (_____)

3. _____   (_____)

Accent Marks

Some words have both a primary accent, shown by a heavy stroke (′), and a secondary accent, shown by a lighter stroke (′). For example, in the word *individual* (in′də-vij′ o͞o əl) the stress, or accent, goes chiefly on the third syllable (vij′), and to a lesser extent on the first syllable (in′).

Use your dictionary to add accent marks to the following words:

prologue   (prō log)   animosity   (an ə mos ə tē)

tacit   (tas it)   magnanimous   (mag nan ə məs)

corroborate   (kə rob ə rāt)

Full Pronunciation

Use your dictionary to write out the full pronunciation (the information given in parentheses) for each of the following words.

binary _____

facsimile _____

vestige _____

antebellum _____

covert _____

euphemism _____

capitulate _____

derisive _____

tenacious _____

vociferous _____

satiate _____

aesthetic _____

anachronism _____

posthumous _____

millennium _____

Now practice pronouncing each word. Use the pronunciation key in your dictionary as an aid to sounding out each syllable. Do *not* try to pronounce a word all at once; instead, work on mastering *one syllable at a time*. When you can pronounce each of the syllables in a word successfully, then say them in sequence, add the accent, and pronounce the entire word.

PARTS OF SPEECH

The next bit of information that the dictionary gives about *tattoo* is *n*. This abbreviation means that the meanings of *tattoo* as a noun will follow.

Use your dictionary if necessary to fill in the meanings of the following abbreviations:

v. = _____

adj. = _____

sing. = _____

pl. = _____

PRINCIPAL PARTS OF IRREGULAR VERBS

Tattoo is a regular verb and forms its principal parts by adding *-ed, -ed,* and *-ing* to the stem of the verb. When a verb is irregular, the dictionary lists its principal parts. For example, with *give* the present tense comes first (the entry itself, *give*). Next comes the past tense (*gave*), and then the past participle (*given*)—the form of the verb used with such helping words as *have, had,* and *was*. Then comes the present participle (*giving*)—the *-ing* form of the verb.

Look up the parts of the following irregular verbs and write them in the spaces provided. The first one is done for you.

Present	Past	Past Participle	Present Participle
swim	swam	swum	swimming
lie			
drink			
freeze			

PLURAL FORMS OF IRREGULAR NOUNS

The dictionary supplies the plural forms of all irregular nouns (regular nouns like *tattoo* form the plural by adding *-s* or *-es*). Give the plurals of the following nouns. If two forms are shown, write down both.

crisis _____

phenomenon _____

library _____

cactus _____

shelf _____

MEANINGS

When a word has more than one meaning, its meanings are numbered in the dictionary, as with the word *tattoo*. In many dictionaries, the most common meanings of a word are presented first. The introductory pages of your dictionary will explain the order in which meanings are presented.

Use the sentence context to try to explain the meaning of the italicized word in each of the following sentences. Write your definition in the space provided. Then look up and record the dictionary meaning of the word. Be sure you pick out the meaning that fits the word as it is used in the sentence.

1. During the hiking trip, we had to *navigate* some difficult trails.

   Your definition _____

   Dictionary definition _____

2. I had a *yen* for ice cream, but I knew I should stick to my diet.

   Your definition _____

   Dictionary definition _____

3. I faced a *gauntlet* of questions from my parents after arriving home at 4 A.M.

   Your definition _____

   Dictionary definition _____

4. Mel tried to *cajole* me into going to the party, but I wasn't in the mood.

   Your definition _____

   Dictionary definition _____

ETYMOLOGY

Etymology refers to the origin and historical development of a word. Such information is usually enclosed in brackets and is more likely to be present in a hardbound dictionary than in a paperback one. Good desk dictionaries include:

The American Heritage Dictionary
Random House Webster's Dictionary
Webster's New Collegiate Dictionary
Webster's New World Dictionary

See if your dictionary gives the origins of each of the following words:

guillotine _____

cereal _____

derrick _____

USAGE LABELS

As a general rule, use only standard English words in your writing. If a word is not standard English, your dictionary will probably give it a usage label like one of the following: *informal, nonstandard, slang, vulgar, obsolete, archaic, rare.*

Look up the following words and record how your dictionary labels them. Remember that a recent hardbound desk dictionary will always be the best source of information about usage.

brass (meaning "rudeness") _____

dope (meaning "very stupid person") _____

beat (meaning "exhausted") _____

croak (meaning "die") _____

snuck (meaning "sneaked") _____

SYNONYMS

A *synonym* is a word that is close in meaning to another word. Using synonyms helps you avoid unnecessary repetition of the same word in a paper. A paperback dictionary is not likely to give you synonyms for words, but a good desk dictionary will.

Consult a desk dictionary that gives you synonyms for the following words and write the synonyms in the space provided.

leave   _____

difficult   _____

important   _____

You might also want to own a *thesaurus,* a book that lists synonyms and *antonyms*—words approximately opposite in meaning to another word. A thesaurus can improve your writing, helping you find the precise word needed to express your thoughts. A thesaurus works much like a dictionary. You look up a word, and instead of definitions provided by a dictionary, you get a list of synonyms for the word. Here are three good thesauruses:

The New American Roget's College Thesaurus in Dictionary Form,
    Paperback Edition
The Random House Thesaurus
Webster's Collegiate Thesaurus

IMPROVING
SPELLING

Poor spelling often results from bad habits developed in the early school years. With work, such habits can be corrected. If you can write your name without misspelling it, there is no reason why you cannot do the same with almost any word in the English language. Following are steps you can take to improve your spelling.

STEP 1: USE THE DICTIONARY

Get into the habit of using the dictionary. When you write a paper, allow yourself time to look up the spelling of all those words you are unsure about. Do not overlook the value of this step just because it is such a simple one. By using the dictionary, you can probably make yourself a 95 percent better speller.

STEP 2: KEEP A PERSONAL SPELLING LIST

Keep a list of words you misspell and study the words regularly. Write the list on the back page of a frequently used notebook or on a separate sheet of paper titled ''Personal Spelling List.''

To master the words on your personal spelling list, do the following:

1   Write down any hint that will help you remember the spelling of a word. For example, you might want to note that *occasion* is spelled with two *c*'s, or that *all right* is two words, not one word.

2   Study a word by looking at it, saying it, and spelling it. You may also want to write out the word one or more times, or ''air write'' it with your finger in large, exaggerated motions.

3   When you have trouble spelling a long word, try to break the word into syllables and see whether you can spell the syllables. For example, *inadvertent* can be spelled easily if you can hear and spell in turn its four syllables: *in ad ver tent.* The word *consternation* can be spelled easily if you hear and spell its four syllables in turn: *con ster na tion.* Remember, then: Try to see, hear, and spell long words in terms of their syllables.

4   Keep in mind that review and repeated self-testing are keys to effective learning. When you are learning a series of words, go back after studying each new word and review all the preceding ones.

STEP 3: MASTER COMMONLY CONFUSED WORDS

Master the meanings and spellings of the commonly confused words on pages 456–466. Your instructor may assign twenty words for you to study at a time and give you a series of quizzes until you have mastered the words.

STEP 4: LEARN KEY WORDS IN MAJOR SUBJECTS

Make up and master lists of words central to the vocabulary of your major subjects. For example, a list of key words in business might include: *economics, management, resources, scarcity, capitalism, decentralization, productivity, enterprise,* and so on; in psychology: *behavior, investigation, experimentation, frustration, cognition, stimulus, response, organism,* and so on. Set aside a specific portion of your various course notebooks to be used only for such lists, and study them using the methods described above for learning words.

STEP 5: STUDY A BASIC WORD LIST

Following is a list of 250 English words that are often misspelled. Study their spellings. Your instructor may assign twenty-five or fifty words for you to study at a time and give you a series of quizzes until you have mastered the entire list.

250 Basic Words

absence	column	hammer
ache	comfortable	handkerchief
achieve	committed	harass
acknowledge	completely	height
advice	conceit	hospital
aisle	conscience	hundred
all right	conscious	husband
already	conversation	imitation
amateur	cruelty	incredible
answer	50 daughter	independent
anxious	deceit	instant
appearance	definite	instead
appetite	deposit	intelligence
attempt	dictionary	interest
attendance	disastrous	interfere
autumn	disease	interrupt
awful	distance	irresistible
bachelor	doctor	January
balance	doubt	kindergarten
bargain	efficient	100 leisure
basically	eighth	library
beautiful	either	lightning
believe	emphasize	likely
beneficial	entrance	livelihood
25 bottom	environment	loneliness
breathe	exaggerate	loose
brilliant	examine	magazine
bureau	existence	making
business	familiar	maintain
cafeteria	fascinate	marriage
calendar	February	material
candidate	financial	mathematics
category	foreign	medicine
ceiling	forty	minute
cemetery	75 friend	mortgage
chief	furniture	muscle
choose	government	naturally
cigarette	grammar	necessary
citizen	grieve	neither
college	guidance	nickel

niece
ninety
noise
obedience
125 obstacle
occasion
occur
occurrence
omission
opinion
opportunity
optimist
ounce
outrageous
pageant
pamphlet
people
perform
persistent
physically
picnic
plausible
pleasant
policeman
possible
precede
prefer
preference
prejudice
150 prescription
probably
psychology
pursue
quantity
quarter
quiet
quiz
raise
really
recede
receive
recognize
recommend

reference
region
reign
relieve
religion
representative
resistance
restaurant
rhythm
ridiculous
right
175 safety
said
salary
scarcely
scholastic
science
scissors
secretary
seize
separate
sergeant
several
severely
shriek
siege
similar
sincerely
sophomore
straight
succeed
suppress
telephone
temperature
tenant
tendency
200 tenth
than
theater
though
thousand
through
tomorrow

tongue
tonight
tournament
toward
transferred
trousers
truly
twelfth
unanimous
until
unusual
usage
used
usual
usually
vacuum
valuable
variety
225 vegetable
vengeance
view
villain
visitor
voice
Washington
wear
weather
Wednesday
weigh
weird
welcome
whether
which
woman
women
won't
writing
written
wrong
yesterday
yolk
your
250 you're

STEP 6: USE ELECTRONIC AIDS

There are three electronic aids that may help your spelling. First, many *electronic typewriters* on the market today will beep automatically when you misspell or mistype a word. They include built-in dictionaries that will then give you the correct spelling. Smith-Corona, for example, has a series of portable typewriters with an "Auto-Spell" feature that start at around $100 at discount stores.

Second, a *computer with a spell-checker* will identify incorrect words and suggest correct spellings. If you know how to write on a computer, you will have no trouble learning how to use the spell-check feature.

Third, *electronic spell-checkers* are pocket-size devices that look much like the pocket calculator you may carry to your math class. They are the latest example of how technology can help the learning process. Electronic spellers can be found in the typewriter or computer section of any discount store, at prices in the $20 range. The checker includes a tiny keyboard. You type out a word the way you think it is spelled, and the checker quickly provides you with the correct spelling of related words. Some of these checkers even *pronounce* the word aloud for you.

VOCABULARY
DEVELOPMENT

A good vocabulary is a vital part of effective communication. A command of many words will make you a better writer, speaker, listener, and reader. Studies have shown that students with strong vocabularies, and students who work to improve a limited vocabulary, are more successful in school. And one research study found that *a good vocabulary, more than any other factor, was common to people who had successful careers.* This section will describe three ways of developing your word power: (1) regular reading, (2) vocabulary wordsheets, and (3) vocabulary study books. You should keep in mind from the start, however, that none of the approaches will help unless you truly decide to make vocabulary development an important goal. Only when you have this attitude can you begin doing the sustained work needed to improve your word power.

REGULAR READING

Through reading a good deal, you will learn words by experiencing them a number of times in a variety of sentences. Repeated exposures to a word in context will eventually make it a part of your working language.

You should develop the habit of reading a daily newspaper and one or more weekly magazines like *Time, Newsweek,* or even *People,* as well as monthly magazines suited to your interests. In addition, you should try to read some books for pleasure. This may be especially difficult at times when you also have textbook reading to do. Try, however, to redirect a regular hour or half hour of your recreational time to reading books, rather than watching television, listening to music, or the like. By doing so, you may eventually reap two rewards: an improved vocabulary *and* the discovery that reading can be truly enjoyable.

WORDSHEETS

Another means of vocabulary development is the use of vocabulary wordsheets. As you read, you should first mark off words that you want to learn. After you have accumulated a number of words, sit down with a dictionary and look up basic information about each of them. Record this information on a wordsheet like the one shown here. Be sure also to write down a sentence in which each word appears. A word is always best learned not in a vacuum but in the context of surrounding words.

Study each word as follows. First, make sure you can correctly pronounce the word and its derivations. (The dictionary pronunciation key that will help you pronounce each word is explained on pages 441–443.) Second, study the main meanings of the word until you can say them without looking at them. Finally, spend a moment looking at the example of the word in context. You should then go on to follow the same process with the second word. Then, after testing yourself on the first and the second words, go on to the third word. Remember, after you learn each new word, continue going back and testing yourself on all the words you have studied. Such repeated self-testing is the key to effective learning.

Activity

Locate four words in your reading that you would like to master. Enter them in the spaces on the vocabulary wordsheet that starts below and fill in all the needed information. Your instructor may then check your wordsheet and perhaps give you a quick oral quiz on selected words.

You may receive a standing assignment to add five words a week to a wordsheet and to study those words. Note that you can create your own wordsheets using loose-leaf paper, or your instructor may give you copies of the wordsheet that appears here.

Vocabulary Wordsheet

1. Word: _tenacious_   Pronunciation: _(tə nā' shəs)_
   Meanings: _1. Keeping a firm hold_
   _____ 2. Persistent; stubborn_

   Other forms of the word: _tenaciously   tenacity_
   Use of the word in context: _I tried to loosen the tick's tenacious grip_
   on my skin.

2. Word: _____   Pronunciation: _____

    Meanings: _____

    _____

    _____

    Other forms of the word: _____

    Use of the word in context: _____

    _____

3. Word: _____   Pronunciation: _____

    Meanings: _____

    _____

    _____

    Other forms of the word: _____

    Use of the word in context: _____

    _____

4. Word: _____   Pronunciation: _____

    Meanings: _____

    _____

    _____

    Other forms of the word: _____

    Use of the word in context: _____

    _____

5. Word: _____   Pronunciation: _____

    Meanings: _____

    _____

    _____

    Other forms of the word: _____

    Use of the word in context: _____

    _____

VOCABULARY STUDY BOOKS

A third means of increasing your word power is the use of vocabulary study books. The most effective of these books help you learn a word by asking you to look at the context—the words around the unfamiliar word—to unlock its meaning. This method is called *using context clues,* or *using word clues.*

Here are some individual vocabulary study books you can find at most bookstores:

1,100 Words You Need to Know (Barron's)—Bromberg and Gordon
30 Days to a More Powerful Vocabulary (Pocket Books)—Funk and Lewis
Instant Word Power (Signet Books)—Lewis
Vocabulary through Pleasurable Reading (Amsco School Publications)

Here is one book you can order:

Building Vocabulary for College, Third Edition, by R. Kent Smith. (For information on ordering this book, write to D.C. Heath and Company, 125 Spring Street, Lexington, MA 02173.)

Many other vocabulary books and programs are available. The best are those which present words in one or more contexts and then provide several reinforcement activities for each word. The books will help you increase your vocabulary *if* you have the determination required to work with them on a regular basis.

COMMONLY CONFUSED WORDS

HOMONYMS

Some words are commonly confused because they have the same sounds but different meanings and spellings; such words are known as *homonyms*. Following are a number of homonyms. Complete the activity for each set of words, and check off and study the words that give you trouble.

all ready   completely prepared
already   previously; before

It was *already* four o'clock by the time I thought about lunch.
My report was *all ready,* but the class was canceled.

Fill in the blanks: David was _____ to sign up for the course when he discovered that it had _____ closed.

brake   stop
break   come apart

The mechanic advised me to add *brake* fluid to my car.
During a commercial *break,* Marie lay on the floor and did fifty sit-ups.

Fill in the blanks: Tim, a poor driver, would always _____ at the last minute and would usually _____ the speed limit as well.

course part of a meal; a school subject; direction
coarse rough

At the movies, I tried to decide on a *course* of action that would put an end to the *coarse* language of the man behind me.

Fill in the blanks: Over the _____ of time, jagged, _____ rocks will be polished to smoothness by the pounding waves.

hear perceive with the ear
here in this place

I can *hear* the performers so well from *here* that I don't want to change my seat.

Fill in the blanks: The chairperson explained that the meeting was held _____ in the auditorium to enable everyone to _____ the debate.

hole   an empty spot
whole entire

A *hole* in the crumbling brick mortar made a convenient home for the small bird and its *whole* family.

Fill in the blanks: The _____ in Dave's arguments wouldn't exist if he put his _____ concentration into his thinking.

its   belonging to it
it's the shortened form for "it is" or "it has"

The tall giraffe lowered *its* head (the head belonging to the giraffe) to the level of the car window and peered in at us.
It's (it is) too late to sign up for the theater trip to New York.

Fill in the blanks: I decided not to take the course because _____ too easy; _____ content offers no challenge whatever.

knew past form of *know*
new not old

No one *knew* our *new* phone number, but the obscene calls continued.

Fill in the blanks: Even people who _____ Charlie well didn't recognize him with his _____ beard.

know to understand
no a negative

By the time students complete that course, they *know* two computer languages and have *no* trouble writing their own programs.

Fill in the blanks: Dogs and cats usually _____ by the tone of the speaker's voice when they are being told "_____."

passed went by; succeeded in; handed to
past a time before the present; by, as in "I drove past the house"

As Yvonne *passed* exit six on the interstate, she knew she had gone *past* the correct turnoff.

Fill in the blanks: Lewis asked for a meeting with his boss to learn why he had been _____ over for promotion twice in the _____ year.

peace calm
piece a part

The best *piece* of advice she ever received was to maintain her own inner *peace*.

Fill in the blanks: Upon hearing that _____ of music, my angry mood was gradually replaced by one of _____.

plain   simple
plane   aircraft

The *plain* box contained a very expensive model *plane* kit.

Fill in the blanks: After unsuccessfully trying to overcome her fear, Sally finally admitted the _____ truth: she was terrified of flying in a _____ .

principal   main; a person in charge of a school
principle   a law or standard

If the *principal* ingredient in this stew is octopus, I'll abandon my *principle* of trying everything at least once.

Fill in the blanks: Our _____ insists that all students adhere to every school _____ regarding dress, tardiness, and smoking.

right   correct; opposite of "left"
write   what you do in English

Without the *right* amount of advance planning, it is difficult to *write* a good research paper.

Fill in the blanks: Connie wanted to send for the records offered on TV, but she could not _____ fast enough to get all the _____ information down before the commercial ended.

than   (thăn)   used in comparisons
then   (thĕn)   at that time

I made more money *then,* but I've never been happier *than* I am now.

Fill in the blanks: When I was in high school, I wanted a racy two-seater convertible more _____ anything else; but _____ my friends pointed out that only one person would be able to ride with me.

their   belonging to them
there   at that place; a neutral word used with verbs like *is, are, was, were, have,* and *had*
they're   the shortened form of "they are"

The tenants *there* are complaining because *they're* being cheated by *their* landlord.

Fill in the blanks: The tomatoes I planted _____ in the back of the garden are finally ripening, but _____ bright red color will attract hungry raccoons, and I fear _____ going to be eaten.

threw   past form of *throw*
through   from one side to the other; finished

As the inexperienced pizza maker *threw* the pie into the air, he punched a hole *through* its thin crust.

Fill in the blanks: As the president moved slowly _____ the cheering crowd, the Secret Service agent suddenly _____ himself at a man waving a small metal object.

to   a verb part, as in *to smile*; toward, as in "I'm going *to* heaven"
too   overly, as in "The pizza was *too* hot"; also, as in "The coffee was hot, *too.*"
two   the number 2

I ran *to* the car *to* roll up the windows.   (The first *to* means "toward"; the second *to* is a verb part that goes with *roll.*)

That amusement park is *too* far away; I hear that it's expensive, *too.*   (The first *too* means "overly"; the second *too* means "also.")

The *two* players (2 players) jumped up to tap the basketball away.

Fill in the blanks: The _____ of them have been dating for a year, but lately they seem _____ be arguing _____ often to pretend nothing is wrong.

wear   to have on
where in what place

Where I will *wear* a purple feather boa is not the point; I just want to buy it.

Fill in the blanks: _____ were we going the night I refused to _____ a tie?

weather   atmospheric conditions
whether   if it happens that; in case; if

Although meteorologists are *weather* specialists, even they can't predict *whether* a hurricane will change course.

Fill in the blanks: The gloomy _____ report in the paper this morning ended all discussion of _____ to pack a picnic lunch for later.

whose   belonging to whom
who's   the shortened form for "who is" and "who has"

"*Who's* the patient *whose* filling fell out?" the dentist's assistant asked.

Fill in the blanks: _____ the salesperson _____ customers are always complaining about his high-pressure tactics?

your   belonging to you
you're the shortened form of "you are"

You're making a fool of yourself; *your* Elvis imitation isn't funny.

Fill in the blanks: If _____ having trouble filling out _____ tax return, why don't you call the IRS's toll-free hot line?

OTHER WORDS FREQUENTLY CONFUSED

Not all frequently confused words are homonyms. Here is a list of other words that people often confuse. Complete the activities for each set of words, and check off and study the words that give you trouble.

a   Both *a* and *an* are used before other words to mean, approximately, "one."
an

Generally you should use *an* before words starting with a vowel (*a, e, i, o u*):

   an orange   an umbrella   an indication   an ape   an effort

Generally you should use *a* before words starting with a consonant (all other letters):

   a genius   a movie   a speech   a study   a typewriter

Fill in the blanks: The morning after the party, I had _____ pounding headache and _____ upset stomach.

accept (ăk sĕpt′)   receive; agree to
except (ĕk sĕpt′)   exclude; but

   It was easy to *accept* the book's plot, *except* for one unlikely coincidence at the very end.

Fill in the blanks: Nan would _____ the position, _____ that it would add twenty minutes to her daily commute.

advice (ăd vīs′)   noun meaning "an opinion"
advise (ăd vīz′)   verb meaning "to counsel, to give advice"

   I have learned not to take my sister's *advice on straightening out my life.*
   A counselor can *advise* you about the courses you'll need next year.

Fill in the blanks: Karen is so troubled about losing her job that I will _____ her to seek the _____ of a professional counselor.

affect (uh fĕkt') verb meaning ''to influence''
effect (ĭ fĕkt') verb meaning ''to cause something''; noun meaning ''result''

The bad weather will definitely *affect* the outcome of the election.

If we can *effect* a change in George's attitude, he may do better in his courses.

One *effect* of the strike will be dwindling supplies in the supermarkets.

Fill in the blanks: Scientists have studied the _____ of large quantities of saccharine on lab animals but have yet to learn how similar amounts _____ human beings.

among implies three or more
between implies only two

After the team of surgeons consulted *among* themselves, they decided that the bullet was lodged *between* two of the patient's ribs.

Fill in the blanks: _____ halves, one enthusiastic fan stood up _____ his equally fanatic friends and took off his coat and shirt.

beside along the side of
besides in addition to

Besides doing daily inventories, I have to stand *beside* the cashier whenever the store gets crowded.

Fill in the blanks: _____ those books on the table, I plan to use these magazines stacked _____ me while doing my research paper.

fewer used with things that can be counted
less refers to amount, value, or degree

I've taken *fewer* classes this semester, so I hope to have *less* trouble finding time to study.

Fill in the blanks: This beer advertises that it has _____ calories and is _____ filling.

former   refers to the first of two items named
latter   refers to the second of two items named

Sue yelled at her sons, Greg and John, when she got home; the *former* had left the refrigerator open and the *latter* had left wet towels all over the bathroom.

Fill in the blanks: Eddy collects coupons and parking tickets: the _____ save him money and the _____ are going to cost him a great deal of money some day.

learn   to gain knowledge
teach   to give knowledge

I can't *learn* a new skill unless someone with lots of patience *teaches* me.

Fill in the blanks: Because she is quick to _____ new things, Mandy has offered to _____ me how to play the latest video games.

loose   (lo͞os)   not fastened; not tight-fitting
lose   (lo͞oz)   misplace; fail to win

In this strong wind, the house may *lose* some of its *loose* roof shingles.

Fill in the blanks: A _____ wire in the television set was causing us to _____ the picture.

quiet   (kwī'ĭt)   peaceful
quite   (kwīt)   entirely; really; rather

Jennifer seems *quiet* and demure, but she has *quite* a temper at times.

Fill in the blanks: Most people think the library is _____ a good place to study, but I find the extreme _____ distracting.

Activity

These sentences check your understanding of *its, it's; there, their, they're; to, too, two;* and *your, you're.* Underline the two incorrect spellings in each sentence. Then spell the words correctly in the spaces provided.

1. ''Its not a very good idea,'' yelled Alexandra's boss, ''to tell you're customer that the striped dress she plans to buy makes her look like a pregnant tiger.''

2. You're long skirt got stuck in the car door, and now its sweeping the highway.

3. When your young, their is a tendency to confuse a crush with true love.

4. After too hours of typing, Lin was to tired to type any longer.

5. It is unusual for a restaurant to lose it's license, but this one had more mice in its' kitchen than cooks.

6. The vampires bought a knife sharpener in order too sharpen there teeth.

7. Your sometimes surprised by who you're friends turn out to be in difficult times.

8. When the children get to quiet, Clare knows their getting into trouble.

9. There friendship developed into love as the years passed, and now, in midlife, their newlyweds.

10. There is no reason to panic if you get a bad grade or too. Its well known that many successful people were not great students.

■ Review Test 1

Underline the correct word in the parentheses. Rather than guessing, look back at the explanations of the words when necessary.

1. I (know, no) that several of the tenants have decided (to, too, two) take (their, there, they're) case to court.
2. (Whose, Who's) the author of that book about the (affects, effects) of eating (to, too, two) much protein?
3. In our supermarket is a counter (where, wear) (your, you're) welcome to sit down and have free coffee and doughnuts.
4. (Its, It's) possible to (loose, lose) friends by constantly giving out unwanted (advice, advise).
5. For a long time, I couldn't (accept, except) the fact that my husband wanted a divorce; (then, than) I decided to stop being angry and get on with life.
6. I spent the (hole, whole) day browsing (threw, through) the chapters in my business textbook, but I didn't really study them.
7. The newly appointed (principal, principle) is (quite, quiet) familiar with the problems (hear, here) at our school.
8. I found that our cat had (all ready, already) had her kittens (among, between) the weeds (beside, besides) the porch.
9. I (advice, advise) you not to take children to that movie; the special (affects, effects) are (to, too, two) frightening.
10. It seems that nobody will ever be able to (learn, teach) Mario to take (fewer, less) chances in his car.

■ Review Test 2

On separate paper, write short sentences using the ten words shown below.

1. accept
2. its
3. you're
4. too
5. then
6. principal
7. their
8. passed
9. fewer
10. who's

EFFECTIVE WORD CHOICE

Choose your words carefully when you write. Always take the time to think about your word choices rather than simply use the first word that comes to mind. You want to develop the habit of selecting words that are precise and appropriate for your purpose. One way you can show sensitivity to language is by avoiding slang, clichés, pretentious words, and wordiness.

SLANG

We often use slang expressions when we talk because they are so vivid and colorful. However, slang is usually out of place in formal writing. Here are some examples of slang:

> Someone *ripped off* Ken's new Adidas running shoes from his locker.
> After the game, we *stuffed our faces* at the diner.
> I finally told my parents to *get off my case.*
> The movie really *grossed me out.*

Slang expressions have a number of drawbacks. They go out of date quickly, they become tiresome if used excessively in writing, and they may communicate clearly to some readers but not to others. Also, the use of slang can be an evasion of the specific details that are often needed to make one's meaning clear in writing. For example, in "The movie really grossed me out," the writer has not provided the specific details about the movie necessary for us to clearly understand the statement. Was it acting, special effects, or violent scenes that the writer found so disgusting? In general, then, you should avoid slang in your writing. If you are in doubt about whether an expression is slang, it may help to check a recently published hardbound dictionary.

Activity

Rewrite the following sentences, replacing the italicized slang words with more formal ones.

Example   When we told the neighbors to *can the noise,* they *freaked out.*
   When we told the neighbors to be quiet, they got upset.

1. I didn't realize how *messed up* Joey was until he stole some money from his parents and *split* for a month.

   _____

   _____

   _____

2. After a hard day, I like to *veg out* in front of the *idiot box.*

   _____

   _____

   _____

3. Paul was so *wiped out* after his workout at the gym that he couldn't *get it together* to defrost a frozen dinner.

   _____

   _____

   _____

4. When Rick tried to *put the move on* Lola at the school party, she told him to *shove off.*

   _____

   _____

   _____

5. My father claims that most *grease monkeys* are *rip-off artists.*

   _____

   _____

   _____

CLICHÉS

A *cliché* is an expression that has been worn out through constant use. Some typical clichés are:

short but sweet	last but not least
drop in the bucket	work like a dog
had a hard time of it	all work and no play
word to the wise	it goes without saying
it dawned on me	at a loss for words
sigh of relief	taking a big chance
too little, too late	took a turn for the worse
singing the blues	easier said than done
in the nick of time	on top of the world
too close for comfort	time and time again
saw the light	make ends meet

Clichés are common in speech but make your writing seem tired and stale. Also, they are often an evasion of the specific details that you must work to provide in your writing. You should, then, avoid clichés and try to express your meaning in fresh, original ways.

Activity 1

Underline the cliché in each of the following sentences. Then substitute specific, fresh words for the trite expression.

Example   My boyfriend has stuck with me <u>through thick and thin</u>.
                through good times and bad

1. As the only girl in an otherwise all-boy family, I got away with murder.

2. When I realized I'd lost my textbook, I knew I was up the creek without a paddle.

3. My suggestion is just a shot in the dark, but it's better than nothing.

_____

4. Janice got more than she bargained for when she offered to help Larry with his math homework.

_____

5. Bob is pushing his luck by driving a car with bald tires.

_____

6. On a hot, sticky midsummer day, iced tea or any frosty drink really hits the spot.

_____

7. Melissa thanks her lucky stars that she was born with brains, beauty, and humility.

_____

8. Anything that involves mathematical ability has always been right up my alley.

_____

9. Your chances of buying a good used car from that dealer are one in a million.

_____

10. Even when we are up to our eyeballs in work, our boss wonders if we have enough to do.

_____

Activity 2

Write a short paragraph describing the kind of day you had. Try to put as many clichés as possible into it. For example, ''I got up at the crack of dawn, ready to take on the world. I grabbed a bite to eat. . . .'' By making yourself aware of clichés in this way, you should lessen the chance that they will appear in your writing.

PRETENTIOUS WORDS

Some people feel that they can improve their writing by using fancy, elevated words rather than simple, natural words. They use artificial, stilted language that more often obscures their meaning than communicates it clearly. Here are some unnatural-sounding sentences:

It was a splendid opportunity to get some slumber.

We relished the delicious repast.

The officer apprehended the intoxicated operator of the vehicle.

This establishment sells women's apparel and children's garments.

The same thoughts can be expressed more clearly and effectively by using plain, natural language, as below:

It was a good chance to get some sleep.

We enjoyed the delicious meal.

The officer arrested the car's drunken driver.

This store sells women's and children's clothes.

Here is a list of some other inflated words, and simpler words that could replace them.

Inflated Words	Simpler Words
subsequent to	after
finalize	finish
transmit	send
facilitate	help
component	part
initiate	begin
delineate	describe
manifested	shown
to endeavor	to try

Activity

Cross out the artificial words in each sentence. Then substitute clear, simple language for the artificial words.

Example   The ~~conflagration~~ was ~~initiated~~ by an arsonist.
The fire was started by an arsonist.

1. Mark and his brother do not interrelate in a harmonious manner.

   _____

2. The meaning of the movie's conclusion eluded my comprehension.

   _____

3. The departmental conference will commence promptly at two o'clock.

   _____

4. A man dressed in odd attire accosted me on the street.

   _____

5. When my writing implement malfunctioned, I asked the professor for another.

   _____

WORDINESS

Wordiness—using more words than necessary to express a meaning—is often a sign of lazy or careless writing. Your readers may resent the extra time and energy they must spend when you have not done the work needed to make your writing direct and concise.

Here are two examples of wordy sentences:

In this paper, I am planning to describe the hobby that I enjoy of collecting old comic books.

In Dan's opinion, he thinks that cable television will change and alter our lives in the future.

Omitting needless words improves these sentences:

I enjoy collecting old comic books.

Dan thinks that cable television will change our lives.

Following is a list of some wordy expressions that could be reduced to single words.

Wordy Form	Short Form
at the present time	now
in the event that	if
in the near future	soon
due to the fact that	because
for the reason that	because
is able to	can
in every instance	always
in this day and age	today
during the time that	while
a large number of	many
big in size	big
red in color	red
five in number	five
return back	return
good benefit	benefit
commute back and forth	commute
postponed until later	postponed

Activity

Rewrite the following sentences, omitting needless words.

1. In conclusion, I would like to end my paper by summarizing each of the major points covered within my report.

   _____

   _____

2. Controlling the quality and level of the television shows that children watch is a continuing challenge to parents that they must meet on a daily basis.

   _____

   _____

3. In general, I am the sort of person who tends to be shy, especially in large crowds or with strangers I don't know well.

    _____

    _____

4. Someone who is analyzing magazine advertising can find hidden messages that, once uncovered, are seen to be clever and persuasive.

    _____

    _____

5. My greatest mistake that I made last week was to hurt my brother's feelings and then not to have the nerve to apologize and say how sorry I was.

    _____

    _____

■ **Review Test 1**

Certain words are italicized in the following sentences. In the space provided at the left, identify the words as slang (S), a cliché (C), or pretentious words (PW). Then replace the words with more effective diction.

_____   1. Losing weight is *easier said than done* for someone with a sweet tooth.

    _____

_____   2. After dinner, we washed the *culinary utensils* and wrapped the *excess* food.

    _____

_____   3. Bruce is so stubborn that talking to him is like *talking to a brick wall.*

    _____

_____   4. Michelle spent the summer *watching the tube* and *catching rays.*

    _____

_____   5. The fans, *all fired up* after the game, *peeled out* of the parking lot and honked their horns.

    _____

_____   6. The stew I made contained *everything but the kitchen sink.*

    _____

_____   7. That *guy* isn't really a criminal; he's just gotten a *bum rap.*

    _____

8. My new *photographic equipment* is so complex that it *hinders my enjoyment* of taking pictures.

   _____

9. I failed the test, and to *add insult to injury,* I got a low grade on my paper.

   _____

10. I *perused* several *periodicals* while I waited for the doctor.

   _____

■ Review Test 2

Rewrite the following sentences, omitting needless words.

1. In today's uncertain economic climate, it is clear that people, namely, average middle-class working people, have great difficulty saving much money or putting anything aside for emergencies.

   _____

   _____

2. He is of the opinion that children should be required by law to attend school until they reach the age of sixteen years old.

   _____

   _____

3. I reached the decision that I did not have quite enough native talent to try out to be one of the players on the basketball team.

   _____

   _____

4. We thought the television program that was on last night was enjoyable, whereas our parents reacted with dislike to the content of the show.

   _____

   _____

5. Because of the bad weather, the school district felt it would be safer to cancel classes and let everyone stay home than risk people having accidents on the way to school.

   _____

   _____

6. It seems to me that all the *Rocky* movies have been overrated, and that many people thought they were much better movies than they actually were.

    _____

    _____

7. I have a strong preference for candy over fruit, which, in my opinion, doesn't taste as good as candy does.

    _____

    _____

8. Lynn is one of those people who rarely admit to being wrong, and it is very unusual to hear her acknowledge that she made a mistake.

    _____

    _____

9. It seems obvious to me, and it should be to everyone else too, that people can be harmed as much by emotional abuse as by physical abuse, even if you don't lay a hand on them.

    _____

    _____

10. Out of all the regrets in my life so far, one of my greatest ones to the present time is that I did not take word processing lessons when I was still in high school and had a chance to do so.

    _____

    _____

SENTENCE VARIETY

One part of effective writing is to vary the kinds of sentences you write. If every sentence follows the same pattern, writing may become monotonous to read. This section of the book explains four ways you can create variety and interest in your writing style. It will also describe coordination and subordination—two important techniques for achieving different kinds of emphasis in writing.

The following are four methods you can use to make simple sentences more complex and sophisticated:

1   Add a second complete thought (coordination).
2   Add a dependent thought (subordination).
3   Begin with a special opening word or phrase.
4   Place adjectives or verbs in a series.

Each method will be discussed in turn.

ADD A SECOND COMPLETE THOUGHT

When you add a second complete thought to a simple sentence, the result is a *compound* (or double) sentence. The two complete statements in a compound sentence are usually connected by a comma plus a joining or coordinating word (*and, but, for, or, nor, so, yet*).

A compound sentence is used when you want to give equal weight to two closely related ideas. The technique of showing that ideas have equal importance is called *coordination*. Following are some compound sentences. In each case, the sentence contains two ideas that the writer considers equal in importance.

Frank worked on the engine for three hours, but the car still wouldn't start.

Bananas were on sale this week, so I bought a bunch for the children's lunches.

We laced up our roller skates, and then we moved cautiously onto the rink.

477

Activity

Combine the following pairs of simple sentences into compound sentences. Use a comma and a logical joining word (*and, but, for, so*) to connect each pair of statements.

Note: If you are not sure what *and, but, for,* and *so* mean, review page 331.

Example ■ The weather was cold and windy.
■ Al brought a thick blanket to the football game.

The weather was cold and windy, so Al brought a thick blanket to

the football game.

1. ■ Stanley was starving.
   ■ He hadn't eaten a thing since breakfast.

   _____

   _____

2. ■ I tried to sleep.
   ■ The thought of tomorrow's math exam kept me awake.

   _____

   _____

3. ■ This diner has its own bakery.
   ■ It has take-out service as well.

   _____

   _____

4. ■ The cardboard storage boxes were soggy.
   ■ Rainwater had seeped into the basement during the storm.

   _____

   _____

5. ■ I didn't have enough money to buy my parents an anniversary present.
   ■ I offered to mow their lawn for the whole summer.

   _____

   _____

ADD A DEPENDENT THOUGHT

When you add a dependent thought to a simple sentence, the result is a *complex sentence*.* A dependent thought begins with one of the following subordinating words:

after	if, even if	when, whenever
although, though	in order that	where, wherever
as	since	whether
because	that, so that	which, whichever
before	unless	while
even though	until	who
how	what, whatever	whose

A complex sentence is used when you want to emphasize one idea over another. Look at the following complex sentence:

Although the exam room was very quiet, I still couldn't concentrate.

The idea that the writer wishes to emphasize here—*I still couldn't concentrate*—is expressed as a complete thought. The less important idea—*Although the exam room was very quiet*—is subordinated to the complete thought. The technique of giving one idea less emphasis than another is called *subordination*.

Following are other examples of complex sentences. In each case, the part starting with the dependent word is the less emphasized part of the sentence.

Even though I was tired, I stayed up to watch the horror movie.

Before I take a bath, I check for spiders in the tub.

When Ivy feels nervous, she pulls on her earlobe.

---

* The two parts of a complex sentence are sometimes called an *independent clause* and a *dependent clause*. A *clause* is simply a word group that contains a subject and a verb. An independent clause expresses a complete thought and can stand alone. A dependent clause does not express a complete thought in itself and ''depends on'' the independent clause to complete its meaning. Dependent clauses always begin with a dependent or subordinating word.

Activity

Use logical subordinating words to combine the following pairs of simple sentences into sentences that contain a dependent thought. Place a comma after a dependent statement when it starts the sentence.

Example ■ Rita bit into the hard taffy.
 ■ She broke a filling.
 When Rita bit into the hard taffy, she broke a filling.

1. ■ I had forgotten to lock the front door.
 ■ I had to drive back to the house.

 _____

 _____

 _____

2. ■ The bear turned over the rotten log.
 ■ Fat white grubs crawled in every direction.

 _____

 _____

 _____

3. ■ Kevin had mailed away for a set of tools.
 ■ He changed his mind about spending the money.

 _____

 _____

 _____

4. ■ Lew is allergic to wool.
 ■ He buys only sweaters made from acrylic.

 _____

 _____

 _____

5. ■ Sara types one hundred words a minute.
 ■ She is having trouble landing a secretarial job.

 _____

 _____

 _____

BEGIN WITH A SPECIAL OPENING WORD OR PHRASE

Among the special openers that can be used to start sentences are *-ed* words, *-ing* words, *-ly* words, *to* word groups, and prepositional phrases. Here are examples of all five kinds of openers:

-ed *word*

Concerned about his son's fever, Paul called a doctor.

-ing *word*

Humming softly, the woman browsed through the rack of dresses.

-ly *word*

Hesitantly, Sue approached the instructor's desk.

to *word group*

To protect her hair, Eva uses the lowest setting on her blow-dryer.

Prepositional phrase

During the exam, drops of water fell from the ceiling.

Activity

Combine each of the following pairs of simple sentences into one sentence by using the opener shown at the left and omitting repeated words. Use a comma to set off the opener from the rest of the sentence.

Example   -ing *word*   ■ The pelican scooped small fish into its baggy bill.
　　　　　　　　　　　　■ It dipped into the waves.

Dipping into the waves, the pelican scooped small fish into

its baggy bill.

-ed *word*　　1. ■ The night sky glittered.
　　　　　　　　　■ It was studded with thousands of stars.

　　　　　　　　　_____

　　　　　　　　　_____

-ing *word*　　2. ■ She wondered how to break the news to the children.
　　　　　　　　　■ She sat in the cold living room.

　　　　　　　　　_____

　　　　　　　　　_____

-ly *word* 3. ■ Shirley signed the repair contract.
            ■ She was reluctant.

_____

to *word* 4. ■ Alan volunteered to work overtime.
group   ■ He wanted to improve his chances of promotion.

_____

Prepositional 5. ■ The accused murderer grinned at the witnesses.
phrase   ■ He did this during the trial.

_____

-ed *word* 6. ■ The vet's office was noisy and confusing.
            ■ It was crowded with nervous pets.

_____

-ing *word* 7. ■ Barry tried to find something worth watching.
            ■ He flipped from channel to channel.

_____

-ly *word* 8. ■ My father asked me where I had been until 5 A.M.
            ■ He was casual.

_____

to *word* 9. ■ Stan stood on the table and tapped a glass with a spoon.
group   ■ He did this to attract everyone's attention.

_____

Prepositional 10. ■ Doctors used leeches to draw blood from sick patients.
phrase   ■ They did this at one time.

_____

PLACE ADJECTIVES OR VERBS IN A SERIES

Various parts of a sentence may be placed in a series. Among these parts are adjectives (descriptive words) and verbs. Here are examples of both in a series:

Adjectives

I gently applied a *sticky new* Band-Aid to the *deep, ragged* cut on my finger.

Verbs

The truck *bounced* off a guardrail, *sideswiped* a tree, and *plunged* down the embankment.

Activity

Combine the simple sentences into one sentence by using adjectives or verbs in a series and by omitting repeated words. In most cases, use a comma between the adjectives or verbs in a series.

Example   ■   Jesse spun the basketball on one finger.
■   He rolled it along his arms.
■   He dribbled it between his legs.

Jesse spun the basketball on one finger, rolled it along his arms,

and dribbled it between his legs.

1. ■   The baby toddled across the rug.
   ■   He picked up a button.
   ■   He put the button in his mouth.

   _____

   _____

2. ■   Water dribbled out of the tap.
   ■   The water was brown.
   ■   The water was foul-tasting.
   ■   The tap was rusty.
   ■   The tap was metal.

   _____

   _____

3. ■   In the dressing room, Pat tried on the swimsuit.
   ■   She looked in the full-length mirror.
   ■   She screamed.

   _____

   _____

4. ■   Art approached the wasps' nests hanging under the eaves.
   ■   The nests were large.
   ■   The nests were papery.
   ■   The eaves were old.
   ■   The eaves were wooden.

   _____

   _____

5. ■   Reeds bordered the pond.
   ■   The reeds were slim.
   ■   The reeds were brown.
   ■   The pond was green.
   ■   The pond was stagnant.

   _____

   _____

■ Review Test 1

On separate paper, use coordination or subordination to combine the following groups of simple sentences into one or more longer sentences. Omit repeated words. Since various combinations are possible, you might want to jot down several combinations in each case. Then read them aloud to find the combination that sounds best.

Keep in mind that, very often, the relationship among ideas in a sentence will be clearer when subordinating rather than coordinating words are used.

Example   ■   Lew arrived at the supermarket.
   ■   Lew had a painful thought.
   ■   He had clipped all the coupons from the paper.
   ■   He had forgotten to bring them.

When Lew arrived at the supermarket, he had a painful thought. He had clipped all the coupons from the paper, but he had forgotten to bring them.

Comma Hints

a   Use a comma at the end of a word group that starts with a subordinating word (as in "When Lew arrived at the supermarket, . . .").

b   Use a comma between independent word groups connected by *and, but, for, or, nor, so, yet* (as in "He had clipped all the coupons from the paper, but . . .").

1. - Dan had repaired his broken watchband with a paper clip.
    - The clip snapped.
    - The watch slid off his wrist.

2. - The therapist watched.
    - Julie tried to stand on her weakened legs.
    - They crumpled under her.

3. - There were spaces on the street.
    - Richie pulled into an expensive parking garage.
    - He had just bought a new car.
    - He was afraid it would get dented.

4. - A sudden cold front hit the area.
    - Temperatures dropped thirty degrees in less than an hour.
    - My teeth began to chatter.
    - I was not wearing a warm jacket.

5. - The verdict was announced.
    - The spectators broke into applause.
    - The defendant looked stunned.
    - Then he let out a whoop of joy.

6. - The teacher watched closely.
    - The second-graders made candles.
    - Suddenly, one boy began to cry.
    - He had spilled hot wax on his arm.

7. - Vern works as a model.
    - He has to look his best.
    - He gained ten pounds recently.
    - He had to take off the extra weight.
    - He would have lost his job.

8. - The ball game was about to begin.
    - A dog ran onto the field.
    - The dog began nipping the infielders' ankles.
    - The game had to be delayed.
    - The dog was chased away.

9. ■ The lion was hungry.
   ■ It watched the herd of gazelle closely.
   ■ A young or sick animal wandered away from the group.
   ■ The lion would move in for the kill.

10. ■ I am a good mechanic.
    ■ My girlfriend is a fast typist.
    ■ We decided to advertise our skills on the college bulletin board.
    ■ Unfortunately, we didn't get any calls at first.
    ■ We had forgotten to include our phone numbers on the notices.

■ Review Test 2

On separate paper, write:

1. Two sentences of your own that begin with *-ed* words
2. Two sentences that begin with *-ing* words
3. Two sentences that begin with *-ly* words
4. Two sentences that begin with *to* word groups
5. Two sentences that begin with prepositional phrases
6. Two sentences that contain a series of adjectives
7. Two sentences that contain a series of verbs

EDITING TESTS

PROOFREADING FOR SENTENCE-SKILLS MISTAKES

The twelve editing tests in this section will give you practice in proofreading for sentence-skills mistakes. People often find it hard to proofread a paper carefully. They have put so much work into their writing, or so little, that it's almost painful for them to look at the paper one more time. You may simply have to *force* yourself to proofread. Remember that eliminating sentence-skills mistakes will improve an average paper and help ensure a strong grade on a good paper. Further, as you get into the habit of ''proofing'' your papers, you will also get into the habit of using sentence skills consistently. They are a basic part of clear, effective writing.

In the first five tests, the spots where errors occur have been underlined; your job is to identify each error. In the last five tests, you must locate as well as identify the errors.

■ Editing Test 1

Identify the five mistakes in essay format in the student paper that follows. From the box below, choose the letters that describe the five mistakes and write those letters in the spaces provided.

a. Title should not be underlined.
b. Title should not be set off in quotation marks.
c. There should not be a period at the end of a title.
d. All major words in a title should be capitalized.
e. Title should be a phrase, not a complete sentence.
f. First line of a paper should stand independent of the title.
g. One line should be skipped between title and first line of the paper.
h. First line of a paper should be indented.
i. Right-hand margin should not be crowded.
j. Hyphenation should occur only between syllables.

> *"eating in fast-food restaurants"*
>
> *Doing so doesn't have to be terrible for your health. Although I often stop at Wendy's or Burger King, I find ways to make healthful choices there. For one thing, I order sandwiches that are as plain as possible. A broiled hamburger or fish sandwich isn't so bad for you, as long as it isn't covered with melted cheese, fatty sauces, bacon, or other "extras" that pile on the fat and calories. Another health-conscious choice is to skip deep-fat-fried potatoes loaded with salt and heavy with cholesterol; instead, I'll order a plain baked potato from Wendy's and add just a bit of butter and salt for taste. In addition, I take advantage of healthy items on menus. For example, most fast-food places now offer green salads and low-fat chicken choices. And finally, I order a sensible beverage—ice water or a diet soda— instead of soda or a milk shake.*

1. _____   2. _____   3. _____   4. _____   5. _____

■ **Editing Test 2**

See if you can locate and correct the ten sentence-skills mistakes in the following passage. The kinds of mistakes are listed in the box below. As you locate each mistake, write the number of the word group containing that mistake and the letter indicating what type of mistake it is. Use the spaces provided. The first answer is given for you as an example.

a. fragment	b. run-on

A Unique Object

¹A unique object in my family's living room is an ashtray. ²Which I made in second grade. ³I can still remember the pride I felt. ⁴When I presented it to my mother. ⁵To my second-grade eyes, it was a thing of beauty. ⁶Now, I'm amazed that my parents didn't hide it away at the back of a shelf it is a remarkably ugly object. ⁷The ashtray is made out of brown clay. ⁸I had tried to mold it into a perfect circle, unfortunately my class was only forty-five minutes long. ⁹The best I could do was to shape it into a lopsided oval. ¹⁰Its most distinctive feature, though, was the grooves sculpted into its rim. ¹¹I had theorized that each groove could hold a cigarette or cigar, I made at least fifty of them. ¹²I somehow failed to consider that the only person who smoked in my family was my father. ¹³Who smoked about five cigars a year. ¹⁴Further, although our living room is decorated in sedate tans and blues, my ashtray is bright purple. ¹⁵My favorite color at the time. ¹⁶Just for variety, it also has stripes around its rim they are colored neon green. ¹⁷For all its shortcomings, my parents have proudly displayed my little masterpiece on their coffee table for the past ten years. ¹⁸If I ever wonder if my parents love me. ¹⁹I look at that ugly ashtray, the answer is plain to see.

1. 2-a   3. _____   5. _____   7. _____   9. _____

2. _____   4. _____   6. _____   8. _____   10. _____

■ **Editing Test 3**

Identify the sentence-skills mistakes at the underlined spots in the selection that follows. From the box below, choose the letter that describes each mistake and write it in the space provided. The same mistake may appear more than once. In one case, there is no mistake.

a. fragment	d. dangling modifier
b. run-on	e. missing comma
c. inconsistent verb tense	f. no mistake

I had a strange experience last <u>winter, I</u> was shopping for Christmas presents when

         1

I came to a small clothing shop. I was going to pass it by. <u>Until I saw a beautiful purple

                    2

robe on a mannequin in the window.</u> <u>Stopping to look at it,</u> the mannequin seemed to

                           3

wink at me. I was really <u>startled, I</u> looked around to see if anyone else was watching.

             4

Shaking my <u>head I</u> stepped closer to the window. Then I really began to question my

       5

<u>sanity, it</u> looked as if the mannequin moved <u>its</u> legs. My face must have shown alarm

   6   7

because the mannequin then <u>smiles.</u> <u>And even waved her arm.</u> I sighed with <u>relief, it</u>

                8   9   10

was a human model after all.

1. _____   3. _____   5. _____   7. _____   9. _____

2. _____   4. _____   6. _____   8. _____   10. _____

■ Editing Test 4

Identify the sentence-skills mistakes at the underlined spots in the selection that follows. From the box below, choose the letter that describes each mistake and write it in the space provided. The same mistake may appear more than once.

a. run-on	d. missing quotation marks
b. mistake in subject-verb agreement	e. wordiness
	f. slang
c. faulty parallelism	g. missing comma

<u>It is this writer's opinion that</u> smokers should quit smoking for the sake of those who
₁

are around them. Perhaps the most helpless creatures that suffer from being near a smoker

<u>is</u> unborn <u>babies, one</u> study suggests that the risk of having an undersized baby is doubled
2   3

if pregnant women are exposed to cigarette smoke for about two hours a day. Pregnant

women both should refrain from smoking and <u>to avoid</u> smoke-filled rooms. Spouses of
4

smokers are also <u>in big trouble.</u> They are more likely than spouses of nonsmokers to die
5

of heart disease and <u>the development of</u> fatal cancers. Office workers are a final group
6

that can be harmed by a smoke-filled environment. The U.S. Surgeon General has <u>said</u>
7

<u>''Workers</u> who smoke are a health risk to their <u>coworkers. While</u> it is <u>undoubtedly true</u>
8   9

<u>that</u> one can argue that smokers have the right to hurt <u>themselves they</u> do not have the
10

right to hurt others. Smokers should abandon their deadly habits for the health of others

at home and at work.

1. _____   3. _____   5. _____   7. _____   9. _____

2. _____   4. _____   6. _____   8. _____   10. _____

■ Editing Test 5

Identify the sentence-skills mistakes at the underlined spots in the selection that follows. From the box below, choose the letter that describes each mistake and write it in the space provided. The same mistake may appear more than once.

a. fragment	e. dangling modifier
b. run-on	f. missing comma
c. mistake in subject-verb agreement	g. wordiness
	h. slang
d. misplaced modifier	

The United States will never be a drug-free <u>society but</u> we could eliminate many of
                                                         1
our drug-related problems by legalizing drugs. Drugs would be sold by companies and

not criminals <u>if they were legal</u>. The drug trade would then take place like any other
                     2
<u>business freeing</u> the police and courts to devote their time to other problems. Lawful
        3
drugs would be sold at a fair <u>price, no</u> one would need to steal in order to buy them.
                                     4
<u>By legalizing drugs,</u> organized crime would lose one of its major sources of revenue.
       5
<u>It goes without saying that</u> we would, instead, create important tax revenues for the
              6
government. Finally, if drugs <u>was</u> sold through legal outlets, we could reduce the drug
                                     7
problem among our young people. It would be illegal to sell drugs to people under a

certain age. <u>Just as is the case now with alcohol.</u> And because the profits on drugs would
                              8
no longer <u>be out of sight,</u> there would be little incentive for drug pushers to sell to young
                9
people. Decriminalizing drugs, in short, could be a solution. <u>To many of the problems</u>
                                                                              10
<u>that result from the illegal drug trade.</u>

1. _____   3. _____   5. _____   7. _____   9. _____

2. _____   4. _____   6. _____   8. _____   10. _____

■ Editing Test 6

Identify the sentence-skills mistakes at the underlined spots in the selection that follows. From the box below, choose the letter that describes each mistake and write it in the space provided. The same mistake may appear more than once. In one case, there is no mistake.

a. fragment	e. mistake with quotation marks
b. run-on	f. mistake in pronoun point of
c. mistake in subject-verb	view
agreement	g. spelling error
d. mistake in verb tense	h. no mistake

One reason that I enjoy the commute to school is that the drive gives me <u>uninterupted</u> ₁ time to myself. The classes and socializing at college <u>is</u> great, and so is the time I spend ₂ with my family, but sometimes all this togetherness keeps <u>you</u> from being able to think. ₃ In fact, I look forward to the time I have <u>alone, it</u> gives me a chance to plan what I'll ₄ accomplish in the day ahead. For example, one Tuesday afternoon my history professor <u>announces</u> that a rough outline for our semester report was due that Friday. <u>Fortunatly,</u> ₅ ₆ I had already done some <u>reading,</u> and I had checked my proposed topic with her the week ₇ before. <u>Therefore, on the way home in the car that evening.</u> I planned the entire history ₈ report in my mind. Then all I had to do when I got home was quickly jot it down before I forgot it. <u>When I handed the professor the outline at 8:30 Wednesday morning.</u> She ₉ asked me <u>''if I had stayed up all night working on it.''</u> She was amazed when I told her ₁₀ that I owed it all to commuting.

1. _____   3. _____   5. _____   7. _____   9. _____

2. _____   4. _____   6. _____   8. _____   10. _____

■ **Editing Test 7**

Identify the sentence-skills mistakes at the underlined spots in the selection that follows. From the box below, choose the letter that describes each mistake and write it in the space provided. The same mistake may appear more than once. In one case, there is no mistake.

a.	fragment	f.	dangling modifier
b.	run-on	g.	homonym mistake
c.	mistake in subject-verb agreement	h.	missing apostrophe
		i.	cliché
d.	missing comma	j.	no mistake
e.	missing capital letter		

Cars can destroy your ego. First of <u>all the</u> kind of car you drive can make you feel
₁
like a second-class citizen. <u>If you can't afford a new, expensive car, and are forced to</u>

drive an old clunker.</u> You'll be the object of pitying stares and nasty sneers. Drivers of
₂

newer-model cars just <u>doesn't</u> appreciate it when a '68 <u>buick</u> with terminal body rust
₃   ₄

lurches into the next parking slot. You may even find that drivers go out of <u>their</u> way not
₅

to park near you. Breakdowns, too, can damage your self-respect. You may be an assistant

bank manager or a job <u>foreman, you'll</u> still feel <u>like two cents</u> when <u>your</u> sitting on the
₆   ₇   ₈

side of the road. As the other cars whiz past, you'll stare helplessly at your <u>cars</u> open
₉

hood or steaming radiator. In cases like this, you may even be turned into that lowest of

creatures, the pedestrian. <u>Shuffling humbly along the highway to the nearest pay phone,</u>
₁₀

your car has delivered another staggering blow to your self-esteem.

1. _____	3. _____	5. _____	7. _____	9. _____
2. _____	4. _____	6. _____	8. _____	10. _____

■ **Editing Test 8**

See if you can locate and correct the ten sentence-skills mistakes in the following passage. The mistakes are listed in the box below. As you locate each mistake, write the number of the word group in the space provided.

---

1 fragment _____

1 run-on _____

1 mistake in verb tense _____

1 nonparallel structure _____

1 dangling modifier _____

1 mistake in pronoun point of

  view _____

1 missing comma after

  introductory material _____

2 missing quotation marks

  _____ _____

1 missing apostrophe _____

---

¹The greatest of my everyday fears is technology. ²Beginning when I couldn't master bike riding and extending to the present day. ³Fear kept me from learning to operate a jigsaw, start an outboard motor, or even using a simple tape recorder. ⁴I almost didn't learn to drive a car. ⁵At age sixteen, Dad lifted the hood of our Chevy and said, All right, you're going to start learning to drive. ⁶Now, this is the distributor. . . When my eyes glazed over he shouted, ''Well, I'm not going to bother if youre not interested!'' ⁷Fortunately, the friend who later taught me to drive skipped what goes on under the hood. ⁸My most recent frustration is the 35 mm camera, I would love to take professional-quality pictures. ⁹But all the numbers and dials and meters confuse me. ¹⁰As a result, my unused camera is hidden away on a shelf in my closet. ¹¹Just last week, my sister gives me a beautiful digital watch for my birthday. ¹²I may have to put it on the shelf with the camera—the alarm keeps going off, and you can't figure out how to stop it.

■ **Editing Test 9**

See if you can locate and correct the ten sentence-skills mistakes in the following passage. The mistakes are listed in the box below. As you locate each mistake, write the number of the word group in the space provided.

1 fragment _____	1 mistake in subject-verb agreement _____
1 run-on _____	
1 missing comma around an interrupter _____	2 missing quotation marks _____ _____
2 apostrophe mistakes _____ _____	1 misplaced modifier _____
	1 nonparallel structure _____

¹I was six years old when, one day, my dog was struck by a car while getting ready for school. ²My mother and I heard the terrifying sound of squealing brake's. ³In a low voice, she said, Oh, my God—Blackie. ⁴I remember trailing her out the door and seeing a car filled with teenagers and a spreading pool of bright blood on our cobblestoned street. ⁵To me, it seemed only a matter of seconds until a police car pulled up. ⁶The officer glanced at the crumpled dog under the car. ⁷And drew his gun. ⁸My mother shouted, ''No!'' ⁹She crawled halfway under the car and took the dog, like a sack of flour, out from under the wheels. ¹⁰Her housedress was splashed with blood, she cradled the limp dog in her arms and ordered the officers to drive her to the vets office. ¹¹It was only then that she remembered me, I think. ¹²She patted my head, was telling me to walk up to school, and reassured me that Blackie would be all right. ¹³The rest of the story including Blackie's slow recovery and few more years of life, are fuzzy and vague now. ¹⁴But the sights and sounds of those few moments are as vivid to me now as they were twenty-five years ago.

■ Editing Test 10

See if you can locate and correct the ten sentence-skills mistakes in the following passage. The mistakes are listed in the box below. As you locate each mistake, write the number of the word group in the spaces provided.

2 fragments _____	1 nonparallel structure _____
_____	2 apostrophe mistakes _____
1 run-on _____	_____
1 mistake in subject-verb	3 missing commas _____
agreement _____	_____ _____

[1]Most products have little or nothing to do with sex a person would never know that by looking at ads'. [2]A television ad for a headache remedy, for example shows the product being useful because it ends a womans throbbing head pain just in time for sex. [3]Now she will not say "Not tonight, Honey." [4]Another ad features a detergent that helps a single woman meet a man in a laundry room. [5]When it comes to products that do relate to sex appeal advertisers often present more obvious sexuality. [6]A recent magazine ad for women's clothing, for instance, make no reference to the quality of or how comfortable are the company's clothes. [7]Instead, the ad features a picture of a woman wearing a low-cut sleeveless T shirt and a very short skirt. [8]Her eyes are partially covered by semi-wild hair. [9]And stare seductively at the reader. [10]A recent television ad for perfume goes even further. [11]In this ad, a boy not older than twelve reaches out to a beautiful woman. [12]Sexily dressed in a dark room filled with sensuous music. [13]With such ads, it is no wonder that young people seem preoccupied with sex.

■ Editing Test 11

See if you can locate and correct the ten sentence-skills mistakes in the following passage. The mistakes are listed in the box below. As you locate each mistake, write the number of the word group in the spaces provided.

---

1 fragment _____   2 missing apostrophes _____

1 run-on _____   _____

1 mistake in subject-verb   1 nonparallel structure _____

  agreement _____   1 dangling modifier _____

2 missing commas after   1 mistake in pronoun point

  introductory material   of view _____

_____ _____

---

¹Being a waitress is an often underrated job. ²A waitress needs the tact of a diplomat, she must be as organized as a business executive, and the ability of an acrobat. ³Serving as the link between customers and kitchen, the most demanding diners must be satisfied and the often-temperamental kitchen help must be kept tamed. ⁴Both groups tend to blame the waitress whenever anything goes wrong. ⁵Somehow, she is held responsible by the customer for any delay (even if it's the kitchens fault), for an overcooked steak, or for an unavailable dessert. ⁶While the kitchen automatically blames her for the diners who change their orders or return those burned steaks. ⁷In addition she must simultaneously keep straight who ordered what at each table, who is yelling for the check, and whether the new arrivals want cocktails or not. ⁸She must be sure empty tables are cleared, everyone has refills of coffee, and no one is scowling because a request for more rolls are going unheard. ⁹Finally the waitress must travel a hazardous route between the busy kitchen and the crowded dining room, she has to dodge a diners leg in the aisle or a swinging kitchen door. ¹⁰And you must do this while balancing a tray heaped with steaming platters. ¹¹The hardest task of the waitress, though, is trying to maintain a decent imitation of a smile on her face—most of the time.

■ Editing Test 12

See if you can locate and correct the ten sentence-skills mistakes in the following passage. The mistakes are listed in the box below. As you locate each mistake, write the number of the word group in the spaces provided.

---

2 fragments _____

_____

1 run-on _____

2 irregular verbs _____

_____

1 misplaced modifier _____

2 missing capital letters

_____ _____

1 mistake in pronoun point of view _____

1 subject pronoun mistake _____

---

¹The thirtieth anniversary party of my uncle and aunt was the worst family gathering I've ever attended. ²On a hot saturday morning in july, Mom and I drived out into the country to Uncle Ted's house. ³It had already rained heavily, and the only place left to park was in a muddy field. ⁴Then, you would not believe the crowd. ⁵There must have been two hundred people in Uncle Ted's small yard, including his five daughters with their husbands and children, all the other relatives, all the neighbors, and the entire congregation of their church. ⁶Since the ground was soaked and light rain was falling. ⁷Mom and me went under the big rented canopy with everybody else. ⁸We couldn't move between the tables, and the humidity fogged my glasses. ⁹After wiping my glasses, I seen that there was a lot of food. ¹⁰It was mainly cold chicken and potato and macaroni salads, I ate a lot just because there was nothing else to do. ¹¹We were surprised that Uncle Ted and his wife were doing all the work themselves. ¹²They ran back and forth with trays of food and gathered trash into plastic bags staggering with exhaustion. ¹³It didn't seem like much of a way to celebrate. ¹⁴Mom was upset that she didn't get to speak with them. ¹⁵When we left, I was hot, sticky, and sick to my stomach from overeating. ¹⁶But quickly pushed our car out of the mud and got us on the road. ¹⁷I have never been happier to leave a party.

PART FIVE

READINGS
FOR
WRITING

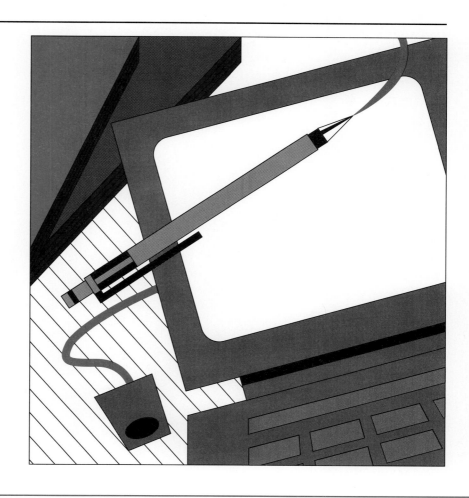

INTRODUCTION
TO THE
READINGS

The reading selections in Part Five will help you find topics for writing. Each selection deals in some way with interesting, often thought-provoking concerns or experiences of contemporary life. One selection, for example, describes new kinds of stress that students face in college; another reminds us of the benefits that can come from expressing appreciation to others; a third discusses the issue of date rape. The varied subjects should inspire lively class discussions as well as serious individual thought. The selections should also provide a continuing source of high-interest material for a wide range of writing assignments.

The selections serve another purpose as well. They will help develop reading skills with direct benefits to you as a writer. One benefit is that, through close reading, you will learn how to recognize the thesis in a selection and to identify and evaluate the supporting material that develops the thesis. In your own writing, you will aim to achieve the same essential structure: an overall thesis followed by detailed and valid support for that thesis. A second benefit is that close reading will also help you explore a selection and its possibilities thoroughly. The more you understand about what is said in a piece, the more ideas and feelings you may have about writing on an assigned topic or a related topic of your own. A third benefit of close reading is becoming more aware of authors' stylistic devices— for example, their introductions and conclusions, their ways of presenting and developing a point, their use of transitions, their choice of language to achieve a particular tone. Recognizing these devices in other people's writing will help you enlarge your own range of ideas and writing techniques.

THE FORMAT OF EACH SELECTION

Each selection begins with a short overview that gives helpful background information and stimulates interest in the piece. The selection is followed by two sets of questions.

- First, there are ten reading comprehension questions to help you measure your understanding of the material. These questions involve several important reading skills: understanding vocabulary in context, recognizing a subject or topic, determining a thesis or main idea, identifying key supporting points, and making references. Answering the questions will enable you and your instructor to check your basic understanding of a selection quickly. More significantly, as you move from one selection to the next, you will sharpen your reading skills as well as strengthen your thinking skills—two key factors in making you a better writer.
- Following the comprehensive questions are seven discussion questions. In addition to dealing with issues of content, these questions focus on matters of structure, style, and tone.

Finally, several writing assignments accompany each selection. The assignments range from personal narratives to expository and persuasive essays about issues in the world at large. Many assignments provide detailed guidelines on how to proceed, including suggestions for prewriting and appropriate methods of development. When writing your essay responses to the readings, you will have opportunities to apply all the methods of development presented in Part Two of this book.

HOW TO READ WELL: FOUR GENERAL STEPS

Skillful reading is an important part of becoming a skillful writer. Following is a series of four steps that will make you a better reader—both of the selections here and in your reading at large.

1 Concentrate As You Read

To improve your concentration, follow these tips:

- First, read in a place where you can be quiet and alone. Don't choose a spot where there is a TV or stereo on or where friends or family are talking nearby.

- Next, sit in an upright position when you read. If your body is in a completely relaxed position, sprawled across a bed or nestled in an easy chair, your mind is also going to be completely relaxed. The light muscular tension that comes from sitting in a straight chair promotes concentration and keeps your mind ready to work.

- Third, consider using your index finger (or a pen) as a pacer while you read. Lightly underline each line of print with your index finger as you read down a page. Hold your hand slightly above the page and move your finger at a speed that is a little too fast for comfort. This pacing with your index finger, like sitting upright on a chair, creates a slight physical tension that will keep your body and mind focused and alert.

2 Skim Material before You Read It

In skimming, you spend about two minutes rapidly surveying a selection, looking for important points and skipping secondary material. Follow this sequence when skimming:

- Begin by reading the overview that precedes the selection.

- Then study the title of the selection for a few moments. A good title is the shortest possible summary of a selection; it often tells you in several words— or even a single word—just what a selection is about. For example, the title ''Shame'' suggests that you're going to read about a deeply embarrassing condition or incident in a person's life.

- Next, form a basic question (or questions) out of the title. For instance, for the selection titled ''Shame,'' you might ask, ''What exactly is the shame?'' ''What caused the shame?'' ''What is the result of the shame?'' Forming questions out of a title is often a key to locating a writer's thesis, your next concern in skimming.

- Read the first and last couple of paragraphs in the selection. Very often a writer's thesis, *if* it is directly stated, will appear in one of these places and will relate to the title. For instance, in ''Why Are Students Turned Off?'' the author says in his second paragraph that ''. . . many students are turned off because they have little power and responsibility for their own education.''

- Finally, look quickly at the rest of the selection for other clues to important points. Are there any subheads you can relate in some way to the title? Are there any words the author has decided to emphasize by setting them off in *italic* or **boldface** type? Are there any major lists of items signaled by words such as *first, second, also, another,* and so on?

3 Read the Selection Straight Through with a Pen in Hand

Read the selection without slowing down or turning back; just aim to understand as much as you can the first time through. Write a check or star beside answers to basic questions you formed from the title, and beside other ideas that seem important. Number lists of important points: 1, 2, 3, ... Circle words you don't understand. Write question marks in the margins next to passages that are unclear and that you will want to reread.

4 Work with the Material

Go back and reread passages that were not clear the first time through. Look up words that block your understanding of ideas and write their meanings in the margin. Also, reread carefully the areas you identified as most important; doing so will enlarge your understanding of the material. Now that you have a sense of the whole, prepare a short written outline of the selection by answering the following questions:

- What is the thesis?
- What key points support the thesis?
- What seem to be other important ideas in the selection?

By working with the material in this way, you will significantly increase your understanding of a selection. Effective reading, just like effective writing, does not happen all at once. Rather, it must be worked on. Often you begin with a general impression of what something means, and then, by working at it, you move to a deeper level of understanding of the material.

HOW TO ANSWER THE COMPREHENSION QUESTIONS: SPECIFIC HINTS

Several important reading skills are involved in the ten reading comprehension questions that follow each selection. The skills are:

- Understanding vocabulary in context
- Summarizing the selection in a title
- Determining the main idea
- Recognizing key supporting details
- Making inferences

The following hints will help you apply each of these reading skills:

- *Vocabulary in context.* To decide on the meaning of an unfamiliar word, consider its context. Ask yourself, ''Are there any clues in the sentence that suggest what this word means?''

- *Subject or title.* Remember that the title should accurately describe the *entire* selection. It should be neither too broad nor too narrow for the material in the selection. It should answer the question ''What is this about?'' as specifically as possible. Note that you may at times find it easier to answer the title question *after* the main-idea question.

- *Main idea.* Choose the statement that you think best expresses the main idea— also known as the *central point* or *thesis*—of the entire selection. Remember that the title will often help you focus on the main idea. Then ask yourself the question, ''Does most of the material in the selection support this statement?'' If you can answer *Yes* to this question, you have found the thesis.

- *Key details.* If you were asked to give a two-minute summary of a selection, the key, or major, details are the ones you would include in that summary. To determine the key details, ask yourself the question, ''What are the major supporting points for the thesis?''

- *Inferences.* Answer these questions by drawing upon the evidence presented in the selection and your own common sense. Ask yourself, ''What reasonable judgments can I make on the basis of the information in the selection?''

On pages 686–687 is a chart on which you can keep track of your performance as you answer the ten questions for each selection. The chart will help you identify reading skills you may need to strengthen.

LOOKING INWARD

Thank You

Alex Haley

 Alex Haley, the author of *Roots*, served in the Coast Guard during World War II. On an especially lonely day at sea—Thanksgiving—he began to give serious thought to a holiday that has become, for most of us, a day of overeating and watching endless games of football. Haley decided to celebrate the true meaning of Thanksgiving, not by remembering the Pilgrims and their turkey dinner, but by writing three very special letters.

It was 1943, during World War II, and I was a young U.S. coastguardsman, serial number 212-548, a number we never seem to forget. My ship, the USS *Murzim*, had been under way for several days. Most of her holds contained thousands of cartons of canned or dried foods. The other holds were loaded with five-hundred-pound bombs packed delicately in padded racks. Our destination was a big base on the island of Tulagi in the South Pacific.

I was one of the *Murzim*'s several cooks and, quite the same as for folk ashore, this Thanksgiving morning had seen us busily preparing a traditional dinner featuring roast turkey.

Well, as any cook knows, it's a lot of hard work to cook and serve a big meal, and clean up and put everything away. But finally, around sundown, with our whole galley crew just bushed, we finished at last and were free to go flop into our bunks in the fo'c'sle. 3

But I decided first to go out on the *Murzim*'s afterdeck for a breath of open air. I made my way out there, breathing in great, deep draughts while walking slowly about, still wearing my white cook's hat and the long apron, my feet sensing the big ship's vibrations from the deep-set, turbine diesels and my ears hearing that slightly hissing sound the sea makes in resisting the skin of a ship. 4

I got to thinking about Thanksgiving. In reflex, my thoughts registered the historic imagery of the Pilgrims, Indians, wild turkeys, pumpkins, corn on the cob and the rest. 5

Yet my mind seemed to be questing for something else—some way that I could personally apply to the waning Thanksgiving. It must have taken me a half hour to sense that maybe some key to an answer could result from reversing the word "Thanksgiving"— at least that suggested a verbal direction, "Giving thanks." 6

Giving thanks—as in praying, thanking God, I thought. Yes, of course. Certainly. 7

Yet my mind continued nagging me. Fine. But something else. 8

After awhile, like a dawn's brightening, a further answer did come—that there were *people* to thank, people who had done so much for me that I could never possibly repay them. The embarrassing truth was I'd always just accepted what they'd done, taken all of it for granted. Not one time had I ever bothered to express to any of them so much as a simple, sincere "Thank you." 9

At least seven people had been particularly and indelibly helpful to me. I realized, with a gulp, that about half of them had since died—so they were forever beyond any possible expression of gratitude from me. The more I thought about it, the more ashamed I became. Then I pictured the three who were still alive and, within minutes, I was down in the fo'c'sle. 10

Sitting at a mess table with writing paper and memories of things each had done, I tried composing genuine statements of heartfelt appreciation and gratitude to my dad, Simon A. Haley, a professor at the old AMNC (Agricultural Mechanical Normal College) in Pine Bluff, Ark., now a branch of the University of Arkansas; to my grandma, Cynthia Palmer, back in our little hometown of Henning, Tenn.; and to the Rev. Lonual Nelson, my grammar school principal, retired and living in Ripley, six miles north of Henning. 11

I couldn't even be certain if they would recall some of their acts of years past, acts that I vividly remembered and saw now as having given me vital training, or inspiration, or directions, if not all of these desirables rolled into one. 12

The texts of my letters began something like, "Here, this Thanksgiving at sea, I find my thoughts upon how much you have done for me, but I have never stopped and said to you how much I feel the need to thank you—" And briefly I recalled for each of them specific acts performed in my behalf. 13

For instance, something uppermost about my father was how he had impressed upon me from boyhood to love books and reading. In fact, this graduated into a family habit of after-dinner quizzes at the table about books read most recently and new words learned. 14

My love of books never diminished and later led me toward writing books myself. So many times I have felt a sadness when exposed to modern children so immersed in the electronic media that they have little to no awareness of the wondrous world to be discovered in books.

I reminded the Reverend Nelson how each morning he would open our little country 15 town's grammar school with a prayer over his assembled students. I told him that whatever positive things I had done since had been influenced at least in part by his morning school prayers.

In the letter to my grandmother, I reminded her of a dozen ways she used to teach 16 me how to tell the truth, to be thrifty, to share, and to be forgiving and considerate of others. (My reminders included how she'd make me pull switches from a peach tree for my needed lesson.) I thanked her for the years of eating her good cooking, the equal of which I had not found since. (By now, though, I've reflected that those peerless dishes are most gloriously flavored with a pinch of nostalgia.) Finally, I thanked her simply for having sprinkled my life with stardust.

Before I slept, my three letters went into our ship's office mail sack. They got mailed 17 when we reached Tulagi Island.

We unloaded cargo, reloaded with something else, then again we put to sea in the 18 routine familar to us, and as the days became weeks, my little personal experience receded. Sometimes, when we were at sea, a mail ship would rendezvous and bring us mail from home, which, of course, we accorded topmost priority.

Every time the ship's loudspeaker rasped, ''Attention! Mail call!'' two-hundred-odd 19 shipmates came pounding up on deck and clustered about the raised hatch atop which two yeomen, standing by those precious bulging gray sacks, were alternately pulling out fistfuls of letters and barking successive names of sailors who were, in turn, hollering ''Here! Here!'' amid the jostling.

One ''mail call'' brought me responses from Grandma, Dad and the Reverend Nel- 20 son—and my reading of their letters left me not only astounded, but more humbled than before.

Rather than saying they would forgive that I hadn't previously thanked them, instead, 21 for Pete's sake, they were thanking *me*—for having remembered, for having considered they had done anything so exceptional.

Always the college professor, my dad had carefully avoided anything he considered 22 too sentimental, so I knew how moved he was to write me that, after having helped educate many young people, he now felt that his best results included his own son.

The Reverend Nelson wrote that his decades as a ''simple, old-fashioned principal'' 23 had ended with grammar schools undergoing such swift changes that he had retired in self-doubt. ''I heard more of what I had done wrong than what I did right,'' he said, adding that my letter had brought him welcome reassurance that his career had been appreciated.

A glance at Grandma's familiar handwriting brought back in a flash memories of 24
standing alongside her white wicker rocking chair, watching her "settin' down" some
letter to relatives. Frequently touching her pencil's tip to pursed lips, character by character,
each between a short, soft grunt, Grandma would slowly accomplish one word, then the
next, so that a finished page would consume hours. I wept over the page representing my
Grandma's recent hours invested in expressing her loving gratefulness to *me*—whom she
used to diaper!

Much later, retired from the Coast Guard and trying to make a living as a writer, I 25
never forgot how those three "thank you" letters gave me an insight into something nigh
mystical in human beings, most of whom go about yearning in secret for more of their
fellows to express appreciation for their efforts.

I discovered in time that, even in the business world, probably no two words are 26
more valued than "thank you," especially among people at stores, airlines, utilities and
others that directly serve the public.

Late one night, I was one of a half-dozen passengers who straggled weary and 27
grumbling off a plane that had been forced to land at the huge Dallas/Fort Worth Airport.
Suddenly, a buoyant, cheerful, red-jacketed airline man waved us away from the regular
waiting room seats, saying, "You sure look bushed. I know a big empty office where
you can stretch out while you wait." And we surely did. When the weather improved
enough for us to leave, "Gene Erickson" was in my notebook and, back home, I wrote
the president of that airline describing his sensitivity and his courtesy. And I received a
thank you!

I travel a good deal on lecture tours and I urge students especially to tell their parents, 28
grandparents, and other living elders simply "thank you" for all they have done to make
possible the lives they now enjoy. Many students have told me they found themselves
moved by the response. It is not really surprising, if one only reflects how it must feel
to be thanked after you have given for years.

Now, approaching Thanksgiving of 1982, I have asked myself what will I wish for 29
all who are reading this, for our nation, indeed for our whole world—since, quoting a
good and wise friend of mine, "In the end we are mightily and merely people, each with
similar needs." First, I wish for us, of course, the simple common sense to achieve world
peace, that being paramount for the very survival of our kind.

And there is something else I wish—so strongly that I have had this line printed 30
across the bottom of all my stationery: "*Find the good—and praise it.*"

■ Reading Comprehension Questions

1. The word *indelibly* in "seven people had been particularly and indelibly
   helpful to me" (paragraph 10) means
   a. partially.
   b. temporarily.
   c. unforgettably.
   d. unhappily.

2. The word *immersed* in "modern children so immersed in the electronic media" (paragraph 14) means
   a. ignorant.
   b. absorbed.
   c. frightened.
   d. misled.

3. Which of the following would be a good alternative title for this selection?
   a. The Importance of Showing Gratitude
   b. The Three Most Important People in My Life
   c. A Lonely Time
   d. Why Letters Are Important

4. Which of the following sentences best expresses the main idea of the selection?
   a. The author took the people he loved for granted.
   b. The author felt grateful to arrive home safely from the war.
   c. The author's father, grandmother, and grammar school principal were delighted to receive letters of thanks.
   d. Writing letters of thanks to the important people in his life taught the author the value of showing appreciation.

5. During World War II, the author served
   a. on a transport ship.
   b. in the Navy.
   c. on an Army base.
   d. on an aircraft carrier.

6. The author encourages his lecture audiences to
   a. make Thanksgiving a special day.
   b. write to company presidents.
   c. thank their elders.
   d. work for world peace.

7. *True or false?* _____ The author's father taught him to love books and reading.

8. The author implies that
   a. children should watch less television.
   b. he disliked his job as a cook aboard ship.
   c. some people do not enjoy being thanked.
   d. his grandmother had never written a letter before.

9. The author implies that
   a. his father was not openly emotional.
   b. the Reverend Lonual Nelson's teaching methods were ineffective.
   c. he never achieved success as a professional writer.
   d. Thanksgiving should be a day of prayer.

10. The author assumed that the people he wrote to would
    a. have expected thanks much sooner.
    b. not reply.
    c. have forgotten the incidents he referred to.
    d. brag about his letters.

■ Discussion Questions

About Content

1. In your opinion, which of the three people Haley wrote to was most influential in his decision to become a writer? Why do you think so?
2. Haley quotes a friend who says, ''In the end we are mightily and merely people, each with similar needs.'' What are two needs Haley says we all share?
3. Alex Haley was far from home when he decided to thank the important people in his life. What might have prevented him from thanking people if he had remained home?

About Structure

4. The technique Haley uses to develop most of his essay is
   a. comparison.
   b. narration.
   c. reasons.
5. How many times does the author use the key word *thank* (or *thanks*) in paragraphs 6 through 9? _____

About Style and Tone

6. When Haley tells us about the letter he wrote to his grandmother, he adds this comment: ''By now, though, I've reflected that those peerless dishes are most gloriously flavored with a pinch of nostalgia.'' What is he implying about her cooking?
7. Does Haley simply want to tell us about a lesson he has learned, or is he trying to persuade us to do something? How can you tell?

■ Writing Assignments

Assignment 1

There's an old Chinese proverb that goes: "Give me a fish, and I will eat for a day. Teach me to fish, and I will eat for a lifetime." Think of someone in your life who taught you something important that you have used (or benefited from) ever since. Write a thank-you letter to this person, telling him or her exactly how you have gained or what you have learned as a result. The person might be a parent, a relative, a family friend, a favorite teacher, an employer, a coach, or a favorite sports hero or movie star.

Organize your letter in the form of a five-paragraph essay. In your introduction, you might mention how you know this person or why you were prompted to write the letter. In your thesis, state that this person has been especially important to you because you learned something important from him or her—and tell what that "something" is. In each of your supporting paragraphs, show one way in which this knowledge or skill has made a difference in your life.

Alternatively, write about three different people, each of whom has taught you something important.

Assignment 2

Pretend that it is Thanksgiving, and one of the members of your family, who is not in a very good mood, says, "I don't have anything to be thankful for this year." Persuade this person that there are some things to be thankful for. Think of at least three and develop each with specific details. Here are some areas you could consider:

Jobs or job opportunities

Educational opportunities

Loved ones

A recent success or triumph in the family

Something beautiful

Recovery from an accident or illness

A prayer that was, or seemed to be, answered

Being together

Sharing a meaningful experience

Learning a valuable lesson

Assignment 3

At the end of his essay, Alex Haley says we should ''Find the good—and praise it.'' Can you think of three kinds of people who do important work yet receive little praise? Such people might include:

Teachers
Nurses
Garbage collectors
Police officers
Fathers or mothers
School maintenance workers
People who keep essential services going

Write an essay about three of these groups, giving specific reasons why each deserves to be praised for good work. Alternatively, write an essay about one of these groups, discussing three specific areas in which it deserves praise.

Shame

Dick Gregory

In this selection, Dick Gregory—the comedian and social critic—narrates two painful experiences from his boyhood. Although the incidents show graphically what it can be like to grow up black and poor, the essay also deals with universal emotions: shame, embarrassment, and the burning desire to hold onto one's self-respect.

I never learned hate at home, or shame. I had to go to school for that. I was about seven   1
years old when I got my first big lesson. I was in love with a little girl named Helene Tucker, a light-complected little girl with pigtails and nice manners. She was always clean and she was smart in school. I think I went to school then mostly to look at her. I brushed my hair and even got me a little old handkerchief. It was a lady's handkerchief, but I didn't want Helene to see me wipe my nose on my hand. The pipes were frozen again, there was no water in the house, but I washed my socks and shirt every night.

I'd get a pot, and go over to Mister Ben's grocery store, and stick my pot down into his soda machine. Scoop out some chopped ice. By evening the ice melted to water for washing. I got sick a lot that winter because the fire would go out at night before the clothes were dry. In the morning I'd put them on, wet or dry, because they were the only clothes I had.

Everybody's got a Helene Tucker, a symbol of everything you want. I loved her for her goodness, her cleanness, her popularity. She'd walk down my street and my brothers and sisters would yell, "Here comes Helene," and I'd rub my tennis sneakers on the back of my pants and wish my hair wasn't so nappy and the white folks' shirt fit me better. I'd run out on the street. If I knew my place and didn't come too close, she'd wink at me and say hello. That was a good feeling. Sometimes I'd follow her all the way home, and shovel the snow off her walk and try to make friends with her Momma and her aunts. I'd drop money on her stoop late at night on my way back from shining shoes in the taverns. And she had a Daddy, and he had a good job. He was a paper hanger. 2

I guess I would have gotten over Helene by summertime, but something happened in that classroom that made her face hang in front of me for the next twenty-two years. When I played the drums in high school it was for Helene and when I broke track records in college it was for Helene and when I started standing behind microphones and heard applause I wished Helene could hear it, too. It wasn't until I was twenty-nine years old and married and making money that I finally got her out of my system. Helene was sitting in that classroom when I learned to be ashamed of myself. 3

It was on a Thursday. I was sitting in the back of the room, in a seat with a chalk circle drawn around it. The idiot's seat, the troublemaker's seat. 4

The teacher thought I was stupid. Couldn't spell, couldn't read, couldn't do arithmetic. Just stupid. Teachers were never interested in finding out that you couldn't concentrate because you were so hungry, because you hadn't had any breakfast. All you could think about was noontime, would it ever come? Maybe you could sneak into the cloakroom and steal a bite of some kid's lunch out of a coat pocket. A bite of something. Paste. You can't really make a meal of paste, or put it on bread for a sandwich, but sometimes I'd scoop a few spoonfuls out of the big paste jar in the back of the room. Pregnant people get strange tastes. I was pregnant with poverty. Pregnant with dirt and pregnant with smells that made people turn away, pregnant with cold and pregnant with shoes that were never bought for me, pregnant with five other people in my bed and no Daddy in the next room, and pregnant with hunger. Paste doesn't taste too bad when you're hungry. 5

The teacher thought I was a troublemaker. All she saw from the front of the room was a little black boy who squirmed in his idiot's seat and made noises and poked the kids around him. I guess she couldn't see a kid who made noises because he wanted someone to know he was there. 6

It was on a Thursday, the day before the Negro payday. The eagle always flew on   7
Friday. The teacher was asking each student how much his father would give to the
Community Chest. On Friday night, each kid would get the money from his father, and
on Monday he would bring it to the school. I decided I was going to buy a Daddy right
then. I had money in my pocket from shining shoes and selling papers, and whatever
Helene Tucker pledged for her Daddy I was going to top it. And I'd hand the money
right in. I wasn't going to wait until Monday to buy me a Daddy.

I was shaking, scared to death. The teacher opened her book and started calling out   8
names alphabetically.

"Helene Tucker?"   9

"My Daddy said he'd give two dollars and fifty cents."   10

"That's very nice, Helene. Very, very nice indeed."   11

That made me feel pretty good. It wouldn't take too much to top that. I had almost   12
three dollars in dimes and quarters in my pocket. I stuck my hand in my pocket and held
onto the money, waiting for her to call my name. But the teacher closed her book after
she called everybody else in the class.

I stood up and raised my hand.   13

"What is it now?"   14

"You forgot me?"   15

She turned toward the blackboard. "I don't have time to be playing with you,   16
Richard."

"My Daddy said he'd . . ."   17

"Sit down, Richard, you're disturbing the class."   18

"My Daddy said he'd give . . . fifteen dollars."   19

She turned around and looked mad. "We are collecting this money for you and your   20
kind, Richard Gregory. If your Daddy can give fifteen dollars you have no business being
on relief."

"I got it right now, I got it right now, my Daddy gave it to me to turn in today, my   21
Daddy said . . ."

"And furthermore," she said, looking right at me, her nostrils getting big and her   22
lips getting thin and her eyes opening wide, "we know you don't have a Daddy."

Helene Tucker turned around, her eyes full of tears. She felt sorry for me. Then I   23
couldn't see her too well because I was crying, too.

"Sit down, Richard."   24

And I always thought the teacher kind of liked me. She always picked me to wash   25
the blackboard on Friday, after school. That was a big thrill, it made me feel important.
If I didn't wash it, come Monday the school might not function right.

"Where are you going, Richard!"   26

I walked out of school that day, and for a long time I didn't go back very often.   27
There was shame there.

Now there was shame everywhere. It seemed like the whole world had been inside 28
that classroom, everyone had heard what the teacher had said, everyone had turned around
and felt sorry for me. There was shame in going to the Worthy Boys Annual Christmas
Dinner for you and your kind, because everybody knew what a worthy boy was. Why
couldn't they just call it the Boys Annual Dinner, why'd they have to give it a name?
There was shame in wearing the brown and orange and white plaid mackinaw the welfare
gave to three thousand boys. Why'd it have to be the same for everybody so when you
walked down the street the people could see you were on relief? It was a nice warm
mackinaw and it had a hood, and my Momma beat me and called me a little rat when
she found out I stuffed it in the bottom of a pail full of garbage way over on Cottage
Street. There was shame in running over to Mister Ben's at the end of the day and asking
for his rotten peaches, there was shame in asking Mrs. Simmons for a spoonful of sugar,
there was shame in running out to meet the relief truck. I hated that truck, full of food
for you and your kind. I ran into the house and hid when it came. And then I started to
sneak through alleys, to take the long way home so the people going into White's Eat
Shop wouldn't see me. Yeah, the whole world heard the teacher that day, we all know
you don't have a Daddy.

It lasted for a while, this kind of numbness. I spent a lot of time feeling sorry for 29
myself. And then one day I met this wino in a restaurant. I'd been out hustling all day,
shining shoes, selling newspapers, and I had googobs of money in my pocket. Bought
me a bowl of chili for fifteen cents, and a cheeseburger for fifteen cents, and a Pepsi for
five cents, and a piece of chocolate cake for ten cents. That was a good meal. I was eating
when this old wino came in. I love winos because they never hurt anyone but themselves.

The old wino sat down at the counter and ordered twenty-six cents worth of food. 30
He ate it like he really enjoyed it. When the owner, Mister Williams, asked him to pay
the check, the old wino didn't lie or go through his pocket like he suddenly found a hole.

He just said: "Don't have no money." 31

The owner yelled: "Why in hell you come in here and eat my food if you don't have 32
no money? That food cost me money."

Mister Williams jumped over the counter and knocked the wino off his stool and 33
beat him over the head with a pop bottle. Then he stepped back and watched the wino
bleed. Then he kicked him. And he kicked him again.

I looked at the wino with blood all over his face and I went over. "Leave him alone, 34
Mister Williams. I'll pay the twenty-six cents."

The wino got up, slowly, pulling himself up to the stool, then up to the counter, 35
holding on for a minute until his legs stopped shaking so bad. He looked at me with pure
hate. "Keep your twenty-six cents. You don't have to pay, not now. I just finished paying
for it."

He started to walk out, and as he passed me, he reached down and touched my 36
shoulder. "Thanks, sonny, but it's too late now. Why didn't you pay it before?"

I was pretty sick about that. I waited too long to help another man. 37

■ Reading Comprehension Questions

1. The word *pregnant* in ''pregnant with poverty'' (paragraph 5) means
   a. full of.
   b. empty of.
   c. sick.
   d. satisfied.

2. The word *hustling* in ''I'd been out hustling all day'' (paragraph 29) means
   a. learning.
   b. stealing.
   c. making friends.
   d. working hard.

3. Which of the following would be a good alternative title for this selection?
   a. Helene Tucker
   b. The Pain of Being Poor
   c. Losing a Father
   d. Mr. Williams and the Wino

4. Which sentence best expresses the main idea of the selection?
   a. Richard felt that being poor was humiliating.
   b. Richard liked Helene Tucker very much.
   c. Richard had to work hard as a child.
   d. The wino refused Richard's money.

5. The teacher disliked Richard because he
   a. was dirty.
   b. liked Helene.
   c. was a troublemaker.
   d. ate paste.

6. *True or false?* _____ Helene Tucker felt sorry for Richard when the teacher embarrassed him.

7. Richard's problems in school were due to his being
   a. hungry.
   b. distracted by Helene.
   c. lonely.
   d. unable to read.

8. The author implies that Richard
   a. was not intelligent.
   b. was proud.
   c. had many friends.
   d. and Helene became friends.

9. The author implies that
   a.   Mr. Williams felt sorry for the wino.
   b.   Richard's teacher was insensitive.
   c.   Richard liked people to feel sorry for him.
   d.   Richard's father was dead.

10. The author implies that
   a.   the mackinaws were poorly made.
   b.   Helene was a sensitive girl.
   c.   Helene disliked Richard.
   d.   the wino was ashamed of his poverty.

■ Discussion Questions

About Content

1.   How might Dick Gregory's teacher have handled the Community Chest incident without making him feel ashamed?

2.   What are some of the lessons Gregory learns from the incident involving the wino at the restaurant?

3.   Where in "Shame" do we find evidence that Dick Gregory finally does escape from poverty?

About Structure

4.   Since Dick Gregory is actually writing about an embarrassing incident in school, why does he devote his first three paragraphs to his feelings about Helene Tucker?

5.   What is the connection between the incident involving the wino at the restaurant and the rest of the essay?

About Style and Tone

6.   In the paragraph beginning, "Now there was shame everywhere," Gregory uses a device called *repetition* when he begins several sentences with the words "There was shame . . ." What is the effect of this repetition?

7.   Why does Gregory use dialog when he narrates the incidents in the classroom and in the restaurant?

■ Writing Assignments

Assignment 1

Dick Gregory tells us in "Shame" that he was ashamed of his poverty and of being on welfare—to the point that he threw away the warm hooded mackinaw he had been given simply because it was obvious proof that he and his family were on relief. Do you think Gregory was justified in feeling so ashamed of his situation? How about other people who are on welfare? Are they justified if they feel ashamed? Choose either of the following thesis statements and develop it in an essay of several paragraphs:

- People on welfare are justified in feeling ashamed.
- People on welfare should not feel ashamed.

Then develop your thesis by thinking of several reasons to support the statement you have chosen.

You might think along the following lines:

Availability of jobs

Education or lack of education

Number of young children at home requiring care

Illness, physical disability

Psychological factors—depression, work habits, expectations, mental illness

Society's attitude toward people on welfare

Assignment 2

At some time in your life, you probably had an experience like Dick Gregory's in "Shame"—something that happened in a classroom, a group of friends or peers, or a family situation that proved to be both embarrassing and educational. At the time, the experience hurt you very much, but you learned from it. Write a narrative essay in which you retell this experience. Try to include vivid details and plenty of conversation so that the incident will come to life.

Assignment 3

Write an essay about three basic things that people must have in order to feel self-respect. In your thesis statement, name these three necessities and state that a person must possess them in order to feel self-respect. Following are some ideas to consider:

A certain number of material possessions

A job

A loving family or a special person

A clear conscience

A feeling of belonging

Freedom from addictions

In your supporting paragraphs, discuss the factors you have chosen, showing specifically why each is so important. In order to avoid falling into the trap of writing generalities, you may want to give examples of people who lack these necessities and show how such people lose self-respect. Your examples may be drawn from personal experience, or they may be hypothetical.

On Being a Mess

Elizabeth Ames

 Do you have any messy habits that are out of control? Does your home, apartment, or bedroom bear an uncomfortable resemblance to the local landfill? If so, you will probably identify with the author of the following essay. On the other hand, if you are compulsively neat, Elizabeth Ames may be able to explain to you why some people just can't get out from under "The Mess."

I am one of those people who simply cannot clean up. To me, the prospect of an orderly living space is as remote—and problematic—as trying to climb Mount Kilimanjaro.   1

There's a definite syndrome of sloppiness. Many people, I've noticed, go about being sloppy in much the same way. I'm not sure what to call us. Messaholics? Mess-addicts? Whatever we are, the one thing we are *not* is slobs. Slobs wallow in their mess. Messy people (for want of a better label) groan over it. We're continually apologizing to the tune of, "My apartment is such a pigsty. My house is such a mess." We are always embarrassed.   2

When my place is at its worst, I frequently invite another Messy Person over. We'll engage in an odd one-upmanship that is both competition and consolation. "I'm sorry, the place is terrible." "You should see *mine*. It's ten times worse." "Oh, no, it isn't." "Yes, it is." Etc.   3

Messy People want to clean up, but we can't. Not that we don't try. We do, and   4
probably more strenuously than most Neat People. I have scoured and dusted my tiny
apartment on more sunny Saturdays than I can count. I have slogged through three-day
marathons (attacking the kitchen, the living room, the bedroom and bathroom in turn).
Yet somehow the apartment will not come to order. Soon after I've thrown in the sponge,
I'm again tripping on the same sneakers and piles of underwear.

Omnivorous. We can never quite conquer the Mess. Rout it from the living room,   5
and it withdraws to the bedroom. From there it may retreat under the bed or into dresser
drawers. A protean monster, it forever changes form to evade us.

To complicate matters, it is also omnivorous. It eats my keys (usually before I go   6
out). It eats my shoes. And worst of all, it eats my bills. That can have sticky consequences
because who, after all, misses bills? Occasionally, it takes the threat of legal action for
me to discover that the Mess devoured my bills before I had a chance to pay them.

Often the Mess seems to rule our lives. I have declined dozens of casual engagements   7
because ''I have to get rid of that Mess.'' Then there are the potential visitors I've had
to meet in restaurants ''because there is a giant Mess in my apartment.''

Other times, the only way to subdue the Mess is to invite people to dinner. But even   8
when I've labored over my apartment all afternoon—even when I think I have it licked—
the Mess rears its ugly head.

''What about the newspapers on the floor?'' a well-meaning friend will chide. ''What   9
about those files and legal pads on the dining room table?''

''But I haven't *finished* those newspapers and I *work* on the dining room table.'' My   10
friends shake their heads sadly. I am surely a lost cause.

And that's on a good day. On bad days, the Mess takes over completely. There is   11
no space at all on that dining-room table, or anywhere else for that matter. Everything I
own is lost under the rubble. On tiptoe, I pick my way around the books and assorted
papers, trying not to step on anything important.

On bad days I frequently cannot decide what to wear, partly because half my ward-   12
robe—the clothes I wore last week—is heaped on the bedroom desk.

As for the kitchen, it can be downright scary. I dread opening the dark refrigerator,   13
certain that some forgotten tomatoes have metamorphosed into new forms of life. Who
knows what lurks in the sink? The dishes there form towers that lean precariously. They
usually manage to fall over between 2 and 3 A.M.

I'm convinced that on one bad day I will enter my apartment and suddenly panic—   14
thinking I've been robbed when I haven't. After all, how could a normal person wreak
such havoc? I must be living with some invisible maniac, or a crazed gorilla.

Perhaps that is why so many Messy People feel ''exposed'' when a stranger glimpses   15
their Mess. Beneath our attempts at denial, we have seen the enemy and he is certainly
no crazed gorilla . . .

Reality, however, is not always easy to face. Thus we have devised several ingenious   16
myths to justify our Mess—and ourselves. They are:

The Clean Mess. This myth is our primary protection against the gruesome label, 17 "slob." Slobs, of course, live in filth. Messy People live amid a profusion of sterile objects. "What's wrong," we ask, "with some basically clean clothes lying around? At least they're not fungus."

The Intellectual Mess. According to this one, we are too busy pondering the state 18 of the universe to bother with such earthly realities as unmade beds. We are creative nonconformists whose order is disorder. People with Intellectual Messes look down their noses at unimaginative organized souls. There's no challenge, they insist, in finding a dictionary *right away*. How routine. How dull.

It's My Mother's Fault. Behind nearly every Messy Person is a Meticulous 19 Mother. We love to recount our childhood torments at her hands and bemoan its effects: "She ordered me to do the bathroom so many times! I now have convulsions at the sight of window cleaner . . . So much talk about eating off her floors warped my subconscious. I'm acting out delusions of being an animal." And so on.

It's My Apartment's Fault. People who rely on this complain, "There's no place 20 left to put anything. My closets are full. What would I do with those things I'm saving for the Salvation Army? What would I do with my stuffed giraffe, Snookie? And those old broiler pans belonged to my grandfather!"

Such are the myths of Mess. Myths, because there are plenty of neat folks with brains, 21 badgering mothers and small apartments. Being a mess is no blessing. The only way out is to probe your true motives, discard the excuses and accept responsibility. For me, that was a gut-wrenching process. It was so powerful, in fact, that I didn't wash dishes for two weeks.

■ **Reading Comprehension Questions**

1. The word *protean* in "a protean monster, it forever changes form to evade us" (paragraph 5) means
   a. horrible.
   b. healthful.
   c. avoidable.
   d. changeable.

2. The word *omnivorous* in "the Mess . . . is also omnivorous" (paragraph 6) means
   a. helpful.
   b. enjoyable.
   c. all-consuming.
   d. easily defeated.

3. Which of the following would be a good alternative title for this selection?
   a. Slobs
   b. The Myths of Messiness
   c. Problems of Working at Home
   d. Messy People

4. Which sentence best expresses the main idea of the selection?
   a. Being a mess has certain advantages.
   b. Being messy creates problems, but messy people can't help themselves.
   c. Messy people don't like strangers to see their messiness.
   d. Messy people fool themselves with myths.

5. *True or false?* _____ The author's apartment has been robbed several times.

6. One thing messy people are not is
   a. competitive.
   b. embarrassed.
   c. disorganized.
   d. content.

7. Which of the following is *not* one of the myths that the author describes as ways messy people justify their messes?
   a. The Clean Mess
   b. It's My Mother's Fault
   c. The Children's Mess
   d. The Intellectual Mess

8. The author implies that
   a. messy people are basically lazy.
   b. messy people are not proud of their bad habits.
   c. neat people are snobs.
   d. small apartments are messier than large homes.

9. The author implies that
   a. she has reformed her messy habits.
   b. friends will overlook her messiness.
   c. she will never change.
   d. her mother caused her messy habits.

10. The author implies that
    a. messy people need myths because they are ashamed of themselves.
    b. she doesn't mind being called a slob.
    c. messy people live in sterile conditions.
    d. she keeps her work separate from the household mess.

■ **Discussion Questions**

About Content

1. Elizabeth Ames offers several excuses for being messy. What are they? Are any of them *good* excuses?
2. Ames insists that she is not a slob, only a messy person. What does she say is the difference between a slob and a messy person? Do you agree that she is not a slob?
3. The author states in the final paragraph that she decided to "accept responsibility" for her messiness. What happened? Do you think that Ames should stay the way she is, or do you think she should try to change?

About Structure

4. What change-of-direction signal is used in paragraph 4? _____
5. To what does the pronoun *it* refer in the first four sentences of paragraph 6? _____

About Style and Tone

6. Why do you think the author always capitalizes the word *mess*?
7. Point out one place in the selection where the author uses exaggeration to make her point.

■ **Writing Assignments**

Assignment 1

Imagine that you are an efficiency expert, and Elizabeth Ames has come to you for help in overcoming her messiness. After you interview her and learn all the details that are in her essay, what suggestions would you make to her for how to be a neater person? What should she do first, second, and third? What routine should she follow to prevent the mess from coming back?

Write a report of several paragraphs in which you explain to Ames a process whereby she can overcome her messy habits and be a neater person.

Start with an introductory paragraph in which you identify the problem she has and make the point that she can cure it if she follows a few simple steps (thesis statement).

Then, in the paragraphs that follow, describe each step in detail, giving specific examples of what she should do to achieve her goal. Refer to some of the same problems she mentions in her essay, and show her how she could clean them up and keep them cleaned up.

In your conclusion, summarize your recommendations, and then encourage Ames by telling her just how much better her life will be once she gets rid of the mess.

Assignment 2

In her essay, Elizabeth Ames is careful to distinguish between being a mess (which she says she is) and being a slob (which she insists she is not). Write your own essay, using as your title ''On Being a Slob.'' What are the character traits of a slob? What kinds of things do slobs do? What would a slob's apartment or house or workplace look like? (One clue Ames gives is the statement ''Slobs wallow in their mess.'' How—and in what ways—would a slob ''wallow''?) Pick out at least three ways in which a slob can be identified and develop each of these ways in a separate paragraph of your essay.

Assignment 3

Think of a word or phrase that you could use to characterize yourself. (Ames calls herself a ''messy person.'') Then write an essay titled ''On Being _____.'' You might, for example, characterize yourself in one of the following ways:

Neat	Compulsive saver
Gullible	Talkative
Too generous	Gambler
Eternal optimist	Dreamer
Suspicious	Helpless
Lucky	Unlucky
Skeptical	Loner

Each of the topic sentences for your supporting paragraphs should make a point about an effect this quality has had on your life. Then you should support the point with specific details. Here, for example, are the thesis statement and topic sentence for an essay titled ''On Being a Compulsive Shopper'':

Thesis: Being a compulsive shopper has caused me many problems.

Topic sentence 1: First, I buy all kinds of things I don't need.

Topic sentence 2: In addition, I can waste hours just drifting around in stores.

Topic sentence 3: Most important, I overspend rather than comparison-shop for the best price.

Only Daughter

Sandra Cisneros

Sandra Cisneros is a well-known Mexican-American writer. Her works include the acclaimed novel *The House on Mango Street.* But to her father, a man of traditional Mexican values, his daughter's success at first meant little compared with the accomplishments of his sons. As Cisneros's essay shows, people often crave approval from those who find it hardest to give.

Once, several years ago, when I was just starting out my writing career, I was asked to write my own contributor's note for an anthology. I wrote: "I am the only daughter in a family of six sons. *That* explains everything." 1

Well, I've thought that ever since, and yes, it explains a lot to me, but for the reader's sake I should have written: "I am the only daughter in a *Mexican* family of six sons." Or even: "I am the only daughter of a Mexican father and a Mexican-American mother." Or: "I am the only daughter of a working-class family of nine." All of these had everything to do with who I am today. 2

I was/am the only daughter and *only* a daughter. Being an only daughter in a family of six sons forced me by circumstance to spend a lot of time by myself because my brothers felt it beneath them to play with a *girl* in public. But that aloneness, that loneliness, was good for a would-be writer—it allowed me time to think and think, to imagine, to read and prepare myself. 3

Being only a daughter for my father meant my destiny would lead me to become someone's wife. That's what he believed. But when I was in the fifth grade and shared my plans for college with him, I was sure he understood. I remember my father saying, "*Que bueno, mi'ja,* that's good." That meant a lot to me, especially since my brothers thought the idea hilarious. What I didn't realize was that my father thought college was good for girls—good for finding a husband. After four years in college and two more in graduate school, and still no husband, my father shakes his head even now and says I wasted all that education. 4

In retrospect, I'm lucky my father believed daughters were meant for husbands. It meant it didn't matter if I majored in something silly like English. After all, I'd find a nice profession eventually, right? This allowed me the liberty to putter about embroidering my little poems and stories without my father interrupting with so much as a "What's that you're writing?" 5

But the truth is, I wanted him to interrupt. I wanted my father to understand what it was I was scribbling, to introduce me as "My only daughter, the writer." Not as "This is my only daughter. She teaches." *Es maestra*—teacher. Not even *profesora.* 6

In a sense, everything I have ever written has been for him, to win his approval even 7
though I know my father can't read English words, even though my father's only reading
includes the brown-ink *Esto* sports magazines from Mexico City and the bloody *¡Alarma!*
magazines that feature yet another sighting of *La Virgen de Guadalupe* on a tortilla or a
wife's revenge on her philandering husband by bashing his skull in with a *molcajete* (a
kitchen mortar made of volcanic rock). Or the *fotonovelas,* the little picture paperbacks
with tragedy and trauma erupting from the characters' mouths in bubbles.

A father represents, then, the public majority. A public who is disinterested in reading, 8
and yet one whom I am writing about and for, and privately trying to woo.

When we were growing up in Chicago, we moved a lot because of my father. He 9
suffered bouts of nostalgia. Then we'd have to let go of our flat, store the furniture with
mother's relatives, load the station wagon with baggage and bologna sandwiches and
head south. To Mexico City.

We came back, of course. To yet another Chicago flat, another Chicago neighborhood, 10
another Catholic school. Each time, my father would seek out the parish priest in order
to get a tuition break, and complain or boast: "I have seven sons."

He meant *siete hijos*, seven children, but he translated it as "sons." "I have seven 11
sons." To anyone who would listen. The Sears Roebuck employee who sold us the washing
machine. The short-order cook where my father ate his ham-and-eggs breakfasts. "I have
seven sons." As if he deserved a medal from the state.

My papa. He didn't mean anything by that mistranslation, I'm sure. But somehow I 12
could feel myself being erased. I'd tug my father's sleeve and whisper: "Not seven sons.
Six! and *one daughter.*"

When my oldest brother graduated from medical school, he fulfilled my father's 13
dream that we study hard and use this—our heads, instead of this—our hands. Even now
my father's hands are thick and yellow, stubbed by a history of hammer and nails and
twine and coils and springs. "Use this," my father said, tapping his head, "and not this,"
showing us those hands. He always looked tired when he said it.

Wasn't college an investment? And hadn't I spent all those years in college? And if 14
I didn't marry, what was it all for? Why would anyone go to college and then choose to
be poor? Especially someone who had always been poor.

Last year, after ten years of writing professionally, the financial rewards started to 15
trickle in. My second National Endowment for the Arts Fellowship. A guest professorship
at the University of California, Berkeley. My book, which sold to a major New York
publishing house.

At Christmas, I flew home to Chicago. The house was throbbing, same as always; 16
hot *tamales* and sweet *tamales* hissing in my mother's pressure cooker, and everybody—
my mother, six brothers, wives, babies, aunts, cousins—talking too loud and at the same
time, like in a Fellini film, because that's just how we are.

I went upstairs to my father's room. One of my stories had just been translated into 17
Spanish and published in an anthology of Chicano writing, and I wanted to show it to
him. Ever since he recovered from a stroke two years ago, my father likes to spend his
leisure hours horizontally. And that's how I found him, watching a Pedro Infante movie
on Galavision and eating rice pudding.

There was a glass filmed with milk on the bedside table. There were several vials of pills and balled Kleenex. And on the floor, one black sock and a plastic urinal that I didn't want to look at but looked at anyway. Pedro Infante was about to burst into song, and my father was laughing. 18

I'm not sure if it was because my story was translated into Spanish, or because it was published in Mexico, or perhaps because the story dealt with Tepeyac, the *colonia* my father was raised in and the house he grew up in, but at any rate, my father punched the mute button on his remote control and read my story. 19

I sat on the bed next to my father and waited. He read it very slowly. As if he were reading each line over and over. He laughed at all the right places and read lines he liked out loud. He pointed and asked questions: "Is this So-and-so?" "Yes," I said. He kept reading. 20

When he was finally finished, after what seemed like hours, my father looked up and asked: "Where can we get more copies of this for the relatives?" 21

Of all the wonderful things that happened to me last year, that was the most wonderful. 22

■ Reading Comprehension Questions

1. The word *destiny* in "Being only a daughter for my father meant my destiny would lead me to become someone's wife" (paragraph 4) means
   a. health.
   b. fate.
   c. beauty.
   d. intelligence.

2. The word *philandering* in "a wife's revenge on her philandering husband by bashing his skull in" (paragraph 7) means
   a. hardworking.
   b. unattractive.
   c. loving.
   d. unfaithful.

3. Which of the following would be a good alternative title for this selection?
   a. Why I Went to College
   b. My First Published Story
   c. Fathers and Daughters
   d. How I Eventually Gained My Father's Approval

4. Which of the following sentences best expresses the main idea of the selection?
   a. Cisneros's father believed daughters were meant for husbands.
   b. Cisneros always wanted to be a writer.
   c. Cisneros wanted her father to recognize her ability, and she finally succeeded.
   d. Despite her successes, Cisneros has remained true to her family and her Mexican heritage.

5. As a child, Cisneros
   a. enjoyed playing outside with her six brothers.
   b. spent a great deal of time alone.
   c. had to go to work to help support her family.
   d. did not want to go to college.

6. *True or false?* _____ Cisneros's father believed that the only reason to go to college was to prepare for a career.

7. Cisneros and her family moved often because
   a. they wanted to live in a neighborhood with good schools.
   b. they disliked living in Chicago.
   c. her father missed his homeland.
   d. they were unable to pay the rent.

8. *True or false?* _____ We can infer that Cisneros's father might have preferred that his daughter were a boy.

9. The author implies that to her father, majoring in English was
   a. acceptable for a daughter, but not for a son.
   b. a waste of education.
   c. an important achievement.
   d. a foolish thing for her to do.

10. We can assume from paragraphs 19–21 that Cisneros's father
    a. did not understand his daughter's story.
    b. understood his daughter's story only after she explained it to him.
    c. was impressed by this particular story because it was related to his life and culture.
    d. did not like the story but wanted to make his daughter feel good about her work.

■ **Discussion Questions**

About Content

1. According to the selection, exactly what did it mean to be "only a daughter" in a Mexican or working-class family? What were Cisneros's family's expectations for her, and how did she appear to live up to them? How didn't she live up to them?

2. Cisneros writes that when she heard her father say, "I have seven sons," she "could feel [herself] being erased." What does she mean by "being erased"? What might parents of all cultures learn from this comment?

3. Cisneros's father doesn't read the sort of material she writes. In fact, he doesn't even read English. Yet his daughter states, "In a sense, everything I have ever written has been for him" (paragraph 7). What does she mean, and why do you think she feels this way?

About Structure

4. Locate the two time signals Cisneros uses in paragraph 9, and write them below.

   _____   _____

5. What does Cisneros's conclusion consist of? How does this conclusion relate to her introduction?

About Style and Tone

6. Cisneros sprinkles her narrative with Spanish words, as when she distinguishes between *maestra* (the way her father introduces her) and *profesora* (her actual profession). What do these word choices add to the narrative? How does Cisneros help her non-Spanish-speaking readers understand those words?

7. Throughout her narrative, Cisneros sometimes uses fragments rather than full sentences. One example is at the end of paragraph 9: "To Mexico City." Find additional examples. Why might a professional writer who majored in English in college include fragments in her published writing? What purpose might they serve?

8. Cisneros includes little dialogue, but she does include some quoted words to emphasize key points. Find some of the quoted remarks. What do they add to the essay?

■ Writing Assignments

Assignment 1

Cisneros ends her essay with the sentence, "Of all the wonderful things that happened to me last year, that was the most wonderful." Make a list of all the wonderful things that have happened to you in the last year or so. These could include such achievements as the following:

Getting a promotion

Doing well in a course you worked hard at

Finding a better job or apartment

Learning a new skill

Maintaining an exercise program

Quitting smoking (or some other harmful practice)

Attending or participating in a very special event, such as a performance or a family gathering

Winning an award or honor on campus, at work, or in your community

Discovering a new friend or relationship or improving an old friendship

Then select from your list the one accomplishment you feel is the most wonderful, and write an essay about it. Include specific details about what motivated you, what you did, and what happened as a result. Feel free to conclude your essay with Cisneros's final sentence or something similar to it.

Alternatively, write an essay that describes three wonderful things that happened to you in the last year or so.

Assignment 2

Cisneros's status as a daughter permitted her to major in English and work at improving her writing. What factors led you to choose your college major, or the major or majors you are considering? Write an essay on why you have chosen or are considering a particular major. Use the outline below in developing support for your thesis statement.

1. Job possibilities the major leads to, and their advantages
2. Talents and skills I have that suit the career I've chosen or am considering
3. Previous work or activities that indicate I'll enjoy this career

Alternatively, write an essay on three majors that you are considering and why.

Assignment 3

Cisneros writes that being the only daughter in her family "had everything to do with who I am today." What has it meant to you to be a son or daughter in your family? Perhaps being a son in your family means a combination of certain responsibilities, privileges, and goals. Maybe being a daughter once meant that your parents had expectations for you that you didn't share. Whatever your situation was or is as a son or daughter, summarize it in your thesis statement, which may be as general as this: "Being an only son in my family had its disadvantages as I grew up." Then support that thesis with points about three key elements of your situation. Following are several such elements for you to consider.

Household chores
Career goals
Financial support
School activities
Work
Responsibilities toward parents
Parental judgment

Remember to provide plenty of examples. Like Cisneros, use rich descriptions, typical reactions, and revealing comments to make those examples come to life for your reader.

I Became Her Target

Roger Wilkins

Any newcomer in school often has an awkward time breaking the ice with classmates. For Roger Wilkins, being the only black student in his new school made the situation considerably worse. He could easily have become the focus of the other students' prejudice and fear. Instead, help came in the form of a teacher who quickly made it clear how she saw him—as a class member with something to contribute.

My favorite teacher's name was "Dead-Eye" Bean. Her real name was Dorothy. She taught American history to eighth graders in the junior high section of Creston, the high school that served the north end of Grand Rapids, Michigan. It was the fall of 1944. Franklin D. Roosevelt was president; American troops were battling their way across France; Joe DiMaggio was still in the service; the Montgomery bus boycott was more than a decade away, and I was a 12-year-old black newcomer in a school that was otherwise all white.

    My mother, who had been a widow in New York, had married my stepfather, a Grand Rapids physician, the year before, and he had bought the best house he could afford for his new family. The problem for our new neighbors was that their neighborhood had

1

2

The prevailing wisdom in the neighborhood was that we were spoiling it and that we ought to go back where we belonged (or alternatively, ought not intrude where we were not wanted). There was a lot of angry talk among the adults, but nothing much came of it.

But some of the kids, those first few weeks, were quite nasty. They threw stones at 3 me, chased me home when I was on foot and spat on my bike seat when I was in class. For a time, I was a pretty lonely, friendless and sometimes frightened kid. I was just transplanted from Harlem, and here in Grand Rapids, the dominant culture was speaking to me insistently. I can see now that those youngsters were bullying and culturally disadvantaged. I knew then that they were bigoted, but the culture spoke to me more powerfully than my mind and I felt ashamed for being different—a nonstandard person.

I now know that Dorothy Bean understood most of that and deplored it. So things 4 began to change when I walked into her classroom. She was a pleasant-looking single woman, who looked old and wrinkled to me at the time, but who was probably about 40. Whereas my other teachers approached the problem of easing in their new black pupil by ignoring him for the first few weeks, Miss Bean went right at me. On the morning after having read our first assignment, she asked me the first question. I later came to know that in Grand Rapids, she was viewed as a very liberal person who believed, among other things, that Negroes were equal.

I gulped and answered her question and the follow-up. They weren't brilliant answers, 5 but they did establish the facts that I had read the assignment and that I could speak English. Later in the hour, when one of my classmates had bungled an answer, Miss Bean came back to me with a question that required me to clean up the girl's mess and established me as a smart person.

Thus, the teacher began to give me human dimensions, though not perfect ones for 6 an eighth grader. It was somewhat better to be an incipient teacher's pet than merely a dark presence in the back of the room onto whose silent form my classmates could fit all the stereotypes they carried in their heads.

A few days later, Miss Bean became the first teacher ever to require me to think. 7 She asked my opinion about something Jefferson had done. In those days, all my opinions were derivative. I was for Roosevelt because my parents were and I was for the Yankees because my older buddy from Harlem was a Yankee fan. Besides, we didn't have opinions about historical figures like Jefferson. Like our high school building or old Mayor Welch, he just was.

After I had stared at her for a few seconds, she said: "Well, should he have bought 8 Louisiana or not?"

"I guess so," I replied tentatively. 9

Why! What kind of question was that, I groused silently. But I ventured an answer. 10 Day after day, she kept doing that to me, and my answers became stronger and more confident. She was the first teacher to give me the sense that thinking was part of education and that I could form opinions that had some value.

Her final service to me came on a day when my mind was wandering and I was 11 idly digging my pencil into the writing surface on the arm of my chair. Miss Bean impulsively threw a hunk of gum eraser at me. By amazing chance, it hit my hand and sent the pencil flying. She gasped, and I crept mortified after my pencil as the class roared.

That was the ice breaker. Afterward, kids came up to me to laugh about "Old Deadeye Bean." The incident became a legend, and I, a part of that story, became a person to talk to. So that's how I became just another kid in school and Dorothy Bean became "Old Dead-Eye."

■ Reading Comprehension Questions

1. The word *deplored* in "But some of the kids, those first few weeks, were quite nasty. . . . Dorothy Bean understood most of that and deplored it" (paragraphs 3–4) means
   a. supported.
   b. imitated.
   c. often taught.
   d. disapproved of.

2. The word *groused* in "Why! What kind of question was that, I groused silently" (paragraph 10) means
   a. complained.
   b. agreed.
   c. answered.
   d. yelled.

3. Which of the following would be a good alternative title for this selection?
   a. Education in the Forties
   b. A True Teacher's Pet
   c. Eighth Grade
   d. A Teacher's Help

4. Which of the following sentences best expresses the main idea of the selection?
   a. After moving from Harlem to Grand Rapids, Michigan, the author had numerous adjustments to make.
   b. Eighth grade can be a challenging time for a new student.
   c. Using unusual methods, Miss Bean helped her eighth-grade students learn to think for themselves.
   d. A teacher helped the first black student in school to be accepted and to learn to think for himself.

5. After moving to Grand Rapids, Wilkins felt ashamed for
   a. having a stepfather.
   b. being smart.
   c. having lived in Harlem.
   d. being different.

6. By involving Wilkins in class discussion, Miss Bean helped the other students see him as more than a
   a. stereotype.
   b. liberal.
   c. legend.
   d. bigot.

7. Wilkins writes that before entering Miss Bean's class, he held
   a. no opinions.
   b. no original opinions.
   c. opinions based on careful thought.
   d. opinions on various historical figures.

8. The author implies that some of the bigotry in Grand Rapids was the result of
   a. anger about the war.
   b. ignorance about black people.
   c. his youth.
   d. ignorance about physicians.

9. In stating "the teacher began to give me human dimensions, though not perfect ones for an eighth grader" (paragraph 6), the imperfection that Wilkins refers to is his
   a. different race.
   b. inadequate answers.
   c. becoming a teacher's pet.
   d. coming from another state.

10. We can conclude that Dorothy Bean threw an eraser at the author because she
    a. knew the event would become an ice breaker for him.
    b. wanted to knock the pencil from his hand.
    c. wanted to ask his opinion about something.
    d. wanted him to pay attention to class.

■ **Discussion Questions**

About Content

1. What does Wilkins mean by the term *nonstandard person* (in paragraph 3)? Do you think he later felt more like a "standard" person? Why or why not?

2. Dorothy Bean had a different approach to the new black student from the other teachers. How did her approach differ from theirs? Why do you think she took this approach?

3. How did Miss Bean give Wilkins "the sense that thinking was part of education and that [he] could form opinions that had some value"?

About Structure

4. Wilkins develops his essay mainly through
   a. definition.
   b. comparison and contrast.
   c. narration.
5. The author uses transition signals to move his story smoothly from one stage to the next. List four such signals:

_____   _____   _____   _____

About Style and Tone

6. In the first paragraph, Wilkins provides some historical background for his story. Why do you think he chose the specific details mentioned there?
7. The word *target* has meanings in the story that aren't obvious just from reading the title. Before reading this essay, what did you think *target* might mean? What meanings do you feel the essay gives to that word?

■ ## Writing Assignments

Assignment 1

Dorothy Bean, Wilkins's favorite teacher, obviously had an important influence on him in more ways than one. She helped him become accepted by the other students, she strengthened his self-image, and she helped him learn to think for himself. Write an essay on one of your favorite teachers and the ways in which he or she influenced you.

Like Wilkins, dramatize specific incidents to show how this teacher affected you. Provide whatever background is necessary to put the teacher's influence into perspective. Your thesis will be a general statement that summarizes the teacher's impact on your life, such as this one: "Mrs. Croson, my sixth-grade teacher, helped me in ways that strengthened all of the rest of my education." Then go on in your introduction to list three specific ways in which the teacher influenced you. An example of such a plan of development is: "She gave me confidence and taught me the joys of reading and writing."

Alternatively, write an essay on three of your favorite teachers. Your thesis might be about the characteristics the three teachers shared or how they influenced you.

Assignment 2

Wilkins suggests that the students in his new school misjudged him because at first they saw him only as a stereotype, a stranger with no particular personal characteristics. Perhaps we are all subject to prejudging people, if not because of their race, then for another reason. Did a person who made a good impression on you ever turn out to be boring or mean? Did a boss you thought was overly strict ever turn out to be supportive and teach you a lot? Write an essay about someone who was really quite different from what you initially thought her or she would be. You may wish to consider the following characteristics that influence people to prejudge each other:

Age
Gender
Race
Sexual preference
Size
Clothing
Job

Begin your essay by explaining in vivid detail your first impression and what caused it. Then go on to narrate some experiences you had with the person and how they changed your mind about him or her.

Alternatively, write about an individual or individuals who have prejudged you. Explain what those people thought of you and why, and describe how they treated you. If they came to change their minds, explain why and how your relationship changed.

Assignment 3

Write an essay in which you contrast your best teacher and your worst teacher. Make a list of the qualities that made one teacher excellent and the other ineffective or worse. Focus on three pairs of contrasting qualities, using either a *one-side-*

at-a-time or a *point-by-point* method of development (see pages 183–184). Following are some elements of teaching to consider as you plan your essay:

Grasp of the subject
Ability to communicate
Ability to motivate
Interest in students
Classroom presentation
Sense of humor

In addition, consider what you or other students learned or did not learn, such as the following:

Subject matter
Ways to learn
Ways to think
Self-confidence
Methods of cooperation

The Ambivalence of Abortion

Linda Bird Francke

 Abortion is an issue almost everyone has strong opinions about. It is both a national question debated by the Supreme Court and a very personal problem confronted by millions of women in the privacy of their own hearts. In the following essay, Linda Bird Francke narrates the story of her decision to have an abortion. As you will see, it was ultimately a very lonely decision—despite the support of her husband. Is the writer for abortion, against abortion, or neither? That is something you, as a reader, will have to decide.

We were sitting in a bar on Lexington Avenue when I told my husband I was pregnant. It is not a memory I like to dwell on. Instead of the champagne and hope which had heralded the impending births of the first, second and third child, the news of this one   1

was greeted with shocked silence and Scotch. ''Jesus,'' my husband kept saying to himself, stirring the ice cubes around and around. ''Oh, Jesus.''

Oh, how we tried to rationalize it that night as the starting time for the movie came and went. My husband talked about his plans for a career change in the next year, to stem the staleness that fourteen years with the same investment-banking firm had brought him. A new baby would preclude that option. 2

The timing wasn't right for me either. Having juggled pregnancies and child care with what free-lance jobs I could fit in between feedings, I had just taken on a full-time job. A new baby would put me right back in the nursery just when our youngest child was finally school age. It was time for *us,* we tried to rationalize. There just wasn't room in our lives now for another baby. We both agreed. And agreed. And agreed. 3

How very considerate they are at the Women's Services, known formally as the Center for Reproductive and Sexual Health. Yes, indeed, I could have an abortion that very Saturday morning and be out in time to drive to the country that afternoon. Bring a first morning urine specimen, a sanitary belt and napkins, a money order or $125 cash— and a friend. 4

My friend turned out to be my husband, standing awkwardly and ill at ease as men always do in places that are exclusively for women, as I checked in at 9 A.M. Other men hovered around just as anxiously, knowing they had to be there, wishing they weren't. No one spoke to each other. When I would be cycled out of there four hours later, the same men would be slumped in their same seats, locked downcast in their cells of embarrassment. 5

The Saturday morning women's group was more disspirited than the men in the waiting room. There were around fifteen of us, a mixture of races, ages and backgrounds. Three didn't speak English at all and a fourth, a pregnant Puerto Rican girl around eighteen, translated for them. 6

There were six black women and a hodgepodge of whites, among them a T-shirted teenager who kept leaving the room to throw up and a puzzled middle-aged woman from Queens with three grown children. 7

''What form of birth control were you using?'' the volunteer asked each one of us. The answer was inevitably ''none.'' She then went on to describe the various forms of birth control available at the clinic, and offered them to each of us. 8

The youngest Puerto Rican girl was asked through the interpreter which she'd like to use: the loop, diaphragm, or pill. She shook her head ''no'' three times. ''You don't want to come back here again, do you?'' the volunteer pressed. The girl's head was so low her chin rested on her breastbone. ''*Sí,*'' she whispered. 9

We had been there two hours by that time, filling out endless forms, giving blood and urine, receiving lectures. But unlike any other group of women I've been in, we didn't talk. Our common denominator, the one which usually floods across language and economic barriers into familiarity, today was one of shame. We were losing life that day, not giving it. 10

The group kept getting cut back to smaller, more workable units, and finally I was put in a small waiting room with just two other women. We changed into paper bathrobes and paper slippers, and we rustled whenever we moved. One of the women in my room was shivering and an aide brought her a blanket. 11

"What's the matter?" the aide asked her. "I'm scared," the woman said. "How 12
much will it hurt?" The aide smiled. "Oh, nothing worse than a couple of bad cramps,"
she said. "This afternoon you'll be dancing a jig."

I began to panic. Suddenly the rhetoric, the abortion marches I'd walked in, the 13
telegrams sent to Albany to counteract the Friends of the Fetus, the Zero Population
Growth buttons I'd worn, peeled away, and I was all alone with my microscopic baby.
There were just the two of us there, and soon, because it was more convenient for me
and my husband, there would be one again.

How could it be that I, who am so neurotic about life that I step over bugs rather 14
than on them, who spend hours planting flowers and vegetables in the spring even though
we rent out the house and never see them, who make sure the children are vaccinated and
inoculated and filled with vitamin C, could so arbitrarily decide that this life shouldn't be?

"It's not a life," my husband had argued, more to convince himself than me. "It's 15
a bunch of cells smaller than my fingernail."

But any woman who has had children knows that certain feeling in her taut, swollen 16
breasts, and the slight but constant ache in her uterus that signals the arrival of a life.
Though I would march myself into blisters for a woman's right to exercise the option of
motherhood, I discovered there in the waiting room that I was not the modern woman I
thought I was.

When my name was called, my body felt so heavy the nurse had to help me into the 17
examining room. I waited for my husband to burst through the door and yell "Stop,"
but of course he didn't. I concentrated on three black spots in the acoustic ceiling until they
grew in size to the shape of saucers, while the doctor swabbed my insides with antiseptic.

"You're going to feel a burning sensation now," he said, injecting Novocain into 18
the neck of the womb. The pain was swift and severe, and I twisted to get away from
him. He was hurting my baby, I reasoned, and the black saucers quivered in the air.
"Stop," I cried. "Please stop." He shook his head, busy with his equipment. "It's too
late to stop now," he said. "It'll just take a few more seconds."

What good sports we women are. And how obedient. Physically the pain passed even 19
before the hum of the machine signaled that the vacuuming of my uterus was
completed, my baby sucked up like ashes after a cocktail party. Ten minutes start to
finish. And I was back on the arm of the nurse.

There were twelve beds in the recovery room. Each one had a gaily flowered draw 20
sheet and a soft green or blue thermal blanket. It was all very feminine. Lying on these
beds for an hour or more were the shocked victims of their sex, their full wombs now
stripped clean, their futures less encumbered.

It was very quiet in that room. The only voice was that of the nurse, locating the 21
new women who had just come in so she could monitor their blood pressure, and checking
out the recovered women who were free to leave.

Juice was being passed about, and I found myself sipping a Dixie cup of Hawaiian 22
Punch. An older woman with tightly curled bleached hair was just getting up from the
next bed. "That was no goddamn snap," she said, resting before putting on her mini-
skirt and high white boots. Other women came and went, some walking out as dazed as
they had entered, others with a bounce that signaled they were going right back to
Bloomingdale's.

Finally then, it was time for me to leave. I checked out, making an appointment to 23
return in two weeks for an IUD insertion. My husband was slumped in the waiting room,
clutching a single yellow rose wrapped in a wet paper towel and stuffed into a Baggie.

We didn't talk the whole way home, but just held hands very tightly. At home there 24
were more yellow roses and a tray in bed for me and the children's curiosity to divert.

It had certainly been a successful operation. I didn't bleed at all for two days just as 25
they had predicted, and then I bled only moderately for another four days. Within a week
my breasts had subsided and the tenderness vanished, and my body felt mine again instead
of the eggshell it becomes when it's protecting someone else.

My husband and I are back to planning our summer vacation and his career switch. 26

And it certainly does make more sense not to be having a baby right now—we say 27
that to each other all the time. But I have this ghost now. A very little ghost that only
appears when I'm seeing something beautiful, like the full moon on the ocean last weekend.
And the baby waves at me. And I wave at the baby. "Of course, we have room," I cry
to the ghost. "Of course, we do."

■ Reading Comprehension Questions

1. The word *preclude* in "A new baby would preclude that option" (paragraph 2) means
   a. include.
   b. prevent.
   c. delay.
   d. force.

2. The word *arbitrarily* in "could so arbitrarily decide that this life shouldn't be" (paragraph 14) means
   a. reluctantly.
   b. unhappily.
   c. thoughtfully.
   d. lightly.

3. Which of the following would be a good alternative title for this selection?
   a. Abortion: A Difficult Decision
   b. The Process of Abortion
   c. Safe Abortions
   d. The Wrong Decision

4. Which sentence best expresses the main idea of the selection?
   a. Abortion clinics today are clean, safe, and friendly.
   b. The author realized that her decision to have an abortion was a selfish one.
   c. Deciding to have an abortion was a painful and unforgettable decision for the author.
   d. Husbands should support wives if they decide to have an abortion.

5. The patients at the clinic are
   a.   mostly black.
   b.   teenagers.
   c.   a mixture of races and ages.
   d.   welfare clients.

6. *True or false?* _____ The abortion clinic was a cold, unfriendly place.

7. Before having her own abortion, the author had
   a.   been opposed to abortion.
   b.   never considered the issue.
   c.   been unable to make up her mind about the issue.
   d.   been actively in favor of abortion.

8. The author implies that
   a.   her career is more important than having another child.
   b.   her husband felt worse about the abortion than she did.
   c.   women can tolerate pain better than men can.
   d.   she will now join an antiabortion group.

9. The author implies that
   a.   career considerations should not enter into a decision to have an abortion.
   b.   birth control is unreliable.
   c.   she still does not feel completely comfortable with her decision.
   d.   the young Puerto Rican girl is irresponsible.

10. *True or false?* _____ The author implies that the men and women at the clinic felt ashamed to be there.

■ Discussion Questions

About Content

1. What reasons does Linda Bird Francke give for her decision to have an abortion? Which are her reasons, and which are her husband's reasons?

2. In what ways are the people at Women's Services considerate to the author? In what ways are they *not* considerate?

3. Why do you think the men are ill at ease and embarrassed?

About Structure

4. What method of introduction does the author use?
   a. Broad to narrow
   b. Anecdote
   c. Questions
5. The author begins and ends her essay with the idea of *ambivalence*: conflicting feelings or thoughts existing at the same time. How is the ambivalence reflected at the end?

About Style and Tone

6. Why does the author repeat the word *agreed* so often at the end of the third paragraph?
7. A *simile* is a figure of speech in which a writer compares one thing to another, very different thing, using the word *like* or *as* to bring out a surprising relationship between the two. In paragraph 19, the author uses a simile when she writes that her baby was ''sucked up like ashes after a cocktail party.'' Why do you think she uses this simile? What is she saying here about her unborn child and her feelings about the abortion?

■ Writing Assignments

Assignment 1

Imagine that a friend comes to you and tells you that she is pregnant. Your friend doesn't know what to do. Write an essay about the three most important questions your friend should ask herself in order to arrive at the best decision. In each supporting paragraph, state what the question is and describe why the answer is so important in the decision-making process. Possible questions are:

What are my goals for the future?
How does the baby's father feel?
How will I support myself and the baby?
What is best for me?
What is best for the baby?
What is the morally right thing to do?
What does my religion teach?
Whom will I hurt by having or not having the baby?
What are the alternatives to abortion?

In your conclusion, you could mention the decision that you hope your friend will come to.

Assignment 2

Think of a difficult decision you are in the process of making now (or one you will soon have to make). Write an essay in which you examine your conflicting feelings. Organize the essay into two supporting paragraphs, covering (1) the arguments in favor of one side, and (2) the arguments for the other side. In your conclusion, you might mention the decision you are leaning toward. Here are a sample thesis, topic sentences, and brief outline for an essay on this topic:

Thesis: Making a decision about whether to continue going to college or get a full-time job has been difficult for me.

Topic sentence 1: Continuing in school might be the best course of action.
    a. Degree means better future earning power
    b. Convenient—my parents available now to baby-sit for my children
    c. Enjoyment of learning

Topic sentence 2: However, getting a full-time job seems urgent now.
    a. Need money to move to larger apartment
    b. Local job opportunity might not be available later
    c. Would have more money for everyday things

Assignment 3

Write a narrative essay on an action you took that you gave considerable thought to but later regretted. The action may be an important one that lends itself to a serious tone (such as filing for divorce, punishing a child, quitting a job, or getting married). Or the action may be one that could be written about in a light, humorous tone (such as getting a haircut, going skiing, wearing a certain outfit, or going out on a particular date).

Smash Thy Neighbor

John McMurtry

We think of football as one of those all-American things, like baseball or apple pie. Children are encouraged to play football from fifth grade through college. Hundreds of hours of network TV are devoted to football coverage. And *Monday Night Football* is almost a patriotic ritual. In this selection, however, a former football player says that football games are cruel contests that injure players and bring out the worst in fans.

A few months ago my neck got a hard crick in it. I couldn't turn my head; to look left or right I had to turn my whole body. But I'd had cricks in my neck since I started playing grade-school football and hockey, so I just ignored it. Then I began to notice that when I reached for any sort of large book (which I do pretty often as a philosophy teacher at the University of Guelph), I had trouble lifting it with one hand. I was losing the strength in my left arm, and I had such a steady pain in my back that I often had to stretch out on the floor to relieve the pressure. 1

Several weeks after my problems with book-lifting, I mentioned to my brother, an orthopedic surgeon, that I'd lost the power in my arm since my neck began to hurt. Twenty-four hours later I was in a Toronto hospital, not sure whether I might end up with a wasted upper limb. Apparently the steady pounding I had received playing college and professional football in the late fifties and early sixties had driven my head into my backbone so that the disks had crumpled together at the neck—''acute herniation''—and had cut the nerves to my left arm like a pinched telephone wire (without nerve stimulation, of course, the muscles atrophy, leaving the arm crippled). So I spent my Christmas holidays in the hospital in heavy traction, and much of the next three months with my neck in a brace. Today most of the pain has gone, and I've recovered most of the strength in my arm. But from time to time I still have to don the brace, and surgery remains a possibility. 2

Not much of this will surprise anyone who knows football. It is a sport in which body wreckage is one of the leading conventions. A few days after I went into the hospital for that crick in my neck, another brother, an outstanding football player in college, was undergoing spinal surgery in the same hospital two floors above me. In his case it was a lower, more massive herniation, which every now and again buckled him so that he was unable to lift himself off his back for days. By the time he entered the hospital for surgery he had already spent several months in bed. The operation was successful, but, as in all such cases, it will take him a year to recover fully. 3

These aren't isolated experiences. Just about anybody who has ever played football for any length of time, in high school, college, or one of the professional leagues, has suffered for it later. 4

Indeed, it is arguable that body shattering is the very *point* of football, as killing and maiming are of war. (In the United States, for example, the game results in fifteen to twenty deaths a year and about fifty thousand major operations on knees alone.) To grasp some of the more conspicuous similarities between football and war, it is instructive to listen to the imperatives most frequently issued to the players by their coaches, teammates, and fans. "Hurt 'em!" "Level 'em!" "Kill 'em!" "Take 'em apart!" Or watch for the plays that are most enthusiastically applauded by the fans, where someone is "smeared," "knocked silly," "creamed," "nailed," "broken in two," or even "crucified." (One of my coaches when I played corner linebacker with the Calgary Stampeders in 1961 elaborated, often very inventively, on this language of destruction: admonishing us to "unjoin" the opponent, "make 'im remember you," and "stomp 'im like a bug.") Just as in hockey, where a fight will bring fans to their feet more often than a skillful play, so in football the mouth waters most of all for the really crippling block or tackle. For the kill. Thus the good teams are "hungry," the best players are "mean," and "casualties" are as much a part of the game as they are of a war.

The family resemblance between football and war is, indeed, striking. Their languages are similar: "field general," "long bomb," "blitz," "take a shot," "front line," "pursuit," "good hit," "the draft," and so on. Their principles and practices are alike: mass hysteria, the art of intimidation, absolute command and total obedience, territorial aggression, censorship, inflated insignia and propaganda, blackboard maneuvers and strategies, drills, uniforms, formations, marching bands, and training camps. And the virtues they celebrate are almost identical: hyperaggressiveness, coolness under fire, and suicidal bravery.

One difference between war and football, though, is that there is little or no protest against football. Perhaps the most extraordinary thing about the game is that the systematic infliction of injuries excites in people not concern, as would be the case if they were sustained at, say, a rock festival, but a collective rejoicing and euphoria. Players and fans alike revel in the spectacle of a combatant felled into semiconsciousness, "blindsided," "clotheslined," or "decapitated." I can remember, in fact, being chided by a coach in pro ball for not "getting my hat" injuriously into a player who was lying helpless on the ground.

After every game, of course, the papers are full of reports on the day's injuries, a sort of post-battle "body count," and the respective teams go to work with doctors and trainers, tape, whirlpool baths, cortisone, and morphine to patch and deaden the wounds before the next game. Then the whole drama is reenacted—injured athletes held together by adhesive, braces, and drugs—and the days following it are filled with even more feverish activity to put on the show yet again at the end of the week. (I remember being so taped up in college that I earned the nickname "Mummy.") The team that survives this merry-go-round spectacle of skilled masochism with the fewest incapacitating injuries usually wins. It is a sort of victory by ordeal: "We hurt them more than they hurt us."

My own initiation into this brutal circus was typical. I loved the game from the moment I could run with a ball. Played shoeless on a green, open field with no one keeping score and in a spirit of reckless abandon and laughter, it's a very different sport. Almost no one gets hurt, and it's rugged, open, and exciting (it still is for me). But, like everything else, it starts to be regulated and institutionalized by adult authorities. And the fun is over.

So it was as I began the long march through organized football. Now there were a 10 coach and elders to make it clear by their behavior that beating other people was the only thing to celebrate and that trying to shake someone up every play was the only thing to be really proud of. Now there were severe rule enforcers, audiences, formally recorded victors and losers, and heavy equipment to permit crippling bodily moves and collisions (according to one survey, more than 80 percent of all football injuries occur to fully equipped players). And now there was the official "given" that the only way to keep playing was to wear suffocating armor, to play to defeat, to follow orders silently, and to renounce spontaneity in favor of joyless drill. The game has been, in short, ruined. But because I loved to play, and play skillfully, I stayed. And progressively and inexorably, as I moved through high school, college, and pro leagues, my body was dismantled. Piece by piece.

I started off with torn ligaments in my knee at thirteen. Then, as the organization 11 and the competition increased, the injuries came faster and harder. Broken nose (three times), broken jaw (fractured in the first half and dismissed as a "bad wisdom tooth," so I played with it for the rest of the game), ripped knee ligaments again. Torn ligaments in one ankle and a fracture in the other (which I remember feeling relieved about because it meant I could honorably stop drill-blocking a 270-pound defensive end). Repeated rib fractures and cartilage tears (usually carried, again, through the remainder of the game). More dislocations of the left shoulder than I can remember (the last one I played with because, as the Calgary Stampeders' doctor said, it "couldn't be damaged any more"). Occasional broken or dislocated fingers and toes. Chronically hurt lower back (I still can't lift with it or change a tire without worrying about folding). Separated right shoulder (as with many other injuries, like badly bruised hips and legs, needled with morphine for the games). And so on. The last pro game I played—against the Winnipeg Blue Bombers in the Western finals in 1961—I had a recently dislocated left shoulder, a more recently wrenched right shoulder, and a chronic pain center in one leg. I was so tied up with soreness that I couldn't drive to the airport. But it never occurred to me that I should miss a play as a corner linebacker.

By the end of my football career, I had learned that physical injury—giving it and 12 taking it—is the real currency of the sport. And that in the final analysis, the "winner" is the man who can hit to kill even if only half his limbs are working. In brief, a warrior game with a warrior ethos into which (like almost everyone I played with) my original boyish enthusiasm had been relentlessly conditioned.

In thinking back on how all this happened, though, I can pick out no villains. As 13 with the social system as a whole, the game has a life of its own. Everyone grows up inside it, accepts it, and fulfills its dictates as obediently as Helots. Far from questioning the principles of the activity, most men simply concentrate on executing these principles more aggressively than anybody else. The result is a group of people who, as the leagues become of a higher and higher class, are progressively insensitive to the possibility that things could be otherwise. Thus, in football, anyone who might question the wisdom or enjoyment of putting on heavy equipment on a hot day and running full speed at someone else with the intention of knocking him senseless would be regarded as not really a devoted athlete and probably "chicken." The choice is made straightforward. Either you, too, do your very utmost to smash efficiently and be smashed, or you admit incompetence or cowardice and quit. Since neither of these admissions is very pleasant, people generally keep any doubts they have to themselves, and carry on.

Of course, it would be a mistake to suppose that there is more blind acceptance of   14 brutal practices in organized football than elsewhere. On the contrary, a recent Harvard study argues that football's characteristics of "impersonal acceptance of inflicted injury," an overriding "organization goal," the "ability to turn oneself on and off," and being, above all, "out to win" are prized by ambitious executives in many large corporations. Clearly, football is no sicker than the rest of our society. Even its organized destruction of physical well-being is not anomalous. A very large part of our wealth, work, and time is, after all, spent in systematically destroying and harming human life; manufacturing, selling, and using weapons that tear opponents to pieces; making ever bigger and faster predator-named cars with which to kill and injure one another by the million every year; and devoting our very lives to outgunning one another for power in an ever-more-destructive rat race. Yet all these practices are accepted without question by most people, even zealously defended and honored. Competitive, organized injuring is integral to our way of life, and football is one of the more intelligible mirrors of the whole process: a sort of colorful morality play showing us how exciting and rewarding it is to Smash Thy Neighbor.

Now, it is fashionable to rationalize our collaboration in all this by arguing that, well,   15 men *like* to fight and injure their fellows, and such games as football should be encouraged to discharge this original-sin urge into less harmful channels than, say, war. Public-show football, this line goes, plays the same sort of cathartic role as Aristotle said stage tragedy does: without real blood (or not much), it releases players and audience from unhealthy feelings stored up inside them.

As an ex-player in this seasonal coast-to-coast drama, I see little to recommend such   16 a view. What organized football did to me was make me *suppress* my natural urges and reexpress them in alienating, vicious form. Spontaneous desires for free bodily exuberance and fraternization with competitors were shamed and forced under ("If it ain't hurtin', it ain't helpin' "), and in their place were demanded armored, mechanical moves, and cool hatred of all opposition. Endless authoritarian drill and dressing-room harangues (ever wonder why competing teams can't prepare for a game in the same dressing room?) were the kinds of mechanisms employed to reconstruct joyful energies into mean and alien shapes. I am quite certain that everyone else around me was being similarly forced into this heavily equipped military precision and angry antagonism, because there was always a mutinous attitude about full-dress practices, and everybody (the pros included) had to concentrate incredibly hard for days to whip himself into just one hour's hostility a week against another club. The players never speak of these things, of course, because everyone is anxious to appear tough.

The claim that men like seriously to battle one another to some sort of finish is a   17 myth. It endures only because it wears one of the oldest and most propagandized of masks—the romantic combatant. I sometimes wonder whether the violence all around us doesn't depend for its survival on the existence and preservation of this tough-guy disguise.

As for the effect of organized football on the spectator, the fans are not so much 18
released from supposed feelings of violent aggression by watching their athletic heroes
perform it as they are encouraged in the view that people-smashing is an admirable mode
of self-expression. The most savage attackers, after all, are, by general agreement, the
most efficient and worthy players of all (the biggest applause I ever received as a football
player occurred when I ran over people or slammed them so hard that they couldn't get
up). . . . Watching well-advertised strong men knock other people around, make them
hurt, is in the end like other tastes. It does not weaken with feeding and variation in form.
It grows.

I got out of football in 1962. In a preseason intersquad game, I ripped the cartilage 19
in my ribs on the hardest block I'd ever thrown. I had trouble breathing, and I had to
shuffle-walk with my torso on a tilt. The doctor in the local hospital said three weeks
rest; the coach said scrimmage in two days. Three days later I was back home reading philosophy.

■ Reading Comprehension Questions

1. The word *atrophy* in ''without nerve stimulation, of course, the muscles
   atrophy, leaving the arm crippled'' (paragraph 2) means
   a. get stronger.
   b. flex.
   c. weaken.
   d. are unaffected.

2. The word *imperatives* in ''It is instructive to listen to the imperatives most
   frequently issued to the players. . . . 'Hurt 'em!' 'Level 'em!' 'Kill 'em!' ''
   (paragraph 5) means
   a. insults.
   b. commands.
   c. compliments.
   d. questions.

3. Which of the following would be a good alternative title for this selection?
   a. The Violence of Football
   b. Football in the United States
   c. A Man Who Played Football
   d. Football and Corporate Competition

4. Which sentence best expresses the main idea of the selection?
   a. Playing football has caused the author much physical pain.
   b. Most football coaches try to make the game less violent.
   c. Football's popularity is a reflection of some negative aspects of society.
   d. Violence is a central part of organized football both for the teams and
      for the fans.

5. The author says that organized football is like
    a. all other sports.
    b. philosophy.
    c. war.
    d. football played without coaches and rules.

6. For the author, football was ruined by
    a. people who play without equipment.
    b. the regulation of adult authorities.
    c. people who dislike its violence.
    d. ambitious executives.

7. According to the author, watching football makes people
    a. believe that ''smashing thy neighbor'' is good.
    b. realize that football is too violent.
    c. feel a great release from their own violent feelings.
    d. escape from the anxieties of their jobs.

8. The author implies that
    a. society is much less brutally competitive than football.
    b. football players never have doubts about the brutality of the game.
    c. the brutal values of football exist in other parts of society.
    d. many people question the violence in football.

9. The author implies that fans
    a. get rid of unhealthy feelings when watching football.
    b. encourage the violence in football.
    c. are unaware of the violence in football.
    d. discourage the really savage attacks in football.

10. In the last paragraph of the selection, the author implies that
    a. his injuries were mild.
    b. the doctor exaggerated the extent of his injuries.
    c. the coach thought that his injuries were mild.
    d. the coach cared more about winning than about his players' injuries.

■ Discussion Questions

About Content

1. According to McMurtry, what qualities of our society are reflected in football?

2. The author makes an analogy between war and football. In what ways are the two activities alike?

3. Do you agree with McMurtry that the violence of football encourages people's taste for ''people-smashing as an admirable mode of self-expression'' (paragraph 18)?

About Structure

4. What method of introduction does the author use?
    a. Anecdote
    b. An opposite
    c. Quotation
5. What method of development is used in paragraphs 5 and 6?
    a. Reasons
    b. Comparison
    c. Examples

About Style and Tone

6. Why does the author call his essay "Smash Thy Neighbor"? To answer, think about how the title may be a play on the words of a familiar biblical command.
7. McMurtry uses terms such as *body wreckage, body shattering,* and *skilled masochism* to describe organized football. What effect does he hope this language will have on the reader? Find three other phrases the author uses to describe football (beginning with paragraph 9), and write them in the spaces below:

    _____

    _____

    _____

■ Writing Assignments

Assignment 1

Imagine that you are a professional football coach (or, if you prefer, the head coach of your school's football team). You have just read "Smash Thy Neighbor" in a national magazine, and you feel angered and hurt by McMurtry's opinion of football. How would you answer his accusations about the sport? Write a letter to the editor of the magazine in which you give three reasons why John McMurtry is wrong about football and its effects on people. You might want to get started with this thesis statement:

I feel John McMurtry is wrong about football for several reasons.

Then continue your letter, describing each reason in detail. Write a separate paragraph for each detail.

Alternatively, imagine that, as a coach, you agree with McMurtry, and write a letter in which you detail three reasons for agreeing.

Assignment 2

Write a narrative essay about a bad experience you had with sports. Among the topics you might write about are:

An injury
Not being chosen for a team
Missing an important point or goal
Being pressured by a parent or coach
Being the clumsiest person in gym class
Being embarrassed while trying to learn a sport

You could begin the essay with a sentence or two about your experience with sports in general—whether sports have been an area of pain or pleasure for you. Your thesis should name the particular experience you will write about and tell your readers that this experience was bad (or embarrassing, or humiliating, or disillusioning, or any other word that seems appropriate).

Then organize your supporting paragraphs by dividing your experience into two or three time phases. You may want to review first the chapter on the narrative essay (pages 137–145).

Assignment 3

Write an essay about a sport you feel is a good one. In each of your supporting paragraphs, give one reason why this sport is good for either players or spectators.

A Hanging

George Orwell

You are about to attend an execution. In this essay, George Orwell (author of *1984*) recalls a hanging he witnessed when he was an English police officer stationed in Burma. Orwell's sensitivity and vividly descriptive writing will make you see and feel what it is like to take the seemingly endless walk from cell to gallows. You will share the guards' uneasiness and the prisoner's terror. And, after you finish the selection, you may also share Orwell's views on capital punishment.

It was in Burma, a sodden morning of the rains. A sickly light, like yellow tinfoil, was slanting over the high walls into the jail yard. We were waiting outside the condemned cells, a row of sheds fronted with double bars, like small animal cages. Each cell measured about ten feet by ten and was quite bare within except for a plank bed and a pot of drinking water. In some of them brown silent men were squatting at the inner bars, with their blankets draped round them. These were the condemned men, due to be hanged within the next week or two. 1

One prisoner had been brought out of his cell. He was a Hindu, a puny wisp of a man, with a shaven head and vague liquid eyes. He had a thick, sprouting moustache, absurdly too big for his body, rather like the moustache of a comic man on the films. Six tall Indian warders were guarding him and getting him ready for the gallows. Two of them stood by with rifles with fixed bayonets, while the others handcuffed him, passed a chain through his handcuffs and fixed it to their belts, and lashed his arms tight to his sides. They crowded very close about him, with their hands always on him in a careful, caressing grip, as though all the while feeling him to make sure he was there. It was like men handling a fish which is still alive and may jump back into the water. But he stood quite unresisting, yielding his arms limply to the ropes, as though he hardly noticed what was happening. 2

Eight o'clock struck and a bugle call, desolately thin in the wet air, floated from the distant barracks. The superintendent of the jail, who was standing apart from the rest of us, moodily prodding the gravel with his stick, raised his head at the sound. He was an army doctor, with a grey toothbrush moustache and a gruff voice. "For God's sake hurry up, Francis," he said irritably. "The man ought to have been dead by this time. Aren't you ready yet?" 3

Francis, the head jailer, a fat Dravidian in a white drill suit and gold spectacles, waved his black hand. "Yes sir, yes sir," he bubbled. "All iss satisfactorily prepared. The hangman iss waiting. We shall proceed." 4

"Well, quick march, then. The prisoners can't get their breakfast till this job's over." 5

We set out for the gallows. Two warders marched on either side of the prisoner, with 6
their files at the slope; two others marched close against him, gripping him by arm and
shoulder, as though at once pushing and supporting him. The rest of us, magistrates and
the like, followed behind. Suddenly, when we had gone ten yards, the procession stopped
short without any order or warning. A dreadful thing had happened—a dog, come goodness
knows whence, had appeared in the yard. It came bounding among us with a loud volley
of barks, and leapt round us wagging its whole body, wild with glee at finding so many
human beings together. It was a large woolly dog, half Airedale, half pariah. For a moment
it pranced round us, and then, before anyone could stop it, it had made a dash for the
prisoner, and jumping up tried to lick his face. Everyone stood aghast, too taken aback
even to grab at the dog.

"Who let that bloody brute in here?" said the superintendent angrily. "Catch it, 7
someone!"

A warder, detached from the escort, charged clumsily after the dog, but it danced 8
and gambolled just out of his reach, taking everything as part of the game. A young
Eurasian jailer picked up a handful of gravel and tried to stone the dog away, but it
dodged the stones and came after us again. Its yaps echoed from the jail walls. The
prisoner, in the grasp of the two warders, looked on incuriously, as though this was
another formality of the hanging. It was several minutes before someone managed to
catch the dog. Then we put my handkerchief through its collar and moved off once more,
with the dog still straining and whimpering.

It was about forty yards to the gallows. I watched the bare brown back of the prisoner 9
marching in front of me. He walked clumsily with his bound arms, but quite steadily,
with that bobbing gait of the Indian who never straightens his knees. At each step his
muscles slid neatly into place, the lock of hair on his scalp danced up and down, his feet
printed themselves on the wet gravel. And once, in spite of the men who gripped him by
each shoulder, he stepped slightly aside to avoid a puddle on the path.

It is curious, but till that moment I had never realised what it means to destroy a 10
healthy, conscious man. When I saw the prisoner step aside to avoid the puddle, I saw
the mystery, the unspeakable wrongness, of cutting a life short when it is in full tide.
This man was not dying; he was alive just as we were alive. All the organs of his
body were working—bowels digesting food, skin renewing itself, nails growing, tissues
forming—all toiling away in solemn foolery. His nails would still be growing when he
stood on the drop, when he was falling through the air with a tenth of a second to live.
His eyes saw the yellow gravel and the grey walls, and his brain still remembered, foresaw,
reasoned—reasoned even about puddles. He and we were a party of men walking together,
seeing, hearing, feeling, understanding the same world; and in two minutes, with a sudden
snap, one of us would be gone—one mind less, one world less.

The gallows stood in a small yard, separate from the main grounds of the prison, 11
and overgrown with tall prickly weeds. It was a brick erection like three sides of a shed,
with planking on top, and above that two beams and a crossbar with the rope dangling.
The hangman, a grey-haired convict in the white uniform of the prison, was waiting beside
his machine. He greeted us with a servile crouch as we entered. At a word from Francis
the two warders, gripping the prisoner more closely than ever, half led, half pushed him

to the gallows and helped him clumsily up the ladder. Then the hangman climbed up and fixed the rope round the prisoner's neck.

We stood waiting, five yards away. The warders had formed in a rough circle round the gallows. And then, when the noose was fixed, the prisoner began crying out to his god. It was a high, reiterated cry of "Ram! Ram! Ram! Ram!" not urgent and fearful like a prayer or a cry for help, but steady, rhythmical, almost like the tolling of a bell. The dog answered the sound with a whine. The hangman, still standing on the gallows, produced a small cotton bag like a flour bag and drew it down over the prisoner's face. But the sound, muffled by the cloth, still persisted, over and over again: "Ram! Ram! Ram! Ram! Ram!"   12

The hangman climbed down and stood ready, holding the lever. Minutes seemed to pass. The steady, muffled crying from the prisoner went on and on, "Ram! Ram! Ram!" never faltering for an instant. The superintendent, his head on his chest, was slowly poking the ground with his stick; perhaps he was counting the cries, allowing the prisoner a fixed number—fifty, perhaps, or a hundred. Everyone had changed colour. The Indians had gone grey like bad coffee, and one or two of the bayonets were wavering. We looked at the lashed, hooded man on the drop, and listened to his cries—each cry another second of life; the same thought was in all our minds: oh, kill him quickly, get it over, stop that abominable noise!   13

Suddenly the superintendent made up his mind. Throwing up his head he made a swift motion with his stick. "Chalo!" he shouted almost fiercely.   14

There was a clanking noise, and then dead silence. The prisoner had vanished, and the rope was twisting on itself. I let go of the dog, and it galloped immediately to the back of the gallows; but when it got there it stopped short, barked, and then retreated into a corner of the yard, where it stood among the weeds, looking timorously out at us. We went round the gallows to inspect the prisoner's body. He was dangling with his toes pointed straight downwards, very slowly revolving, as dead as a stone.   15

The superintendent reached out with his stick and poked the bare body; it oscillated, slightly. "*He's* all right," said the superintendent. He backed out from under the gallows, and blew out a deep breath. The moody look had gone out of his face quite suddenly. He glanced at his wristwatch. "Eight minutes past eight. Well, that's all for this morning, thank God."   16

The warders unfixed bayonets and marched away. The dog, sobered and conscious of having misbehaved itself, slipped after them. We walked out of the gallows yard, past the condemned cells with their waiting prisoners, into the big central yard of the prison. The convicts, under the command of warders armed with lathis, were already receiving their breakfast. They squatted in long rows, each man holding a tin pannikin, while two warders with buckets marched round ladling out rice; it seemed quite a homely, jolly scene, after the hanging. An enormous relief had come upon us now that the job was done. One felt an impulse to sing, to break into a run, to snigger. All at once everyone began chattering gaily.   17

The Eurasian boy walking beside me nodded towards the way we had come, with a knowing smile: "Do you know, sir, our friend (he meant the dead man), when he heard his appeal had been dismissed, he pissed on the floor of his cell. From fright.—Kindly   18 take one of my cigarettes, sir. Do you not admire my new silver case, sir? From the boxwallah, two rupees eight annas. Classy European style.''

Several people laughed—at what, nobody seemed certain.   19

Francis was walking by the superintendent, talking garrulously: "Well, sir, all hass   20
passed off with the utmost satisfactoriness. It wass all finished—flick! like that. It iss not
always so—oah, no! I have known cases where the doctor wass obliged to go beneath
the gallows and pull the prisoner's legs to ensure decease. Most disagreeable!''

"Wriggling about, eh? That's bad,'' said the superintendent.   21

"Ach, sir, it iss worse when they become refractory! One man, I recall, clung to the   22
bars of hiss cage when we went to take him out. You will scarcely credit, sir, that it took
six warders to dislodge him, three pulling at each leg. We reasoned with him. 'My dear
fellow,' we said, 'think of all the pain and trouble you are causing to us!' But no, he
would not listen! Ach, he wass very troublesome!''

I found that I was laughing quite loudly. Everyone was laughing. Even the superinten-   23
dent grinned in a tolerant way. "You'd better all come out and have a drink,'' he said
quite genially. "I've got a bottle of whisky in the car. We could do with it.''

We went through the big double gates of the prison, into the road. "Pulling at his   24
legs!'' exclaimed a Burmese magistrate suddenly, and burst into a loud chuckling. We
all began laughing again. At that moment Francis's anecdote seemed extraordinarily funny.
We all had a drink together, native and European alike, quite amicably. The dead man
was a hundred yards away.

■ Reading Comprehension Questions

1. The word *reiterated* in "the high, reiterated cry of 'Ram! Ram!' '' (paragraph 12) means
   a. reluctant.
   b. lonely.
   c. repeated.
   d. useless.

2. The word *amicably* in "we all had a drink together, ... quite amicably''
   (paragraph 24) means
   a. with hostility.
   b. unnecessarily.
   c. quietly.
   d. in a friendly way.

3. Which of the following would be a good alternative title for this selection?
   a. A Burmese Prisoner
   b. Capital Punishment
   c. Eyewitness to an Execution
   d. What It Means to Take a Life

4. Which sentence best expresses the main idea of the selection?
   a. Capital punishment is unpleasant to carry out, but it is necessary in some cases.
   b. Executions in Burma were done in an inefficient and amateurish way.
   c. Taking another person's life, no matter why, is morally wrong.
   d. No one cared about the Burmese prisoner who was hanged.

5. Just before he was executed, the prisoner
   a. protested his innocence.
   b. cried out to his god.
   c. tried to escape from the gallows.
   d. said a quiet prayer.

6. *True or false?* _____ The prisoner had been convicted of murder.

7. After the execution, the author and the other authorities
   a. felt relief.
   b. became very depressed.
   c. realized they had done something wrong.
   d. couldn't speak for a long while.

8. The author implies that
   a. the dog that interrupted the march to the gallows belonged to the prisoner.
   b. no one has the right to take another person's life.
   c. the authorities knew the prisoner was innocent.
   d. other methods of execution are more humane than hanging.

9. The author implies that
   a. the prisoner would have escaped if he had not been so heavily guarded.
   b. the prisoner did not die immediately.
   c. the hangman had volunteered for the job.
   d. the superintendent of the jail was nervous and upset about the hanging.

10. The author implies that
    a. the people who witnessed the hanging later laughed and joked to cover up the uneasiness they felt.
    b. the native people and the Europeans felt differently about the hanging.
    c. he had become friends with the prisoner before the execution.
    d. Burmese officials were corrupt.

■ Discussion Questions

About Content

1. How does the prisoner act as he is led out to be hanged? On the basis of his actions, what state of mind do you feel he is in?
2. Why does everyone stand ''aghast'' when the stray dog licks the prisoner's face? Why is this incident important? (To answer, you might consider what qualities the dog represents or symbolizes.)
3. The author has a moment of understanding when the prisoner steps ''slightly aside to avoid a puddle on the path.'' What realization does the author come to? How is this realization related to the small incident of avoiding a puddle?

About Structure

4. The best statement of the author's thesis is in paragraph 10. Find it and write it in the spaces below:

   _____

   _____

About Style and Tone

5. Why do you think Orwell ends the narrative with the statement, ''The dead man was a hundred yards away''?
6. Orwell uses several *similes* (comparisons using the words *like* or *as*) to add vividness to the narrative. He says, for example, that the guards handled the prisoner ''like men handling a fish which is still alive and may jump back into the water.'' Find two more similes and write them here:

   _____

   _____

7. In part, Orwell uses dialog to tell his story; we hear the actual voices of the superintendent, Francis, the prisoners, and others. Find and underline all the lines spoken by the superintendent. Discuss how the words the superintendent speaks (and the tone of voice he speaks them in) reflect the emotional changes the superintendent goes through.

■ **Writing Assignments**

Assignment 1

Use examples and details from ''A Hanging'' to support the following thesis statement:

> In ''A Hanging,'' George Orwell constantly contrasts death with life in order to show us how wrong it is to kill another human being.

You might organize your supporting paragraphs by showing how death is contrasted with life (1) on the way to the gallows; (2) at the gallows; (3) after the hanging.

To get started, reread the selection closely, noting words and incidents that seem to be closely related to either death or life. For example, in paragraph 2, Orwell describes the prisoner as ''quite unresisting, yielding his arms limply to the ropes.'' It is as if the prisoner is already dead. In contrast, the guards are filled with life and action: they handcuff the prisoner, lash his arms, and keep a ''careful, caressing grip'' on him. At many other points in the story, this strong contrast between death and life is described.

Use a point-by-point method of contrast in developing your essay. You may want to look first at the example of this method on page 184.

Assignment 2

Find out (1) if capital punishment is legal in your state, and, if so, (2) which method of execution is used. (You could find this information by calling your city or county library.) Then imagine that a statewide vote will soon be taken to find out if voters want to change this law. Decide if you would (or would not) change the law. Give reasons for your decision. For example, if your state does have capital punishment, and you would vote not to change the law, you might give the reasons in the following essay outline:

> Thesis: Our state law allows a jury to vote for ''death by lethal injection'' for convicted criminals, and I would not vote to change this law.
>
> Topic sentences:
> (a) First of all, the death penalty saves thousands of tax dollars that would be spent to keep criminals in prison for life.
> (b) In addition, the punishment acts as a deterrent to other criminals.
> (c) Most important, death is an appropriate punishment for someone who commits a terrible crime.

In order to avoid writing in vague, general terms, you may want to use specific examples of cases or crimes currently being discussed in the news. You may also need facts and statistics you can find by consulting the card catalog in your college library under the subject heading *Capital Punishment* and by skimming the appropriate books.

Assignment 3

On the basis of the knowledge you have gained by reading this selection, write an essay with *either* of the thesis statements below:

- Executions today are as brutal as the one described in ''A Hanging.''
- Executions today are humane compared with the one described in ''A Hanging.''

You may want to write about each of the following areas in your supporting paragraphs:

Methods of execution and atmosphere in which executions are conducted

Kinds of people who are executed

Fairness of the trials and judges

In My Day

Russell Baker

''Other people can become frail and break, but not parents.'' In the essay that follows, Russell Baker describes how he comes to see the error of that statement. Watching his ill mother drift further and further away in time, he recognizes ways in which we are linked to and isolated from our parents and our children.

At the age of eighty my mother had her last bad fall, and after that her mind wandered free through time. Some days she went to weddings and funerals that had taken place half a century earlier. On others she presided over family dinners cooked on Sunday   1 afternoons for children who were now gray with age. Through all this she lay in bed but moved across time, traveling among the dead decades with a speed and ease beyond the gift of physical science.

"Where's Russell?" she asked one day when I came to visit at the nursing home. 2

"I'm Russell," I said. 3

She gazed at this improbably overgrown figure out of an inconceivable future and promptly dismissed it. 4

"Russell's only this big," she said, holding her hand, palm down, two feet from the floor. That day she was a young country wife with chickens in the backyard and a view of hazy blue Virginia mountains behind the apple orchard, and I was a stranger old enough to be her father. 5

Early one morning she phoned me in New York. "Are you coming to my funeral today?" she asked. 6

It was an awkward question with which to be awakened. "What are you talking about, for God's sake?" was the best reply I could manage. 7

"I'm being buried today," she declared briskly, as though announcing an important social event. 8

"I'll phone you back," I said and hung up, and when I did phone back she was all right, although she wasn't all right, of course, and we all knew she wasn't. 9

She had always been a small woman—short, light-boned, delicately structured—but now, under the white hospital sheet, she was becoming tiny. I thought of a doll with huge, fierce eyes. There had always been a fierceness in her. It showed in that angry, challenging thrust of the chin when she issued an opinion, and a great one she had always been for issuing opinions. 10

"I tell people exactly what's on my mind," she has been fond of boasting. "I tell them what I think, whether they like it or not." Often they had not liked it. She could be sarcastic to people in whom she detected evidence of the ignoramus or the fool. 11

"It's not always good policy to tell people exactly what's on your mind," I used to caution her. 12

"If they don't like it, that's too bad," was her customary reply, "because that's the way I am." 13

And so she was. A formidable woman. Determined to speak her mind, determined to have her way, determined to bend those who opposed her. In that time when I had known her best, my mother had hurled herself at life with chin thrust forward, eyes blazing, and an energy that made her seem always on the run. 14

She ran after squawking chickens, an axe in her hand, determined on a beheading that would put dinner in the pot. She ran when she made the beds, ran when she set the table. One Thanksgiving she burned herself badly when, running up from the cellar oven with the ceremonial turkey, she tripped on the stairs and tumbled back down, ending at the bottom in the debris of giblets, hot gravy, and battered turkey. Life was combat, and victory was not to the lazy, the timid, the slugabed, the drugstore cowboy, the libertine, the mushmouth afraid to tell people exactly what was on his mind whether people liked it or not. She ran. 15

But now the running was over. For a time I could not accept the inevitable. As I sat 16
by her bed, my impulse was to argue her back to reality. On my first visit to the hospital
in Baltimore, she asked who I was.

"Russell," I said. 17

"Russell's way out west," she advised me. 18

"No, I'm right here." 19

"Guess where I came from today?" was her response. 20

"Where?" 21

"All the way from New Jersey." 22

"When?" 23

"Tonight." 24

"No. You've been in the hospital for three days," I insisted. 25

"I suggest the thing to do is calm down a little bit," she replied. "Go over to the 26
house and shut the door."

Now she was years deep into the past, living in the neighborhood where she had 27
settled forty years earlier, and she had just been talking with Mrs. Hoffman, a neighbor
across the street.

"It's like Mrs. Hoffman said today: The children always wander back to where they 28
come from," she remarked.

"Mrs. Hoffman has been dead for fifteen years." 29

"Russ got married today," she replied. 30

"I got married in 1950," I said, which was the fact. 31

"The house is unlocked," she said. 32

So it went until a doctor came by to give one of those oral quizzes that medical men 33
apply in such cases. She failed catastrophically, giving wrong answers or none at all to
"What day is this?" "Do you know where you are?" "How old are you?" and so on.
Then, a surprise.

"When is your birthday?" he asked. 34

"November 5, 1897," she said. Correct. Absolutely correct. 35

"How do you remember that?" the doctor asked. 36

"Because I was born on Guy Fawkes Day," she said. 37

"Guy Fawkes?" asked the doctor, "Who is Guy Fawkes?" 38

She replied with a rhyme I had heard her recite time and again over the years when 39
the subject of her birth date arose:

"Please to remember the Fifth of November,
Gunpowder treason and plot.
I see no reason why gunpowder treason
Should ever be forgot."

Then she glared at this young doctor so ill informed about Guy Fawkes's failed scheme
to blow King James off his throne with barrels of gunpowder in 1605. She had been a
schoolteacher, after all, and knew how to glare at a dolt. "You may know a lot about
medicine, but you obviously don't know any history," she said. Having told him exactly
what was on her mind, she left us again.

The doctors diagnosed a hopeless senility. Not unusual, they said. ''Hardening of the 40
arteries'' was the explanation for laymen. I thought it was more complicated than that.
For ten years or more the ferocity with which she had once attacked life had been turning
to a rage against the weakness, the boredom, and the absence of love that too much age
had brought her. Now, after the last bad fall, she seemed to have broken chains that
imprisoned her in a life she had come to hate and to return to a time inhabited by people
who loved her, a time in which she was needed. Gradually I understood. It was the first
time in years I had seen her happy.

She had written a letter three years earlier which explained more than ''hardening 41
of the arteries.'' I had gone down from New York to Baltimore, where she lived, for one
of my infrequent visits and, afterwards, had written her with some banal advice to look
for the silver lining, to count her blessings instead of burdening others with her miseries.
I suppose what it really amounted to was a threat that if she was not more cheerful during
my visits I would not come to see her very often. Sons are capable of such letters. This
one was written out of a childish faith in the eternal strength of parents, a naive belief
that age and wear could be overcome by an effort of will, that all she needed was a good
pep talk to recharge a flagging spirit. It was such a foolish, innocent idea, but one thinks
of parents differently from other people. Other people can become frail and break, but
not parents.

She wrote back in an unusually cheery vein intended to demonstrate, I suppose, that 42
she was mending her ways. She was never a woman to apologize, but for one moment
with the pen in her hand she came very close. Referring to my visit, she wrote: ''If I
seemed unhappy to you at times—'' Here she drew back, reconsidered, and said something
quite different:

''If I seemed unhappy to you at times, I am, but there's really nothing anyone can 43
do about it, because I'm just so very tired and lonely that I'll just go to sleep and forget
it.'' She was then seventy-eight.

Now, three years later, after the last bad fall, she had managed to forget the fatigue 44
and loneliness and, in these free-wheeling excursions back through time, to recapture
happiness. I soon stopped trying to wrest her back to what I considered the real world
and tried to travel along with her on those fantastic swoops into the past. One day when
I arrived at her bedside she was radiant.

''Feeling good today,'' I said. 45

''Why shouldn't I feel good?'' she asked. ''Papa's going to take me up to Baltimore 46
on the boat today.''

At that moment she was a young girl standing on a wharf at Merry Point, Virginia, 47
waiting for the Chesapeake Bay steamer with her father, who had been dead sixty-one
years. William Howard Taft was in the White House, Europe still drowsed in the dusk
of the great century of peace, America was a young country, and the future stretched
before it in beams of crystal sunlight. ''The greatest country on God's green earth,'' her
father might have said, if I had been able to step into my mother's time machine and join
him on the wharf with the satchels packed for Baltimore.

I could imagine her there quite clearly. She was wearing a blue dress with big puffy 48
sleeves and long black stockings. There was a ribbon in her hair and a big bow tied on
the side of her head. There had been a childhood photograph in her bedroom which
showed all this, although the colors of course had been added years later by a restorer
who tinted the picture.

About her father, my grandfather, I could only guess, and indeed, about the girl on   49
the wharf with the bow in her hair, I was merely sentimentalizing. Of my mother's
childhood and her people, of their time and place, I knew very little. A world had lived
and died, and though it was part of my blood and bone I knew little more about it than
I knew of the world of the pharaohs. It was useless now to ask for help from my mother.
The orbits of her mind rarely touched present interrogators for more than a moment.

Sitting at her bedside, forever out of touch with her, I wondered about my own   50
children, and their children, and children in general, and about the disconnections between
children and parents that prevent them from knowing each other. Children rarely want to
know who their parents were before they were parents, and when age finally stirs their
curiosity there is no parent left to tell them. If a parent does lift the curtain a bit, it is
often only to stun the young with some exemplary tale of how much harder life was in
the old days.

I had been guilty of this when my children were small in the early 1960s and living   51
the affluent life. It galled me that their childhoods should be, as I thought, so easy when
my own had been, as I thought, so hard. I had developed the habit, when they complained
about the steak being overcooked or the television being cut off, of lecturing them on the
harshness of life in my day.

"In my day all we got for dinner was macaroni and cheese, and we were glad to get it."   52
"In my day we didn't have any television."   53
"In my day . . . "   54
"In my day . . . "   55

At dinner one evening a son had offended me with an inadequate report card, and   56
as I leaned back and cleared my throat to lecture, he gazed at me with an expression of
unutterable resignation and said, "Tell me how it was in your day, Dad."

I was angry with him for that, but angrier with myself for having become one of   57
those ancient bores whose highly selective memories of the past become transparently
dishonest even to small children. I tried to break the habit, but must have failed. A few
years later my son was referring to me when I was out of earshot as "the old-timer."
Between us there was a dispute about time. He looked upon the time that had been my
future in a disturbing way. My future was his past, and being young, he was indifferent
to the past.

As I hovered over my mother's bed listening for muffled signals from her childhood,   58
I realized that this same dispute had existed between her and me. When she was young,
with life ahead of her, I had been her future and resented it. Instinctively, I wanted to
break free, cease being a creature defined by her time, consign her future to the past, and
create my own. Well, I had finally done that, and then with my own children I had seen
my exciting future become their boring past.

These hopeless end-of-line visits with my mother made me wish I had not thrown   59
off my own past so carelessly. We all come from the past, and children ought to know
what it was that went into their making, to know that life is a braided cord of humanity
stretching up from time long gone, and that it cannot be defined by the span of a single
journey from diaper to shroud.

■   **Reading Comprehension Questions**

1. The word *formidable* in "And so she was. A formidable woman. Determined to speak her mind, determined to have her way, determined to bend those who opposed her" (paragraph 14) means
   a. gentle.
   b. forgetful.
   c. difficult and demanding.
   d. mean and violent.

2. The word *dolt* in "she had been a schoolteacher . . . and knew how to glare at a dolt. '. . . you obviously don't know any history,' she said" (paragraph 39) means
   a. stupid person.
   b. spot on the wall.
   c. genius.
   d. son.

3. Which of the following would be a good alternative title for this selection?
   a. Bringing Up Children
   b. Losing Touch with Our Past
   c. A Hopeless Senility
   d. A Woman's Life

4. Which sentence best expresses the main idea of the selection?
   a. A bad fall led to the mental deterioration of the author's mother.
   b. Aging parents are a problem for adult children.
   c. Children ought to know their family's past and know that they are connected to a series of generations.
   d. There is often conflict within a family.

5. *True or false?* _____ Baker's mother had been unhappy before her senility set in.

6. Toward the end of her life, Baker's mother
   a. remained physically strong.
   b. revealed family secrets to the author.
   c. mentally wandered through her past.
   d. refused to go to the hospital.

7. Eventually, Baker decided
   a. to stop visiting his mother.
   b. to move to Baltimore.
   c. that he was right to lecture his children on the harshness of life in his day.
   d. to try to join his mother on her mental journeys to the past.

8. From the reading, we can conclude that Baker's mother
   a. would recover.
   b. believed she was really living the events she was remembering.
   c. actually predicted the day of her own funeral.
   d. had been unhappy most of her life.

9. From the details Baker selects to describe his mother, we can conclude that his description of her is
   a. overly sentimental.
   b. without insight.
   c. realistic.
   d. totally unsympathetic.

10. *True or false?* _____ The author implies that parents and children tend to understand each other well.

■ **Discussion Questions**

About Content

1. In both his own words and those of his mother, the author reveals why she was unhappy during the last years of her life. What are the reasons either stated or suggested by Baker for her unhappiness?

2. When his mother's mind began to wander, Baker's first impulse was to ''argue her back to reality.'' Later he instead ''tried to travel along with her on those fantastic swoops into the past.'' What does the reading suggest about why he at first wanted to bring his mother back to reality? And why did he change his mind?

3. Does Baker believe he has been a good son to his mother? A good father to his children? Do you? Do you feel primarily sympathetic or critical toward Baker?

About Structure

4. The author's thesis is a general point that he derives from his personal family experiences. Where does he first mention that thesis? Why might he have chosen to state his thesis at that point in the piece?

About Style and Tone

5. Baker uses repetition and parallel wording in three places (paragraph 14, paragraph 15, and paragraphs 52–55). Find these instances of repetition and parallel wording. What does Baker achieve with these stylistic elements?

6. Baker paints a vivid, unsentimental picture of his mother. His description is of a woman who could be difficult, even unlikable. Write below three adjectives he uses about his mother that contribute to this image:

_____   _____   _____

7. The tone of paragraph 51 can be described as
   a. tolerant.
   b. regretful.
   c. unsure.
   d. indignant.

■ **Writing Assignments**

Assignment 1

Is there an elderly person in your life of whom you could say, "When I grow old, I hope I do it just like him, or her?" Write an essay describing that person, using descriptions and anecdotes to make your points dramatically and colorfully. It will be helpful to review the explanation of descriptive essays on page 128.

Assignment 2

Baker provides us with a sharp picture of his mother at several stages of her life. Choose a member of your own family and write about him or her at one particular time of life. Your essay might be about "my grandfather in his eighties," "my sister at fifteen," or "my mother after her children had all left home." Select the most significant details you can to create a vivid word portrait of that person. Incorporate one or more of these elements used by Baker:

Physical description
Anecdotes
Dialogue
First-person point of view
Repetition for emphasis and dramatic effect
Stating the thesis *after* providing the evidence

Assignment 3

Crises such as a family member's illness or death have significant effects, as they did in Baker's case. Write an essay about a crisis in your family's life in which you explore the effects the crisis had on individual family members, on the family as a unit, or on both. Common family crises include illness, death, loss of a job, and disasters such as fires, floods, and earthquakes.

An example of a thesis statement for this essay is: ''My grandfather's death was a significant experience for me in several ways.'' Support for this thesis would be a few ways in which the experience was significant: for example, seeing a grieving parent in a different light—as a child, not a parent; personally realizing the finality of death; and learning significant pieces of family history from the family's reminiscing about the grandfather.

Here are two more possible thesis statements for this assignment:

My father's heart disease has changed our family's lifestyle.

While having our house burn down was a terrible event, it had several surprisingly positive effects.

Alternatively, you can write about the influence of an important *positive* event in your family's life, perhaps a wedding or a birth.

OBSERVING OTHERS

On the Meaning of Plumbing and Poverty

Melanie Scheller

It's bad enough that the poor must suffer from material deprivation—inadequate food, clothing, housing, and health services.   But a poverty of pride accompanies the material inadequacies.   No one can know just what this means unless he or she has experienced it, and Melanie Scheller has.   She knows all too well how the psychological effects last long after one has overcome the material problems of poverty.   In this essay, plumbing represents for Scheller both the physical and the psychological pain of being poor in this rich country.

Several years ago I spent some time as a volunteer on the geriatric ward of a psychiatric hospital. I was fascinated by the behavior of one of the patients, an elderly woman who shuffled at regular intervals to the bathroom, where she methodically flushed the toilet. Again and again she carried out her sacred mission as if summoned by some supernatural force, until the flush of the toilet became a rhythmic counterpoint for the ward's activity. If someone blocked her path or if, God forbid, the bathroom was in use when she reached it, she became agitated and confused. 1

Obviously, that elderly patient was a sick woman. And yet I felt a certain kinship with her, for I too have suffered from an obsession with toilets. I spent much of my childhood living in houses without indoor plumbing, and while I don't feel compelled to flush a toilet at regular intervals, I sometimes feel that toilets, or the lack thereof, have shaped my identity in ways that are painful to admit. 2

I'm not a child of the Depression, but I grew up in an area of the South that had   3
changed little since the days of the New Deal. My mother was a widow with six children
to support, not an easy task under any circumstances, but especially difficult in rural
North Carolina during the 1960s. To her credit, we were never seriously in danger of
going hungry. Our vegetable garden kept us stocked with tomatoes and string beans. We
kept a few chickens and sometimes a cow. Blackberries were free for the picking in the
fields nearby. Neighbors did their good Christian duty by bringing us donations of fresh
fruit and candy at Christmastime. But a roof over our heads—that wasn't so easily
improvised.

Like rural Southern gypsies, we moved from one dilapidated Southern farmhouse to   4
another in a constant search for a decent place to live. Sometimes we moved when the
rent increased beyond the 30 or 40 dollars my mother could afford. Or the house burned
down, not an unusual occurrence in substandard housing. One year when we were gathered
together for Thanksgiving dinner, a stranger walked in without knocking and announced
that we were being evicted. The house had been sold without our knowledge and the new
owner wanted to start remodeling immediately. We tried to finish our meal with an attitude
of thanksgiving while he worked around us with his tape measure.

Usually we rented from farm families who'd moved from the old home place to one   5
of the brick boxes that are now the standard in rural Southern architecture. The old
farmhouse wasn't worth fixing up with a septic tank and flush toilet, but it was good
enough to rent for a few dollars a month to families like mine. The idea of tenants' rights
hadn't trickled down yet from the far reaches of the liberal North. It never occurred to
us to demand improvements in the facilities. The ethic of the land said we should take
what we could get and be grateful for it.

Without indoor plumbing, getting clean is a tiring and time-consuming ritual. At one   6
point I lived in a five-room house with six or more people, all of whom congregated in
the one heated room to eat, do homework, watch television, dress and undress, argue,
wash dishes. During cold weather we dragged mattresses from the unheated rooms and
slept huddled together on the floor by the woodstove. For my bathing routine, I first
pinned a sheet to a piece of twine strung across the kitchen. That gave me some degree
of privacy from the six other people in the room. At that time our house had an indoor
cold-water faucet, from which I filled a pot of water to heat on the kitchen stove. It took
several pots of hot water to fill the metal washtub we used.

Since I was a teenager and prone to sulkiness if I didn't get special treatment, I got   7
to take the first bath while the water was still clean. The others used the water I left
behind, freshened up with hot water from the pot on the stove. Then the tub had to be
dragged to the door and the bath water dumped outside. I longed to be like the woman
in the Calgon bath oil commercials, luxuriating in a marble tub full of scented water with
bubbles piled high and stacks of thick, clean towels nearby.

People raised in the land of the bath-and-a-half may wonder why I make such a fuss   8
about plumbing. Maybe they spent a year in the Peace Corps, or they back-packed across
India, or they worked at a summer camp and, gosh, using a latrine isn't all that bad. And

of course it's *not* that bad. Not when you can catch the next plane out of the country, or pick up your duffel bag and head for home, or call mom and dad to come and get you when things get too tedious. A sojourn in a Third World country, where everyone shares the same primitive facilities, may cause some temporary discomfort, but the experience is soon converted into amusing anecdotes for cocktail-party conversation. It doesn't corrode your self-esteem with a sense of shame the way a childhood spent in chronic unrelenting poverty can.

In the South of my childhood, not having indoor plumbing was the indelible mark 9 of poor white trash. The phrase ''so poor they didn't have a pot to piss in'' said it all. Poor white trash were viciously stereotyped, and never more viciously than on the playground. White-trash children had cooties—everybody knew that. They had ringworm and pinkeye—don't get near them or you might catch it. They picked their noses. They messed in their pants. If a white-trash child made the mistake of catching a softball during recess, the other children made an elaborate show of wiping it clean before they would touch it.

Once a story circulated at school about a family whose infant daughter had fallen 10 into the ''slop jar'' and drowned. When I saw the smirks and heard the laughter with which the story was told, I felt sick and afraid in the pit of my stomach. A little girl had died, but people were laughing. What had she done to deserve that laughter? I could only assume that using a chamber pot was something so disgusting, so shameful, that it made a person less than human.

My family was visibly and undeniably poor. My clothes were obviously hand-me- 11 downs. I got free lunches at school. I went to the health department for immunizations. Surely it was equally obvious that we didn't have a flush toilet. But like an alcoholic who believes no one will know he has a problem as long as he doesn't drink in public, I convinced myself that no one knew my family's little secret. It was a form of denial that would color my relationships with the outside world for years to come.

Having a friend from school spend the night at my house was out of the question. 12 Better to be friendless than to have my classmates know my shameful secret. Home visits from teachers or ministers left me in a dither of anticipatory anxiety. As they chattered on and on with Southern small talk about tomato plants and relish recipes, I sat on the edge of my seat, tensed against the dreaded words, ''May I use your bathroom, please?'' When I began dating in high school, I'd lie in wait behind the front door, ready to dash out as soon as my date pulled in the driveway, never giving him a chance to hear the call of nature while on our property.

With the help of a scholarship I was able to go away to college, where I could choose 13 from dozens of dormitory toilets and take as many hot showers as I wanted, but I could never openly express my joy in using the facilities. My roommates, each a pampered only child from a well-to-do family, whined and complained about having to share a bathroom. I knew that if I expressed delight in simply having a bathroom, I would immediately be labeled as a hick. The need to conceal my real self by stifling my emotions created a barrier around me and I spent my college years in a vacuum of isolation.

Almost 20 years have passed since I first tried to leave my family's chamber pot 14
behind. For many of those years it followed behind me—the ghost of chamber pots past—
clanging and banging and threatening to spill its humiliating contents at any moment. I
was convinced that everyone could see it, could smell it even. No college degree or job
title seemed capable of banishing it.

If finances had permitted, I might have become an Elvis Presley or a Tammy Faye 15
Bakker, easing the pain of remembered poverty with gold-plated bathtub fixtures and
leopard-skinned toilet seats. I feel blessed that gradually, ever so gradually, the shame of
poverty has begun to fade. The pleasures of the present now take priority over where a
long-ago bowel movement did or did not take place. But for many Southerners, chamber
pots and outhouses are more than just memories.

In North Carolina alone, 200,000 people still live without indoor plumbing. People 16
who haul their drinking water home from a neighbor's house or catch rainwater in barrels.
People who can't wash their hands before handling food, the way restaurant employees
are required by state law to do. People who sneak into public restrooms every day to
wash, shave, and brush their teeth before going to work or to school. People who sacrifice
their dignity and self-respect when forced to choose between going homeless and going
to an outhouse. People whose children think they deserve the conditions in which they
live and hold their heads low to hide the shame. But they're not the ones who should
feel ashamed. No, they're not the ones who should feel ashamed.

■ **Reading Comprehension Questions**

1. The word *corrode* in "A sojourn in a Third World country, where everyone
   shares the same primitive facilities, may cause some temporary discomfort,
   but . . . It doesn't corrode your self-esteem with a sense of shame the way a
   childhood spent in . . . poverty can" (paragraph 8) means
   a. build up.
   b. take into account.
   c. imitate.
   d. wear away.

2. The word *stifling* in "I knew that if I expressed delight in simply having a
   bathroom, I would immediately be labeled as a hick. The need to conceal my
   real self by stifling my emotions created a barrier around me" (paragraph
   13) means
   a. showing.
   b. writing about.
   c. learning about.
   d. holding back.

3. Which of the following would be a good alternative title for this selection?
   a. Fighting Poverty with Vegetable Gardens
   b. The Myth of White Trash
   c. How Society Should Fight Poverty
   d. The Shame of Poverty

4. Which sentence best expresses the main idea of the selection?
   a. Many poor people in the South do not have indoor plumbing.
   b. Going to college changed the author's life.
   c. While the poor feel shame, the shame is really not theirs.
   d. As a child, the author was ashamed of not having indoor plumbing.

5. The author grew up
   a. moving from one run-down farmhouse to another.
   b. during the Depression.
   c. in a small family.
   d. always hungry.

6. *True or false?* _____ As a child, the author didn't care if people knew that she was poor.

7. The author didn't have
   a. enough food to eat.
   b. the proper immunizations.
   c. any dates in high school.
   d. the use of an indoor bathroom until she went away to college.

8. *True or false?* _____ We can conclude from the selection that in order to maintain an appearance of dignity as a child and as a college student, Scheller could not truly be herself among her friends.

9. The author implies that she
   a. is angry that people are still forced to live without indoor plumbing.
   b. is a social worker.
   c. no longer lives in the South.
   d. now lives in a luxurious home.

10. The author implies that those who should feel ashamed about poverty are
    a. poor children.
    b. the homeless.
    c. people who have temporarily used a latrine and feel it's not so bad.
    d. those who look down on the poor and those who allow them to live so poorly.

■ **Discussion Questions**

About Content

1. What evidence does Scheller give us to support her statement that a childhood of poverty "corrodes your self-esteem with a sense of shame"?

2. In the final line in her essay, Scheller writes of poor children, "No, they're not the ones who should feel ashamed." Of the other persons Scheller mentions in the reading, who does she seem to believe *should* feel ashamed? Who else might she believe should feel ashamed?

3. Judging from the selection, how does society's attitude toward the poor influence their feelings about themselves? For example, consider the attitudes Scheller describes toward "poor white trash" and what she supposes her college roommates' attitudes toward her background would be.

About Structure

4. What method of introduction does Scheller use in this essay?
   a. Quotation
   b. Incident or brief story
   c. Explaining the importance of the topic

5. What change-of-direction signal is used in paragraph 11?

   _____

6. Scheller uses many vivid details to help us see and feel the shame of poverty. She mentions, for example, that if a poor child caught a softball during recess, the other children would make "an elaborate show of wiping it clean before they would touch it." What are two details that you consider very effective in showing us how deeply she felt her shame?

   _____

   _____

About Style and Tone

7. In the last paragraph of her essay, Scheller repeats herself. What do you think this adds to her conclusion?

■ **Writing Assignments**

Assignment 1

At Melanie Scheller's childhood school, "poor white trash" without indoor plumbing were despised and made fun of. Were there children at your school who were looked down upon by their classmates? Write an essay describing the following:

   Why these children were disliked
   How their classmates acted toward them
   What effect being so disliked seemed to have on the children

Assignment 2

How (if at all) should our society make life easier for the poor? Write an essay describing ways in which you feel we should help the poor. Your topic sentence might be something like this: ''Society should help the poor through both government and private efforts.'' Following are some possibilities for topic sentences of supporting paragraphs for this essay.

> State governments must legislate minimum standards in rental property.
>
> The media must educate the public about the poor.
>
> More public works projects should be established to provide work and income to the poor while accomplishing needed work.
>
> Government and charities must find more and better ways of giving needed products and service to the poor without shaming them.

Assignment 3

In ''Shame'' (pages 515–518), Dick Gregory also discusses childhood feelings of shame because of poverty. Compare Gregory's and Scheller's feelings of shame and what each of them suggests about how society and individuals treat the poor. In addition, compare Gregory's and Scheller's references to the shame others should feel because of how they treat the poor.

Your thesis statement might be one of the following:

- There are some marked similarities in Melanie Scheller's and Dick Gregory's memories of their childhood experiences of poverty.
- There are both similarities and differences in Melanie Scheller's and Dick Gregory's treatments of their childhood experiences of poverty.

A Kite

James Herndon

In the following selection from James Herndon's book *How to Survive in Your Native Land*, you'll meet a truly unforgettable student named Piston. Piston outrages the administration, baffles teachers, and angers his fellow students. But Piston's most rebellious act is building a monster and unleashing it on the entire school. You'll see in this selection how Piston's creation lives only for a moment but has a profound impact on all who experience it.

I might as well begin with Piston. Piston was, as a matter of description, a redheaded   1
medium-sized chubby eighth-grader; his definitive characteristic was, however, stubbornness. Without going into a lot of detail, it became clear right away that what Piston didn't
want to do, Piston didn't do; what Piston did want to do, Piston did.

It really wasn't much of a problem. Piston wanted mainly to paint, draw monsters,   2
scratch designs on mimeograph blanks and print them up, write an occasional horror
story—some kids referred to him as The Ghoul—and when he didn't want to do any of
those, he wanted to roam the halls and on occasion (we heard) investigate the girls' bathrooms.

We had minor confrontations. Once I wanted everyone to sit down and listen to what   3
I had to say—something about the way they had been acting in the halls. I was letting
them come and go freely and it was up to them (I planned to point out) not to raise hell
so that I had to hear about it from other teachers. Sitting down was the issue—I was
determined everyone was going to do it first, then I'd talk. Piston remained standing. I
reordered. He paid no attention. I pointed out that I was talking to him. He indicated he
heard me. I inquired then why in hell didn't he sit down. He said he didn't want to. I
said I did want him to. He said that didn't matter to him. I said do it anyway. He said
why? I said because I said so. He said he wouldn't. I said Look I want you to sit down
and listen to what I'm going to say. He said he *was* listening. I'll listen but I won't sit down.

Well, that's the way it goes sometimes in schools. You as teacher become obsessed   4
with an issue—I was the injured party, conferring, as usual, unheard-of freedoms, and
here they were as usual taking advantage. It ain't pleasant coming in the teachers' room
for coffee and having to hear somebody say that so-and-so and so-and-so from *your* class
were out in the halls *without a pass* and *making faces* and *giving the finger* to kids in *my*
class during the most *important* part of *my* lesson about *Egypt*—and you ought to be
allowed your tendentious speech, and most everyone will allow it, sit down for it, but
occasionally someone wises you up by refusing to submit where it isn't necessary. But
anyway, it's not the present point, which is really only Piston's stubbornness. Another
kid told me that when Piston's father got mad at him and punished him, as Piston thought,
unjustly (one cannot imagine Piston considering any punishment just), Piston got up in
the middle of the night, went into the garage and revenged himself on his father's car.
Once he took out and threw away two spark plugs. Another time he managed to remove
all the door handles. You get a nice picture of Piston sitting quiet all evening long brooding
about not being allowed to watch some favorite science-fiction program because he'd
brought home a note about unsatisfactory this-or-that at school, sitting there unresponding
and impassive, and then his father getting up in the morning to go to work, perhaps in a
hurry or not feeling well, trying to start the car or looking at the locked doors and rolled
up windows and the places where the door handles had been pried off. How did any of
us get into this? we ought to be asking ourselves.

It was probably Frank Ramirez who brought up the idea of making kites. Frank was   5
a teacher, not a kid; we were working together. All the kids were making them suddenly;
they scrounged the schoolrooms and maddened the shop teachers looking for suitable
lengths of wood. Frank brought in fancy paper. The kites were wonderful. Naturally we
plunged down to the lower field to fly them. They flew well, or badly, or not at all,

crashed and were broken, sailed away, got caught in overhead wires, the kids ran and yelled and cried and accused one another. It went on for several days and of course we heard a lot about classes overlooking the lower field being interrupted in the most important parts of the lessons about Egypt, for after all those kids wanted to know why they couldn't be flying kites instead of having Egypt, and Frank and I were cocky enough to state aloud that indeed we also wondered why they couldn't be flying kites too, after all who was stopping them? Piston, up in Room 45, was preparing our comeuppance.

Piston had been making a kite for several days. He continued making it while others 6 were flying theirs. It had only one definitive characteristic too; it was huge. The cross-pieces were 1 × 2 boards. The covering was heavy butcher paper, made heavier by three coats of poster paint in monstrous designs. The cord was clothesline rope. It was twenty feet long. Piston was finished with his kite about the time when everyone else had finished with the whole business of making and flying kites and had settled down in the room anticipating a couple of weeks of doing nothing, resting up for some future adventure. Piston produced his finished product, which was universally acclaimed a masterpiece. It was. Pictorially monstrous as usual, its *size,* its heavy *boards,* its *rope,* aroused a certain amount of real awe. Piston was really something else, we could see that. None of us had had such a concept.

But when Piston announced he was prepared to fly it, we all hooted, relieved. It was 7 easier to have Piston-the-nut back again than to put up with Piston-the-genius-artist. No one had thought of it as something to fly—only as something to look at and admire. In any case, it clearly would not fly. It was too big, too heavy, too awkward, unbalanced, there wasn't enough wind, you couldn't run with it—we had lots of reasons. Stubborn Piston hauled it down to the field past amazed windows of classbound kids ignoring Egypt once again to goggle and exclaim. Down on the grass we all gathered around the inert monster. If nothing else, Frank and I thought, Piston had prepared a real scene, something memorable—David being drawn through the streets of Florence.

The kite flew. Piston had prepared no great scene. Instead he had (I think) commanded 8 the monster kite to fly. So it flew. Of course it flew. Two of the biggest and strongest boys were persuaded to run with the kite; Piston ran with the rope. Everyone participated in what was believed to be a charade. We would act as if we thought the kite would fly. It would be in itself a gas. They ran; he pulled. The kite lumbered into the air, where it stayed aloft menacingly for perhaps four or five minutes. Then it dove, or rather just fell like a stone (like an avalanche!), with a crash. When it crashed, everyone was seized with a madness and rushed to the kite, jumped on it, stomped it, tore it . . . all except Frank and I, and we wanted to. (Great difficulties at that very moment were angrily reported to us later by teachers of Egypt classes.)

The kite was saved, though. Piston repaired and repapered it, repainted it. Frank and 9 I hung it in the room and admired it, and forgot it. But next week, Lou, the principal, approached us at lunchtime with great excitement. What about Piston? he wanted to know, and what about that Kite? Whose idea . . . ? and so on. His concern was not Egypt, but the fact that Piston and others had taken it out to the playground during lunch and flown it again. So? So! screamed Lou, the goddamn thing was a menace! It weighed a hundred pounds. It fell down and damn near killed thirty or forty seventh-grade girls, and their mothers were calling him up and was this Piston crazy or were we, or what? And he wanted it made clear that flying that kite was out! O-U-T, out! He had enough troubles with our goddamn class running around all over the place and other teachers griping and smoking in the bathrooms and parents complaining they weren't learning nothing and he'd always supported us but he couldn't have that giant kite. Couldn't have it! We soothed him, agreeing to tell Piston in no uncertain terms and so on. We walked outside with Lou, who had calmed down and had begun admiring the kite in retrospect, realizing that there was no way such a creation could fly (*aerodynamically speaking,* he said), and yet it did fly and this Piston or whatever his name was must be a pretty exceptional kid, and we were agreeing and realizing what a great guy Lou was for a principal even if, we reminded him, he had goofed up our schedule for this marvelous class we'd planned which had resulted in that extraordinary kite and other grand exploits, along with, we admitted, a certain amount of difficulty for him, Lou, and how well he'd handled it and supported us and . . . when Lou suddenly screamed Aarrghhh! and fell back. I thought he'd been stung by a bee—we'd had a lot of bees that year, which also interrupted Egypt quite a bit, flying in the classroom where kids could scream with fake or real fear or try to kill them by throwing objects, often Egypt books, at them, exempt from retribution by the claim that they were just trying to save some *allergic kid* from *death*—but then he screamed There it is again! and pointed up, and there was The Monster from Outer Space, seventy-five feet up, plunging and wheeling and lurching through the thin air, a ton of boards and heavy paper and ghouls and toothy vampires leering down at an amazed lunchtime populace of little seventh-grade girls, all with mothers and phones. Jesus Christ, look out! yelled Lou, and rushed for the playground, just as the giant came hurtling down like a dead flying mountain. It crashed; seventh-grade girls scattered. (Their mothers reached for the phones.) Kids rushed from every direction and hurled themselves at the kite. They stomped it and tore it and killed it in wildest glee. They lynched it and murdered it and executed it and mercy-killed it and put it out of its misery, and when it was over and Lou had everyone pulled off the scattered corpse of the kite and sitting down on benches and shut up there was nothing left of it but bits and pieces of painted butcher paper and 1 × 2 boards and clothesline rope.

■ **Reading Comprehension Questions**

1. The word *definitive* in "It had only one definitive characteristic" (paragraph 6) means
   a. hidden.
   b. puzzling.
   c. ridiculous.
   d. essential.

2. The word *retribution* in "exempt from retribution" (paragraph 9) means
   a. confusion.
   b. enjoyment.
   c. punishment.
   d. repetition.

3. Which of the following would be a good alternative title for this selection?
    a. Piston and His Monster Kite
    b. Chaos in the Classroom
    c. Different Types of Teachers
    d. Stubbornness in Students
4. Which sentence best expresses the main idea of the selection?
    a. Piston's kite was the biggest one made in the class.
    b. The author and the ''Egypt'' teachers had different teaching methods.
    c. Piston's falling kites threatened children's lives.
    d. Piston represented a threat to established school practices.

5. *True or false?* _____ At one point, the author himself wanted to destroy Piston's kite.
6. When people saw the kite Piston had made, they
    a. felt a little awed by it.
    b. thought it had a chance of flying.
    c. were frightened by it.
    d. were proud of Piston.
7. According to the author, Piston's main characteristic was
    a. originality.
    b. disobedience.
    c. stubbornness.
    d. intelligence.
8. We can conclude that the other children attacked Piston's kite because
    a. the kite was ugly.
    b. their teachers wanted them to.
    c. Piston's behavior confused and angered them.
    d. they wanted to disturb the ''Egypt'' teachers.
9. From the selection we can conclude that
    a. the author was not an effective teacher.
    b. the author believes that education should involve more than ''Egypt'' classes.
    c. most students preferred ''Egypt'' classes to making kites.
    d. the author would rather have taught ''Egypt'' classes.
10. From the selection we can conclude that
    a. the students in the ''Egypt'' classes were getting a better education.
    b. the principal would have liked to fire the author and his friend Frank Ramirez.
    c. the other teachers began to adopt the author's methods.
    d. the other teachers disapproved of the author's methods.

■ **Discussion Questions**

About Content

1. In what ways is Piston stubborn? Give examples from the reading selection.
2. Why did the students want to wreck the kite? What might the kite represent?
3. What seems to be Herndon's attitude toward Piston?

About Structure

4. What synonym for *kite* is used in paragraph 7?
5. In paragraph 3, what do the pronouns *they* and *them* refer to?

About Style and Tone

6. Why does Herndon refer to lessons about Egypt so often? Since it would be highly unlikely that all the other classes in Herndon's school were studying Egypt, Herndon is probably using Egypt as a symbol—something that stands for something else. What might Egypt stand for?
7. The kite is obviously a symbol as well. What is the kite a symbol of? In what ways does the kite reflect Piston's personality?

■ **Writing Assignments**

Assignment 1

Write an essay in which you present three reasons to support *either* of the following thesis statements:

■ Piston would be an asset to any school.
■ Piston would be a detriment to any school.

If you choose the first statement, think of several ways in which Piston would be good for a school. Here are possible topic sentences for such an essay. (You might use some of them or think of your own.)

> Piston, first of all, would make teachers question some of their more meaningless rules and regulations.
>
> In addition, Piston might inspire students with his originality and ambition.
>
> Finally, Piston would teach other students to respect people who are ''different.''

You should support each of your reasons why Piston would be an asset to a school with examples drawn from ''A Kite'' as well as with ideas based on your own understanding of Piston's personality.

If you choose the second statement, think of reasons why Piston would be a bad student for a school to have. Again, here are possible topic sentences for this kind of essay:

> For one thing, Piston would disrupt all his classes and prevent other students from learning.
>
> Also, Piston might encourage other students to misbehave.
>
> Worst of all, Piston might endanger people's lives.

As before, support your reasons with details and examples from ''A Kite'' and ideas based on your own understanding of Piston.

Assignment 2

James Herndon obviously considered Piston one of the most unforgettable characters he had ever met. Whom do you know, or whom have you known at some time in your life, who is equally unforgettable—or just as much of a ''character'' as Piston? In an introductory paragraph, describe exactly who the person is and how long you have known him or her. Also, express in your thesis exactly what qualities make this person so vivid for you. (If Herndon had used a thesis statement, he might have said, ''One of my eighth-grade students is the most stubborn, vengeful, and daring person I have ever known.'') Then support your reasons by giving specific examples of the character's words and actions. Provide the details needed for your readers to see for themselves why that person is so colorful and special.

Assignment 3

Piston was an unusual person, but so was his teacher. Why was Herndon an unusual kind of schoolteacher? Think of several reasons and develop each in a separate paragraph. Alternatively, compare or contrast Herndon with some teacher you know.

Brett Hauser:
Supermarket Box Boy

Studs Terkel

For his book *Working,* Studs Terkel interviewed dozens of people about their jobs—what they did, what they liked about their jobs, what made them unhappy about their work. In this selection, a teenage box boy at a supermarket (a person who packs the groceries and often carries them out to the customer's car) talks about his job.   You may never have been a box boy, but you will understand some of his complaints about his work: the impersonal atmosphere, the concern with trivial details, and the office politics.

He is seventeen. He had worked as a box boy at a supermarket in a middle-class suburb on the outskirts of Los Angeles. "People come to the counter and you put things in their bags for them. And carry things to their cars. It was a grind."   1

You have to be terribly subservient to people: "Ma'am, can I take your bag?" "Can I do this?" It was at a time when the grape strikers were passing out leaflets. They were very respectful people. People'd come into the check stand, they'd say, "I just bought grapes for the first time because of those idiots outside." I had to put their grapes in the bag and thank them for coming and take them outside to the car. Being subservient made me very resentful.   2

It's one of a chain of supermarkets. They're huge complexes with bakeries in them and canned music over those loudspeakers—Muzak. So people would relax while they shopped. They played selections from *Hair.* They'd play "Guantanamera," the Cuban Revolution song. They had *Soul on Ice,* the Cleaver book, on sale. They had everything dressed up and very nice. People wouldn't pay any attention to the music. They'd go shopping and hit their kids and talk about those idiots passing out anti-grape petitions.   3

Everything looks fresh and nice. You're not aware that in the back room it stinks and there's crates all over the place and the walls are messed up. There's graffiti and people are swearing and yelling at each other. You walk through the door, the music starts playing, and everything is pretty. You talk in hushed tones and are very respectful.   4

You wear a badge with your name on it. I once met someone I knew years ago. I remembered his name and said, "Mr. Castle, how are you?" We talked about this and that. As he left, he said, "It was nice talking to you, Brett." I felt great, he remembered me. Then I looked down at my name plate. Oh shit. He didn't remember me at all, he just read the name plate. I wish I put "Irving" down on my name plate. If he'd have said, "Oh yes, Irving, how could I forget you . . . ?" I'd have been ready for him. There's nothing personal here.   5

You have to be very respectful to everyone—to the customers, to the manager, to the checkers. There's a sign on the cash register that says: Smile at the customer. Say hello to the customer. It's assumed if you're a box boy, you're really there 'cause you want to be a manager some day. So you learn all the little things you have absolutely no interest in learning. 6

The big thing there is to be an assistant manager and eventually manager. The male checkers had dreams of being manager, too. It was like an internship. They enjoyed watching how the milk was packed. Each manager had his own domain. There was the ice cream manager, the grocery manager, the dairy case manager. . . . They had a sign in the back: Be good to your job and your job will be good to you. So you take an overriding concern on how the ice cream is packed. You just die if something falls off a shelf. I saw so much crap there I just couldn't take. There was a black boy, an Oriental box boy, and a kid who had a Texas drawl. They needed the job to subsist. I guess I had the luxury to hate it and quit. 7

When I first started there, the manager said, "Cut your hair. Come in a white shirt, black shoes, a tie. Be here on time." You get there, but he isn't there. I just didn't know what to do. The checker turns around and says, "You new? What's your name?" "Brett." "I'm Peggy." And that's all they say and they keep throwing this down to you. They'll say, "Don't put it in that, put it in there." But they wouldn't help you. 8

You had to keep your apron clean. You couldn't lean back on the railings. You couldn't talk to the checkers. You couldn't accept tips. Okay, I'm outside and I put it in the car. For a lot of people, the natural reaction is to take a quarter and give it to me. I'd say, "I'm sorry, I can't." They'd get offended. When you give someone a tip, you're sort of suave. You take a quarter and you put it in their palm and you expect them to say, "Oh, thanks a lot." When you say, "I'm sorry, I can't," they feel a little put down. They say, "No one will know." And they put it in your pocket. You say, "I really can't." It gets to a point where you have to do physical violence to a person to avoid being tipped. It was not consistent with the store's philosophy of being cordial. Accepting tips was a cordial thing and made the customer feel good. I just couldn't understand the incongruity. One lady actually put it in my pocket, got in the car, and drove away. I would have had to throw the quarter at her or eaten it or something. 9

When it got slow, the checkers would talk about funny things that happened. About Us and Them. Us being the people who worked there, Them being the stupid fools who didn't know where anything was—just came through and messed everything up and shopped. We serve them but we don't like them. We know where everything is. We know what time the market closes and they don't. We know what you do with coupons and they don't. There was a camaraderie of sorts. It wasn't healthy, though. It was a put-down of the others. 10

There was this one checker who was absolutely vicious. He took great delight in making every little problem into a major crisis from which he had to emerge victorious. A customer would give him a coupon. He'd say, "You were supposed to give me that at the beginning." She'd say, "Oh, I'm sorry." He'd say, "Now I gotta open the cash register and go through the whole thing. Madam, I don't watch out for every customer. I can't manage your life." A put-down. 11

It never bothered me when I would put something in the bag wrong. In the general 12
scheme of things, in the large questions of the universe, putting a can of dog food in the
bag wrong is not of great consequence. For them it was.

There were a few checkers who were nice. There was one that was incredibly sad. 13
She could be unpleasant at times, but she talked to everybody. She was one of the few
people who genuinely wanted to talk to people. She was saying how she wanted to go
to school and take courses so she could get teaching credit. Someone asked her, "Why
don't you?" She said, "I have to work here. My hours are wrong. I'd have to get my
hours changed." They said, "Why don't you?" She's worked there for years. She had
seniority. She said, "Jim won't let me." Jim was the manager. He didn't give a damn.
She wanted to go to school, to teach, but she can't because every day she's got to go
back to the supermarket and load groceries. Yet she wasn't bitter. If she died a checker
and never enriched her life, that was okay, because those were her hours.

She was extreme in her unpleasantness and her consideration. Once I dropped some 14
grape juice and she was squawking like a bird. I came back and mopped it up. She kept
saying to me, "Don't worry about it. It happens to all of us." She'd say to the customers,
"If I had a dime for all the grape juice I dropped . . ."

Jim's the boss. A fish-type handshake. He was balding and in his forties. A lot of 15
managers are these young, clean-shaven, neatly cropped people in their twenties. So Jim
would say things like "groovy." You were supposed to get a ten-minute break every two
hours. I lived for that break. You'd go outside, take your shoes off, and be human again.
You had to request it. And when you took it, they'd make you feel guilty.

You'd go up and say "Jim, can I have a break?" He'd say, "A break? You want a 16
break? Make it a quick one, nine and a half minutes." Ha ha ha. One time I asked the
assistant manager, Henry. He was even older than Jim. "Do you think I can have a
break?" He'd say, "You got a break when you were hired." Ha ha ha. Even when they
joked it was a put-down.

The guys who load the shelves are a step above the box boys. It's like upperclassmen 17
at an officer candidate's school. They would make sure that you conformed to all the
prescribed rules, because they were once box boys. They know what you're going through,
your anxieties. But instead of making it easier for you, they'd make it harder. It's like a
military institution.

I kept getting box boys who came up to me, "Has Jim talked to you about your hair? 18
He's going to because it's getting too long. You better get it cut or grease it back or
something." They took delight in it. They'd come to me before Jim had told me. Everybody
was out putting everybody down. . . .

■ Reading Comprehension Questions

1. The word *subservient* in "You have to be terribly subservient to people"
   (paragraph 2) means
   a. sneaky.
   b. submissive.
   c. firm.
   d. pushy.

2. The word *incongruity* in ''I just couldn't understand the incongruity'' (paragraph 9) means
   a. contrast.
   b. attitude.
   c. anger.
   d. saving.

3. Which of the following would be a good alternative title for this selection?
   a. The Value of Hard Work
   b. Why I Quit My Job
   c. The Trouble with Bosses
   d. Getting Along with Customers

4. Which sentence best expresses the main idea of the selection?
   a. Brett Hauser hated his job.
   b. Supermarket workers have to be nice to everybody.
   c. Working as a box boy is a dead-end job.
   d. Brett Hauser's boss was unfair to his employees.

5. One complaint Brett had about his job was that he
   a. had to get a haircut.
   b. had to wear a uniform.
   c. was not allowed breaks.
   d. was not promoted to assistant manager.

6. One supermarket checker liked to put down customers by
   a. refusing to accept tips from them.
   b. criticizing them for giving him coupons at the end of the order.
   c. calling them stupid.
   d. taking a break whenever a customer appeared.

7. When Brett talks of *Us* and *Them, Them* refers to
   a. customers.
   b. bosses.
   c. grape strikers.
   d. checkers.

8. We can assume that Brett did not like
   a. being nice to people he did not respect.
   b. carrying heavy bags to people's cars.
   c. listening to music all day long.
   d. customers who forgot to give him a tip.

9. What seems to have bothered Brett the most about his job was the
   a. hours.
   b. routine.
   c. pay.
   d. people.

10. *True or false?* _____ We can assume that Brett needed a job very badly.

■ **Discussion Questions**

About Content

1. Which does Brett dislike more, the job itself or the people he must deal with? How can you tell?
2. Do you think Brett was justified in quitting his job? Why or why not?
3. What qualities does Brett dislike in the checker who wants to be a teacher but says she can't go to school? Is Brett also afraid of being trapped?

About Structure

4. As Brett Hauser describes his job, he jumps around from topic to topic, with little attention to transitions or other methods of organization—as most people do when they talk. (The interview was originally tape-recorded.) If Brett were to write up his interview as an organized essay, what are three areas he might divide it into and discuss one at a time?
5. In the fifth sentence of paragraph 9, the pronoun *it* has no reference word. To what does this pronoun refer?

About Style and Tone

6. Brett uses some slang words and phrases. List three:

   _____   _____   _____

7. Brett also has a good vocabulary of more difficult standard English words, such as *subservient* and *domain*. List three other words that show that Brett has an extensive vocabulary:

   _____   _____   _____

■ **Writing Assignments**

Assignment 1

Perhaps, at some point in your life, you have held a job about which you had strong feelings (positive or negative). Or maybe you know someone who is presently holding a job and loves it—or, like Brett, hates it. Write a description of this job, focusing on at least three different aspects of it. Have *either* of these thesis statements in your introduction:

- I really enjoyed working as a _____.
- When I worked as a _____, I couldn't wait for quitting time.

Then describe the job. As in Studs Terkel's selection, use vivid details that make your (or your friend's) attitude toward the job very clear.

Alternatively, if you have never worked at a job about which you have strong feelings, rewrite ''Brett Hauser'' as a well-organized five-hundred-word essay. Include an introduction, three supporting paragraphs for the thesis that ''Working as a supermarket box boy is the worst job I have ever had,'' and a conclusion. Feel free to invent added details you might need to round out your supporting paragraphs.

Assignment 2

Compare or contrast Brett's job with a summer or part-time job you have had. (If you have never worked outside the home, compare or contrast Brett's job with that of being a homemaker—or a full-time student.) Here are some of the areas on which you might want to focus:

Hours
Pay
Working conditions
Coworkers
Customers
Bosses—how they treated employees
Chances for advancement

In your conclusion, decide which job, yours or Brett's, is better—and why.

Assignment 3

Studs Terkel gathered his information by interviewing different kinds of workers. Interview a person you know about his or her job. Use the material to write an essay about that person's job.

You could organize the essay into paragraphs dealing with the following:

What the person does on the job
Reasons why the person likes the job
Reasons why the person dislikes the job

Or you might decide to write about three of the following (in separate paragraphs):

Things the person likes or dislikes about the duties of the job
Things the person likes or dislikes about the employer
Things the person likes or dislikes about the coworkers
Things the person likes or dislikes about the working conditions

Defense Mechanisms

Ronald B. Adler and Neil Towne

The ancient Greeks understood defense mechanisms. In the Greek fable of the fox and the grapes, a fox who cannot reach the topmost grapes on a vine tells himself that they were probably sour anyway. As you will see in the following textbook selection, the fox was using a defense mechanism—rationalization—to protect his self-image. As you read, you will probably be able to identify defense mechanisms that both you and people you know use.

How do we manage self-deception? In the following pages you'll read about some of the methods we use. They are generally referred to as defense mechanisms. Just as the two methods of protecting yourself from physical attack are to flee or to fight, the mechanisms for psychological defense involve either avoidance or counterattack. The fact that these defense mechanisms operate unconsciously and have as their goal the avoidance of, or escape from, threat and anxiety makes them difficult to recognize in ourselves. And when we fail to realize that we're distorting the reality that makes up our lives, communication with others suffers. 1

Defense mechanisms are not always undesirable. There are times when protecting a private self is desirable, particularly when such disclosure would be treated cruelly by others. Also, confronting too many unpleasant truths or perceptions of one's self too quickly can be unmanageable, and thus these mechanisms serve as protective gear for handling the process of self-discovery at a safe rate. However, your own experience will show that, most often, acting in the following defensive ways can damage your relationships with others. We therefore believe that acquainting you with some of the most common defense mechanisms—with the hope of reducing them in your life—is a valuable step in helping you become a better communicator. 2

Rationalization. One of the most common ways of avoiding a threat to our self-concept is to *rationalize,* that is, to think up a logical but untrue explanation that protects the unrealistic picture we hold of ourselves. 3

Have you ever justified cheating in school by saying the information you were tested on wasn't important anyway or that everybody cheats a little? Were those your real reasons, or just excuses? Have you ever shrugged off hurting someone's feelings by saying she'll soon forget what you've done? In cases like these it's often tempting to explain behavior you feel guilty about by justifying it in terms that fit your self-concept. . . . 4

Rationalization Reader for Students

Situation	What to say
When the course is the lecture type:	We never get a chance to say anything.
When the course is the discussion type:	The professor just sits there. We don't know how to teach the course.
When all aspects of the course are covered in class:	All he does is follow the text.
When you're responsible for covering part of the course outside class:	He never covers half the things we're tested on.
When you're given objective tests:	They don't allow for any individuality for us.
When you're given essay tests:	They're too vague. We never know what's expected.
When the instructor gives no tests:	It isn't fair! He can't tell how much we really know.
When you have a lot of quizzes instead of a midterm and final:	We need major exams. Quizzes don't cover enough to really tell anything.
When you have only two exams for the whole course:	Too much rides on each one. You can just have a bad day.

Reaction Formation. People who use reaction formation avoid facing an unpleasant   5
truth by acting exactly opposite from the way they truly feel. The common expression
that describes this behavior is "whistling in the dark."

For example, you may have known somebody who acts like the life of the party,   6
always laughing and making jokes, but who you suspect is trying to fool everybody—
including himself—into missing the fact that he is sad and lonely. Another example of
reaction formation involves the person who goes overboard to be open-minded, insisting,
"I'm not prejudiced! Why, some of my best friends are ———!" It's easy to suspect
that someone who makes such a fuss about being tolerant may be unwilling to admit that
just the opposite is true. . . .

Projection. In projection you avoid an unpleasant part of yourself by disowning 7
that part and attributing it to others. For instance, on the days when as instructors we
aren't as prepared for class as we might be, it's tempting to claim that the hour hasn't
gone well because the students didn't do *their* homework. Similarly, you may have found
yourself accusing others of being dishonest, lazy, or inconsiderate when in fact such
descriptions fit your behavior quite well. In all of these cases we project an unpleasant
trait of our own onto another, and in so doing we avoid facing it in ourselves. It doesn't
matter whether the accusation you make about others is true or not: In projection the
important point is that you are escaping from having to face the truth about yourself.

The mechanism of projection explains the common experience of taking an instant 8
dislike to someone you've just met and realizing later that the traits you found so distasteful
in that person are precisely those you dislike in yourself. By criticizing the new acquaintance you can put the undesirable characteristic ''out there,'' and not have to admit it
belongs to you.

A surefire test to determine whether you are using projection to fool yourself is to 9
take every attack you make on others and substitute ''I'' for the words you use to identify
the other person. For example, ''She talks too much'' becomes ''I talk too much,'' or
''They're being unfair'' is instead ''I'm being unfair.'' When you try this simple experiment and your accusation of another seems to be true of you, you are projecting. . . .

Fantasy. When a person's desires or ambitions are frustrated, he often resorts to a 10
fantasy world to satisfy them. We often daydream ourselves out of our ''real'' world into
one that is more satisfying. A good example of this is the young career woman who finds
herself bored with her dull life as a typist. To insulate herself from this unbearable
existence she escapes into the excitement of her own fantasies. She becomes the leading
lady in the romance magazine stories, the television dramas, and the movies she frequents.
No matter how exciting and glamorous these fantasies are, they're not connected to the
problem of her reality and therefore can't help her make changes to improve her life.

There is much to be said for the short daydream that lifts the boredom of an unpleasant 11
task, or the fantasies that can be creative tools to help us think up new solutions to
problems. But as with all defense mechanisms, the danger of fantasizing is that it keeps
us from dealing squarely with what's bothering us by providing a temporary escape which
doesn't really solve the problem.

Repression. Sometimes rather than facing up to an unpleasant situation and trying 12
to deal with it, we protect ourselves by denying its existence. Quite simply, we ''forget''
what would otherwise be painful. Take a couple, for example, who can't seem to agree
about how to handle their finances. One partner thinks that money is meant to be spent,
while the other believes that it's important to save for the future. Rather than working to
solve this important problem, the husband and wife pretend nothing is wrong. This charade
may work for a while, but as time goes by, each partner will probably begin to feel more

and more uncomfortable and will likely begin to build up resentments about the way the other one uses their common money. Eventually these resentments are almost sure to leak into other areas of the marriage.

In the same way, we've seen families with serious problems—an alcoholic parent, a 13 teenager into drugs, a conflict between members—try to pretend that everything is perfectly all right, as if acting that way will make it so. Of course, it's unlikely that they'll solve these problems without admitting that they exist. . . .

Emotional Insulation and Apathy. Often, rather than face an unpleasant situation, 14 people will avoid hurt by not getting involved or pretending they don't care. Probably the most common example of *emotional insulation* is the person who develops a strong attachment to someone only to have the relationship break up. The pain is so great that the sufferer refuses to become involved like this again. At other times people who are hurt in this way defend their feeling of self-worth by becoming *apathetic,* by saying they don't care about whoever hurt them.

The sad thing about emotional insulation and apathy is that they prevent the person 15 who uses them from doing anything about dealing with the cause of the defensiveness. As long as I say I don't care about dating when I really do, I can't go out with anyone because this would be inconsistent with my artificial self-concept. As long as I don't admit that I care about you, our relationship has little chance of growing.

Displacement. This occurs when we vent aggressive or hostile feelings against 16 people or objects that are seen as less dangerous than the person or persons who caused the feelings originally. The child who is reminded that she has to clean up her room before she can play may get rid of some of her hostility by slamming the door to her bedroom or beating up a younger brother or sister. She knows it might cause her more pain if she expressed this hostility against her parents. In the same way, displacement occurs when, for example, a workman gets angry at the boss but doesn't want to risk getting fired and so takes out his frustration by yelling at his family. . . .

Verbal Aggression. Sometimes, when we can get away with it, the easiest way to 17 avoid facing criticism is to drown it out. Verbal aggression illustrates the old saying "The best defense is a good offense." Counterattacking somebody who threatens our self-concept tends to relieve tension and helps the defensive person feel better because his fireworks probably cover up whatever it was in the original remark that threatened him.

A good example of verbal aggression is the "so are you" defensive maneuver. When 18 a person says something we feel is too critical, we counterattack by telling her all her faults. Our remarks may be true, but they don't answer her criticism and only wind up making her more defensive.

Temper tantrums, hitting below the belt, and bringing up past grievances are some 19 other types of verbal aggression.

Now that you've had a look at several ways people defend an unrealistic self-concept, 20 we hope you'll be able to detect the role defense mechanisms play in your life. We want to repeat that these mechanisms aren't usually destructive unless they're practiced to the point where an individual's view of reality becomes distorted. . . . Our hope is that you can look at *yourself* with a little more knowledge of how you operate when you detect a threat to your self-concept.

Finally, you'll find defense mechanisms don't usually appear as simple, clear-cut 21 behaviors. We usually use them in combination because it's only natural to protect one's self in as many ways as possible.

■ Reading Comprehension Questions

1. The word *charade* in "the husband and wife pretend nothing is wrong. . . . This charade may work for a while" (paragraph 12) means
   a. problem.
   b. game.
   c. solution.
   d. discussion.

2. The word *vent* in "when we vent aggressive or hostile feelings" (paragraph 16) means
   a. repress.
   b. protect.
   c. let out.
   d. list.

3. Which of the following would be a good alternative title for this selection?
   a. Undesirable Behaviors
   b. Facing the Truth
   c. Ways We Avoid Reality
   d. How We Communicate

4. Which sentence best expresses the main idea of the selection?
   a. Defense mechanisms are dangerous when carried to an extreme.
   b. A good communicator never uses defense mechanisms.
   c. People use various defense mechanisms to protect their self-image.
   d. Rationalization and projection are the most dangerous kinds of defense mechanisms.

5. Bringing up past grievances and throwing temper tantrums are examples of
   a. repression.
   b. rationalization.
   c. emotional insulation.
   d. verbal aggression.

6. *True or false?* _____ Taking a dislike to someone because he or she has some negative traits you see in yourself is an example of reaction formation.

7. Using defense mechanisms can be healthy when you are
   a. defending your private self from the cruelty of others.
   b. looking for an escape from your problems.
   c. trying to forget about a parent's alcoholism.
   d. trying to get over a broken relationship.

8. The authors imply that
   a. repression is a way to solve some marital problems.
   b. apathetic people have lost their self-worth.
   c. students using rationalization will criticize a class no matter how it is conducted.
   d. people who are outgoing and sociable at parties are really covering up the fact that they are sad and lonely.

9. We can conclude that a woman who argues with her husband and then releases her anger by driving recklessly is using
   a. displacement.
   b. apathy.
   c. projection.
   d. fantasy.

10. The authors imply that
    a. instructors use projection more than any other defense mechanism.
    b. a good communicator deals with reality.
    c. defense mechanisms are more helpful than harmful.
    d. some people never need to use defense mechanisms.

■ Discussion Questions

About Content

1. In what two instances, according to Adler and Towne, is the use of defense mechanisms desirable? When do defense mechanisms become psychologically destructive?

2. What do you think is probably the most common defense mechanism that people use in everyday life? Give examples.

3. The authors say that we often use defense mechanisms in combination. Give an example of a situation in which a person would be using two defense mechanisms.

4. What are the benefits, if any, of fantasizing? What are the drawbacks?

About Structure

5. What is the method of development used for most paragraphs in the selection?

6. Paragraph 2 contains three types of transition signals: an addition signal, change-of-direction signal, and conclusion signal. What are they?

_____

_____

_____

About Style and Tone

7. One of the ways the authors of this selection achieve a friendly, helpful tone is by speaking directly to the reader. For example, in paragraph 4, the authors ask the reader questions: ''Have you ever justified cheating in school . . . ? Were those your real reasons . . . ? Have you ever shrugged off hurting someone's feelings . . . ?'' Find two other places in the selection where the authors use the ''you'' point of view to speak directly to their audience. Write

   the numbers of those paragraphs here: _____   _____

■ **Writing Assignments**

Assignment 1

You may have recognized your own behavior in several of these descriptions of defense mechanisms. Write an essay about the three defense mechanisms you use most often. In your thesis, state that you rely on three kinds of defense mechanisms in everyday life. Then, in each of your supporting paragraphs, give examples (or an extended example) of times you found yourself using that particular defense mechanism.

Assignment 2

Write an essay about three defense mechanisms you see someone else using. (The person should be someone you know well, such as a family member, friend, or coworker.) As in Assignment 1, use examples to develop your supporting paragraphs.

Assignment 3

Write an essay proving that some students often use rationalization, fantasy, and repression (*or* regression) to cope with school. Develop your supporting paragraphs with hypothetical examples of fictional students. In each supporting paragraph, describe how your fictional student uses one of the defense mechanisms to cope with academic, social, or personal problems.

Why Are Students Turned Off?

Casey Banas

A teacher pretends to be a student and sits in on several classes. What does she find in the typical class? Boredom. Routine. Apathy. Manipulation. Discouragement. If this depressing list sounds familiar, you will be interested in the following analysis of why classes often seem to be more about killing time than about learning.

Ellen Glanz lied to her teacher about why she hadn't done her homework; but, of course, many students have lied to their teachers. The difference is that Ellen Glanz was a twenty-eight-year-old high school social studies teacher who was a student for six months to improve her teaching by gaining a fresh perspective of her school. 1

She found many classes boring, students doing as little as necessary to pass tests and get good grades, students using ruses to avoid assignments, and students manipulating teachers to do the work for them. She concluded that many students are turned off because they have little power and responsibility for their own education. 2

Ellen Glanz found herself doing the same things as the students. There was the day when Glanz wanted to join her husband in helping friends celebrate the purchase of a house, but she had homework for a math class. For the first time, she knew how teenagers feel when they think something is more important than homework. 3

She found a way out and confided: "I considered my options: Confess openly to the teacher, copy someone else's sheet, or make up an excuse." Glanz chose the third option—the one most widely used—and told the teacher that the pages needed to complete the assignment had been ripped from the book. The teacher accepted the story, never checking the book. In class, nobody else did the homework; and student after student mumbled responses when called upon. 4

"Finally," Glanz said, "the teacher, thinking that the assignment must have been difficult, went over each question at the board while students copied the problems at their seats. The teacher had 'covered' the material and the students had listened to the explanation. But had anything been learned? I don't think so." 5

Glanz found this kind of thing common. "In many classes," she said, "people simply didn't do the work assignment, but copied from someone else or manipulated the teacher into doing the work for them." 6

"The system encourages incredible passivity," Glanz said. "In most classes one sits and listens. A teacher, whose role is activity, simply cannot understand the passivity of the student's role," she said. "When I taught," Glanz recalled, "my mind was going constantly—figuring out how to best present an idea, thinking about whom to call on, whom to draw out, whom to shut up; how to get students involved, how to make my point clearer, how to respond; when to be funny, when serious. As a student, I experienced little of this. Everything was done to me." 7

Class methods promote the feeling that students have little control over or responsibility for their own education because the agenda is the teacher's, Glanz said. The teacher is convinced the subject matter is worth knowing, but the student may not agree. Many students, Glanz said, are not convinced they need to know what teachers teach; but they believe good grades are needed to get into college. 8

Students, obsessed with getting good grades to help qualify for the college of their choice, believe the primary responsibility for their achievement rests with the teacher, Glanz said. "It was his responsibility to teach well rather than their responsibility to learn carefully." 9

Teachers were regarded by students, Glanz said, not as "people," but as "role-players" who dispensed information needed to pass a test. "I often heard students describing teachers as drips, bores, and numerous varieties of idiots," she said. "Yet I knew that many of the same people had travelled the world over, conducted fascinating experiments or learned three languages, or were accomplished musicians, artists, or athletes." 10

But the sad reality, Glanz said, is the failure of teachers to recognize their tremendous communications gap with students. Some students, she explained, believe that effort has little value. Some have heard reports of unemployment among college graduates and others, and after seeing political corruption they conclude that honesty takes a back seat to getting ahead any way one can, she said. "I sometimes estimated that half to two-thirds of a class cheated on a given test," Glanz said. "Worse, I've encountered students who feel no remorse about cheating but are annoyed that a teacher has confronted them on their actions." 11

Glanz has since returned to teaching at Lincoln-Sudbury. Before her stint as a student, she would worry that perhaps she was demanding too much. "Now I know I should have demanded more," she said. Before, she was quick to accept the excuses of students who came to class unprepared. Now she says, "You are responsible for learning it." But a crackdown is only a small part of the solution. 12

The larger issue, Glanz said, is that educators must recognize that teachers and students, though physically in the same school, are in separate worlds and have an on-going power struggle. "A first step toward ending this battle is to convince students that what we attempt to teach them is genuinely worth knowing," Glanz said. "We must be sure, ourselves, that what we are teaching is worth knowing." No longer, she emphasized, do students assume that "teacher knows best." 13

■ **Reading Comprehension Questions**

1. The word *agenda* in "the agenda is the teacher's" (paragraph 8) means
   a. program.
   b. boredom.
   c. happiness.
   d. book.

2. The word *ruses* in "students using ruses to avoid assignments" (paragraph 2) means
   a. questions.
   b. sicknesses.
   c. parents.
   d. tricks.

3. Which of the following would be a good alternative title for this selection?
   a. How to Get Good Grades
   b. Why Students Dislike School
   c. Cheating in Our School Systems
   d. Students Who Manipulate Teachers

4. Which sentence best expresses the main idea of the selection?
   a. Ellen Glanz is a burned-out teacher.
   b. Ellen Glanz lied to her math teacher.
   c. Students need good grades to get into college.
   d. Teachers and students feel differently about schooling.

5. How much of a class, according to the author's estimate, would often cheat on a test?
   a. One-quarter or less
   b. One-half or less
   c. One-half to two-thirds
   d. Almost everyone

6. *True or false?* _____ As a result of her experience, Glanz now accepts more of her students' excuses.

7. Glanz found that the school system encourages an incredible amount of
   a. false expectations.
   b. passivity.
   c. temporary learning.
   d. hostility.

8. The author implies that
   a. few students cheat on tests.
   b. most students enjoy schoolwork.
   c. classroom teaching methods should be changed.
   d. Glanz had a lazy math teacher.

9. The author implies that
   a.   Glanz should not have become a student again.
   b.   Glanz is a better teacher than she was before.
   c.   Glanz later told her math teacher that she lied.
   d.   social studies is an unimportant subject.

10. The author implies that
   a.   most students who cheat on tests are caught by their teachers.
   b.   most teachers demand too little of their students.
   c.   students who get good grades in high school do so in college.
   d.   students never question what teachers say.

■ Discussion Questions

About Content

1.   Are you surprised that a twenty-eight-year-old high school teacher would become as ''turned off'' as a high school student? Why or why not?

2.   Glanz feels that nothing is learned when a teacher goes over an assignment that nobody has done—in effect doing the students' homework for them. Do you agree with her? If so, what do you feel should be done about the problem?

3.   Glanz feels that students have little power and responsibility where their own education is concerned. What examples of this situation does she give? Can you think of others?

About Structure

4.   What method of introduction is used in paragraph 1?
   a.   Brief anecdote
   b.   Quotation
   c.   Questions

5.   The last paragraph uses a combination of conclusion techniques. What are they?
   a.   Recommendation and quotation
   b.   Prediction and anecdote
   c.   Questions and summary

About Style and Tone

6. The author of this article focuses on Ellen Glanz. Glanz wants to persuade us of the importance of her observations. But what is the *author's* purpose in writing this selection?
   a. To report Ellen Glanz's story
   b. To agree with Ellen Glanz
   c. To disagree with Ellen Glanz

7. Parallel structure can create a smooth, readable style (see page 392). For example, note the series of *-ing* verbs in the following sentence from paragraph 2: "... students *doing* as little as necessary to pass tests and get good grades, students *using* ruses to avoid assignments, and students *manipulating* teachers to do the work for them." Find two other places where parallelism is used in this selection and write the sentences in the spaces below.

_____

_____

_____

_____

_____

■ Writing Assignments

Assignment 1

Play the role of student observer in one of your college classes. Then write an essay with *either* of the following theses:

- In my _____ class, students are turned off.
- In my _____ class, students are active and interested.

In each supporting paragraph, state and detail one reason why the atmosphere in that particular class is either boring or interesting. You might want to consider areas such as

Instructor: presentation, tone of voice, level of interest and enthusiasm, teaching aids used, ability to handle questions, sense of humor, and so on

Students: level of enthusiasm, participation in class, attitude (as shown by body language and other actions), and so on

Other factors: condition of classroom, length of class period, noise level in classroom, and so on

Assignment 2

Glanz says that students like to describe their teachers as "drips, bores, and numerous varieties of idiots." Write a description of one of your high school teachers or college instructors who either *does* or *does not* fit that description. Show, in your essay, that your teacher or instructor was as weak, boring, and idiotic as Glanz says—or just the opposite (dynamic, creative, and bright). In either case, your focus should be on providing specific details that *enable your readers to see for themselves* that your thesis is valid.

Assignment 3

How does the classroom situation Ellen Glanz describes compare with a classroom situation with which you are familiar—either one from the high school you attended or one from the school in which you are presently enrolled? Select one class you were or are a part of, and write an essay in which you compare or contrast your class with the ones Ellen Glanz describes. Here are some areas you might wish to include in your essay:

How interesting the class was

How many of the students did their assignments

What the teaching methods were

How much was actually learned

How active the teacher or instructor was

How passive the students were

What the students thought of the teacher or instructor

Choose any three of the above areas, or three other areas. Then decide whether you are going to use a *one-side-at-a-time* or a *point-by-point* method of development (see pages 183–184).

Five Parenting Styles

Mary Ann Lamanna and Agnes Reidmann

Parenting has been called "the biggest on-the-job training program ever." Parents have to raise children without much guidance or advance instruction, and sometimes this results in a "parenting style" that causes problems. In the following textbook selection, the authors discuss five parenting styles. See if you can identify your parents—or yourself—in one of the classifications.

Considering the lack of consensus about how to raise children today, it may seem difficult to single out styles of parenting. From one point of view there are as many parenting styles as there are parents. . . . Yet certain elements in relating to children can be broadly classified. One helpful grouping is provided in E. E. LeMasters' listing of five parenting styles: the martyr, the pal, the police officer, the teacher-counselor, and the athletic coach. . . . We will discuss each of these.

1

The Parent as Martyr. Martyring parents believe "I would do anything for my child." . . . Some common examples of martyring are parents who habitually wait on their children or pick up after them; parents who nag children rather than letting them remember things for themselves; parents who buy virtually anything the child asks for; and parents who always do what the children want to do.

2

This parenting style presents some problems. First, the goals the martyring parent sets are impossible to carry out, and so the parent must always feel guilty. Also, . . . martyring tends to be reciprocated by manipulating. In addition, it is useful to ask if persons who consistently deny their own needs can enjoy the role of parenting and if closeness between parent and child is possible under these conditions.

3

The Parent as Pal. Some modern parents, mainly those of older children and adolescents, feel that they should be pals to their children. They adopt a **laissez-faire** policy, *letting their children set their own goals, rules, and limits,* with little or no guidance from parents. . . . According to LeMasters, "pal" parents apparently believe that they can avoid the conflict caused by the generation gap in this way.

4

Pal parenting is unrealistic. For one thing, parents in our society *are* responsible for guiding their children's development. Children deserve to benefit from the greater knowledge and experience of their parents, and at all ages they need some rules and limits, although these change as children grow older. Much research points to the conclusion that laissez-faire parenting is related to juvenile delinquency, heavy drug use, and runaway behavior in children. . . .

5

LeMasters points out that there are also relationship risks in the pal-parent model. If things don't go well, parents may want to retreat to a more formal, authoritarian style of parenting. But once they've established a buddy relationship, it is difficult to regain authority. . . .

6

The Parent as Police Officer. The police officer (or drill sergeant) model is just   7
the opposite of the pal. These parents make sure the child obeys all the rules at all times,
and they punish their children for even minor offenses. Being a police officer doesn't
work very well today, however, and **autocratic discipline,** *which places the entire power
of determining rules and limits in the parents' hands*—like laissez-faire parenting—has
been associated with juvenile delinquency, drug use, and runaway teen-agers. . . .

There are several reasons for this. First, Americans have tended to resist anything   8
that smacks of tyranny ever since the days of the Boston Tea Party. Hence, children are
socialized to demand a share of independence at an early age.

A second reason why policing children doesn't work well today is that rapid social   9
change gives the old and the young different values and points of view and even different
knowledge. In our complex culture, youth learn attitudes from specialized professionals,
such as teachers and school counselors, who often ''widen the intellectual gap between
parent and child.'' . . . For example, many young people today may advocate Judy Blume's
novel for teens, *Forever* (1975), which is explicit about and accepting of premarital sex.
Many parents, however, disapprove of the book.

A third reason why the police officer role doesn't work is that children, who find   10
support from their adolescent peers, will eventually confront and challenge their parents.
LeMasters points out that the adolescent peer group is ''a formidable opponent'' to any
cop who insists on strict allegiance to autocratic authority. . . .

A fourth reason is that autocratic policing just isn't very effective in molding children's   11
values. One study of 451 college freshmen and sophomores at a large western university
found that adolescents were far more likely to be influenced by their parents' referent or
expert power . . . than by coercive or legitimate power. The key was respect and a close
relationship; habitual punishment or the ''policing'' of adolescents were far less effective
modes of socialization. . . .

The Parent as Teacher-Counselor. The parent as teacher-counselor acts in accord   12
with the **developmental model of child rearing,** *in which the child is viewed as an
extremely plastic organism with virtually unlimited potential for growth and development.*
The limits to this rich potential are seen as encompassed in the limits of the parent to tap
and encourage it. . . . This model conceptualizes the parent(s) as almost omnipotent in
guiding children's development. . . . If they do the right things at the right time, their
children will more than likely be happy, intelligent, and successful.

Particularly during the 1960s and 1970s, authorities have stressed the ability of parents   13
to influence their children's intellectual growth. Psychologist J. McVicker Hunt, for
example, stated that he believes ''you could raise a middle-class child's I.Q. by twenty
points with what we know about child-rearing.'' . . .

The teacher-counselor approach has many fine features, and children do benefit from   14
environmental stimulation. Yet this parenting style also poses problems. First, it puts the
needs of the child above the parents' needs. It may be unrealistic for most parents to
always be there, ready to stimulate the child's intellect or to act as a sounding board.
Also, parents who respond as if each of their child's discoveries is wonderful may give
the child the mistaken impression that he or she is the center of everyone's universe. . . .

A second difficulty is that this approach expects parents to be experts—an expectation 15 that can easily produce guilt. Parents can never learn all that psychologists, sociologists, and specialized educators know. Yet if anything goes wrong, teacher-counselor parents are likely to feel they have only themselves to blame. . . .

Finally, contemporary research suggests more and more that this view greatly exagger- 16 ates the power of the parent and the passivity of children. Children also have inherited intellectual capacities and needs. Recent observers point instead to an **interactive perspective,** *which regards the influence between parent and child as mutual and reciprocal,* not just a "one-way street." . . .

The "athletic coach" model proceeds from this perspective. 17

The Parent as Athletic Coach. Athletic-coach parenting incorporates aspects of 18 the developmental point of view. The coach (parent) is expected to have sufficient ability and knowledge of the game (life) and to be prepared and confident to lead players (children) to do their best and, it is hoped, to succeed.

This parenting style recognizes that parents, like coaches, have their own personalities 19 and needs. They establish team rules, or *house rules* (and this can be done somewhat democratically with help from the players), and teach these rules to their children. They enforce the appropriate penalties when rules are broken, but policing is not their primary concern. Children, like team members, must be willing to accept discipline and, at least sometimes, to subordinate their own interests to the needs of the family team.

Coaching parents encourage their children to practice and to work hard to develop 20 their own talents. But they realize that they can not play the game for their players. LeMasters says:

> The coach's position here is quite analogous to that of parents; once the game has begun it is up to the players to win or lose it. . . . [He] faces the same prospect as parents of sitting on the sidelines and watching players make mistakes that may prove disastrous.

LeMasters also points out that coaches can put uncooperative players off the team 21 or even quit, but no such option is available to parents.

■ Reading Comprehension Questions

1. The word *plastic* in "an extremely plastic organism" (paragraph 12) means
   a. sickly.
   b. stiff.
   c. transparent.
   d. pliable.

2. The word *autocratic* in "autocratic discipline, which places the entire power . . . in the parents' hands" (paragraph 7) means
   a. unfocused.
   b. independent.
   c. dictatorial.
   d. generous.

3. Which of the following would be a good alternative title for this selection?
   a. Mistakes Parents Make
   b. How to Be a Good Parent
   c. Kinds of Parents
   d. Parents as Coaches

4. Which sentence best expresses the main idea of the selection?
   a. There are as many parenting styles as there are parents.
   b. Styles of parenting can be broadly classified into five groups.
   c. The "police officer" parenting approach can lead to delinquency.
   d. The influence between parent and child must be mutual.

5. Martyr parents
   a. act as buddies to their children.
   b. buy anything the child asks for.
   c. insist on strict obedience.
   d. establish house rules.

6. *True or false?* _____ The athletic-coach approach regards the parent-child relationship as a one-way street.

7. Teacher-counselor parents
   a. often blame themselves if something goes wrong.
   b. use autocratic discipline.
   c. insist on strict obedience.
   d. let their children set their own limits.

8. The authors imply that
   a. the teacher-counselor style of parenting is most effective.
   b. the athletic-coach style of parenting is most effective.
   c. "pal" parents have solved the problem of the generation gap.
   d. parents should set all the rules for the household.

9. *True or false?* _____ Sometimes children learn different values at school.

10. We might conclude from this selection that
    a. parenting is a complex and difficult role.
    b. the best parents are unsophisticated ones.
    c. different parenting styles are appropriate at different stages of growth.
    d. the authors favor the parent as teacher-counselor.

■ **Discussion Questions**

About Content

1. What reasons do the authors give for saying that parents cannot be pals to their children? Do you agree?

2. Which parenting style do you think the authors prefer? How can you tell?

3. Why is it difficult for parents to act as teacher-counselors? Give examples from your own experience.

About Structure

4. What method of development is used in the section ''The Parent as Police Officer''?
   a. Reasons
   b. Contrast
   c. Narrative

5. Analyze paragraph 14 (the third paragraph of ''The Parent as Teacher-Counselor''). Where is the topic sentence? What kind of support is given for this topic sentence?

6. What are three transition words used in paragraph 3?

   _____   _____   _____

7. Find at least four terms that are defined in the selection. Write the terms in the spaces below:

   _____   _____

   _____   _____

About Style and Tone

8. Below are aids to understanding often used in textbooks. Which *three* appear in this selection?
   a. Preview and summary
   b. Charts
   c. Heads and subheads
   d. Definitions and examples
   e. Boldface and italic type
   f. Graphs

■ Writing Assignments

Assignment 1

Write a description of ''Three Childing Styles.'' In other words, write an essay similar to ''Five Parenting Styles'' in which you discuss three different behavior patterns of children in families. Choose from the following behavior patterns, or others that may occur to you.

The child as:

Prima donna or spoiled brat
Miniature adult
Helpless baby
"Daddy's girl" or "Mama's boy"
Tough kid
Rebel
Showoff
Carbon copy of parent
Little angel

In separate supporting paragraphs, describe in detail how each of your three types behaves.

Assignment 2

Write an essay that uses the following thesis statement:

My parents were (tried to be) _____.

Fill in the blank with one of the five parenting styles described in the article (or with another one that you think up). Then present three different incidents that show your parents acting according to that style. (You may, of course, choose to write about only one parent.)

Assignment 3

Write an essay in which you argue that "a _____ (name a particular parenting style described in the selection) is the ideal parent." Develop the essay by giving three reasons why such parents are best.

Feel free to use any of the styles the authors describe; you could, for example, come up with a convincing argument that "police officer" parents are best, based on your own experience or reasoning.

Propaganda Techniques in Today's Advertising

Ann McClintock

Do you cheer for "America's team"? Are you convinced that "Coke is it"? Have you ever picked up your phone to "reach out and touch someone"? If you've responded to such ad slogans, you have been swayed by the effective use of propaganda. If you associate the word *propaganda* with the tactics used by strong-arm governments to brainwash their citizens, you may be surprised by McClintock's evidence that we are the targets of propaganda every day, and that propaganda techniques shape many of our opinions and decisions.

We Americans, adults and children alike, are being seduced. We are being brainwashed. And few of us protest. Why? Because the seducers and the brainwashers are the advertisers we willingly invite into our homes. We are victims, seemingly content—even eager—to be victimized. One study reports that each of us, during an average day, is exposed to over *five hundred* advertising claims of various types. This bombardment may even increase in the future since current trends include ads on movie screens, shopping carts, videocassettes, even public television. We read advertisers' messages in newspapers and magazines; we watch their alluring images on television. We absorb their messages into our subconscious.

Advertisers lean heavily on propaganda to sell their products, whether the "product" is a brand of toothpaste, a candidate for office, or a political viewpoint. *Propaganda* is a systematic effort to influence people's opinions, to win them over to a certain view or side. Propaganda is not necessarily concerned with what is true or false, good or bad. Propagandists simply want people to believe the messages being sent. Advertisers often use subtle deceptions to sway people's opinions; they may even use what amount to outright lies.

What kind of propaganda techniques do advertisers use? There are seven common types:

1. Name-Calling. Name-calling is a propaganda tactic in which a competitor is referred to with negatively charged names or comments. By using such negative associations, propagandists try to arouse feelings of mistrust, fear, and even hate in their audiences. For example, a political advertisement may label an opposing candidate a "loser," "fence-sitter," or "warmonger." Depending on the advertiser's target market, labels such as "a friend of big business" or "a dues-paying member of the party in power" can be the epithets that damage an opponent. Ads for products also ofen use name-calling. An American manufacturer may refer in its commercial, for instance, to a "foreign car"— not an "imported one." The label of foreignness will have unpleasant connotations in many people's minds. Another example is the MasterCard ad that shows a man trying unsuccessfully to get some cash with his American Express card. A childhood rhyme claims that "names can never hurt me," but name-calling is an effective way to damage the opposition, whether it is another credit card company or a congressional candidate.

2. Glittering Generalities. A glittering generality is an important-sounding but general claim for which no explanation or proof is offered. It is the opposite of name-calling. Advertisers who use glittering generalities surround their products with attractive—and slippery—words and phrases. They use vague terms that are difficult to define and that may have different meanings to different people, such as *great, progress, beautiful,* and *super.* This kind of language stirs positive feelings in people, feelings that may spill over to the product or idea being pitched. As with name-calling, the emotional response may overwhelm logic. Target audiences accept the product without thinking very much about what the glittering generalities really mean.

The ads for politicians and political causes often use glittering generalities because such buzzwords can influence votes. Election slogans include high-sounding but basically empty phrases like the following:

> "He cares about people." (That's nice, but is he a better candidate than his opponent?)
> "Vote for progress." (Progress by *whose* standards?)
> "They'll make this country great again." (Does "great" mean the same thing to the candidate as it does to me?)
> "Vote for the future." (What kind of future?)

Ads for consumer goods are also sprinkled with generalities. Product names, for instance, are often designed to evoke good feelings: *Luvs* diapers, *New Freedom* feminine hygiene products, *Joy* liquid detergent, and *Loving Care* hair color. Product slogans lean heavily on vague but comforting phrases: Kinney is "The Great American Shoe Store," General Electric "brings good things to life," and Dow Chemical "lets you do great things." We are also told that Chevrolet is the "heartbeat of America" and Coke is "the real thing."

3. Transfer. In transfer, advertisers try to improve the image of a product by associating it with a symbol or image most people respect and admire, like the American flag or Uncle Sam. The advertisers hope that the trust and prestige attached to the symbol or image will carry over to the product. Many companies use transfer devices to identify their products: Lincoln Insurance shows a profile of the president; Continental Insurance portrays a Revolutionary War Minuteman; Amtrak's logo is red, white, and blue; Liberty Mutual's corporate symbol is the Statue of Liberty; Allstate's name is cradled by a pair of protective, fatherly hands.

Corporations also use the transfer technique when they sponsor prestigious shows on radio and television. These shows function as symbols of dignity and class. Kraft Corporation, for instance, sponsored a "Leonard Bernstein Conducts Beethoven" concert, while Gulf Oil is the sponsor of *National Geographic* specials and Mobil supports public television's *Masterpiece Theater*. In this way, corporations reach an educated, influential audience and improve their public image by associating themselves with quality programming.

Political candidates, of course, practically wrap themselves in the flag. Ads for a candidate often show either the Washington Monument, a Fourth of July parade, the Stars and Stripes, or a bald eagle soaring over the mountains. The national anthem or "America the Beautiful" may play softly in the background. Such appeals to Americans' love of country surround the candidate with an aura of patriotism and integrity. **10**

4. Testimonial. The testimonial is one of advertisers' most-used propaganda techniques. Similar to the transfer device, the testimonial capitalizes on the admiration people have for a celebrity—even though the celebrity is not an expert on the product being sold. **11**

Print and television ads offer a nonstop parade of testimonials: here's Cher for Holiday Spas; here's basketball star Michael Jordan eating Wheaties; Michael Jackson sings about Pepsi; American Express features a slew of well-known people who assure us that they never go anywhere without their American Express card. Testimonials can sell movies, too; newspaper ads for films often feature favorable comments by well-known reviewers. And, in recent years, testimonials have played an important role in pitching books; the backs of paperbacks frequently list complimentary blurbs by celebrities. **12**

Political candidates, as well as their ad agencies, know the value of testimonials. Barbra Streisand lent her star appeal to the presidential campaign of Bill Clinton, while Arnold Schwarzenegger endorsed George Bush. **13**

As illogical as testimonials sometimes are (Pepsi's Michael Jackson, for instance, is a health-food adherent who does not drink soft drinks), they are effective propaganda. We like the *person* so much we like the *product* too. **14**

5. Plain Folks. The plain folks approach says, in effect, "Buy me or vote for me. I'm just like you." Regular folks will surely like Bob Evans's Down on the Farm Country Sausage or good old-fashioned Country Time lemonade. Some ads emphasize the idea that "we're all in the same boat." We see people making long-distance calls for just the reasons we do—to put the baby on the phone to Grandma or to tell Mom we love her. And how do these folksy, warmhearted scenes affect us? They're supposed to make us feel that AT&T—the multinational corporate giant—has the same values we do. Similarly, we are introduced to the little people at Ford, the ordinary folks who work on the assembly line, not to bigwigs in their executive offices. What's the purpose of such an approach? To encourage us to buy a car built by these honest, hardworking "everyday Joes" who care about quality as much as we do. **15**

Political advertisements make almost as much use of the "plain folks" appeal as they do of transfer devices. Candidates wear hard hats, farmers' caps, and assembly-line coveralls. They jog around the block and carry their own luggage through the airport. The idea is to convince voters that the candidates are at heart average people with the same values, goals and needs as you and I have. **16**

6. Card Stacking. When people say that "the cards were stacked against me," they 17
mean that they were never given a fair chance. Applied to propaganda, card stacking
means telling half-truths—misrepresenting the facts by suppressing relevant evidence.
Card stacking is a difficult form of propaganda both to detect and to combat. When a
candidate claims that an opponent has "changed his mind three times on this important
issue," we tend to accept the claim without investigating whether the candidate had good
reasons for changing his mind. Many people are simply swayed by the implication that
the candidate is "waffling" on the issue.

Advertisers also use a card-stacking trick when they make an unfinished claim. For 18
example, they will say that their product has "twice as much pain reliever." We are left
with a favorable impression. We don't usually ask, "Twice as much pain reliever as
what?" When Ford claimed that its LTD model was "400 percent quieter," many people
assumed that the LTD must be quieter than all other cars. When taken to court, however,
Ford admitted that the phrase referred to the difference between the noise level inside
and outside the LTD.

7. Bandwagon. In the bandwagon technique, advertisers urge, "Everyone's doing 19
it. Why don't you?" This kind of propaganda appeals to the deep desire many have not
to be different. Political ads tell us to vote for the "winning candidate." Advertisers know
we tend to feel comfortable doing what others do; we want to be on the winning team.
Or ads show a series of people proclaiming, "I'm voting for the Senator. I don't know
why anyone wouldn't." Again, the audience feels under pressure to conform.

The bandwagon approach is also a staple of consumer ads. They tell us, for example, 20
that "nobody doesn't like Sara Lee" (the message is that you must be weird if you don't).
They tell us that "most people prefer Brand X two to one over other leading brands" (to
be like the majority, we should buy Brand X). If we don't drink Pepsi, we're left out of
"the Pepsi generation." To take part in "America's favorite health kick," the National
Dairy Council urges us to drink milk. And Honda motorcycle ads, praising the virtues of
being a follower, tell us, "Follow the leader. He's on a Honda."

Why do these propaganda techniques work? Why do so many of us buy the products, 21
viewpoints, and candidates urged on us by propaganda messages? They work because
they appeal to our emotions, not to our minds. Clear thinking requires hard work: analyzing
a claim, researching the facts, examining both sides of an issue, using logic to see the
flaws in an argument. Many of us would rather let the propagandists do our thinking for us.

Because propaganda is so effective, it is important to detect it and understand how
it is used. We may conclude, after close examination, that some propaganda sends a
truthful, worthwhile message. Some advertising, for instance, urges us not to drive drunk,
to become volunteers, to contribute to charity. We may even agree that a particular soap
or soda is "super." Even so, we must be aware that propaganda is being used. Otherwise,
we will have consented to handing over to others our independence of thought and action.

■ Reading Comprehension Questions

1. The word *epithets* in "labels such as 'a friend of big business' or 'a dues-paying member of the party in power' can be the epithets that damage an opponent" (paragraph 4) means
   a. courtesies.
   b. descriptive labels.
   c. assurances.
   d. delays.

2. The word *capitalizes on* in "the testimonial capitalizes on the admiration people have for a celebrity" (paragraph 11) mean
   a. reports about.
   b. ignores.
   c. cuts back on.
   d. takes advantage of.

3. Which of the following would be a good alternative title for this selection?
   a. The World of Advertising
   b. Common Persuasion Techniques in Advertising
   c. Propaganda in Politics
   d. Common Advertising Techniques in Television

4. Which sentence best expresses the central point of this essay?
   a. Americans may be exposed daily to over five hundred advertising claims of some sort.
   b. The testimonial takes advantage of the admiration people have for celebrities, even though they have no expertise on the product being sold.
   c. People should detect and understand common propaganda techniques, which appeal to the emotions rather than to logic.
   d. Americans need to understand that advertising, a huge industry, affects their lives in numerous ways.

5. The propaganda technique in which a product is associated with a symbol or image most people admire and respect is
   a. glittering generalities.
   b. transfer.
   c. testimonials.
   d. bandwagon.

6. The technique in which evidence is withheld or distorted is called
   a. glittering generalities.
   b. bandwagon.
   c. plain folks.
   d. card stacking.

7. The technique that makes a political candidate seem to be just like the people an ad is aimed at is
   a. glittering generalities.
   b. bandwagon.
   c. plain folks.
   d. card stacking.

8. A way to avoid being taken in by propaganda is to use
   a. our emotions.
   b. name-calling.
   c. clear thinking.
   d. our subconscious.

9. The author implies in paragraph 2 that propagandists may not care about
   a. financial success.
   b. presenting a balanced view.
   c. the products they sell.
   d. the political candidates they promote.

10. From paragraphs 21–22, we can conclude the author feels
    a. we are unlikely to analyze advertising logically unless we recognize it as propaganda.
    b. propaganda should not be allowed.
    c. if we don't want to hand over to others our independence, we should ignore all propaganda.
    d. we should not support the "products, viewpoints, and candidates urged on us by propaganda messages."

■ Discussion Questions

About Content

1. Some of the propaganda techniques listed in the selection have contrasting appeals. How do name-calling and glittering generalities contrast with each other? Testimonial and plain folks?

2. Why are ads with a bandwagon appeal so effective? What ads have you seen lately that use this technique?

3. McClintock states, "We are victims, seemingly content—even eager—to be victimized." Why do you think she says this, and do you agree? Do you think this article will change how you view ads in the future?

About Structure

4. The selection can be said to employ several modes of essay development. What parts are developed through division and classification and through definition? What roles do examples and cause and effect play?

5. The author uses the first two paragraphs to explain her views of advertisers and their public and to explain propaganda. What does she use the last two paragraphs for?

About Style and Tone

6. What kind of audience do you think this selection was written for? Explain your answer.
   a. General public
   b. Instructors and students
   c. Advertisers

7. In paragraph 1, McClintock's choice of words shows her attitudes toward both propagandists and the public. Which specific words reveal her attitudes, and what attitudes do they represent?

■ Writing Assignments

Assignment 1

Choose three ads currently used on television or in print. Show that each ad uses one or more of the propaganda techniques that McClintock discusses. Be specific about product names, what the ad looks like, kinds of characters in the ad, and so on. Don't forget that all your specific details should back up your point that each ad uses a certain propaganda technique (or techniques) to sell a product. Your thesis will make some overall statement about the three ads, such as either of these:

> Beer advertisements use a variety of propaganda techniques.
> Glittering generalities are used to sell very different types of products.

Assignment 2

Imagine that you work for an ad agency and have been asked to come up with at least three possible campaigns for a new product (for example, a car, a perfume, a detergent, jeans, beer, a toothpaste, a deodorant, or an appliance). Write an essay in which you describe three different propaganda techniques that might be used to sell the product and how these claims could persuade the public to buy. Be specific about the general looks, the characters, and the wording of your ads and about how they fit in with the techniques you suggest.

Assignment 3

Do some informal "market research" on why people buy the products they do. Begin by asking at least ten people why they bought a particular brand-name item. You might question them about something they're wearing (designer jeans, for example). Or you might ask them what toothpaste they use, what car they drive, what pain reliever they take, or what chicken they eat—or ask about any other product people use. Take notes on the reasons people give for their purchases.

Then write an essay with the thesis "My research suggests that people often buy products for three reasons." Include in your introductory paragraph your plan of development—a list of the three reasons that were mentioned most often by the people you interviewed. Develop your supporting paragraphs with examples drawn from the interviews. As part of your support, use quotations from the people you spoke with.

CONFRONTING PROBLEMS

Date Rape

Ellen Sweet

Not so long ago, many Americans had not even heard of date rape; yet according to experts, it is by far the most common form of rape in this country. How can something so common and so important have been ignored for so long? And what can be done about it? To help our society understand the problem, *Ms.* magazine conducted a study of sexual assault. The coordinator of the project was Ellen Sweet, who wrote this selection on the nature and causes of date rape, as well as responses to the problem.

It was the beginning of spring break when I was a junior. I was in good spirits and had been out to dinner with an old friend. We returned to his college [dorm]. There were some seniors on the ground floor, drinking beer, playing bridge. I'm an avid player, so we joined them, joked around a lot. One of them, John, wasn't playing, but he was interested in the game. I found him attractive. We talked, and it turned out we had a mutual friend, shared experiences. It was getting late, and my friend had gone up to bed, so John offered to see me safely home. We took our time, sat outside talking for a while. Then he said we could get inside one of the most beautiful campus buildings, which was usually locked at night. I went with him. Once we were inside, he kissed me. I didn't resist, I was excited. He kissed me again. But when he tried for more, I said no. He just grew completely silent. I couldn't get him to talk to me any more. He pinned me down and ripped off my pants. *I couldn't believe it was happening to me....*

Let's call this Yale graduate Judy. Her experience and her disbelief, as she describes   1
them, are not unique. Gretchen, another student victim of date rape (or acquaintance rape,
as it is also called), had known for five years the man who invited her to an isolated
vacation cabin and then raped her. "I considered him my best friend," she says on a
Stanford University videotape used in discussions of the problem. "I couldn't believe it.
I couldn't believe it was actually happening to me."

Such denial, the inability to believe that someone they know could have raped them,   2
is a common reaction of victims of date rape, say psychologists and counselors who have
researched the topic and treated these women. In fact, so much silence surrounds this
kind of crime that many women are not even aware that they have been raped. In one
study, Mary P. Koss, a psychology professor at Kent State University, Ohio, asked female
students if they had had sexual intercourse against their will through use of or threat of
force (the minimal legal definition of rape). Of those who answered yes, only 57 percent
went on to identify their experience as rape. Koss also identified the other group (43
percent) as those who hadn't even acknowledged the rape to themselves.

"I can't believe it's happening on our campus," is usually the initial response to   3
reports such as Koss's. She also found that one in eight women students had been raped,
and another one in four were victims of attempted rape. Since only 4 percent of all those
reported the attack, Koss concluded that "at least ten times more rapes occur among
college students than are reflected in official crime statistics." (Rape is recognized to be
the most underreported of all crimes, and date rape is among the least reported, least
believed, and most difficult to prosecute, second only to spouse rape.)

Working independently of Koss, researchers at Auburn University, Alabama, and   4
more recently, University of South Dakota and St. Cloud State University, Minnesota,
all have found that one in five women students were raped by men they knew.

Koss also found a core group of highly sexually aggressive men (4.3 percent) who   5
use physical force to compel women to have intercourse but who are unlikely to see their
act as rape. These "hidden rapists" have "oversubscribed" to traditional male roles, she
says. They believe that aggression is normal and that women don't really mean it when
they say no to sexual advances. Such men answer "True" to statements like "most
women are sly and manipulating when they want to attract a man," "a woman will only
respect a man who will lay down the law to her," and "a man's got to show the woman
who's boss right from the start or he'll end up henpecked."

In Koss's current study, one respondent who answered yes to a question about   6
obtaining intercourse through physical force wrote in the comment, "I didn't rape the
chick, she was enjoying it and responding," and later, "I feel that sex is a very pleasant
way to relieve stress. Especially when there are no strings attached."

"He acted like he had a right, like he *didn't believe me*," says a coed from Auburn   7
University on a videotaped dramatization of date rape experiences. And several weeks
later, when she confronts him, saying he forced her, he says no, she wanted it. "You
raped me," she finally tells him. And the picture freezes on his look of incredulity.

Barry Burkhart, a professor of psychology at Auburn, who has also studied sexual   8
aggression among college men, found that 10 percent had used physical force to have
intercourse with a woman against her will, and a large majority admitted to various other
kinds of aggression. "These are ordinary males operating in an ordinary social context,"
he says. "So what we conclude is that there's something wrong with that social context."

The something wrong is that our culture fosters a "rape supportive belief system," 9 according to social psychologist Martha Burt. She thinks that "there's a large category of 'real' rapes, and a much smaller category of what our culture is willing to call a 'real' rape. The question is, how does the culture manage to write off all those other rapes?" The way it's done, says Burt, currently director of the Social Services Research Center at the Urban Institute in Washington, D.C., is by believing in a series of myths about rape, including:

■ It didn't really happen (the woman was lying).

■ Women like rape (so there's no such thing as rape).

■ Yes, it happened, but no harm was done (she wasn't a virgin; she wasn't white).

■ Women provoke it (men can't control themselves).

■ Women deserve it anyway.

It's easy to write off date rapes with such myths, coupled with what Burt calls our 10 culture's "adversarial sexual beliefs": the gamesmanship theory that everybody is out for what they can get, and that all sexual relationships are basically exploitive and predatory. In fact, most victims of date rape initially blame themselves for what happened, and almost none report it to campus authorities. And most academic institutions prefer to keep it that way, judging from the lack of surveys on date rape—all of which makes one wonder if they don't actually blame the victim, too.

As long as such attacks continue to be a "hidden" campus phenomenon, unreported 11 and unacknowledged by many college administrators, law enforcement personnel, and students, the problem will persist. Of course, the term has become much better known in the three years since *Ms.* reported on the prevalence of experiences such as Judy's and Gretchen's. It has been the subject of talk shows such as *The Donahue Show* and TV dramas (*Cagney and Lacey*). But for most people it remains a contradiction in terms. "Everybody has a stake in denying that it's happening so often," says Martha Burt. "For women, it's self-protective. . . . If only bad girls get raped, then I'm personally safe. For men, it's the denial that 'nice' people like them do it."

The fault has not entirely been that of the institutions. "Ten years ago, we were 12 telling women to look over your shoulder when you go out at night and lock your doors," says Py Bateman, director of a nationally known rape education program in Seattle, Alternatives to Fear. The prevailing myth was that most rapes were committed by strangers in dark alleys.

"If you have to think that sixty to eighty percent of rape is by people you know— 13 that's hard to deal with," says Sylvia Callaway, who directed the Austin, Texas, Rape Crisis Center for more than eight years before leaving last July. "No rape center in a university community would be surprised that the university is not willing to deal with the problem."

Statistics alone will not solve the problem of date rape, but they could help bring it 14 out into the open. Which is why *Ms.* undertook the first nationwide survey on college campuses. The *Ms.* Magazine Campus Project on Sexual Assault, directed by Mary P. Koss at Kent State and funded by the National Center for the Prevention and Control of Rape, reached more than seven thousand students at a nationally representative sample of thirty-five schools to find out how often, under what circumstances, and with what aftereffects a wide range of sexual assaults, including date rape, took place.

Preliminary results are now ready, and the information is no surprise. Participating schools were promised anonymity, but each will receive the results applying to its student body. Our hope is that the reaction of "we can't believe it's happening on our campus" will be followed by "what can we do about it—now."   15

Just how entrenched is denial of this problem today? One gauge might be the difficulty our own researchers had in persuading schools to let us on campus. For every college that approved our study, two others rejected it. Their reasons (in writing and in telephone conversations) were themselves instructive: "we don't want to get involved," "limited foreseeable benefit," "too volatile a topic," "have not had any problems in this area," "worried about publicity," "can't allow surveys in classroom," "just can't invest the time now," "would be overintrusive," "don't want to be left holding the bag if something goes wrong."   16

Several schools rejected the study on the basis that filling out the questionnaire might upset some students, and that we were not providing adequate follow-up counseling. (Researchers stayed on campus for at least a day after the distribution of the questionnaire, gave students listings of counselors or rape crisis centers to consult if anything upset them, and offered to meet with school personnel to brief them.) But isn't it less upsetting for a student to recognize and admit that she has been the victim of an acquaintance rape than to have buried the trauma of that rape deep inside herself?   17

"It's a Catch-22 situation. You want a survey to publicize a problem that has tremendous psychological implications. And the school says, 'Don't do it, because it will get people psychologically upset,'" admits John Jung, who heads the human subjects review committee at California State University/Long Beach (a school that declined our study).   18

One wonders just who are the "people" who will get most psychologically upset: the students, or their parents who pay for their educations, or the administrators who are concerned about the school's image. "There may have been an episode here," said John Hose, executive assistant to the president of Brandeis University, "but there is no *cause célèbre* surrounding the issue. In such cases, the reaction of Student Affairs is to encourage the student to be in touch with her parents and to take legal action."   19

"Student Affairs" at Brandeis is headed by Rodger Crafts, who moved to this post about a year ago from the University of Rhode Island. "I don't think we have a significant problem here because we have a sophisticated and intelligent group of students," said Dean Crafts. As for the University of Rhode Island, more students there are "first generation college attenders," as he put it, and therefore have "less respect" for other people. Vandalism and physical harm are more likely to occur with "lower educational levels." Respect for other people goes along with "intelligence level."   20

Back at the University of Rhode Island, the counseling center is sponsoring a twelve-week support and therapy group this fall for male students who are coercive and abusive in their relationships with women. Even though Nancy Carlson, director of Counseling and Career Services, is enthusiastic about such programs and workshops, she notes, "the awareness about date rape has been a long time coming."   21

Another school where administrators were the last to confront the challenge to their   22
school's self-image is Yale. Last year, two student publications reported instances of date
rape on campus that surprised students, faculty, and administration. "There are no full
statistics available on rape between students at Yale anywhere. . . . There is no mention
of rape in the 1983–1984 Undergraduate Regulations. There is no procedure for a victim
to file a formal complaint of rape with the university. But there is rape between students
at Yale," wrote Sarah Oates in the *Yale Daily News.* Partly in response to such charges,
current Yale undergraduate regulations now list "sexual harassment" under "offenses
that are subject to disciplinary action"—but still no mention of rape.

Yale students brave enough to bring a charge of sexual harassment may go before   23
the Yale College Executive Committee, a specially convened group of faculty, administrators, and students that can impose a series of penalties, graduated in severity, culminating
in expulsion. All its hearings and decisions are kept secret (but can in theory be subpoenaed
in a court of law). But Michael McBride, current chair of the committee, told me that
cases of date rape have come up during the past year, leading in one instance to a student
being asked to "resign" from the university, and in another, the conclusion that there
was not "sufficient evidence." (In Judy's case, described at the beginning of this article,
the senior she charged was penalized by being denied the privilege of graduating with
his class. But she claims that after he demanded that the case be reconsidered, he was
fully exonerated.) Said McBride, "What surprised me the most was how complicated
these cases are. It's only one person's word against another's. It's amazing how different
their perceptions can be."

Judy chose to take her case before the Executive Committee rather than report it to   24
the local police, because she felt she would have complete confidentiality and quick action.
Actually, there were many delays. And then, because the man she accused hired a lawyer,
she was forced to hire one too. As a result, the meeting felt very much like a jury trial
to her, complete with cross-examinations that challenged her truthfulness and raised
excruciatingly embarrassing questions.

Judy's lawyer felt that such painful questions were necessary. But it seems as if the   25
lesson feminists in the sixties and seventies worked so hard and successfully to make
understood—not to blame the victim for stranger rape—is one that will have to be learned
all over again in the case of acquaintance rape. Only this time, the woman who reports
the rape suffers a triple victimization. Not only is she attacked and then not believed, but
she carries the added burden of losing faith in her own judgment and trust in other people.

In a recently published study of jurors in rape trials, University of Illinois sociologist   26
Barbara Reskin found that jurors were less likely to convict a man if the victim knew
him. "Consent is the preferred rape defense and gets the highest acquittal rates," Reskin
observes. "In a date rape situation, I would think the jury would assume that the woman
had already accepted his invitation in a romantic sense. It would be a matter of how *much*
did she consent to."

Personal characteristics also influence jurors, Reskin says. Those she studied couldn't   27
imagine that certain men would commit a rape: if they were attractive, had access to
sexual partners such as a girlfriend or a wife. More often than not, they'd say, "But he
doesn't look like a rapist." Reskin imagines that this pattern would be "magnified in
date rape, because these are men who could get a date, they're not complete losers."

It may turn out that solutions to the problem will turn up at places with a less genteel 28 image to protect. Jan Strout, director of the Montana State Women's Resource Center, wonders if schools such as hers, which recognize that they are dealing with a more conservative student body and a "macho cowboy image," aren't more willing to take the first step toward acknowledging the problem. A group called Students Against Sexual Assault was formed there two-and-a-half years ago after several students who were raped or resisted an attempted rape "went public." With men and women sharing leadership, this group is cosponsored by the Women's Resource Center and the student government.

Admitting to the problem isn't easy even when data is available, as doctoral student 29 Genny Sandberg found at the University of South Dakota. Last spring, she announced the results of a dating survey she coauthored with psychologists Tom Jackson and Patricia Petretic-Jackson. The most shocking statistic: 20 percent of the students (most from rural backgrounds and living in a rural campus setting) had been raped in a dating situation. The state board of regents couldn't believe it. "I just think that that's absolutely ridiculous," former regent Michael Rost said, according to the Brookings *Daily Register,* "I can't believe we would allow that to occur. If it is true, it's a very serious problem." Regent William Srstka agreed, "If this is true it's absolutely intolerable."

Following testimony by one of the researchers, the board changed its tune. Members 30 are now discussing how to begin a statewide education and prevention program.

An inspiring example of how an administration can be led to new levels of 31 consciousness took place at the University of Michigan earlier this year. Spurred by an article in *Metropolitan Detroit* magazine, a group of students staged a sit-in at the office of a university vice-president who had been quoted as saying that "Rape is a red flag word. . . . [The university] wants to present an image that is receptive and palatable to the potential student cohort," and also that "Rape is an issue like Alzheimer's disease or mental retardation [which] impacts on a small but sizable part of the population. . . . Perhaps it has to become a crisis that is commonly shared in order to get things done."

The students who spent the entire day in Vice-President Henry Johnson's office 32 claimed that rape had already become a crisis on their campus. They presented a list of twelve demands, ranging from a rape crisis center on campus to better lighting and installation of outdoor emergency phones. By the end of the day, Johnson had started to change his mind. Although he insisted that he had been misquoted and quoted out of context in the press, he told me that "I did not realize [before that] acquaintance rape was so much of a problem, that it was the most prevalent type of rape. There is a heightened awareness now on this campus. Whether we as a faculty and administration are as sensitive as we should be is another issue—and that will take some time."

In the meantime, members of the Michigan Student Assembly Women's Issues Com- 33 mittee (one of the groups active in organizing the protest) took their demands before the school's board of regents. The result: a $75,000 program for rape prevention and education on campus, directly reporting to Johnson's office. "We'll now be in a position to document the problem and to be proactive," says Johnson. Jennifer Faigel, an organizer of the protest, acknowledges a change in the administration's awareness but says the students themselves, disappointed in the amount of funding promised for the program, have already formed a group (Students Organized Against Rape) to develop programs in the dorms.

In just the three years since *Ms.* first reported on date rape, several new campus 34
organizations have sprung up and other ongoing programs have surfaced.

But the real measure of a school's commitment to dealing with this problem is the 35
range of services it provides, says Mary Harvey, who did a nationwide study of exemplary
rape programs for the National Center for the Prevention and Control of Rape. ''It
should have preventive services, crisis intervention, possibilities for long-term treatment,
advocacy, and women's studies programs that educate about violence. The quality of a
university's services to rape victims can be measured by the degree to which these other
things are in place.''

Minimally, rape counselors and educators feel, students need to be exposed to informa- 36
tion about date rape as soon as they enter college. Studies show that the group most
vulnerable to acquaintance rape are college freshmen, followed by high school seniors.
In Koss's original survey, for example, the average age of the victim was eighteen.

''I'd like a program where no first-year students could finish their starting week at 37
college without being informed about the problem of acquaintance rape,'' says Andrea
Parrot, a lecturer in human service studies at Cornell University, who is developing a
program to train students and dorm resident advisers as date rape awareness counselors.
Parrot and others admit that this would be a bare minimum. Handing out a brochure to
read, even conducting a workshop on the subject during the busy orientation week and
counting on students voluntarily attending, needs to be followed up with sessions in
dormitories or other living units. These are the most common settings for date rapes,
according to a study by Parrot and Robin Lynk.

So how do we go about changing attitudes? And how do we do it without ''setting 38
student against student?'' asks Gretchen Mieszkowski, chair of the Sexual Assault Prevention Committee at the University of Houston/Clear Lake. Chiefly a commuter campus,
with a majority of married women students, Clear Lake nevertheless had seventeen
acquaintance rapes reported to the local crisis hot line last year. ''We had always focused
on traditional solutions like lighting and escort services at night,'' Mieszkowski says.
''But changing lighting in the parking lot is easy; it's only money.''

Many who have studied the problem of rape education believe it has to begin with 39
college-age women and men talking to each other more frankly about their beliefs and
expectations about sex. Py Bateman of Alternatives to Fear thinks it has to start earlier,
among teenagers, by developing rudimentary dating skills at the lower end of the sexual
activity scale. ''We need to learn more about holding hands than about sexual intercourse.''

Bateman continues: ''We've got to work on both sides. Boys don't know what they 40
want any more than girls do. The way our sexual interaction is set up is that boys are
supposed to push. Their peers tell them that scoring is what counts. They're as divorced
from intimacy as girls.''

Gail Abarbanel of the Rape Treatment Center at Santa Monica Hospital agrees. Her 41
center conducts educational programs for schools in Los Angeles County. In a recent
survey of more than five thousand teenagers, she found a high degree of misconception
and lack of information about rape: ''Most boys say yes to the question, 'If a girl goes
back to a guy's house when she knows no one is home, is she consenting to sex?' And
most boys believe that girls don't mean no when they say it.''

Women clearly need to get more convincing, and men clearly need to believe them 42
more. But until that ideal time, Montana State's Jan Strout warns, "Because men have
been socialized to hear yes when women say no, we have to scream it."

■ Reading Comprehension Questions

1. The word *incredulity* in "when she confronts him, saying he forced her, he
   says no, she wanted it. 'You raped me,' she finally tells him. And the picture
   freezes on his look of incredulity" (paragraph 7) means
   a. playfulness.
   b. warmth.
   c. disbelief.
   d. intelligence.

2. The word *fosters* in "our culture fosters a 'rape supportive belief system,'
   according to social psychologist Martha Burt" (paragraph 9) means
   a. delays.
   b. promotes.
   c. avoids.
   d. admits.

3. Which of the following would be a good alternative title for this selection?
   a. Rape in Our Society
   b. Date Rape on Campuses
   c. Myths about Rape
   d. Rape Crisis Centers

4. Which sentence best expresses the main idea of the selection?
   a. School administrators find it difficult to acknowledge the problem of
      date rate.
   b. Date rape on campuses is common, yet solutions are slow in coming.
   c. In 60 to 80 percent of all rapes, the rapist is known by the victim.
   d. Most women do not report date rapes to campus authorities.

5. A common reaction by victims of date rape is
   a. immediately reporting the rape to officials.
   b. sympathizing with the rapist.
   c. disbelief.
   d. suicide.

6. *True or false?* _____ A sociologist's study of jurors in rape trials found
   that jurors were more likely to convict a man accused of rape if he knew the
   woman than if he didn't.

7. *True or false?* _____ The best time for college students to learn about date
   rape, according to rape counselors and educators, is by the end of their first year.

8. The author implies that dealing with the problem of date rape
   a. will be easy.
   b. is impossible.
   c. is mainly the responsibility of the court system.
   d. requires a broad range of programs and services.

9. The author implies that colleges don't want to know how much date rape occurs on their campuses because
   a. the school's image will be harmed.
   b. attendance would go down at sports events.
   c. female students will be afraid to go to class.
   d. students don't care about social issues.

10. From the reading, we might conclude that to combat date rape successfully,
    a. men and women cannot share the same dormitories.
    b. men and women must change their attitudes.
    c. campus buildings must have better locks.
    d. law enforcement agencies must have a higher profile on campus.

■ **Discussion Questions**

About Content

1. According to the article, why is a victim of date rape so often not believed?
2. Paragraph 9 of the essay lists five common myths about rape, including ''women like rape'' and ''men can't control themselves.'' How do you respond to those beliefs? Are you aware of other beliefs about rape that you consider false?
3. Are first-year students informed about the problem of acquaintance rape on your campus? Does your campus have any other preventive services, such as educational sessions in dormitories, good lighting, and escort services?

About Structure

4. To support her main idea, the author uses
   a. studies and figures.
   b. opinions.
   c. anecdotes.
   d. all of the above.
5. What method of conclusion is used in the final paragraph?
   a. Recommendation
   b. Anecdote
   c. Questions

About Style and Tone

6. Why do you think the author begins the article with specific details of Judy's and Gretchen's stories?
7. The author writes, "Participating schools [in the *Ms.* survey] were promised anonymity." But in discussing those who *refused* to participate in the study, Sweet names schools and individuals. What might be her reasons for doing so?

■ Writing Assignments

Assignment 1

Write a letter to your college's student services office requesting the establishment of a date rape education program on your campus. Raise and discuss several points in support of your suggestion. You might want to consider:

Statistics from this article
Your own or a friend's experience with date rape or attempted rape
Personal knowledge about attitudes toward sex on your campus
Other such programs you know of, and their effects

In preparation for this letter, you might informally survey a few of the male and female students you know, or find out about programs at other schools in your area, or both.

Assignment 2

Write an essay using *one* of the following as your thesis statement:

■ While men should be held responsible for their own behavior, there are a few ways women can help protect themselves against date rape.
■ There are several ways our school can help to prevent date rape.
■ Men and women should both take steps to make dating less of a minefield for the two sexes.
■ Men who commit date rape should be held accountable for their actions in several ways.
■ People should understand common myths about rape and know what to say and do to help dispel those myths.

To help yourself decide on a thesis, make a list of possible supporting details for several of the above options. Then consider developing the option for which you have the most promising supporting details.

Assignment 3

Write an essay on ways in which our culture may encourage overly aggressive male behavior and overly submissive female behavior. In listing possible points for this essay, consider how male-female relationships and male and female images in general are portrayed and viewed in our society. You might want to consider, for example, how males and females are depicted in any of the following: television shows, films, rock videos, and advertisements.

Here's to Your Health

Joan Dunayer

Dunayer contrasts the glamorous "myth" about alcohol, as presented in advertising and popular culture, with the reality—which is often far less appealing. After reading her essay, you will be more aware of how we are encouraged to think of alcohol as being tied to happiness and success. You may also become a more critical observer of images presented by advertisers.

As the only freshman on his high school's varsity wrestling team, Tod was anxious to fit in with his older teammates. One night after a match, he was offered a tequila bottle on the ride home. Tod felt he had to accept, or he would seem like a sissy. He took a swallow, and every time the bottle was passed back to him, he took another swallow. After seven swallows, he passed out. His terrified teammates carried him into his home, and his mother then rushed him to the hospital. After his stomach was pumped, Tod learned that his blood alcohol level had been so high that he was lucky not to be in a coma or dead.   1

Although alcohol sometimes causes rapid poisoning, frequently leads to long-term addiction, and always threatens self-control, our society encourages drinking. Many parents, by their example, give children the impression that alcohol is an essential ingredient of social gatherings. Peer pressure turns bachelor parties, fraternity initiations, and spring-semester beach vacations into competitions in "getting trashed." In soap operas, glamorous characters pour Scotch whiskey from crystal decanters as readily as most people turn on the faucet for tap water. In films and rock videos, trend-setters party in nightclubs and bars. And who can recall a televised baseball or basketball game without a beer commercial? By the age of 21, the average American has seen drinking on TV about 75,000 times. Alcohol ads appear with pounding frequency—in magazines, on billboards, in college newspapers—contributing to a harmful myth about drinking.   2

Part of the myth is that liquor signals professional success. In a slick men's magazine, one full-page ad for Scotch whiskey shows two men seated in an elegant restaurant. Both are in their thirties, perfectly groomed, and wearing expensive-looking gray suits. The windows are draped with velvet, the table with spotless white linen. Each place-setting consists of a long-stemmed water goblet, silver utensils, and thick silver plates. On each plate is a half-empty cocktail glass. The two men are grinning and shaking hands, as if they've just concluded a business deal. The caption reads, ''The taste of success.'' 3

Contrary to what the liquor company would have us believe, drinking is more closely related to lack of success than to achievement. Among students, the heaviest drinkers have the lowest grades. In the work force, alcoholics are frequently late or absent, tend to perform poorly, and often get fired. Although alcohol abuse occurs in all economic classes, it remains most severe among the poor. 4

Another part of the alcohol myth is that drinking makes you more attractive to the opposite sex. ''Hot, hot, hot,'' one commercial's soundtrack begins, as the camera scans a crowd of college-age beachgoers. Next it follows the curve of a woman's leg up to her bare hip and lingers there. She is young, beautiful, wearing a bikini. A young guy, carrying an ice chest, positions himself near to where she sits. He is tan, muscular. She doesn't show much interest—until he opens the chest and takes out a beer. Now she smiles over at him. He raises his eyebrows and, invitingly, holds up another can. She joins him. This beer, the song concludes, ''attracts like no other.'' 5

Beer doesn't make anyone sexier. Like all alcohol, it lowers the levels of male hormones in men and of female hormones in women—even when taken in small amounts. In substantial amounts, alcohol can cause infertility in women and impotence in men. Some alcoholic men even develop enlarged breasts, from their increased female hormones. 6

The alcohol myth also creates the illusion that beer and athletics are a perfect combination. One billboard features three high-action images: a baseball player running at top speed, a surfer riding a wave, and a basketball player leaping to make a dunk shot. A particular light beer, the billboard promises, ''won't slow you down.'' 7

''Slow you down'' is exactly what alcohol does. Drinking plays a role in over six million injuries each year—not counting automobile accidents. Even in small amounts, alcohol dulls the brain, reducing muscle coordination and slowing reaction time. It also interferes with the ability to focus the eyes and adjust to a sudden change in brightness—such as the flash of a car's headlights. Drinking and driving, responsible for over half of all automobile deaths, is the leading cause of death among teenagers. Continued alcohol abuse can physically alter the brain, permanently impairing learning and memory. Long-term drinking is related to malnutrition, weakening of the bones, and ulcers. It increases the risk of liver failure, heart disease, and stomach cancer. 8

Finally, according to the myth fostered by the media in our culture, alcohol generates a warm glow of happiness that unifies the family. In one popular film, the only food visible at a wedding reception is an untouched wedding cake, but beer, whiskey, and vodka flow freely. Most of the guests are drunk. After shouting into the microphone to get everyone's attention, the band leader asks the bride and groom to come forward. They are presented with two wine-filled silver drinking cups branching out from a single stem. ''If you can drink your cups without spilling any wine,'' the band leader tells them, ''you will have good luck for the rest of your lives.'' The couple drain their cups without taking a breath, and the crowd cheers. 9

A marriage, however, is unlikely to be ''lucky'' if alcohol plays a major role in it. 10
Nearly two-thirds of domestic violence involves drinking. Alcohol abuse by parents is
strongly tied to child neglect and juvenile delinquency. Drinking during pregnancy can
lead to miscarriage and is a major cause of such birth defects as deformed limbs and
mental retardation. Those who depend on alcohol are far from happy: over a fourth of
the patients in state and county mental institutions have alcohol problems; more than half
of all violent crimes are alcohol-related; the rate of suicide among alcoholics is fifteen
times higher than among the general population.

Alcohol, some would have us believe, is part of being successful, sexy, healthy, and 11
happy. But those who have suffered from it—directly or indirectly—know otherwise. For
alcohol's victims, ''Here's to your health'' rings with a terrible irony when it is accompanied by the clink of liquor glasses.

■ ## Reading Comprehension Questions

1. The word *caption* in ''In a slick men's magazine, one full-page ad for Scotch
   whiskey shows two men seated in an elegant restaurant. . . . The caption
   reads 'the taste of success''' (paragraph 3) means
   a. menu.
   b. man.
   c. words accompanying the picture.
   d. contract that seals the business deal.

2. The word *impairing* in ''Continued alcohol abuse can physically alter the
   brain, permanently impairing learning and memory'' (paragraph 8) means
   a. postponing.
   b. doubling.
   c. damaging.
   d. teaching.

3. Which one of the following would be a good alternative title for this selection?
   a. The Taste of Success
   b. Alcohol and Your Social Life
   c. Too Much Tequila
   d. Alcohol: Image and Reality

4. Which sentence best expresses the main idea of the selection?
   a. Sports and alcohol don't mix.
   b. The media and our culture promote false images about success and hap-
      piness.
   c. The media and our culture promote false beliefs about alcohol.
   d. Liquor companies should not be allowed to use misleading ads about
      alcohol.

5. According to the selection, drinking can
   a. actually unify a family.
   b. lower hormone levels.
   c. temporarily improve performance in sports.
   d. increase the likelihood of pregnancy.

6. *True or false?* _____ Alcohol abuse is most severe among middle-class people.

7. *True or false?* _____ The leading cause of death among teenagers is drinking and driving.

8. From the first paragraph of the essay, we can conclude that
   a. even one encounter with alcohol can actually lead to death.
   b. tequila is the worst type of alcohol to drink.
   c. wrestlers tend to drink more than other athletes.
   d. by the time students reach high school, peer pressure doesn't influence them.

9. *True or false?* _____ The author implies that one or two drinks a day are probably harmless.

10. The author implies that heavy drinking can lead to
    a. poor grades.
    b. getting fired.
    c. heart disease.
    d. all of the above.

■ **Discussion Questions**

About Content

1. According to Dunayer, how many parts are there to the myth about alcohol? Which part do you consider the most dangerous?

2. Drawing on your own experience, provide examples of ways in which our culture encourages drinking.

About Structure

3. What method does Dunayer use to begin her essay?
   a. Broad to narrow
   b. Idea that is contrary to what will be developed
   c. Incident

4. The body of Dunayer's essay is made up of four pairs of paragraphs (paragraphs 3 and 4; 5 and 6; 7 and 8; 9 and 10) that serve to introduce and develop each of her four main supporting points. What is the pattern by which she divides each point into two paragraphs?

5. Dunayer introduces the first part of the myth about alcohol with the words "Part of the myth is . . . " (See the first sentence of paragraph 3.) Then she goes on to use an addition transition to introduce each of the three other parts of the myth—in the first sentences of paragraphs 5, 7, and 9. Write those addition transitions here:

_____   _____   _____

6. What method does Dunayer use to conclude her essay?
   a. Prediction or recommendation
   b. Summary and a final thought
   c. Thought-provoking question

About Style and Tone

7. Why is the title of the essay appropriate?

■ Writing Assignments

Assignment 1

Describe and analyze several recent advertisements for wine, beer, or liquor on television or radio, in newspapers or magazines, or on billboards. Argue whether the ads are socially and humanly responsible or irresponsible in the way that they portray drinking. Your thesis might be something like one of the following examples:

> In three recent ads, ad agencies and liquor companies have acted irresponsibly in their portrayal of alcohol.

> In three recent ads, ad agencies and liquor companies have acted with a measure of responsibility in their portrayal of alcohol.

Alternatively, write about what you consider responsible or irresponsible advertising for some other product or service: cigarettes, weight loss, and cosmetics are possibilities to consider.

Assignment 2

If you have a friend, relative, or classmate who drinks a lot, write a letter warning him or her about the dangers of alcohol. If appropriate, use information from Dunayer's essay. Remember that since your purpose is to get someone you care about to control or break a dangerous habit, you should make your writing very personal. Don't bother explaining how alcoholism affects people in general. Instead, focus directly on what you see it doing to your reader.

Divide your argument into at least three supporting paragraphs. You might, for instance, talk about how your reader is jeopardizing his or her relationship with three of the following: family, friends, boss and coworkers, instructors and classmates.

Assignment 3

Dunayer describes how alcohol advertisements promote false beliefs, such as the idea that alcohol will make you successful. Imagine that you work for a public service ad agency given the job of presenting the negative side of alcohol. What images would you choose to include in your ads?

Write a report to your boss in which you propose in detail three antialcohol ads. Choose from among the following:

Ad counteracting the idea that alcohol leads to success
Ad counteracting the idea that alcohol is sexy
Ad counteracting the idea that alcohol goes well with athletics
Ad counteracting the idea that alcohol makes for happy families

How to Make It in College, Now That You're Here

Brian O'Keeney

The author of this selection presents a compact guide to being a successful student. He will show you how to pass tests, how to avoid becoming a student zombie, how to find time to fit in everything you want to do, and how to deal with personal problems while keeping up with your studies. These and other helpful tips have been culled from the author's own experience and his candid interviews with fellow students.

Today is your first day on campus. You were a high school senior three months ago. Or maybe you've been at home with your children for the last ten years. Or maybe you work full time and you're coming to school to start the process that leads to a better job. Whatever your background is, you're probably not too concerned today with staying in college. After all, you just got over the hurdle (and the paperwork) of applying to this place and organizing your life so that you could attend. And today, you're confused and tired. Everything is a hassle, from finding the classrooms to standing in line at the bookstore. But read my advice anyway. And if you don't read it today, clip and save this article. You might want to look at it a little further down the road. 1

By the way, if this isn't your very first day, don't skip this article. Maybe you haven't been doing as well in your studies as you'd hoped. Or perhaps you've had problems juggling your work schedule, your class schedule, and your social life. If so, read on. You're about to get the inside story on making it in college. On the basis of my own experience as a final-year student, and on dozens of interviews with successful students, I've worked out a no-fail system for coping with college. These are the inside tips every student needs to do well in school. I've put myself in your place, and I'm going to answer the questions that will cross (or have already crossed) your mind during your stay here. 2

What's the Secret of Getting Good Grades?

It all comes down to getting those grades, doesn't it? After all, you came here for some reason, and you're going to need passing grades to get the credits or degree you want. Many of us never did much studying in high school; most of the learning we did took place in the classroom. College, however, is a lot different. You're really on your own when it comes to passing courses. In fact, sometimes you'll feel as if nobody cares if you make it or not. Therefore, you've got to figure out a study system that gets results. Sooner or later, you'll be alone with those books. After that, you'll be sitting in a classroom with an exam sheet on your desk. Whether you stare at that exam with a queasy stomach or whip through it fairly confidently depends on your study techniques. Most of the successful students I talked to agreed that the following eight study tips deliver solid results. 3

1. Set Up a Study Place. Those students you see ''studying'' in the cafeteria or game room aren't learning much. You just can't learn when you're distracted by people and noise. Even the library can be a bad place to study if you constantly find yourself watching the clouds outside or the students walking through the stacks. It takes guts to sit, alone, in a quiet place in order to study. But you have to do it. Find a room at home or a spot in the library that's relatively quiet—and boring. When you sit there, you won't have much to do except study. 4

2. Get into a Study Frame of Mind. When you sit down, do it with the attitude that you're going to get this studying done. You're not going to doodle in your notebook or make a list for the supermarket. Decide that you're going to study and learn *now,* so that you can move on to more interesting things as soon as possible. 5

3. Give Yourself Rewards. If you sweat out a block of study time, and do a good   6
job on it, treat yourself. You deserve it. You can "psych" yourself up for studying by
promising to reward yourself afterwards. A present for yourself can be anything from a
favorite TV show to a relaxing bath to a dish of double chocolate ice cream.

4. Skim the Textbook First. Lots of students sit down with an assignment like   7
"read chapter five, pages 125–150" and do just that. They turn to page 125 and start to
read. After a while, they find that they have no idea what they just read. For the last ten
minutes, they've been thinking about their five-year-old or what they're going to eat for
dinner. Eventually, they plod through all the pages but don't remember much afterwards.

In order to prevent this problem, skim the textbook chapter first. This means: look   8
at the title, the subtitles, the headings, the pictures, the first and last paragraphs. Try to
find out what the person who wrote the book had in mind when he or she organized the
chapter. What was important enough to set off as a title or in bold type? After skimming,
you should be able to explain to yourself what the main points of the chapter are. Unless
you're the kind of person who would step into an empty elevator shaft without looking
first, you'll soon discover the value of skimming.

5. Take Notes on What You're Studying. This sounds like a hassle, but it   9
works. Go back over the material after you've read it, and jot down key words and phrases
in the margins. When you review the chapter for a test, you'll have handy little things
like "definition of rationalization" or "example of assimilation" in the margins. If the
material is especially tough, organize a separate sheet of notes. Write down definitions,
examples, lists, and main ideas. The idea is to have a single sheet that boils the entire
chapter down to a digestible lump.

6. Review after You've Read and Taken Notes. Some people swear that talking   10
to yourself works. Tell yourself about the most important points in the chapter. Once
you've said them out loud, they seem to stick better in your mind. If you can't talk to
yourself about the material after reading it, that's a sure sign you don't really know it.

7. Give Up. This may sound contradictory, but give up when you've had enough.   11
You should try to make it through at least an hour, though. Ten minutes here and there
are useless. When your head starts to pound and your eyes develop spidery red lines,
quit. You won't do much learning when you're exhausted.

8. Take a College Skills Course If You Need It. Don't hesitate or feel embar-   12
rassed about enrolling in a study skills course. Many students say they wouldn't have
made it without one.

How Can I Keep Up with All My Responsibilities without Going Crazy?

You've got a class schedule. You're supposed to study. You've got a family. You've got   13
a husband, wife, boyfriend, girlfriend, child. You've got a job. How are you possibly
going to cover all the bases in your life and maintain your sanity? This is one of the

toughest problems students face. Even if they start the semester with the best of intentions, they eventually find themselves tearing their hair out trying to do everything they're supposed to do. Believe it or not, though, it is possible to meet all your responsibilities. And you don't have to turn into a hermit or give up your loved ones to do it.

The secret here is to organize your time. But don't just sit around half the semester planning to get everything together soon. Before you know it, you'll be confronted with midterms, papers, family, and work all at once. Don't let yourself reach that breaking point. Instead, try these three tactics.   14

1. Monthly Calendar. Get one of those calendars with big blocks around the dates. Give yourself an overview of the whole term by marking down the due dates for papers and projects. Circle test and exam days. This way those days don't sneak up on you unexpectedly.   15

2. Study Schedule. Sit down during the first few days of this semester and make up a sheet listing the days and hours of the week. Fill in your work and class hours first. Then try to block out some study hours. It's better to study a little every day than to create a huge once-or-twice-a-week marathon session. Schedule study hours for your hardest classes for the times when you feel most energetic. For example, I battled my tax law textbook in the mornings; when I looked at it after 7:00 P.M., I might as well have been reading Chinese. The usual proportion, by the way, is one hour of study time for every class hour.   16

In case you're one of those people who get carried away, remember to leave blocks of free time, too. You won't be any good to yourself or anyone else if you don't relax and pack in the studying once in a while.   17

3. "To-Do" List. This is the secret that single-handedly got me through college. Once a week (or every day if you want to), write a list of what you have to do. Write down everything from "write English paper" to "buy cold cuts for lunches." The best thing about a "to do" list is that it seems to tame all those stray "I have to" thoughts that nag at your mind. Just making the list seems to make the tasks "doable." After you finish something on the list, cross it off. Don't be compulsive about finishing everything; you're not Superman or Wonder Woman. Get the important things done first. The secondary things you don't finish can simply be moved to your next "to do" list.   18

What Can I Do If Personal Problems Get in the Way of My Studies?

One student, Roger, told me this story: 19

> Everything was going OK for me until the middle of the spring semester. I went through a terrible time when I broke up with my girlfriend and started seeing her best friend. I was trying to deal with my ex-girlfriend's hurt and anger, my new girlfriend's guilt, and my own worries and anxieties at the same time. In addition to this, my mother was sick and on a medication that made her really irritable. I hated to go home because the atmosphere was

so uncomfortable. Soon, I started missing classes because I couldn't deal with the academic pressures as well as my own personal problems. It seemed easier to hang around my girl-friend's apartment than to face all my problems at home and at school.

Another student, Marian, told me: 20

I'd been married for eight years and the relationship wasn't going too well. I saw the hand-writing on the wall, and I decided to prepare for the future. I enrolled in college, because I knew I'd need a decent job to support myself. Well, my husband had a fit be-cause I was going to school. We were arguing a lot anyway, and he made it almost impossi-ble for me to study at home. I think he was angry and almost jealous because I was draw-ing away from him. It got so bad that I thought about quitting college for a while. I wasn't getting any support at home and it was just too hard to go on.

Personal troubles like these are overwhelming when you're going through them.   21 School seems like the least important thing in your life. The two students above are perfect examples of this. But if you think about it, quitting or failing school would be the worst thing for these two students. Roger's problems, at least with his girlfriends, would simmer down eventually, and then he'd regret having left school. Marian had to finish college if she wanted to be able to live independently. Sometimes, you've just got to hang tough.

But what do you do while you're trying to live through a lousy time? First of all, do   22 something difficult. Ask yourself, honestly, if you're exaggerating small problems as an excuse to avoid classes and studying. It takes strength to admit this, but there's no sense in kidding yourself. If your problems are serious, and real, try to make some human contacts at school. Lots of students hide inside a miserable shell made of their own troubles and feel isolated and lonely. Believe me, there are plenty of students with problems. Not everyone is getting A's and having a fabulous social and home life at the same time. As you go through the term, you'll pick up some vibrations about the students in your classes. Perhaps someone strikes you as a compatible person. Why not speak to that person after class? Share a cup of coffee in the cafeteria or walk to the parking lot together. You're not looking for a best friend or the love of your life. You just want to build a little network of support for yourself. Sharing your difficulties, questions, and complaints with a friendly person on campus can make a world of difference in how you feel.

Finally, if your problems are overwhelming, get some professional help. Why do you   23 think colleges spend countless dollars on counseling departments and campus psychiatric services? More than ever, students all over the country are taking advantage of the help offered by support groups and therapy sessions. There's no shame attached to asking for help, either; in fact, almost 40 percent of college students (according to one survey) will use counseling services during their time in school. Just walk into a student center or counseling office and ask for an appointment. You wouldn't think twice about asking a dentist to help you get rid of your toothache. Counselors are paid—and want—to help you with your problems.

Why Do Some People Make It and Some Drop Out?

Anyone who spends at least one semester in college notices that some students give up 24
on their classes. The person who sits behind you in accounting, for example, begins to
miss a lot of class meetings and eventually vanishes. Or another student comes to class
without the assignment, doodles in a notebook during the lecture, and leaves during the
break. What's the difference between students like this and the ones who succeed in
school? My survey may be nonscientific, but everyone I asked said the same thing: attitude.
A positive attitude is the key to everything else—good study habits, smart time scheduling,
and coping with personal difficulties.

What does "a positive attitude" mean? Well, for one thing, it means avoiding the 25
zombie syndrome. It means not only showing up for your classes, but also doing something
while you're there. Really listen. Take notes. Ask a question if you want to. Don't just
walk into a class, put your mind in neutral, and drift away to never-never land.

Having a positive attitude goes deeper than this, though. It means being mature about 26
college as an institution. Too many students approach college classes like six-year-olds
who expect first grade to be as much fun as *Sesame Street*. First grade, as we all know,
isn't as much fun as *Sesame Street*. And college classes can sometimes be downright dull
and boring. If you let a boring class discourage you so much that you want to leave
school, you'll lose in the long run. Look at your priorities. You want a degree, or a
certificate, or a career. If you have to, you can make it through a less-than-interesting
class in order to achieve what you want. Get whatever you can out of every class. But
if you simply can't stand a certain class, be determined to fulfill its requirements and be
done with it once and for all.

After the initial high of starting school, you have to settle in for the long haul. If you 27
follow the advice here, you'll be prepared to face the academic crunch. You'll also live
through the semester without giving up your family, your job, or *Monday Night Football*.
Finally, going to college can be an exciting time. You do learn. And when you learn
things, the world becomes a more interesting place.

■ Reading Comprehension Questions

1. The word *queasy* in "with a queasy stomach" (paragraph 3) means
   a. intelligent.
   b. healthy.
   c. full.
   d. nervous.

2. The word *tactics* in "try these three tactics" (paragraph 14) means
   a. proofs.
   b. problems.
   c. methods.
   d. questions.

3. Which of the following would be a good alternative title for this selection?
   a. Your First Day on Campus
   b. Coping with College
   c. How to Budget Your Time
   d. The Benefits of College Skills Courses

4. Which sentence expresses the main idea of the selection?
   a. In high school, most of us did little homework.
   b. You should give yourself rewards for studying well.
   c. Sometimes personal problems interfere with studying.
   d. You can succeed in college by following certain guidelines.

5. According to the author, ''making it'' in college means
   a. studying whenever you have any free time.
   b. getting a degree by barely passing your courses.
   c. quitting school until you solve your personal problems.
   d. getting good grades without making your life miserable.

6. If your personal problems seem overwhelming, you should
   a. drop out for a while.
   b. try to ignore them.
   c. tell another student.
   d. seek professional help.

7. Which of the following is *not* described by the author as a means of time control?
   a. Monthly calendar
   b. To-do list
   c. Study schedule
   d. Flexible job hours

8. We might infer that the author
   a. is a writer for the school newspaper.
   b. is president of his class.
   c. has taken a study skills course.
   d. was not a successful student in his first year of college.

9. From the selection we can conclude that
   a. college textbooks are very expensive.
   b. it is a good practice to write notes in your textbook.
   c. taking notes on your reading takes too much time.
   d. a student should never mark up an expensive textbook.

10. The author implies that
    a. fewer people than before are attending college.
    b. most students think that college is easy.
    c. most students dislike college.
    d. coping with college is difficult.

■ Discussion Questions

About Content

1. What pitfalls does O'Keeney think are waiting for students just starting college? Are there other pitfalls not mentioned in the article?
2. What is the secret that the author says got him through college? What do you think is the most helpful or important suggestion the author makes in the selection?
3. Do you agree with the author that Roger and Marian should stay in school? Are there any situations where it would be better for students to quit school or leave temporarily?

About Structure

4. What is the thesis of the selection? Write here the number of the paragraph in which it is stated: _____
5. Why does the article begin with the first day on campus?
6. What method of introduction does the author use in the section on personal problems (starting on page 635)? What is the value of using this method?

About Style and Tone

7. This essay is obviously written for college students. Can you guess where an essay like this one would appear? (*Hint:* Reread the first paragraph.)

■ Writing Assignments

Assignment 1

Write a process essay similar to the one you've just read that explains how to succeed in some other field—for example, a job, a sport, marriage, child rearing. First, brainstorm three or four problem areas a newcomer to this experience might encounter. Then, under each area you have listed, jot down some helpful hints and techniques for overcoming these problems. For example, a process paper on "How to Succeed as a Waitress" might describe the following problem areas in this kind of job:

Developing a good memory
Learning to do tasks quickly
Coping with troublesome customers

Each supporting paragraph in this paper would discuss specific techniques for dealing with these problems. Be sure that the advice you give is detailed and specific enough to really help a person in such a situation.

You may find it helpful to look over the process essays on pages 158–161.

Assignment 2

Write a letter to Roger or Marian, giving advice on how to deal with the personal problem mentioned in the article. You could recommend any or all of the following:

Face the problem realistically. (By doing what?)

Make other contacts at school. (How? Where?)

See a counselor. (Where? What should this person be told?)

Realize that the problem is not so serious. (Why not?)

Ignore the problem. (How? By doing what instead?)

In your introductory paragraph, explain why you are writing the letter. Include a thesis statement that says what plan of action you are recommending. Then, in the rest of the paper, explain the plan of action (or plans of action) in detail.

Assignment 3

Write an essay contrasting college *as you thought it would be* with college *as it is.* You can organize the essay by focusing on three specific things that are different from what you expected. Or you can cover three areas of difference. For instance, you may decide to contrast your expectations about (1) a college dorm room, (2) your roommate, and (3) dining hall food with reality. Or you could contrast your expectations about (1) fellow students, (2) college professors, and (3) college courses with reality.

Refer to the section on comparison and contrast essays in this book (pages 178–193) to review point-by-point and one-side-at-a-time methods of development. Be sure to make an outline of your essay before you begin to write.

College Lectures:
Is Anybody Listening?

David Daniels

College students are doodling in their notebooks or gazing off into space as their instructor lectures for fifty minutes. What is wrong with this picture? Many would say that what is wrong is the students. However, the educator and author David Daniels would say that the lecture itself is the problem. As you read this article, see if you agree with his analysis of lectures and their place in a college education.

1   A former teacher of mine, Robert A. Fowkes of New York University, likes to tell the story of a class he took in Old Welsh while studying in Germany during the 1930s. On the first day the professor strode up to the podium, shuffled his notes, coughed, and began, *''Guten Tag, Meine Damen und Herren''* (''Good day, ladies and gentlemen''). Fowkes glanced around uneasily. He was the only student in the course.

2   Toward the middle of the semester, Fowkes fell ill and missed a class. When he returned, the professor nodded vaguely and, to Fowkes's astonishment, began to deliver not the next lecture in the sequence but the one after. Had he, in fact, lectured to an empty hall in the absence of his solitary student? Fowkes thought it perfectly possible.

3   Today, American colleges and universities (originally modeled on German ones) are under strong attack from many quarters. Teachers, it is charged, are not doing a good job of teaching, and students are not doing a good job of learning. American businesses and industries suffer from unenterprising, uncreative executives educated not to think for themselves but to mouth outdated truisms the rest of the world has long discarded. College graduates lack both basic skills and general culture. Studies are conducted and reports are issued on the status of higher education, but any changes that result either are largely cosmetic or make a bad situation worse.

4   One aspect of American education too seldom challenged is the lecture system. Professors continue to lecture and students to take notes much as they did in the thirteenth century, when books were so scarce and expensive that few students could own them. The time is long overdue for us to abandon the lecture system and turn to methods that really work.

5   To understand the inadequacy of the present system, it is enough to follow a single imaginary first-year student—let's call her Mary—through a term of lectures on, say, introductory psychology (although any other subject would do as well). She arrives on the first day and looks around the huge lecture hall, taken a little aback to see how large the class is. Once the hundred or more students enrolled in the course discover that the professor never takes attendance (how can he?—calling the role would take far too much time), the class shrinks to a less imposing size.

Some days Mary sits in the front row, from where she can watch the professor read 6
from a stack of yellowed notes that seem nearly as old as he is. She is bored by the
lectures, and so are most of the other students, to judge by the way they are nodding off
or doodling in their notebooks. Gradually she realizes the professor is as bored as his
audience. At the end of each lecture he asks, ''Are there any questions?'' in a tone of
voice that makes it plain he would much rather there weren't. He needn't worry—the
students are as relieved as he is that the class is over.

Mary knows very well she should read an assignment before every lecture. However, 7
as the professor gives no quizzes and asks no questions, she soon realizes she needn't
prepare. At the end of the term she catches up by skimming her notes and memorizing
a list of facts and dates. After the final exam, she promptly forgets much of what she has
memorized. Some of her fellow students, disappointed at the impersonality of it all, drop
out of college altogether. Others, like Mary, stick it out, grow resigned to the system and
await better days when, as juniors and seniors, they will attend smaller classes and at last
get the kind of personal attention real learning requires.

I admit this picture is overdrawn—most universities supplement lecture courses with 8
discussion groups, usually led by graduate students, and some classes, such as first-year
English, are always relatively small. Nevertheless, far too many courses rely principally
or entirely on lectures, an arrangement much loved by faculty and administrators but
scarcely designed to benefit the students.

One problem with lectures is that listening intelligently is hard work. Reading the 9
same material in a textbook is a more efficient way to learn because students can proceed
as slowly as they need to until the subject matter becomes clear to them. Even simply
paying attention is very difficult: people can listen at a rate of four hundred to six hundred
words a minute, while the most impassioned professor talks at scarcely a third of that
speed. This time lag between speech and comprehension leads to daydreaming. Many
students believe years of watching television have sabotaged their attention span, but their
real problem is that listening attentively is much harder than they think.

Worse still, attending lectures is passive learning, at least for inexperienced listeners. 10
Active learning, in which students write essays or perform experiments and then have
their work evaluated by an instructor, is far more beneficial for those who have not yet
fully learned how to learn. While it's true that techniques of active listening, such as
trying to anticipate the speaker's next point or taking notes selectively, can enhance the
value of a lecture, few students possess such skills at the beginning of their college careers.
More commonly, students try to write everything down and even bring tape recorders to
class in a clumsy effort to capture every word.

Students need to question their professors and to have their ideas taken seriously. 11
Only then will they develop the analytical skills required to think intelligently and cre-
atively. Most students learn best by engaging in frequent and even heated debate, not by
scribbling down a professor's often unsatisfactory summary of complicated issues. They
need small discussion classes that demand the common labors of teacher and students
rather than classes in which one person, however learned, propounds his or her own ideas.

The lecture system ultimately harms professors as well. It reduces feedback to a 12
minimum, so that the lecturer can neither judge how well students understand the material

nor benefit from their questions or comments. Questions that require the speaker to clarify obscure points and comments that challenge sloppily constructed arguments are indispensable to scholarship. Without them, the liveliest mind can atrophy. Undergraduates may not be able to make telling contributions very often, but lecturing insulates a professor even from the beginner's naive question that could have triggered a fruitful line of thought.

If lectures make so little sense, why have they been allowed to continue? Administrators love them, of course. They can cram far more students into a lecture hall than into a discussion class, and for many administrators that is almost the end of the story. But the truth is that faculty members, and even students, conspire with them to keep the lecture system alive and well. Lectures are easier on everyone than debates. Professors can pretend to teach by lecturing just as students can pretend to learn by attending lectures, with no one the wiser, including the participants. Moreover, if lectures afford some students an opportunity to sit back and let the professor run the show, they offer some professors an irresistible forum for showing off. In a classroom where everyone contributes, students are less able to hide and professors less tempted to engage in intellectual exhibitionism. 13

Smaller classes in which students are required to involve themselves in discussion put an end to students' passivity. Students become actively involved when forced to question their own ideas as well as their instructor's. Their listening skills improve dramatically in the excitement of intellectual give and take with their instructors and fellow students. Such interchanges help professors do their job better because they allow them to discover who knows what—before final exams, not after. When exams are given in this type of course, they can require analysis and synthesis from the students, not empty memorization. Classes like this require energy, imagination, and commitment from professors, all of which can be exhausting. But they compel students to share responsibility for their own intellectual growth. 14

Lectures will never entirely disappear from the university scene both because they seem to be economically necessary and because they spring from a long tradition in a setting that rightly values tradition for its own sake. But the lectures too frequently come at the wrong end of the students' educational careers—during the first two years, when they most need close, even individual, instruction. If lecture classes were restricted to junior and senior undergraduates and to graduate students, who are less in need of scholarly nurturing and more able to prepare work on their own, they would be far less destructive of students' interests and enthusiasms than the present system. After all, students must learn to listen before they can listen to learn. 15

■ Reading Comprehension Questions

1. The word *enhance* in "techniques of active listening . . . can enhance the value of a lecture" (paragraph 10) means
   a. ruin.
   b. ignore.
   c. increase.
   d. claim.

2. The word *atrophy* in "Without [questions and comments], the liveliest mind can atrophy" (paragraph 12) means
   a.   waste away.
   b.   be unchanged.
   c.   compete.
   d.   strengthen.

3. Which of the following would be a good alternative title for this selection?
   a.   How to Benefit from Lecture Classes
   b.   Passive Learning
   c.   Problems with Lecture Classes
   d.   Lectures: An Academic Tradition

4. Which sentence best expresses the main idea of the selection?
   a.   American colleges and universities are being attacked from many sides.
   b.   Colleges and universities should offer interactive, not lecture, classes to first-year and second-year students.
   c.   College graduates lack basic skills and general culture.
   d.   American colleges and universities are modeled on German ones.

5. According to the author, the lecture system
   a.   encourages efficient learning.
   b.   encourages students to ask questions.
   c.   helps professors teach better.
   d.   discourages students' attendance and preparation.

6. An example of passive learning is
   a.   attending lectures.
   b.   writing essays.
   c.   doing experiments.
   d.   debating a point.

7. To develop their thinking skills, students do *not* need to
   a.   bring tape recorders to class.
   b.   question professors.
   c.   debate.
   d.   attend small discussion classes.

8. The author implies that large lecture classes
   a.   require students to have well-developed listening skills.
   b.   encourage participation.
   c.   are more harmful for juniors and seniors than for first-year students.
   d.   are a modern invention.

9. *True or false?* _____ Daniels suggests that small classes demand greater effort from both faculty and students.

10. The author implies that administrators love lectures because
    a. students learn better in lectures.
    b. professors teach better through lecturing.
    c. schools make more money on lecture classes.
    d. professors can show off in lectures.

■ Discussion Questions

About Content

1. How do your experiences in lecture classes and smaller classes compare with Daniels's descriptions of such classes?
2. What reasons are given to explain why lectures are ''much loved by faculty and administrators''?
3. What are the disadvantages of lectures, according to the author?

About Structure

4. In which early paragraph does the thesis of this selection appear? Write its number here: _____
5. What method of introduction does the author use in this essay?

About Style and Tone

6. The author supports his main point with
    a. research and statistics.
    b. experts' opinions.
    c. students' opinions.
    d. personal observations.
7. What is the tone of Daniels's comments on administrators, professors, and students in paragraph 13? Back up your choice with details from the paragraph.
    a. Peaceful
    b. Critical
    c. Affectionate
    d. Humorous

■ Writing Assignments

Assignment 1

Write an essay in which you contrast a lecture class with a smaller, more interactive class. First make a list of the differences between the two classes. Following are some possible areas of difference you might consider:

Interest level
Demands on students
Opportunities for asking questions
Opportunities for discussions
Quality of feedback from the instructor

Choose three of the differences you found, and then decide which class you learned more in. You will then have the basis for a thesis statement and three supporting topic sentences. An example of a thesis statement for this essay is:

Because of the different approaches to students' questions, class discussion, and feedback from the instructor in grading papers, I learned a lot more in my first-year English class than in my business lecture class.

That thesis statement could be shortened to:

I learned a lot more in my first-year English class than in my business lecture class.

The three supporting points for this thesis statement are about:

Different approaches to students' questions
Class discussion
Personal feedback on assignments

Change each of the points listed above into a sentence, and you have your three topic sentences. A topic sentence based on the last point above might be: ''While my English instructor gave me a lot of useful feedback on my assignments, my business instructor put only a grade on papers.'' Use specific details from your experience to develop your supporting paragraphs.

Here is another possible thesis for this assignment:

While my business principles class was a large lecture class, I learned a lot more in it than in my American literature class because of the quality of the instructor's presentations, time set aside for attention to individual students, and use of audiovisual and computer materials.

If you haven't as yet taken any lecture classes, compare any two classes in college or high school.

Assignment 2

In this selection, Daniels has given some disadvantages of lectures. Write an essay on the advantages of lectures. Use examples from your personal experience and the experience of others to support your points. Begin by jotting down a list of advantages. Then choose the advantages you have the most to say about and develop those in your essay.

Assignment 3

Which teachers or instructors have you had who were not in a rut, who conducted classes that made you glad to learn? Write a description of your idea of a very good teacher or instructor. Your description may be of someone who actually taught you, or it may be of a fictional person who combines all the traits you have enjoyed (or missed) in your teachers and instructors through the years. Be sure to include plenty of specific examples of classroom activities and their effects on students. Following is a list of various aspects of teaching that you may wish to use in your description.

Mastery of subject matter
Ability to excite students about subject
Types of activities used
Relationships with students
Feedback to students
Homework and tests

Seven Ways to Keep the Peace at Home

Daniel A. Sugarman

We like to think of our homes as havens of peace and security, but they more often resemble battlegrounds. Living together in close quarters, family members must cope with each other's moods, problems, worries, and pressures. The author of this selection presents several helpful suggestions for defusing tense situations in the home. You may discover the underlying reasons for some of your own recurring family quarrels.

Not long ago, the parents of a seven-year-old girl consulted me because their daughter 1
was on her way to becoming a full-fledged hypochondriac. The girl's father was a physician,
and both parents were busy, involved people. During an early session with the family,
the reasons behind the girl's problems became clear. Dad arrived late and was preoccupied
and worried. He started to speak to me when his daughter interrupted: ''My throat hurts
a lot. I feel sick.'' Automatically he produced a tongue depressor and looked into her
throat. As he reassured her about her health, I realized the girl's complaints represented
the *only* way that she could engage her father's full attention.

When I pointed out that it was *he* who was unconsciously turning his daughter into 2
a chronic complainer, the father altered his behavior. He began giving her more attention
when she was *not* complaining about her health, and treating her physical complaints
very lightly when they occur. The girl began to improve. Soon, she hardly complained
about her health at all.

In the course of my clinical practice, I have seen hundreds of families in conflict, 3
and I am astounded at how frequently families unwittingly perpetuate tension-causing
behavior. Explosions just seem to happen again and again, until family members can be
helped to understand their interactions and learn to meet their mutual needs in less
destructive ways.

Although conflicts may be so ingrained for some families that outside professional 4
help is needed, certain principles of Family First Aid can go a long way in reducing
friction for most families. Here are seven steps that I have found to be helpful for
diminishing family tension.

1. Give Up the Myth of the Perfect Family. A couple of years ago, an unhappy 5
teen-ager came to my office with her family and announced, ''Well, here we are! The *Shady,*
not the *Brady,* Bunch!'' I find that many people, like this girl, resent their own families for
not living up to some romanticized notion of family life that can be found only on television.
In contrast to TV, *real* families go through periods of crisis that strain everyone's nerves.
During these trying times, most families' feelings and actions bear little resemblance to the
sanitized, prepackaged, half-hour comedy routines on TV.

Some months ago, for example, Grace and Lew Martin* brought their sixteen-year- 6
old son to me. Frank was an angry, sullen boy who had been doing poorly in school and
been caught smoking pot there. When Frank took his father's car out and was caught
speeding at ninety miles per hour, his parents insisted he come for treatment.

During our first session, it became evident that Frank's problem was certainly not 7
the only one in the family. Mr. Martin had been consistently passed over for promotion
at work. Mrs. Martin worked long hours trying to sell real estate, but because of high
mortgage rates she was having little success. Frank's fourteen-year-old sister had fractured
her leg the previous winter, and several operations had been required before it was set
properly. Mr. Martin had become angry and withdrawn, and was criticizing Mrs. Martin's
ability to manage the household. She, in turn, spent more time away from home and
began to drink heavily. Family fights became more and more frequent. Everyone tried to
bolster his or her own tottering sense of self-esteem by shattering the self-esteem of a
loved one.

---

*All names in this article have been changed to protect patients' privacy.

As I listened to this troubled family, I became aware that it wasn't the real problems 8
that were about to do them in. It was their self-hate. Mr. Martin was furious at himself
for not having gotten his promotion and because his wife had to work. Mrs. Martin was
furious with herself because she wasn't selling houses and because she couldn't stay at
home and care for her daughter. Frank was angry at them all, and so guilty about his
angry feelings that I suspect his ninety-mile-per-hour ride partially represented an attempt
at self-execution.

Once the Martin family understood how they were punishing themselves for not 9
being a perfect family, they began to show compassion toward themselves. They rapidly
began to solve the real problems.

The idea of the typical, happy family is becoming an anachronism. As the national 10
divorce rate approaches 50 percent, increasing numbers of people will live in single-parent
families. Should these people hate themselves because they aren't part of a typical family?
Unfortunately, too many do just that. As high interest rates nibble away at the American
dream of owning one's own home, should people hate themselves because they don't have
a ''typical'' single-family dwelling—or because everyone in the family has to work to
support this home? Unfortunately, too many do that, too.

I often wonder if the perfect American family ever did exist. If it did, I haven't met 11
it often in the past few years. As a matter of fact, research suggests that growing up in
a perfectly happy family is not as important as psychologists once thought. In one continuing study of 248 children, Jean Macfarlane at the University of California Institute of
Human Development has found that children who grew up in troubled homes do *not*
necessarily grow up to be troubled adults. Children who grew up in happy homes are *not*
necessarily better adjusted by the age of thirty.

When you give up the myth of the perfect family and deal with your real problems 12
in a spirit of compassion, psychological growth begins to take place.

2. Tell It Like You Feel It. Have you heard the story of the fifteen-year-old boy 13
who had never said a word in his whole life? He came to breakfast one day and suddenly
yelled, ''This oatmeal is cold!'' His astounded mother replied, ''You can *talk!* Why haven't
you spoken before?'' The boy shrugged and said, ''Before this, everything was okay.''

Funny story. Not so funny when situations like this occur in real families. And they 14
do. All too frequently I encounter people in families who, for one reason or another, feel
they must hide their feelings.

A few months ago, I saw an unhappy couple. Mrs. Raymond was almost always 15
depressed. Sometimes she couldn't even take care of her home and children. Mr. Raymond
was quite protective of his wife—but at the same time he was having an affair.

Together in my office, the Raymonds had little to say to each other. Each was very 16
solicitous, but wary of saying something that might upset the other. By not saying what
they felt, they managed to upset each other more than if they had communicated their
feelings directly.

It's odd how many people believe that when they stop verbalizing, communication 17
ceases. Nothing, of course, is further from the truth, because communication consists of
much more than words. Angry silence, sighs, headaches, impotence and arrests for drunken
driving can often be forms of distorted communication.

For his vacation, Mr. Raymond made plans to take his family on a two-week camping 18 trip. Mrs. Raymond told me she *dreaded* the idea of camping. When I urged her to express her displeasure so a mutually satisfying vacation could be arranged, she replied, ''But he works so hard. He deserves to go where he wants for vacation.'' Once at the campsite, she developed headaches and nausea. After two days of misery, she went to a local doctor, who failed to find any physical reason for her discomfort. During the rest of the vacation she tortured both herself and her husband with her physical complaints. It would have been much kinder had she told him how she felt before they left home.

Each time we conceal something from someone close to us, the relationship becomes 19 poorer. So, if you want to reduce family tensions, one of the most important ways to start is to send honest communications to those you love.

3. Don't Play Telephone. Do you remember the game ''Telephone''? A message 20 gets passed from person to person, and everyone laughs at how distorted it becomes. As a game, telephone can be fun. In real life, sending messages through third parties fouls things up. It's important for family members who have ''business'' with other family members to take it up *directly*.

When tension mounts in a relationship between two people, a frequent way of dealing 21 with this is to send messages through a third person. Family therapists refer to the process as ''triangulation.'' Following a spat, a mother may say to her son, ''Tell your father to pass the salt,'' which may be answered by, ''Tell your mother to get her own salt.'' In many chronic cases of triangulation, the middleman becomes severely disturbed.

Two years ago, Ruth and Ralph Gordon brought their seventeen-year-old daughter 22 for treatment. Lucille was not doing well in school, using drugs heavily and becoming blatantly promiscuous. When I began to work with her, she was uncommunicative and hostile. After some time, however, she opened up and told me her parents rarely talked to each other—but both used her as a confidante. Mrs. Gordon was sexually unsatisfied and suggested to Lucille that she ask her father to go for marital counseling. Mr. Gordon told Lucille that he was seeing another woman, and he urged Lucille to speak to her mother about improving her grooming. Caught in this tangle of feelings, Lucille became more and more troubled. It wasn't until she refused to play middleman that she began to improve. When either parent began to send a message through her, she learned to say, ''Tell him/her yourself!''

You'll find that when family members learn to dial each other directly, there's rarely 23 a busy signal or wrong number. With direct dealing, a sense of freshness is engendered.

4. Make Your Blueprints Flexible. Almost all parents have a secret master plan 24 for their children. Sometimes this calls for a child to grow up exactly like a parent—or, more often, for the child to become an improved version of the parent. In our culture, with its emphasis on getting ahead and self-fulfillment, it's tempting to hope that our children will realize many of our own desires. Whether we like it or not, though, children have a habit of spinning their own dreams. When a child's plans become different from his parents' blueprint, the family is on a collision course that can be avoided only by understanding and flexibility.

Most parents don't even realize how much they push and pull. I think you would 25 be surprised, too, at how frequently children will say things to their parents only to placate them.

One teenage girl assured her parents that she was going to study harder and prepare   26
for college. This girl told me, ''I don't plan to go to college, but I can't tell them yet.
They are disappointed enough, and I don't want to rip up any more of their dreams for
me.'' Caught in a web of parental expectations, this girl was miserable, and didn't
feel free enough to explore her own potential and channel her abilities into realistic
vocational goals.

An experienced parent knows that different children require different handling. When   27
we become wise and willing enough to revise our blueprints so that they incorporate the
child's realistic needs and aptitudes, we are on the road to a less tension-filled family life.

5. Learn to Use Contracts. Psychologists say that when two people marry, they   28
agree to a contract. Sometimes, a couple has a strong emotional investment in keeping
the not-so-pretty clauses of the contract hidden from everyone—including themselves.
Gina and Tom Butler were married twenty-five years before their hidden contract
caused problems.

When Tom met Gina, he was a skinny kid from a poor family who had a burning   29
desire to become financially successful. He was, under his bravado, painfully anxious and
felt very inadequate. Gina was the prettiest girl in town. She was also desperately unhappy
at home and couldn't wait to get away from the constant bickering there. When she was
sixteen, she had an abortion. At seventeen, she met Tom. As they dated they unwittingly
began to draft their contract. Gina, unconsciously, agreed to make Tom feel adequate to
reduce his anxieties. Tom, for his part, agreed never to discuss Gina's abortion, and to
remove her from her hostile home situation by marrying her.

For many years their contract worked well. Gina massaged Tom's ego. She encour-   30
aged, reassured, supported him. When the children went off to college, however, she felt
she needed to grow. She attended a local college, graduated with honors and accepted a
position with a well-known company. As Gina became successful, Tom became irritable
and angry. He accused her of not being interested in the family. Eventually, he accused
her of having a lover and of being ''a tramp, like you were when I met you and like
you'll always be.'' With these words, their contract was breached, and both sought the
services of attorneys. Fortunately, Gina's lawyer suggested counseling before divorce.
Once in treatment, the hidden aspects of Gina and Tom's contract were uncovered, and
they negotiated a more mature contract based upon mutual respect.

Many family contracts, like the Butlers', tend to disintegrate when one member of   31
the family begins to grow. And that's really all right, if the family can use the anxiety
that inevitably results as a catalyst to foster healthy mutual growth.

I find it helps a lot if you can face up to your hidden contracts and then update them.   32
It's also fruitful when you set clear provisions for the many minor vicissitudes of daily
living that can vex the family. Coats not hung up in the closet, hedges left untrimmed—
these are the raw materials that fuel family explosions. Frequently, an annoying, persistent
source of tension can be cleared away by drafting a new contract, whose terms are clearly
understood by all parties.

One teenager agreed to wash the dishes in exchange for transportation to cheerleading   33
practice. One husband agreed not to smoke when he was with his wife, in exchange for
her maintaining her weight loss. In these cases, all involved felt they had gotten a good
deal, and niggling sources of family tension were eliminated by negotiation.

6. Stop the "Good Guy"–"Bad Guy" Routine. Sometimes, the greatest 34 problems in families arise when people classify children as Good Guys and Bad Guys. These families tend to make a scapegoat of one of their members, who from that point on becomes "it" in a never-ending game of tag.

The Freemonts had four children. Brett, the third child, resembled Mrs. Freemont's 35 uncle Mark, who was serving time for embezzlement. "He's just like Uncle Mark," the Freemonts proclaimed when Brett came home from nursery school with a toy giraffe that he had taken, and again when Brett was eight and got into a fight with another third-grader. By the time Brett was fifteen, he had far more serious problems. "I'm just like my uncle Mark," he told me: the label had become a self-fulfilling prophecy. Brett felt doomed to replicate his uncle's life. But once you realize that no two people are exactly alike, you can free members of your family to be themselves.

Curiously, sometimes the Bad Guy of the family really serves to hold that family 36 together. I once worked with an eighteen-year-old girl who was constantly involved in mischief. As I began to understand her family situation, I realized that this girl's parents were emotionally estranged and the constant turmoil her behavior produced was an attempt to get her parents to form a united front. Indeed, she was partially successful. Her bizarre antics were at times so extreme that her parents barely had time to examine their own problems.

The next time you're in the midst of a family problem, resist your natural urge to 37 think in terms of *right* and *wrong*. Rather, ask yourself, "What is going on here and why?" In our era of no-fault car insurance and no-fault divorce, it makes increasing sense to have no-fault (or all-fault) family problems.

7. Get Rid of Old Emotional Baggage. When people enter into any new relation- 38 ship, they come to the new with a lot of old fears and unhealed emotional wounds. Unless you look at your own history honestly, you're likely to unwittingly re-create the same unhappy mess that gave you so much pain in the past.

Rachel Dorton grew up in an unhappy household in which her father frequently had 39 affairs. When *she* married, with fidelity her top priority, Rachel chose Mal, a hardworking, earnest accountant. For a time, all went well. After several months of marriage, however, Rachel became increasingly suspicious when Mal did audits in distant cities. She made his life miserable with constant suspicion and pleas for reassurance. After several sessions of counseling, Rachel came to realize that, without conscious intent, she was recreating the very experiences she had hated so much as a child. As she faced her feelings squarely, she was able to become less provocative, and she came to understand that *some* men— particularly Mal—could indeed be trusted.

During periods of severe stress, it's astounding how people may treat others the same 40 way they were treated by their parents. Ed Richardson had had a rough childhood. His father, a hardworking train conductor, would often take abuse from passengers and arrive home irritable and tense. Sometimes he would beat Ed severely. "You're no good," his father would proclaim. "You're a nothing."

Ed resolved that he would never hit his own children or call them names. For years 41 his resolve held, but then Ed's company went bankrupt and he was forced to take a job he despised. The family had to retrench and move to a smaller home. During this crisis, Ed's oldest boy cut school and was caught shoplifting. Ed brought the boy home and began to beat him. To his horror he found himself yelling, "You're no good . . . you're a nothing." Shaken by this experience, Ed got professional help. It took him a while to put things back together, but it helped when he realized that, when the chips are down, most people do unto others what has been done unto them.

At its best, a nourishing family serves as a safe haven enclosed by invisible walls of love 42
and concern. In such a family, individuals can replenish diminished feelings of self-esteem.

At its worst, a family can become a red-hot crucible in which ancient conflicts brew 43
and boil and are reenacted again and again. Most frequently, however, families just seem
to bumble along with little emotional insight into how the family itself may be responsible
for intensifying or perpetuating a family member's problem.

Solving family problems has never been easy. As a practicing psychologist, I know 44
that good intentions alone are usually not enough. Effective action most often follows
accurate understanding. With a little practice, care and use of these seven steps, the
chances are good that you'll be able to lower the tension level in the best family of all—
your own.

■ Reading Comprehension Questions

1. The word *anachronism* in "The idea of the typical, happy family is becoming an anachronism" (paragraph 10) means
   a. an ideal.
   b. an injustice.
   c. a disease.
   d. something out of its time.

2. The word *catalyst* in "the family can use the anxiety . . . as a catalyst to foster healthy mutual growth" (paragraph 31) means
   a. something which brings about change.
   b. an unfortunate accident.
   c. criticism.
   d. a form of destruction.

3. Which of the following would be a good alternative title for this selection?
   a. Creating Family Blueprints
   b. How to Reduce Family Tension
   c. Hidden Contracts
   d. Troubled Families

4. Which sentence best expresses the main idea of the selection?
   a. Believing myths about the perfect family can cause problems.
   b. When people marry, they agree to a contract.
   c. Following certain steps can help keep peace in a family.
   d. Family members play psychological games with each other.

5. One way for a family to stop playing ''telephone'' would be to
   a. get rid of old emotional baggage.
   b. negotiate better contracts.
   c. communicate directly.
   d. create flexible blueprints.

6. *True or false?* _____ Children who grow up in happy homes are not necessarily better adjusted as adults.

7. The ''Good Guy/Bad Guy'' routine means that
   a. family members feel they must be perfect.
   b. family members refuse to communicate with each other directly.
   c. families make scapegoats of one of their members.
   d. parents create secret master plans for their children.

8. The author implies that
   a. ''triangulation'' can be a helpful way for family members to communicate.
   b. making a scapegoat of a family member can unite a family.
   c. people need to identify their problems before they can act to help themselves.
   d. fidelity is essential in marriage.

9. The author implies that
   a. the perfect American family existed until fairly recently.
   b. creating family contracts inevitably leads to problems.
   c. how a parent treats a child can affect the following generations.
   d. families need ''middlemen'' to pass along communications.

10. *True or false?* _____ The author implies that all families need professional help at times.

■ **Discussion Questions**

About Content

1. According to Sugarman, who is more to blame for family problems, parents or children? Give examples from the selection to prove your point. Do you agree with him?

2. What are some ways, according to the selection, that family members take out their frustrations on each other? Can you think of any other ways?

3. At the end of the third section of the selection, Sugarman writes, ''You'll find that when family members learn to dial each other directly, there's rarely a busy signal or wrong number'' (paragraph 23). What does he mean? Do you think he is correct?

4. What does Sugarman mean by a ''hidden contract'' in a relationship (paragraph 28)? Give examples of such hidden contracts from the article or from your own knowledge.

About Structure

5. What method of introduction does the author use?
   a. Broad to narrow
   b. Anecdote
   c. Questions

6. Which method of introduction does the author use to begin the section on step 1?
   a. Beginning with an opposite
   b. Anecdote
   c. Broad to narrow

   Which method does he use to begin the section on step 3?
   a. Question
   b. Anecdote
   c. Quotation

About Style and Tone

7. In the concluding three paragraphs, the author compares a nourishing family to a ''haven enclosed by invisible walls of love and concern.'' He compares a tension-filled family to a ''red-hot crucible in which ancient conflicts brew and boil.'' See if you can think of two other comparisons that could be used to describe a loving family and a fighting family.

■ Writing Assignments

Assignment 1

Write about the three ways that would be most appropriate for keeping peace at your home. Following are examples of how the three supporting paragraphs in your essay might begin.

First supporting paragraph:

> One way our family would benefit is if we would stop playing the game of telephone. All too often, one family member uses another to . . .

Second supporting paragraph:

> Another step our family should take is to "Tell it like you feel it." My mother, for example, sometimes hides her true feelings about . . .

Third supporting paragraph:

> Perhaps most important, our family needs to stop the "Good-Guy/Bad-Guy" routine. Two people in my family seem to have been cast in these roles . . .

Develop the ways you choose with specific examples that involve the actual members of your family.

Assignment 2

Sugarman tells us seven ways to keep the peace at home. However, there are other places where it is important to keep the peace—for instance, at school, at the workplace, in the dormitory room. Choose one of these other places and write your own guide to how to keep the peace there. Use three of the rules discussed in the article or think of other rules, and develop each paragraph by giving specific examples of the rule you are suggesting. Try to include appropriate stories, as Sugarman does, to show what you mean.

Assignment 3

Write an essay-length summary of the selection. Your goal is to write a shortened and condensed—but accurate—version of the selection in about five hundred words. To do this, you should do the following:

> In each supporting paragraph of your summary, cover two or three of the peacekeeping methods.
>
> Include only *key* ideas.
>
> Shorten examples (or eliminate extra examples).
>
> Eliminate dialog and repeated ideas.

Most important, remember that a summary should be *in your own words,* not the original author's. Therefore, don't simply copy material from the selection. You should, instead, put the author's ideas into your own words.

Below is an introduction that you can use to begin the essay:

> A Summary of "Seven Ways to Keep the Peace at Home"
>
> Family is a word associated with warmth, affection, caring, love, and peace. In reality, though, family life can be very different. Tension, anger, and frustration take over, at times, in almost every household. In his article, "Seven Ways to Keep the Peace at Home," Daniel A. Sugarman describes several techniques people can use to prevent or resolve family conflicts.

In Praise of the F Word

Mary Sherry

What does it take to get by in high school? Too little, according to the author, a teacher in an "educational-repair shop." In this article which originally appeared in *Newsweek,* Mary Sherry describes the ways she sees students being cheated by their schools and proposes a remedy you may find surprising.

Tens of thousands of 18-year-olds will graduate this year and be handed meaningless diplomas. These diplomas won't look any different from those awarded their luckier classmates. Their validity will be questioned only when their employers discover that these graduates are semiliterate.   1

Eventually a fortunate few will find their way into educational-repair shops—adult-literacy programs, such as the one where I teach basic grammar and writing. There, high school graduates and high school dropouts pursuing graduate-equivalency certificates will learn the skills they should have learned in school. They will also discover they have been cheated by our educational system.   2

As I teach, I learn a lot about our schools. Early in each session I ask my students to write about an unpleasant experience they had in school. No writers' block here! "I wish someone would have had made me stop doing drugs and made me study." "I liked to party and no one seemed to care." "I was a good kid and didn't cause any trouble, so they just passed me along even though I didn't read well and couldn't write." And so on.   3

I am your basic do-gooder, and prior to teaching this class I blamed the poor academic skills our kids have today on drugs, divorce and other impediments to concentration necessary for doing well in school. But, as I rediscover each time I walk into the classroom, before a teacher can expect students to concentrate, he has to get their attention, no matter what distractions may be at hand. There are many ways to do this, and they have much to do with teaching style. However, if style alone won't do it, there is another way to show who holds the winning hand in the classroom. That is to reveal the trump card of failure.   4

I will never forget a teacher who played that card to get the attention of one of my children. Our youngest, a world-class charmer, did little to develop his intellectual talents but always got by. Until Mrs. Stifter.   5

Our son was a high school senior when he had her for English. "He sits in the back of the room talking to his friends," she told me. "Why don't you move him to the front row?" I urged, believing the embarrassment would get him to settle down. Mrs. Stifter looked at me steely-eyed over her glasses. "I don't move seniors," she said. "I flunk them." I was flustered. Our son's academic life flashed before my eyes. No teacher had ever threatened him with that before. I regained my composure and managed to say that I thought she was right. By the time I got home I was feeling pretty good about this. It   6 was a radical approach for these times, but, well, why not? "She's going to flunk you," I told my son. I did not discuss it any further. Suddenly English became a priority in his life. He finished out the semester with an A.

I know one example doesn't make a case, but at night I see a parade of students who are angry and resentful for having been passed along until they could no longer even pretend to keep up. Of average intelligence or better, they eventually quit school, concluding they were too dumb to finish. "I should have been held back," is a comment I hear frequently. Even sadder are those students who are high school graduates who say to me after a few weeks of class, "I don't know how I ever got a high school diploma."

Passing students who have not mastered the work cheats them and the employers who expect graduates to have basic skills. We excuse this dishonest behavior by saying kids can't learn if they come from terrible environments. No one seems to stop to think that—no matter what environments they come from—most kids don't put school first on their list unless they perceive something is at stake. They'd rather be sailing.

Many students I see at night could give expert testimony on unemployment, chemical dependency, abusive relationships. In spite of these difficulties, they have decided to make education a priority. They are motivated by the desire for a better job or the need to hang on to the one they've got. They have a healthy fear of failure.

People of all ages can rise above their problems, but they need to have a reason to do so. Young people generally don't have the maturity to value education in the same way my adult students value it. But fear of failure, whether economic or academic, can motivate both.

Flunking as a regular policy has just as much merit today as it did two generations ago. We must review the threat of flunking and see it as it really is—a positive teaching tool. It is an expression of confidence by both teachers and parents that the students have the ability to learn the material presented to them. However, making it work again would take a dedicated, caring conspiracy between teachers and parents. It would mean facing the tough reality that passing kids who haven't learned the material—while it might save them grief for the short term—dooms them to long-term illiteracy. It would mean that teachers would have to follow through on their threats, and parents would have to stand behind them, knowing their children's best interests are indeed at stake. This means no more doing Scott's assignments for him because he might fail. No more passing Jodi because she's such a nice kid.

This is a policy that worked in the past and can work today. A wise teacher, with the support of his parents, gave our son the opportunity to succeed—or fail. It's time we return this choice to all students.

■ Reading Comprehension Questions

1. The word *validity* in "[the diplomas'] validity will be questioned . . . when . . . employers discover that these graduates are semiliterate" (paragraph 1) means
   a. soundness.
   b. dates.
   c. age.
   d. supply.

2. The word *impediments* in "I blamed the poor academic skills our kids have today on drugs, divorce and other impediments to concentration" (paragraph 4) means
   a. questions.
   b. paths.
   c. skills.
   d. obstacles.

3. Which one of the following would be a good alternative title for this selection?
   a. Learning to Concentrate in School
   b. Teaching English Skills
   c. A Useful Tool for Motivating Students
   d. Adult Literacy Programs

4. Which sentence best expresses the main idea of the selection?
   a. Many adults cannot read or write well.
   b. English skills can be learned through adult literacy programs.
   c. Schools should include flunking students as part of their regular policy.
   d. Before students will concentrate, the teacher must get their attention.

5. Sherry's night students are
   a. usually unemployed.
   b. poor students.
   c. motivated to learn.
   d. doing drugs.

6. According to the author, many students who get "passed along"
   a. are lucky.
   b. never find a job.
   c. don't get into trouble.
   d. eventually feel angry and resentful.

7. Sherry feels that to succeed, flunking students as a regular policy requires
   a. adult-literacy programs.
   b. graduate-equivalency certificates.
   c. the total cooperation of teachers and parents.
   d. a strong teaching style.

8. The author implies that our present educational system is
   a. the best in the world.
   b. doing the best that it can.
   c. very short of teachers.
   d. not demanding enough of students.

9. *True or false?* _____ Sherry implies that high school students often don't realize the value of academic skills.

10. From the selection, we may conclude that the author based her opinion on
    a. statistics.
    b. educational research.
    c. her personal and professional experiences.
    d. expert professional testimony.

■ **Discussion Questions**

About Content

1. Sherry writes that ''before a teacher can expect students to concentrate, he has to get their attention, no matter what distractions may be at hand.'' What distractions does she mention in the article? Can you think of any others?

2. Do you feel your high school made an honest effort to give you the skills you need—and to make you aware of the importance of those skills? If not, what should your school have done that it did not do?

About Structure

3. The main method of development of this selection is
   a. narration.
   b. description.
   c. argumentation and persuasion.

4. In which paragraph does the author first state her main idea? Paragraph _____. What are the other paragraphs in which she states her main idea? _____ _____

5. What contrast transitions are used in the first sentences of paragraphs 7 and 10? What ideas are being contrasted in those sentences?

About Style and Tone

6. Why do you think Sherry titles her essay ''In Praise of the F Word''? Why doesn't she simply use the word *fail*?

7. What stylistic method does Sherry use in paragraph 11 to add rhythm and force to her points about flunking as a regular policy?

■ Writing Assignments

Assignment 1

Write an essay which has as its thesis *one* of the following points:

- In my opinion, students have no one to blame but themselves if they leave school without having learned basic skills.
- When students graduate or quit school lacking basic skills, they are the victims of an inadequate educational system.
- Flunking students has more disadvantages than advantages.

Support your thesis with several points, each developed in its own paragraph.

Assignment 2

Sherry proposes using "flunking as a regular policy" as a way to encourage students to work harder. What else might school systems do to help students? Write an essay in which you suggest a few policies for our public schools and give the reasons you think those changes will be beneficial. Following are some possible policies you may wish to consider:

> More writing in all classes
> Shorter summer vacations
> Less emphasis on memorization and more on thinking skills
> A language requirement
> A daily quiet reading session in elementary grades

Assignment 3

Here are two letters sent to *Newsweek* by teachers in response to Sherry's article:

Letter 1

Mary Sherry's essay advocating the use of flunking as a teaching tool was well intentioned but naive. In the first place, my local school district—and I doubt it's unique—discourages the practice by compiling teachers' failure rates for comparison (would you want to rank first?). More important though, F's don't even register on many kids' Richter scales. When your spirit has been numbed—as some of my students' spirits have—by physical, sexual, and psychological abuse, it's hard to notice an F. Walk a mile in one of my kids' shoes. Real fear has little to do with school.

> Kay Keglovits
> Arlington, Texas

Letter 2

Sherry is right: flunking poor students makes sense. But, as she notes, "making it work again would take a dedicated, caring conspiracy between teachers and parents." I once failed a high school junior for the year. I received a furious call from the student's mother. I was called to a meeting with the school superintendent, the principal, the mother, and the student. There it was decided that I would tutor the student for four months so that the F could be replaced with a passing grade. This was a total sham; the student did nothing during this remedial work, but she was given a passing grade. No wonder education is in the condition that we find it today.

Arthur J. Hochhalter
Minot, North Dakota

These letters suggest that schools that want to try flunking as a regular policy will have to plan carefully. Write an essay in which you discuss ways to make failing poor students work as a regular policy. Your thesis statement can be something like this: "In order for a policy of flunking to work, certain policies and attitudes would need to be changed in many schools." As support in your essay, use the ideas in these letters, Sherry's ideas, and any other ideas you have heard or thought of. Describe your supporting ideas in detail and explain why each is necessary or useful.

The Plug-In Drug

Marie Winn

What effect has television had on American family life? In the following selection, Marie Winn argues that TV is the most significant—and possibly most damaging—influence in children's lives today. If you have ever seen a family sitting hypnotized in front of the TV set, eyes glazed, unable to communicate with each other, you may agree with her. After you read the selection, you might also think twice before you use TV as a baby-sitter.

A quarter of a century after the introduction of television into American society, a period   1
that has seen the medium become so deeply ingrained in American life that in at least one state the television set has attained the rank of a legal necessity, safe from repossession in case of debt along with clothes, cooking utensils, and the like, television viewing has become an inevitable and ordinary part of daily life. Only in the early years of television did writers and commentators have sufficient perspective to separate the activity of watching

television from the actual content it offers the viewer. In those early days writers frequently discussed the effects of television on family life. However, a curious myopia afflicted those early observers: almost without exception they regarded television as a favorable, beneficial, indeed, wondrous influence upon the family.

"Television is going to be a real asset in every home where there are children," predicts a writer in 1949.   2

"Television will take over your way of living and change your children's habits, but this change can be a wonderful improvement," claims another commentator.   3

"No survey's needed, of course, to establish that television has brought the family together in one room," writes *The New York Times* television critic in 1949.   4

Each of the early articles about television is invariably accompanied by a photograph or illustration showing a family cozily sitting together before the television set, Sis on Mom's lap, Buddy perched on the arm of Dad's chair, Dad with his arm around Mom's shoulder. Who could have guessed that twenty or so years later Mom would be watching a drama in the kitchen, the kids would be looking at cartoons in their rooms, while Dad would be taking in the ball game in the living room?   5

Of course television sets were enormously expensive in those early days. The idea that by 1975 more than 60 percent of American families would own two or more sets was preposterous. The splintering of the multiple-set family was something the early writers could not foresee. Nor did anyone imagine the number of hours children would eventually devote to television, the common use of television by parents as a child pacifier, the changes television would effect upon child-rearing methods, the increasing domination of family schedules by children's viewing requirements—in short, the *power* of the new medium to dominate family life.   6

After the first years, as children's consumption of the new medium increased, together with parental concern about the possible effects of so much television viewing, a steady refrain helped to soothe and reassure anxious parents. "Television always enters a pattern of influences that already exist: the home, the peer group, the school, the church and culture generally," write the authors of an early and influential study of television's effects on children. In other words, if the child's home life is all right, parents need not worry about the effects of all that television watching.   7

But television does not merely influence the child; it deeply influences that "pattern of influences" that is meant to ameliorate its effects. Home and family life have changed in important ways since the advent of television. The peer group has become television-oriented, and much of the time children spend together is occupied by television viewing. Culture generally has been transformed by television. Therefore it is improper to assign to television the subsidiary role its many apologists (too often members of the television industry) insist it plays. Television is not merely one of a number of important influences upon today's child. Through the changes it has made in family life, television emerges as *the* important influence in children's lives today.   8

Television's contribution to family life has been an equivocal one. For while it has, indeed, kept the members of the family from dispersing, it has not served to bring them *together.* By its domination of the time families spend together, it destroys the special quality that distinguishes one family from another, a quality that depends to a great extent on what a family *does,* what special rituals, games, recurrent jokes, familiar songs, and shared activities it accumulates. . . .   9

Yet parents have accepted a television-dominated family so completely that they cannot see how the medium is involved in whatever problems they might be having. A first-grade teacher reports: 10

''I have one child in the group who's an only child. I wanted to find out more about her family life because this little girl was quite isolated from the group, didn't make friends, so I talked to her mother. Well, they don't have time to do anything in the evening, the mother said. The parents come home after picking up the child at the baby-sitter's. Then the mother fixes dinner while the child watches TV. Then they have dinner and the child goes to bed. I said to this mother, 'Well, couldn't she help you fix dinner? That would be a nice time for the two of you to talk,' and the mother said, 'Oh, but I'd hate to have her miss *Zoom*. It's such a good program!' '' 11

Even when families make efforts to control television, too often its very presence counterbalances the positive features of family life. A writer and mother of two boys aged three and seven described her family's television schedule in an article in *The New York Times*: 12

> We were in the midst of a full-scale War. Every day was a new battle and every program was a major skirmish. We agreed it was a bad scene all around and were ready to enter diplomatic negotiations. . . . In principle we have agreed on 2½ hours of TV a day, *Sesame Street, Electric Company* (with dinner gobbled up in between) and two half-hour shows between 7 and 8:30 which enables the grown-ups to eat in peace and prevents the two boys from destroying one another. Their pre-bedtime choice is dreadful, because, as Josh recently admitted, ''There's nothing much on I really like.'' So . . . it's *What's My Line* or *To Tell the Truth.* . . . Clearly there is a need for first-rate children's shows at this time. . . .

Consider the ''family life'' described here: Presumably the father comes home from work during the *Sesame Street—Electric Company* stint. The children are either watching television, gobbling their dinner, or both. While the parents eat their dinner in peaceful privacy, the children watch another hour of television. Then there is only a half-hour left before bedtime, just enough time for baths, getting pajamas on, brushing teeth, and so on. The children's evening is regimented with an almost military precision. They watch their favorite programs, and when there is ''nothing much on I really like,'' they watch whatever else is on—because *watching* is the important thing. Their mother does not see anything amiss with watching programs just for the sake of watching; she only wishes there were some first-rate children's shows on at those times. 13

Without conjuring up memories of the Victorian era with family games and long, leisurely meals, and large families, the question arises: isn't there a better family life available than this dismal, mechanized arrangement of children watching television for however long is allowed them, evening after evening? 14

Of course, families today still do *special* things together at times: go camping in the summer, go to the zoo on a nice Sunday, take various trips and expeditions. But their *ordinary* daily life together is diminished—that sitting around at the dinner table, that spontaneous taking up of an activity, those little games invented by children on the spur of the moment when there is nothing else to do, the scribbling, the chatting, and even the quarreling, all the things that form the fabric of a family, that define a childhood. Instead, the children have their regular schedule of television programs and bedtime, and the parents have their peaceful dinner together. 15

The author of the article in *The Times* notes that "keeping a family sane means 16 mediating between the needs of both children and adults." But surely the needs of adults are being better met than the needs of the children, who are effectively shunted away and rendered untroublesome, while their parents enjoy a life as undemanding as that of any childless couple. In reality, it is those very demands that young children make upon a family that lead to growth, and it is the way parents accede to those demands that builds the relationships upon which the future of the family depends. If the family does not accumulate its backlog of shared experiences, shared *everyday* experiences that occur and recur and change and develop, then it is not likely to survive as anything other than a caretaking institution.

Family Rituals. Ritual is defined by sociologists as "that part of family life that 17 the family likes about itself, is proud of and wants formally to continue." Another text notes that "the development of a ritual by a family is an index of the common interest of its members in the family as a group."

What has happened to family rituals, those regular, dependable, recurrent happenings 18 that gave members of a family a feeling of *belonging* to a home rather than living in it merely for the sake of convenience, those experiences that act as the adhesive of family unity far more than any material advantages?

Mealtime rituals, going-to-bed rituals, illness rituals, holiday rituals, how many of 19 these have survived the inroads of the television set?

A young woman who grew up near Chicago reminisces about her childhood and 20 gives an idea of the effects of television upon family rituals:

"As a child I had millions of relatives around—my parents both come from relatively 21 large families. My father had nine brothers and sisters. And so every holiday there was this great swoop-down of aunts, uncles, and millions of cousins. I just remember how wonderful it used to be. These thousands of cousins would come and everyone would play and ultimately, after dinner, all the women would be in the front of the house, drinking coffee and talking, all the men would be in the back of the house, drinking and smoking, and all the kids would be all over the place, playing hide and seek. Christmas time was particularly nice because everyone always brought all their toys and games. Our house had a couple of rooms with go-through closets, so there were always kids running in a great circle route. I remember it was just wonderful.

"And then all of a sudden one year I remember becoming suddenly aware of how 22 different everything had become. The kids were no longer playing Monopoly or Clue or the other games we used to play together. It was because we had a television set which had been turned on for a football game. All of that socializing that had gone on previously had ended. Now everyone was sitting in front of the television set, on a holiday, at a family party! I remember being stunned by how awful that was. Somehow the television had become more attractive."

As families have come to spend more and more of their time together engaged in 23 the single activity of television watching, those rituals and pastimes that once gave family life its special quality have become more and more uncommon. Not since prehistoric times when cave families hunted, gathered, ate, and slept, with little time remaining to accumulate a culture of any significance, have families been reduced to such a sameness.

Real People. It is not only the activities that a family might engage in together that are diminished by the powerful presence of television in the home. The relationships of the family members to each other are also affected, in both obvious and subtle ways. The hours that the young child spends in a one-way relationship with television people, an involvement that allows for no communication or interaction, surely affect his relationships with real-life people. 24

Studies show the importance of eye-to-eye contact, for instance, in real-life relationships, and indicate that the nature of a person's eye-contact patterns, whether he looks another squarely in the eye or looks to the side or shifts his gaze from side to side, may play a significant role in his success or failure in human relationships. But no eye contact is possible in the child-television relationship, although in certain children's programs people purport to speak directly to the child and the camera fosters this illusion by focusing directly upon the person being filmed. (Mr. Rogers is an example, telling the child ''I like you, you're special,'' etc.) How might such a distortion of real-life relationships affect a child's development of trust, of openness, of an ability to relate well to other *real* people? . . . 25

A family therapist discusses the use of television as an avoidance mechanism: 26

''In a family I know the father comes home from work and turns on the television set. The children come and watch with him and the wife serves them their meal in front of the set. He then goes and takes a shower, or works on the car or something. She then goes and has her own dinner in front of the television set. It's a symptom of a deeper-rooted problem, sure. But it would help them all to get rid of the set. It would be far easier to work on what the symptom really means without the television. This television simply encourages a double avoidance of each other. They'd find out more quickly what was going on if they weren't able to hide behind the TV. Things wouldn't necessarily be better, of course, but they wouldn't be anesthetized.'' . . .

A number of research studies substantiate the assumption that television interferes with family activities and the formation of family relationships. One survey shows that 78 percent of the respondents indicated no conversation taking place during viewing except at specified times such as commercials. The study notes: ''The television atmosphere in most households is one of quiet absorption on the part of family members who are present. The nature of the family social life during a program could be described as 'parallel' rather than interactive, and the set does seem to dominate family life when it is on.'' Thirty-six percent of the respondents in another study indicated that television viewing was the only family activity participated in during the week. . . . 27

Undermining the Family. In its effect on family relationships, in its facilitation of parental withdrawal from an active role in the socialization of their children, and in its replacement of family rituals and special events, television has played an important role in the disintegration of the American family. But of course it has not been the only contributing factor, perhaps not even the most important one. The steadily rising divorce rate, the increase in the number of working mothers, the decline of the extended family, the breakdown of neighborhoods and communities, the growing isolation of the nuclear family—all have seriously affected the family. . . . 28

And so the American family muddles on, dimly aware that something is amiss but   29
distracted from an understanding of its plight by an endless stream of television images.
As family ties grow weaker and vaguer, as children's lives become more separate from
their parents', as parents' educational role in their children's lives is taken over by
television and schools, family life becomes increasingly more unsatisfying for both parents
and children. All that seems to be left is Love, an abstraction that family members *know*
is necessary but find great difficulty giving each other because the traditional opportunities
for expressing love within the family have been reduced or destroyed.

For contemporary parents, love toward each other has increasingly come to mean   30
successful sexual relations, as witnessed by the proliferation of sex manuals and sex
therapists. Opportunities for manifesting other forms of love through supporting, understanding, nurturing, even, to use an unpopular word, *serving* each other, are less and less
available as mothers and fathers seek independent destinies outside the family.

As for love of children, this love is increasingly expressed through supplying material   31
comforts, amusements, and educational opportunities. Parents show their love for their
children by sending them to good schools and camps, by providing them with good food
and good doctors, by buying them toys, books, games, and a television set of their very
own. Parents will even go further and express their love by attending PTA meetings to
improve their children's schools, or by joining groups that are acting to improve the
quality of their children's television programs.

But this is love at a remove, and is rarely understood by children. The more direct   32
forms of parental love require time and patience, steady, dependable, ungrudgingly given
time actually spent *with* a child, reading to him, comforting him, playing, joking, and
working with him. But even if a parent were eager and willing to demonstrate that sort
of direct love to his children today, the opportunities are diminished. What with school
and Little League and piano lessons and, of course, the inevitable television programs, a
day seems to offer just enough time for a good-night kiss.

■ Reading Comprehension Questions

1. The word *ameliorate* in ''that pattern . . . that is meant to ameliorate its
   effects'' (paragraph 8) means
   a. improve.
   b. process.
   c. begin.
   d. model.

2. The word *equivocal* in ''television's contribution . . . has been an equivocal
   one'' (paragraph 9) means
   a. temporary.
   b. equal.
   c. uncertain.
   d. unusual.

3. Which of the following would be a good alternative title for this selection?
   a. Television's Influence on America
   b. How Television Changes People
   c. Children and Television
   d. Television's Harmful Influence on the Family

4. Which sentence best expresses the main idea of the selection?
   a. Modern parents are using television as a baby-sitter.
   b. The domination of television has led to a breakdown in family relationships.
   c. Family rituals have been destroyed by TV.
   d. Parents can fight TV's influence by giving children strong values.

5. According to the author, the demands that young children make on their parents
   a. can tear a family apart.
   b. add to a stressful atmosphere.
   c. are caused by watching TV.
   d. can lead to growth.

6. *True or false?* _____ Research studies show that families talk about TV shows while they are watching them.

7. According to the author, parents can best show their love for children by
   a. providing good food and good doctors.
   b. sending them to good schools.
   c. spending time with children in activities other than watching TV.
   d. improving the quality of children's TV programs.

8. The author implies that
   a. the influence of TV can be effectively offset by limiting children to two hours or less of TV a day.
   b. peers, not TV, are the most important influence on a child's life.
   c. Mister Rogers is an example of TV's positive influence.
   d. today's parents are more selfish about their need for private time.

9. The author implies that
   a. teachers should use TV in the classroom.
   b. TV prevents families from expressing their love for each other.
   c. watching TV can help children settle their quarrels.
   d. TV is the main factor in the disintegration of the American family.

10. The author implies that
   a. by watching quality TV shows, children can learn to handle real-life relationships.
   b. TV cannot influence a child who already has strong values.
   c. parents are dangerously unaware of the effect of TV on their children.
   d. it is all right to allow children to watch TV so that parents can enjoy a peaceful dinner.

■ Discussion Questions

About Content

1. Why were early observers of television's effect on the family wrong in their conclusions?
2. How has television destroyed the "special quality that distinguishes one family from another"?
3. How do hours of watching TV affect a child's interactions with real-life people?

About Structure

4. What method of development is used in paragraph 5?
   a. Contrast
   b. Reasons
   c. Classification

About Style and Tone

5. Why do you think Winn titled her essay "The Plug-In Drug"? What does her title imply about her attitude toward television?
6. Reread the last paragraph of the selection. In the last sentence, the author talks about piano lessons and Little League. How does she feel about these activities?
   a. They are necessary to a child's growth.
   b. They are a waste of time.
   c. They are not as important as things families do together.

   On the basis of your answer, what would you say is the tone of this sentence?
   a. Slightly sarcastic
   b. Straightforward
   c. Humorous
7. The author uses the words *domination, destroy, danger,* and *dismal,* among others, to describe television. What is the effect of these words on the reader? List three additional negative words the author uses to describe TV:

   _____   _____   _____

■ Writing Assignments

Assignment 1

In paragraph 3 of "The Plug-In Drug," Marie Winn quotes an early prediction: "Television will take over your way of living and change your children's habits." Is this true? Think about some ways in which television has taken over your way of living and affected your (or your children's) habits. Then organize your thoughts into an essay of several paragraphs. You might want to use as your thesis a sentence similar to the following example:

Television has affected my life in several ways.

Then devote a paragraph to each way, supporting your points with details and examples.

Assignment 2

Winn devotes her essay to discussing the negative effects of television on family life. Can you think of any positive effects television can have (or has had) on your family life—or on families in general? Make a list of these positive effects. Then choose the best ones and arrange them in order of importance, saving the most important one for last. In an essay, develop each one in its own paragraph. The following list will give you some ideas of possible *good* things about television:

Educational value

Moral value—some programs do teach lessons

Role models—we see people on television we admire

Eases loneliness

Keeps us up-to-date on current events

Takes us to places we would never be able to visit; allows us to see events we didn't see in person

Visual impact—beautiful or exciting to watch

Assignment 3

Write an essay contrasting how one of your family rituals is conducted *with television* and how it might be *without television.* You might write about:

Family celebration

Holiday

Saturday morning or Sunday afternoon

Getting ready for school or work

Bedtime

Dinnertime

Organize the essay into two supporting paragraphs using a one-side-at-a-time method of development (see page 183). In the first supporting paragraph, describe your particular ritual as it is with television. Then, in the second supporting paragraph, imagine how it would be without TV. Be sure that each detail in the first supporting paragraph is covered in the second supporting paragraph; for example, if you state that the first thing you do in the morning now is turn on the *Today* show, you should describe in the second supporting paragraph what you *could* do instead—play soft music to start the day, perhaps.

How to Deal with a Difficult Boss

Donna Brown Hogarty

The "bad boss" is a familiar character of TV sitcoms and cartoons. But when you're dealing with a real-life bad boss, the situation is hardly amusing. According to this essay, difficult bosses fall into several categories. Learning to recognize these types can give you some guidance on how to work successfully in a challenging situation.

Harvey Gittler knew his new boss was high-strung—the two had worked together on the factory floor. But Gittler was not prepared for his coworker's personality change when the man was promoted to plant manager. 1

Just two days later, the boss angrily ordered a standing desk removed because he'd seen a worker leaning on it to look up an order. He routinely dressed down employees at the top of his lungs. At one time or another he threatened to fire almost everyone in the plant. And after employees went home, he searched through trash cans for evidence of treason. 2

For many workers, Gittler's experience is frighteningly familiar. Millions of Americans have temperamental bosses. In a 1984 Center for Creative Leadership study of corporate executives, nearly 75 percent of the subjects reported having had at least one intolerable boss. 3

"Virtually all bosses are problem bosses, in one way or another," says psychologist Mardy Grothe, coauthor with Peter Wylie of *Problem Bosses: Who They Are and How to Deal with Them*. The reason, he said, lies in lack of training. Most bosses were promoted to management because they excelled at earlier jobs—not because they have experience motivating others. 4

Uncertain economic times worsen the bad-boss syndrome. "There is an acceptance of getting results at any price," says Stanley Bing, a business executive and author of 5

Crazy Bosses. "As a result, the people corporations select to be bosses are the most rigid and demanding, and the least able to roll with the punches."

Bad bosses often have a recognizable modus operandi. Harry Levinson, a management   6
psychologist in Waltham, Massachusetts, has catalogued problem bosses, from the bully to the jellyfish to the disapproving perfectionist. If you're suffering from a bad boss, chances are he or she combines several of these traits and can be dealt with effectively if you use the right strategy.

The Bully. During his first week on the job, a new account manager at a small   7
Pennsylvania advertising agency agreed to return some materials to a client. When he mentioned this at a staff meeting, the boss turned beet red, his lips began to quiver and he shouted that the new employee should call his client and confess he didn't know anything about the advertising business, and would not be returning the materials.

Over the next few months, as the account manager watched coworkers cower under   8
the boss's browbeating, he realized that the tyrant fed on fear. Employees who tried hardest to avoid his ire were most likely to catch it. "He was like a schoolyard bully," the manager recalls, "and I've known since childhood that, when confronted, most bullies back down."

Armed with newfound confidence and growing knowledge of the ad business, he   9
matched his boss's behavior. "If he raised his voice, I'd raise mine," the manager recalls. True to type, the boss started to treat him with grudging respect. Eventually, the young man moved up the ranks and was rarely subjected to his boss's outbursts.

Although standing up to the bully often works, it could make matters worse. Mardy   10
Grothe recommends a different strategy: reasoning with him after he's calmed down. "Some bosses have had a problem with temper control all their lives, and are not pleased with this aspect of their personality," he explains. Want a litmus test? If the boss attempts to compensate for his outburst by overreacting and trying to "make nice" the next day, says Grothe, he or she feels guilty about yesterday's bad behavior.

Grothe suggests explaining to your boss how his temper affects you. For instance,   11
you might say, "I know you're trying to improve my performance, but yelling makes me less productive because it upsets me."

Whatever strategy you choose, deal with the bully as soon as possible, because "once   12
a dominant/subservient relationship is established, it becomes difficult to loosen," warns industrial psychologist James Fisher. Fisher also suggests confronting your boss behind closed doors whenever possible, to avoid being disrespectful. If your boss continues to be overbearing, try these strategies from psychologist Leonard Felder, author of *Does Someone at Work Treat You Badly?*

- To keep your composure while the boss is screaming, repeat a calming phrase to yourself, such as "Ignore the anger. It isn't yours."

- Focus on a humorous aspect of your boss's appearance. If she's got a double chin, watch her flesh shake while she's yammering. "By realizing that even the most intimidating people are vulnerable, you can more easily relax," explains Felder.

- Wait for your boss to take a breath, then try this comeback line: "I want to hear what you're saying. You've got to slow down."

Finally, never relax with an abusive boss, no matter how charming he or she can be, 13 says Stanley Bing. "The bully will worm his or her way into your heart as a way of positioning your face under his foot."

The Workaholic. "Some bosses don't know the difference between work and play," 14 says Nancy Ahlrichs, vice president of client services at the Indianapolis office of Right Associates, an international outplacement firm. "If you want to reach them at night or on a Saturday, just call the office." Worse, such a boss invades your every waking hour, making it all but impossible to separate your own home life from the office.

Ahlrichs advises setting limits on your availability. Make sure the boss knows you 15 can be reached in a crisis, but as a matter of practice go home at a set time. If he responds angrily, reassure him that you will tackle any project first thing in the morning. Get him to set the priorities, so you can decide which tasks can wait.

If you have good rapport with the boss, says Mardy Grothe, consider discussing the 16 problem openly. Your goal is to convince him that just as he needs to meet deadlines, you have personal responsibilities that are equally important.

The Jellyfish. "My boss hires people with the assumption that we all know our 17 jobs," says a woman who works for a small firm in New England. "Unfortunately, he hates conflict. If someone makes a mistake, we have to tiptoe around instead of moving to correct it, so we don't hurt anyone's feelings."

Her boss is a jellyfish. He has refused to establish even a basic pecking order in his 18 office. As a result, a secretary sat on important correspondence for over a month, risking a client's tax write-offs. Because no one supervises the firm's support staff, the secretary never received a reprimand, and nobody was able to prevent such mishaps from recurring. The jellyfish simply can't take charge because he's afraid of creating conflicts.

So "you must take charge," suggests Lee Colby, a Minneapolis-based management 19 consultant. "Tell the jellyfish: 'This is what I think I ought to be doing. What do you think?' You are taking the first step, without stepping on your boss's toes."

Building an indecisive supervisor's confidence is another good strategy. For example, 20 if you can supply hard facts and figures, you can then use them to justify any course you recommend—and gently ease the jellyfish into taking a firmer position.

The Perfectionist. When Nancy Ahlrichs was fresh out of college, she landed her 21 first full-time job, supervising the advertising design and layout of a small-town newspaper. On deadline day, the paper's irritable general manager would suddenly appear over her shoulder, inspecting her work for errors. Then he'd ask a barrage of questions, ending with the one Ahlrichs dreaded most: "Are you sure you'll make the deadline?"

"I never missed a single deadline," Ahlrichs says, "yet every week he'd ask the same 22 question. I felt belittled by his lack of confidence in me."

Ironically, the general manager was lowering the staff's productivity. To paraphrase 23 Voltaire, the perfect is the enemy of the good. According to psychiatrist Allan Mallinger, coauthor with Jeannette DeWyze of *Too Perfect: When Being in Control Gets Out of Control*, "the perfectionist's overconcern for thoroughness slows down everyone's work.

When everything has to be done perfectly, tasks loom larger." The nit-picking boss who is behind schedule becomes even more difficult, making subordinates ever more miserable.

"Remember," says Leonard Felder, "the perfectionist needs to find something to worry about." To improve your lot with a perfectionist boss, get her to focus on the big picture. If she demands that you redo a task you've just completed, mention your other assignments, and ask her to prioritize. Often, a boss will let the work you've completed stand—especially when she realizes another project may be put on hold. If your boss is nervous about a particular project, offer regular reports. By keeping the perfectionist posted, you might circumvent constant supervision. 24

Finally, protect yourself emotionally. "You can't depend on the perfectionist for encouragement," says Mallinger. "You owe it to yourself to get a second opinion of your work by asking others." 25

The Aloof Boss. When Gene Bergoffen, now CEO of the National Private Truck Council, worked for another trade association and asked to be included in the decision-making process, his boss was brusque and inattentive. The boss made decisions alone, and very quickly. "We used to call him 'Ready, Fire, Aim,' " says Bergoffen. 26

Many workers feel frozen out by their boss in subtle ways. Perhaps he doesn't invite them to key meetings or he might never be available to discuss projects. "At the core of every good boss is the ability to communicate expectations clearly," says Gerard Roche, chairman of Heidrick & Struggles, an executive search firm. "Employees should never have to wonder what's on a boss's mind." 27

If your boss fails to give you direction, Roche says, "the worst thing you can do is nothing. Determine the best course of action, then say to your boss: 'Unless I hear otherwise, here's what I'm going to do.' " 28

Other strategies: When your boss does not invite you to meetings or include you in decision making, speak up. "Tell her you have information that might prove to be valuable," suggests Lee Colby. If that approach doesn't work, find an intermediary who respects your work and can persuade the boss to listen to your views. 29

To understand your boss's inability to communicate, it's vital to examine his work style. "Some like hard data, logically arranged in writing," says Colby. "Others prefer face-to-face meetings. Find out what makes your boss tick—and speak in his or her language." 30

Understanding your boss can make your job more bearable in a number of ways. For instance, try offering the boss two solutions to a problem—one that will make him happy, and one that will help you to reach your goals. Even the most difficult boss will usually allow you to solve problems in your own way—as long as he's convinced of your loyalty to him. 31

No matter which type of bad boss you have, think twice before going over his head. Try forming a committee with your colleagues and approaching the boss all together. The difficult boss is usually unaware of the problem and often is eager to make amends. 32

Before embarking on any course of action, engage in some self-analysis. Chances are, no matter how difficult your boss is, you are also contributing to the conflict. "Talk to people who know you both, and get some honest feedback," suggests Mardy Grothe. 33

"If you can fix the ways in which you're contributing to the problem, you'll be more likely to get your boss to change."

Even if you can't, there's a silver lining: the worst bosses often have the most 34 to teach you. Bullies, for example, are frequently masters at reaching difficult goals. Perfectionists can often prod you into exceeding your own expectations.

As a young resident psychologist at the Menninger psychiatric hospital in Topeka, 35 Kansas, Harry Levinson was initially overwhelmed by the high standards of founder Karl Menninger. "I felt I was never going to be able to diagnose patients as well as he did or perform to such high academic requirements," Levinson recalls. He even considered quitting. But in the end, he rose to the challenge, and today he believes he owes much of his success to what he learned during that critical period.

Dealing with a difficult boss forces you to set priorities, to overcome fears, to stay 36 calm under the gun, and to negotiate for better working conditions. And the skills you sharpen to ease a tense relationship will stand you in good stead throughout your career. "Employees who are able to survive a trying boss often earn the respect of higher-ups for their ability to manage a situation," says Levinson. "And because a difficult boss can cause rapid turnover, those who stick it out often advance quickly."

Your bad boss can also teach you what not to do with subordinates as you move 37 up—and one day enable you to be a better boss yourself.

■ Reading Comprehension Questions

1. The words *compensate for* in "If the boss attempts to compensate for his outburst by overreacting and trying to 'make nice' the next day, says Grothe, he or she feels guilty about yesterday's bad behavior" (paragraph 10) mean
   a. make up for.
   b. deny.
   c. point to.
   d. emphasize.

2. The word *circumvent* in "If your boss is nervous about a particular project, offer regular reports. By keeping the perfectionist posted, you might circumvent constant supervision" (paragraph 24) means
   a. cause.
   b. avoid.
   c. welcome
   d. promote.

3. Which of the following would be a good alternative title for this selection?
   a. Dealing with Bosses Who Bully
   b. Problems at Work
   c. How to Be a Better Boss
   d. Handling Bad Bosses

4. Which sentence best expresses the main idea of the selection?
   a. Human interaction is extremely complicated.
   b. Bosses are often poor at their jobs because they don't know how to motivate people.
   c. Methods are available to deal with different kinds of difficult bosses.
   d. Most bullies will back down when they meet someone who stands up to them.

5. According to the selection, most bosses have been promoted to management because they
   a. are better educated than their coworkers.
   b. have close personal relationships with their supervisors.
   c. are good at motivating other workers.
   d. excelled at jobs they held earlier.

6. The new account manager at an advertising firm dealt with his bullying boss by
   a. making the boss see he was really trying to do a good job.
   b. taking the boss to lunch and talking honestly about the situation.
   c. raising his voice at the boss when the boss raised his voice.
   d. going over the boss's head and complaining to the company president.

7. According to Hogarty, a bad boss can help you
   a. learn to reach difficult goals.
   b. exceed your own expectations.
   c. overcome fears.
   d. all of the above.

8. We can infer that workaholic bosses
   a. want their employees to be workaholics too.
   b. are the worst of all the categories described in the essay.
   c. are quite rare.
   d. always become angry when asked to discuss their problem openly.

9. We can infer that Nancy Ahlrichs's perfectionist manager at the newspaper
   a. thought that Nancy was trying to steal his job.
   b. was only teasing Nancy with his questions.
   c. was not able to relax and trust employees who had proven themselves.
   d. wanted Nancy to quit her job.

10. The author suggests that most employees with bad bosses
    a. should quit their jobs.
    b. are better off learning to cope with the bad boss than quitting.
    c. deserve the bad treatment they receive.
    d. would prefer to work for a perfectionist boss than a jellyfish boss.

■ **Discussion Questions**

About Content

1. What strategies does Hogarty suggest for dealing with each of the five types of bosses she mentions?

2. Hogarty claims that "the worst bosses often have the most to teach you" (paragraph 34). What examples does she give to support that point? Have you ever had a bad boss from whom you learned something? If so, what did you learn, and how?

About Structure

3. What method of introduction does Hogarty use in her essay?
   a. Incident or brief story
   b. Broad general statement of the topic
   c. Idea or situation that is the opposite of the one developed

4. Where in the selection does Hogarty most clearly state her thesis? Locate the paragraph and write its number here: _____

5. Hogarty introduces the five types of bosses with
   a. addition signals.
   b. illustration signals.
   c. headings.

6. What type of conclusion does Hogarty use?
   a. Summary
   b. Thought-provoking question
   c. Thought about the future

About Style and Tone

7. In general, is Hogarty's tone in discussing how to deal with difficult bosses pessimistic or optimistic? What specific details support your answer?

■ **Writing Assignments**

Assignment 1

Write an essay about a difficult boss you have had. Place your bad boss in a category with a special name like those Hogarty uses. Use one of Hogarty's types—bully, workaholic, jellyfish, perfectionist, or aloof boss—or come up with another type of your own. If appropriate, use two or more such labels, as in this thesis statement: "Fred, my boss at Allied Plastics, was both a classic bully and an ego crusher." Support your thesis by narrating in detail three specificic incidents in which your boss acted badly.

Alternatively, write about what you have learned from your bosses, good or bad.

Assignment 2

Hogarty lists five types of difficult bosses. Naturally, there are difficult workers as well. What are several kinds of difficult workers that you have known? Write an essay in which you list and describe in detail several types of difficult workers. You may also want to include advice on dealing with such employees. Using examples from your or other people's experiences (or both), include numerous specific details. (Review the selection to see the specific details that Hogarty uses, including brief narrations, quotations, and explanations.) Following are some qualities of difficult workers to consider:

Tries to get away with doing as little work as possible

Frequently calls in sick just to miss work

Has no interest in learning

Has no interest in the company's goals

Often makes excuses for poor performance

Interferes with other people's work

Tries to advance himself or herself at the expense of other workers

Assignment 3

Write an essay on your ideal boss. Drawing on a list of the qualities you would look for in an ideal boss, choose three that you think are most important. Here are some characteristics many workers seek in a boss:

Teaches skills to help workers grow

Is tolerant of mistakes

Offers help when an error is made

Welcomes ideas from others

Provides opportunities for workers to contribute

Helps workers attend helpful seminars and classes

Your essay should support a thesis statement such as either of the following:

My ideal boss would have three key qualities.

If I became the head of my own company, I would try to develop characteristics that helped both the company and my workers.

Is Sex All That Matters?

Joyce Garity

From the skimpy clothing in ads to the suggestive themes in many of today's TV comedies, our young people are bombarded with sexuality. How does the constant stream of sexual images influence their behavior and dreams? In considering that question, social worker Joyce Garity focuses on one young woman named Elaine, alone and pregnant with her second child.

1   A few years ago, a young girl lived with me, my husband, and our children for several months. The circumstances of Elaine's coming to us don't matter here; suffice it to say that she was troubled and nearly alone in the world. She was also pregnant—hugely, clumsily pregnant with her second child. Elaine was seventeen. Her pregnancy, she said, was an accident; she also said she wasn't sure who had fathered her child. There had been several sex partners and no contraception. Yet, she repeated blandly, gazing at me with clear blue eyes, the pregnancy was an accident, and one she would certainly never repeat.

2   Eventually I asked Elaine, after we had grown to know each other well enough for such conversations, why neither she nor her lovers had used birth control. She blushed— porcelain-skinned girl with one child in foster care and another swelling the bib of her fashionably faded overalls—stammered, and blushed some more. Birth control, she finally got out, was "embarrassing." It wasn't "romantic." You couldn't be really passionate, she explained, and worry about birth control at the same time.

3   I haven't seen Elaine for quite a long time. I think about her often, though. I think of her as I page through teen fashion magazines in the salon where I have my hair cut. Although mainstream and relatively wholesome, these magazines trumpet sexuality page after leering page. On the inside front cover, an advertisement for Guess jeans features junior fashion models in snug denim dresses, their legs bared to just below the crotch. An advertisement for Liz Claiborne fragrances shows a barely clad young couple sprawled on a bed, him painting her toenails. An advertisement for Obsession cologne displays a waif-thin girl draped stomach-down across a couch, naked, her startled expression suggesting helplessness in the face of an unseen yet approaching threat.

4   I think of Elaine because I know she would love these ads. "They're so beautiful," she would croon, and of course they are. The faces and bodies they show are lovely. The lighting is superb. The hair and makeup are faultless. In the Claiborne ad, the laughing girl whose toenails are being painted by her handsome lover is obviously having the time of her life. She stretches luxuriously on a bed heaped with clean white linen and fluffy pillows. Beyond the sheer blowing curtains of her room, we can glimpse a graceful wrought-iron balcony. Looking at the ad, Elaine could only want to be her. Any girl would want to be her. Heck, *I* want to be her.

But my momentary desire to move into the Claiborne picture, to trade lives with the 5 exquisite young creature pictured there, is just that—momentary. I've lived long enough to know that what I see is a marketing invention. A moment after the photo session was over, the beautiful room was dismantled, and the models moved on to their next job. Later, the technicians took over the task of doctoring the photograph until it reached full-blown fantasy proportions.

Not so Elaine. After months of living together and countless hours of watching her 6 yearn after magazine images, soap-opera heroines, and rock goddesses, I have a pretty good idea of why she looks at ads like Claiborne's. She sees the way life—her life—is supposed to be. She sees a world characterized by sexual spontaneity, playfulness, and abandon. She sees people who don't worry about such unsexy details as birth control. Nor, apparently, do they spend much time thinking about such pedestrian topics as commitment or whether they should act on their sexual impulses. Their clean sunlit rooms are never invaded by the fear of AIDS, of unwanted pregnancy, of shattered lives. For all her apparent lack of defense, the girl on the couch in the Obsession ad will surely never experience the brutality of rape.

Years of exposure to this media-invented, sex-saturated universe have done their 7 work on Elaine. She is, I'm sure, completely unaware of the irony in her situation: She melts over images from a sexual Shangri-la, never realizing that her attempts to mirror those images left her pregnant, abandoned, living in the spare bedroom of a stranger's house, relying on charity for rides to the welfare office and supervised visits with her toddler daughter.

Of course, Elaine is not the first to be suckered by the cynical practice of using sex 8 to sell underwear, rock groups, or sneakers. Using sex as a sales tool is hardly new. At the beginning of this century, British actress Lily Langtry shocked her contemporaries by posing, clothed somewhat scantily, with a bar of Pear's soap. The advertisers have always known that the masses are susceptible to the notion that a particular product will make them more sexually attractive. In the past, however, ads used euphemisms, claiming that certain products would make people "more lovable" or "more popular." What is a recent development is the abandonment of any such polite double-talk. Advertising today leaves no question about what is being sold along with the roasted peanuts or artificial sweetener. "Tell us about your first time," coyly invites the innuendo-filled magazine advertisement for Campari liquor. A billboard for Levi's shows two jeans-clad young men on the beach, hoisting a girl in the air. The boys' perfect, tan bodies are matched by hers, although we see a lot more of hers: bare midriff, short shorts, cleavage. She caresses their hair; they stroke her legs. A jolly gang-bang fantasy in the making. And a TV commercial promoting the Irish pop group The Cranberries blares nonstop the suggestive title of their latest album: "Everybody else is doing it, so why can't we?"

Indeed, just about everybody is doing it. Studies show that by the age of 20, 75 9 percent of Americans have lost their virginity. In many high schools—and an increasing number of junior highs—virginity is regarded as an embarrassing vestige of childhood, to be disposed of as quickly as possible. Young people are immersed from their earliest days in a culture that parades sexuality at every turn and makes heroes of the advocates of sexual excess. Girls, from toddlerhood on up, shop in stores packed with clothing once thought suitable only for streetwalkers—lace leggings, crop tops, and wedge-heeled boots. Parents drop their children off at Madonna or Michael Jackson concerts, featuring simulated on-stage masturbation, or at Bobby Brown's show, where a fan drawn out of the audience is treated to a pretended act of copulation. Young boys idolize sports stars like Wilt Chamberlain, who claims to have bedded 20,000 women. And when the "Spur Posse," eight California high school athletes, were charged with systematically raping girls as young as 10 as part of a "scoring" ritual, the beefy young jocks were rewarded with a publicity tour of talk shows, while one father boasted to reporters about his son's "manhood."

In a late, lame attempt to counterbalance this sexual overload, most schools offer sex 10
education as part of their curriculums. (In 1993, forty-seven states recommended or required such courses.) But sex ed classes are heavy on the mechanics of fertilization and birth control—sperm, eggs, and condoms—and light on any discussion of sexuality as only one part of a well-balanced life. There is passing reference to abstinence as a method of contraception, but little discussion of abstinence as an emotionally or spiritually satisfying option. Promiscuity is discussed for its role in spreading sexually transmitted diseases. But the concept of rejecting casual sex in favor of reserving sex for an emotionally intimate, exclusive, trusting relationship—much less any mention of waiting until marriage—is foreign to most public school settings. "Love and stuff like that really wasn't discussed" is the way one Spur Posse member remembers his high school sex education class.

Surely teenagers need the factual information provided by sex education courses. But 11
where is "love and stuff like that" talked about? Where can they turn for a more balanced view of sexuality? Who is telling young people like Elaine, my former houseguest, that sex is not an adequate basis for a healthy, respectful relationship? Along with warnings to keep condoms on hand, is anyone teaching kids that they have a right to be valued for something other than their sexuality? Madison Avenue, Hollywood, and the TV, music, and fashion industries won't tell them that. Who will?

No one has told Elaine—at least, not in a way she comprehends. I haven't seen her 12
for a long time, but I hear of her occasionally. The baby boy she bore while living in my house is in a foster home, a few miles from his older half-sister, who is also in foster care. Elaine herself is working in a local convenience store—and she is pregnant again. This time, I understand, she is carrying twins.

■ **Reading Comprehension Questions**

1. The word *dismantled* in "A moment after the photo session was over, the beautiful room was dismantled, and the models moved on to their next job" (paragraph 5) means
   a. used.
   b. photographed.
   c. taken apart.
   d. perfected.

2. The word *vestige* in "In many high schools—and an increasing number of junior highs—virginity is regarded as an embarrassing vestige of childhood" (paragraph 9) means

   a. reversal.
   b. activity.
   c. remainder.
   d. error.

3. Which of the following would be a good alternative title for this selection?

   a. Teens and Birth Control
   b. The Use of Sex to Sell Products
   c. An Unbalanced View of Sexuality
   d. The Advantages of Casual Sex

4. Which sentence best expresses the main idea of the selection?

   a. Sexual images have helped our society become more open and understanding about a natural part of life.
   b. We live in a society ruled by Madison Avenue, Hollywood, and the TV, music, and fashion industries.
   c. Sex education courses, required in most states, have not done enough to teach our children about sexuality and responsible behavior.
   d. Nothing, not even sex education, is counteracting the numerous sexual images in our society that encourage irresponsible, casual sex.

5. According to the author, Elaine probably likes to look at sexy magazine ads because

   a. she doesn't have high moral standards.
   b. she wishes she could afford the products being advertised.
   c. they portray the kind of life she'd like to lead.
   d. they remind her of her life before she had children.

6. In contrast to Elaine, the author

   a. understands that most ads portray an unreal world.
   b. finds ads like the Claiborne ad distasteful.
   c. never looks at fashion magazines.
   d. does not have children.

7. Elaine

   a. wanted to become pregnant.
   b. thinks birth control isn't romantic.
   c. never finished high school.
   d. has a healthy fear of AIDS.

8. We can conclude the author believes that

   a. sex is a private matter that should not be discussed.

   b. many young people view sex as an adequate basis for a relationship.

   c. Madison Avenue, Hollywood, and the TV, music, and fashion industries have completely destroyed all morality in America.

   d. virginity is an embarrassing vestige of childhood.

9. The author implies that

   a. sexy ads should be illegal.

   b. schools should teach contraception at an earlier age.

   c. sex should be reserved for an exclusive, loving relationship.

   d. casual sex is sometimes, though not always, a good idea.

10. The author suggests that sex education classes

   a. are a major cause of casual, unprotected sex.

   b. should include the role of sex in a meaningful relationship.

   c. should not include the mechanics of fertilization and birth control.

   d. have a role that rightfully belongs to parents.

■ Discussion Questions

About Content

1. Garity suggests that our society's messages about sex leave out some important points. What does she feel is missing? Do you agree or disagree with her analysis?

2. The author lists numerous examples to illustrate and support her claim that "young people are immersed from their earliest days in a culture that parades sexuality at every turn and makes heroes of advocates of sexual excess." What examples can you think of to add to her list? Describe and explain them.

3. In paragraph 7, the author says that Elaine is "completely unaware of the irony of her situation." In an ironic situation, there is an inconsistency between what might be expected and what actually happens. What about Elaine's situation is ironic?

About Structure

4. Look at the first few sentences of paragraph 3. How does the author bring us from "a few years ago" into the present?

5. At first, this reading seems to focus solely on the influence of advertising. At what point does the reading introduce other influences? What are they?

About Style and Tone

6. What is Garity's purpose in writing "Is Sex All That Matters"?
    a. To entertain readers with discussions of interesting people and events.
    b. To give readers practical factual information on such topics as birth control and pregnancy.
    c. To persuade readers that changes are needed in how sexuality is treated in our society.
7. Why has Garity chosen to focus so much of her essay on Elaine? What would have been lost if Garity had omitted Elaine from the essay?

■ Writing Assignments

Assignment 1

Garity accuses the advertising, film, TV, music, and fashion industries of contributing to our sex-saturated society by parading "sexuality at every turn." Choose one industry from that list, and write your own essay about how it portrays sexuality.

There is more than one way you can approach this assignment. In an essay on the fashion industry, for instance, you could focus on types of clothing being promoted, ads in print, and ads on TV. In an essay on the music industry, you might discuss three musicians and how their lyrics and their performances promote a particular view of sex. Whatever your choice, include specific, colorful descriptions, as Garity does when discussing ads and fashions. (See, for example, paragraphs 3 and 8.)

Assignment 2

Garity suggests that sex education courses should include more than the "mechanics of fertilization and birth control" (paragraph 10). Write an essay describing several ways you feel sex education classes could incorporate "love and stuff like that." Begin by selecting three general approaches that could be used in a sex education class to get students to think about what a rich, balanced romantic relationship is made of. For example, you might focus on three of the following:

Discussion of what students seek in a relationship

Discussion of a fictional relationship, such as that of Romeo and Juliet or two characters in a TV show

Discussion of the lyrics of a popular song

Bringing into class a psychologist who deals with problems in relationships

Bringing into class one or more couples who have been together for many years

Discuss each method you choose in a separate paragraph. Describe in detail how the method would work, using hypothetical examples to illustrate your points.

Assignment 3

Advertisements represent many elements of our society. Choose an element other than sexuality, and analyze the way ads of any kind (in magazines and newspapers, on billboards and buses, on TV and radio) portray that subject. Following are some areas of our lives that are commonly represented in ads:

Family life
Women's roles
Men's roles
Possessions
Looks
Health

In analyzing an ad, consider what images and words are used, how they are intended to appeal to the audience, and what values they promote. Use the conclusion you come to as the thesis of your essay. For example, an essay on men's roles might make this point: "Many of today's TV ads promote participation of fathers in domestic activities."

Support your conclusion with colorful descriptions of several ads. Make your descriptions detailed enough so your readers can "see" the elements of ads you refer to. Be sure to focus on the parts of the ads that support the point you are trying to make. You could organize your essay by devoting a paragraph each to three significant ads. Or you could devote each supporting paragraph to one of several important points about the subject you've chosen. For instance, an essay about fathers helping at home might discuss child care, cleaning, and cooking. A paragraph on each of those topics might refer to two or more ads.

READING
COMPREHENSION
CHART

Write an X through the numbers of any questions you missed while answering the comprehension questions for each selection in Part Five, Readings for Writing. Then write in your comprehension score. If you repeatedly miss questions in any particular skill, the chart will make that clear. Then you can pay special attention to that skill in the future.

Selection	Subject or Title	Thesis or Main Idea	Key Details			Inferences			Vocabulary in Context		Comprehension Score
Haley	1	2	3	4	5	6	7	8	9	10	%
Gregory	1	2	3	4	5	6	7	8	9	10	%
Ames	1	2	3	4	5	6	7	8	9	10	%
Cisneros	1	2	3	4	5	6	7	8	9	10	%
Wilkins	1	2	3	4	5	6	7	8	9	10	%
Francke	1	2	3	4	5	6	7	8	9	10	%
McMurtry	1	2	3	4	5	6	7	8	9	10	%
Orwell	1	2	3	4	5	6	7	8	9	10	%
Baker	1	2	3	4	5	6	7	8	9	10	%
Scheller	1	2	3	4	5	6	7	8	9	10	%

Selection	Subject or Title	Thesis or Main Idea	Key Details			Inferences			Vocabulary in Context		Comprehension Score
Herndon	1	2	3	4	5	6	7	8	9	10	%
Terkel	1	2	3	4	5	6	7	8	9	10	%
Adler	1	2	3	4	5	6	7	8	9	10	%
Banas	1	2	3	4	5	6	7	8	9	10	%
Lamanna	1	2	3	4	5	6	7	8	9	10	%
McClintock	1	2	3	4	5	6	7	8	9	10	%
Sweet	1	2	3	4	5	6	7	8	9	10	%
Dunayer	1	2	3	4	5	6	7	8	9	10	%
O'Keeney	1	2	3	4	5	6	7	8	9	10	%
Daniels	1	2	3	4	5	6	7	8	9	10	%
Sugarman	1	2	3	4	5	6	7	8	9	10	%
Sherry	1	2	3	4	5	6	7	8	9	10	%
Winn	1	2	3	4	5	6	7	8	9	10	%
Hogarty	1	2	3	4	5	6	7	8	9	10	%
Garity	1	2	3	4	5	6	7	8	9	10	%

ACKNOWLEDGMENTS

"The Ambivalence of Abortion." Linda Bird Francke, from *The New York Times*, May 1976. Copyright © 1976 by The New York Times Company. Reprinted by permission of the author's agent. Selection on pages 540–543.

"Brett Hauser: Supermarket Box Boy." Studs Terkel, from *Working: People Talk about What They Do All Day and How They Feel about What They Do*. Copyright © 1972, 1974 by Studs Terkel. Reprinted by permission of Pantheon Books, a division of Random House, Inc. Selection on pages 584–586.

"College Lectures: Is Anybody Listening?" David Daniels. Reprinted with permission from *Trend* magazine, November, 1987. Selection on pages 641–643.

"Date Rape." Ellen Sweet, from *Ms.* magazine, October 1985. Reprinted by permission. Selection on pages 617–624.

"Defense Mechanisms." Ronald B. Adler and Neil Towne, abridged from *Looking Out/Looking In*, 3d ed. Copyright © 1981 by Holt, Rinehart and Winston. Reprinted by permission of Holt, Rinehart and Winston, CBS College Publishing. Selection on pages 590–594.

"Five Parenting Styles." Mary Ann Lamanna and Agnes Reidmann, from *Marriages and Families: Making Choices throughout the Life Cycle*. Copyright © 1981 by Wadsworth, Inc. Reprinted by permission of Wadsworth Publishing Company, Belmont, California 94004. Selection on pages 603–605.

"A Hanging." George Orwell, from *Shooting an Elephant and Other Essays*. Copyright © 1945, 1946, 1949, 1950 by Sonia Brownell Orwell; renewed 1973, 1974 by Sonia Orwell. Reprinted by permission of Harcourt Brace Jovanovich, Inc. Selection on pages 555–558.

"Here's to Your Health." Joan Dunayer. Reprinted by permission of Townsend Press. Selection on pages 627–628.

"How to Deal with a Difficult Boss." Donna Brown Hogarty, from *Reader's Digest*, July 1993. Reprinted by permission. Selection on pages 671–675.

"How to Make It in College, Now That You're Here." Brian O'Keeney. Reprinted by permission. Selection on pages 632–637.

"I Became Her Target." Roger Wilkins, originally published in *Newsday*, September 6, 1987. Reprinted by permission. Selection on pages 534–536.

"In My Day." Russell Baker, from *Growing Up*. Copyright © 1982 by Russell Baker. Reprinted with permission of Congdon & Weed, Chicago, Ill. Selection on pages 562–566.

"In Praise of the F Word." From the "My Turn" column in *Newsweek*. Reprinted by permission of Mary Sherry. Selection on pages 657–658.

"Is Sex All That Matters?" Joyce Garity. Reprinted by permission of Townsend Press. Selection on pages 679–681.

"A Kite." James Herndon, from *How to Survive in Your Native Land*. Copyright © 1971 by James Herndon. Reprinted by permission of Simon and Schuster, Inc. Selection on pages 577–580.

"On Being a Mess." Elizabeth Ames, from *Newsweek*, issue of July 7, 1980. Reprinted by permission. Selection on pages 522–524.

"Only Daughter." Sandra Cisneros, orginally published in *Glamour*, November 1990. Copyright © by Sandra Cisnerof 1990. Reprinted by permission. Selection on pages 528–530.

On the Meaning of "Plumbing and Poverty." Melanie Scheller, from *Independent Weekly*, January 4, 1990. Reprinted by permission. Selection on pages 571–574.

"The Plug-In Drug." Marie Winn, adapted from the chapter "Family Life" in *The Plug-In Drug*. Copyright © 1977 by Marie Winn Miller. Reprinted by permission of Viking-Penguin, Inc. Selection on pages 662–667.

"Propaganda Techniques." Ann McClintock. Reprinted by permission. Selection on pages 609–612.

"Seven Ways to Keep the Peace at Home." Daniel A. Sugarman, from *Families* magazine, issue of March 1982. Reprinted by permission of the author. Selection on pages 647–653.

"Shame." Dick Gregory with Robert Lipsyte, from *Nigger: An Autobiography*. Copyright © 1964 by Dick Gregory Enterprises, Inc. Reprinted by permission of the publisher, E. P. Dutton, Inc. Selection on pages 515–518.

"Smash Thy Neighbor." John McMurtry, from *Maclean's*. Reprinted by permission. Selection on pages 547–551.

"Thank You." Alex Haley, from *Parade* magazine, issue of November 21, 1982. Copyright © 1982 by Alex Haley. Reprinted by permission. Selection on pages 508–511.

"Why Are Students Turned Off?" Casey Banas, from *Chicago Tribune*, issue of August 5, 1979. Copyright © 1979 by the Chicago Tribune. Used with permission. Selection on pages 597–598.

INDEX